D
848
.C38
1988

Caute, David.

The year of the
barricades

$7.98

THE YEAR OF THE BARRICADES

Also by David Caute:

Political Studies

Communism and the French Intellectuals
The Left in Europe Since 1789
Frantz Fanon
The Fellow-Travellers
The Great Fear:
The Anti-Communist Campaign
under Truman and Eisenhower
Under the Skin:
The Death of White Rhodesia

Other Works

The Illusion:
An Essay on Politics, Theatre and the Novel
Collisions: Essays and Reviews
Cuba, Yes?
The Espionage of the Saints: Two Essays on Silence and the State

Novels

At Fever Pitch
Comrade Jacob
The Decline of the West
The Occupation
The K-Factor
News from Nowhere

THE YEAR OF THE BARRICADES

— ☮ —

A Journey Through 1968

David Caute

1817

Harper & Row, Publishers, New York
Cambridge, Philadelphia, San Francisco, Washington
London, Mexico City, São Paulo, Singapore, Sydney

FIRST EDITION

Copyeditor: Carole Berglie
Designer: C. Linda Dingler
Photo research: Vincent Virga

Library of Congress Cataloging-in-Publication Data

Caute, David.
  The year of the barricades.

  Bibliography: p.
Includes index.
    1. History, Modern—1945–   . 2. Radicalism—History—20th century. 3. Insurgency—History—20th century. 4. Government, Resistance to—History—20th century. 5. Revolutions—History—20th century.
I. Title.
D848.C38   1988   909.83   87-45605
ISBN 0-06-015870-0

---

87 88 89 90 91 RRD 10 9 8 7 6 5 4 3 2 1

CONTENTS

ACKNOWLEDGMENTS

I am much indebted to the following for kindly putting their knowledge of the period at my disposal and for their helpful comments on various chapters:

Robin Blackburn, Percy Cohen, Meghdad Desai, Milan Hauner, Laurence Harris, Richard Kuper, Karel Kyncl, Annette Lavers, Gerald Rabkin, Martin Shaw, George Theiner.

They are not, of course, responsible for the opinions expressed or for any inaccuracies.

I owe a special debt to my British and American editors, Christopher Sinclair-Stevenson and Ted Solotaroff, for their close reading of the text and many valuable suggestions.

INTRODUCTION

The year 1968 was the most turbulent since the end of World War II. The entire postwar order was challenged in a chain of insurrections extending from America to Western Europe and Czechoslovakia, yet nowhere was the challenge successful.

The revolutionary movements of 1967–69 marked, in one respect at least, a break with history: in a period of unprecedented material prosperity and cultural tolerance, the sons and daughters of the most privileged sections of the population rebelled. It was a moral revolt generated by "alienation" from dominant values, but it did not, on the whole, extend to the working class. The iconoclasm and mounting violence of the New Left outraged the mass of citizens, reinforcing the paternalistic values of "law and order."

Only black America provided a revolt by those who were exploited as well as alienated. But here again the reaction of the white majority was hostile and punitive—a more entrenched racism.

In the vanguard of rebellion were the students, scornful of representative democracy and consensus politics, distrustful of capitalist technocracy and the media-manipulated "consumer society," unimpressed by time-honored hierarchies of authority. They marched, demonstrated, occupied universities, and courted police repression, driving university presidents, deans, vice-chancellors, rectors, and directors to distraction and, not infrequently, to premature retirement. The majority of university teachers, while often initially sympathetic to student demands, finally rejected the whole movement, equated Student Power with antirational Left-fascism—and welcomed its repression.

What were they—courageous visionaries or romantic utopians? Genuine revolutionaries or posturing spoiled brats? An authentic resistance movement or a frivolous carnival by kids who had never known poverty and the fear of unemployment? An idealistic challenge to imperialism or a pantomime of rhetorical gestures? A rebirth of the critical intelligence or a long, drugged "trip" into fashionable incoherence? This book aims to provide a history that will yield tentative answers to these questions.

If one factor sustained the international fever of 1968 it was the war in Vietnam. Worse than a blunder, it was a crime. Not only were the architects (the Kennedy and Johnson administrations) compromised by this murderous exercise in *force majeure* but also the loyal apologists, the governments of Europe, social democrats, and conservatives alike. The New Left rapidly shed its initial optimism, bitterly concluding that these governments were the ones the majority of their citizens deserved.

The Vietnamese paid the highest price for the war, but the cost in domestic friction among the Western democracies was unprecedented. Draft evasion became a major enterprise in the United States; an ambitious president, eager for a second term of office, abandoned his claim; his most dangerous rival was assassinated. Bullets also felled the most famous black American of his time and Germany's most influential student leader (though he survived). The Democratic National Convention in Chicago was accompanied by scenes of violence more suggestive of war than of a civil society bonded by shared values. The French government was temporarily paralyzed by the most severe revolt since the Paris Commune of 1871; night after night a pall of tear gas hung over the streets of the Latin Quarter. A citadel of Ivy League serenity, Columbia University, witnessed physical violence previously unimaginable, while San Francisco State College was reduced to protracted anarchy. London University's elite School of Economics succumbed to almost continuous insurrection. West Berlin was divided by burning animosities and rioting spread across the Federal Republic admired for its stable democracy and "economic miracle."

The grim scenes in Chicago's streets and parks followed close on the heels of the Soviet tanks entering Prague. The Czechoslovak "Spring," that extraordinary cry for liberty and "socialism with a human face," was snuffed out by half a million invading soldiers. A small country was raped while the world sat on its hands. The Prague Spring is not only of acute interest on its own account; it also provokes speculation about the nature of the New Left in the capitalist democracies. The Czechoslovak reform movement, students included, was working for precisely the freedoms that Western radicals were rejecting as bogus and manipulative; the Czechs desired a liberal government and a more open society, but the New Left wanted either no government at all or a form of libertarian "participatory democracy" retrieved from state power and bureaucracy.

Only those who have enjoyed constitutional democracy can learn to despise the formal freedoms. "Repressive tolerance" (in Herbert Marcuse's celebrated phrase) meant nothing to the students of Prague. Should we therefore conclude that the Czechoslovak students, raised under an oppressive dictatorship, were "mature" in values and judgments while their pampered Western colleagues were incapable of distinguishing the bad from the worse? We shall see that the innovative ideas of the New Left—frequently, though not invariably, expressed with clarity and sophistication—constitute a treasury whose present dilapidation impoverishes us.

A central theme of this book is the relationship of the New Left to the sixties' "counterculture," a term that embraces a plethora of disparate motions: dropout hippies, obscene language, acid trips, underground newspapers and films, "alternative theatre" with attendant "happenings," anti-universities, surrealist street politics, communal self-help, folk and rock music alien to ears attuned to Beethoven or the Palm Court Orchestra, mystical cults, aggressive sexuality, flamboyant clothing, ecological awareness, rejection of ambition and careerism. But how "counter" was the counterculture in practice? Despite the punitive legislation introduced to check the use of drugs, the open, commercial societies of the West were able to accommodate outrageous cultural gestures—and very often to turn them to profit. In fact there was plenty of careerism and profit-taking within the counterculture itself; for this reason (among others) the political platoons of the New Left distrusted excessive hedonism and the vaporous notion that the world will be changed if each does his "own thing." This distrust reveals the more sober face of the New Left, its sense of social responsibility, its anchorage in the ancient harbor of socialist tradition. But such was the turmoil of 1968 that the majority of solid citizens neither knew nor cared about such distinctions; the upstart young simply needed to be taught a lesson.

By the end of 1970, the high tide of campus rebellion had receded, the Western democracies were back to business-as-usual, and the New Left generation had either come to terms with the ways of the world or confined its residual idealism to local projects: ecology, people's lawyers, communalism. The major exception was the women's movement, but that was both a product and a rejection of the male-dominated New Left. Fundamental to all New Left movements was a vision of a world undivided by race, class, or gender; the feminists, like the Black Panthers, took the separatist road to equality. The white male radicals of the mid-sixties accepted that they were historically branded by the crimes of their race; ten years later their successors accepted—though less unequivocally—that they were also branded by the crimes of their sex. This fracture in the bonding vision of the sixties proved fatal.

Twenty years later we have seen the detritus of a mass movement degenerate into elitist strategies of terrorism. The Panthers apart, no one in the New Left of 1967–68 ever carried a gun or a bomb; the bullets and tear gas belonged to the State alone. But by 1969–70 the Weathermen were addicted to dynamite, and the embittered European ultras were also going underground: the Red Brigades in Italy, the Red Army Faction (Baader-Meinhoff) in Germany, the Angry Brigade in Britain. The urban guerrilla was not the rural guerrilla transplanted from countryside to town; he (or frequently she) was a terrorist cut off from the surrounding human landscape. Daniel Cohn-Bendit may have tried to hijack Paris, but his only weapon was force of argument and personal commitment; it's inconceivable that he would have hijacked an airliner or threatened to kill its passengers if his demands were not met.

Another major change, two decades on, is the almost complete disappearance among Western students of what one might call "Third World idealism." There are no longer any Che Guevaras, Ho Chi Minhs, or Chinese Red Guards, or any solemn quotes from Little Red Books to be plastered on living-room walls or chanted in the streets. There are still anti-imperialist demonstrations on behalf of Nicaragua or Libya and a resurgence of conscience about apartheid, but Nelson Mandela is a symbol of suffering rather than a charismatic idol. There is no Cuba today, no born-again guerrilla society exciting romantic emulation. Almost every Western radical knows in 1988 what the New Left did not comprehend in 1968: In the postcolonial Third World, the new elites are rarely interested in either democracy (of whatever model) or liberty. Much preferred is presidential populism.

In the West itself, criticism of reactionary governments now assumes the low murmur of servants grumbling below stairs about their masters, but the inevitability of rulers and ruled, rich and poor, is accepted. The New Left believed otherwise. For that alone they deserve our renewed attention.

PROLOGUE:
THE PENTAGON

"Emboldened, the hippie girls began placing flowers in gun barrels as tokens of peace..."

WASHINGTON, Saturday, October 21, 1967—The citadel and nerve-center of the American war machine, a vast, five-sided edifice set on 583 acres of lawn and parking lots, is under siege. In the sunshine of an Indian summer a vast crowd of 90,000 has gathered in the capital, around the reflecting pool beneath the Lincoln Memorial, to hear the speeches on "a staggeringly beautiful day." This is America's seventh national protest against the Vietnam War, and many of the speeches touch familiar chords in frustrated ears. "Welcome to another dull peace march with dull speeches," quips the folksinger Phil Ochs, before singing his own composition, "I Declare the War is Over."

United in its abhorrence of the war, this American gathering was deeply divided in philosophy and life-style. The sober ranks of middle-aged dissenters had been shaken by the flamboyant disrespect of the New Left for the American flag, representative democracy, and the rule of law. The most outrageously disruptive apostles of the counterculture, the Yippies, were liable to turn any purposeful protest into a scandalous happening; their sense of theatre ensured that they would claim the headlines and the television coverage. Yippie spokesman Jerry Rubin had promised "wholesale disruption" of American society. "We're going to raise the Pentagon three hundred feet in the air," added his clowning colleague Abbie Hoffman. "A thousand children will stage Loot-ins at department stores to strike at the property fetish that underlies genocidal war," had predicted Keith Lampe (who also raised the question, "Does LBJ suck?").

Such obscenity and iconoclasm left moderate peace groups shocked, fearful, and antagonistic. As the radical journalist Andrew Kopkind put it, they "wanted a pleasant autumn walk with the right mixture of moral outrage and prayerful persuasion." The new generation of young radicals were through with all that. What had it ever achieved? But the Mobilization's coordinator, David Dellinger, had diplomatically rebuilt the bridges, and October 21 brought the level-headed liberals and Old Leftists to Washington. They were all there: reform Democrats, SANE, Women Strike for Peace, American Friends Service Committee, CORE, Inter-University Christian Movement, Catholic Peace Fellowship, Martin Luther King's Southern Christian Leadership Conference, National Lawyers' Guild, National Conference for a New Politics. "The vast majority," observed the London *Times*'s correspondent, "looked as if they had decamped temporarily from Ivy League campuses." Most of them were ready to chant nothing more obscene than "Hell, no, we won't go" and "LBJ, how many kids did you kill today?" Perched above the crowd at the Lincoln Memorial, a black held aloft a poignant placard: "No Vietnamese Ever Called Me a Nigger." Few could quarrel with that.

A message of solidarity from North Vietnam was being read when the announcement was made that the crowd could proceed to cross the bridge over the Potomac into Virginia. The Mobilization had a (heavily negotiated) permit to demonstrate at the Defense Department, and now the crowd began to walk toward the Pentagon.

It was the climax of a week of national protest and civil disobedience, much—but not all—of it conducted with dignity and decorum. During Stop the Draft Week thousands had demonstrated at induction centers and many were arrested. At the Church of the Reformation, 212 East Capitol Street, thirty or forty young men representing the twenty-four Resistance groups in the country gathered on the lawn. Passing from hand to hand were a few loaves of bread, a jar of peanut butter, and a couple quarts of milk—meager rations, but more than enough since no one took much. The Resisters then moved in procession to the Justice Department to face the media, after which they filed up the steps to deposit their draft cards in the bag. Norman Mailer, the most energetic literary intelligence of his time, observed the ceremony with sympathy as each man came up, gave his name and the state or area or college he represented, and then proceeded to name the number of draft cards he had been entrusted to turn in. Mailer reflected that these young men were committing their futures to prison, emigration, or "at best, years where everything must be unknown. . . ."

Some were scholarly and dressed conservatively, resembling clerks; others wore dungarees. Noticing a sharp kid who wore dark glasses because his eyes were recovering from Oakland police mace, Mailer reflected: "This student had a Berkeley style which Mailer did not like altogether: it was cocky, knowledgeable, and quick to mock the generations over thirty." Then came "the faculty"—academics with careers and families, many of whom hovered irresolutely near the Justice Department steps before finally moving up them. The leaders of the delegation, Dr. Benjamin Spock and the Reverend William Sloane

Coffin, had already entered the Justice Department carrying 994 cards, but had encountered much difficulty in persuading the officials to receive them.

At Harvard and Yale, clergymen and seminarians had staged solemn ceremonies of draft-card burning with accompanying hymns and candlelit processions. Across the nation those bearing witness had embarked on vigils and symbolic occupations. But the thousands now crossing the bridge over the Potomac under a brilliant October sun had cause to reflect that not all the protests had been conducted so politely. In Oakland, California, 10,000 demonstrators, many of them students from the University of California at Berkeley, had roamed streets thick with police tear gas in a renewed effort to close down the army's induction center. At the University of Wisconsin, a minor demonstration had escalated into a major revolt. The underlying temper was raw.

As soon as the New Left vanguard reached the precincts of the Pentagon, probing actions began and a flying column broke through the chicken-wire fences erected the previous day. The assault party consisted of Students for a Democratic Society (SDS) and an amorphous, quarreling assortment of high-density radicals called the Revolutionary Contingent. Together they charged across one of the Pentagon's vast parking lots, bearing aloft flags of the Vietnamese National Liberation Front (NLF) and attacking the military police barrier. The MPs countercharged with rifles and sheathed bayonets; the authorities were nothing if not prepared, having deployed 1,500 Metropolitan police, 2,500 National Guardsmen, 200 U.S. Marshals, and 6,000 troops of the 82nd Airborne Division, fresh from invading Santo Domingo and curbing the Detroit riots. But, once through the wire barrier, several hundred guerrillas began scaling a twenty-foot-high wall up to the terrace level of the fortress; by sundown 2,000 of the intrepid had invaded forbidden territory. Some even gained access to the building, a Kafkaesque maze of identical corridors, but they were hemmed in by ranks of troops.

The militants of SDS, the hippies, and the Yippies squatted down directly in front of the Pentagon, singing, holding discussions, and listening to an ex–Green Beret testify about his defection. The clean-cut boys in khaki found themselves face to face with a long-haired rabble decked out in all manner of provocative costumes: Sgt. Pepper's Band, Arab sheiks, Park Avenue doormen, Wyatt Earp, Indians, Batman, Martians, Roman senators. As Mailer put it, the troops did not know whether to expect "a hairy kiss on their lips or a bomb between their knees." Emboldened, the hippie girls began placing flowers in gun barrels as tokens of peace; some bared their breasts.

The soldiers suffered constant taunts from the massed ranks of young demonstrators, who had temporarily transferred their loathing from the invisible warlords to the visible working-class sons of Middle America confronting them. The taunting continued through the afternoon and evening, the soldiers under strict orders to remain silent, many of them trembling. A captain in the Airborne kept calling out through his bullhorn, "A Company, hold your ground, A Company. Nobody comes and nobody goes."

The brasher kids began to kick at the soldiers, confident now that they would not retaliate. James Reston, of the *New York Times,* was appalled by what he saw: "They spat on some of the soldiers in the front line and goaded them with the most vicious personal slander."

Rifles were now pointed at the demonstrators. The kids were horrified—this was their America! Gerald Long, of the *National Guardian,* watched a girl trying to reason with a soldier, "We're just like you. You're like us." Then she brought her two fingers to her mouth, kissed them, and touched the soldier's lips. Four soldiers dragged her away. Some of the girls were gentle and sweet—true flower girls; others displayed what Mailer called "the well-seasoned and high-spiced bitch air of fifty Harlem pickup lovers in a year. . . ." A startling disproportion of women were arrested and many were beaten. When such distinguished notables as Dr. Spock, Noam Chomsky, Sidney Lens, Robert Lowell, and Dwight Macdonald appeared on the scene, the one who got the beating was Dagmar Wilson, of Women Strike for Peace. She was also fined and given a thirty-day suspended jail sentence.

Then the military assault began. Margie Stamberg, of the Washington *Free Press,* described it: "Slowly the wedge began to move in on people. With bayonets and rifle butts, they moved first on the girls in the front line, kicking them, jabbing at them again and again with the guns, busting their heads and arms to break the chain of locked arms. The crowd appealed to the paratroopers to back off, to join them, to just act human. They sang the 'Star-Spangled Banner' and other songs. . . . And so we sat. Some individuals left but most remained." Beating and dragging away their victims, the paratroopers moved through the ranks of seated demonstrators. Harvey Mayes, of the English Department at Hunter College, saw a girl beaten as she lay covering her head with her arms. A soldier thrust his club swordlike between her hands into her face. "She twisted her body so we could see her face. But there was no face there. . . ." She vomited blood.

One or two military detachments threw tear gas. The Pentagon later denied it, but, according to Andrew Kopkind, "reporters and demonstrators saw the soldiers in the act." A Pentagon spokesman justified the degree of force used as "consistent with objectives of security and control faced with varying levels of dissent."

Those who had occupied a corner of the Pentagon stayed overnight to spray-paint the stone wall of the mall, the pier, and the sides of the ramp—offering further hostages to a hostile press. The flamboyant Jerry Rubin claimed to have been pissing at the time of his arrest, "a sacramental gesture." But the best-publicized arrest, much earlier (he wanted to get back to New York for a party), had been that of Norman Mailer. With a BBC documentary film crew in attendance, Mailer had transgressed a line of marshals (watched by young people who might not have read him or might not believe in celebrities) while Dwight Macdonald hovered uncertainly in the background, calling Mailer back, then beating a retreat.

Mailer missed the New York party and spent the night in prison, but it was all good copy, worth a National Book Award (the brilliant *Armies of the Night*). With the help of an adroit lawyer he escaped the prison sentence (thirty days, twenty-five of them suspended) that the commissioner believed Mailer's maturity and influence on young people merited. Others stayed inside, obstructed prison work, and suffered solitary confinement. A Quaker group from Connecticut, who refused food and water, were fed intraveneously. Men who would not wear prison clothing were thrown, naked, into the "hole" and confined to cells so small that not all of them could lie down at once to sleep.

The day after the Pentagon demonstration, on Sunday, October 22, 5,000 people marched across London, from Trafalgar Square to Grosvenor Square, behind the Vietnam Solidarity Campaign's slogan, "Get Out of Vietnam Now." The target was the American embassy, and the battle that developed in Grosvenor Square—there were forty-seven arrests after repeated charges by mounted police—was regarded as a disturbing break with British tradition.

The bastion of British tradition, the BBC, despatched Dick Fontaine's cameras into an all-American bar where the customers were watching Norman Mailer on television; the novelist was calling the war obscene, and the mind of General Westmoreland (U.S. Military Commander in Vietnam) more obscene than all the dirty books you heard so much about (including Mailer's novel, *Why Are We in Vietnam?*). The studio audience booed while the drinkers in the bar growled about communist tendencies. Then a black man in the bar pulled out the TV plug with the explanation that it was a white man's war and Mailer and Fontaine had no right to oppose it; only blacks should oppose it.

These episodes tell us a good deal about the year ahead, 1968.

— 1 —

THE VIETNAM WAR—TET

"In Saigon, Vietcong guerrillas penetrate the U.S. embassy; the press carries pictures of American soldiers lying dead within the compound."

"Thousands of refugees were in flight from the battle zones."

TET

SOUTH VIETNAM, January 30–31, 1968—National Liberation Front (Vietcong) guerrillas, supported by conventional forces from North Vietnam, launch a massive offensive to mark Tet, the Vietnamese New Year. Thirty-six of forty-four provincial towns come under attack. Fierce fighting extends from Da Nang in the north through the Central Highlands to Can Tho in the Mekong Delta. North Vietnamese regulars bombard their way into the ancient city of Hue, at terrible cost to its inhabitants. In Saigon, Vietcong guerrillas penetrate the U.S. embassy; the press carries pictures of American soldiers lying dead within the compound.

On the day the Tet offensive was launched, Defense Secretary Robert McNamara reported to the Senate Armed Services Committee that Vietcong "combat efficiency and morale" were falling. But now fierce fighting extended along a 600-mile front and Communist tanks appeared at Langvei, sending South Vietnamese forces and civilian refugees in flight to the American base at Khe Sanh. Here they were disarmed, refused shelter, and driven away. Colonel Lownds, the commander at Khe Sanh, told Newbold Noyes of the Washington *Star:* "This thing can come back to haunt me—all of us. If these people say when the chips were down, after getting us to fight for you, you wouldn't protect them, then the whole civic action business here goes down the drain." Despite the jumbled pronouns, the colonel clearly believed that the South Vietnamese had been fighting for the Americans.

Between January 29 and February 1—four days—the American forces suffered 281 dead and 1,195 wounded. The South Vietnamese dead during the same period numbered 632. The Pentagon lacquered the coffins by announcing that the Communist offensive had been a complete failure. A few weeks later Clark Clifford replaced McNamara as defense secretary, and an additional 10,500 troops were rushed to

Vietnam, bringing the American military contingent there to over half a million.

Massive slaughter took place in the ancient city of Hue as it was stormed by the Vietcong and North Vietnamese, then slowly recaptured, inch by inch, by the Americans. According to Gabriel Kolko, American air strikes reduced 80 percent of the city to rubble. The Americans pounded the area around the Citadel to dust with air strikes, napalm runs, artillery, and naval gunfire. By early March at least 1,000 civilians had died, and unburied bodies sprawled on the banks of the Perfume River. Thousands of refugees were in flight from the battle zones. Fires raged in the Cholon district of Saigon. Even Under Secretary of the U.S. Air Force Townsend Hoopes was appalled by the American military response. In Saigon artillery and air strikes were repeatedly used against densely populated areas of the city. According to Hoopes, on February 7, at least 1,000 civilians were killed and 1,500 wounded in an effort to dislodge 2,500 Vietcong from Ben Tre.

The secretary-general of the United Nations, U Thant, continued to press for a halt to the bombing of North Vietnam. But Lyndon Johnson was adamant. Either Hanoi must suffer the fury of the most powerful nation on earth or it must accept the "San Antonio formula," the president's four conditions for a cease-fire. The Communists would never agree to one of those conditions: that the National Liberation Front evacuate the 20 percent of South Vietnam it currently controlled.

But the American public was deeply shaken, and confidence in the president plummeted. Simultaneously a gold and dollar crisis preoccupied the administration and made it impossible for Johnson to grant the Pentagon's demand for 206,000 more men in Vietnam. The Tet offensive also unleashed the greatest wave of anti-American feeling around the world ever experienced.

THE WAR

The greatest evil of the age was the Vietnam War. Many other furies surfaced in the late sixties, but it was the systematic destruction of a people and its habitat, the moral collusion of European governments, which "overdetermined" the fusion of other angers, political and cultural, into the international insurrection which is our subject.

The Vietnam War received media coverage more extensive and more intense than any in history. This was the first television war. Reporters from all over the world swarmed in. The army laid on facility trips like a travel bureau. The open society offered an open war—but not quite. Eighteen months elapsed between the massacre at My Lai in March 1968 and its exposure.

The draft brought the war home to the United States, but the impact was primarily moral. Revulsion and rebellion most affected the young members of the social class least affected by the draft. As David Tuck, a black soldier who had served in Vietnam with the 3rd Brigade of the 25th Infantry Division, from January 1966 to February 1967, told the Russell War Crimes Tribunal, "In my particular outfit 117 out of 156 were black soldiers. It is a common practice to put the people whom they consider expendable in the infantry. This is [sic] the black soldiers, the Puerto Ricans and the hillbillies." Although the Black Panthers denounced the war, it was not a major issue in the ghettos; indeed, many young blacks volunteered as an escape from poverty.

The absolute necessity and virtue of the global struggle against communism had been planted so deep in the American psyche during the late 1940s and the 1950s that it required a new, disenchanted generation to unravel the surreal logic of fighting totalitarianism by supporting corrupt dictatorships, of combating "aggression" by massive displays of firepower across vast empires of indirect rule. A generation determined to disbelieve the claims of corporate liberalism found itself psychologically incapable of confronting the totalitarian nature of Vietnamese communism, and the repressive facets of Third World liberation movements in general.

France's desperate attempt to retain possession of her Indo-Chinese colony had been increasingly underwritten by the Eisenhower-Dulles administration. However, military disaster finally forced France to the conference table. On May 7, 1954, Dien Bien Phu fell to the Vietminh, who now controlled about three-quarters of the country. Negotiations took place at Geneva from May to July. The Vietnamese Communist delegation called for early, nationwide elections, but the Soviet Union pressed its ally to make concessions—the most fatal one being the provisional zonal demarcation of Vietnam along the 17th Parallel. Thus were born "North" and "South" Vietnam, although the Final Declaration of the Conference, issued on July 21, 1954, stressed that "the military demarcation line is provisional and should not in any way be interpreted as constituting a political or territorial boundary." Indeed, to consolidate the unity of Vietnam it was agreed that "general elections be held in July 1956, under the supervision of an international control commission." The authorities of the two zones, North and South, were to begin consultations about the elections from July 20, 1955.

In January 1955, the Democratic Republic of Vietnam, led by President Ho Chi Minh, began pressing for the scheduled joint elections. In July the American secretary of state, John Foster Dulles, responded: Neither the United States nor the government of Ngo Dinh Diem in the South had signed the Geneva accords or was bound by it. Dulles claimed that the United States was "not afraid at all of elections, provided they are held under conditions of genuine freedom. . . ." Diem organized a fraudulent referendum in the South, installed himself as president, and set about liquidating the pro-Communist National Liberation Front, whose leader, Nguyen Huu Tho, was imprisoned. The British and French washed their hands of responsibility and refused Hanoi's repeated demands for a reconvened Geneva Conference.

Despite Dulles's denial, Washington was, indeed, afraid of nation-wide elections. According to President Eisenhower himself, "I have never talked or corresponded with a person knowledgeable in Indo-Chinese affairs who did not agree that had elections been held [in 1956] . . . possibly 80 per cent of the people would have voted for the communist Ho Chi Minh." The president had explained his position to a conference of state governors, in Seattle, on August 4, 1953: "Let us assume we lose Indo-China. . . . The tin and tungsten that we so greatly value from that area would cease coming. . . . So when the United States votes 400 million dollars to help that war, we are not voting a give-away program. We are voting for the cheapest way [to protect] . . . our security, our power and ability to get certain things we need from the riches of the Indo-Chinese territory and from Southeast Asia."

By 1958 there were an estimated 40,000 political prisoners in Diem's jails; by the end of 1961, 150,000. The arrival of the Kennedy administration in Washington accelerated, rather than reduced, America's commitment. Meanwhile Roman Catholics, fleeing from persecution in the North, flowed south.

The NLF proposed a five-point program: independence, democracy, peace, neutrality, and reunification. But how could the last two items be reconciled? Interviewing Nguyen Van Tien, chief of the permanent delegation of the NLF in Hanoi, early in 1967, the radical American writer John Gerassi asked him "how he envisaged the 'reunification' of a neutral part of the country with a Communist part." The reply was hardly convincing: " 'By keeping each section independent in policy but united in a federation. The body at the top will sit over both regimes. Whether it will be an assembly or council or whatever will be discussed later, that is after the reunification. . . . This general policy of ours has been approved by the Government of the North. . . . Each section [of Vietnam] will be independent internally. . . .' "

Washington and Saigon both knew that a unified Vietnam would be a Communist Vietnam. Determined to thwart this denouement, Kennedy and Johnson poured in aid, advisers, and troops. In March 1962, American troops became engaged in combat with Vietcong guerrillas for the first time. By December 1965, there were at least fourteen major U.S. air bases in Vietnam and 166,000 troops; a year later the manpower had more than doubled.

The policy of removing the rural population from its normal habitat to deprive the guerrillas of support had been practiced by the British in Malaya. It was repeated with new zeal, and on a vaster scale, in Vietnam. Early in 1962, Operation Sunrise was launched with the aim of razing villages and regrouping entire populations. By 1967, the NLF claimed that 14 million inhabitants had been forcibly evacuated into 17,000 concentration camps.

The Diem regime, meanwhile, had fallen to a military coup in October 1963. Diem's personal corruption, his policy of repression, his persecution of the Buddhists, the failure of the strategic hamlet program, and the incompetence of his drafted troops, had all combined to precipitate a crisis and the first of a succession of coups perpetrated by the power-hungry warlords of the South. On December 20, 1964, yet another coup took place in Saigon. By January 1965, the desertion rate within the South Vietnamese army reached 30 percent among draftees within six weeks of induction, and a large proportion of the remainder would not fight. In 1967, Lt.-General Nguyen Van Thieu was confirmed as president of South Vietnam by virtually meaningless elections.

The Johnson administration propounded the "domino" theory; Defense Secretary Robert McNamara described Vietnam as "a major test of communism's new strategy" of local revolution which, if not foiled, might be extended rapidly from one country to the next. Secretary of State Dean Rusk repeated the warning. The logic of this philosophy, and of Washington's claim that South Vietnam was the victim of "external aggression," dictated a major escalation of the war: the bombing of North Vietnam.

(But "external" aggression? We might imagine that the British had sent in troops to support the Confederate states during the American Civil War. Union troops had moved across the Mason-Dixon line in support of guerrillas loyal to the Union; London had then accused President Lincoln and General Grant—that is, Ho Chi Minh and General Giap—of "external aggression.")

On August 4, 1964, Johnson announced that North Vietnamese torpedo boats had wantonly attacked the U.S. destroyer *Maddox* in the international waters of the Bay of Tonkin; in reprisal he had ordered the bombing of the North Vietnamese installations supporting the torpedo boats. The following day the president requested, and promptly was granted, a congressional resolution authorizing him to take all necessary action "to protect our Armed Forces." Jet planes of the U.S. Seventh Fleet strafed and bombed a number of targets north of the 17th Parallel. The truth of the matter, however, emerged later: on the 30th of July, South Vietnamese patrol boats, protected by the *Maddox*, had raided North Vietnamese fishing vessels and bombarded two islands.

The systematic bombing of North Vietnam began in February 1965, shortly after Lyndon Johnson, the "peace candidate," had won a landslide victory over his hawkish Republican opponent, Barry Goldwater. The major cities of Hanoi and Haiphong were now targeted, the Pentagon insisting that only "military targets" were hit. The distinguished correspondent Harrison Salisbury, of the *New York Times*, personally observed that a significant portion of Nam Dinh had been destroyed: ". . . intensive destruction of civilian housing and ordinary business streets . . . an appearance familiar to anyone who saw blitzed London, devastated Berlin and Warsaw, or smashed Soviet cities like Stalingrad and Kharkov."

In January 1967, John Gerassi visited Nam Dinh. En route he passed through Phu Ly, which "used to be a throbbing little agricultural and artefact centre, a provincial headquarters with 7,600 inhabitants. Today it has none. It used to have 1,230 houses. Today it has 245, and they have been abandoned." The Americans claimed that the town was a rallying point for supplies going south to the NLF. Twelve miles from the sea, and connected to it by small canals and feeder rivers crammed with junks and sampans, lay Phat Dam, a town of 5,700 inhabitants, 4,200 of them Roman Catholic. According to Gerassi's North Vietnamese hosts, Phat Dam had been bombed fifty-seven times between March 1965 and January 1967. On Sunday, April 24, 1966, seventy-two people were killed when bombs struck the church of St. Francis Xavier while mass was in progress.

Prominent among the targets of the American bombers were the dikes, extending for 4,000 kilometers and performing a vital role in the rice-growing economy on the alluvial flats of the Red, Chu, Ma, and Ca rivers. The Russell Tribunal's Second Japanese Investigation Team provided a long, detailed catalogue of bombing attacks on specific dikes and on the teams repairing them. Fragmentation bombs designed to kill or injure human beings were regularly employed. Napalm caused ghastly injuries.

But the suffering of the South was even greater. Nguyen Van Dong of the NLF told the Russell Tribunal that, "Up to 1965, twenty-six out of forty-three provinces in South Vietnam have been submitted to raids which used toxic chemicals. Seven hundred thousand hectares of fields

and forests have been devastated, 146,274 persons have been poisoned."
A particularly devastating weapon was napalm, a jelly obtained from
the salts of aluminum, palmitic or other fatty acids, and naphthenate
acids. The acids give a viscous consistency to gasoline so that a highly
incendiary jelly results. In 1967, forty-nine members of International
Voluntary Services, all of whom had worked in South Vietnam, wrote
to Johnson describing the war as "an overwhelming atrocity." They
referred to "the free strike zones, the refugees, the spraying of herbicide
on crops, the napalm . . . the deserted villages, the sterile valleys, the
forests with huge swathes cut out." They spoke of refugees "forcibly
resettled, landless, in isolated desolate places which are turned into
colonies of mendicants."

Two American reporters, Orville and Jonathan Schell, reported a
visit to Quang Ngai Province. "We flew daily with the Forward Air
Control. What we saw was a province utterly destroyed. In August
1967, during Operation Benton, the 'pacification' camps became so full
that Army units were ordered not to 'generate' any more refugees.
. . . Every civilian on the ground was assumed to be the enemy by the
pilots by nature of living in Quang Ngai, which was largely a fire-free
zone. . . . Village after village was destroyed from the air. . . . Air strikes
on civilians became a matter of routine. . . ."

The Russell Tribunal heard the testimony of Americans who had
fought in the war. The Vietnam veteran David Tuck claimed he had
seen a prisoner thrown out of a helicopter, and many others casually
executed: ". . . it was the standard policy in my outfit not to take any
prisoners" unless they happened to be Vietcong officers. Ears were
commonly cut from the dead and collected as trophies. Tuck also
described the phenomenon of "the mad minute" when unlimited firepower would be poured into a village.

Another young witness before the tribunal was Peter Martinsen,
who had trained as an interrogator at the Fort Holabird Army Intelligence School in Maryland before being posted to Vietnam in September
1966. Attached to the 541st Military Intelligence detachment (11th
Armored Cavalry Regiment), Martinsen described how in November
1966 he interrogated and tortured a prisoner in Lon Giao camp, and
another such incident in May 1967 during Operation Manhattan, a few
kilometers from a Michelin plantation. American officers, said Martinsen, were well aware of the brutal methods used during interroga-
tions, but normally kept out of the way: "I had the man dig his own
grave with a gun at his head. . . . I counted off the minutes. . . . I counted
them off in Vietnamese so he knew I wasn't kidding. He broke down
and cried. . . . I described what death he was going to have. . . . This
is what is known as 'breaking the prisoner.' " Electrical torture had

been standard for a time, "but was not common towards the end of our assignment." Although Martinsen concluded by reaffirming his own opposition to communism—"Of course, the Tribunal will be used for Communist propaganda"—he nevertheless wanted to inform his fellow countrymen that "war causes war crimes"—crimes committed by "Mrs. Jones's son down the street."

The last word belonged to President Lyndon Johnson, obsessed by the fear that if he got out of Vietnam he would be judged

> . . . a coward. An unmanly man. A man without a spine. Oh, I could see it coming, all right. Every night when I fell asleep I could see myself tied to the ground in the middle of a long, open space. In the distance I could hear the voices of thousands of people. They were all shouting at me and running toward me: "Coward! Traitor! Weakling!"

Evidently those large ears had closed out "Murderer!"

2

THE ANTIWAR MOVEMENT:
America, Europe, and Japan

"The VDC [Vietnam Day Committee] picketed Johnson in San Francisco, demonstrated in front of troop trains, and confronted the police outside the Oakland army base."

"The [International War Crimes] tribunal convened...Jean-Paul Sartre as executive president, Vladimir Dedijer as chairman and president of sessions."

A BLUNDER AND A CRIME

Beginning in 1965, the New Left's public demonstrations against the war initially alienated mainstream public opinion, but they presented a consciousness-raising challenge which, during the period from 1967 to 1969, contributed to a remarkable conversion in American attitudes. In August 1965, only 14 percent of young Americans, aged twenty-one to twenty-nine, regarded the war as a "mistake." By July 1967, the corresponding figure was 32 percent; by August 1968, 48 percent; by October 1969, 58 percent. Among the middle-aged (thirty to forty-nine), the same movement of disillusion was visible: 22 percent in 1965, 37 percent in 1967, 48 percent in 1968, 54 percent by the end of 1969. The high cost of the war itself, the failure to achieve any kind of military victory, gradually alienated public opinion, allowing the moral arguments to take shelter under the roof of pragmatism: It was not so much a crime as a "mistake." By 1968, the young demonstrators' moral protests were making an impact on Main Street that their anti-imperialist rhetoric could never achieve.

The swing of opinion was most dramatic among students. According to a Gallup poll in the spring of 1967, 35 percent of students identified themselves as "doves," 49 percent as "hawks." By the fall of 1969, the corresponding figures were 69 and 20 percent.

On April 17, 1965, Students for a Democratic Society (SDS) had sponsored a national protest against the war in Washington, which exposed the inhibitions of the Old Left. Several "adult" peace groups hastened to dissociate themselves; Turn Towards Peace issued a statement challenging "activity which is in fact more hostile to America than to war." On the eve of the SDS march, eleven veterans of American socialism, including Norman Thomas, Bayard Rustin, H. Stuart Hughes, and A. J. Muste, issued a statement explaining that they would join hands only with those who believed in an "independent peace movement, not committed to any form of totalitarianism nor drawing

inspiration or direction from the foreign policy of any government."
The New Left reacted with contempt.

Out of the Berkeley Free Speech Movement—the *fons et origo* of
the international student insurrection, born at the University of California at Berkeley in the fall of 1964—emerged the Vietnam Day Committee (VDC) and a massive campus teach-in on May 21 and 22, 1965. The
VDC picketed Johnson in San Francisco, demonstrated in front of
troop trains, and confronted the police outside the Oakland army base.
On October 15 and 16, 1965, an estimated 100,000 people in fifty
different cities marched in a protest called by the VDC and coordinated
by an ad hoc student group in Madison, Wisconsin. Referring to Johnson and his circle of advisers, Carl Oglesby, SDS's president, commented sardonically: "They are not moral monsters. They are all
honorable men." Oglesby invited his audience to imagine Thomas Jefferson and Tom Paine in puzzled conversation with their liberal heirs,
McGeorge Bundy, Robert McNamara, Dean Rusk, and Arthur Gold-
berg. So the Vietcong were receiving outside help? Did they not remember Lafayette, or the 3,000 British freighters that the French obligingly
sank on behalf of the American rebels? So the Vietcong were guilty of
terrorizing the population? Did they never hear about the treatment
handed out to Loyalist collaborators by the American insurgents?

The October demonstrations were angrily denounced in Washington. On the Senate floor, Majority Leader Mike Mansfield condemned
their "utter irresponsibility," while Attorney General Nicholas Katzen-
bach announced a Justice Department investigation of the SDS. The
president joined in the attack and the media, too, were almost universally hostile.

Troop trains to the Oakland army terminal ran along the Santa Fe
Railroad through a suburb of Berkeley, only five blocks from the headquarters of the Vietnam Day Committee. Alerted by scouts who telephoned news of approaching trains, the VDC's guerrillas swarmed
across the rails. Soon these ambushes were attended not only by the
police, but also by the press and television cameras recording the running fights along the track. The VDC's "Attention All Military Personnel"—an eloquent appeal to soldiers to defect—was distributed at
induction centers and military bases: "When the South Vietnamese
people see you in your foreign uniform, they think of you as *their*
enemy. You are the ones bombing their towns. They don't know
whether you're a draftee or a volunteer, whether you're for the war or
against it; but they're not taking any chances either."

In November 1965, Norman Morrison, a Quaker deeply moved by
the self-immolating Buddhists of South Vietnam, set himself on fire in
front of the Pentagon and died. Dead, he became an iconographic figure
in North Vietnam.

At the close of 1965, socialist intellectuals of the Old Left, including Irving Howe, Michael Harrington, Bayard Rustin, and Lewis Coser, signed a statement. Their intention was "to end a cruel and futile war, not to give explicit or covert political support to the Vietcong"; such a declaration was imperative if they were to deserve the support of large numbers of Americans. They demanded an immediate end to the bombing of the North; a declaration of American readiness to negotiate with the NLF; a negotiated cease-fire; and self-determination for the South Vietnamese without the interference of foreign troops. The intellectuals of the Old Left thus subscribed to America's *de facto* division of Vietnam into two political entities, North and South, even though such a division had no historical foundation and had been expressly rejected in the Geneva Agreement. Indeed, Irving Howe admitted elsewhere that "the Vietcong rests upon very considerable indigenous support"; the United States was "trying to act in the name of a South Vietnamese nation which has all but crumbled and now consists of little more than a military apparatus. . . ." (He may have meant *state,* not *nation.* A nation is its people.)

But the anti-Communist fixation survived, and in April 1967 SANE, a pressure group dedicated to nuclear arms reduction, refused to support the Spring Mobilization (the ad hoc coalition responsible for antiwar agitation through the late sixties) on the ground that it was anti-American, and it refused to pin equal responsibility for the war on Hanoi. Dr. Benjamin Spock, a figure totally alien to communism, registered his protest by resigning as co-chairman of SANE.

By 1967, the American New Left was receiving welcome moral support from European intellectuals and students (the first British university teach-ins on Vietnam, at the London School of Economics and at Oxford, had taken place in the summer of 1965). No European troops were despatched to Vietnam, but the governments of NATO gave Washington loyal support throughout the war. That a Labour government should condone "genocide" (a much-used term) with scarcely a murmur of dissent from its backbench MPs angered the young and sharpened their contempt for the reformist Left. From 1966, the German Social Democratic Party was the prisoner of a pro-American Grand Coalition in Bonn; as foreign minister in the government of Chancellor Kurt Kiesinger, Willy Brandt's position was indistinguishable from that of the British prime minister, Harold Wilson. Even Charles de Gaulle, who had tried to reconvene the Geneva Conference in 1965, and sent NATO packing from France, refused to allow the International War Crimes Tribunal, sponsored by Bertrand Russell and Jean-Paul Sartre, to hold its hearings in Paris. Wilson had already refused visas to foreign members of the tribunal.

Bertrand Russell, who had publicly torn up his Labour Party card, condemned, "the nauseous opportunism of Wilson and [Foreign Secretary] Brown." The government retaliated by refusing an entry permit to Ralph Schoenmann, the young American who served as Russell's private secretary and coordinator of the International War Crimes Tribunal. Schoenmann slipped back into Britain but was arrested in Hyde Park on June 27, 1968 and was deported. When Russell died in February 1970, Prime Minister Wilson called him, "the British Voltaire." Voltaire was in the air; de Gaulle had recently refused to sanction Sartre's arrest on the grounds that, "One doesn't imprison Voltaire." Yet the two "Voltaires" had been prevented from inviting foreigners of like mind and kindred spirit to London and Paris.

Russell launched the tribunal in November 1966: "We do not represent any state power, nor can we compel the policy makers responsible for crimes against the people of Vietnam to stand accused before us. We lack *force majeure.*" Ninety-three years old, the philosopher inserted an autobiographical note: "I have lived through the Dreyfus case and been party to the investigation of the crimes committed by King Leopold in the Congo. I can recall many wars. . . . In my own experience I cannot discover a situation quite comparable [to Vietnam]. I cannot recall a people so tormented, yet so devoid of the failings of their tormentors. I do not know any other conflict in which the disparity in physical power was so vast." Russell financed his Peace Foundation and the tribunal by publishing successive volumes of his best-selling *Autobiography.* Volume 2, covering the years 1914–44, appeared in April 1968; volume 3 (1944–67), in May 1969.

The tribunal* convened in full session in the Folkets Hus, Stockholm, in May 1967, under a glare of television lights. Russell himself, too old to attend, served as honorary president, Jean-Paul Sartre as executive president, Vladimir Dedijer as chairman and president of sessions. American members of the tribunal were only four: the writer James Baldwin, the black radical Stokely Carmichael, the veteran pacifist organizer David Dellinger, and Carl Oglesby, writer and past president of SDS. (Other Americans, like Professor Gabriel Kolko, served as expert witnesses.) Sartre, who had taken a leading role in protests against French brutality in Algeria, complained that the principles laid down at Nuremberg had been allowed to vanish "into thin air." For thirty years, the Third World had struggled for freedom against the victors of 1945, yet no one had applied the Nuremberg principles. The War Crimes Tribunal, argued Sartre, derived its legality

*The International War Crimes Tribunal consisted of three officers and twenty-three members from Germany, Sweden, Turkey, Italy, France, Mexico, Britain, Yugoslavia, the Philippines, Cuba, Pakistan, Japan, and the United States. Except for Cuba, the Communist world was not represented.

"from both its absolute powerlessness and its universality." Despite an invitation to the United States government to submit its own evidence and witnesses, there was no response, apart from a disparaging personal reference to Russell by Secretary of State Dean Rusk.

After hearing evidence for a week, the eleven members of the tribunal present and voting were unanimous: "We find the government and armed forces of the United States are guilty of the deliberate, systematic and large-scale bombardment of civilian targets, including civilian populations, dwellings, villages, dams, dikes, medical establishments, leper colonies, schools, churches, pagodas." The tribunal also concluded unanimously that the United States was guilty of genocide, that its treatment of prisoners contravened the Geneva Convention, and that it had used weapons, including napalm, prohibited by the laws of war. Sartre said: "Here, in the shadowy and robot-like souls of the soldiers, we find the truth about the war in Vietnam: it matches all of Hitler's declarations. He killed the Jews because they were Jews. The armed forces of the United States torture and kill men, women and children in Vietnam *because they are Vietnamese.* . . . This is their way of enduring the genocidal situation in which their government has put them." Foreign intellectuals visiting the United States reinforced the abhorrence increasingly felt by American students. In February 1968, the German writer Hans Magnus Enzensberger abandoned his fellowship at Wesleyan University in Connecticut, in protest against American global policy. Conor Cruise O'Brien, the Irish incumbent of the Schweitzer Chair of Humanities at New York University, spoke from many platforms: "Dean Rusk likes to talk about Chinese aggression but the hundreds of thousands of foreign troops now laying waste in Vietnam are neither Chinese nor Russian. They are the troops of the United States and her allies. The task they are attempting is the subjugation of the national resistance of a peasant country, through the fullest possible application of the intellectual, scientific, industrial and military resources of the wealthiest country in the world."

By 1967, the antiwar movement was increasingly devoted to the armed struggle of the National Liberation Front. Vietcong flags abounded in street demonstrations, and the joys of sloganeering had buried subtler, more humane perceptions. The Tet offensive of January 1968 brought the war cries—"Ho-Ho-Ho Chi Minh!"—to a new pitch. David Dellinger, editor of *Liberation* and a pacifist prisoner of conscience during World War II, hailed the "heroic forces" of the NLF, while even the radical historian Staughton Lynd, returning from North Vietnam, argued that his commitment to nonviolence was compatible with support for the "just war" waged by the Vietcong.

Nigel Young, of the School of Peace Studies at Britain's University of Bradford, and a committed pacifist, lamented the new war cries: "Yet it is a tragic irony that . . . the Resistance failed to make stronger trans-national links with those resisters in Vietnam closest to them in spirit and action, e.g., the young, militant and neutralist Buddhists, often monks, using nonviolent techniques against successive Saigon regimes. Calling for immediate ceasefire, the 'Third Way' monks, nuns and social workers encouraged draft resistance against both armies, refusing to fight themselves and sheltering thousands of deserters." As a consequence they suffered the destruction of pagodas, assassination, execution, or imprisonment.

The New Left conspicuously ignored abundant evidence that the Communist forces in Vietnam were increasingly practicing forms of conventional warfare, including artillery bombardments of towns, which put victory at 100 on the scale of priorities and the sparing of human life at 0. The style of the Tet offensive in January–February 1968 left no room for doubt, but doubt is an intolerable burden in the knapsack of campaigning soldiers and political militants alike.

Visiting South Vietnam was as easy as vacationing in Japan and generally no more dangerous, but no more than fifty Americans had reached Hanoi by mid-1968. Tom Hayden and Staughton Lynd had blazed the trail in 1965, but the North Vietnamese by no means confined their invitations to ultraradicals, preferring liberal intellectuals who enjoyed a wider constituency of influence. Foreign guests were accommodated in the Thong Nhat Hotel and got what was known as "the tour"—a round of formal interviews and visits to the villages in a motorized procession. The tight controls (and the embarrassingly luxurious meals) which visiting radicals experienced caused some resentment; Susan Sontag would have liked to walk, or even bicycle, around Hanoi, but two Volgas were always on hand to transport her down the street.

Many of the visitors were sensitive to the difference between traveling and fellow traveling; between a decent sympathy and gullibility. One difficulty encountered was language itself—not the foreign *langue,* but the stereotyped *langage,* the prefabricated phrases with which the Vietnamese Communists welded together their steel sentences. Sontag, who flew to Hanoi in May 1968, soon found herself referring to the Saigon army as the "puppet troops"—but she balked at "the socialist camp." Her traveling companion, Andrew Kopkind, also wondered at what point to inject his own skepticism, as when the North Vietnamese insisted they had not deployed any troops south of the border (apart from southern-born Viet Minh, who had come north after the Geneva accords but subsequently returned to fight for the NLF).

The black American writer Julius Lester was beset by no such inhibitions when he reached Hanoi: "To be in a country and not to be surrounded by white people. What a joy. . . . In Vietnam I felt completely free for the first time in my life . . . their gentleness was mine, and their enemy was mine." Father Daniel Berrigan, SJ, who arrived in Hanoi shortly after the Tet offensive with the mission of bringing home three captured American pilots, experienced a poet's enchantment: "a dreamlike trance seemed to lie gently upon people and trees and animals." It struck Berrigan that the American ghetto and the Hanoi bombings were aspects of a single enterprise—"a total war in both cases." Bracketing Ho Chi Minh with the saints and martyrs of the Roman Catholic Church, he found North Vietnamese society suffused with a "naïve faith in human goodness."

By 1967–68, the television networks were drenching the living rooms of America with coverage of the war. NBC and CBS were each reported to be spending $2 million a year on Vietnam. Scenes of combat were doctored to exclude what was visually unbearable (a GI with his leg shot away, screaming obscenities at the medic, pleading to be shot) and morally awkward (the torturing of prisoners, the napalming of villages, the concentration camps of the pacification program). There were occasional moments of truth: Walter Cronkite showed a CBS film of American soldiers cutting off the ears of dead Vietcong as souvenirs; CBS also broadcast Morley Safer's report of marines setting fire to huts with cigarette lighters. Angered, the Pentagon tried to pressure CBS into withdrawing this Canadian reporter from Vietnam.

The radical filmmakers had to be content with college and peace-group audiences. Emile de Antonio (director of *Point of Order* and *Rush to Judgment*) compiled an indictment of American policy out of documentary footage and interviews for *In the Year of the Pig*. But the kind of investigative reporting preferred by the networks was Bernard Kalb's *Vietcong* (CBS), demonstrating the enemy's ruthless tactics during the Tet offensive. Meanwhile, on wider screens, John Wayne gave mainstream America *The Green Berets* (1968), in which Wayne dealt the "Commies" some of their own medicine, and more, while celebrating American heroism and compassion (a small, Asiatic child lifted in his strong, caring arms). Wayne himself had the distinction of never having served a day in the armed forces.

The most influential television commentators either supported administration policy (as did Chet Huntley) or concealed their disillusionment. David Brinkley told *TV Guide* in June 1967 that the war was a mistake and America should get out, but he did not repeat this view on screen. In May 1967, the "Huntley-Brinkley Report" began with Brinkley's announcing that Martin Luther King, Jr., had alienated other civil rights leaders by denouncing the war; the program then went on to "interview" Hubert Humphrey, who sorrowfully chastised King without intervention from any audible "interviewer."

JAPAN

TOKYO, January 19, 1968—Japanese students break into the foreign ministry, hurling stones through windows, in a climactic demonstration against the visit of the U.S.S. *Enterprise* and an American military hospital for soldiers wounded in Vietnam.

The Japanese student movement had led the world in the tactics of mass confrontation and synchronized disruption in an industrialized country, although its direct impact on American and European students owed more to television coverage than to intellectual bonding. By January 1968, the Vietnam War had become the major issue in Japan. In the course of a week some three hundred students, mainly from the "Trotskyist" Sampa faction of Zengakuren, were arrested. The Peace for Vietnam Committee (Baheiren) broadcast megaphone appeals to the crew of the *Enterprise,* berthed in Sasebo Harbor, to desert.

Preparations for combat were always thorough: sharp-edged sticks, bags of stones, motorcycle helmets, gas masks—and the young women organized into first-aid squads. On the appointed day the two armies met as if by mutual agreement at a strategic street intersection where demonstrations were forbidden. The television cameras were waiting; the fighting began at precisely the hour already announced on the newscasts. Students and police phalanxes then engaged in close combat like extras in a medieval film by Kurosawa. The year 1967–68 was one of mounting turmoil: repeated riots, ammunition trains blocked, television programs dominated by the students, demonstrations in front of the prime minister's office, pitched battles at American bases. In mid-March, five hundred Tokyo high school students demonstrated against the Vietnam War and the new U.S. Army Field Hospital at Oji.

Their violence notwithstanding, the demonstrating students received support from the Socialist and Communist parties, both of which not only opposed visits by American nuclear warships but also maintained local "struggle" headquarters at Sasebo Naval Base. In mid-March, a major debate took place in the House of Representatives as to whether the Antisubversive Activities Law should be employed against the demonstrators. In April, the National Public Safety Commission called for severe measures.

Formed in 1948, Zengakuren (All-Japan Federation of Student

Self-Government Associations) had been originally dominated by the pro-Soviet, "revisionist," Communist Party (JPC), but had moved sharply to the left from the mid-fifties, simultaneously suffering sectarian splintering; by 1968 at least a dozen radical factions were engaged in open competition. To sort them out is the historian's burden; the casual reader is unlikely to shoulder it.

Numerically dominant but not always able to set the pace was the pro-Communist faction of Zengakuren, known as Minsei (Democratic Youth League). It controlled 65 percent of Zengakuren's 519 Student Self-Government Associations (to which 61 percent of Japan's 1.4 million students belonged). Cautious in its tactics, it was fiercely and scornfully challenged by at least six left-wing anti-Communist student groups, pride of place belonging to Sampa Rengo (Three-Faction Alliance) and Kakumaru (Japan Marxist Student League). The Marxist Sampa, led by its fast-talking chairman Katsuyuki Akiyama, controlled 20 percent of Zengakuren's associations; Kakumaru, only 6 percent.

However, such was the pugnacious factionalism of the Japanese student Left, that by early July 1968 Sampa Rengo itself was divided in four directions, thus:

- Chukaku—(white helmet), strong in Hosei University, Yokohama National University, and the University of Tokyo Institute of Technology. Main enemy: "Japanese imperialism." Tactics: All-out armed clashes with the police whenever possible. Leader: The above-mentioned Katsuyuki Akiyama.
- Shagakudo—(red helmet), centered on the private universities of Tokyo and Kansai, committed to "worldwide proletarian revolution." Tactics: Seizure of university buildings.
- Shaseido (blue helmet); quite similar to Shagakudo.
- Kakumuru (white helmet with "Z"). Aim: A revolutionary socialist Japan.

All of these groups were furiously anti-American and opposed to the U.S. base on Okinawa. But, when Chukaku invited the other factions to a national convention of reconciliation on July 15, 1968, two of the subfactions of Shagakudo (one of them affiliated with the Trotskyist Fourth International) refused to attend. As the year 1968 progressed, the left-wing factions displayed as much zeal for fighting one another as for assaulting the police. As we shall see in a later chapter, this was particularly in evidence on the campus of the University of Tokyo.

According to a resident journalist, funds came in from "nostalgic businessmen who used to be Zengakuren themselves" and from companies hoping to be involved in the lucrative Japanese trade with China.

Many of the larger firms made special attempts to recruit radical students, who often proved to be "aggressive salesmen and good organizers." But there is also evidence pointing in the opposite—and more obvious—direction. In October 1968—following massive violence against government buildings and Tokyo's busiest railway station, Shinjuku, accompanied by anti-American slogans and chants of praise to Che Guevara, Mao Tse-tung, and Ho Chi Minh—the students received a warning from big business. On November 10, the voice of the corporations was heard: Those arrested during riots would not be hired. The Kawasaki Heavy Industry Company had already rescinded offers of employment to students who had been arrested.

Despite the dramatic impact of the radical student riots, the vast majority of Japanese students were indifferent or hostile. Miniskirts had come to Tokyo, couples now embraced in public, gigs were played in psychedelic underground dance halls, couples roared off for the weekend in sports cars or on motorbikes. Electric guitars, pinball, and bowling—even hippie decadence—exercised a greater fascination than did American imperialism. So, also, did the prospect of a good job with Sony or Honda. Not only would Japanese capitalism survive, but the Liberal Democratic Party would maintain its hegemony indefinitely.

During the early part of 1968 the liberal wing of the American antiwar movement was temporarily captivated by the rainbow of electoral politics; the McCarthy and Kennedy campaigns briefly offered hope of a more enlightened White House. The New Left fought the illusion all the way to the Democratic National Convention in August. But what is meant by the "New Left"?

3

THE NEW POLITICS
OF THE YOUNG

"The young Trotskyists, Maoists, and Black Panthers also shared the wider *zeitgeist* of the New Left, the romantic admiration for Che Guevara and the guerrilla insurgent…"

NEW LEFT, OLD LEFT

What was the "New Left"—and what the "Old Left"? Unlike Whigs and Tories, Democrats and Republicans (or Jonathan Swift's High Heels and Low Heels), the answer is not to be found in a formal allegiance. The distinction between the New and Old Lefts was one of outlook, temperament, and style. Generation also played a part—the idealistic exuberance of youth, the crusted caution of middle age—but many individuals were able to cross that frontier.

The Old Left was by no means an alliance of sympathetic parties. Democratic Socialists and Communists with common memories of the 1930s and the Cold War were habitually locked in mutual enmity; the hostility between Stalinists and Trotskyists was legendary. Within the New Left, too, there were dramatic divergences. A gentle "flower-power" girl appealing to soldiers to "make love not war" bore little affinity to a hardened Weatherman engaged in militaristic confrontations with the police or in planting bombs.

Where, then, resided the frontiers between the Old and New Lefts? The Old Left, whether revolutionary or reformist, accepted the necessity of political parties, each competing with the others for control of the State. Adversarial politics inevitably involved leadership, hierarchy, discipline. The most fundamental characteristic of the New Left was its libertarian distrust of state power, parties, competition, leadership, bureaucracies, and, finally, representative government.

The New Left demanded "participatory democracy," not only in the universities (where its influence was most conspicuous), but in the wider society as well. This vision, part anarchist, part Rousseauesque, was generally derided by the Old Left as both aggravatingly utopian and a free ride for charismatic orators seeking power without responsibility.

The Old Left accepted that the modern State, with its corporate economy, inescapably concentrates power at the center. Not only the

Bolsheviks but the Western European Communists and Socialists amalgamated expropriated capitalist enterprises into *nationalized* industries administered by governments through large bureaucracies. The New Left rejected political and economic concentrations of power in favor of a decentralized society with power vested at a local level among producers, community associations, and student unions. A key phrase during the French events of May and June 1968 was *auto-gestion,* or self-management. It was a "cellular" movement, whereas the Old Left stressed the primacy of the whole over the parts.

The Old Left issued plans, programs, and manifestos. Each of its parties offered codified remedies (of which the most important was "vote for us"); the New Left laid more emphasis on spontaneity, on discovering solutions through direct experience and action—the parents of perception.

The Old Left, whether Leninist or Social Democratic, tended to view society in terms of class conflict (though the reformist wing of social democracy and the American labor unions were already converted to redistribution of wealth within a new social consensus). The European New Left displayed a high level of class consciousness, but the movement as a whole was more passionately concerned about racial discrimination and the exploitation of the Third World—about which white working-class attitudes varied from indifference to conservatism. The New Left remained a middle-class movement that made no headway within the trade unions, the backbone of the old Communist, Socialist, and Labour parties.

Jürgen Habermas noted that student protesters were almost exclusively bourgeois youth, representing neither the working class, nor the blacks, nor the underdeveloped countries, yet eager to act on their behalf. They set no store by bourgeois rights and constitutions. As for the achievements of the past, the radical students dismissed them as models of integration, which had absorbed only too effectively all oppositional forces. "So we are confronted here with the first bourgeois revolt against the principles of a bourgeois society that is almost successfully functioning according to its own standards."

The young radicals regarded the Third World not only with concern, but also with sentimental reverence. When Gregory Calvert, national secretary of SDS, addressed its Princeton Conference in February 1967, he began with a story about Guatemalan guerrillas who, on entering a village, did not teach Mao, or anti-imperialism, or dialectical materialism, but rather brought all the people together. After each guerrilla fighter had testified about his own life and longings, the villagers were encouraged to do the same and to discover their common humanity. (Here Calvert quoted Sartre.) Thus Third World liberation movements were pictured as mirrors of the humane, nondogmatic, existential New Left, versed in the post-Brechtian theatre of therapy and happening. It was a distorted view, but politics can never encompass the totality of truth, only discern what most urgently needs to be done and who most urgently deserves support. It was in this respect that the New Left's vision was most penetrating.

The Old Left fully accepted industrial and technological progress: more consumer goods for everyone, and the deadening assembly lines which produced them. Its quarrel was with "exploitation" rather than "alienation." The Blakean, pastoral, ecological, media-conscious counterculture of the New Left, by contrast, was at war with a corporate technology enslaving human beings to the cycle of production and consumption: "the system." Not only Madison Avenue but also the dominant academic ideology were held guilty of manipulating popular consciousness into acquiescence. "Alienation" was the crucial term in the vocabulary of the New Left.

For the Old Left, politics was a part of life strictly bounded by trade union meetings, occasional demonstrations, sending small checks to good causes. It was "out there" rather than "in here." Normally politics did not extend to the family, to private life; returning home, the worker resumed his role as patriarch. New Left politics were "existential" and directly related to the individual's immediate environment, whether factory, college, or ghetto—here and now. (Even so, it was rampantly male chauvinist.)

Socialists of the Old Left rarely challenged the paternalism of the schools and universities they attended, the moral right of administrators and faculty to lay down the law on curriculum, examinations, and rules for personal conduct. Nor did they question competition at the service of personal ambition. They demanded "equality of opportunity," the great legacy of the universal bourgeois revolution. The most far-reaching innovation of the New Left was to challenge these time-honored hierarchies. For the Old Left, the existence of elites—whether based on power or skills—was a fact of life. For the New Left, it was an unacceptable fact of corporate society: power and privilege invariably corrupt. Hence the influence of C. Wright Mills's books, *New Men of Power, The Power Elite,* and *Listen, Yankee.* The road to liberation was interpreted as the long march through the institutions.

Despite its insurrectionary phase and its guerrilla image, the New Left was essentially a gradualist movement employing theatrical shock tactics to turn tigers into paper tigers. The New Left enveloped the Pentagon and burned the Paris Bourse, but the point of storming the presidential palace (wherever) was merely to be seen smoking the old man's cigars.

The Old Left was not without passion (and anger), but held that the mind must govern the heart. Many commentators have argued that the New Left was "antirational," Sorelian, bonded to myth. This is a mistake. The New Left must be divided between its intensely intellectual platoons—preponderant in Europe—and the apostles of instinct and feeling, whose sacramental playground was America, where the prevailing mood came closer to the spirit of "witness" more commonly associated with committed religious communities.

The Old Left was typically conventional in its life-style and social attitudes. Its adherents conducted themselves in a socially respectable manner and had long since abandoned any thought of an alternative culture. The New Left's relaxed, permissive attitude to sex and drugs often offended the adult Old Left, who in turn seemed "square," "hung up," and therefore repressive to the young. Happenings, ensemble theatre, audience participation, underground papers, and rock concerts remained alien terrain to the Old Left throughout the sixties.

Despite the common sensibility joining the New Left to the counterculture, they were by no means identical. Between the "politicos" and the hippies there was tension, even animosity. Many of the militant students of 1968 who occupied universities and confronted the police in the streets wore short hair and would rather have swallowed castor oil than LSD. The role of young Trotskyists and Maoists within the New Left complicated the libertarian image, for they had inherited the historical claim of the Marxist vanguard parties to seize centralized state power. The Black Panthers in America were likewise more Leninist than libertarian. Why, then, accord Maoists, Trotskyists, and Black Panthers a place within the New Left? A common composite enemy— the Vietnam War, racism, global imperialism—was the prime unifying force, leading to shared demonstrations and occupations (though sometimes not). The young Trotskyists, Maoists, and Black Panthers also shared the wider *zeitgeist* of the New Left, the romantic admiration for Che Guevara and the guerrilla insurgent, the communal spirit, the willingness to "do it here and now" and to break the law, bait the police, and challenge authority at every opportunity.

The alteration of attitudes was particularly dramatic in America. The journalist Jack Newfield recalled student life at Hunter College in the fifties, when politics involved running for student council on an innocuous platform, and dissent implied "a vague, emotional yearning for Adlai Stevenson." The life pattern that the campus rebels of the sixties recoiled from in disgust had been "deified" by Newfield's generation: "Marry well and early, don't be a troublemaker, start a career in daddy's business or in a large corporation, and save up for a split-level home in the lily-white suburbs. . . ." To receive college loans, they signed loyalty oaths without complaint.

The first phase of the New Left, from 1960 to 1965, really belonged to America alone, despite the marginal influence of the post-1956 intellectual "New Left" in Britain and of the British Campaign for Nuclear Disarmament, a movement of the Old Left led by clergymen and Labour MPs of the Tribune Group, with many youthful followers and with a brief civil-disobedience component, the Committee of 100. The early American New Left, inspired by the Cuban revolution and deeply concerned about atomic weapons, took shape mainly in the segregationist states of the South, where small groups of dedicated white activists arrived to support black students' demands for desegregation of lunch counters and bus stations, the right to vote, and genuine equality before the law. It was essentially a movement of personal commitment, of young idealists operating outside the political machines and more influenced by Albert Camus's existential humanism than by Jean-Paul Sartre's socialist ideology. The mood was warm, generous, self-sacrificial; it lacked the rancorous tone, the spirit of enmity characteristic not only of European political crusades but also of the New Left in its final confrontation, from 1967 to 1969, with imperial "Amerika."

The nuclear issue was (and remains) vitally important on its own account. But it also drew attention to the irrationality of advanced technocratic systems committed to rational social engineering. As Theodore Roszak commented in *The Making of a Counter Culture,* all the automobiles and television sets were one minute from midnight all the time. The debate about nuclear weapons broke the seal of the stifling Cold War consensus of the fifties and subverted Daniel Bell's "end of ideology" (which denotes a fundamentally conflict-free society cemented by consensus about goals and values, intellectually dominated by pragmatic arguments among problem-solving experts). In Roszak's words, men and women awoke in rebellion against "an evil which is not defined by the mere facts of the bomb, but by the total ethos of the bomb, in which our politics, our public morality, our economic life, our intellectual endeavor are now embedded with the wealth of ingenious rationalization." Whether one agrees with him or not, this perception was crucial to the emergent New Left.

The most influential voice in the new philosophy of alienation belonged, perhaps paradoxically, to a veteran Marxist of the Frankfurt school who had emigrated to the United States, Herbert Marcuse. The word "influential," however, begs several questions. Marcuse's abstract formulations were less accessible than, for example, the urgent, fact-intensive polemics of C. Wright Mills, and mainly appealed to an intellectual elite versed in Marxian dialectics, particularly in Germany.

In *Eros and Civilization* (1955), and more intensively in *One-Dimensional Man* (1964), Marcuse had argued that man could avoid the fate of a Welfare-through-Warfare state only by reconstructing the productive apparatus without the repressed asceticism that provided the basis for a system of domination. The erotic energy of the life instincts could not be freed under the dehumanizing conditions of profitable affluence. Marcuse rejected Freud's insistence on an inherent conflict between the reality principle and the pleasure principle, offering instead the perspective of a nonrepressive sublimation, allowing the pleasure principle to liberate man from the performance principle (non-stop automated work) and to discover himself as both subject and object of his needs and desires. (On the other hand, Marcuse saw no hope in the pleasure principles and unbridled libido of the new Bohemia; beatniks, hipsters, and hippies had become the pathetic refuge of a deformed humanity. Existentialism and Zen were harmless revolts, easily assimilated.)

Marcuse's most provocative thesis dismissed pluralistic capitalist democracy as a sham, a system of false needs and illusory freedoms designed not only to turn people into mere commodity producers but, further, to induce them to recognize themselves as commodities. He also poured scorn on the empiricism and positivism of bourgeois social theory, which had abandoned the critical tradition in its abject eagerness to serve the system's values by presenting man's domination of nature as inseparable from man's domination of man ("progress," "experts," "representative government"). Every alternative perspective had been dismissed as utopian, totalitarian, or inconsistent with the "facts." But these "facts" were merely those understood by robots. Contemporary ideology thus ensured that the cycle of production and consumption reproduced political domination and perpetuated man's alienation from his own potential.

SDS

Founded in 1960, Students for a Democratic Society (SDS) was originally the renamed student section of the League for Industrial Democracy. Its first convention was not held until June 1962, when SDS articulated its philosophy through the marvelous Port Huron Statement: "We are people of this generation, bred in at least modest comfort, housed now in universities, looking uncomfortably at the world we inherit. . . . Many of us began maturing in complacency." But then came awareness of degradation in the South and "the enclosing fact of the Cold War, symbolized by the presence of the Bomb. . . ."

The Port Huron Statement expressed in embryo most of the ideas and attitudes that were to characterize SDS and the New Left throughout the sixties. It attacked nuclear deterrence theory; capitalism and the paternalistic welfare state; the military-industrial complex; the university *in loco parentis;* the Soviet Union because of its "total suppression of organized opposition"; and America's support of right-wing dictatorships.

Here was the beginning of the search for a synthesis of individual idealism and mass activity, but without the fetters of a programmatic orthodoxy. The Movement was reaching out for a "third way"; as the historian Staughton Lynd expressed it, "So long as revolution is pictured as a violent insurrection it seems to me both distasteful and unreal. The traditional alternative, the Social Democratic vision of electing more and more radical legislators until power passes peacefully to the Left, seems equally illusory." What Lynd proposed was a series of challenges to the system at its morally most vulnerable points: refusals of the heart, mind, and body, which should remain nonviolent but not necessarily legal.

In the mid-sixties occurred a second phase of American New Left activity, based on community projects in the North and the demand for free speech in the universities. This may prove to be the most enduring legacy of the New Left and the counterculture: the project of an "alternative" society composed of grassroots, "counter institutions" designed both to challenge the bureaucratic structures of official society and to endow common people with an awakening sense of their own capacity.

The European New Left surfaced in the mid-sixties as the horror of the Vietnam War became a global issue. Paradoxically, the accession to power, or shared power, of social democracy in Britain, Germany, and Italy after a decade and a half of uninterrupted conservative governance only accelerated the radicalization of the young. The new growth was fertilized by a powerful chemical—a sense of betrayal. The Marxian critique of capitalism had yielded to the revisionism of social democrats, who redefined socialism as a "welfare state" founded on a capitalist "mixed economy" in which the public sector served as a kind of hospital for sick or nonprofitable industries and services. This third and final period of the New Left, the *Götterdämmerung,* was intensely ideological, confrontational, and violent; waves of protest swept across the advanced countries, each intensely conscious of its solidarity with the others. Indeed, a new "International" was born among students. It is by the street scenes and campus occupations of 1967–69 that the New Left is remembered—and rejected—by the population at large.

Friction, sometimes enmity, characterized the New Left's relationship with the Old throughout the sixties. As the decade progressed, fraternal arguments gave way to fratricidal knifeplay: In Britain, the New Left and the Wilson government; in Germany, the SDS and the Social Democratic Party within the coalition government; in France, Cohn-Bendit and the Communists; in Italy, the rioting students and Pietro Nenni. Only where pluralistic democracy had not yet been achieved—in Czechoslovakia, Poland, Yugoslavia, and Spain—did this not occur; the New Left is almost by definition a product of pluralistic democracy.

In America, the quarrel between the Old and New Lefts (which must include not only the beleaguered socialists but also the liberal wing of the Democratic Party, whose role in American political life was analogous to that of social democracy in Europe) had begun early. The Port Huron Statement of 1962 immediately got SDS into hot water with its parent body, the League for Industrial Democracy. Anti-communism was the main bone of contention. The essays and memoirs of Irving Howe, the distinguished literary critic and editor of *Dissent,* provide a sensitive commentary on the long-running battle, as well as a large window onto the mind and sensibility of the Old Left abruptly confronted by the New. No one else wrote so perceptively, yet with such cancerous animosity, about the fatal moat separating two generations of radicals.

Howe was exasperated both by the New Left's "anti-anti-communism" and by its loose, informal, libertarian style. As Howe recalled, several founding figures of SDS came in for a chat with the editorial board of *Dissent:* "At this meeting two generations sat facing each other, fumbling to reach across the spaces of time. We were scarred, they untouched. . . . We had pulled ourselves out of an immigrant working class, an experience not likely to induce romantic views about the poor; they, children of warm liberals and cooled radicals, were hoping to find a way into the lives and wisdom of the oppressed." The young idealists seemed to be presenting "participatory democracy" as an alternative to "representative democracy" rather than as its complement. "We winced." And why, if they were libertarians, did they insist on admiring Castro's Cuba?

Return visits were paid. Attending SDS board meetings, Howe found them "interminable and structureless. . . . In the blur of fraternity nothing was thought through." The ideal community seemed to be "an anarchy of pals, in which anyone dropping in at a meeting could speak as long as they [sic] wished. . . ." Howe didn't like the prevailing cultural styles either: "the wish to shock" and to say "fuck." By the mid-sixties, Howe was complaining that the New Left had merely reversed the blind ultrapatriotism of the 1950s; their anti-Americanism, it seemed to him, went hand in hand with uncritical admiration for Third World nationalist movements of the Communist-authoritarian variety.

In 1966–67, the New Left's rejection of the coalition between socialists and liberal Democrats (recommended by Irving Howe, Michael Harrington, Bayard Rustin, and Norman Thomas as America's way forward) was sharpened by revelations about the Central Intelligence Agency's (CIA) covert funding and penetration of liberal organizations; the National Student Association, the Institute of International Labor Research, the American Newspaper Guild, the National Council of Churches, the Congress for Cultural Freedom, and the London magazine *Encounter* had all been compromised (as was first revealed in the *New York Times* in April 1966, and later, in more detail, by the *Ramparts* issue of March 1967).

Compromised, also, were the liberal intellectuals who had served in the Kennedy administration: John Kenneth Galbraith and Arthur Schlesinger, Jr., did not now deny that they had known about CIA funding of the Congress for Cultural Freedom. The grand old man of American socialism, Norman Thomas, was likewise tarred. The *New York Times* published a letter from Thomas on February 22, 1967, claiming that he had not known where the money for his Institute of International Labor Research was coming from. However, Diana Trilling, the literary critic and essayist, recalled a meeting of the executive board of the American Committee for Cultural Freedom, when its chairman, the same Norman Thomas, reported insolvency and suggested that he should "phone Allen." He did, returning with the news that a check for $1,000 would be mailed the next morning. They all knew that "Allen" was Allen Dulles, director of the CIA: "None of us, myself included, protested," reflected Trilling. She was unrepentant.

The CIA revelations brought the New Left a fringe of fellow travelers from the ranks of the middle-aged intellectuals who felt themselves to have been cruelly duped. Some of them hauled stiffening limbs through the windows of occupied universities in search of rejuvenation. Stephen Spender, who had indignantly resigned as co-editor of *Encounter*, found himself in President Grayson Kirk's occupied office at Columbia. Dwight Macdonald, a prominent New York intellectual and a regular contributor to *Encounter*, hurried up to Columbia on news of the insurrection in April 1968. "I've never been in or near a revolution before," he reported. "I guess I like them. There was an atmosphere of exhilaration, excitement. . . ." Once a Trotskyist, he saw Mathematics Hall as "the Smolny Institute of the revolution. . . ."

Irving Howe regarded Herbert Marcuse and other professorial

friends of the New Left as bandwaggoners flattered by juvenile applause. Professor Edward Shils, of the University of Chicago, was equally contemptuous of the "middle-aged courtiers who offer their legitimatory services. . . . From Sartre and Marcuse to Paul Goodman and Dwight Macdonald, they provide agreeable but unsought applause." The angry divide separating the Cold War generation from the New Left persisted. Diana Trilling, although increasingly convinced that the Vietnam War was a tragic mistake, had to ask herself why she had taken part in no march or demonstration. The answer was obvious: The protest movement had been preempted by anti-Americanism, by those who talked of genocidal imperialism, "as if America were uniquely greedy and rapacious among nations." She added: "I will not march under the flag of the Viet Cong, and where has there been a protest against American error under an American flag?" The poet Robert Lowell (imprisoned during World War II as a conscientious objector) damned her as a "housekeeping goddess of reason, preferring the confines of her mind to experience, and pronouncing on the confusion of the crowd. . . ." She seemed to him "more preoccupied with the little violence of the student uprisings than with the great violence of the nation at war."

As the decade progressed and the New Left embarked on dramatic acts of insurrection, Irving Howe's temper burned on a shorter fuse. Theatrical violence had nothing to do with creating a better America, so why did they do it? One reason, he suspected, was that the New Left was so utterly American. "It took to the arts of publicity like Tom Sawyer to games of deceit, offering the mass media the verbal, sometimes actual violence on which it dotes." Himself a born polemicist with a Talmudic gift for disputation, Howe began to feel the scars of too many arrows. There was something peculiarly wounding in the New Left attacks on older liberals and radicals. "They wanted to deny our past, annul our history, wipe out our integrity, and not as people mistaken or even pusillanimous but as people who were 'finished,' 'used up.' " In 1968, finding himself on a platform at the University of Kansas with the SDS leader he increasingly distrusted, Tom Hayden, Howe "taunted" [his word] Hayden about the recent Soviet invasion of Czechoslovakia. "And he says he isn't prepared to condemn the Russians since there may well be 'counter-revolutionaries' among the Czechs. We spar viciously." The audience was mainly with Hayden.

Howe felt the spirit of fraternity yielding to dogmatism and a romantic-nihilistic fascination with the "politics of the deed." The New Left had caught the habit of breaking up meetings and hobbling speakers they disapproved of. On December 5, 1968, for example, members of SDS closed down two meetings at the Loeb Student Center of New York University, wrapping South Vietnam's representative to the United Nations in a Nazi flag and pouring water over his head, then invading the platform from which James Reston was addressing an audience of five hundred and tearing up his notes. Howe himself suffered verbal abuse on campus; in his bitter retrospective judgment, the movement "burned itself out in the ecstasy of its own delusions."

Herbert Marcuse did not agree. On December 4, 1968, he spoke at a meeting in New York to celebrate the twentieth anniversary of the Marxist monthly, the *Guardian*. Although the majority of Americans and Europeans remained content with the prevailing system and were unaware of their own self-alienation, Marcuse believed that the integration of the working class would not continue indefinitely. The New Left must work patiently, at the local level, to demonstrate what libertarian socialism meant in practice, setting itself the "superhuman" task of combating the false consciousness fostered by the media monopolies. "I believe," he concluded, "that the New Left today is the only hope we have." Marcuse's *Essay on Liberation,* published in 1969, marked a startling change of emphasis (which further angered the liberals). He now embraced the youth culture as the authentic agency of change and applauded the revolutionary potential not only of its politics but also of its life-style. In the context of the Great Refusal, obscenities ruptured the false definitions of Establishment language, while catchphrases such as "flower power" and "black is beautiful" reversed traditional symbolic values: ". . . the exotic belligerency in the songs of protest; the sensuousness of long hair, of the body unsoiled by plastic cleanliness. . . ." Humor was now a revolutionary weapon.

CUBA, SÍ

The Havana Cultural Congress of January 1968 lasted for two weeks and attracted some four hundred intellectuals from Latin America, Europe, and the United States (despite State Department harassment). After nine years the Cuban revolution continued to exercise its fascination. Boldly defiant of the United States, it had recently given the life of its most admired spirit, Ernesto "Che" Guevara, to the cause of transcontinental revolution. Cuba was also admired for its nonbureaucratic style, for Castro's impassioned rhetoric, its modernist films and bold poster art, lithographs and lino-cuts, its innovative architecture, its Teatro Nacional de Guinol, the vigorous patronage disbursed through La Casa de las Américas. Cuba's exuberant sense of display made a refreshing contrast with the dour puritanism of Moscow and Peking.

In the Third World Exhibition at Havana, old American advertising signs were grouped together, sterile and useless, like items from some twenty-first-century museum. Mickey Mouse and Donald Duck stared up at a grotesque roof mural of Lyndon Johnson creating the world, while elaborate photomontages of GIs in Vietnam blotted out the sun. Some nightclubs and cabarets were functioning, the daiquiris were delicious, the calypso music enchanting. The playwright Arnold Wesker spent the first three months of 1968 in Cuba, directing his play *The Four Seasons* in Spanish. "It was just marvelous. I've never known anything like it. . . ."

The legend of Cuba was inscribed on the heart of the young radicals. It was *the* revolution of its time, and its spirit both inspired and echoed the New Left's own. Cuba had been a client state of the United States since the Spanish-American War of 1898. The ruthless dictatorship of Fulgencio Batista had suited Washington, the sugar-plantation magnates, the owners of the great ranches, and the tourists in search of sunshine, gambling, and prostitution. Yet within a year of taking power, the Castro government was faced with urgent American concern for democratic elections. The reason was clear: Castro had expropriated American-owned land and property on a large scale. In April 1961, a covert, CIA-sponsored military operation, for which President John F. Kennedy took responsibility, came to grief at Playa Givón in the Bay of Pigs.

Three weeks before the Bay of Pigs, Kennedy had announced the Alliance for Progress: "Let us once again awaken our American revolution until it guides the struggles of peoples everywhere." Yet Kennedy granted diplomatic recognition to five of the seven military coups against constitutional regimes that took place in Latin America during his thousand days in office. In March 1965, Lyndon Johnson sent American troops into the Dominican Republic "to prevent a Communist takeover."

The Fair Play for Cuba Committee had been formed in 1960. Visiting authors like Jean-Paul Sartre and C. Wright Mills explained in sympathetic terms the historical dynamics and praxis of the Cuban revolution. Mills's *Listen, Yankee* exercised a profound influence on the young American radicals of the New Left. He depicted the new Cuba as genuinely and urgently committed to the emancipation of illiterate peasants, blacks, women—"the people." Castro's government expropriated the bloated landlords, slashed rents, sent teachers and doctors out of Havana into the countryside, armed the workers and peasantry, and talked of abolishing not only the profit motive but money itself. The Cubans appealed to the New Left because their philosophy seemed to be hurrying in pursuit of their actions. As Norman Mailer noted, the New Left was drawing its political aesthetic from Cuba, first creating the revolution and then learning from it. The future of the revolution existed "in the nerves and cells of the people . . . rather than in the sanctity of the original idea."

Che Guevara told Americans who defied the State Department's ban on visiting Cuba that he would like to become an urban guerrilla in the United States, to fight "in the belly of the beast." Then, in an existential gesture irresistibly appealing to the New Left, he resigned his ministerial posts and committed his fate to the jungles of the Congo and Bolivia. On October 8, 1967, the Bolivian military captured and shot him; a photograph of his corpse flashed around the world, followed by the publication of his war diary. The younger generation had its supreme martyr, its Jesus. No idealized medieval portrait of Christ achieved a greater beauty and serenity than resided in Che's perfect features and dark, lustrous eyes. Posters of Che plastered the walls of a generation: Che alone, Che with Fidel, Che in China, Che playing chess, Che deep-sea fishing with Fidel, Che moving among the Cuban people with long hair and rifle, Che pacing his ministerial office, Che cutting sugarcane, Che orating, Che reading, and Che dead.

Shortly before Guevara's death, the Italian publisher Giangiacomo Feltrinelli flew into La Paz loaded with bank notes, spread out an array of maps in the Hotel Capablanca, and pondered how to rescue two of his authors: Guevara, still at liberty with his dwindling band of guerrillas, and the French intellectual Régis Debray, arrested in April 1967 after spending forty-three days in the mountains with Guevara's guerrillas and now facing a possible death sentence by a military court. The Bertrand Russell Peace Foundation despatched a team of young intellectuals disguised as journalists. One of them, Tariq Ali, explained: "My task was to photograph all the top military officers in Camiri so that we could identify the men in charge of the anti-guerrilla operation." Heady stuff, but easier said than done; as soon as he pulled out his camera, an officer pulled out his revolver.

Other members of the mission, Robin Blackburn and Perry Anderson (of *New Left Review*) did succeed in interviewing Debray in prison, while Russell's secretary, Ralph Schoenmann, attended the young French Marxist's trial, denounced the court procedures, and was deported. After Guevara's death, Debray told the Bolivian court that he shared responsibility with the guerrillas and regretted not having died at Che's side. The revolutionary vanguard-elite recommended in Debray's book *Revolution in the Revolution,* actually ran counter to New

Left libertarianism, but nobody seemed to notice, and Grove Press's paperback edition sold handsomely. Appreciations of Che came from famous pens: John Berger, Italo Calvino, Julio Cortazar, André Gorz, Graham Greene, Robert Lowell, David Mercer, Thomas Merton, Herbert Read, Jean-Paul Sartre (who described Guevara as "the most complete human being of our age"), Jorge Semprun, Alan Sillitoe, Susan Sontag and Peter Weiss, to name a few.

Susan Sontag had visited Cuba for three months in 1960; since then Fidel and Che had been "heroes and cherished models" to her. Sontag found in Cuba a rare symbiosis of political radicalism, avant-garde art, and liberty of artistic expression. While regretting the absence of a free press, she described Cuba as "in some respects the most genuinely democratic country in the world today . . . [a country] astonishingly free of repression," which, unlike previous revolutions, had not begun to consume its own children. (One may dissent. Not all of Castro's 20,000 political prisoners had been henchmen of Batista; Hubert Matos was only one of many who had fought alongside Castro and Guevara for his vision of a democratic Cuba.)

Sontag noticed certain paradoxes involved in the New Left's love affair with Cuba. In "Some Thoughts on the Right Way (for us) to Love the Cuban Revolution," she argued that overdevelopment had driven the American Movement to search for the authentic "self" against public and official values, whereas Bohemianism, long hair, drugs, pornography, and homosexuality were condemned in Cuba as relics of underdevelopment. The Protestant work ethic (careers, competition) was now suspect in the United States, whereas the Cuban voluntary work brigades demanded manual labor of everyone, and Castro constantly exhorted his people to overcome lethargy and unpunctuality. The American Movement distrusted all forms of patriotism, while Cuba proudly paraded its militia and tanks.

So why did the love affair endure? A common enemy was no doubt one factor, but there was also an affinity of style. The Cubans were warm, outgoing, talkative, informal—so unlike the stolid, regimented Eastern Europeans or the chillingly uniform, disturbingly predictable, and seemingly sexless North Vietnamese. To Cuba came the young American idealists of the Venceremos Brigade, cutting sugarcane, engaging in savage existential politics among themselves, and purging racial and sexual guilt (but not always) in the current iconoclastic slang of disillusion and exaggeration; they were refugees from "total fascism."

A succession of black American visitors, from Robert Williams and Leroi Jones to Julius Lester came to Cuba, saw, and were conquered. Sound judgment did not always prevail. "The West says a 'cult of personality' exists in the figures of Mao and Fidel," wrote Lester. "That is not true. Revolutionary consciousness and revolutionary commitment have destroyed the ego in Mao and Fidel, and in that destruction, they as men became free." One could doubt this—and doubt it even more on reading Lester's next line: "Fidel is Cuba. China is Mao. Cuba is Fidel."

4

CHILDREN OF PLEASURE— THE COUNTERCULTURE

"The most notorious prophet of LSD, the great charlatan of the sacramental underground, was Dr. Timothy Leary."

"The coming of the Stones was dreaded by city fathers across Europe..."

MUSIC: FROM FOLK TO ROCK

LONDON, February 1968—As the Tet battles rage in Vietnam, four of the most famous young men in the world board a flight for India to study with the Maharishi Mahesh Yogi, president of the Academy of Transcendental Meditation. A screaming crowd of teenyboppers in miniskirts sees them off at Heathrow, and the world's press dutifully camps outside the Maharishi's academy in the Himalayan foothills, filling the idle days with stories about temples, beggars, and lepers.

The Beatles—John, Paul, George, and Ringo—remind us that 1968 did not belong to war, napalm, insurrection, barricades, and tear gas alone; nor did the young invariably embrace the doctrinaire idealism of the New Left. The year 1968 was also the heyday of hedonism, of private pleasures gift wrapped in permissiveness, of an alternative "revolution" of the spirit and senses with a wider youthful constituency than the New Left—and scarcely less outrageous to the middle-aged guardians of order.

Not that popular music in the sixties ignored the darker stresses of social conflict or the uprush of bonding idealism. Folk music had been the bridge between the populist Old and the New Lefts; the guitar was the sound of existential humanism, of peace through persuasion. Pete Seeger's "This Land Is My Land" carried the message of peace from the Old Left era to the New. The gentle radicalism of Bob Dylan's "Blowin' in the Wind," the sardonic thrust of Joan Baez's rendition of Dylan's "With God on Our Side," the serene message of Dylan's "Do What the Spirit Say Do"—this was the voice of the early sixties, the civil rights campaigns, the new sense of community. Shortly before the police stormed into Sproul Hall at Berkeley in December 1964, Joan Baez appealed to the students to remain nonviolent. "Muster all the love of which you are capable."

On the back cover of her album *Farewell Angelina* (1965), Baez offered a passionate appeal: ". . . here we are, waiting on the eve of destruction with all the odds against any of us living to see the sun rise one day soon. . . . Only you and I can help the sun rise each coming morning." She had parted company with Dylan, who had abruptly renounced protest and one of whose songs, "My Back Pages," clearly derided commitment: "Ah, but I was so much older then, I'm younger than that now." Baez conveyed her lament in her song "To Bobby":

> You left us marching on the road,
> And said how heavy was the load—
> The years were young,
>   the struggle barely at its start.

When Dylan appeared at the Newport Folk Festival in July 1965 armed with an electric guitar, his audience was outraged.

The Beatles, too, represented the benign and persuasive face of pop music; Prime Minister Harold Wilson had cashed in on his own Liverpool connection by having them honored as Members of the British Empire at Buckingham Palace. The raucous Rolling Stones, by contrast, were iconoclasts with throats of hot metal; as the London *Times* reflected following Mick Jagger's conviction on a drugs charge, "Mr Jagger will become an MBE the day General Moshe Dayan has lunch with President Nasser."

Largish politico-cultural claims were advanced on behalf of the Beatles, few of them (apart from the quality of their music) sustainable on scrutiny. "They robbed the pop world of its violence," wrote Jeff Nuttall, "they robbed the protest world of its terrible, self-righteous drabness." The poet Allen Ginsberg made a pilgrimage to their native Liverpool, found a roaring, seedy, half-Irish, working-class port brimming with poetry readings, drugs, and happenings, and he acclaimed it "the center of the consciousness of the human universe." But wealth and fame are the shifting centers of the universe; in August 1968, the Beatles' shop Apple gave away its stock of clothes, records, pretty green carrier bags—one item for each supplicant in the long line stretching down Baker Street. A month later Hunter Davies published his biography of the Beatles, and some illusions went to the junkyard. John Lennon was quoted: "I'm not worried about the political situation in Greece, as long as it doesn't affect us. I don't care if the Government is all fascist, or communist." George Harrison said: "You go on being reincarnated, till you reach the absolute truth . . . we were made John, Paul, George and Ringo because of what we did last time, it was all there for us on a plate." Ringo said: "Everything that Government does turns to crap, not gold. The railways made a profit when they were private firms, didn't they? It's like Vietnam, England, our Government. Outdated."

John Hoyland's message to Lennon in the radical paper *Black Dwarf* was "Come and join us," despite the amusing complaint that the song "Revolution" was as revolutionary as the radio serial *Mrs. Dale's Diary.* Hoyland preferred the Rolling Stones: "they refuse to accept the system that's fucking up our lives." (Every part of the system except its money?)

Musically innovative, utopian, wistful, Edenic, the Beatles brilliantly synthesized the exotic fads of the counterculture, commanding not only the adulation of the teenyboppers but also (with the *Sgt. Pepper* album) the admiration of music critics and intellectuals. But fame and fortune and acid had carried them safely past the dangerous headland of genuine political radicalism. Yoko Ono entered the scene—Japanese by birth, educated at Sarah Lawrence, an artist; she and Lennon staged a joint show at the Arts Lab in London in May 1968. Having filmed John Lennon smiling for ninety minutes, Yoko Ono told the press in July that she wanted to make a film of everybody in the whole world smiling. After their marriage the couple staged a Bed-In for Peace in various cities, attended by the press. If Lennon later chose to spend a fragment of his fortune on a *New York Times* advertisement, "War is over if you want it," the war machine could live with that. During 1969, the Beatles disintegrated as a group.

Joan Baez remained loyal to the Movement. At Christmas 1972, she was in Hanoi during one of the heaviest aerial bombardments in history. Meanwhile another bombardment had descended on the affluent West: electronic rock, brash, frenetic and aggressive, the wilder voice of the psychedelic counterculture. From 1966 a new wave of irreverent, "radical" groups stormed underground London: Pink Floyd, the Cream, Soft Machine, the Social Deviants, Arthur Brown (a university dropout who electrified audiences by his frenetic performances with the Exploding Galaxy). The commercial promoters moved in smartly, and the gigs were promoted from coterie cellars to vast auditoriums like Alexandra Palace, packed with naïve, hero-worshipping children.

In his book *Gates of Eden,* Morris Dickstein has argued that the shift from folk to rock music—an intensely urban, deafening total environment created by manipulated energy and violent ritual—reflected a massive desertion from existential witness to the "Fuck you!" of the violent collective actions of the late sixties. Underground papers like the *Los Angeles Free Press* and the *Berkeley Barb* served up a mixed dish of rock, dope, sex, and revolution. Rock was promoted not merely for its gut pleasures, but as the vanguard of existential and political liberation. Yet rock was not a political force in the West, although the Communist regimes' reaction to groups like Prague's Plastic People was indeed political. The new rock, housed in vast new emporia like the Fillmore in San Francisco and the Fillmore East in lower Manhattan, obliterated words and ideas or amplified them to extinction, releasing the force of the subconscious in furious displays of fantasy. Throbbing light shows accompanied the music, serving as the visual counterpart to the new electric sound. Some rock groups teased half-radical themes out of the counterculture, but the wider audience was not invariably interested in Vietnam, the ghettos, or the "system."

The San Francisco rock paper *Rolling Stone,* launched by Jan Wenner in November 1967, projected rock as the authentic revolutionary consciousness of a generation; politics was "out." The commercial promoters were glad to agree, as they swooped to scoop the takings—hence CBS's ads, "The Revolutionaries Are on Columbia" and "The Man Can't Bust Our Music." Supported by the record companies, *Rolling Stone* was unwilling to break with the star system.

The real life of idolized rock groups like the Rolling Stones centered on Decca, Swiss bank accounts, hard deals with promoters, fast cars, servants, retinues of gofers, bodyguards, and drug peddlers—the flashy, stoned display of the new rich. As the critic Michael Lydon wrote: "The Stones are STARS—on tour if not elsewhere, automatically the center of attention and privilege. . . . All non-Stones are relatively insecure, and in a constant struggle to maintain their own egos, and their own place, in the graded orbits round the Stones."

The coming of the Stones was dreaded by city fathers across Europe; their concerts could precipitate major disturbances. Harassed and searched by immigration officials, the stars found it tempting to regard themselves as more subversive than Che Guevara. According to an insider's *kitsch* account of Mick Jagger's political fantasy, "He leaped at the chance of joining the revolution when tens of thousands of angry young people stormed into Grosvenor Square to demonstrate their hatred of American imperialism and the Vietnam War." At first Jagger went unnoticed. Linking arms with a young man on one side and a young woman on the other, "he felt a part of what was happening, as though he were really contributing." But then he was recognized, fans demanded his autograph, and reporters jostled one another for an interview. "He fled, bitterly realizing that his fame and wealth precluded him from the revolution—he was a distraction, not a leader. . . ." Out of this chastening experience came the song "Street Fighting Man," bemoaning "that summer has arrived and it's time for revolution, but he's only a rock 'n' roll singer." *Black Dwarf* invited Jagger to write out the words of that song, which it printed in his own fair hand.

Nor could greater political claims be made—although they *were* made—for Vanilla Fudge, Strawberry Alarm Clock, Dow Jones and the Industrials, Jefferson Airplane, the Grateful Dead, Blood, Sweat and Tears, or the Doors. The rock festivals satisfied hungers that were both communitarian and vaguely mystical. Despite the frenetic music, young people passed joints around with love and tenderness, not unlike a Quaker meeting waiting for the spirit.

DRUG CULTURE

There were plenty of drugs to share, and there was scarcely a music group or "underground" minstrel who did not use them, frequently in debilitating doses.

But a basic distinction must be made between the occasional drug users, the "seekers," and the habitual addicts, or "heads." The former on the whole remained outside the hippie, dropout culture, and were capable performers, intellectual in outlook, widely read, able to separate thought from feeling, but rather ambivalent about career values. The "head" by contrast was more deeply into morbid self-exploration, and typically disappeared into a hippie enclave, either returning to family or college after a year or becoming a long-term dropout.

How widespread was the use of drugs? In 1969 a Roper poll reported that 76 percent of American college seniors said they had never tried marijuana, and that 96 percent had never used LSD. A Gallup survey reached similar conclusions: 68 percent said they had never tried pot, 88 percent that they had not taken barbiturates, 92 percent that they had never used LSD. A Gilbert national survey of American youth (February 1970) found that only 10 percent reported the regular use of any drug.

Nevertheless, drug use had spread despite often draconian attempts by legislators and narcotics squads to stamp it out. In 1967 there were 2,393 prosecutions for cannabis offenses in Britain; in 1968, 3,071 (including John Lennon and Yoko Ono); and in 1970, 7,250 prosecutions. Alabama prescribed a mandatory sentence of five years for first offense of possession, forty years for a second offense; Missouri introduced a life sentence for the first offense of selling cannabis, and for the second offense of possessing it. In Massachusetts there was a five-year sentence for being in the company of anyone possessing it.

Legislators and judges did not on the whole use drugs, or obtained them on a doctor's prescription. Their own "drugs" were tobacco and alcohol. (On January 8, 1969, the London *Times* reported: "The findings of the report on cannabis by the Advisory Committee on Drug

Dependence point to the general conclusion that, in the light of present knowledge, the drug is no more, perhaps less, harmful than alcohol.") In a celebrated case, two stars of the Rolling Stones rock group, Mick Jagger and Keith Richard, were prosecuted. The judge sentenced Jagger to three months in prison. The editor of the London *Times,* no less, protested in a long leader: "There must remain a suspicion in this case that Mr. Jagger received a more severe sentence than would have been thought proper for any purely anonymous young man." That this was indeed the judicial frame of mind was confirmed on appeal, when Lord Chief Justice Hubert Parker, although substituting a conditional discharge for imprisonment, declared: ". . . you are, whether you like it or not, an idol of a large number of young people in this country—being in that position you have very grave responsibilities, and if you do come to be punished it is only natural that those responsibilities should carry a higher penalty."

The drugged hippies of San Francisco's Haight-Ashbury became incapable of helping a kindred spirit suffering violence. If someone collapsed in the middle of the street, no one moved. Among the underground poets, psychiatrists, art dealers, and rock stars, the claimed journeys to "inner truth" degenerate, on inspection, into puddles of vomit. However corrupt ("bent") London's vice squad and the Chelsea constabulary, no one was destroying the Rolling Stones except the Stones. Brian Jones, original inspiration of the group but later a desperate, debauched addict corrupted by fame and wealth, died in a swimming pool. Tony Sanchez, who by his own account constantly supplied the group with drugs, reports that by the late sixties many of them were "strung out on smack" (heroin), while cocaine was snorted regularly, producing an instant high and overspill of energy, as did "speedballs," mixtures of heroin and cocaine. Sanchez paints a sordid but convincing picture of a new, overnight aristocracy too immature to cope with sudden fame and wealth, drug-torturing their minds and bodies.

Among the middle-aged—the parents—heroin and LSD ("acid") caused the greatest alarm. LSD was first discovered by the Swiss chemist Dr. Albert Hoffman in the early 1940s, and subsequently was used in the treatment of psychiatric patients and, by the CIA, on prisoners, addicts, and prostitutes unaware of their role as guinea pigs. LSD affects the region of the brain that receives signals from the senses, inducing what Hoffman calls "reality uncensored"; it heightens colors, transforms sounds, and turns motion into a "web of frozen moments." Aldous Huxley, experimenting with the hallucinogen mescaline, was dazzled by "the miracle, moment by moment, of naked existence"; the drug opened "the doors of perception." Dr. Richard Blum and his associates at Stanford University claimed that LSD was a means "for

enhancing values or expanding the self, a road to love and better relationships, a device for art appreciation or a spur to creative endeavors,
a means of insight and a door to religious experience."

Ken Kesey, thirty-two years old in 1968, author of *One Flew Over
the Cuckoo's Nest,* rambled about the West Coast in a Day-Glo bus
packed with microphones, amplifying equipment, and devotees known
as the Merry Pranksters. According to one commentator, Kesey may
have "turned on" at least 10,000 young people to LSD during his
twenty-four presentations of the acid test. The writer Tom Wolfe
claimed that acid was demonstrably destroying the political culture of
the West Coast: "The political thing, the whole New Left, is all of a
sudden like *over* on the hip circuit around San Francisco, even at
Berkeley, the very citadel of the Student Revolution and all." A young
radical who had championed the grape workers or campaigned for civil
rights in Mississippi would reappear on the campus—"and immediately
everybody knows he has become a head . . . he now has a very tolerant
and therefore withering attitude toward all those who are still . . .
trapped in the old 'political games'. . . ."

The most notorious prophet of LSD, the great charlatan of the
sacramental underground, was Dr. Timothy Leary. Dismissed by Harvard in 1963, Leary was patronized by a young New York millionaire
and veteran LSD voyager, William Hitchcock, who turned over his
4,000-acre estate at Millbrook, New York. Here Leary administered
LSD to groups of paying guests and to children as young as nine years
old, scandalizing the medical profession by taking the drug himself at
the same time as his wards. (Leary promised that the kids who had
taken acid would fight no war and join no corporation.) Dr. Hoffman
reports that Leary wrote to Sandoz Laboratories in Switzerland, requesting one hundred grams—enough for two million people.

In April 1966, Millbrook was raided and Leary was charged with
possessing marijuana. The previous April he had been arrested with his
daughter, found guilty of transporting half an ounce of cannabis, fined
$30,000, and given a sentence of five to thirty years (later quashed by
the Supreme Court). By 1966 Leary's eighteen-year-old daughter and
sixteen-year-old son had both been in jail, his son (according to Leary)
ten times.

Leary pitched his tent within the nonpolitical counterculture, although he liked to be friendly with anybody who was anybody. He
contemptuously dismissed conventional political action; the Free
Speech Movement at Berkeley, for example, was "playing right onto the
game boards of the administration and the police." Indeed, any social
action, "unless it's based on expanded consciousness," was simply
"robot behavior." Why attempt to create a better university? The only

way was to "turn on, tune in and drop out." Leary's language was laced with minor vulgarities. "Game" was a favorite word. The radical psychoanalyst Dr. Ronald Laing, perhaps the most influential "anti-psychiatrist" of the sixties, was accorded this accolade: "He weaves science-religion-art-experience into the slickest board game of our time." Laing was a member of the advisory panel of SOMA, whose stated project was to examine the scientific, social, and moral implications of "psychotropic drug use and methods of altering consciousness in general."

Leary spliced the pseudoreligious ("sacramental") into the pseudoscientific. "The temple of God is your own body—the Orientals teach us that." Here was a religion involving no tension between the senses and spirit, between the id and the ego—merely *The Politics of Ecstasy,* as Leary called his book. "The deep psychedelic experience is a death-rebirth flip. You turn on the ancient rhythm and you become its beat." And: "The visionary revelation answers the escape question. There is no death. Ecstatic, mirthful relief. . . . There is just off–on, in–out, start–stop, light–dark, flash–delay."

Leary told *Playboy* magazine: "The three inevitable goals of the LSD session are to discover and make love with God, to discover and make love with yourself, and to discover and make love with a woman." He further explained that, "In a carefully prepared, loving LSD session, a woman will inevitably have several hundred orgasms." But nothing of this was heard from Leary when he addressed middle-aged audiences; no word of taking the vote away from everyone over fifty. The journalist Warren Hinckle reported Leary playing the Bay Area in a Brooks Brothers '59 suit and paisley tie, selling $4 seats mainly to squares: "Dr. Leary's pitch is to the straight world."

One of the straight world's discriminating intelligences, Diana Trilling, went down to the Village Barn to observe Dr. Leary's Psychedelic Celebration; there was no admission charge. Under indictment for illegal possession of marijuana, Leary was primed to plead freedom of religion under the First Amendment; hence his show on the night of Trilling's visit was called "The Incarnation of Christ," but an "Illumination of the Buddha" was also available. Background music included the *Missa Luba,* a Congo version of the Roman Catholic mass, and Verdi's *Requiem.* Leary's incantatory voice came and went and came: "Let's return to the twentieth century and reincarnate Jesus Christ, let's do it everyone right now. . . . You have to take on all the sin, guilt and wretchedness of the world. . . ." Leary then invited someone to come up from the audience, take off his clothes, and be nailed to the cross. "Let's look in the bag. There are some nails here and a crown of thorns." No takers. Apparently Leary expected none.

By 1967–68, the authorities were reacting with alarm. A million Americans were estimated to have taken LSD by 1968. And in Britain, the minister of state at the Home Office, Alice Bacon, told the House of Commons that she had been horrified to read, under the hair dryer, a copy of *Queen,* which quoted Paul McCartney saying "God is in everything and everywhere and everyone. It's just that I realized all this through acid, but it could have been done through anything." President Johnson went before Congress: "The time has come to stop the sale of slavery to the young."

Timothy Leary was a prime target; arrested in December 1968 at Laguna Beach, California (headquarters of his Brotherhood of Eternal Love), on a marijuana charge, he received a sentence of six months to ten years, and was denied bail on the ground that he represented a danger to the community. Transferred to San Luis Obispo, where he was held for eight months, and facing another trial in New York, Leary escaped by climbing a twelve-foot-high chain-link fence with the help of daily gymnastics and some Robin Hood Weatherpeople. Their communiqué praised Leary "for the work he did in helping us begin the task of creating a new culture on the barren wasteland. . . . LSD and grass . . . will help us make a future world where it will be possible to live in peace."

Leary reached Algeria, moved to Switzerland, walked into a U.S. government trap in Afghanistan in 1972, then found himself back in an American prison. Recanting after his fashion, he denounced Eastern religions and was accused by former colleagues of "singing."

THE UNDERGROUND

Drugs and illicit sex brought the self-styled literary underground of the sixties into constant conflict with conventional morality and frequent violation of the law. From the coast of California to the metropolitan centers of Europe, the youthful Bohemia of the sixties was high most of the time and in the horizontal position much of the time. According to Jeff Nuttall's *Bomb Culture* (1968), the duplicated magazines, happenings, and home movies produced by the avant-garde underground (a term first coined in New York about 1964) were in essence a response to "the spiritual bankruptcy which begat the bomb." Certainly there were radical spirits among underground editors and poets, but the movement as a whole was about drugs and personal contact ads.

International Times (London), *Berkeley Barb, East Village Other,*

Los Angeles Free Press, Other Scenes, San Francisco Oracle, and *Open City* all employed bright, discordant colors, neo–art nouveau drawings, and vivacious cartoons that conveyed not so much fear of the bomb or social radicalism, as the image of gentle grass, "psychedelic" acid trips, and guilt-free sex whether straight or gay. New York's leading underground guru, Ed Sanders, a poet and antibomb demonstrator who had served a prison sentence for his part in the New York Harbor swim-ins, produced *Fuck You: A Magazine of the Arts.* Its editorials, choking with expletives, exhorted "queers," junkies, and dropouts to defend themselves against police harassment through effective legal channels. *International Times* reproduced a plug for LSD from *The Oracle of Southern California:* "Man's need to surrender is helped by psychedelic sacraments. Psychedelics are more aphrodisiac than scientific studies of fucking can ever show. The sexual energy aroused on acid is general, god-like, cosmic. Hence most people are not interested in merely genital fucking on an acid trip; they are fucking the universe."

There was no lack of persuasive voices from the underground to convince the young that only through mind-releasing drugs could existential fulfillment be achieved. Dr. Joseph Berke, a prophet of the counterculture, explained that the Apollonian culture of the West (rational, materialistic, repressed, straight) feared the Dionysian ethos (emotional, hedonistic, communal—and curved). Marijuana and hashish, he said, were medically harmless and much easier to abandon than opiates, tobacco, or alcohol. Jeff Nuttall quoted Dr. Berke when high: "Let the bombs fall, the biggest bombs, and so a great mandala will unfold, and in a micro moment, all that can be, will be. . . ." Nuttall himself was finally disillusioned: the "hunger for regenerative spirituality becomes discolored into a vapid pseudo-oriental antimaterialism, 'Why worry about the world and the human species? They're not real anyway.' "

The writer William Burroughs, author of *The Soft Machine* and *Naked Lunch,* and a luminary of the drug culture, complained in *International Times* that the sensational commercial press not only lumped all drugs together, but falsely alleged that cannabis led to heroin. According to Burroughs, it was the mission of the underground press to explain that marijuana entailed no ill effects; that speed and cocaine could kill; and that opiates are addictive. The Yippie spokesman Jerry Rubin—advocate of marijuana, LSD, and mescaline—struck a pseudoradical note by describing heroin as "the government's most powerful counter revolutionary agent, a form of germ warfare. Since they can't get us back into their system, they try to destroy us through heroin."

Drugs and sex (or "obscenity"), rather than politics, led to police harassment of underground magazines and shops. Frequently production was disrupted by raids and fines. In London, where mail order was the principal means of dissemination, the drugs squad moved ahead of the vice squad, raiding *International Times* (which had to rename itself *IT* under protest from Times Newspapers, Ltd.) and arresting Jim Lowell of the Asphodel bookshop. Jeff Nuttall expressed his indignation: "They arrest and imprison Hoppy. . . . They do the same to Robert Fraser, the only really adventurous art dealer in London. They confiscate the Dine-Paolozzi prick pictures and charge Fraser with *vagrancy* for showing them. They arrest Sigma artists for drawing on the pavement and they arrest John Latham for protesting about it."

Having raised £500 from Victor Herbert, "the underground millionaire," Jim Haynes and two colleagues, Barry Miles and John Hopkins, had launched *International Times* in October 1966. Miles was managing director of Indica bookshop and the victim of a punitive police raid; Hopkins was a dropout from the Harwell Atomic Research Station, who arrived in jail on a marijuana charge via the Campaign for Nuclear Disarmament, Centre 42, and Pink Floyd. Haynes and his colleagues went overground into the gilded worlds of fashion and show business to splash-launch *IT* with a huge party at the Round House attended by everyone who was anyone. The drugs squad gave it a miss.

Tom McGrath, poet and editor of *IT,* put down his thoughts about the Movement (which he doubted was really a movement) after the paper was raided in March 1967. Compressed (as they perhaps deserve to be), these ruminations sound familiar to students of dada and surrealism:

> Inner directed. . . . A new way of looking at things, not an ideology. . . . The revolution takes place within the minds of the young. . . . You either have the attitude or you don't. . . . The search for pleasure (orgasm) covers every field of human activity. . . . Abolish money. . . . Not a movement of protest but of celebration. . . . Grooving. . . . No leaders. . . . Crazy. . . . The squares sneer. . . . Don't forget the bomb, but begin the revolution with love and McLuhan-style media theory.

Exploiting the new cheapness of offset photolithography, *IT* achieved a print run of 50,000 copies per issue in 1968, but the tensions with the New Left mounted when the paper trashed the Vietnam marches, the "fights, arrests and the destruction of the beautiful green lawn at Grosvenor Square." As an alternative, *IT* proposed the Design Revolution, Spiritual Evolution, Inner Space Adventure, and Work Democracy. Apparently all answers lay within the head.

Jeff Nuttall's retrospective on the original aims of the underground projected not only an artist's personal vision, but also a synthesis of political and countercultural values that was closer to the exception than the rule. In awarding this vision to the Movement as a whole, Nuttall fostered an illusion:

> The spread of an ego-dissolving delirium wherein a tribal telepathic understanding could grow up among men . . . to cultivate aesthetic perception in the face of utilitarian perception, to reinstate the metalled road as a silken ribbon . . . to outflank police, educationalists, moralists through whom the death machine is maintained . . . dislocate . . . punctuality, servility, and property . . . [allow] people to fuck freely and guiltlessly, dance wildly and wear fancy dress all the time. To eradicate . . . the pauline lie . . . that people neither shit, piss nor fuck . . . to reinstate a sense of health and beauty pertaining to the genitals and the arsehole.

There was also a watered down version peddled to kids with a few pounds in their jeans and a vague urge to "do their thing" or "be themselves." Richard Neville, editor of *Oz,* conveyed its eclectic banality all too perfectly in the first month of 1968: ". . . as anyone who has bummed his way through Europe or Asia will testify, the Movement is casually international. No one sews flags on rucksacks anymore." The new society was to have no clocks, no money, no Wimpyburgers. "Already the Underground boasts its own boutiques, newspapers, restaurants, literature, music, poetry, cinema, clubs, designers. . . . Now, if you're busted, you can dial 603-8654 for help 'day or night with love.' "

Underground writers rarely rejected offers of publication by mainstream magazines or publishers—the Penguin Modern Poets Series, for example. Writers, musicians, and artists came up for the takings like star amateur boxers turning professional. In swinging London, the frontier between affluent "radical chic" and genuine rejection of the dominant culture was as fluid as the fast-fashion garment industry. The career of Jim Haynes, a young American of legendary charm, energy, and talent, incarnates the relaxed, politically agnostic, passage to and fro across that frontier.

Haynes's Arts Laboratory in Covent Garden was supported by a galaxy of overground celebrities; television companies arrived from all over the world to film the Arts Lab. Everybody came, including the wife of the American ambassador, the Cuban ambassador, and twelve Soviet directors hosted by the British Council. Haynes not only received support from Marion Javits, wife of the New York senator, but was assigned as escort to one of Lyndon Johnson's daughters—soon after selling *IT* to audiences leaving Peter Brook's production of *US,* a play aimed at her daddy's genocidal war. Shadowed by the Secret Service, Haynes took Miss Johnson to the Royal Court.

But the Arts Lab was increasingly filled with twenty-year-old kids carrying rucksacks, which put the smarter set off. Haynes was deeply committed to low-cost culture, to interfacing the different arts under a single roof, and, indeed, to finding unoccupied premises for the roofless to squat in. Finally succumbing to piles of bills, the Arts Lab closed forever; Haynes went off to Paris to teach and to launch the magazine *Suck* in Amsterdam, where the police didn't interfere. Haynes argues that *Suck* was more underground than its New York counterpart, *Screw,* but a dispute about nude photographs of Germaine Greer set the limit to ethical debate, and the annual "Wet Dream Festivals" in Holland were patronized mainly by the jet set. New money carried all before it.

CONSENTING ADULTS

The classified ads columns of the underground served a genuinely liberating function by challenging both traditional Puritanism and heterosexual repression of gay rights. The prevailing style was conveyed in this ad from the *East Village Other:*

- THREE STUDENTS, 2 CHICKS, 1 GUY, WANT WELL-HUNG GUYS AND STACKED CHICKS FOR GANG BANGS. IF YOU FUCK, SUCK, OR TAKE UP THE ASS, SEND SEXY PICTURE AND ADDRESS.

Taste apart, what was at stake was the civil liberty of consenting adults to pursue their own inclinations in full light of day. The backlash duly created martyrs. In January 1970, *IT* was prosecuted for conspiring to corrupt public decency and morals; fines and legal costs ensured the demise of the paper. *Oz* (whose editor, Richard Neville, had announced that "The weapons of revolution are obscenity, blasphemy and drugs") suffered the same fate, though the law was indifferent to Neville's perennial offense: trivializing language. The crunch came with *Oz 28,* "A Schoolkids' Issue," in which guilt-free sex and soft drugs were demanded as the right of every adolescent, with supporting cartoons showing repressed schoolmasters whacking each other's naked buttocks, plus the cartoon character Rupert Bear, a symbol of virtue to little children, engaged in a dirty rampage. The sentences handed down by Judge Michael Argyle were savage (although suspended by the appeal court) and the costs closed *Oz* down.

The underground theatre, no less than the magazines, rushed headlong into uninhibited eroticism. Repression inevitably obscured the issue of authenticity (just as it transformed student revolutionaries from lieutenants into brigadiers). In March 1969, police in New York pounced on the author, director-producer, and entire cast of *Che,* a fantasy about the last hours of Guevara that was playing at the Free Store Theatre in Cooper Square. Not so much the politics as the fondling and grappling of nude actors provoked the "bust" under a warrant from Judge Amos Basel. But the genuine offense was the exploitation of the Guevara legend; pseudoradical America was spraying its porn with Third World symbols the way mediocre cooks use Oriental spices.

COUNTERCULTURE

The years 1967–70 marked the peak of the counterculture. Western society had witnessed a rapid drift from work-based Puritanism to consumer-boom permissiveness. "Repressive sublimation" (pleasures morally forbidden) yielded to "repressive desublimation" (a cornucopia of indulgences on credit). The hippie-rock-drug culture disturbed the Puritan ethic, but it also served as an experimental space station for the new, dynamic capitalism. Thousands of artisan workshops emerged to pioneer products and pleasures that big business would later mop up. As the British sociologist Stuart Hall observed, "The counter-culture did not arise from the experience of repression, but rather from the 'repressive tolerance' of the liberal-capitalist state. It *redefined* this liberalism, this tolerance, this pluralism, this consensus as *repressive*. It renamed 'consensus' as 'coercive'; it called 'freedom' 'domination'; it redefined its own relative affluence as a kind of alienated, spiritual poverty."

Within the counterculture there was no lack of heavy jargon, nor of revolutionary posturing, as when Louis Kampf, a professor at MIT and president of the Modern Language Association, wrote: "The movement should have harrassed [*sic*] Lincoln Center from the beginning. Not a performance should go by without disruption. The fountains should be dried with calcium chloride, the statuary pissed on, the walls smeared with shit." Reveling in "Let's hate ourselves," Kampf offered a logic much in fashion: "Had the advocates of black power who damaged a Rembrandt at the New York Metropolitan Museum been caught, they would have been read a lesson on the values of the culture by a philistine judge. More than likely they would have been jailed; a piece of canvas is obviously more valuable than a man's freedom."

At a less pretentious level, kids were rejecting TV, comics, grade school, father-knows-best, and the-policeman-is-your-friend. This lighter side would blow with the wind and eventually settle on the TV screens as hip blacks cavorting through commercials. The caricature of the mainstream counterculture was the earnest English teacher who urged his high school students to reject all texts in favor of fondling whatever came to hand: "the tactile universe, the empire of the senses," and all that. Literacy was the boa constrictor.

Sociologists speak of working-class "subcultures" as distinct from the "alternative" and "counter" cultures adopted by young middle-class rebels, whose inheritance involves a sense of responsibility for the prevailing social order. Teds, Mods, Rockers, Angels, Skinheads, Greasers, and Punks propose a delinquency that entertains no thought of changing society and, indeed, derives its vicarious pleasures from the hostility of an unalterable *status quo.* Motorcycle gangs may stage drive-ins to protest crash-helmet regulations, but the challenge is no more radical than that of French peasants blockading roads to protest falling farm prices. The counterculture, by contrast, was the work of an alternative elite torn between the "red" and the "green."

The classic texts were Theodore Roszak's *The Making of a Counter Culture,* first published in 1968, and *Where the Wasteland Ends* (1972). Both books challenged a single-vision civilization of experts and technicians dedicated to an idolatrous reality principle, which destroyed the ancient animist covenant between man and nature, equated truth with utility, and divorced knowledge from wisdom. Roszak traced the historical roots of the redeeming counterculture to the romantic tradition of Blake and Shelley, Wordsworth and Goethe. The hostile technocratic ideology extended back to Bacon's New Atlantis, through Hobbes, Saint-Simon, Bentham, Marx, Veblen, and Comte—the social engineers, positivists, behaviorists, and manipulators.

To escape the wasteland, said Roszak, we must cease to censor our dreams, annihilate the stopwatch, and open the doors of perception. He called for a communitarian approach to work, a participatory democracy that could not be blueprinted but would certainly involve de-urbanization, a return to Mother Earth, and—with the help of dissenting technicians, dropped-out professionals, and people's architects—a new kind of society combining modern knowhow with ancient animism, a world where (with Blake) "every particle of dust breathes forth its joy." In short, "Blake, not Marx, is the prophet of our historical horizon."

Rozsak believed that the New Left had imparted political dignity to the tenderer emotions. Herbert Marcuse agreed that the "disaffiliation" of the young now provided the major lever for change. It was the students who had taken up Allen Ginsberg's fight against the deity of power and greed, Moloch, while the working class sat tight and played safe, "the stoutest prop of the established order." Roszak was into poetry, communes, resource groups, and organic homesteading, but his prescription too neatly perforated the contemporary counterculture at the point where the Arcadian impulses were deafened by the electronic ego of the ear-splitting amplifiers. Despite the rural communes, the big city was "where it was at."

THE FREE SCHOOL OF NEW YORK

The highbrow version of the counterculture incarnated itself at the Free School (originally "University") of New York; the more popular, middlebrow version was purveyed by the long-running show, *Hair*. The Free School (founded in 1965 and located in a suitably derelict building at 20 East 14 Street, New York City) declared itself to have been "forged in response to the intellectual bankruptcy and spiritual emptiness of the American educational establishment," which treated students as "raw material to be processed for the university's clients—business, government and military bureaucracies." FUNY was compelled to restyle itself the Free School after the state of New York warned that legal adoption of the word "university" required Department of Education approval and proof of assets worth $500,000.

The dynamo and manager of the Free School was Allen Krebs, who had been fired from his post at Adelphi University after traveling to Cuba in 1964. Subpoenaed by the House Committee on Un-American Activities in the summer of 1966, Krebs was also fired by the New School. Granting no credits or degrees, the Free School offered such courses as Perspectives for American Radicals, Culture Against Man, Latin America—The Next Vietnams?, Community Organization, Mao and Black Power, Sociology for a Revolutionary World, Improvisation Workshop ("a non-verbal exchange of ideas about ourselves and society"), Ethics and Reality, Elementary Course in Marxist Economics, Self-Defense for Radicals, and Psychoanalysis and Marxism.

The squarer members of the faculty credited themselves with Ph.Ds when possible, even though such titles derived from the despised corporate monsters. The traditional divisions between subjects were also accepted: history, drama, fiction, economics, philosophy, psychology, science, math, sociology, international affairs. When unable to attend, Staughton Lynd would send in his lecture to be read by a student, but not all the faculty were so keen on formal literacy. Ed Sanders, for example, offered Revolutionary Egyptology, which got into finding God through mushrooms, acid, strobes, grass, orgasm, and his magazine *Fuck You*.

According to Joseph Berke, the Free School was split down the middle between "the politicos and the culture wizards," the former dominated by the Maoist May 2 Movement, the wizards dismissing political stuff as sheer illusion. For them the media were where it was at—the system's black box. The Maoists were still in search of the working class, but Berke dismissed the American blue-collar worker as a "pig" grunting for material goods and (inexcusably) upward mobility; the genuinely alienated class was the kids who understood what "alienation" really meant.

The media's version of the Free School was the Liberation News Service, which by 1967–68 was servicing about three-quarters of America's four hundred alternative newspapers and magazines. As one of its founders, Raymond Mungo (himself a draft resister), explained, LNS's sources opened up news of "Havana, Hanoi, Peking, South Africa, university insurgency, sexual freedom, serious psychedelic research" ignored by the commercial agencies. LNS formed part of the New Media Project, which included ghetto radio stations, high school newsletters, and radio stations "with a conscience," like WBAI–FM in New York.

5

INSURRECTION IN EUROPE, I: Poland, Italy, Spain, France, and Britain

"During the academic year 1967–68, nineteen of thirty-three Italian state universities were affected by student unrest…"

"The speech provoked a storm of controversy and [Enoch] Powell's rapid dismissal from the Conservative Shadow Cabinet."

"…a new clash took place in White-hall when left-wing groups demonstrating against racism encountered Smithfield Market porters marching in support of immigration control."

POLAND: A PLAY

WARSAW, January 30, 1968—Police arrest some fifty out of two hundred students protesting the forced closure of a play. Anti-Russian references in Adam Mickiewicz's nineteenth-century drama *Dziady* ("The Forefathers") have been drawing applause from Warsaw audiences. Chanting "Free art, free theatre!," the fifty students are arrested while marching to the censor's office. Party leader Wladyslaw Gomulka—citing offending lines from *Dziady* such as "All that Moscow sends us are spies, jackasses and fools"—has personally ordered the production at the Narodwy Theatre to close.

The irony lay in the fact that this long and complex play had been required reading in Poland's high schools since 1918, and had been staged at least sixteen times since 1945. But the irony may have been lost on two of the arrested students, Adam Michnik and Henryk Szlaifer, who were promptly expelled from Warsaw University. This action detonated an explosion: throughout 1968 it was the young who emboldened their liberal parents.

On February 29, the Warsaw branch of the Writers' Union boldly passed a motion by secret ballot requesting that the ban on the play be lifted. Indeed, they went further, calling for curbs on censorship in general and for the participation of working writers in formulating cultural policy. The Polish United Workers Party responded by importing workers' delegations to intimidate the writers; Jerzy Putrament, secretary of the Party cell in the Warsaw Writers' branch, threatened tighter Party control unless some of its members were expelled. Demanding clear "commitment" from artists, the Party paper, *Trybuna Ludu,* attacked decadent theatre productions.

On March 8, students marched to the university rector's building and demonstrated for two hours on behalf of their dismissed colleagues. Following scuffles between the students and plainclothes auxiliaries, truckloads of armed police were sent onto the campus. On March 9, fighting spread to Warsaw Polytechnic; the police resorted to tear gas. The students, expressing solidarity with Warsaw's writers, responded with a seventeen-point resolution and marched on the offices of the government newspaper, *Zycie Warszawy,* which had described them as "scum." (Conflict between students and the press was to figure prominently also in Italy, Germany, Yugoslavia, France, and Britain.) The resolution passed at the Warsaw Polytechnic on March 13 affirmed the following:

1. Article 71 of the Constitution guaranteed freedom of speech, of assembly, and of the press.
2. All students arrested should be listed and released.
3. Those responsible for police brutality should be punished.
4. Workers should not be set against students.
5. The press, radio, and television should provide a true account of student demands and actions.
6. No measures should be taken against "academic workers" (teachers) who had supported the students.
7. The Citizens' Militia should be withdrawn from campuses.
8. Dissociation must be made from both anti-Semitism and Zionism.

All of Poland's universities went on strike. For three days, Warsaw University was a battleground, with the fighting spreading across the city. Students sheltering on the steps of the Holy Cross Church were clubbed by police. But police who tried to break up a meeting in the Electronics Faculty of the Polytechnic were driven out with shouts of "Long live Czechoslovakia!" (Although the Prague Spring was still in its infancy, its message was already clear. Two Czech correspondents covering the demonstrations had their notes and films confiscated; Miroslav Pavel, of the liberal *Mladá Fronta,* was unable to transmit a single report to Prague.)

In Poland, as in Yugoslavia three months later, the solidarity of youth overwhelmed Party allegiance. Both the official Socialist Youth Union and the official Union of Rural Youth passed liberal resolutions deploring the rising anti-Semitism. Fighting spread to Krakow, where 5,000 students from the Jagiellonian University marched with placards saying, "Warsaw is not alone." Students in Poznan clashed with police while on their way to petition the university rector. On March 16, riot police with water hoses and clubs attacked demonstrators who had gathered in the Ring marketplace in Katowice to demand democratization and an end to mendacious reporting in the press. Poland was perhaps the first country to experience, during 1968, the epidemic fever of freedom.

The state-controlled daily, *Zycie Warszawy,* printed a list of the student demands, but with a dismissive reply to each one. Free speech and assembly could not "be used against the character of our socialist system." As for allegations of police brutality, "When chopping wood, splinters must fly." State television showed factory meetings unanimously condemning the students and demanding "Purge the Party of Zionists."

On March 19, Gomulka himself delivered a speech in the Palace of Culture. He made certain conciliatory gestures, promising to discuss student demands and not to set workers against them in the streets (as had repeatedly happened). As for freedom of speech and demonstration, they could not be judged "in the abstract," said Gomulka (a formula favored by Communist leaders under pressure). Noting that Jewish students had been prominent in the disturbances, he denounced by name certain "revisionist" professors, and invited Zionists to leave the country. He was continually interrupted by shouts of the traditional "Long live, long live," which were heard on radio and television and were accorded varying interpretations by foreign newspapers.

Gomulka's speech did not end the disturbances. A twenty-four-hour strike at Warsaw Polytechnic went ahead, with 5,000 students spending the night on the premises to the strains of Chopin. A kitty of 5,000 *zlotys* helped to provide blankets, food, and candles, but vodka and other hard liquor were forbidden. On March 22, the police started clearing the area around the Polytechnic, pushing back thousands of people applauding the students. Big chants of "General strike!" and the sound of the "Internationale" suggested a physical confrontation, but at 2 A.M., the students abandoned their sit-in following an ultimatum heard over the radio. On the 24th, the London *Times* found the Polytechnic almost deserted and the city relaxed "in Spring Sunday calm."

A day later, six prominent professors in the humanities departments of Warsaw University—all of them named by Gomulka—were dismissed: Bronislaw Baczko, a specialist in eighteenth-century French philosophy; Zygmunt Bauman, accused in the press of being influenced by American sociology and the structuralism of Claude Lévi-Strauss; the philosopher Leszek Kolakowski, a leading figure in the upheaval of 1956; and Stefan Morawski, Maria Hortszowicz, and Wlodzimierz Brus. Stefan Zolkiewski, a literary theorist and former minister of education, was fired as secretary of the Social Sciences Department of the Academy of Sciences. He was a Jew.

Liberal Prague made clear its opposition. The Philosophy Faculty of the Charles University responded by inviting Kolakowski and Baczko to lecture; the Czech Writers' Union protested to the Polish ambassador; and even the (normally conservative) Slovak Academy of Sciences wrote to the rector of Warsaw University demanding an explanation of the dismissals. Declared the journal *Literární Listy:* "The young people who demonstrate were born in Socialist Poland and defend freedom of speech against police repression. . . ." (Only four months later Gomulka sent his answer, when Polish troops invaded Czechoslovakia.) The Yugoslav journal *Praxis* also defended the six Polish professors.

On March 28, 2,000 Warsaw University students defied warnings and gathered to demand the reinstatement of the six professors. Many wore white caps, the new symbol of student defiance. The rector, Dr. Stanislaw Furski, threatened "severe measures," then expelled thirty-four students, suspended eleven others, and closed eight departments. All 1,616 affected students were obliged to reapply for admission (seventy were eventually rejected). In April, the army newspaper, *Sztandar Mlodyck,* confirmed that the victimized students had been conscripted, although it provided no figures. The rector of the Higher School of Rural Economy, Professor Antoni Kleszczynski, set the tone when he complained that students were too well off: They should do their military service before their higher education, as prior to 1939. "We maintain for each student dormitory armies of administrators, cleaning women, plumbers, locksmiths and even gardeners." And what do we get in return? (This voice is familiar: although a Communist, Professor K. had his *Doppelgänger* in the shape of Falangist rectors in Spain and Conservative vice-chancellors in Britain.)

By April, with examinations approaching, the Polish universities were subdued. But the spirit of revolt was not extinguished. In June, the Polish press revealed for the first time that the May Day ceremonies in Wroclaw had been disrupted; in reprisal, forty-seven students were expelled from the university.

The Party embarked on a drastic campaign to isolate the students from the workers, resorting to virulent anti-Semitism orchestrated by the minister of the interior, General Mieczyslaw Moczar, leader of the so-called Partisan faction within the Party and chairman of Zbowid, a war veterans' organization which linked student demonstrations to subversion by West Germany, America, and Israel. The Soviet bloc had embraced the Arab cause during the Six-Day War of 1967, which gave a boost to Moczar's anti-Semitic campaign against liberal Jews and prompted Gomulka to keep pace by linking Jews with subversion. The Polish press now accused the wartime Judenrat and the ghetto leaders of collaboration with the Nazis in exterminating the Jews (whose numbers had been reduced from 3.5 million to about 27,000). Two Party secretaries, Joseph Kepa of Warsaw and Edward Gierek of Silesia (the future successor to Gomulka as general secretary), denounced "Zionist agitators" while Gomulka himself advised Jews "who loved Israel" (that is, Jews) to leave Poland. From early March the press was blaming Jews for the student rioting; an article in *Slowo Powszechne,* a pseudo-Catholic paper subsidized by the Party to undermine the Church, named the alleged Zionist student agitators and their fathers.* The Babel Club of the Jewish Cultural Association was "revealed" by *Trybuna Ludu* and Warsaw Party Secretary Kepa to be the center of the plot. The "anti-Zionist" purge removed almost all of Poland's few remaining Jews from leading positions in the Party, the administration, and the universities.

In mid-July, Gomulka warned that the anti-Zionist campaign had gotten out of hand, while the official ideologist Zenon Kliszko admitted that "the Jew and the Zionist are being made identical." But of course that had always been the intention; the Jew was not only symbolic of the critical intelligence and cosmopolitan liberal values feared by the Party, but was also a time-honored scapegoat, for there is no doubt that the anti-Semitic campaign was popular among workers and peasants. Although far-reaching workers' uprisings took place in Poland in 1956, 1970, 1976, and 1980–81, the student-intellectual revolt of 1968, inspired by the banning of *Dziady,* remained isolated from the workers.

ITALY

ROME, March 1, 1968—Two hundred people are injured, including 147 policemen, and hundreds are arrested when students who have assembled on the Spanish Steps and marched to the Faculty of Architecture in the northeast quarter do battle with police. The capital is paralyzed by monstrous traffic jams extending from the city center to the Villa Borghese. As the students hurl rocks at the police jeeps, Communist city councilors observe without comment the burning vehi-

---

*Three senior Jewish officials, whose children had been involved in the student demonstrations, were discharged: Fryderyk Topolski, director of urban dispersal; Jan Grudzinski, of the Foreign Ministry; and Jan Gorecki, director-general of the Finance Ministry. At the end of April, Julius Katz-Suchy, professor of diplomatic history at Warsaw University and previously ambassador to India, was prematurely retired, having been accused by *Trybuna Ludu* of "ambivalence" toward student demonstrations. Two economics professors—Ignacy Sachs and Kazimierz Laski, both Jews—were dismissed at Warsaw University, while two Jewish history professors at Lodz—Leon Tadeusz-Blaszczyk and Pavel Korzel—were accused of pro-Israel sympathies and suffered the same fate. In May, Professor Stefan Amsterdamsky, head of the Philosophy of History Department of Lodz University, was dismissed and expelled from the Party. At the end of that month, E. Etler, director of the documentary film *Judaika,* a tribute to the Jewish faith and the murdered Jews, was dismissed from the Polish Film School at Lodz at the same time as Professor Jerzy Toeplitz, an eminent Jewish film historian and rector of the Film School. The Jewish film director Aleksandr Ford was expelled from the Party and the dissolution of eight film units within Film Polski was demanded. Jerzy Bossak, also Jewish, was dismissed as head of the State Documentary Film Studio in Warsaw.

cles and cracked heads. The students are demanding the passage of a university reform bill through the Italian parliament. A group of professors sympathetic to their cause call for the dismissal of the Magnificent Rector of Rome University, Professor Pietro d'Avack. These calls are echoed by the Left in Parliament.

During the academic year 1967–68, nineteen of thirty-three Italian state universities were affected by student unrest; thirteen buildings were occupied. The revolt came out of the blue, without alert-signals of cultural alienation or rebellion against the traditional Roman Catholic social and sexual values still dominating Italian society.

The conflagration began at the universities of Trento and Turin, which experienced a month's occupation from November 27 to December 27, 1967, then continued with a series of battles, evictions, lockouts, and demonstrations of student solidarity with Fiat workers. Student revolts in Milan, Rome, and Naples followed rapidly. The Naples Faculties of Agriculture and Architecture were the first to be occupied in December, with the occupation spreading to all the faculties and involving what Maria Antonietta Macciocchi (elected a Communist deputy for the city the following May) called the "sequestration" of the rector.

Throughout Italy counter-courses were organized on guerrilla warfare, repression in the family, and other radical subjects. Renewed occupations during the early months of 1968 culminated in March with the closing of many arts faculties. The "Red Guard" militants at Turin demanded the election of professors and the grading of examinations under the supervision of student committees. By April, Turin University had conceded "the right to speak during lessons," the creation of seminar groups involving full professors, the abolition of signatures of presence and roll calls at lectures, and the provision of a hall for student meetings. But the rector of Turin rejected a student voice in the selection of professors and in the spending of funds.

Delegations arrived from all over Italy to learn from the Turin experience. Student unrest was epidemic at Pisa, Milan, Florence, Rome, Naples, Venice, Catania, Palermo, and Trento. Five million dollars in damage was inflicted at the universities of Rome, Pisa, Milan, and Trento. Slogans celebrating Che and Mao appeared everywhere. In the vanguard of the insurrection were the Student Movement (the largest group), the Maoist Guardie Rosse, and a Situationist group called Uccelli (the Birds). A faction adopting the position of the German SDS was concentrated in Turin, where Luigi Bobbio and Guido Viale laid stress on the institutional structures of capitalism and the students' role as "detonator" in forging an advanced revolutionary consciousness.

Italian universities were bursting at the seams with 530,000 students and an average staff-student ratio of only one-to-forty. Rome boasted only three hundred professors for 60,000 registered students, a ratio of 200:1; according to one estimate the university could properly accommodate only 18,000 students. Personal and intellectual contacts were minimal. Professors, unremovable emperors of their departments, habitually neglected their academic duties to pursue parallel careers, notably in politics. The leading Christian Democratic politician, Amintore Fanfani—sometime prime minister and foreign minister in the Center-Left government of Aldo Moro—held the chair of economic history in Rome's Law Faculty. Frequently the professors dished up stale courses from manuals written by themselves, then set the examinations. The curricula were notoriously antiquated; the political science syllabus at Rome University stopped dead at Rousseau. According to one estimate, only 30 percent of 1967's graduates found jobs.

Students and underpaid junior faculty were now demanding new teaching schedules, revised examination methods, and increased power to faculty councils. But the rigid hierarchies remained unresponsive. On February 17, 1968, the *Corriera Della Sera* published "A Manifesto of Illustrious Teachers," demanding a return to legality, an end to the occupations by extremists, and a resumption of the "instruction desired by the majority." The government had a university reform bill in the pipeline, but Parliament dissolved itself before its passage into law. The debates had shown the general inability of the deputies to comprehend student demands; at the eleventh hour, the Right and the Communists—the one protesting "too much!," the other "too little!"—combined to thwart a bill authorizing the creation of student-faculty joint committees.

By March, twenty-six universities had experienced demonstrations and half a million students were estimated to be on strike or not at work. In Turin students attempted to storm the premises of the newspaper *Stampa* to complain about its biased reporting. Unrest spread to the schools. At the elite Parini School in Milan, pupils met in general assembly and voted to strike. When their headmaster, Professor Daniele Mattalia, defended their right to do so and refused to call in the police, he was suspended by the director of schools. A noted Dante scholar, Mattalia spoke enthusiastically of the need for self-government and self-discovery. The Parini pupils, demanding the admission of more working-class kids to their school, voted their head "the most democratic in Milan." The school was closed.

Student occupations closed Rome University from March 1 to 12, but no sooner was it reopened than new demonstrations took place. On March 16, clashes occurred when police blocked the route of 5,000 students marching on the American embassy to protest the Vietnam War. Meanwhile, the radical Right was mobilizing. Four hundred self-styled "Nazis" had arrived from northern Italy, holding up tricolor flags and large banners inscribed "Duce" and "Italian Socialist Republic" (founded by Mussolini and the Germans after Italy's armistice with the Allies in 1943). These northern Nazis proceeded to take over the occupied Law Faculty from a neo-fascist group of similar stripe to the Occident Movement in France, and then dispersed the left-wing students; the latter regrouped, wearing plastic helmets, and attempted in vain to dislodge them. After thirteen hours, the rector called in the police: one hundred students were hurt during the day, thirty-four of them hospitalized.

Under severe duress, the university administration agreed to hold the scheduled examinations under conditions laid down by the students. This code: (1) permitted each candidate to abandon the examination if he or she wished to take it again later; (2) made provision for the examination board to discuss the papers in the presence of the candidates; and (3) entitled students to request examination on alternative questions not set in the papers. (In fact, these demands were in accordance with the official statutes, which had never been put into effect.) The examinations started and continued normally for two weeks, but then d'Avack, the Magnificent Rector, sallied out into the central courtyard and ordered the students, by megaphone, to evacuate the buildings. When this was ignored, he declared the examinations annulled (rendering the men liable to military conscription), met the minister of education, Luigi Gui, and called in the police, who cleared the buildings with a display of brutality.

The next day 4,000 students gathered in the Piazza di Spagna and marched to the Architecture Faculty, their numbers growing. The police were waiting and attacked immediately. Richard Davy, of the London *Times,* commented that "they seemed to feel that they have a mission not just to clear the streets but to punish and injure anyone found walking in them." On April 27, in the Piazza Cavour, the police charged when a student demonstration was almost over, injuring 50 and arresting 160. Lawyers denounced the police brutality that took place outside and on the steps of the Palace of Justice itself. Exclaimed the *Corriera della Sera:* "For four hours the capital was chaos." Meanwhile, unrest continued in Turin, Milan, Venice, Bologna, and Bari. Members of the Student Movement attempted to block trucks carrying newspapers to Venice—a conscious imitation of SDS tactics in Germany against the Springer newspaper empire.

On May 1, with a general election scheduled for May 19, the student banners attacked Pietro Nenni, the veteran Socialist who had finally amalgamated his party with the right-wing Social Democrats and thrown in his lot with Aldo Moro's Center-Left coalition government. "Nenni, Your Police are like the Gestapo," one banner proclaimed. Regiments of carabinieri, supported by the green-uniformed riot squads of the Public Security and black-capped paratroops, were deployed in Rome.

Although Nenni's "historic compromise" with the center parties provoked the same anger among Italian students as did Brandt's in Germany, the Italian Communist Party (PCI) had remained wary of the student demonstrations. Facing an election, the PCI did not wish to be associated with mob violence. Many workers were relatively *integrati* with Fiat's consumer society and preferred a plate of May Day *fettuccine* at home to a demonstration. A PCI document circulating in April warned against the notion of an autonomous student movement in rebellion against technocratic society. Clearly the Party was ill at ease with radical student ideology, which now looked to Mao, Castro, or the radical priest Camillo Torres, rather than to Gramsci and Togliatti (the great deans of Italian communism). However, unlike the intransigent and generally contemptuous attitude of the French Communist Party toward the student movement, the Italian Communists made strenuous efforts to understand the new radical pantheism; in February and March the journal *Contemporaneo-Rinascita* devoted several generous discussions to the youth revolt. But the PCI's theoreticians invariably reverted to the necessity of a revolutionary *party*— perhaps the highest barrier between the New and Old Lefts.

In April, the PCI's general secretary, Luigi Longo, invited student leaders of all persuasions to confer with him for four hours. Subsequently he published an article in the Party journal *Rinascita* on May 3, in which he spoke of a new historic bloc of progressive forces including youth and students. Longo admitted errors in the Party's attitude toward the student movement, and a lack of information about the Cuban, Latin-American, and the Chinese Cultural revolutions—all areas of symbolic appeal to European students. The comparative breadth of the Italian Communist perspective was expressed by Maria Antonietta Macciocchi, when she wrote of the "Vietnam generation" as "an entire movement which is part of the Party but which is also outside the Party, and for whom *the* important fact of their lifetime is the defeat inflicted on the American Cyclops by the tiny Vietnamese nation." Rossana Rossanda, a member of the Central Committee of the PCI and its national spokeswoman on education, even wrote sympathetically of Daniel Cohn-Bendit, a deviation that no French Communist official attempted. Longo's gesture, however, was implicitly repudiated in June by the Party theoretician, Giorgio Amendola, who published a polemic in *Rinascita,* accusing students of "extremist infantilism" and "nineteenth-century revolutionary barricades tactics." To make things worse, Longo later praised the "realism" displayed by the French Communist Party during the events of May and June, adding that the French student movement was divided by everything except hostility to Gaullism.

In the general election, Nenni's Socialists suffered a rebuff, their share of the national vote falling to 14.5 percent, compared with 20 percent in 1963. Although the center of political gravity had shifted very little, the Socialists took note of minor Communist gains, and promptly pulled out of the Center-Left coalition, throwing Italy into a protracted government crisis. The PCI marginally improved its share of the vote.

With the reopening of Milan State University under police protection on May 29, the storm center moved to the Catholic University of the Sacred Heart (La Cattolica), occupied by two hundred students wearing miners' helmets and armed with staves and fire extinguishers. The rector, besieged in his office, had his meals sent in but was given leave to attend mass. The leaders of the revolt petitioned the archbishop of Milan to allow students full freedom of discussion. (At the Cattolica, the Left invoked Pope John XXIII; the Right, Pius XII.) Student reinforcements from Rome, Genoa, Venice, and Trento arrived and an attack was launched on the offices of the *Corriera della Sera* (whose reporting angered Italian students much as *Le Figaro* did in France and the Springer newspapers in Germany). The demonstrators overturned cars to form barricades around the Via Solferino; at dawn they assembled again in the Fuoro Buonaparte and Via Dante, smashing windows. On June 8, police stormed the Catholic University, the Polytechnic University, and the triennial exhibition of decorative arts, arresting 250 and putting 30 in the hospital. (Later in the year the Church imposed on all new students an oath of loyalty to the university's rules and hierarchy. Students were forbidden to take part in demonstrations or movements not approved by the Church—the democratic image offered by the Church in Poland was hardly in evidence in Italy or Spain.)

Just as the Cannes Film Festival had been disrupted, so on May 31, the Milan Triennale Exhibition, The World of Tomorrow, was closed by students and artists a few minutes after the ribbon was cut.

Concurrent and spectacular events in France quickly made their impact. The Student Movement distributed handbills in working-class areas, calling for worker-student collaboration against privilege in education. On June 3, some three hundred right-wing students attacked the radicals who had reoccupied Rome University three days earlier. At the request of the Magnificent Rector, the police reoccupied the university.

In Florence, radicals denouncing Gaullism marched under NLF flags and portraits of Mao. In downtown Genoa, a thousand workers and students marched in tenuous alliance and in solidarity with the French comrades. In Turin, red and black flags were raised on the steps of the Palazzo Campana, the university's main administration building. Ten universities remained under occupation, and such was the breakdown that some cut their losses by declaring the academic year to be terminated.

SPAIN

MADRID, March 28, 1968—General Franco's government closes Madrid University *en bloc,* indefinitely. Twenty-three students are expelled from Seville, and Valencia becomes the third Spanish university to be shut down. The U.S. embassy in the capital is ringed by police reacting to major demonstrations against the Vietnam War accompanied by a flamboyant display of NLF flags, a rash of Ho and Che posters, and slogans aimed at the American military bases in Spain. Despite Franco, young Spain has rejoined the world. Vietnam is secondary to the native issue: democracy.

The strength of the Spanish student movement lay in its collaboration with the militant sections of the working class (Communist, Socialist, and anarchist). Franco's regime had tightly limited the number of university students, only 3 percent of whom came from working-class or peasant backgrounds. Fees were high and grants minimal. Junior lecturers earned only 3,000 *pesetas* ($45) a month. Between 40 and 50 percent of students entering the universities dropped out before their final examinations. Feudal structures of authority prevailed.

A member of a workers' commission told *Le Monde*'s correspondent, Daniel Garric, that Spain was the only country in Europe where workers and students, Catholic and Communist, collaborated. "The country continues to live in 1936," remarked a clandestine student official. Invited to name their *maîtres à penser,* Spanish radicals nominated several French Marxists, including Jean-Paul Sartre, Louis Althusser, and André Gorz, as well as Che Guevara and "above all Herbert Marcuse." (But one may be skeptical about the latter's appeal in a predemocratic society.)

In 1962 radical students had formed their own clandestine organization, the Democratic University Federation, which opposed not only the official students' union, the SEU, but the whole authoritarian regime. The first confrontation came in Madrid on February 24, 1965, when a silent march to the university rectorate, protesting government control of the SEU elections, was broken up by the police. The government closed the Faculties of Philosophy and Medicine and suspended four professors. In 1966 the focus of the struggle switched to Barcelona; police stormed a Capuchin monastery, where a convention of free students was in progress; sixty-eight professors were suspended and numerous students were banned and fined. Barcelona University was closed.

In December 1967, Madrid University's Faculty of Political and Economic Science was closed on account of what the rector called "open rebellion." Rioting students had hurled stones and shouted "Liberty!" and "Death to Franco!" The University of Salamanca was also affected. In Barcelona, police dispersed two hundred students demonstrating their solidarity with Madrid. In January 1968, the government installed a permanent police force, the Policía Universitaria, on the campus; on January 15, thirty-five police jeeps, two platoons of cavalry, and water cannon were moved into the university city, but the government was nevertheless forced to close Madrid's Faculty of Philosophy and Letters after desks, chairs, bottles, and bricks were hurled from upper windows. A protest meeting was held at the Law Faculty, a bus was set on fire, and traffic was blocked. The minister of education, Manuel Lora Tamayo, closed the affected faculties until March 1, forcing its students to reapply for entry (the same tactic was employed a month later in Warsaw) and to lose their enrollment fees. The burning of offending newspapers provided another link with the students of Warsaw (and, later, with Belgrade).

The neo-fascist mentality characteristic of Franco's thirty-year reign was reflected in a decision taken early in the year to close the Center of Higher Studies and Sociological Research (with 1,500 students) and to fine the director 25,000 *pesetas.* The charge against him was "political activity against the Government" and the main instance provided was an unauthorized lecture by the eminent French political scientist, Professor Maurice Duverger.

Meanwhile at Bilbao, professors of the Faculty of Economic Sciences and Politics presided at an assembly of 1,800 students, during which an illegal autonomous union was formed. Strikes hit the universities of Oviedo, Granada, and Valencia. The minister of information showed his mettle by bringing a case against Rafael Gonzales, director of a Roman Catholic periodical, who had described the closure of the Madrid faculties as illegal. Police hosed Madrid students in green dye on January 21. On January 25, the Faculty of Sciences was closed for twenty-four hours after an illegal meeting; the following day the police invaded the Medical School, already paralyzed by lockouts and riots.

Madrid's School of Technical Sciences (with 10,000 students) was closed. Twenty-two Barcelona students were expelled at the end of January, following a campus battle. All 15,000 Barcelona students responded by boycotting classes. The lawyers' association protested to the rector over the imposition of penalties without a proper hearing. Varying sanctions were taken against twenty-seven Madrid students.

The Ministry of Education announced that from January 29, special police agents would be stationed on the campus at the disposal of the rector and deans. But three-quarters of the professors in the Law Faculty adamantly refused to give classes under such conditions. The same principled reaction occurred at the Faculty of Medicine, where professors declined to supervise clinical work under a police presence. In the relentless cycle of retaliation and counter-retaliation, four medical professors were suspended by the rector of Madrid, Isodoro Martín. Professor Hernández Tejero, dean of the Law Faculty, and his deputy, Professor García Gallo, resigned in protest. Pressures on the government's yes-men within the administration were now intense: the university's vice-rector, Professor García Trevijano, resigned after being censured by professors of the Political Science Faculty for approving certain sanctions against students. Professor Arellano, of Seville, boldly associated the general university turmoil with the crisis of a nation deprived of elementary liberty and freedom of association. Professor Carlos Ollero, of Madrid, publicly hailed the events as a sign of hope for a democratic future.

In mid-February, Madrid's Faculties of Economics and Political Science were no sooner opened than students gathered in "illegal" assemblies to support their victimized colleagues. Police chased them through corridors and classrooms, arresting forty students inside three Madrid faculties. Fifteen hundred students gathered in the Faculty of Law to declare Rector Martín *persona non grata.* Pursued by the police, some took refuge in the university chapel, while others sought sanctuary with Torres López, dean of the Law Faculty, who refused to hand over their identity cards to the police. Soon afterwards another dean, Prieto Castro, resigned after the police had hosed him in colored dye when he tried to defuse a tense confrontation outside his own office. Castro threatened to bring suit against the chief of police.

In no other country was the intensity and sheer persistence of protest action so remarkable. The iron fist of an authoritarian state merely intensified it. In Spain, as in other countries where basic democracy was lacking (Poland, Czechoslovakia, Yugoslavia) or where corruption, overcrowding, and administrative breakdown dominated students' lives, technocracy and consumer capitalism were not the main issues. Situationists and Yippies—the apostles of cultural revolution—

thrived only in the affluent bourgeois democracies of Western Europe and the United States.

The cycle of repression and protest in Spain was unique; it was almost ceremonial, despite its violence and despite the passionate animosities behind the ritual. The arrest of student delegates elected at "illegal" meetings was the constant pattern. Five hundred Madrid students boycotted classes to protest the arrest of their delegate, Roman Oria, and a fine of $700 imposed by the minister of education on Don Andrés Garrigo, editor of a popular student periodical. Seven hundred Salamanca students demonstrated outside the police station demanding the release of arrested colleagues. In short, a formidable proportion of Spain's 175,000 students were in a state of permanent rebellion.

At the end of February, the government stepped back, removing police agents from the university. On Wednesday, February 28, classes took place normally for the first time in five months. But early in March, Seville University was closed and further gatherings took place in Madrid to protest police actions in Seville and Pamplona. Inevitably police on foot and horseback broke up the meeting, snatching the "ringleaders" into detention. Unrest spread to Zaragoza and the private Catholic University of Navarre Opus Dei, with Bilbao in ferment. A thousand students barricaded themselves into Santiago de Compostela, demanding the resignation of the dean of the Faculty of Science, who had denounced thirteen students to the police. The rector had issued a stern warning deterring professors who wished to express solidarity by attending the student meetings.

In April, Education Minister Manuel Lora Tamayo, a "moderate," informed Spain's tame legislature, the Cortes, that the student movement had subversive international roots. But on April 21, Rector Martín of Madrid resigned. He had forwarded to the minister a letter from his Council of Professors demanding that certain cabinet measures be rescinded, notably the decision to station police on the campus. When the cabinet offered no concession, Martín felt obliged to resign along with two vice-rectors. Almost simultaneously, the minister's head also rolled after repeated clashes in the cabinet with the hard-line interior minister, Camilo Alonso Vega, who controlled the police.

On April 30, four days of heavy rioting began in the Spanish capital, prompted by an economic recession, a pay freeze, and the agitational activity of the clandestine Communist Party. Columns of workers, organized by the illegal "workers' commissions," converged on the Plaza Atocha, leading to running battles with civil guards in the suburb of Getafe. A strike and boycott of public transport hit Madrid as heavy detachments of security forces were drafted into the capital to confront mobile shock commandos of workers and students operating from light vehicles and coordinated by clandestine radio. Clashes also occurred in many provincial towns, including Seville, Bilbao, and Alicante.

As soon as Madrid University reopened its doors on May 6, after a thirty-six-day lockout, a rash of posters called for a resumption of the struggle. A meeting held to denounce the "fascist press" on May 14 resulted in another clash with the police. The temperature continued to rise. Violent battles in the city involved firebombs and barricades; the message from Paris was inspirational. On May 17, as the strike wave spread through France, the red flag flew for three hours over Madrid's Faculty of Letters. Riots followed Rector José Botella's ban (Martín's successor was a gynecologist still encased in the atavistic womb of a moribund authoritarianism) on a talk by Professor García Calvo, a Latinist who had been dismissed in 1965 for advocating student rights and, more recently, arrested while marching in the van of a May Day demonstration. On the fourth consecutive day of turmoil in Madrid, May 20, rioting continued across the city. When the illegal Democratic University Federation sponsored a concert by the Catalan protest singer Raimon, 5,000 people turned up.

On May 22, the government announced reforms. (A day later de Gaulle also announced reforms.) But they fell far short of student expectations: three new universities and two polytechnics would be created. The new education minister, Luis Villar Palasi (a professor of law), was able to insist that police be withdrawn from campuses and that restrictions be removed from student assemblies. Any sort of poster would be permissible except personal insults to Generalísimo Francisco Franco, the Caudillo. Palasi also pressed for legalization of the independent student associations—that would come later in the year.

In May, seventy-three students went on trial as a consequence of the rioting in Madrid. More than a thousand students who barricaded themselves in the School of Philosophy after the arrest of the Marxist student leader Pedro Giral were beaten, sprayed with dye from fire hoses and, in some cases, sent to military service (basically the fate that Columbia University in New York granted its own troublemakers). On June 2, the police raided student union offices in the closed Political and Economic Science Faculty in order to seize radical literature. No end was in sight.

NANTERRE (PARIS)

NANTERRE, March 22, 1968—Following the arrest of six members of the National Vietnam Committee, radical students decide to occupy the administrative building in protest. The activists take the elevator to the eighth floor, stage a token occupation of the professorial council chamber, and invade Dean Grappin's empty office. Walls are plastered with slogans: "Professors, you are past it and so is your culture!" "When examined, answer with questions!" "Please leave the Communist Party as clean on departing as you would like to find it on entering." (In France, public toilets are customarily protected by such *prière de laisser* notices.) From this demonstration the March 22 Movement takes its name. Its nucleus consists of virtually inseparable comrades united by friendship and belief, moving to and fro between Nanterre and the Latin Quarter of Paris.

The Nanterre campus of the University of Paris, opened in 1964, consisted of ultramodern, ultrafunctional buildings of steel and glass set in the midst of tar-paper–hut slums and raw, unfinished low-cost housing, crammed with immigrant Algerians. By 1968 the campus accommodated 12,000 students, many of them suffering from acute alienation. Dancing once a week, *ciné* club twice a week, and television every night were no substitute for the warmth and pulsing life of the Latin Quarter. Furniture could neither be added to nor changed; no cooking was allowed; and boys were forbidden to visit girls in their rooms. (The reverse journey was allowed if the girl was over twenty-one or had her parents' written permission.)

In April 1967, a group of male students at Nanterre had camped in the entrance hall of one of the women's dormitories. Among them was a freckled, red-haired sociology student with something of a reputation as a beatnik, Daniel Cohn-Bendit. (In fact, he wore his hair short and often wore a conventional jacket.) By early next morning a ring of police had surrounded the dormitory block.

In November, Nanterre went on strike. Cohn-Bendit reported: ". . . the first term of the 'historic' year 1967–68 saw a student strike which went far beyond the traditional political and union framework. Some 10,000 to 12,000 of us boycotted all lectures in order to force the authorities to improve our working conditions . . . a protest against overcrowding, which had been exacerbated by the recent Fouchet reforms and the consequent reorganization of lecture halls." Sleek, conspicuously anonymous men were spotted strolling around the campus, studying faces and intently reading student notice boards. The anarchists began to photograph these plainclothes policemen and pin their portraits to the same notice boards.

On January 8, 1968, an earnest and amiable minister for youth, François Missoffe, the editor of a massive anthology on the problems of French youth, arrived at the *cité universitaire* of Nanterre to open a new swimming pool. Jeered by a group of anarchists, including a young man with a cheeky air, the minister chose to confront them; Daniel Cohn-Bendit complained that his book said nothing about the sexual problems of the young. Missoffe recommended a dip in the swimming pool as a cure for such problems, whereupon Cohn-Bendit accused him of talking like a Hitler Youth. The minister shrugged this off, but a zealous official began proceedings to deport the twenty-one-year-old foreign student. (Born in France in 1945 of émigré German Jews who had fled the Nazis, Cohn-Bendit had been registered as stateless at birth. He adopted German citizenship in 1959 to avoid French military service. His brother Gabriel, born in Paris in 1936 as a French citizen, shared Daniel's libertarian outlook.)

With the "swimming pool" incident, the movement of the *enragés* had begun. On January 26, forty activists marched up and down the main hall carrying banners ridiculing the plainclothes police plaguing the campus. Panicking, the administration called in the uniformed police. A thousand students gathered to repel them.

Toward the middle of March, students of social psychology decided to boycott their examinations, and they distributed a pamphlet, "Why Do We Need Sociologists?" written by Cohn-Bendit, Jean-Pierre Duteuil, Bertrand Gérard, and Bernard Granautier. The main thrust of their argument was that modern sociology, "a belated import from across the Atlantic," was purpose-built to condition students to the functional requirements of the capitalist system.

On March 28, one week after the founding of the March 22 Movement (and the closure of the University of Warsaw), Dean Grappin ordered a four-day suspension of lectures and laboratory work. A police cordon ringed the campus while five hundred students divided into discussion groups on the lawn. Three days later, second-year sociology students decided to boycott their exams, condemning sociology as a capitalist fraud. By now the teaching faculty was split. Professors in the Faculty of Letters and Social Science (notably Guy Michaud, professor of French literature) supported the demand that a lecture hall be made permanently available for political discussions, while professors in the Faculty of History wanted the ringleaders arrested. Dean Grappin did provide a small room, but the students took over a large lecture theatre on April 2 for a meeting of 1,200, attended by Karl-Dietrich Wolff of the German Socialist Students League, whose theory and practice exercised a vital influence on the Nanterre activists, notably Cohn-Bendit who, equally fluent in German and French, had made Frankfurt his home.

The dean of Nanterre, Pierre Grappin, an active, respected liberal, was a man of the Left, a former Resistance hero who had escaped while in transit to a Nazi concentration camp. His academic council was not confined to *professeurs titulaires* (full professors), but included *maîtres de conférence* and *chargés d'enseignement* (assistant professors and instructors). Grappin deplored the rising violence at Nanterre as a form of left-wing fascism; on April 4, he yielded to pressure from the right-wing minister of education, Alain Peyrefitte, to close the campus. Peyrefitte later (May 9) told the National Assembly: "What were these daily agitations all about? In the name of a 'university critique' the most stupid rhetoric was poured out in lecture theatres which, for the night, had been christened Fidel Castro, Che Guevara, Mao Tse-tung, or Leon Trotsky."

When militant activity resumed after the Easter break, the fever was heightened by the attempted assassination of Germany's most influential student leader, Rudi Dutschke, whom Cohn-Bendit had met in 1967 and much admired. The dean issued a notice: Examinations scheduled for May and October would be held on schedule. On April 22, 1,500 students occupied the B1 Lecture Theatre, while study commissions met in C Building. The resulting manifesto reflected the rising influence of the March 22 Movement: outright rejection of the capitalist-technocratic university, of the division of labor and of so-called neutral knowledge—supplemented by a call for solidarity with the working class.

The university now embarked on disciplinary action against eight students, including Cohn-Bendit, summoning them to appear before a Disciplinary Committee at the Sorbonne on May 3. Four Nanterre professors (Lefèvre, Touraine, Michaud, and Ricoeur) volunteered to undertake their defense. In Professor Alain Touraine's opinion, the student movement at Nanterre would not have turned into a national crisis if its adversaries in the university and the government had been less blind. The strike of November 1967 had no more interested the Ministry of Education, said Touraine, than the major industrial strikes of 1967 at Rhodiaceta and Saviem enterprises had interested the minister of social affairs. *"Les Français n'intéressaient pas leurs dirigeants"*—the French did not interest their leaders. Christian Fouchet, the minister of education whose proposed reforms had excited widespread agitation in the universities, had become minister of the interior by the time of the May insurrection. In terms of Touraine's comment, it was a symbolic promotion.

Touraine's affection and respect for his pupil Cohn-Bendit were reciprocated. "During the sociology course," Touraine wrote, "he constantly intervened, discussing, commenting, criticizing. He did not re-

ject teaching or study, but could only take part at the top of his voice.
. . . [An] orator and peace-maker of assemblies, but capable, an instant
after a grand collision, of calmly discussing a situation or action, he was
above all an awaker, provoking fear, reserve, often hesitation, but almost always sympathy." Cohn-Bendit particularly enjoyed ridiculing
the standardized slogans of the sectarian Left. For his part, Cohn-
Bendit praised Touraine as "that exceptional professor" who understood the need for political and ideological commitment. It was a rare
compliment.

BRITAIN: VIETNAM

LONDON, March 17, 1968—25,000 march on the American embassy
in Grosvenor Square. The police deploy 1,300 men, 800 of them in the
vicinity of the square, including a mounted contingent. Taking over the
entire width of Oxford Street, the young radicals hop-hop to the chant
of "Ho-Ho-Ho Chi Minh! We will fight, We will win!"

After thirteen years of Tory rule, the Labour government elected
in 1964 had raised expectations among the young which soon turned
to bitter disillusionment. The Campaign for Nuclear Disarmament
(CND), since 1958 the symbolic rallying point for every duffle-coated
"good cause" and humane guitar, collapsed after the Wilson government adopted Britain's bomb and the Tribune Group MPs—stalwarts
of the Aldermaston marches like Anthony Greenwood—found their
cabinet duties to be incompatible with membership in CND's national
council. By 1967 the nuclear issue had been delivered into the hands
of a revolutionary New Left contemptuous of parliamentary politics
and convinced that the function of the Labour Party was to preserve
the capitalist system by effecting minor reforms and diverting the working class into sterile trade unionism and electoral games. In March
1968, Cambridge students attempted to overturn a car carrying Labour
Defence Secretary Denis Healey. The May Day Manifesto of 1968 (the
work of socialist intellectuals) echoed the disillusionment: "We are
faced with something alien and thwarting: a manipulative politics
. . . which has taken our meanings and changed them . . . which seems
our creation, but now stands against us, as the agent of the priorities
of money and power."

Attempting to storm the American embassy on March 17, the
demonstrators encountered flailing truncheons and a charge by
mounted police—but no tear gas. Such were the clashes that 117 policemen and 45 demonstrators received medical treatment. Charges were

brought against 246 people. The police commander on the spot blamed the Vietnam Ad Hoc Committee for failing to issue precise instructions, appoint marshals, and generally make clear its objectives. An alternative perspective was voiced by journalist Peter Fryer, who had witnessed the Soviet suppression of the Hungarian revolt in 1956. He reported that a young policeman had three times punched his wife in the small of the back. Later Fryer himself was kicked in the head by four or five policemen; lifted off the ground; kicked in the thigh, the buttock, and the testicles; then thrown over a railing and low hedge.

Up front and "Ho-Hoing" was the radical student best known to the British public in the late sixties, Tariq Ali. A Pakistani of flamboyant charm and a former president of the Oxford Union, he had visited North Vietnam as a member of an investigating team despatched by the Russell Peace Foundation. Tariq Ali shared the disgust of his generation at the "utterly servile and prostrate" posture of British and German social democracy. A Gerald Scarfe cartoon of the period depicted Wilson's long, forked tongue licking the posterior of LBJ, with the simple caption: "Special relationship." A Trotskyist of the International Marxist Group and intellectually indebted (like others of his generation) to the historian Isaac Deutscher, Tariq Ali was depicted in the British popular press (with some encouragement from the orator himself) as the demon of insurrectionary street warfare.

But what of "Ho-Ho-Ho Chi Minh"? Another Stalinist, surely. Why chant one leader's name to symbolize a whole people's struggle against foreign domination? Does a cause require a personification? A decade later, after the unification of Vietnam on Hanoi's terms, Tariq Ali wrote: "The National Liberation Front of Vietnam fought the war not just for national independence, but also for 'democracy.' It was committed to holding free elections, to freedom of the press, of trade unions, of political parties, of creed, of demonstration. All of this was unambiguously stated by the NLF. But it didn't happen. All the talk about 'democracy' turns out to be a subterfuge, a manoeuvre to obtain mass support. Nothing more."

The attempted assassination of Rudi Dutschke brought further demonstrations in London. Eight hundred police formed a cordon six men deep to hold off a thousand demonstrators chanting "Rudi Dutschke!" outside the Springer offices in the *Daily Mirror* building. Led by the Vietnam Solidarity Campaign (Tariq Ali and David Barrymore, a London fashion photographer wearing a red steel helmet), International Socialist, and some anarchists, the demonstrators had surged up from Trafalgar Square, outflanking the tail of the CND's Easter march, which was on its sober way to St. Paul's to pay tribute to Martin Luther King, Jr. Leaping and hopping in a *Zorba the Greek* dance, chanting the names of Ho and Rudi, this crowd incurred the displeasure of Axel Springer's Fleet Street colleagues. The London *Times* deplored the violence of those "for whom protest is a means of self-expression," but congratulated the London police on their restraint: "The worst thing the police can do is to take it upon themselves to inflict punishment on the demonstrators," as recently in Warsaw and West Berlin. The *Observer* extended its congratulations to the students of Madrid and Warsaw, "who seek to win freedoms like ours from repressive regimes," but withheld it from the rioters of Tokyo, West Berlin, and London, who did not represent, "serious political movements pursuing real aims: they are more like a highbrow version of football hooliganism." Speaking for the Old Left Tribune Group, Frank Allaun, MP, drew a distinction between the legitimate German SDS protests against the Springer newspaper empire, and the "pathetic and ill-considered" sympathy demonstrations staged in London, which merely succeeded in snatching the headlines "from the enormous and moving protest which was made by the Aldermaston marchers." It seemed that student revolt was always a good idea—if somewhere else.

On May 1 appeared a pilot sheet for the first issue of *Black Dwarf* (May 15), edited by Tariq Ali and turned down (he reported) by some thirty printers. On June 1, the *Dwarf* announced in banner headlines: "WE SHALL FIGHT WE WILL WIN—PARIS LONDON ROME BERLIN." The playwright David Mercer's leading article denounced the "respectable citizen" who "lives rooted in his smug individual interests. . . . He makes money out of everything and everyone, given the chance—not stopping short at the most barbarous means of destruction. He produces and consumes at random, wastefully. He builds ugly cities and makes the air stink and throb from the pursuit of his wretched palliatives: loot, territory, petty power."

The *Black Dwarf* issue of July 5 suggested that Tariq Ali was under various stresses; apparently some comrades were accusing him of cultivating his own personality. He promised to stop traveling around and addressing four meetings a week: "I have decided to abandon the more public aspects of my political life." The playwright Dennis Potter was quoted as including Tariq Ali among the "impotent, squawking, posturing, finger jabbing nincompoops" who were doing nobody any good. The *Dwarf,* however, continued to attract writers of high quality (including David Mercer, John Berger, and Eric Hobsbawm) and remained refreshingly free of sectarianism.

BRITAIN: RACE

BIRMINGHAM, April 20, 1968—Enoch Powell, MP, delivers a speech that will become both famous and notorious. "Those whom the gods wish to destroy they first make mad. We must be mad, literally mad, as a nation to be permitting the annual inflow of some 50,000 dependants, who are for the most part the material of the future growth of the immigrant-descended population. . . . Like the Roman, I seem to see 'the river Tiber foaming with much blood.' "

In Britain workers and radical students were deeply divided. Race was the most abrasive issue.

Powell was a well-educated man who had been appointed professor of Greek at Sydney University, Australia, at the age of twenty-five (with a special interest in Thucydides and Herodotus). Having held various junior government posts, he had stood for the leadership of his party in 1965, but received the support of only fifteen Conservative MPs out of 298. Now, in 1968, Powell capitalized on the recent ghetto riots in the United States: "That tragic and intractable phenomenon which we watch with horror on the other side of the Atlantic, but which there is interwoven with the history and existence of the States itself, is coming upon us here by our own volition and our own neglect."

The speech provoked a storm of controversy and Powell's rapid dismissal from the Conservative Shadow Cabinet. But the popular reaction was alarming: "The only man in this country with the guts to say it!"

In February the Labour government had responded to racial pressure about a threatened influx of Kenya Asians, by rushing the Commonwealth Immigration Act through the Commons in three days. The act, which fixed annual quotas and limited the right of entry of certain categories of British passport holders, was described by the *New Statesman* as "the first incontestably racialist law to be placed on the statute book"—despite Home Secretary James Callaghan's "pitiful sophistries" and his claims that the basis of the act was "geographical not racial." The columnist Alan Watkins asked: "But where are the ministerial anti-racialists today?" Where were Richard Crossman, Anthony Wedgwood Benn, and Barbara Castle? Even the London *Times* called the bill "panic and prejudice . . . shameful."

Four days after Powell's speech in Birmingham the London *Times* printed an ugly picture of a dignified Sikh gentleman walking past a crowd of yelling dockworkers gathered outside Parliament in support of Powell. At the West India dock a thousand men signed a petition complaining about the "threat to our living standards by this blind policy of unlimited immigrants being imposed on us." On April 26, more than 4,000 London dockworkers staged a strike in support of

Powell. Clearly the mythology of racial fear was reinforced by slum housing conditions in the inner cities.

May Day 1968 was marred by angry clashes outside Parliament between left-wing students and Powellite workers, including dockworkers and porters from the meat and fish markets at Smithfield and Billingsgate. A counter-demonstration, featuring the ubiquitous student leader Tariq Ali, demanded Powell's prosecution under Section 6 of the Race Relations Act (which banned the public use of words likely to create racial hatred). Tariq Ali wrote of "the sickening display of malice towards coloured workers. . . ." This only proved that "it's easy for upper-class racists to brainwash the most backward and mean-minded elements of the working class into a hideous mob."

Racial tension poisoned the year, further dividing the New Left from the working class. Powell, the people's tribune, was repeatedly prevented from speaking on university platforms. In March his car was attacked at Essex University; on May 3, the wife of a pro-Rhodesia, pro-apartheid Tory MP, Patrick Wall, was thrown to the ground and kicked at Leeds University. In June an invitation to speak at Birmingham University was withdrawn on the ground that Powell's safety could not be guaranteed. After a fuss the invitation was renewed. (Tories were not the only visiting speakers at risk; Prime Minister Harold Wilson now required unprecedented security protection wherever he went. As the Tory *Sunday Telegraph* happily reported, "His mere appearance is enough to provoke fury.")

On July 7, a new clash took place in Whitehall when left-wing groups demonstrating against racism encountered Smithfield Market porters marching in support of immigration control. The race issue was symptomatic of the failure of the New Left in Britain to achieve even a shadow of unity with the unionized workers. Although the late sixties witnessed a sharp rise in industrial strikes, and a clash between the government and the unions over the legislation proposed in the White Paper, "In Place of Strife," the sociologist Peter Sedgwick's summary of the period was accurate: "The Instant Left was abstract, brave, verbally fluent and powerless. The working-class protest was concrete, cautious, verbally stereotyped and often successful."

6

INSURRECTION IN EUROPE, II:
Germany and West Berlin, Belgium, and Yugoslavia

"The attempted assassination of Rudi Dutschke precipitated furious rioting not only in West Berlin, but throughout West Germany."

GERMANY/WEST BERLIN

WEST BERLIN, April 11, 1968—Six days after the assassination of Martin Luther King, Jr., a man called Josef Bachmann fires a succession of shots at the student leader Rudi Dutschke. Hit twice in the head and once in the chest while riding his bicycle, Dutschke almost dies.

Less than a year had passed since another student at the Free University of Berlin had been shot dead by a plainclothes policeman during a demonstration against the Shah of Iran outside the Berlin opera house. Benno Ohnesorg, married and with a pregnant wife, had never before taken part in a demonstration. Outrage at his death touched every university in West Germany. Twelve thousand Berlin students marched behind his coffin. June 2, 1967 was a decisive event in the radicalization of the German student movement. But an opinion poll showed that a majority of the wider public believed the dead student got no more than he deserved.

It transpired that Dutschke's assailant was a "loner," twenty-three years old, politically unaffiliated, but influenced by the Springer press and the mayor of Berlin's denunciations of the radical students at the Free University. Bachmann kept a painting of Hitler in his room (the police reported) and, like Hitler, was a house painter. Dutschke, who had recently appeared on the cover of the magazine *Capital* looking like one of the less glamourous villains in a Western movie, was due to stand trial for "severe disturbances of the peace," arising out of his disruption of a Christmas Eve service in Berlin's Kaiser Wilhelm Memorial Church. Having delivered a speech against the Vietnam War from the chancel, he had been struck on the head by a member of the congregation and taken to a hospital. Thirty Evangelical pastors from Bremen had then compared Dutschke's action to that of Christ driving the money changers from the temple. Josef Bachmann reportedly told the police, "I read about Martin Luther King and I said to myself I must do this too."

Twenty-eight years old, the son of a Lutheran family living in the eastern part of Germany, Rudi Dutschke had moved to West Berlin in 1961 shortly before the building of the wall, and enrolled at the Free University. Passionately opposed to the authoritarian, bureaucratic socialism practiced in the Soviet Union and the German Democratic Republic (DDR)—where he had refused military service on Christian socialist grounds, accepting three years' factory work instead—he diagnosed the root of the deformation not merely in Stalinist "excesses," but in Leninism itself: in the rule of the Party rather than of the proletariat. It followed that all enterprises should be owned and controlled by workers' councils; for students and workers alike, the struggle must assume the form of the "long march through the institutions." Dutschke had recently carried this message to Prague, when he spoke and answered questions for six hours at the Charles University. While in Prague he told a British interviewer: "We must hate certain elements in society, but we must feel guilty about doing so. I have advocated the use of violence in practical instances, yes, but only against objects and property, not people."

With a lank forelock hanging down over intent eyes, sometimes short of a shave, Rudi carried an air of Celtic ferocity; when a Prague hotel waiter objected to his jeans and jerkin and his black-jowled appearance, Dutschke replied that he assumed this was not the Prague of the Emperor Franz Josef. An inspired orator described by the Springer newspapers as the mad axeman of the East German Party leader Walter Ulbricht, Dutschke had addressed crowds in a score of German and foreign cities, denouncing liberalism and party politics. A tribune of the politics of total belief, he justified the strategy of provoking the public as the only way of advertising the New Left's ideas and needs. "Without provocation we wouldn't be noticed at all." An ascetic impervious to liquor, tobacco, and material comforts, Dutschke had married an American and had an infant son named Hosea Che.

"Bourgeois democracy" was unacceptable. Even before the Coalition of 1966, the ruling Christian Democrats (CDU) and the Social Democratic opposition (SDP) had reached bipartisan agreement on the essentials of foreign and military policy. On December 1, 1966, came the news of a coalition government in Bonn, strengthening the case for an extraparliamentary opposition in the eyes of Rudi Dutschke and the New Left. The novelist Günter Grass, author of *The Tin Drum* and a dedicated Social Democrat, denounced the coalition with the warning that, "The youth of our country will turn its back on the state and will move either to the Left or the Right as soon as this wretched marriage has been agreed upon."

Grass, however, accorded the extraparliamentary Left a sardonic gaze: "Wherefrom come these all-or-nothing demands, if not from the well fertilized small gardens of German idealistic philosophy, and has not this German idealism always been a youthful extravaganza, to be followed by an exhausted reclining on the conservative plush sofa?" He predicted that the young "revolutionaries" would soon be voting Christian Democrat and pursuing careers while occasionally reminiscing about their escapades over a glass of Moselle.

THE FREE UNIVERSITY OF BERLIN

The Free University was founded in 1948 as West Berlin's answer to the Humboldt University, located since 1945 in the Soviet sector. The "Free" carried two connotations: political and educational. The plan was to break with the old, feudal model of lordly professors, subservient assistants, and supine students; indeed, the support given to radical students by their teachers was a conspicuous feature of the Free University in the 1960s. So, too, was the failure of the anti-Communist factor to divert student indignation from the Vietnam War, Third World poverty, the evils of the consumer society, and the "betrayal" of the Grand Coalition of 1966.

The student body had changed in composition. In the academic year 1956–57, almost one-third came from the East, bringing with them a stable anticommunism. By 1964–65, only 5 percent came from the Communist side of the wall, and the radical quotient was reinforced by students evading West German conscription.

Of West Germany's 271,000 students, between 4,000 and 6,000 were reckoned to be highly politicized radical activists. The most influential organization was the German Socialist Students League (SDS), founded in 1946 by the Social Democratic Party, but increasingly in conflict with the parent body until they split in 1961. This rift accelerated the SDS's radicalization, which continued until it dissolved in March 1970. By 1968 the SDS's membership stood at 2,500, according to its chairman, Karl-Dietrich Wolff, a law student born in 1943. Wolff had spent a year working with civil rights groups in the United States and spoke fluent English and French. Influenced by Rosa Luxemburg and Herbert Marcuse to the point of rejecting the concept of a political party, the SDS was dedicated to the commune as the unit of workers' control and decentralization. The SDS had fifty-six groups, exerted strong influence on between 10 and 25 percent of the students (depending on the university), and contained within it a faction from the banned Communist Party. In Berlin, about 600 students belonged to the SDS (out of the 16,000 at the Free University, and the 34,000 in the city as a whole).

Ideological reinforcement was offered by young dons in Göttingen (eight of whom published a letter in defense of the SDS in February 1968) and at the Free University—notably Ekkehart Krippendorff, Klaus Meschkat, and Johannes Agnoli, who adopted a Marcusean approach to late capitalist society. (Marcuse himself had been warmly received when he lectured at the Free University in 1967; he returned to visit Rudi Dutschke in the hospital as he recovered from his injuries.)

Despite tensions about the internal structure of the university, its curricula, and its examination system, the main issue at the Free University was always the wider society and the wider world: Vietnam, the Congo, Cuba, Iran, Rhodesia. Speeches often ended with Castro's battle cry, *"Venceremos!"* Third World guerrilla movements were regarded as the vanguard of the "permanent revolution"; reversing the traditional Marxist teleology, the SDS expected the liberation of the underdeveloped world to precipitate the revolution in the advanced capitalist states. Dutschke expressed disgust at the contradiction between America's posture as guarantor of Berlin's freedom and its attempts to extinguish liberation movements.

In November 1967, concurrent with the founding of the Anti-University in London, some six hundred radical students and sixty staff drawn from all the institutions of higher education in West Berlin set up a Critical University (Kritische Universität) composed of thirty-three work circles whose focus varied from the obvious, political themes (Cuba, Methods of Direct Action, and so on) to Architecture and Society, Theology and Politics, and the Ideology of Science. An "anti-authoritarian kindergarten" was created "to release the mother to work, study, take a lover, and teach young children anything but the moral lesson of sit down, don't talk, eat what's on your plate." The Berlin student movement led the way in self-help, setting up committees of inquiry into police conduct and city politics, launching its own counter-propaganda service (Offentlichkeitskomitee), and generally steeling theory with practice.

Jürgen Habermas, professor of philosophy and sociology at the University of Frankfurt-am-Main, noted in 1967 that the most active student radicals were no longer pursuing university reform. "Instead they desire the immediate overthrow of social structures. . . . For the first time in the history of the Federal Republic of Germany, students are playing a political role that must be taken seriously."

The values of possessive individualism (money and power) were now rejected. Productivity was viewed by students from affluent homes through the filter of manipulated consumerism. Achievement and competition were bourgeois devices for maintaining a hierarchical, inegalitarian society. Unlike in the United States, German society suffered neither from a racial underclass nor direct involvement in the Vietnam War: no ghettos and no draft. The radical position in Germany was therefore intellectual and isolated; Habermas pointed to the "almost unbroken theoretical tradition influenced by Hegel and Marx." But the student's subject of study was as closely correlated with political attitudes in Germany as elsewhere. A survey undertaken in 1968 found "very radical" attitudes among 19 percent of biology students, 23.6 percent of physicists, 31.7 percent of psychologists, 33.5 percent of those studying political science, and 49.2 percent of sociology students. By 1968 the radicalization of students had reached its peak, affecting the younger generation as a whole. One poll showed three-quarters of all German students and 67 percent of all those aged fifteen to twenty-five sympathetic to student demonstrations—a wider constituency than the "very radical" one mentioned above.

But the hostility of the wider public was no less extensive. A survey by the Institute for Applied Sociology in Bad Godesberg before the Easter 1968 demonstrations found that 66 percent of nonstudents questioned the right of students to express political opinions publicly; one-third wanted to ban all student demonstrations. The belief was widespread that students were parasites on the taxpayer (in fact 58 percent were mainly supported by their parents while 13 percent paid their way by getting jobs).

The scale of the demonstrations after the attempt on Rudi Dutschke's life temporarily rescued the radical students from their isolation. In Essen, where there was no university, young workers staged an anti-Springer demonstration. The SDS made constant attempts to bridge the gap to the proletariat, which contributed a mere 5 percent of German students and which bore the brunt of military conscription, as in the United States and Italy. But the shooting of a Benno Ohnesorg or a Rudi Dutschke generated a deceptive and strictly transitory sympathy; in the long term, worker-student collaboration proved possible only under authoritarian regimes (Spain, Greece, Czechoslovakia after the Soviet invasion). Klaus Mehnert cites the testimony of Michael Schneider, a philosophy and sociology graduate who went to work in a Berlin factory to nurture Leninist consciousness among the workers, only to discover that the knowall attitude of students annoyed them. The constant slogan "Destroy" (destroy the state, destroy the hierarchies) created resistance and anxiety. One young worker told Schneider, "Shut up; all you want is to make everything *kaput!*" The students of Berlin managed to win the transitory sympathy of wage earners on only one occasion—in August 1967, when the city decided to keep the big stores open for longer hours in honor of a festival. The students responded promptly to the anger of employees and unions over the refusal to pay the full overtime rate.

All demonstrations, but most particularly anti-American ones, angered the citizens of West Berlin, encircled as they were by the DDR and mainly dependent on the United States for the city's independent status. The students came and went, enjoying a liberty of demonstration unavailable on the other side of the wall, yet periodically breaking windows in America House, pulling the U.S. flag to half-mast, hoisting the banner of the Vietcong, and disrupting the visit of Vice-President Humphrey in the spring of 1967. Local trade union leaders condemned demonstrations against the Vietnam War as giving comfort to communism. As the taxi driver remarked to the London *Times*'s correspondent, "Hitler would have soon stopped all these students."

An international Congress on Vietnam had been organized by the SDS in West Berlin two months before the shooting of Rudi Dutschke. The march that followed the congress blocked the Kurfürstendamm under a forest of alien flags. Mayor Klaus Schutz, having tried to ban the march, but having been overruled in court, retaliated by organizing a pro–United States rally and calling a public holiday for the purpose. Hysteria swept the city. During the counter-demonstration solid, middle-aged burghers attacked heckling students with cries of "Cut off her [i.e., his] hair!" and "Lynch him, hang him!" After a long delay, a committee of inquiry set up by the Berlin Senate confirmed many charges of police brutality. The chief of police was sent on permanent leave. Jürgen Habermas summed up the city's record: "All organs of the Government, the police, administration of justice, House of Representatives, and the Mayor himself distinguished and compromised themselves by foolish prejudice and repression: illegal prohibitions of demonstrations, dubious confiscations and problematic arrests, indefensible court proceedings, open police terror, and a Mayor who even thanked the police after Ohnesorg was shot."

Violence during February was not confined to Berlin; it occurred in Freiburg, in Hamburg (where a thousand marched on America House), in Munich (where the SDS stormed an America House art exhibition with spray paint, unfurling the NLF flag); in Bremen (where rioting high school students joined forces with young workers to make a political issue out of planned fare increases, wrecking buses and trams and forcing the Senate to capitulate); in Duisburg, Kiel, and Bochun over the same issue; in Frankfurt (where the U.S. consulate came under attack); in Bonn (where students broke into the rector's study and defaced the university's Golden Book). A British journalist, Neal Ascherson, reported: "All over the country, nicely dressed middle-class schoolboys and young girls with blonde fringes [bangs] talk about 'unmasking the apparatus' and 'institutionalized violence under late capitalism.' " According to a poll, over half the high school and university students approved of the demonstrations. During the second week of March, anti-Vietnam demonstrations in Stuttgart provoked the police to confiscate a leaflet stigmatizing Chancellor Kurt Kiesinger's record under the Nazis. The Social Democratic minister of justice, Gustav Heinemann (a future president of the Federal Republic) defended the right of demonstration; Kiesinger himself granted the students' sincere commitment—but to an error as old as the world: utopia.

The answer of the annual convention of the Federation of German Student Associations (Verband Deutscher Studentschaften), representing 108 universities and colleges, was to: (1) condemn American policy in Vietnam; (2) demand recognition of the DDR; (3) call for the resignation of President Lubke; and (4) insist on the "democratization" of education. The association's new chairman, Christoph Ermann, a political science student at Marburg, rejected the West German state outright in the name of a "permanent revolution" (but eschewing force).

The attempted assassination of Dutschke precipitated furious rioting not only in West Berlin, but throughout West Germany. Thousands of student demonstrators marching under red flags and portraits of Rosa Luxemburg and Karl Liebknecht, the Spartacist martyrs of 1919, fought with police while attempting to invade City Hall. Berlin's fashionable Kurfürstendamm swarmed with police and armored cars, the loudspeakers urging the demonstrators to "Stop this play acting" and "Stop acting like monkeys." Disorders struck Düsseldorf, Cologne, Munich (where two were killed), Heidelberg, Mannheim, Freiburg, Essen, Baden-Baden, and Frankfurt, where students drowned the Good Friday hymns in St. Peter's Church with the "Internationale."

The main target, in Hamburg and other cities, was the newspaper chain owned by the right-wing millionaire Axel Springer, Cold War Warrior and scourge of the Left. Attempts were made to block the distribution of his magazine *Bild Zeitung* (circulation: 5 million), forcing police in some instances to drive the Springer delivery vans. In West Berlin an area of ten square blocks around the Springer premises was sealed off by barbed wire and police carrying submachine guns. The "Extraparliamentary Opposition"—the key term in current use—demanded not only the breakup of the Springer empire, but a city council containing significant numbers of workers and students, as well as an hour a day of free time on television.

Axel Springer owned 70 percent of the Berlin and Hamburg daily press, 85 percent of all Sunday newspapers. In West Berlin the Springer papers had whipped up a hysterical backlash against the students, describing them as beatniks, wastrels, gangsters, Communists, and sex maniacs. Typical headlines in *Bild Zeitung* read: "Stop the Young Reds' Terror Now," "We Shouldn't Leave all the Dirty Work to the Police and their Water Cannons," "Dutschke, No. 1 Enemy of the People—Throw the Gang Out." Springer wanted a German A-bomb and a government led by the right-wing Bavarian politician, Franz Josef Strauss. The SDS retaliated by launching a national campaign for the expropriation of the Springer empire, and set up a Springer Tribunal modeled on the Russell War Crimes Tribunal. The nonpolitical Students Federation, to whom 300,000 were affiliated, justified the sabotage of Springer's distribution network. Theological support arrived from the Protestant bishop of Berlin.

On April 14, the Berlin police achieved new levels of brutality as they broke up an Easter peace march of 4,000. Over 350 people had been jailed in three days. Rhythmically chanting "Rudi Dutschke!" interspersed with cries of "Nazi swine!," the demonstrators threw rocks, apples, and firecrackers. Inside the Technical University, Wolfgang Lefevre, a twenty-six-year-old leader and theoretician of the SDS, asked: "Why is it that we were beaten up and dispersed? Why is it that there were only twenty cars to block the delivery of the Springer publications when we had counted on six hundred to eight hundred? Is it because most students fear for their property and do not want their automobiles demolished?" Lefevre's abashed audience nodded in shame. A physics student, Pieter Mieciak, wearing the bushy moustache favored by radicals, confessed: "My father lets me use his car and obviously I could not go and wreck it."

The German press was haunted by memories of 1919, of the street fighting and murders that blighted the Weimar Republic. The young generally held capitalism and their parents responsible for the triumph of Nazism, although underlying the youthful radicalism was a desire to atone for Hitler and the death camps. A poll taken after Easter showed that 84 percent of West German adults deplored the student demonstrations, with only 6 percent registering positive approval. Mayor Schutz of West Berlin had explained that the violence had not really been about Vietnam or Springer, "but to make the free democratic state incapable of action." But there were signs that the radical students also recoiled from the escalating violence (if only in theory); in the neon-lit "Audi Maxi" at Berlin's Technical University, a long teach-in voted in favor of nonviolence.

Among the 180 students arrested in Berlin was Peter Brandt, the nineteen-year-old son of Foreign Minister Willy Brandt, leader of the Social Democrats and formerly the most famous of West Berlin's mayors. The previous month Willy Brandt had been roughed up by radical demonstrators when arriving for the SDP's annual conference in Nuremberg. Peter Brandt described himself as a revolutionary Marxist and the Springer chain as a sort of national drug; as for the parliamentary system, it should be replaced by councils of workers and intellectuals. Returning from Africa, Willy Brandt, the nation's vice-chancellor, wrote to Burgermaster Schutz that violence must be "stifled in the egg" and the SDS prevented from planning sedition. But Peter Brandt, while expressing personally friendly sentiments toward his parents—he described their home as a tolerant place with plenty of laughter—felt that his father and the SDP were guilty of betrayal by joining the Grand Coalition. (Later in the year he was fined 400 *deutsche marks* for rioting in November 1967 and April 1968.)

KOMMUNE I

Scandalous or surrealistic happenings were not encouraged by the SDS. Nevertheless, inspired by the libertarian blend of direct action and drugs practiced by the Dutch Provo movement, Fritz Teufel (meaning "Devil") and Rainer Langhans (recently a lieutenant in the West German army) launched Kommune I in March 1967. A month later, eleven members of Kommune I were arrested on charges of planning attempts against the life or health of U.S. Vice-President Humphrey. Teufel was incarcerated in Moabit Prison. Twenty-four years old and notorious for his escapades, both real and apocryphal, Teufel had burst into the university rector's room; seized his cigars and seal of office; donned his cap, gown, and chain; and then ridden off on a small-wheeled bicycle to the big hall, the "Audi Maxi," where students cheered him and elected him rector—whereupon he "dismissed" all the unpopular professors. Arrested half an hour before the arrival of the Shah of Iran at the Berlin opera house, then released, Teufel demanded his own reincarceration, achieving his aim by staging a "go-in" to the Berlin State Parliament with a following of disciples and witnesses.

Kommune I loved to outrage the public, even to the point of exploiting a tragic department-store fire in Brussels, which cost three hundred lives. Four spoof pamphlets were published on May 24, 1967, attributing the blaze to anti–Vietnam War cells, and suggesting the example might be imitated in Germany, thus: ". . . three hundred satiated citizens and their exciting lives came to an end, and Brussels became Hanoi. Now no one needs to shed tears for the poor Vietnamese people over his breakfast paper. As from today he can simply walk into the made-to-measure department of KaDeWe, Hertie, Woolworth, Bilka, or Neckermann and discreetly light a cigarette in the dressing room. . . ."

A trial followed on charges of incitement to arson. Teufel and Langhans (like Jerry Rubin and Abbie Hoffman in America) ensured that the exchanges in the Berlin court were less than dignified.

LANGHANS: Don't shout like that!
TANKE (court official):   I thought you might not hear too well under that hair.
LANGHANS: Now I can't hear you.
TANKE: So I'll come a little closer.
SCHWERDTNER (judge):   I'd rather you didn't, Tanke.
LANGHANS: Why not, do I stink?
SCHWERDTNER: Yes, you do.

Teufel and Langhans were acquitted in April 1968. A few days later, two members of Kommune I, Andreas Baader and Gundrun Ensslin, staged a real arson attempt in the Schneider store in Munich. Put on trial in October, they disrupted the proceedings and refused to plead. The arsonists were hailed in anarchist circles and among the *Schili,* or "radical chic."

An American proponent of the counterculture and the free university movement, Joseph Berke, visited Kommune I at Stephanstrasse 60. At six in the evening, no one had yet risen from his or her mattress to face the long day's night. Two television sets, permanently turned on but silent, absorbed the communards as they awoke. The Kommune was now totally drugged "on hash, tea and acid," even though it had originally rejected drugs as bourgeois diversions of mind and energy from the political revolution.

Kommune I lived by constant provocation and contained more than its share of spoiled-brat exhibitionists, but provocation was central to the strategy of the New Left in general. Jürgen Habermas noted: "Demonstrations have taken the form of obvious provocations that produce immediately consumable offenses or counter-aggressions." These in turn excited not only indignation, but pleasure, releasing the agitators from the burden of proving where it all might lead. Protest became a permanent way of life. The American Black Panther leader Stokely Carmichael was quite explicit about the tactic: "You create disturbances, you keep pushing the system . . . until they have to hit back; once your enemy hits back, then your revolution starts. If your enemy does not hit back, then you do not have a revolution."

According to Habermas, the young German radicals, like their American counterparts, were not normally in rebellion against their own parents. Jürgen Habermas and Kenneth Keniston came to the same conclusions: The young activists were emphatically committed to living out expressed but unimplemented parental values. The typical home background was liberal and rationalist—but indecisive about converting values into civic action. Conflict with the strong, authoritarian father was no longer the issue, although radicals did tend to identify with the mother, frequently regarded as the embodiment of concern and compassion.

THE EMERGENCY LAWS

During the weekend of May 12, over 40,000 people demonstrated in Bonn against the Emergency Bills due to have their second reading in the Federal Parliament (Bundestag). The central proposal of the bills was an "Emergency Parliament" of only twenty-two members, plus eleven from the provincial Länder, which would assume full executive powers in the event of an emergency. In a strange sequel to this demonstration, eight hundred students returning to West Berlin by train staged a sit-in in an East German railway station to discuss how they could help their insurgent colleagues in Paris, where the "night of the barricades" had occurred only twenty-four hours earlier.

The most conspicuous *enragé* of the Paris insurrection, Daniel Cohn-Bendit, came from Frankfurt, and it was in that city that the SDS had blockaded the university on May 16. A counter-group of three hundred, wishing to attend lectures, stormed a side entrance, leading to violent struggles. The rector, Professor Walter Ruegg, accompanied by Hesse's minister of culture, addressed a teach-in of 4,000 students as an alternative to calling in the police.

But patience has its limits. As the passage of the Emergency Laws approached, Frankfurt University officials prudently locked the doors of the red sandstone building housing the administration. It was to no avail; the students got in with the help of battering rams. Amid a sea of broken glass, a throng of shouting, high-spirited militants spilled through the offices. A professor took the *Christian Science Monitor*'s correspondent to his office: "What bothers me is that the rebels tend to bring about the very conditions they oppose. . . . This strengthens the forces of the Right." Back at Frankfurt's SDS headquarters, where Mao posters decorated Chairman Wolff's office—as a joke with a strain of seriousness, Wolff explained—students planning to travel to Paris were warned about the type of tear gas being used: "I ran into it myself in Paris and for ten minutes I thought I was going to die. Sucking lemons seems to help." As inspiration, Daniel Cohn-Bendit was on hand; but three days later, when the SDS headquarters in Frankfurt were raided by the police, he was back in Paris, illegally, with or without lemons.

When the Bundestag passed the Emergency Laws on May 30, by 384 votes to 100, Ruegg finally summoned the police to end the four-day occupation. In Giessen, the turmoil was such that the university had to be closed. In Munich, Bonn, and Hamburg students invaded public theatres and attempted to debate the Emergency Laws with bemused audiences who had paid good money for an evening's *kultur*. In Bonn, President Lubke (who had made good money out of building concentration camps for the Nazis) had to leave the opera by an emergency exit. But, when 2,000 Berlin students approached several factories in the hope of fraternizing with the workers on the French model, they were received coldly.

At the end of June the insurrection resumed at the Free University in Berlin, with the occupation of the rector's office and the main lecture hall. As so often, this was an act of retaliation; the rector had called in the police to end a five-week-old occupation of the Far East Institute. Daniel Cohn-Bendit, back in West Germany, proposed that the action be extended to the political science and sociology institutes, but it was Fritz Teufel (Germany's version of Abbie Hoffman) who stole the show by installing himself as "rector."

The real victory that June brought to the Free University was of the kind already won by Cohn-Bendit and his sexually liberated comrades at Nanterre; by prearrangement, groups of men and women moved with Germanic precision from their segregated hostels into those reserved for the other sex. Despite management threats, this *blitzkrieg* was successful; sixteen out of twenty modernistic dormitories, built out of Ford Foundation money a decade earlier, became desegregated. Thus was the revolution diverted.

BELGIUM

The anti-Springer demonstrations in Germany sparked a sympathetic response among radicals at the Free University of Brussels on April 14, 1968. On May 13, the Greek actress Melina Mercouri moved hearts and minds with a denunciation of the Greek military regime. Eight days later, 2,000 students and some friendly professors gathered to demand participatory democracy. This "General Assembly" despatched forty representatives to occupy the offices of the Administrative Council (twenty-five worthies, mainly politicians, bankers, and industrialists self-elected by cooptation). A banner hanging from the main building on Franklin Roosevelt Avenue declared: "This university is open to the entire population." Within, red and black flags were attached to the statue of Theodore Verhaegen, who had founded the university in 1834 as a free-thinking institution to serve as a counterweight to the Catholic University of Louvain.

Learning from Paris, the authorities did not call in the police. The threat came from rallies of right-wing students in crew cuts, black shirts, and leather jackets who gave a tumultuous reception to Léopold Flamme, professor of industrial legislation, when he denounced small sects who arrogantly seized power.

The rector, Marcel V. Homes, a biologist, humbly and intelligently sought permission to address the "General Assembly" on May 25. He promised reforms and a revision of the current year's examination schedules. "But can we have confidence in the Council?" a student asked. "That is not for me to answer," the rector responded. "All I can say is that in society one is not free to do everything one wants to do." (Clearly Homes was not a disciple of "Take your dreams for realities," but few rectors were.)

On May 29, with militants still occupying the administrative offices, the Academic Council offered to abolish itself in favor of an elected body. The forty-six-day occupation, however, did not end until an all-night debate on June 30, with the radicals promising to continue the struggle against a society corrupted by the profit motive.

In December, the new rector, André Jaumotte, suffered the wrecking of his office after Belgium's monarch, King Baudouin, attended a lecture surrounded by police. This offended; more police were called to prevent an imminent battle between left- and right-wing students, and there was greater violence on this occasion than during the summer occupation; Molotov cocktails were hurled from rooftops during serious rioting. The arrest of two students inevitably protracted the unrest until Christmas saved the day. The calendar alone guaranteed peace in Europe's universities.

YUGOSLAVIA

BELGRADE, June 2, 1968—A group of actors and musicians have been hired to perform to "Youth-Action" workers camped near the student dormitories in New Belgrade. The free concert is reserved for these volunteers assisting in the erection of an apartment block. Other students are deliberately excluded. A crowd gathers in front of the theatre, windows are broken, a fire truck is set aflame, cars are overturned. The following day 3,000 or 4,000 students set out on a march, to find themselves confronted by police rushed in to the capital from all over Serbia. The president of the Serbian Parliament and the president of the League of Communists step forward and offer to negotiate with the students. They do so in good faith, but then, inexplicably, the police allegedly open fire and many people are wounded, including the two negotiating officials.*

That afternoon, June 3, a thousand students occupied the Faculty of Philosophy and Sociology and issued seven demands, including the dismissal of the Federal and Serbian interior ministers, plus Belgrade's police chief, plus—for good measure—the newspaper and radio editors whose reports had travestied the events. The revolt immediately spread to other faculties. In the spirit of Paris, the students soon took control of their "Left Bank," handing out literature and directing the traffic. From trams, buses, and cars, eager hands reached out to snatch the leaflets protesting economic inequalities and Yugoslavia's unemployment problem which forced young workers, whether unskilled or technicians, to work in Germany and other capitalist countries. From one of the buildings hung a huge banner: "We Have Had Enough of the Red Bourgeoisie."

In the city center the authorities behaved in Gaullist fashion, lining the streets with riot police. Yugoslavia's Communist League excelled itself in warning workers not to fraternize with students, and in engineering a torrent of synchronized resolutions from the workers' councils expressing confidence in their leaders and denouncing irresponsible violence. *Borba* and other newspapers displayed as much hostility as the Warsaw press in February–March, the Springer press in April, or the Paris press in May.

This suggests that the real confrontation lay not between the two Cold War social systems but between power elites jealous of gerontocratic privilege and the ardor of democratic youth. Indeed, the Zagreb student leader Zlatko Markus had recently written in the Belgrade periodical *Gledista* that throughout the world the young were asked to show loyalty and devotion, but were not offered reason for doing so with conviction. A meeting in the Belgrade Law Faculty resolved that the existing university "suits the existing society and does not suit the proclaimed principles" of socialism. A few professors stirred the

---

*The facts were soon in dispute. According to the London *Times,* and the *New York Times,* citing student sources, 137 were injured, of whom 105 were students, including an unspecified number suffering bullet wounds. But the police were reported as denying that they had opened fire.

mounting unrest, which began in April: Dr. Stevan Vracar heretically proposed a two-party system; Professor Ljubomir Tadic advised the students to press for a free and critical university.

Following the decision of the Ministry of the Interior to ban and confiscate the weekly publication *Student,* students of the Law Faculty installed loudspeakers in the city center and began addressing the crowds. The prevailing mood was closer to Paris than to Prague. The journalist Lajos Lederer saw slogans in University Square, in the city center, such as "Down with Communist Princes." A series of interviews by D. Plamenic with workers drinking slivovitz in the open-air cafés suggested that most of them wished the students luck, but did not dare transform their sympathy into solidarity strikes because of poverty and terror of unemployment. The students themselves contrasted—and perhaps exaggerated—the fraternization taking place in France, blaming the Yugoslav League of Communists for intimidating the factories into isolating the students.

Faculty support strengthened. The dean and acting dean of the Theatre and Television Academy resigned in sympathy with students who occupied it. Many prominent politicians came to fraternize and discuss the way ahead. A cheerful meeting in the quadrangle of the Philosophy Faculty was attended by a large number of teachers. The university rectorate (administration building) in the city center remained occupied. On June 5, Belgrade University's Committee of Professors from all the faculties conferred for seven hours and came out solidly in support of the students' complaints and demands.

A professor of engineering recalled the transformation of his own students: "I found a group of young people that I didn't know existed. It was as if they had all at once woken up. They didn't ask, they demanded. They told me to choose their side or get out of my office. That is what I liked best." But the professor was far from being an advocate of Student Power: "The students must realize that as engineers they cannot begin to fathom the details of social and economic policy. They cannot butt their heads against the system; instead they must strive to make it more effective." His students curtly characterized this as "shit." Anatole Shub reported that the students had forced every Yugoslav to commit himself: "Yugoslav democrats of all ages now know exactly who their friends are." (But such knowledge was likely to prove transitory; many students derided "chameleons.")

A crisis had been reached on June 9 (police encircling the faculties, the press demanding severe punishments), when President Tito addressed the nation on television, boldly endorsing the students' Action Program and their political awareness. (The four points of the Action Program: (1) demanded the abolition of privileges and of nonsocialist accumulation of wealth; (2) protested against the national disease of unemployment; (3) called for the democratization of the Party, the Socialist Alliance, the unions, and the youth organization; and (4) insisted on university reform linked to an improvement in the material position of students.) Said Tito: "We were overtaken by events because our ears were not tuned sharply enough." Even though he did not refer to the demand for the dismissal of the interior ministers and police chief, two hundred students in the Law Faculty broke into ten minutes' applause and sang, "Comrade Tito, blue flower, you struggle for the people's rights." Jonathan Randal, of the *New York Times,* reported comments such as, "Can you imagine President Johnson accepting the Columbia students's demands?" As in Prague, students in Belgrade emerged with an image of themselves as practical and mature. A girl told Randal, "I think student romantics in France and West Germany are wrong because they think they can change half of Europe." A fine arts student unwittingly echoed the professor of engineering when he argued that "Western students want to destroy their order, but we want to perfect ours."

Tito having spoken, the police immediately evaporated, the press groveled, the students paraded in triumph. The majority then went back to work.

But general assemblies in the radical Philosophy and Sociology Faculty continued to advance subversive propositions directed against Yugoslavia's privileged elite. Tito made a second speech against extremism, and on July 20, the police cleared the building; the Faculty Committee was promptly expelled from the League of Communists, and soon it was business as usual—almost the universal dénouement of 1968.

7

THE USA:
The Democratic Primaries and
Draft Resistance

"...Bobby drove among blacks and Mexicans and college kids, swaying precariously at the apex of a pyramid of oustretched hands."

"Eugene McCarthy...had relapsed into what looked like a sulk."

THE DEMOCRATIC PRIMARIES

Defeating an incumbent president hungry for his party's renomination seemed a remoter prospect in 1967 than landing on the moon—not least a president with a formidable record of Great Society welfare reform and civil rights legislation under his belt, labor and the blacks solidly behind him, and a grip on the South that no Northern liberal could hope to challenge.

But these calculations overlooked the deadly cancer of the Vietnam War and the dynamic activity of a young political astronaut named Allard Lowenstein—the man, in David Halberstam's words, "who ran against Lyndon Johnson." Lowenstein was also the young man who walked into the mine field between the New Left and liberal Democratic machine politics. Thirty-nine years of age, the son of upper-middle-class Jews who supported the New Deal and passionately admired Eleanor Roosevelt, by 1967 Al Lowenstein was at Yale, organizing an "LBJ Must Go" campaign. Advertisements appeared in the *New York Times*: "Mister President, College Editors Protest Your War"; "Mister President, Student Council Presidents Reject Your War."

On August 15, 1967 he addressed the National Student Association (NSA). He claimed to have been the last president of the NSA before it became tied to the CIA, but SDS picketed him with placards: "Don't Listen to the CIA Agent Downstairs." Lowenstein wanted to convince his audience that the existing political system could be made to work for radicals, if only Bobby would run. No message could have been less acceptable to the New Left, nor did it move Robert Kennedy, who told Lowenstein (and every other courtier) that he had talked with Mayor Daley and Chairman X and Governor Y, all of whom said, "No, this isn't your year; wait until '72." When Senator Eugene McCarthy almost casually stepped into the ring to face the heavyweight champion of the political world, Lowenstein's machine of liberal contacts and caucuses across the nation was immediately in McCarthy's corner, orchestrating the punches.*

Jack Newfield expressed the anguish of Kennedy's supporters on December 28: "If Kennedy does not run in 1968, the best side of his character will die. He will kill it every time he butchers his conscience and makes a speech for Johnson next autumn." Apparently Kennedy carried this clipping around with him, but he was less pleased by a placard at Brooklyn College, "Bobby Kennedy: Hawk, Dove or Chicken?" None of the Senate doves wanted Kennedy to run.

McCarthy's ridicule of the Pentagon's claimed successes during the Communist Tet offensive merely stung the White House; the senator from Minnesota was regarded as a lightweight maverick posing no serious threat to the president's renomination in August. A Gallup poll published early in February showed the president ahead of McCarthy by a massive 71 to 18 percent and also leading Robert Kennedy by 52 to 40 percent. Kennedy told a Chicago audience on February 8 that the Tet offensive had "finally shattered the mask of official illusion with which we have concealed our true circumstances, even from ourselves." But Kennedy remained in his Hamlet role, haunted by the blunder he had made the day before the Tet offensive opened when, speaking to the press, he said: "I have told friends and supporters who are urging me to run that I would not oppose Lyndon Johnson under any foreseeable circumstances."

Eugene McCarthy was campaigning in the New Hampshire primary, supported by Harvard kids who took it seriously enough to shave off their beards. "McCarthy's speeches are dull, vague and without either poetry or balls. He is lazy and vain...." wrote the *Village Voice*'s Jack Newfield. Jeremy Larner, who worked on McCarthy's campaign staff, recalled his "slate-stone eyes which bore down hard and registered nothing." He had a habit of throwing away speeches carefully researched and scripted by his aides in favor of a few casual remarks off the cuff. As David Halberstam put it, "one sensed that if elected President he might abolish the U.S. Government...."

Likewise, McCarthy's aversion to ethnic politics broke all the campaign rules in the Democratic book. He was ill at ease in the ghettos—the blacks had never heard of him—and it was somewhat sourly that he mocked Bobby Kennedy for setting up committees to

*Allard Lowenstein was murdered in his New York City law office on March 14, 1980 by a deranged friend who had been a civil rights worker, a revolutionary, a dropout. Since Lowenstein's death a bitter controversy has raged about the nature of his anticommunism, his role in the NSA in 1949–50, and whether he had been a CIA agent, a fantasist, the recipient of South African money, and more.

deal with "twenty-six varieties of Americans—like twenty-six varieties of ice cream. Like a jigsaw puzzle." McCarthy proposed four new "civil rights": (1) to have a job that returns a decent living; (2) to receive an education relevant to one's potential to learn; (3) to enjoy adequate health; and (4) to occupy a decent house in a neighborhood that is properly part of the United States.

McCarthy was at his most formidable when blitzing the Vietnam War: The Pentagon and the CIA were beyond civilian control, foreign policy had become militarized, all restraint had been abandoned in an orgy of counterinsurgency. "If elected," he said, "I would go to the Pentagon"—an echo of Eisenhower's pledge in 1952 that "If elected I would go to Korea." That "go to" carried a vague patrician promise, which McCarthy made more specific when he threatened to fire Secretary of State Dean Rusk, FBI Director J. Edgar Hoover, and General Lewis B. Hershey, head of the draft—threats Kennedy would never utter. McCarthy's young campaigners cried out, "Right on!" Perhaps the system could, after all, be redeemed.

But could it? What was McCarthy's own legislative record? Why had he so often supported special-interest lobbies and subsidies: for the Daughters of the American Revolution, for the free sale of firearms, and, most egregiously, the Foreign Investor Act of 1966, loaded with riders for the benefit of mutual funds? McCarthy had also voted for the notorious Gulf of Tonkin Resolution in 1964, although he was later one of only five senators who voted to repeal that resolution (William Fulbright, the chairman of the Foreign Relations Committee, being another), while Kennedy went with the majority. Carl Oglesby drew up a list of McCarthy's betrayals of liberalism: In 1959 he had voted for the Student Loyalty Oath Bill; two years later he had voted against withholding funds from segregated schools; he had voted for every Vietnam War appropriations bill; he had constantly opposed the admission of Communist China to the United Nations. Oglesby mocked the young idealists working for McCarthy: "Don't demand socialism tomorrow. Demand, instead, that capitalism . . . begin creating for itself a more human heart . . . demand that the old elites at once start behaving better."

The result of the Democratic primary in the sparsely populated and predominantly Republican state of New Hampshire was an event of global interest: Johnson squeezed home against McCarthy by only 49 to 42 percent. The Senate Foreign Relations Committee's hearings on Vietnam, which were televised in New Hampshire, had undoubtedly damaged the president. Robert Kennedy waited and watched; on

March 13 he told the press he would make a decision within a few days. Three days later a company of American soldiers in Vietnam made a different kind of decision, but no one told the press.

MY LAI

VIETNAM, March 16, 1968—The scene is Quang Ngai Province, on the northeast coast of South Vietnam, an area of green rice paddies. American strategy since 1966 has been to "sanitize" the area, that is, kill the Vietcong and remove the civilian population. Bombs, rockets, napalm, and cannon fire have poured in, rendering 138,000 civilians homeless and destroying 70 percent of the dwellings.

Charlie Company, First Battalion, 20th Infantry, arrived on the scene in December 1967, commanded by Captain Ernest Medina, a Mexican-American; among his platoon commanders was Second Lieutenant William L. Calley, Jr., wh) is generally held to have lacked the respect of his men. On February 25, 1968, Charlie Company lost six men killed and twelve wounded when it walked into a mine field. On March 14, a booby trap killed a sergeant and badly wounded one of his men. By this time, Calley's platoon was casually murdering civilians. Gregory Olsen, of Ohio, a devout Mormon, wrote to his father on the 14th: "They are all seemingly normal guys; some were friends of mine. For a while they were like wild animals. It was murder, and I'm ashamed of myself for not trying to do anything about it. This isn't the first time, dad."

On March 16, Calley's platoon attacked My Lai 4, a hamlet of about seven hundred people. Captain Medina's precise orders that day are in dispute. According to some members of the platoon, the command was to kill everyone and take no prisoners: "They're all VCs, now go and get them." But Olsen and another soldier said Medina had ordered the destruction of the village itself and of "anybody that was running from us, hiding from us, or who appeared to us to be the enemy." Either way, the U.S. Army had abandoned any attempt to distinguish between civilians and combatants among a hostile population of Asiatics.

Seymour Hersh broke the story with a definitive account of the massacre in *Harper's* magazine (May 1970).

The killings began without warning. A member of Calley's platoon stabbed a man with his bayonet, killed him with another thrust, then picked up a middle-aged man and threw him down a well. Soldiers began shooting women and children who were kneeling, weeping, and praying around a temple. Calley later shot people from ten to fifteen feet; he called this "wasting" them. Some women cried "No VC"; others, "No, no, no."

Villagers were killed in their homes. Helicopters shot down those who fled. People were herded into bunkers and killed with hand grenades and M79 grenade launchers. Many of the GIs were laughing: "Hey, I got me another one." "Chalk up one for me." Villagers were driven toward a large drainage ditch at the eastern end of the hamlet, where Calley organized further slaughter. Soldiers took breaks to rest and smoke before resuming the killing. Bodies were mutilated, cut up, tossed about.

A helicopter pilot, Chief Warrant Officer Hugh C. Thompson of Georgia, was so incensed by what he saw that he reported it by radio to Brigade Headquarters. Lt.-Colonel Frank A. Barker, head of Task Force Barker, intercepted the message and called through to Medina. The captain replied that he had a body count of 310: "I don't know what they're doing. The first platoon's in the lead. I'm trying to stop it." But helicopter pilot Thompson had seen Medina kill a wounded woman.

Medina called Calley: "That's enough for today." But Calley then organized the murder of a further twenty-five to thirty people in the drainage ditch. Women threw themselves across children. Calley shot plenty of children, including a two-year-old boy who had miraculously crawled out of the ditch, crying. Thompson brought his helicopter down and rescued nine Vietnamese, five of them children, while he and Calley exchanged furious words. Thompson landed again and plucked a child out of a ditch.

Not the least astonishing aspect of this journey into hell was the presence, from start to finish, of a newspaper reporter, Jay Roberts, and a photographer, Ron Haeberle. The third platoon of C Company, commanded by Charles A. West, continued with the massacre while Haeberle took photographs. West said later: "It's hard to distinguish a mama-san from a papa-san when everybody has on black pyjamas."

Later, much later, when the inquiry was under way, the surviving villagers themselves testified. Nguyen Thi Ngoc Tuyet, age nineteen, recalled how she watched a baby trying to open her slain mother's blouse to nurse. A soldier shot the infant, then slashed it with a bayonet. Nguyen Khoa, a peasant, told of a thirteen-year-old girl who was raped before being killed. Soldiers then attacked Khoa's wife, tearing off her clothes, but before they could rape her, her six-year-old son fell riddled with bullets and saturated the soldiers with blood.

Immediately after the operation, the *New York Times* ran a front-page story claiming that 128 "Vietcong" had been killed. General

Westmoreland sent C Company a message of congratulations. Although a reporter and a photographer had recorded a systematic act of genocide, which had also been witnessed by Colonel Oran K. Henderson, the officer commanding the 11th Brigade, while cruising above My Lai, and by at least sixty army men in a dozen helicopters, the only report of the massacre appeared in the French-language *Bulletin de Vietnam,* published by the North Vietnamese delegation to the Paris peace talks. No American paper attempted to follow up or check out the story. As for photographer Ron Haeberle, by early 1969 he was back in the United States showing slides of the My Lai slaughter to Rotary Club luncheons.

The story eventually came out because a former GI, Ronald Ridenhout, began writing letters to congressmen and senators. Ridenhout had not been involved, but he had flown over My Lai a few days after the massacre and had picked up information from soldiers of C Company. Late in August, President Nixon put a "hold" on all investigations, but incensed army legal officers pressed ahead with charges against Calley. Army investigators did not get to My Lai until November 1969, twenty months after the event. On arrival they found three mass graves, a ditch full of bodies, and a total body count of 450 to 500 people, mostly women, children, and old men. The story then broke in the press. Seymour Hersh's book, *My Lai 4,* followed.

It emerged that refusal to obey Calley's orders had been perfectly feasible. A few of his men had in fact refused to shoot or made themselves scarce; they suffered no retribution nor, indeed, did they expect to. The courageous intervention of the helicopter pilot, Warrant Officer Thompson, spoke for itself.

The army's judicial system singled out Calley for blame and punishment. Neither Medina nor the enlisted men who committed the massacre were ever charged. As Bertrand Russell and Jean-Paul Sartre had pointed out, no "Nuremberg" War Crimes Tribunal existed to bring flagrant breaches of the Geneva Convention to justice.

BOBBY

A younger son of the Boston-Irish millionaire Joseph Kennedy, who was prewar ambassador to Britain, Robert Kennedy had served as junior counsel to the Democratic minority on Joseph McCarthy's notorious Senate Permanent Subcommittee on Investigations at the time of the Wisconsin senator's bullish onslaughts on the Voice of America and the U.S. Army. Appointed assistant counsel to the Senate rackets committee, he hounded the gangster boss of the Teamsters Union, Jimmy Hoffa. Bobby ran his elder brother's presidential campaign with ruthless energy, judging people (David Halberstam recalled) in terms of their loyalty and "toughness," and was rewarded, although only thirty-five years of age, with the post of attorney general. When faced with the challenge of Southern governors, legislatures, and courts acting in open defiance of federal laws, Robert Kennedy tended to back off. The president would need the white South in 1964. After the assassination of JFK in November 1963, Bobby behaved like a man in shock. He offered himself as ambassador to Vietnam, but was rejected. He went to Poland and then sought the vice-presidential nomination in 1964. Johnson again said no. Bobby rushed to New York, secured the Democratic nomination for senator to cries of "opportunist!," ran against the incumbent Republican, and won. Entering the Senate, Kennedy joined the Democratic caucus, which was beginning to voice qualified criticism of the war to which JFK had committed American troops. It was at this juncture that Bobby suddenly emerged as an outspoken champion of the poor and the ethnic minorities.

The Camelot tradition of JFK's administration also persisted. Among guests invited to Bobby's forty-second birthday breakfast were the Soviet poets Yevgeny Yevtushenko and Andrey Voznesensky; Allen Ginsberg came too, as did Robert Lowell, who had given Jacqueline Kennedy a copy of Plutarch which Bobby borrowed and read. Lowell later wrote:

> For them, like a prince, you daily lift your tower
> to walk through dirt in your best cloth.

Radical intellectuals were leading a double mental life, supporting draft resistance, withholding taxes, applauding the campus revolts, yet fascinated by dreams of real power and a resurrected court of Camelot.

Now, in mid-March, Bobby entered the race. He made an early run into California, where the Kennedy magic sprang to life. Often he was surrounded by teenage girls in Day-Glo toreador pants and emitting "Beatle" squeals. When he reached Hollywood it was touch-and-go whether people would be killed in the stampede. Arriving in the Watts ghetto of Los Angeles, Kennedy told a friendly crowd of blacks that he would end the war. A slim figure in a gray suit perched on the back of a car, Bobby drove among blacks and Mexicans and college kids, swaying precariously at the apex of a pyramid of outstretched hands. Andrew Young, executive director of Martin Luther King's Southern Christian Leadership Conference, told reporters that Kennedy was now more popular among blacks than the president.

Sixty reporters followed him everywhere, the targets of lavish hospitality. Even journalists more sympathetic to the New Left than to any known version of Democratic politics felt the gravitational pull of the Kennedy mystique. Andrew Kopkind, soon to visit Hanoi, began his *New Statesman* report of March 29 with a scathing attack on both Jack and Bobby Kennedy, only to change gear in the final paragraph: "It is impossible to reject the Bobby phenomenon, even if it is equally impossible to enjoy it. Kennedy is real. The radical protests, the Senate doves and even the McCarthy campaign are not. They have all helped to create the atmosphere in which a political alternative to Johnson could develop, but are no alternatives themselves. Bobby alone can make it."

The media monitored the onrush of the Kennedy campaign. *Time* magazine noted that college kids too young to remember the political balance sheet of the JFK administration were moved in memory "by the lucency of the thousand days, the bravura of Jack's life and the trauma of his death. Bobby has made it all historic and contemporary at the same time. . . ." Bobby's style and physical presence strengthened the association: the Harvard-trained Boston diction; the rhetorical, rising cadences. His key phrases—"We can do better" and "This is a time to begin again"—echoed JFK's speeches in 1960. Like his elder brother, Bobby offered a persona more adventurous than his explicit policy commitments.

Robert Kennedy later admitted that Eugene McCarthy got the support of the "A" kids (with the energetic help of Al Lowenstein), whereas he himself picked up the "B" and "C" streams. McCarthy's youngsters were inclined to romanticize the NLF, Che Guevara, or Malcolm X, yet recoiled from the violent anti-Americanism of the New Left. (Besides, a presidential election year is a national festival; to remain aloof, as SDS did, was like denying the flesh.) Though they hated the war and the draft, McCarthy's army of idealists still believed in the possibility of the good father. They talked door-to-door to older people, considerately, respectfully; the older people liked them.

The McCarthy students who loved Gene regarded Bobby as both opportunistic (having hung back) and ruthless; they distrusted the senior knights who were reviving Camelot in armor tarnished by a decade of betrayed liberal ideals—Larry O'Brien, Pierre Salinger, Ted Sorensen—and the endorsement from former Defense Secretary Robert McNamara, which was played on TV every night. Likewise, ads announced that law enforcement officers all over America endorsed Kennedy. Jeremy Larner conveyed the distaste felt by the "Gene generation" for the scene at Bobby's headquarters: "Crowds of twitchy celebrity hunters in the lobby . . . . Upstairs, middle-aged politicians wander the halls with dead cigars. . . . Ethnic people looking ethnic, chosen and paid specimens of every variety. . . . Into the elevator goes a clutch of silken society people, tanned heads held at elegant angles. . . ."

Arthur Schlesinger, Jr. noted the rise of anti-Bobby sentiment among the intelligentsia; his fortune, his Irish mafia machine, his service on Joseph McCarthy's committee in the fifties were all held against him. The professor found himself "hissed at practically every public appearance in the city." Kennedy told Jack Newfield, "I just feel that those New York liberals are sick . . . so filled up with hate and envy." James Reston noted that, "The opposition to him is personal, almost chemical, and sometimes borders on the irrational."

At the end of March, encouragement for Bobby and a further blow to Johnson came from New York, when the Democratic State Committee voted 58 to 30 percent to support a Kennedy man, Eugene Nickerson, for the U.S. Senate. But it was Eugene McCarthy who brought the president down by defeating Johnson by 57 to 35 percent in the Wisconsin primary. The president now had no appetite for the battle. A Gallup poll showed a dramatic decline in his popularity, with only 36 percent of the American public approving his conduct of affairs. On March 31, he broadcast to the nation, announcing that he had ordered a halt to the bombing of 90 percent of North Vietnam, including all populated areas. (The State Department clarified: the 20th Parallel would be the limit.) Johnson called for peace talks.

Then he added: "I shall not seek and I will not accept the nomination of my party for another term as President."

It was a Sunday. People ran out of their apartments and brownstones in Greenwich Village, New York, to whoop and shake hands. It was perhaps the most personal political event since the assassination of President Kennedy. A hippie came up to Andrew Kopkind and said softly, "Johnson said uncle exclamation point."

Bobby Kennedy sent the president a telegram describing his decision as "truly magnanimous" and asking for a meeting "to discuss how we might work together in the interests of national unity during the coming months." The president, whom he had only recently accused of "calling upon the darker impulses of the American spirit," he now lauded as the man "who brought to final fulfillment the [Democratic Party's] policies of thirty years." Bobby was hustling to close out Vice-President Hubert Humphrey and secure for himself the endorsement of the Party machine. On April 2, at a fund-raising dinner in Philadelphia, he described the hack machine politician, James Tate, as "one of the greatest mayors in the United States." But Johnson wasn't having Bobby in 1964, and he wasn't having him now. Bitterly he told a Chicago audience that the media were better at conveying war and conflict than efforts to build peace. The president detested the Kennedy clan and despised the wider radical-liberal consensus, which applauded David Levine's two cartoons, the first showing LBJ with crocodiles falling from his eyes and the second showing LBJs falling from a crocodile's eyes. Jules Feiffer, a playwright and cartoonist with an enthusiastic following in New York and London, had written of Johnson: "We have come to see him as not vital but violent, not clever but devious, not shrewd but cynical. . . ."

Kennedy told 10,000 enthusiastic students at the University of Pennsylvania that America must negotiate with the NLF in Vietnam. McCarthy, criticizing the continued bombing north of the demilitarized zone, called for a coalition government in Saigon. Neither candidate suggested that the United States should simply quit.

THE WAR

On April 1, following Eugene McCarthy's success in the New Hampshire and Wisconsin primaries, Johnson limited the bombing to the southern part of North Vietnam. But on April 19, American planes flew 145 missions against the North, the highest total of the year. Despite the opening of peace talks in Paris (or deadlocked talks about talks; the United States refused to recognize the NLF, while Hanoi refused to recognize the Saigon regime as legitimate participants), mid-May brought the worst week of the war for American forces: 562 killed and 1,100 wounded. Furious fighting had again broken out in Saigon; District 4, the habitat of 300,000 people, lying within a mile of the National Assembly and the big hotels crammed with journalists, was so heavily infiltrated that American planes bombed it.

In Paris the North Vietnamese demanded a complete bombing halt before they would negotiate. The leader of the American delegation, Averell Harriman, countered by linking the bombing to the scale of North Vietnamese infiltration across the border and down the Ho Chi Minh Trail through Laos. According to Washington, Hanoi had sent 85,000 regular troops to the South, of whom 15,000 were attached to Vietcong units and the rest deployed in nine divisions consisting of ninety-nine infantry battalions and forty-three combat support battalions. Four regular North Vietnamese regiments had been involved in the attacks on Saigon at the beginning of May.

Washington, meanwhile, continued to defend the democratic credentials of President Thieu's regime in Saigon. These were not enhanced by the imprisonment of Truong Dinh Dzu, the lawyer who had run second to Thieu in the presidential election of 1967. Campaigning for peace and neutrality, Truong had won 800,000 votes against Thieu's purported 1,650,000 in yet another rigged election. Detained after the Tet offensive, then released on April 13, but rearrested on May 1, Truong was sentenced by a military court at the end of July to five years' hard labor. His crime? Mere advocacy of negotiations with the NLF when interviewed by the London *Times* and UPI in April. This was construed as "conduct detrimental to the anti-Communist spirit of the people and the armed forces." The London *Times* asked: "How can any non-Communist democratic force take shape if no man of repute any longer dares to declare himself?"

Even the South Vietnamese minister of information protested at "the way the Americans fight their war. . . . Our peasants will remember their cratered rice fields and defoliated forests, devastated by an alien air force that seems at war with the very land of Vietnam."

THE ROAD TO CALIFORNIA

After Martin Luther King, Jr., was assassinated on April 4, Robert Kennedy joined in the long march through Atlanta from the church to the grave, evoking a warm response from blacks along the way. But, entering the Indiana primary, Kennedy had to tread carefully between the state's large black population and the white backlash generated by the ghetto rioting that followed the murder of King. To the blue-collar workers of Gary, he denounced violence; in Indianapolis, black crowds gathered round to take his hand.

But youthful idealism was to be frustrated, as the New Left had warned. Hubert Humphrey, once a famous liberal senator but now the Humpty-Dumpty of American politics, was in the race (although he did not declare himself until the end of April), supported by the majority of the nation's twenty-four Democratic governors and still loyal to his crippled president: ". . . the man of peace that I see in this country—but peace may I say with justice and peace with freedom—is President Lyndon Johnson." The Party machine and the union bosses duly transferred the franchise. The AFL-CIO, headed by the loyal George Meany, launched the National Labor Committee for Humphrey, chaired by I. W. Abel, president of United Steel Workers, and backed by a veritable Who's Who of American labor. So efficiently did the machine come behind Humphrey that by the end of April his managers could already claim 900 of the 1,312 delegates needed to secure the presidential nomination. "Here we are," Humphrey said, "the way politics ought to be in America, the politics of happiness, the politics of purpose, the politics of joy. . . ." The time had come, he announced, for every American to say, "I love my country."

On May 8, Kennedy scored his first clear victory in the primaries, taking 42 percent of the Democratic vote in Indiana, against 31 percent for Governor Roger Branigin (Humphrey's front man) and a crushing 27 percent for Eugene McCarthy. Robert Kennedy told Jack Newfield: "I prefer many of the poor white people I've met in Indiana. . . . I think I just like the Poles in Gary better than those New York reformers. . . ."

Norman Mailer met Bobby Kennedy just once—in May, after Kennedy's victory in Indiana—describing him as "somewhere between a blade of grass and a blade of steel, fine, finely drawn, finely honed . . . attractive as a movie star." During their conversation Kennedy refused to trade in ideas unless they were attached to bills, platforms, or specific debates—Mailer had no mind for such details—and finally advised the writer that McCarthy "seems more like your sort of guy, Mr. Mailer."

Nebraska followed on May 15, another Kennedy victory: 52 percent for Bobby, 31 percent for McCarthy, and an 8 percent write-in vote for Humphrey. McCarthy looked down and out, but on May 29 his despondent yet still beavering young activists received the boost they needed: victory in Oregon by 45 percent to Kennedy's 39 percent and Humphrey's write-in of 4 percent. Oregon was prime McCarthy territory—middle-class, white, and liberal—and it was here that he most sarcastically ridiculed Bobby's advisers, his astronaut, his dog, his advocacy of federal gun control, and, above all, his refusal to debate. "Bobby threatened to hold his breath unless the people of Oregon voted for him." Kennedy admitted, "I do my best with people who have problems."

California was the showdown, a state where liberal and radical sentiment was strong and noisy, an exhilarating terrain for both McCarthy and Kennedy camps. "We hopped through sunny California," Larner recalled, "the airports, the campuses, the freeways and shopping centers. Everywhere we had bands and blues groups playing "When the Saints Come Marching In" and crowds of students who kept McCarthy happy." It looked neck and neck; finally Kennedy was forced into a television debate on June 2.

The long-awaited confrontation began with Kennedy accusing McCarthy of proposing to force a coalition government on Saigon, "a coalition with the Communists even before we begin the negotiations." For his part, Bobby would give the Vietcong only "some role" in the future, transferring more of the combat duties to the South Vietnamese. Both candidates agreed that the United States could not simply pull out, and both wished to maintain a wide range of foreign commitments: to NATO, to Israel, to Formosa, and to Japan, South Korea, and India. The New Left watched their TV screens, their suspicions confirmed.

McCarthy offered a more radical challenge than Kennedy to the power of the FBI, the CIA, and the Defense Department, whose directors, he said, enjoyed too much latitude and protection from scrutiny. Kennedy's line was almost complacent; as attorney general he had never ordered any kind of wiretap—a lie—and his own experience in the National Security Council had confirmed that the president always made the decisions. (But neither John F. Kennedy nor Lyndon Johnson had dared to challenge J. Edgar Hoover's autocratic and paranoid grip on the FBI.)

A Los Angeles *Times* telephone poll gave victory in the television debate to Kennedy by 2.5 to one, and Kennedy went on to win the California primary by the finest of margins—46 to 42 percent for McCarthy. It may not have mattered; *Newsweek* estimated that Humphrey was only 32.5 delegates short of the number required to secure the nomination. A Gallup poll of Democratic county chairmen (who influence the selection of delegates and are frequently delegates themselves) showed that 70 percent backed Humphrey, only 16 percent Kennedy, and a mere 6 percent McCarthy.

The day of his narrow victory in California, June 5, Senator Robert Kennedy was assassinated.

THE DRAFT

BOSTON, May 1968—The Spock trial opens. Most famous of the defendants is every young mother's mentor and guide, Dr. Benjamin Spock.

Between August 1964 and the departure of the last U.S. combat forces from Vietnam in March 1973, 26.8 million American men came of draft age. But, of these, less than 11 million were actually drafted into the armed forces. An astonishing 57.5 percent were exempted, or disqualified, or escaped through deferment.

The middle classes evaded the draft legally. In 1965–66, college graduates accounted for only 2 percent of all inductees. The II-S was the magic classification that guaranteed deferment for college students. Graduate schools were also II-S sanctuaries until 1968, when the Selective Service lifted this blanket exemption. Of the Harvard class of 1970, only 56 men served in the military, two of them in Vietnam. A report published that year showed that 234 sons of senators and congressmen had come of age since the United States became involved in Vietnam; of these, 118 had received deferments, and only 28 had gone to Vietnam. One had been wounded. Among those disqualified for military service on medical grounds were the sons of such ultra-Hawks as Barry Goldwater, Ronald Reagan, and Thomas Dodd.

The white middle classes knew how to fail their medicals. A loophole in the law gave every registrant the right to choose the site of his pre-induction physical examination. Butte, Montana, was considered the spot for anyone with a doctor's letter; Little Rock, Arkansas, was for anyone with a note from a psychiatrist; Seattle, Washington, was for anyone carrying a medical message, "regardless of what the letter said."

Patriotic college men too fit to flunk their medicals lined up to join the National Guard (which mainly stayed at home). In 1968 the guard had a waiting list of 100,000. One Pentagon study concluded that 71 percent of all reserve and 90 percent of all guard enlistments wanted to avoid the draft. Professional athletes, most of them superpatriots, loved the guard. Ten members of the Dallas Cowboys were assigned to one division, the backfield of the Philadelphia Eagles to the same reserve unit. Blacks accounted for only 1 percent of the guard.

The first draft-card burnings occurred in 1965. David Mitchell, of End the Draft, burned his card during the Fifth Avenue Parade in New York, invoking in his defense the principles of Nuremberg. Congress retaliated with a law that made the destruction of a draft card punishable by five years in prison and a $5,000 fine. In December 1966, SDS's national council approved the creation of local unions and committees of draft resisters. A Cornell student tore up his card in December 1966, and precipitated the Draft Resistance Union. Resistance was born in San Francisco, New England Resistance in Boston, Cadre in Chicago, and Draft Denial in New York, where 175 young men enacted the first collective ceremony by burning their cards in Central Park, before the Easter 1967 march organized by the Spring Mobilization Committee.

In the summer of 1967, Congress altered the draft regulations, dropping deferment for graduate students starting the following year; about 650,000 male students would be affected. Steven Kelman, a Harvard student, recalled: "A peaceful campus, only marginally concerned with Vietnam, suddenly became desperate. We felt boxed in." During the fall semester what Kelman called "burning frenzy" seized Harvard. By the end of 1967, some 2,000 Americans had turned in their draft cards; by the time of the Spock trial, the figure was closer to 4,000. But a much greater number had taken the indirect road of evasion: an estimated 20,000 had departed for Canada.

The Justice Department figures for draft evasion prosecutions were: 380 in 1964–65; 663 in 1965–66; 1,335 in 1966–67; 1,826 in 1967–68; 3,305 in 1968–69. More than 2,000 prison sentences were handed down. But the actual number of draft refusals was far higher; between July 1, 1968 and June 30, 1969, 27,444 draft cases were reported to U.S. attorneys. It has been estimated that about 10,000 men burned their draft cards in public or defiantly turned them in to the authorities.

Not that draft-refusal was accorded universal approval among the radical Left; the Socialist Workers Party, the Progressive Labor Party, and the Young Socialist Alliance—well aware that the working-class boys were in no position to take part in these inflammatory festivities—urged socialists to get into the army and agitate within its ranks. Norman Mailer, himself an old soldier, also wondered whether it wasn't better to go into the army. Deprived of dissenters, "the armed forces could more easily become Glamour State for the more mindless regions of the proletariat if indeed the proletariat was not halfway to Storm Troop Junction already." On the other hand, a soldier who could not in good conscience fire on the enemy was a liability to his colleagues; iron logic dictated that if you disapproved of the war too much to shoot Vietcong, "then your draft card was for burning."

A big burn-in took place in October 1967 at the Arlington Street Church, Boston. The Reverend William Sloane Coffin, Presbyterian chaplain of Yale, preached the sermon. Four thousand people joined the rally on the Common, and some 250 draftees turned their cards over to Coffin and other ministers. Fifty burned their cards. Embryo support organizations sprang up: Support in Action, launched by the writers Grace Paley and Paul Goodman; Conscientious Resistance, a response to Mitchell Goodman's call in the summer of 1967; Clergy and Laymen Concerned about the War in Vietnam, sponsored by Reverend Coffin and Professor Seymour Melman, of Columbia; Resist, supported by Noam Chomsky and Dwight Macdonald. All these worthy bodies incarnated the wholesome conscience of decent liberalism, known to their enemies as "bleeding hearts."

Stop the Draft Week incensed the administration. On October 26, 1967, General Lewis B. Hershey, head of the Selective Service, retaliated by writing to the 4,081 local draft boards recommending that "misguided registrants," who took part in "illegal demonstrations" or who interfered with recruiting, should forthwith be reclassified 1-A and immediately inducted. This was justified on the grounds that deferments were granted only in the national interest. Uproar ensued. Hershey's letter was denounced by the *New York Times,* the American Association of University Professors, the National Student Association, and Supreme Court Justice Abe Fortas, who described Hershey as "a law unto himself [who] responds only to his own conversation." Kingman Brewster, Jr., president of Yale, called Hershey's letter "an absolutely outrageous usurpation of power." Several colleges announced they would ban army recruiters from their campuses until the directive was revoked.

On December 5, Dr. Spock got himself arrested outside the Whitehall Street induction center in New York City. The following day a larger, more vigorous crowd of 2,000 people turned up. In Philadelphia, seven hundred demonstrated and seventy were arrested. On December 7, angry dockworkers spoiling for a fight arrived at Whitehall Street; on this occasion, three hundred demonstrators were arrested in New York and some more in Cincinnati who broke into the federal building to occupy its recruiting center. Again the administration retaliated; the Justice Department announced the formation of a special unit in the Criminal Division to speed up prosecutions of violations of the Selective Service Act, with special attention to the "counsel, aid or abet" provisions and those covering "obstruction of recruiting." The Spock trial was on its way.

The issue of graduate deferments had raised a fever and inspired the Moratorium Day of February 16. At Columbia, 75 percent of the classes were cancelled so that students could hear experts and moral counselors answer questions about the draft. Among the invited speakers were Dwight Macdonald, Robert Lowell, Professor John Fried, and the redoubtable Noam Chomsky, the most formidable intellectual critic of the *pax Americana*.

Among the class of '68, the candidates for martyrdom were few, whether at the hands of the Vietcong or in American jails. According to a Gallup poll released in June, only 7 percent of students said they would refuse to serve if drafted. The majority of those determined to evade conscription settled for a storm of paperwork to get themselves installed in foreign universities. Young men were leaving for Canada each week, with the prospect of obtaining Canadian citizenship after spending five years out of any eight in that country. Mexico was a poor alternative because of the risk of extradition to the United States. None of the Western European countries presented a danger of legal action against American draft evaders, but the chances of obtaining a permit to remain in those countries varied; Sweden, France, and Switzerland were considered the most sympathetic. It is estimated that 150,000 young men emigrated during the war.

Some stayed to face the music. Peter Irons served three years in prison, from 1967 to 1969, for refusing military service. A former editor of the UAW paper, and active in the Student Peace Union, he had founded an SDS chapter at the University of New Hampshire, where he refused the teacher's loyalty oath and was responsible for getting it declared unconstitutional. In June 1968, David Harris, who had joined the Student Nonviolent Coordinating Committee (SNCC) civil rights campaign in the South, went on trial in San Francisco for refusing induction. Twenty-three years of age and married to Joan Baez, Harris had stepped down from the presidency of the Stanford University student body to devote himself to organizing war resistance. His message had been widely circulated: the draft system was not simply "them"; it was "all of us who alienate ourselves into the power of the state." Harris added: "I find no more honorable position in modern America than that of criminal. . . ." The atmosphere in the San Francisco courtroom was hopeful. There were seven women on the jury, including a member of Women Strike for Peace, and the judge was sharp with the prosecution but courteous to the defense, praising Harris's high motivation. But the verdict was guilty, and the sentence was three years in jail. In 1976 Harris ran as a Democrat for Congress, but without success.

THE SPOCK TRIAL

While serving as a psychiatist in naval hospitals during World War II, Benjamin Spock had filled in time writing *The Common Sense Book of Baby and Child Care,* which became the biggest seller in American publishing history, apart from the other, less practical Bible. Later, having campaigned for John Kennedy, Spock became increasingly alarmed by the nuclear arms race and joined the national board of SANE. In 1964 he appeared on television for the Doctors for Johnson Committee. Two days after his victory, LBJ telephoned: "He said in a voice of great humility, 'Dr. Spock, I hope I will be worthy of your trust.' "

Within three months Spock was peppering the White House with letters protesting the betrayal of campaign promises. Replies came from McGeorge Bundy, Walter W. Rostow, and other top aides, all very respectful and promising continuing study, careful attention. Then Spock took to the streets. At first, Jessica Mitford reports, he found marching embarrassing, "like one of those bad dreams," he said, "when you are downtown without any clothes on."

Spock and Coffin courted prosecution in August 1967, when they published "A Call to Resist Illegitimate Authority,"* in which they

*Marcus Raskin and Arthur Waskow wrote the final text of the "Call to Resist Illegitimate Authority." Among those who signed the Call were Nelson Aldrich, Emilo de Antonio, Rev. Philip Berrigan SSJ, Norman Birnbaum, Robert Brustein, Alexander Calder, Noam Chomsky,

declared the Vietnam War to be "unconstitutional and illegal," as well as contrary to the United Nations Charter and the Geneva accords of 1954, "which our government pledged to support." The methods used in the war amounted to "crimes against humanity," prohibited by the Geneva Convention of 1949. "These are commitments to other countries and to Mankind, and they would claim our allegiance even if Congress should declare war." The authors of "A Call to Resist" promised to raise funds "to organize draft resistance unions, to supply legal defense and bail, to support families and otherwise aid resistance to the war in whatever ways may seem appropriate."

On October 20, 1967, Benjamin Spock, Rev. Coffin, Marcus Raskin, Mitchell Goodman, and Michael Ferber—the five men later indicted and brought to trial—accompanied Selective Service registrants to the Justice Department in Washington, where 185 registration certificates and 172 notices of classification were dumped on distressed officials of the department in "a fabricoid briefcase."

On December 5, 1967, Dr. Spock gathered with other demonstrators (including Allen Ginsberg, Susan Sontag, and Conor Cruise O'Brien) outside the Whitehall Street induction center. Spock's arrest was prearranged; he and four others were allowed through a police barrier to seat themselves symbolically on the steps. "I have come to commit civil disobedience," Spock told reporters. Two hundred and sixty-four arrests were made. In January the Boston 5 were indicted for "conspiracy to counsel evasion and violation of the Universal Military Training Act."

At the end of January 1968, Spock received a standing ovation from an audience of 4,000 when he appeared at a Manhattan rally along with many of the 437 prominent liberals who had pledged themselves, in defiance of Section 7203 of the Internal Revenue Code, to withhold the 10 percent war tax surcharge and the estimated 23 percent of income tax related to war expenditure. Among those risking a year in prison—highly unlikely—and/or a $10,000 fine were Nelson Algren, James Baldwin, Norman Mailer, William Styron, Susan Sontag, Leslie Fiedler, and Thomas Pynchon.

The government's indictment included "A Call to Resist Illegitimate Authority" and the demonstration at the Justice Department on October 20.

Rev. William Sloane Coffin, Robert Coover, Frederick Crews, Lawrence Ferlinghetti, Allen Ginsberg, Mitchell Goodman, Paul Goodman, Nat Hentoff, Leo Huberman, Gabriel Kolko, Hans Koningsberger, Jean-Claude van Itallie, Christopher Lasch, Sidney Lens, Robert Lowell, Staughton Lynd, Dwight Macdonald, Herbert Marcuse, Thomas Merton, Barrington Moore, Jr., Jack Newfield, Conor Cruise O'Brien, Carl Oglesby, Grace Paley, Linus Pauling, Richard H. Popkin, Philip Rahv, Philip Roth, Wilfred Sheed, Edgar Snow, Theodore Solotaroff, Susan Sontag, Dr. Benjamin Spock, Paul Sweezy, Richard Wilbur, and Sol Yurick.

Spock's co-defendant, the Reverend William Sloane Coffin, had been a Cold War man, having served from 1945 to 1947 as a liaison officer with the Red Army. Graduating from Yale in 1949, he entered Union Theological Seminary, then quit to join the CIA, where he served until 1953. Coffin's radicalism took wing when he witnessed college students flocking south in the early sixties to fight the Jim Crow laws. He followed and was jailed more than once—in Baltimore for protesting segregation in an amusement park; in St. Augustine, Florida, for joining a sit-in. Presbyterian chaplain of Yale for the past ten years, Coffin had offered Battell Chapel as a sanctuary for draft violators, without consulting his deacons, causing some fluttering in the dovecote, but he enjoyed the protection of Yale's president, Kingman Brewster, a firm civil libertarian.

Jessica Mitford observed Coffin in action at the Yale draft-card turn-in, part of a nationwide demonstration called by the Resistance for April 3, 1968. Walking through the streets of New Haven with Coffin, Mitford likened the experience to "being in a movie about a small-town folk hero. People come up to shake his hand, students run after him with urgent questions, old folks stop their cars to call out, 'Good luck, Bill!' and 'Howdy, Reverend!' " Norman Mailer remarked that Coffin had the sort of face that one expected to find on the cover of *Time* or *Fortune* as Young Executive of the Year. In 1972 Coffin would fly to Hanoi to receive three more American pilots released by the Vietnamese; by that time he would be on comradely terms with former Attorney General Ramsey Clark, responsible for indicting Spock and Coffin, but in due course a visitor to Hanoi himself. Explained Clark: "I had to uphold the law of the land. I believe in civil disobedience and for civil disobedience to take place the law has to hold firm." Said like a man—and Coffin was a man, too, with a huge handshake, not least for Catholics like Daniel Berrigan.

A third defendant, Marcus Raskin, had served on President Kennedy's staff as disarmament adviser, but soon became disillusioned with the New Frontier, not least because of its extension to Vietnam. He saw Washington moving "more and more in the direction of Satrapism, the imperialist manipulation of small nations and of power groups within those nations, the Diems and the Kys." After Raskin left the government in 1963 and helped set up the Institute for Policy Studies, he and Bernard Fall edited *The Vietnam Reader,* which was rejected by eleven publishers before achieving a powerful impact in university circles.

At twenty-three, Michael Ferber was the youngest of those indicted. His decision to join the Resistance came after an unsuccessful application to his local draft board to change his student deferment status to that of conscientious objector. He tried to explain Unitarianism to the board, "the religious dimensions of man that can exist with or without a belief in God—Tillich's definition of religion as one's ultimate commitment or concern." (Perhaps understandably, American humanists were inclined to take refuge behind phoney pantheisms and fake churches, rather than state their case strictly in terms of human relationships.) But the board "couldn't understand the idea of a church without a creed." Ferber turned in his draft card on October 16, 1967.

The fifth defendant in the Spock trial, Mitchell Goodman, had served as an artillery lieutenant in World War II. While teaching at Stanford in May 1967, he had circulated a pledge of mass civil disobedience and was astonished when fifty faculty members signed it, including eight full professors in the medical school. Much emboldened, Goodman bombarded the East Coast intelligentsia with mailings and was one of the architects of the Pentagon demonstration in October 1967.

A fierce argument broke out within the American Civil Liberties Union between those who wished merely to submit an *amicus curiae* brief arguing that the conspiracy charges violated free speech under the First Amendment, and more radical elements eager to provide the five accused with defense lawyers. By the time the national board finally voted 26 to 20 to offer legal and financial aid to the Boston 5, most of the defendants had arranged for their own legal representation.

District Judge Francis J. W. Ford, eighty-five years old and blatantly biased toward the government, curtly dismissed the plea of Spock's counsel, Leonard Boudin, that the jury should take into account the sincerity of the defendants' belief that the Vietnam War was illegal and the draft unconstitutional. The strategy of the defense lawyers—to plead that the defendants had merely exercised their constitutional right of advocacy—was probably futile. Clearly those defendants who had been present at draft-card burnings were guilty of more than mere advocacy. Equally barren was the attempt to argue, without support from Congress or the courts, that the draft and the Vietnam War were "illegal." A more impressive stand would have stressed the citizen's moral duty to defy the law when higher, humanitarian considerations so dictate. "Aw, fuck, Mitch. . . ." wrote the Yippie leader Jerry Rubin in an open letter to Mitchell Goodman, "within hours Spock's arrest became an accepted part of American pluralism . . . just another court case and trial, buried in legalisms."

All were found guilty except Marcus Raskin. Passing sentence, Judge Ford declared that their crimes had been "in the nature of treason" (a word never employed during the trial by the prosecution), worthy of two years in prison and a fine. The poet Robert Lowell presented 28,000 signatures on a "statement of complicity" promising to replicate the offenses.

Spock and Ferber later had their convictions set aside by the U.S. Court of Appeals for the First Circuit. A retrial was ordered for Coffin and Goodman, but no further action was taken.

CIVIL DISOBEDIENCE

Can civil disobedience be justified in a democratic society subject to the rule of law?

Professor George F. Kennan, a former ambassador to the Soviet Union (1952) and Yugoslavia (1961–63), then a professor at the Princeton Institute for Advanced Study, was disgusted by the outbreak of civil disobedience, and made himself clear in an article published in the *New York Times Magazine* on January 21, 1968. "Respect for the law," wrote Kennan, "is not an obligation which is exhausted or obliterated by willingness to accept the penalty for breaking it."

W. H. Auden took up the challenge in a letter to the *New York Times,* quoting Dr. Johnson: "The magistrate has a right to enforce what he thinks, and he who is conscious of the truth has a right to suffer." Modifying his stand in his subsequent book, *Democracy and the Student Left,* Kennan offered a distinction between a citizen's (justifiable) refusal to perform repugnant actions and a more general lawlessness against authority and the state (intolerable). But Kennan got himself into difficulties when he insisted that the burning of a draft card was an "extravagant and indefensible act" because the conscript had no idea what kind of service he would be required to perform in the armed forces. Kennan's logic was remote from reality. A conscript who suspended his refusal until he found himself in the Vietnam War would require exceptional courage to lay down his arms, and would inevitably be regarded as a coward by his fellow soldiers. Conversely, his refusal to accept conscription—if widely imitated—might persuade the government to discontinue an unjust war.

Determined to press logical perversity to its limit, Kennan argued that any young man currently refusing military service must be prepared "to condemn not just the war his Government is at this moment conducting, but every one that it has conducted in the past, including that which established its political independence. . . ." But why? Would a French conscript who refused to serve in Algeria in 1960 be guilty, by implication, of failing to defend his country against Hitler in 1940 or the monarchies of Europe in 1792?

As the flood of eloquent replies to Kennan's "Rebels without a Program" attested, the prime intellectual influence on younger resisters was Thoreau's essay, "Civil Disobedience." But Thoreau was a libertarian distrustful of all government, even when founded on the counting of votes; the draft-resistance movement of the late sixties required a moral foundation enabling it to disobey particular commands by a government it recognized as lawful. The formula most widely adopted was the Nuremberg principle.

By this code a person is not only entitled but *legally obliged* to refuse a criminal order from higher authority. Professor John Fried, of City College, New York, who spoke on many campuses, summarized the findings of a group of American lawyers, namely that American policy in Vietnam violated a number of international treaties and conventions. As we have seen, the defendants in the Spock trial vigorously adopted this line of defense, but the argument is gravely flawed. When the Nuremberg Tribunal established by the Allies referred to war crimes, it did not mean the violation of international treaties—otherwise every German soldier who crossed into Poland and Russia would have become a felon. The second objection is that any valid framework of law requires a judicial process; yet the individual American citizen, or conscript, enjoyed no status as litigant with regard to the United States' alleged violations of international treaties. The judicial process at Nuremberg had been conducted by governments enjoying *force majeure;* they took care to install no permanent court before which they themselves might be arraigned in the future by their own citizens. Bertrand Russell and Jean-Paul Sartre had to invent their own.

The only forum available to Americans for challenging the legality of executive orders was the U.S. Supreme Court, but the court had upheld the conviction of David O'Brien for burning his draft card. Even the sole dissenting judge, William O. Douglas, had not entertained the broader issues of international conventions.

In short, draft resisters did not have a legal leg to stand on. But they had a moral leg. In certain exceptional circumstances, under force of conscience, the individual may disobey a law he or she recognizes as valid—and take the consequences. It was just as Dr. Johnson had said.

DISSENT IN THE ARMED FORCES

The Reverend William Sloane Coffin condemned as absurd the regulation requiring conscientious objectors to believe in God. Indeed, Coffin maintained that conscientious objection to a particular war was as deserving of respect as objection to every war. Few agreed. In the meantime, what was a religion? Muhammad Ali, alias Cassius Clay, heavyweight boxing champion of the world, had pleaded Black Muslim religious objections when resisting the draft, but failed to impress an all-white jury in Houston in June 1967. Facing a five-year prison sentence, Ali was stripped of his title, but kept himself out of jail on appeal.

In March 1968, Captain Dale Noyd of the U.S. Air Force was court-martialed at Cannon Air Force Base in New Mexico. The case attracted national media attention; NBC-TV was in court throughout. A decorated officer from the state of Washington with combat experience in Korea, Noyd's studies in experimental psychology at the University of Michigan had put him in touch with radical folk music (Joan Baez) and humanistic existentialism. Noyd had subsequently composed a long letter resigning his commission on the ground that the Vietnam War violated the Constitution and the U.N. Charter. The air force, unmoved, appointed him housing officer at Cannon. Noyd then filed an application as a conscientious objector, claiming that the war violated his humanist beliefs. But this was rejected on the ground that he was not a "universal pacifist." Noyd's next application for conscientious-objector status quoted such Christian luminaries as Paul Tillich, Karl Barth, and Pierre Teilhard de Chardin, alongside their humanist counterparts: Albert Camus, Bertrand Russell, John Dewey, and Erich Fromm. The air force was losing patience. Noyd was assigned to retrain on the F-100 aircraft, and on December 4, 1967, his squadron commander ordered him in writing to instruct a student pilot who would probably later serve in Vietnam. Noyd refused.

Battered by a phalanx of theologians, for some of whom belief in God was merely an option in the religious syllabus, the military court retreated to the point where it would accept Noyd's refusal if avowedly based on an inner compulsion so powerful it rendered him "mentally incapable" of obeying these orders. This was a hard one for Noyd, whose existentialism persuaded him that he was making a moral choice by the exercise of free will. The officers of the court, meanwhile, had upgraded the military vocation to religious status. As one major put it, "It's not the military against his religion. It's the conflict of two different religions." Noyd got one year's hard labor and was dismissed from the air force.

On April 1, 1969, Boston Chief District Judge Charles Wyzanski raised the spirits of the Resistance when he ruled that legislation which restricted conscientious objection to religious grounds violated the First Amendment, which forbade Congress from making any law respecting the establishment of religion or prohibiting the free exercise of religion.

Resistance to the Vietnam War within the armed forces was of course the exception, but dissident activity and desertion gathered momentum during 1967–69. In June 1966, three Fort Hood soldiers had challenged their orders on the basis of the specific illegality of the war in Vietnam. The case of the Presidio 27 grew out of a peace march in San Francisco during October 1968. Not only were servicemen forbidden to take part in demonstrations while in uniform, but the accused were mainly stockade prisoners who had gone AWOL in order to do so. The majority received prison sentences.

Despite the ban, four hundred soldiers staged a peace march in Seattle in February 1969. On June 5, a rebellion occurred in the Fort Dix stockade. Thirty-eight men were court-martialed, including Terry Klug, who had been placed in the stockade after going AWOL from Fort Bragg from June 1967 to January 1969—time which he spent promoting resistance in the U.S. armed forces stationed in Europe. The Workers' Defense League provided legal assistance.

Political agitation within the armed forces was protected by the First Amendment, provided it remained strictly verbal. *Open Sights,* produced in the army barracks at Fort Belvoir, Virginia, was one of approximately ten underground antiwar papers circulating in the camps. Published every two weeks and printed by photo-offset, it was distributed free and financed by advertisements. The Fort Dix *Shakedown,* an eight-page tabloid printed in New York, was widely distributed in rail and bus stations and was also folded into copies of the *New York Times* on sale at Fort Dix. In the South, resistance papers written by enlisted men appeared at Fort Jackson, South Carolina; at Fort Hood, Texas; and at Fort Gordon, Georgia. Despite the constitutional protection, Dennis Davis, editor of *The Last Harass* at Fort Gordon, was given an Undesirable Discharge two weeks before he was due to leave the army.

THE ULTRAS

The ultra-Resistance was something else: the physical sabotage of the Selective Service system without violence to persons.

In March 1968, Barry Bondus came out of jail after serving eighteen months in Sandstone Prison. Two years earlier, Bondus—then a nineteen-year-old Big Lake, Minnesota, farm boy—had broken into the local draft board and dumped two large bucketfuls of human feces into the filing cabinet, defiling several hundred 1-A draft records. His eleven brothers had worked hard with him to fill the buckets. The writer Francine du Plessix Gray later referred to this combined fraternal effort as "the movement that started the Movement."

The Baltimore 4 (Father Philip Berrigan, Reverend James Mengel, David Eberhardt, and Thomas Lewis) defiled six hundred draft records by drenching them with blood in October 1967. Berrigan, curate of Baltimore's largest black parish and totally dedicated to the black cause, received a six-year sentence. He spent the summer of 1968 in Allenwood Penitentiary, Pennsylvania.

The Catonsville 9 staged their first act on May 17, 1968, when they entered a local draft board in Catonsville, a lily-white suburb of Baltimore, Maryland, and burned up its files with napalm they had manufactured with the help of a recipe from *Ramparts* magazine. "Our apologies, good friends," declared Father Daniel Berrigan, the poet-priest who was one of their leaders, "for the fracture of good order, the burning of paper instead of children." The nine were all Roman Catholics, clergy and lay. In October they came before Chief Judge Roszel C. Thomsen in Baltimore. I. F. Stone recognized in them "the stuff of which saints are made. . . . They joyfully admitted their guilt, like early brethren preparing for the lions." Indeed, the trial attracted some 2,000 zealots from across the nation, with SDS on hand, peace amulets, arm bands, and the upside-down *Y* symbol of the peace movement abounding.

"The priests," wrote Francine Gray, "were young, beautiful, and terrifying." They displayed a stamina, endurance, and fanaticism that she found more threatening than that of the most incendiary SDS leaders. A platoon of priests held up a placard: "To speak of God and remain silent on Vietnam is blasphemy, blasphemy, blasphemy." This was Irish Catholic rhetoric, but Protestant dissenters were also on hand, notably Bishop James Pike, flamboyantly displaying a huge peace amulet from Haight-Ashbury. "You Catholics are getting greater and greater!" he cried, and the crowd shouted back, "Sock it to 'em, Jim baby!" Pike loved an audience: "The Government is chicken. . . . You're chicken not to indict me for inciting and abetting young men to resist the war." Maybe the Justice Department felt that loss of headlines was punishment enough for Pike. But the Protestant churches also produced serious voices of protest: the Baptist Harvard theologian, Harvey Cox, who had launched the ceremony of receiving draft cards on collection plates at war-protest services; and the Lutheran Pastor Richard Neuhaus, an elected McCarthy delegate to the Democratic Convention, who was jailed for leading a protest march through Chicago in August 1968, after the defeat of the peace plank.

The team of defense lawyers was led by the tall, leonine William Kunstler, who argued that the Catonsville 9 were being prosecuted for the sort of protest that the German defendants at Nuremberg were prosecuted for not making—a masterpiece of historical distortion. "They are not more guilty than Socrates or Jesus when brought before the courts," said Kunstler. Did he know that Socrates and Jesus were both guilty? Judge Thomsen allowed the defendants extraordinary latitude in explaining why they did it, before sentencing the majority of them to three years in prison. The Catonsville 9 were freed on appeal, except for the already-jailed Philip Berrigan and Thomas Lewis. In March 1970, the Supreme Court rejected the group's appeal.

Both the Berrigan brothers, the superstars of the Roman Catholic New Left, subsequently defied the law by going underground. Daniel Berrigan, born in 1921 and a Jesuit, was at that time the hip chaplain of Cornell University, with experience of the French worker-priest movement in the 1950s and of periods of exile decreed by his own church. "Shalom, man" was one of his ecumenical greetings. He had been jailed for a week after the Pentagon demonstration in October 1967, but he was at ease with the powerful, gave the Benediction at the opening session of the U.N. General Assembly, and celebrated liturgies in Kennedy living rooms.

The vice-president of riot-torn Cornell had nothing but praise for Daniel Berrigan's influence on the campus: "Before Dan came to Cornell, each time I went to the coffee house, I'd get the hate load: vituperation, cynicism, hostility, angry arguments. . . . Dan has infused charity into our SDS." Berrigan's entrances into the Baltimore courtroom were theatrical; as he strode toward the bar he stopped frequently to autograph copies of his latest book, *Night Flight to Hanoi.*

But the courts were not moved, and the time came, in March 1970, to go to jail. The Berrigans decided, with six others, to vanish. Philip Berrigan was the first to be caught by the FBI. Interviewed in hiding, Daniel Berrigan described himself as the object not of a traditional manhunt, but of a Vietnam-type search-and-destroy mission. Quoting from his master text, St. John of the Cross's *The Dark Night of the Soul,* Father Berrigan disowned, but did not deplore, the current wave of bomb attacks by the Weathermen. "And I can excuse the violence of these people as a temporary thing, I don't see a hardened, long-term ideological violence operating, as in the case of the Klansmen." Daniel Berrigan was finally arrested in August 1970.

Napalm caught on. Although the Boston 2 (students Suzi Williams and Frank Femia) settled for black paint when they went into action on June 1968, the spectacular Milwaukee 14 employed napalm when destroying 10,000 draft records in September. They were brought to trial in Milwaukee County Court on charges of burglary, arson, and theft—a federal trial for interference with the Selective Service would follow. The oldest of the defendants, at forty-seven, was Christian Brother Basil O'Leary, head of the Economics Department of St. Mary's College, Minnesota. Alongside him sat Father James Honey, twenty-eight, a hot-tempered Boston-Irish curate who kept saying, "Don't cut us up, Judge." Father Robert Cunnane, thirty-five, from Boston, jovially remarked at one point in the proceedings: "This is like being stoned to death with marshmallows." He spent idle moments reading *The Gospel According to Peanuts*.

The two young prosecuting district attorneys, one Jewish and one black, were both supporters of Eugene McCarthy and made it clear that they abhorred the Vietnam War. "I'm more violently anti-war than anyone in the courtroom," announced District Attorney Allen Sansom, "but I don't burn draft records, it's bad for the Peace Movement." The black district attorney, Harold Jackson, Jr., who had made his way from East Harlem via the Groton School and Colgate University on scholarships, declared: "Our draft laws are obscene. The Wyzanski decision was great. . . . But these draft-file burners are the worst thing that could happen to us liberals." Eventually both district attorneys cracked. Jackson, himself a Roman Catholic, finally asked that the jury be dismissed while he made his own personal submission: "It is impossible for the State represented by human beings to sit here any longer having it said that they believe in and of themselves that poverty and the war are irrelevant." After the trial Harold Jackson, Jr., quit as district attorney to work exclusively with black civil rights cases.

On May 26, 1969, the eleventh day of the trial, the jury took only seventy minutes to find all the defendants guilty. Sister Joanna Malone of the DC 9 (she specialized in liturgical dancing) cried out from the public gallery: "We thank you, men and women of the jury, for finding Jesus Christ guilty again!" The audience of two hundred sobbed, wept, clenched fists, linked arms, and sang "We Shall Overcome." (Francine Gray noted that the ultra-Resistance was predominantly Irish and had "a streak of the IRA in the viscerality of its emotions and tactics." On June 6, Judge Larsen handed down two-year prison sentences.

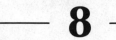

8

THE USA:
Black Power

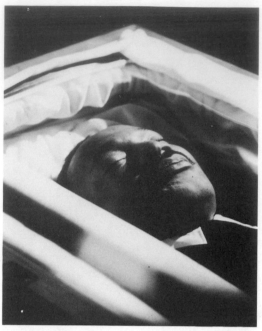

"April 4, 1968—The most respected black leader in the United States, Martin Luther King, Jr., is shot dead on the balcony of a [Memphis] motel."

"...black rioting breaks out in the South, spreading rapidly to 110 cities..."

"Out of the fires emerged...the Black Panther Party, and the voice of H. Rap Brown hailing the riots as a 'rehearsal for revolution.'"

MARTIN LUTHER KING, JR.

MEMPHIS, April 4, 1968—The most respected black leader in the United States, Martin Luther King, Jr., is shot dead on the balcony of a motel. King has come to Memphis to support a strike by black garbage workers demanding union recognition. The unknown assassin vanishes. A plot is suspected—November 1963 all over again—and black rioting breaks out in the South, spreading rapidly to 110 cities including Baltimore, New York City's Harlem and Brooklyn, Newark, Chicago, Detroit, Boston—everywhere. Seventy-five thousand National Guardsmen are deployed on the streets; the final casualty count is 39 dead and 2,500 injured.

Troops were deployed around the White House and the Capitol as rioting and arson spread through Washington, D.C. By mid-afternoon more than seventy fires were burning in the District of Columbia, and the young black gangs had reached the corner of 14th and F streets, a central shopping area less than two hundred yards from the White House. The London *Times* correspondent Louis Heren found himself surrounded "by a pushing and menacing ring of Negroes. An older Negro, lounging against a traffic light, told them to cool it, and they did. For a few minutes they sauntered over to a broken window, and casually outfitted themselves in bright clothes suitable for a Caribbean winter. . . . There was no anger. An observer could swear on oath that most of the youngsters had never heard of Dr. Martin Luther King, let alone his murder. They radiated the supreme happiness of the irresponsible, glorying in their sudden power."

Another journalist watched the riots from the safer vantage point of a television set. He saw a woman staggering under a monster case of Kleenex, then a man pushing a cumbrous dressing table with a huge mirror along the street; he waved to the watching millions at home. Another sat among splintered glass trying on a pair of banana-yellow boots. "In Manhattan," reported Alan Brien in the *New Statesman,* "rumour was full of tongues, pandering to that guilty thrill in anticipating the apocalypse which is one of the deep excitements of modern metropolitans."

The ferocious ghetto riots of the mid-sixties left an ugly scorch across consensus politics in an era of rising prosperity and unprecedented antipoverty programs: twenty riots in 1964, eighty-two in the nightmarish summer of 1967. Thirty-four people died during the Watts (Los Angeles) riots of August 1965. According to the Kerner Report, the typical ghetto rioter was an unmarried male, aged fifteen to twenty-four, somewhat better educated than the average inner-city black, incensed about limited job opportunities, resentful toward middle-class blacks, and furiously hostile to whites. Out of the fires emerged a new, though fragmented radicalism: the Sons of Watts, the Young Men for Total Democracy, the Black Panther Party, and the voice of H. Rap Brown hailing the riots as a "rehearsal for revolution." SDS's leading militant, Tom Hayden, was more cautious: "There is little revolutionary consciousness or commitment to violence *per se* in the ghetto. Most people in the Newark riot were afraid, unorganized, and helpless when directly facing the automatic weapons. . . ." He nevertheless concluded that the riots marked a first step toward "an American form of guerrilla warfare in the slums." Rioting offered the blacks their only way of entering and making history.

Martin Luther King, Jr., had striven for a better version of history. Tributes to him poured in from all over the world. On April 9, he was buried in Atlanta. Between 60,000 and 100,000 people followed the funeral cortege as the coffin was drawn, symbolically, by two Georgia mules along its four-mile journey from the Ebenezer Baptist Church to the memorial service at Morehouse College. Jacqueline Kennedy was greeted at the King family home. Robert Kennedy also came. Congress immediately passed Lyndon Johnson's civil rights bill, banning racial discrimination in the sale, purchase, or renting of domestic property. The provisions, which applied to banks and housing agencies, were designed to cover 80 percent of housing.

Martin Luther King, Jr., had first come to national prominence with the year-long Montgomery bus boycott that began in 1955. Pastor of the Ebenezer Baptist Church in Atlanta (and son of the previous incumbent), he occupied a pivotal position; the Southern churches provided *the* cultural base for the black civil rights movement. The Kings of Atlanta enjoyed a primacy greater than that of the Lodges among Boston's Yankees or the Kennedys among its Irish. But what gave King his distinction, apart from personal courage and dedication, was his oratorical prowess, his melodious voice, his close, compelling communion with the Christian congregations of the black South. He was *the* preacher for love and justice, urging his flock to resist but remain stoical in their suffering, "for we shall reach the Promised Land, O Lord." Abused, assaulted, imprisoned, King was the Gandhi of black American resistance.

King's strategy of nonviolent civil disobedience was dictated not only by his Christian beliefs, but also by pragmatism; successive federal governments in Washington wrung their hands while Southern senators filibustered, Southern governors refused to implement civil rights, and Southern sheriffs like Bull Connor and Ross Barnett used clubs, water hoses, dogs, and cattle prods against blacks demanding equality before the law. Local vigilantes committed murder almost with impunity; even if brought to trial, they could always count on an all-white jury. Under its racist director, J. Edgar Hoover, the FBI did not want to know.

King's Southern Christian Leadership Conference (SCLC) shared with the National Association for the Advancement of Colored People (NAACP) a firm commitment to nonviolent resistance, but the young radicals of the Student Nonviolent Coordinating Committee (SNCC), aware that 85 percent of black children in the South still sat in segregated classrooms, aware that the 1965 Civil Rights Act had been feebly implemented (what Professor Martin Duberman called "little more than federally approved tokenism, a continuation of paper promises and ancient inequities"), aware that even in 1966 an energetic voter-registration drive and political campaign by the SNCC/Black Panther party among the 12,000 blacks of Lowndes County, Alabama, had failed to defeat a racist machine representing only 3,000 whites—aware of all this, the young radicals had turned their backs on Martin Luther King, Jr., to heed the revolutionary voices of Malcolm X, Frantz Fanon, and the Black Panthers. Some even called King an "Uncle Tom," including those who promised vengeance when he was assassinated. The voice of the immediate future belonged to the black radical Stokely Carmichael, even though the Nobel Peace Prize was King's.

King had turned north, toward the ghettos. Attempting to mediate during the Watts riots of 1965, he was mainly ignored or scorned. Mayors like Yorty of Los Angeles, Locker of Cleveland, and Daley of Chicago rebuffed him. "Why, this Mayor Locker . . . he's damning me now and calling me an extremist, and three years ago he gave me the key to the city and said I was the greatest man of the century." King's team moved into Chicago in 1966—into the black slums of the South Side and the pitiful squalor of the West Side. Thirty percent of the city was black, yet blacks held less than 3 percent of policy-making posts in local government and finance. The Polish, Ukrainian, and Irish neighborhoods were hostile to civil rights, school busing, and to "niggers," period. The fattened black-ward politicians in Daley's machine played it the mayor's way: docility in return for patronage. A year later, in Cleveland, King's men found themselves thwarted by hostile Black Muslims, alienated youth, and a cynical urban disrespect for elders.

After much agonizing, King came out unequivocally against the Vietnam War, called LBJ's war on poverty "scarcely a skirmish," and described the American government as "the greatest purveyor of violence in the world today." This was a bold step for a man schooled to believe that blacks could claim their place in the sun only if they left unchallenged America's stance in the wider world. (The earlier persecution of the actor Paul Robeson, who didn't, was a lesson to them all.) A gulf opened up between King and the moderates of the NAACP and the Urban League, like Whitney Young, who warned King that communism had to be stopped and friendship maintained with the president responsible for the Civil Rights Act and the most far-reaching antipoverty programs in American history. King told Young, "Whitney, what you're saying may get you a foundation grant but it won't get you into the kingdom of truth."

In April 1967, King addressed a huge antiwar rally at the United Nations Plaza in New York City. Why send young blacks 8,000 miles to guarantee liberties "they had not found in Southwest Georgia and East Harlem"? Why send black and white boys to fight together "for a nation that has been unable to seat them together in the same schools"?

Arriving in radical Berkeley, California, King found signs hailing a "King–Spock" Peace and Freedom ticket for the 1968 elections. It was the white students who wanted King, but he was wise to say no; in the rift valley between the Promised Land and Vote for Me, legions of supporters would be lost. He would have emerged from the presidential campaign detested by the Democratic establishment, despised by the young radical blacks, and a loser.

Up to the moment of King's death the Washington establishment had been working to keep his Poor People's March out of the capital. Now they heaped praises upon his memory—not only Bobby Kennedy but also Eugene McCarthy, Hubert Humphrey, Richard Nixon, and Nelson Rockefeller hurried to Atlanta for the funeral. Well-informed reporters could be forgiven a smile at the general atmosphere of pious outrage and Christian dedication on that scorching day. Under pressure from J. Edgar Hoover, Attorney General Robert Kennedy had finally given permission in October 1963 for the wiretapping of King's phone; tapes and bugs had been installed not only in his office, but in the motels he used around the country. Later—and not by accident only three weeks before King was due to receive the Nobel Prize—Coretta King opened an anonymous package sent by Hoover, containing a tape of one of the drunken sex parties that her husband (*Time* magazine's Man of the Year) and his colleagues frequently engaged in with local women and prostitutes. The tape had arrived with a note clearly inviting King to commit suicide.

Undeflected by the establishment's postmortem homage, the Poor People's Campaign insisted on marching from Memphis to Washington, arriving on May 13 and setting up a squatter camp called Resurrection City. On June 24, King's successor as leader of the SCLC, the Reverend Dr. Ralph Abernathy, and 343 of his followers were arrested on the steps of the Capitol after the police—with 1,600 regular troops on standby—had expelled them from their plywood encampment. About 350 of the refugees vanished into the ghetto, and the expected rioting began. Mayor Commissioner Walter Washington imposed a curfew. The intersection of 14th and U streets was smothered in tear gas. Shopkeepers who had been looted in April after King's death armed themselves with staves and banded into vigilante groups. It was a hot, sultry night.

Almost a year after King's assassination, James Earl Ray, a small-time escaped convict extradited from Britain, pleaded guilty to King's murder and was sentenced to ninety-nine years in prison. A review of the assassination ordered by Attorney General Edward H. Levi in November 1976 confirmed the FBI's harassment of King, but found no evidence of an assassination plot.

THE PANTHERS: BLACK POWER

The day after King's death Eldridge Cleaver was arrested in Oakland, and a colleague in the Black Panther Party was shot dead. It was, perhaps, no coincidence.

Nineteen sixty-eight was to be the most dramatic year in Eldridge Cleaver's life: literary fame, a shoot-out, jail, a presidential candidate, exile. At 3 A.M. on January 16, the San Francisco Tac Squad had kicked down Cleaver's door and ransacked his apartment. On April 5, he addressed a rally at Berkeley, warned that King would be avenged (he despised King), and later that day was trapped by police in a burning house on 12th Street in Oakland. By Cleaver's account, his colleague Bobby Hutton was shot five times as they emerged with their hands up. Eight Black Panthers were arrested. According to Cleaver's wife, Kathleen, he was beaten in the ambulance and in Alameda County Jail. When she found him in Vacaville Hospital (where he spent the next two months), he was a trembling wreck.

Eldridge Cleaver had joined the Black Muslims while imprisoned in San Quentin, where he had been held since 1956. When his hero Malcolm X broke with Elijah Muhammad, Cleaver also saw the light, then joined the Black Panthers after Malcolm's assassination. The Panthers' Marxist-Leninist version of black power represented an advance, morally and intellectually, on the conservative separatism of Elijah Muhammad's Nation of Islam, with its fantastical brew of pseudo-anthropology and *ersatz* racist theology. The sociology was no more edifying: "The reason I drive a Cadillac is obvious," Elijah Muhammad explained. "Negroes place a high value on things like this."

Malcolm X had come out of the Muslim movement. Black was beautiful: "Yes, that raping, red-headed devil was my *grandfather!* . . . If I could drain away *his* blood that polluted *my* body, and pollutes *my* complexion, I'd do it!" Having learned from Elijah Muhammad that "separation" is the voluntary version of the "segregation" imposed by the white man, Malcolm broke with Elijah Muhammad in 1963 and set up the Muslim Mosque, Inc., in New York. His pilgrimage to Mecca and his journeys abroad excited his interest in Arab and African independence movements, but he was equally honored to be received by His Eminence Prince Faisal of Saudi Arabia and the Osagyefo Dr. Kwame Nkrumah of pseudosocialist Ghana. Frantz Fanon's analysis of the betrayal of the African masses by the power-hungry elites who dominated the bourgeois nationalist parties of the former colonies was ignored by Malcolm X, as indeed by Stokely Carmichael, who shrewdly confined himself to quoting Fanon's call for violent insurrection against the colonists. Carmichael also quoted Camus: When a slave stops accepting his master's definitions, he begins to create his own life.

Cleaver was released from Soledad Prison in December 1966, but on parole and with four years of his sentence hanging over him if he violated its terms. Formed in Oakland in October 1966, the Black Panther Party drew its cadres from disparate black elements: SNCC, CORE, the Deacons, the Muslims, the followers of Malcolm X. The Panthers called themselves "revolutionary nationalists." In 1966, Stokely Carmichael and SNCC's black militants had turned bitterly from electoral frustration in the South toward the Northern ghettos—and, simultaneously, turned on the devoted white activists who had worked with them. "They were on the run from sterile, irrelevant, middle-class white America, and they rendered themselves useless, in many instances, by their inability to come to grips with the bare harshness and embedded racism of the society," wrote Carmichael's colleague, Charles V. Hamilton. Black power was born. Said Carmichael: "When you talk of black power you talk of bringing the country to its knees, of building a movement that will smash everything Western civilization has created."

The Panthers believed in organization, hierarchy (adopting British-style ministerial and military ranks, like the Mau Mau in Kenya) and power; the libertarianism of SDS and the white New Left was dismissed as playground stuff for middle-class kids still enacting nursery rebellions. Unlike the white radicals, the Panthers carried guns; after every shoot-out and arrest it was the duty of white radicals to believe the Panthers' version of events. In 1967, Panthers burst into the California state legislature at Sacramento armed to the teeth. The Panthers had a flair for publicity (they had seen many, many movies), and they demanded the right to carry guns for "self-defense" against the police—the pigs—whose arbitrary, racist harassment must be replaced by black community policing. Armed patrols shadowed the police, acted as witnesses to incidents, and informed those accosted of their rights. The Panthers demanded the release of all black convicts from prison for retrial by all-black juries.

Also in the Panther program was control of local PTAs, radio stations, and slum-clearance projects. Helping poor tenants to fight slum landlords was a torch passed from the community projects of the early New Left to the Panthers and the Latino Young Lords of Chicago and New York City.

Declaring their solidarity with colonized peoples, the Panthers applied to the United Nations for recognition as a nongoverning organization like the Palestinians—and demanded the exemption of blacks from military service. The director of the FBI, J. Edgar Hoover, called the Panthers the "greatest threat to the internal security of the country" during 1968. Senator John L. McClellan's Permanent Subcommittee on Investigations provided a sympathetic forum for police officers and informants to denounce the Panthers.

How much influence did the Panthers exert in the ghettos? Tom Wolfe found that almost "any young ace" admired the Panthers for their courage. "They ripped off the white man and blew his mind and fucked him around like nobody has ever done it." The black berets, dark shades, and leather swagger of the Panthers inevitably reinforced the ghetto's traditional respect for the toughest group on the block. And yet the Panthers failed to achieve solid organizational authority in the ghettos of San Francisco, even though their national headquarters were just over the Bay Bridge in Oakland. A major problem was the absence of a culture amenable to socialistic endeavor. Solid work was so scarce, or so unremunerative, that prestige fell to the gang leader who prospered most ostentatiously without working. Thorstein Veblen had identified the "spurious aristocracy" that exists below the working class and the honest poor; Wolfe updated the model as the pimp in beautiful clothes who "drives the customized sun-roof Eldorado with the Jaguar radiator cap." The Panthers' breakfast program for poor people was introduced belatedly and seems to have been penetrated by gang criminals and hustlers, at the expense of local black traders. There were murders and executions.

Panthers strove to demonstrate to the local youths that they were not just another gang in the game of looting and retribution; their twenty-six rules for members included not carrying narcotics or weed while doing Party work. But it was the poverty programs, not a Marxist black independent state somewhere sometime, that caught the imagination of the gangs. The poverty program professionals funneling funds into "community organizing" were always on the lookout for what Wolfe called "the bad-acting dudes who were the 'real leaders,' the 'natural leaders,' the 'charismatic figures' in the ghetto jungle." Going downtown to "mau-mau" the bureaucrats at City Hall and in the Office of Economic Opportunity had become the routine practice in San Francisco. They gave out the poverty grants and paid organizing jobs. Not only blacks were in on the act, but also Chicanos, Latinos, Chinese, Filipinos, American Indians, Samoans.

The subtlest disease afflicting black radicalism was the temptation to extract large sums of money by working on white liberal guilt. The churches were a sitting target. Take the case of the Interreligious Foundation of Community Organizations' Black National Economic Conference held in Detroit in April of 1968. A noisy SNCC rhetorician, James Forman, hectored the delegates with the news that "only armed, well-disciplined, black-controlled government can insure the stamping out of racism." As a first step, Forman demanded that churches and synagogues fork up a mere $500 million "in reparations" to be spent on: (1) a Southern land bank; (2) four publishing and printing enterprises; (3) four "futuristic" audiovisual networks; and (4) a black labor strike and defense fund. And more. Although Forman explicitly promised the physical disruption of "racist" synagogues and churches, his manifesto was endorsed by 187 votes to 63, while some six hundred other delegates sat mute. Murray Kempton's diagnosis of the mood was no doubt accurate: "They have learned, living with these pieties and neglects, that nothing is noticed unless it is outrageous." James Forman and his followers duly interrupted church services and staged a sit-in at New York's Union Theological Seminary with demands for the payment of the aforementioned $500 million.

"Black Power" was a useful tactical slogan, but futile as long-term aspiration. The white New Left fervently embraced it, but socialists of the Old Left remained unconvinced. As Martin Duberman noted, centralization, oligopoly, and the growth of huge conglomerates would defeat Black Power. Lamenting the slide into rhetoric and defiant gestures, Christopher Lasch quoted from *The Crisis of the Negro Intellectual* the recently published work of a black writer, Harold Cruse: "The black ghettoes are in even more dire need of every possible kind of economic and self-help organization, and a buyers and consumers council, but the most militant young nationalists openly ridicule such efforts as reformist and a waste of time. . . . What they do consider revolutionary are Watts-type uprisings—which lead nowhere." However, Lasch did acknowledge that the ghetto lumpen-proletariat, unorganized and unrepresented by unions or political parties, required something other than the traditional demands for civil rights. Black Power offered a vigorous formula for ethnic solidarity and self-help. But it soon became a cliché for opportunists; old-line politicians used it to shore up their ghetto machines, business people exploited it to expand all-black markets, preachers preached it to hold on to congregations. Even the Yippie spokesman Abbie Hoffman was struck by the paradoxes: " 'Black Power!' yells the seventeen-year-old as he kicks in the store window in Newark and grabs the TV set. 'Black Power!' says the chairman of Negroes for Wallace in Los Angeles. 'Black Power!' shouts Stokely, the international revolutionist."

Black Power ideology stressed the ethnic and historical separatism of Afro-Americans. "From now on," wrote Carmichael and Hamilton, "we shall view ourselves as African-Americans and as black people who are in fact energetic, determined, intelligent, beautiful and peace-loving." According to William Melvin Kelley, a black writer: "We remained African because in Africa we had possessed a complex and highly developed oral tradition. . . . We missed the sounds of each of our languages, but the content, its meanings, stayed with us." White intellectuals were not impressed. "American Negro culture," wrote Christopher Lasch, "grew not out of African survivals nor even out of the legacy of slavery but out of the experience of the Negro people in the South after the Civil War." Black Americans wanted education, housing, upward mobility, status, consumer goods, and U.S. passports. Peter Schrag commented in *Partisan Review:* "Every black Peace Corps volunteer in Senegal or Tanzania has discovered that in every respect that matters he is not an African come home, but an American abroad."

Norman Mailer, on the other hand, recognized the political significance of body language; he reckoned that the black no longer wanted equality. Despite inferior food and less fresh air, light and sanitation, he had achieved a physical superiority which endowed him with genuine style: "Let us brood, brothers, on the superior cool of the Negro in public places. For the cool comes from a comprehensive vision, a relaxation before the dangers of life, a readiness to meet death, philosophy, or amusement at any turn."

Norman Mailer's hip existentialism corresponded to Eldridge Cleaver's; indeed Cleaver praised Mailer's essay, "The White Negro." White liberals found both a challenge and some comfort in Cleaver's best-selling *Soul on Ice;* it generated a pleasant *Schadenfreude.* Militant rhetoric was softened by the confessions of a long-term prisoner who had fallen in love with his white woman lawyer. For every page of Marxist menace, there was a passage of sexual psychology. Cleaver blasted the white culture while flattering it. Although he scorned Martin Luther King's creeping Christian compromises, preferring the lethal rage of Bigger Thomas (the menial rebel in Richard Wright's novel *Native Son*) as an authentic response to "the stifling, murderous, totalitarian white world," he nevertheless rejected "the racist strait-jacket demonology of Elijah Muhammad." Cleaver quoted Fanon and Aimé Césaire on the necessity of anti-imperialist struggle, yet consolingly assured his readers that "there is in America today a generation of white youth that is totally worthy of a black man's respect."

Cleaver was ultramacho and something of a showman, at ease with the flamboyant iconoclasm of Jerry Rubin and California's white Yippies. Around the Bay Area, *Soul on Ice* became gospel-of-the-day. The sardonic Tom Wolfe reported the case of an English class at San Francisco State College, where the white woman teacher, "one of those Peter, Paul, and Mary–type intellectuals," was reading the book to her class. The white kids were all murmuring and sighing, "Far out . . . too much. . . . Wow, that's heavy . . ." until one of the blacks, "a funky character with electric hair," raised his hand and told her that Cleaver's book was written to give a thrill and maybe Buick Estate Wagon backseat rape fantasies to white women in Palo Alto and Marin County. The teacher and her white students stared at him "with congealed faces."

Early in 1968 a rift opened up within the Black Panthers on the issue of strategy during the election year. In February, Stokely Carmichael, appointed acting prime minister of the Panthers while Huey Newton was in jail, delivered a speech in Oakland, which he called "A Declaration of War." Explicitly racist, it seemed designed to thwart any collaboration with white radicals and liberals within the Peace and Freedom Party.

Carmichael was no less forceful a character than Cleaver; no party was big enough for both of them. Carmichael was not American-born; he had passed the rigorous entrance examination for Bronx High School of Science after his parents brought him from Trinidad in 1952. Jack Newfield recalled his first meeting with Carmichael in August 1961, when Carmichael had just emerged from the Parchmann State Reformatory in Mississippi after serving forty-nine days as a freedom rider. "You know how dumb them crackers are? In jail they took away all my books—stuff by Du Bois, King, Camus. But they let me keep Mills's book about Castro, *Listen, Yankee,* because they thought it was against Northern agitators." Newfield next met him in 1965, in Lowndes County, where Carmichael, then twenty-five years of age, was breaking the ancient paralytic fear among the blacks by openly taunting the sheriff, mocking his stride, cursing him in Yiddish. "The lean, tall athletic body was beginning to develop the 'starch fat' of the poor."

Now, in February 1968, Carmichael began his speech by recalling how the white man wiped out the American Indians ("the Red Man"), and how he brought the blacks to America to pick cotton. But that service was no longer needed, and genocide was imminent (like Hiroshima, like Vietnam). He advised his audience to "check out the white race. Wherever they have gone they have ruled, conquered, murdered and plagued—whether they are the majority or the minority they *always* rule. They always rule, always rule." So: "The major enemy is the honky. . . ." Black people everywhere, even Uncle Toms and merchants, were brothers. "It is a question of color. It is a question of color." Calling for a black united front of all classes (those who refused to collaborate would be "offed"), Carmichael ended: "We are an African people with an African ideology."

Cleaver rejected this approach. While subscribing to the Panthers' utopian demand for a U.N.-supervised plebiscite of America's blacks, his tactical preference was for a united front of radical forces. "I think there is a danger in the great desire for black unity." Cleaver accused Carmichael of forgetting his Marxism by papering over the class struggle within the black community. In a remarkable prison interview, Huey Newton—the Panthers' prime minister—implicitly endorsed Cleaver's position and contemptuously likened the black bourgeoisie to the tame "house nigger" who would always betray the more embittered and radical "field niggers." Remarkably, Newton now rejected the notion of African roots and culture, praising the recent role played by young white radicals in America, the Yippies included. "Okay, I can dig it. I can see how it makes the pigs over-react, and then whites begin to defend themselves collectively." Carmichael, in short, was on his own.

On June 11, 1968, Cleaver was released by a county court judge on $50,000 bail, four days before the trial of Huey Newton, who was charged with shooting a policeman the previous October. Patrolman John Frey had stopped Newton's car; a passing black bus driver testified that he saw Newton pull out a gun and start shooting, but no gun belonging to Newton had been found. Experts for the prosecution claimed that Frey had been shot with his own gun from behind. On

September 8, Newton was convicted, but only of manslaughter—a political compromise. The poster of Newton, rifle in one hand, spear in the other, stayed up on dormitory walls alongside Che Guevara.

The prevailing state of war between the police and the Panthers—exacerbated by the successful rent strikes that the Panthers had organized during the summer—was dramatized by an incident at the Kings County Courthouse in September. A dozen Panthers wearing black berets and necklaces of machine gun bullets, charged with assaulting three policemen and with holding an unauthorized rally, were set upon and beaten up in the lobby by 150 whites, mainly off-duty policemen belonging to the so-called Law Enforcement Group, a right-wing lobby within the New York City Patrolmen's Benevolent Association, who happened to be carrying their truncheons, though out of uniform. As they lashed out at the Panthers, there were yells of "White Power!" and "Wallace for President!" Mayor John Lindsay protested, but seven months later none of the assailants had been charged.* The alarming escalation of racial conflict panicked the moderate NAACP's journal, *Crisis* (November 1968), into a vehement attack on black extremists who espoused "apartheid," preached racism and anti-Semitism, and advocated violent revolution.

Cleaver was nominated as presidential candidate for the disintegrating Peace and Freedom Party when it convened at Ann Arbor, Michigan, in August. But the prospects for an effective interracial radical coalition were far from promising; they were indeed dead. The seedbed of the PFP, the National Conference for New Politics (NCNP), had suffered a traumatic experience at its Chicago convention in September 1967, when the black delegations stormed around the conference hall and the black caucus met in continuous succession behind closed doors guarded by bodyguards with shaven heads. Whites were excluded from the caucus rooms with shouts of "Human beings only, honkies and animals not admitted." The caucus, reported Richard Blumenthal, included nationalists in Afro shirts and *faletas,* Northern ghetto militants in blue jeans and rimless tinted glasses, King's SCLC representatives in expensive suits, women from the Mississippi Freedom Democratic Party in cotton dresses, SNCC men in Black Power T-shirts, and more.

The blacks demanded, for starters, that the thirteen points of their resolution be endorsed without amendment. The 2,100 delegates duly obliged, by a vote of 3 to 1, and then voted by the same margin to give the black caucus 50 percent of the convention votes (effective control,

---

*During 1969–70, President Nixon's attorney general, John Mitchell, directed a massive judicial process against the Panthers, with indictments in New York, Cleveland, Chicago, and New Haven; police raids on Panthers offices across the country; and further shoot-outs.

since the caucus voted as a block). Particularly persuasive was the cultural argument that whites had been "defining" blacks for three hundred years, and would continue to do so if they attempted to amend black resolutions. Speaking on behalf of the blacks' demands, Bertram Garskoff, of Ann Arbor Citizens for Peace, declared, "We are just a little tail on the end of a very powerful black panther. And I want to be on that tail—if they'll let me." But Arthur Waskow, a founding member of NCNP, was appalled: "One thousand liberals are trying to become good radicals and they think they can do it by castrating themselves." Martin Peretz, a Harvard instructor who was a major contributor to NCNP, walked out after the passage of a black resolution condemning Israel. Disgusted by populist anti-Semitism and angered by Carmichael's role as ambassador for Havana, Hanoi and the Arabs, Peretz ventilated his disillusionment in *Commentary* and never looked back.

As a broad-Left coalition, the PFP was now doomed. By the time the party held its founding convention in March, King had refused to run as its presidential candidate and PFP's liberals were deserting to Eugene McCarthy. The alliance with the local Oakland Panthers now dominated the PFP rump. The imprisoned Huey Newton was nominated for the 7th Congressional District, Cleaver was adopted as presidential candidate, and the PFP's campaign (condemned by the *Guardian,* organ of the New Left) degenerated into a fiasco.

Governor Ronald Reagan raised a storm when Cleaver was invited to teach a small, experimental course at Berkeley, and on September 27 the State Court of Appeals gave him sixty days to return to Vacaville to face charges of violating parole (a tactful interval to allow his election as president of the United States?). Haunted by the prospect of reincarceration, Cleaver vanished in November, escaped abroad, spent eight months on the move, and finally found asylum in Algeria. Here he wrote his "Open Letter to Stokely Carmichael," who had resigned from the Panthers and exiled himself in Guinea. Cleaver accused him of "SNCC paranoia" and of putting racial solidarity before Marxism.

RADICAL CHIC

A British Labour MP visiting the United States in January 1968 noted that Black Power people were much in demand at liberal white parties in North Beach, San Francisco, and Georgetown, Washington D.C. Referring to themselves guiltily as Caucasians, the whites seemed both to expect and to want to be threatened with black violence, nodding respectfully as they heard how all the highway ramps in Detroit and all the bridges in Washington would soon be dynamited. The MP visited a popular off-off-Broadway play, *Christmas Turkey,* during which a white girl lay naked on a table throughout most of the action, asking the black Nats to eat her and so end race hatred. This, of course, was youthful idealism and sentimentality engaging in the politics of gesture which, when the appurtenances of wealth are added, become radical chic.

At the 1968 London Film Festival, similar vibrations were apparent in the audience's reaction to Agnes Varda's film, *Black Panther,* shot in August outside the Oakland courthouse during a demonstration calling for the release of Huey Newton. Young Panthers in identical black-leather jackets marched forward in step, carrying walkie-talkies, then spaced themselves out dramatically on the courthouse steps. When Kathleen Cleaver, wearing an Afro hairstyle, explained that black women must be beautiful in a *black* way, a white member of the London audience cried out "Right on!" and there was an outbreak of applause a few yards from the Thames.

Agnes Varda was able to film-interview Huey Newton in Alameda County Jail. Joan Didion went to see him because she was "interested in the alchemy of issues, for an issue is what Huey Newton had then become." She also called on Cleaver—another "issue"—when he was out on parole, felt herself being "visually frisked" before being admitted to his apartment, and discussed the commercial prospects of his book, *Soul on Ice.* Earlier in the year (Didion recalls) she had watched Robert Kennedy's funeral while sitting on a verandah of the Royal Hawaiian Hotel in Honolulu, in between rereading "all of George Orwell." Of the year 1968, Didion remarked: "I did no good works but I tried to keep in touch. I was responsible. I recognized my name when I saw it." This was the California-hip variety of radical chic.

Didion lived in the soft-centered, liberal belt which "kept in touch" with the many revolutions and happenings in the air. Huey Newton, Eldridge Cleaver, and San Francisco State College were all "flash pictures in variable sequence, images with no 'meaning' beyond their temporary arrangement, not a movie but a cutting room experience." This cutting room extended up to Bel Air, where Roman Polanski accidentally spilled red wine on her dress, some time before Didion, sitting at the shallow end of a Beverly Hills swimming pool on August 9, 1969, received a phone call about the murders of Polanski's wife Sharon Tate and other victims at his house on Cielo Drive. Another happening, another "issue." Later, Didion bought a dress for Linda Kasabian, which she wore to begin her testimony at the murder trial of Charles Manson.

Tom Wolfe's essay "Radical Chic" was directed at a group of

wealthy New Yorkers who entertained, if not embraced, the Black Panthers because they were, at that moment, "it." The conductor Leonard Bernstein's wife Felicia gave a party for the Panthers, twenty-one of whose comrades faced trial (and needed money) on charges of conspiring to blow up five department stores, railroad facilities, a police station and—bizarrely—the Bronx Botanical Gardens. Bernstein offered his fee for the next performance of *Cavalleria Rusticana,* adding, "I *hope* that will be four figures!" In Wolfe's view, the rich were not really interested in the black cause while it was embodied by square, worthy, Southern clergymen like Martin Luther King. They got socially excited only when the blacks produced revolutionary leaders with cosmopolitan connections, modern tongues, and menacing electric hairdos. Stokely Carmichael and Eldridge Cleaver, LeRoi Jones and H. Rap Brown—any one of them *made* a party. The wealthy people gathered in the Bernsteins' apartment had heard that the Panthers were Marxists—but aren't we all? All, that is against the "booooozh-wah" and the "petty-boooozwah" in the white power structure. Fine! Not one of the Bernsteins' invited guests doubted that being bourgeois was a state of mind—something like dull and philistine and Mayor Daley— rather than a way of making money.

The word "capitalist," however, made Bernstein's white guests nervous. They wondered whether the Panthers planned to strip them of their jewels. The thing to be was rich, but a champion of the poor. The poor deserved to be rich too—almost. It was the mean-spirited, Republican Middle-American booooozwah who—lacking imagination, culture, and breeding—hated and feared the poor. Only the people with genuine style understood *guilt,* without which you were spiritually lost. Leonard Bernstein wanted to know whether the Panther spokesman, Field-Marshal Don Cox, didn't feel "infuriated" when he walked into a house as lavish as his own. Cox replied: "I'm over that." "Well," said Bernstein, disappointed but slightly relieved, "it makes *me* mad."

Encouraged, Cox reported how he had been coming out of the courthouse the other day when an off-duty pig gave him the finger. Tom Wolfe reports Bernstein's reaction: " 'God,' says Lenny, and he swings his head around toward the rest of the room, 'most of the people in this room have had a problem about being unwanted.' "

Wolfe's snarl is perfect: "He has done it. He has just steered the Black Panther movement into a 1955 Jules Feiffer cartoon. Rejection, Security, Anxiety, Oedipus, Electra . . . the era of the great cresting tide of Freud, Jung, Adler. . . ."

The Bernstein party got slaughtered in the *New York Times,* which spoke of the Panthers as "the romanticized darlings of the politico-cultural jet set. . . ." The editorial went on to blast "Mao-Marxist ideology and Fascist para-militarism," none of which was any good to "those blacks and whites seriously working for complete equality and social justice." But the *New York Review of Books,* understandably sensitive about radical chic, gave Wolfe's essay no mercy: "Cruel and shallow . . . low comedy nastiness . . ." wrote Jason Epstein. What Wolfe called "radical chic" was in reality "only the unhappy residue of the broken promises and defeated politics of the Kennedys."

BLACK AND WHITE ARTS

There was plenty of theatre in black politics and as much politics in black theatre—but a different version for black audiences and white. The fieriest of black writers, Leroi Jones, had laagered himself away in Newark's black community theatre, Spirit House, where Muslim customs prevailed and Jones reportedly gave no outside interview except (according to report) for a large fee. A brilliant talent was that of Ed Bullins, resident playwright at Harlem's New Lafayette Theater (and the Panthers' minister of culture), whose *Electronic Nigger* offered forty-five minutes of intellectual farce that picked off the white bourgeoisie with a deadly aim while exposing the clash between technology and humanist values from a black standpoint.

White writers occasionally found acceptance with black companies, but it was rare. Joseph Dolan Tuotti, an alumnus of the Watts Writers' Workshop, depicted the poverty program in his play *Big Time Buck White.* In the office of BAD, a "poverty gig," blacks battle over funds and insult each other ("Who you callin' nigger, nigger?") until an Afro-style leader takes over and teaches them to reserve their fire for the whites. The mainly white audience was invited to ask questions: "Can white people help?" And then treated to scornful answers: "Yes, after you've cleaned up your own neighborhood."

Heavier on the international cultural scales was the work of another white writer, Peter Weiss, whose *Song of the Lusitanian Bogey* was performed by the Negro Ensemble Company (the term "Negro" was fast yielding to "black") at St. Mark's Playhouse during 1968 and subsequently on tour in London. Playing with disciplined ferocity, the company writhed and railed before a monstrous metal zombie, the "bogey" of the title, whose ravenous jaws opened to disgorge a succession of raging Portuguese authoritarians holding colonial Angola in subjection. Weiss's new Marxist formula—loads of statistical information conveyed within a ramshackle epic form—was not redeemed by the slick virtuosity of a company floating on a Ford Foundation grant midway between Harlem and Bedford-Stuyvesant, but a long way from either.

Productions attempting to bridge the gap between black and white perspectives were generally resented. Stanley Kramer's film *Guess Who's Coming to Dinner* portrayed a white liberal couple (Katharine Hepburn and Spencer Tracy) who find themselves severely tested when their daughter brings home a black fiancé (Sidney Poitier), although he is as well integrated in middle-class society as Ralph Bunche. Robert Kotlowitz, the astute film critic of *Harper's* magazine, remarked that he wouldn't want to watch the film in Harlem or Watts, "where it may well be stoned by young Negroes who know better about miscegenation."

The major black critical confrontation with white liberal culture followed the publication of William Styron's novel, *The Confessions of Nat Turner,* a fictional autobiography of the Negro leader of a slave revolt in Virginia who was hanged for the deaths of more than fifty whites. Styron's liberal imagination equally offended the white South— Styron is himself a Southerner—and the black North. The real Nat Turner had killed a white woman; Styron had taken the liberty of depicting Nat overcoming a strong sexual passion for his kind and gentle victim, even though she had "showed me Him whose presence I had not fathomed or maybe never even known."

Ten black writers responded in a volume of essays that—charged with the raw racial voltage of the time—accused Styron, variously, of racism, falsification of history, and a masked apologia for slavery, and of transforming the revolutionary general Nat Turner into a hesitant, pampered "house nigger" capable of cowardice. Styron had also depicted slaves loyal to their masters helping to shoot down the insurgents; the black writers claimed that this never happened. Rallying in support of Styron, the Marxist historian of American slavery, Eugene Genovese, demonstrated that such loyalty was a common feature of slave revolts in the Caribbean and in Brazil.

Two of the black scholars, Mike Thelwell and Vincent Harding, accused Styron of creating a Nat Turner besotted by white culture, white language, and white dreams. (But, as Genovese pointed out, Frantz Fanon had depicted this common phenomenon in his admired essay, "Black Skin, White Mask.") Styron's Nat has a homosexual experience and afterwards remains continent; the black critics objected that Styron had deprived him of his manhood. To compound the offense, Styron had invented a black character, Will, who is bloodthirsty, nihilistic, consumed by hate, and hungry for rape—a smear, said the critics, on their race. Genovese argued that such types "appeared in the noblest of uprisings and revolutions throughout history."

On the other hand, no rape did occur during the real Nat Turner's slave revolt, so why inject this element?

Several works by black authors that might have given comfort to Styron appeared during 1968. William H. Grier and Price M. Cobbs argued that because power and money—symbols of masculinity in capitalist society—are denied to blacks, they become obsessed with sexual potency. Reared in the ghetto by a matriarchy that anxiously suppresses all masculine assertiveness as fatally dangerous, the sons compensate by a cult of ultramasculinity, embracing the stereotype of Negro-male muscular-sexual prowess and dreaming of imposing it by screwing or raping white women. (Ed Bullins's play, *The Wine Time,* performed in Harlem, showed a pregnant wife berating her husband for being unemployed; again and again she tells him he's no man. Goaded, the male section of the audience joined in the action with shouts of "Give it to her!")

Eldridge Cleaver described how he stuck a white glamour girl from *Esquire* on his prison wall. Preferring white women, as did most of his friends, he had become a rapist, first of black girls, then of white ones. "Rape was an insurrectionary act." But his lust for white women filled him with guilt and shame, because he came to realize how the driving force of it was rooted in the psychology of a class-ridden, racist society in which sexual aspiration mirrored social dominance and subordination. Given Cleaver's sexual phenomenology (the omnipotent but physically frail white male Administrator; the fragile, beautiful, ultrafeminine white woman; the virile Negro supermasculine Menial; the rejected, slaving Amazonian Negress), Styron could well have cited this radical black author in defense of his novel.

— 9 —

COLUMBIA

"Columbia University, April 23, 1968—The student revolution comes to New York City when an elite private school of the Ivy League is occupied by black and white students."

UP AGAINST THE WALL . . .

COLUMBIA UNIVERSITY, April 23, 1968—The student revolution comes to New York City when an elite private school of the Ivy League is occupied by black and white students.

The early activity of SDS at Columbia in the fall of 1966 grew out of opposition to CIA and military recruiters on the campus. In the spring of 1967, students had voted 1,333 to 563 that Columbia College should not release class ranks to the draft boards; the College's faculty agreed. (Seventy percent of them believed the United States should get out of Vietnam.) In April, there were major confrontations over recruiting on campus by the U.S. Marines, with faculty and deans intervening to keep opposing student factions apart.

Grayson Kirk, president of Columbia, was a target for the New Left. A director of Socony Mobil Oil, Con Edison, IBM, and various financial institutions, he also sat on the boards of two foundations that had received covert CIA funds. Kirk ran a tight ship; the crew's job was to work hard and play hard and be proud to be on boards—not to question the commodore's strategy. For eight months Kirk had refused to release a report that he himself had commissioned on student life, rules, and decision making. The president showed the color of his eyes when he told an audience in Virginia, only thirteen days before the revolt, "Our young people, in disturbing numbers, appear to reject all forms of authority, from whatever source derived, and they have taken refuge in a turbulent and inchoate nihilism whose sole objectives are destruction."

But Kirk's "nihilism" was "freedom" to the new generation; his conception of order was oppressive. A week before the outbreak, Linda St. Clair, a student at Barnard (Columbia College's female associate college) was put on trial before the faculty student board for having concealed a misdemeanor: she lived with her boyfriend. Sixty other women then came forward to testify that they were equally guilty.

Trouble was coming from two directions. A year before the revolt, the London *Times* reported that the university's seventy-two black undergraduates, many of whom had joined the new Afro-American Society (A-AS), felt themselves part of a separate culture, alienated and yet simultaneously afraid of assimilation—"A thirty-second vice-niggership at General Motors," as Marvin Kelly, a first-year student, put it. A storm was brewing around Columbia's gymnasium project (to be built on an adjoining derelict park site), which had a long and contentious history. New York City Mayor John Lindsay and Parks Commissioner Thomas Hoving had both criticized the project. The A-AS had taken up the issue, accusing Columbia of being a rapacious slum landlord bent on ripping off the ghetto's scarce land resources. On April 4, Martin Luther King was assassinated and the temperature rose. A memorial service for King in St. Paul's Chapel at Columbia was disrupted by SDS students, who rushed the pulpit and seized the microphone from the chaplain, claiming that it was hypocrisy for a racist institution to pay tribute to a black civil rights leader.

Columbia's SDS had recently come under the leadership of intransigent guerrillas headed by Mark Rudd, "a tall, hulking, slack-faced young man with a prognathic jaw and blue-gray eyes so translucent that his gaze seems hypnotic," to quote Professor Daniel Bell. Having recently returned from Cuba and written an enthusiastic report in Columbia's student newspaper, Rudd was on the warpath soon after his election as Columbia SDS's new president. Defying President Grayson Kirk's rule against indoor demonstrations, a radical group known as the IDA 6 gathered in Low Library to protest Columbia's collaboration with the Institute for Defense Analysis, a consortium of some dozen universities which supervised the distribution of government contracts for university research projects. Kirk was a member of the IDA's board. The IDA 6—five undergraduates and one graduate student— were ordered to report to their deans. They not only refused, but threw down the gauntlet in the shape of an open letter from Mark Rudd to Grayson Kirk. By any standards it was insulting: "There is only one thing left to say. It may sound nihilistic to you, since it is the opening shot in a war of liberation. I'll use the words of LeRoi Jones, whom I'm sure you don't like a whole lot: 'Up against the wall, motherfucker, this is a stick-up.' Yours for freedom, Mark." (The phrase "Up against the wall, motherfucker" originated in the ghettos, where it was commonly employed by cops when searching people. An SDS chapter on the Lower East Side composed of hippies, artists, dropouts, and local people had recently styled themselves the Motherfuckers; Columbia SDS picked it up in time for the April 22 issue of its paper and for Rudd's letter to Kirk.)

At noon on April 23, the IDA 6 and their supporters gathered at the campus sundial for a rally. After some confused discussion the demonstrators converged on the site of the proposed new gymnasium on Morningside Drive and 112 Street, and tore down the fence surrounding the excavation. The scene was chaotic, with SDS temporarily losing control, Assistant Dean Erwin Glikes pulling at Rudd's sleeve, Dean Platt running alongside the demonstrators, and Professor Orest Ranum yelling "Come on now, come *on* now!" in an attempt to restrain them. When the crowd reached the gym site, a policeman who moved to arrest a white student was punched and kicked. Bill Sales, a black graduate, made a speech linking the gym to Vietnam, German students, Martin Luther King, Angola, Mozambique, Zimbabwe, and South Africa.

Scattered by the police, the demonstrators re-formed at the sundial and decided to hold an indoor demonstration in Hamilton Hall at the office of Acting Dean Harry Coleman. The dean was taken hostage. Vice-President David Truman, meanwhile, was resisting President Kirk's inclination to send the police into Hamilton Hall.

At 2 A.M. the steering committee of the Hamilton Hall occupation finally broke along racial lines after a long black-caucus meeting. The blacks felt they must make their own demands in their own way and wanted the whites out. At 5:30 A.M. the fatigued white students led by Rudd left the building, while the blacks began to barricade themselves in. The beleaguered Dean Coleman and two colleagues, meanwhile, did some barricading of their own by pushing heavy furniture against his office door. (Coleman was released twenty-six hours after his incarceration.) The SDS contingent expelled from Hamilton, about 130 of them, wandered the campus at a loss, then smashed a window in Low Library, Columbia's administrative center; gained entry; broke a glass pane in President Kirk's door; and occupied his office. It contained a $450,000 Rembrandt, *Portrait of a Dutch Admiral,* and a sculptured ebony lion statuette.

The police were finally summoned and began to break through the barricades to Low Library. It was a time for heroes, but the group occupying the president's office dropped out of the window one by one (including Mark Rudd) until only 27 were left to face the music. (One of the participants estimated that 173 jumped out of the window.) The police, however, refused Truman's request to arrest only the whites in Low Library without rendering the same service to the blacks in Hamilton Hall (which Truman would not permit). In a bizarre turn, the police shrugged and abandoned Low Library, taking the Rembrandt with them, while SDS began climbing back through President Kirk's window.

Five buildings were occupied: Hamilton by the black students; Fayerweather mainly by graduate students, many of them in history; Avery for the most part by students in the School of Architecture; and Low Library and Mathematics by the most radical, hard-line SDS. Tom Hayden, the founding father of SDS and its most experienced revolutionary, immediately arrived on the campus and, according to Daniel Bell, advised SDS to accept black leadership. But the blacks had embarked on separatism, and Hayden was soon leading the occupation of Mathematics Hall—"A maestro of participatory democracy, he conducted the mass meetings that night with consummate skill," reported the editors of Columbia's student newspaper.

HAYDEN

Tom Hayden was born in 1939. Graduating from the University of Michigan, where he edited the *Michigan Daily,* he became a founding member of SDS, its first president, and draftsman of the eloquent Port Huron Statement. Hayden went South with the civil rights movement, and was imprisoned in Georgia. Later he became the main architect of the Newark Community Union project. "We are saying ordinary, common people should make decisions about urban renewal and the war on poverty." What did not interest him was "charismatic leaders, synthetic crises . . . flashy demonstrations." In Newark he was arrested on a trumped-up charge during struggles with local landlords and politicians. A gifted writer who served as contributing editor to *Liberation* and *Studies on the Left,* Hayden held contempt for Democratic coalition politics that was total; he could list the foundations, banks, and corporations that owned "lock, stock and barrel, the major enterprises in Mississippi." Jack Newfield noted that Hayden harbored "an overwhelming sense" of the sinfulness of the affluent society.

Tom Hayden traveled to Cuba and twice to North Vietnam, then turned up in Cambodia as an escort for three servicemen released by the Vietcong. During 1968 he acted as coordinator of the National Mobilization Committee Against the War in Vietnam. Following his experience with the Columbia insurrection, he published "Two, Three, Many Columbias" in *Ramparts* (June 15, 1968), arguing that Columbia had opened "a new tactical stage" in the Resistance, that of "permanent occupation, revolutionary committees, barricaded resistance." He also recommended hit-and-run tactics between strikes: "raids on the offices of professors doing weapons research could win substantial support among students while making the university more blatantly repressive." The aim of SDS at Columbia was clear: "They want a new and independent university standing against the mainstream of American society, or they want no university at all."

Diana Trilling observed Hayden during the Columbia occupation, for which she felt nothing but hostility, and was struck by a quality of "nervousness under practical control, almost to the point of rigidity. . . . The face is long, thin, narrowed-eyed, tight-lipped, with little flexibility—here is someone who has gone beyond the need for ordinary human, ordinary social responsiveness; there is no charm, only intention and discipline and an overcast of hard dreariness." Hot on the heels of the Columbia insurrection, Diana Trilling was tartly surprised to read a newspaper report that when Robert Kennedy's body lay in state in St. Patrick's, Hayden came to the cathedral to mourn. Jack Newfield was in the cathedral, waiting for his turn to stand vigil, when he noticed Tom Hayden slumped in the shadows, alone in an empty pew, tears forming in his eyes. A green cap from Havana protruded from his pants pocket. Also weeping, head bowed, the cords of his neck swollen, was Mayor Richard Daley of Chicago. Less than three months later, Hayden and Daley would be at war in the streets of Chicago.

Using Newfield as an intermediary, Robert Kennedy had set up a meeting with Hayden and Staughton Lynd, authors of *The Other Side,* one of the earliest first-hand reports from Hanoi. Afterwards, Lynd told Newfield that he found Kennedy "Very fair-minded. Sort of detached. And not authoritarian at all." Hayden judged Kennedy to be superior to "Reuther or Rauh or any of those guys," and was reminded of Pierre Mendès-France. Unaware of this episode, Diana Trilling found Hayden's performance in St. Patrick's odd. After all, she reasoned, everything that Hayden lived and worked for was "directed to the destruction of everything that Kennedy most significantly lived and worked for. . . ." Kennedy believed in "the possibility of our society," whereas Hayden "believes that our society must be destroyed." Indeed it was odd, not least in light of an anecdote by Jeremy Larner, who worked for Eugene McCarthy during the 1968 campaign. Over dinner in California, Hayden asked him, "Why are you a whore for McCarthy?" He then predicted that all "this McCarthy–Robert Kennedy crap" would be resolved by the emergence of a National Liberation Front in the United States. People like Larner (reported Larner) would be killed.

Jack Newfield admired Hayden, but Trilling's animosity was more typical of the reaction Hayden evoked in the older generation of Left and liberal intellectuals, even though (or perhaps because) he did what he believed in, whereas they believed in what they would have done had circumstances not conspired to prevent them. Irving Howe spoke of

Hayden's "clenched style—that air of distance suggesting reserves of power—one could already see the beginnings of a commissar." Each encounter left Howe impressed by the younger man's gifts, "yet also persuaded that some authoritarian poisons of this century had seeped into the depths of his mind." Murray Kempton, reviewing Hayden's account of the Chicago 7 trial, displayed relentless animosity: "We do not believe what Hayden remembers or have faith in what he promises . . . in poor Hayden, we hear the mechanical beat of what sounds like the revolutionary heart and we gaze into what seems all too suspiciously like the liberal eye."

COLUMBIA OCCUPIED

Columbia's Strike Coordinating Committee represented all of the occupied buildings (or "communes") except Hamilton Hall, on the basis of one representative for every seventy students. Decisions required the assent of all the "communes," involving hours of discussions, day and night. The appeal to "community" was tireless, through microphones, bullhorns, and typewritten, Xeroxed or mimeographed notices posted on placards on the barred gates of the university. Written on the walls was the exhortation, "Create two, three, many Columbias"—a deliberate echo of Che Guevara's "Create two, three, many Vietnams in Latin America."

Despite the regular meetings in each occupied building, and the highly democratic structure of representation, the initiative was held by the SDS leadership in Strike Central, which operated from Ferris Booth Hall, the student activities building. But SDS's intransigence and determination to regard Columbia as a coincidental field of battle in the wider war created tensions with the liberal members of the Strike Coordinating Committee, who were impressed by the proposals and goodwill of the Ad Hoc Faculty Committee, and who were themselves keener to reform Columbia than to overthrow capitalism. The inevitable split came in May, when the liberals peeled away to form Students for a Restructured University.

Meanwhile, in President Kirk's office (whose shelves were lined with unopened books and French titles never cut), David Shapiro of SDS sat in Kirk's high-backed leather chair, wearing dark glasses, smoking one of the president's cigars, and posing for press photographers. Incriminating documents found in the president's files were rapidly published. One of these, "A Brief Account of Columbia University in the City of New York," had been written by a prominent trustee in December 1967. It referred to a grant of $5 million from the U.S. Air Force for studies on ballistic missiles, and a further $5 million from the navy for basic research on underwater transmission of sound. Kirk had written in the margin: "I question the tactical wisdom of using this illustration. We have avoided emphasis or publicity about this project because we have so many students and faculty opposed to all forms of research for the Defense Department. How about using some of the oceanographic or medical projects?"

A total of 750 occupiers had to be fed. In revolution, as in war, eating loses none of its appeal. Friendly stores sent in food, money was easily raised by collection, physicians and medical students from the city's hospitals set up an infirmary. Food from Harlem CORE was taken into Hamilton Hall. Black politicians and notables came and went. But then angry members of the faculty and the conservative student Majority Coalition began to enforce a food blockade of Low Library.

Occupied Columbia, like the occupied Sorbonne three weeks later, became a magnet for intellectual tourists. Stephen Spender was one of them. Offered a helping hand up onto the sill of Grayson Kirk's window, Spender found himself in the president's office. Someone asked him if this was like Spain during the civil war. Spender declined an offer of one of the president's cigars. To raise money on behalf of the students, Norman Mailer threw a party and Dwight Macdonald wrote a letter; Professor Daniel Bell sourly commented that what he called the New York literary "establishment" were "ecstatic at having a real revolution on their doorstep."

One professor who turned down an invitation to visit the rebel campus at Columbia was Herbert Marcuse, widely held by his liberal contemporaries to be the evil genius of the New Left. Marcuse commented: "I have never suggested or advocated or supported destroying the established universities and building new anti-institutions instead. I have always said that no matter how radical the demands of the students, and no matter how justified, they should be pressed within the existing universities. I believe—and this is where the finkdom comes—that American universities, at least quite a few of them, today are still enclaves of relatively critical thought and relatively free thought. ... But this is one of the very rare cases in which I think you can achieve what you want to achieve within the existing institutions." Diana Trilling nevertheless held that Marcuse's "spirit presided over the boiling campus" at Columbia. Reporters and cameras roamed the campus. Mark Rudd, twenty years old, the son of Lituanian and Polish immigrants (his father was a colonel in the reserve who had worked for the Defense Department until he moved into suburban real estate), mocked the *New York Times* for putting forward three possible interpretations of the Motherfucker slogan and for printing the word as "mother-blank." Rudd's analysis of the prehistory of the revolt laid stress on the Vietnam War, the change in the draft regulations, the assassination of Martin Luther King—"perhaps *the* most important critical event"—and the emergence of Eugene McCarthy. "The first day the McCarthy committee set up on campus, 650 people signed up," which was positive in its way, but also represented the lure of cooptation back into the electoral system. "And the moment we began to *act*—to act directly against racism and imperialism—the McCarthy buttons disappeared."

Rudd was not impressed by Herbert Marcuse's depiction of the universities as centers for "relatively free," critical, open thought. The "relatively" part reminded him of a "temporary, partial bombing halt." His SDS colleague Lewis Cole was not so sure: ". . . it finally becomes a question of whether you're going to let the critical thought factory and the murder factory be in the same building." For Rudd, *"the* primary goal of radicals" was long-term illumination: "And the harvest of this planting will not be seen this year when we get a modicum of student power, not in ten years when students have all the bipartite committees they want, but sometime in the future when this understanding of capitalist society bears fruit in much higher level struggle. In revolution."

David Truman, Columbia's vice-president and provost, called Rudd "totally unscrupulous and morally very dangerous." Within a few weeks his name and truculent personality symbolized everything liberal opinion loathed and feared in the white student revolution. As evidence, both Diana Trilling and Professor S. M. Lipset quoted a notorious speech Rudd gave in Boston after the Columbia insurrection: "We manufactured the issues. The Institute for Defense Analysis is nothing at Columbia. Just three professors. . . . And the gym issue is bull. It doesn't mean anything to anybody. I had never been to the gym site before the demonstrations began. I didn't even know how to get there." As his colleague Dotson Rader put it, "We wanted them to act irrevocably. We wanted a response *to us.* . . . They could give nothing without endangering the whole fucking System. . . . I wanted them . . . to reveal themselves for what they are—a stinking, rotten group of venal men. . . ."

The problem for SDS was that many Columbia students who joined the uprising did, indeed, concentrate their hopes on reforming the university. On April 29, six days after the occupation began, the Columbia *Spectator* announced the results of a referendum in which 5,500 students took part. This revealed broad support for the rebels' demands and broad opposition to their tactics. A huge majority wanted to end construction of the gym, while the majority who called for ending all ties with the IDA was roughly 2 to 1. But the tactics used by SDS and the Afro-American Society were supported by 1,325 and condemned by 4,124—indeed 3,466 actually opposed an amnesty, with only 2,054 wanting one. (The radicals would answer that but for their physical dramatization of the gym and IDA issues, many students might never have given them a moment's thought.)

The black students occupying Hamilton Hall stated their own demands: (1) no gymnasium; (2) the dropping of charges against those arrested in previous demonstrations at the gym site; (3) the severance of all ties with the Institute for Defense Analysis; and (4) an amnesty for all those involved in the occupation. Ray Brown, a senior majoring in history, believed the most significant issue was the building "of a Jim Crow gymnasium on public park land in Harlem." The university had colluded with the city to acquire the land in nearby Morningside Park without the community's assent; and the community was to have access "to only 15 percent" of the gym facility. "Our immediate concern is not with the restructuring of Columbia University." Bill Sales, a graduate student in Public Law and Government, explained why the blacks did not go along with the general demand for "student power": The press had defined the issue as "a problem involving young student rebels, alienated from their parents and from society in general, striking out in random fashion against authority." As a result, the basic issue of the university's relationship to the black community was ignored.

Diana Trilling, a resident of the neighborhood, fearful that the university might be overrun or burned down by the blacks of Harlem, lived behind bolted doors, sitting up late into the night, "the unceasing campus radio at my side, straining for the unfamiliar sound on the street beneath my shaded windows, the tramp or rush or scuffle of invasion." However, the black population of Harlem took very little part in the events, even though such bogeymen as Stokely Carmichael, Charles 37X Kenyatta, and H. Rap Brown did visit their brothers in Hamilton Hall.

The distinguished faculty of Columbia responded to the crisis in a variety of ways, but the immediate reaction was a desire to mediate between rebels and administration. The Ad Hoc Faculty Group formed itself into a special constabulary of volunteers, patrolling the campus wearing arm bands, squeezing through windows to negotiate with the "communes," and keeping the peace. Immanuel Wallerstein, associate professor of sociology and a member of the group's steering committee, regarded the race issue as crucial in precipitating an "all-out struggle," although Vietnam and the governance of the university were important.

The steering committee (all except one of whom were tenured

professors) came up with compromise proposals: (1) to suspend work on the gymnasium; (2) to vest disciplinary power in a tripartite judiciary body; and (3) to ensure that strike leaders should not be victimized, although there would have to be collective punishment for all involved in so flagrant a violation of the rules (including the detention of a dean).

Neither President Kirk nor the SDS was buying the package, even though 2,500 students had endorsed the proposals within hours of their formulation. Kirk refused to accept community review of any future decision on the gymnasium, nor would the president yield any of his disciplinary powers. Rudd had told an audience of two hundred faculty that their conciliatory efforts were "bullshit."

The issue that most divided and perplexed the faculty members was the insurgents' demand for amnesty. Professor Peter Gay, historian of the Enlightenment, did not approve of the Ad Hoc Faculty Group's attempts at mediation and rejected the demands for amnesty: The students were attempting to offend and even overthrow authority "without ever being punished for it." Adult civil disobedience "should take upon itself whatever consequences it may have." Professor Lionel Trilling felt that a complete amnesty would be "to declare that the university was not a polity or a community, that there were no social bonds among its members." Eric Bentley, professor of dramatic literature and translator of Brecht, disagreed. There had been no violence against persons (this was forgetful): a piece of fence at the gym site had been broken, that was all. Grayson Kirk had embarked on "a very personal, vindictive attempt to destroy Mark Rudd." If you believe in reforms, why punish those people who precipitated them? "There are a lot of people who now want the reform of Columbia. Most of them didn't until a month ago. . . ."

At 3:30 A.M. on Friday, April 26, with more than a thousand students and some faculty members outside Low Library chanting "Kirk must go!," Vice-President Truman announced through a megaphone that plans to develop the gym site would be suspended; he also promised that the police would not be called in. On April 30, the administration called the police. An assault force of 1,000 men was assembled, few of them friendly toward privileged students who burned the American flag. Rudd and Strike Central were out on campus coordinating the defenses with walkie-talkies. In Mathematics Hall, the occupiers rubbed slippery green soap on the stairs, although, according to Professor Daniel Bell, "in Mathematics Hall which was dominated by the Maoists, kooks, and hippies, there was little resistance and few students were hurt." In Fayerweather, students were marshaled into separate areas: those who intended active resistance, and those who would merely offer a token protest. In the latter, the resistance was bitter, with each room barricaded, provoking the worst incidents of police brutality. Two hundred and fifty students and faculty stood outside Low Library, blocking the police passively; other pickets protectively surrounded Avery Hall and Fayerweather.

The police charged, wielding flashlights and blackjacks. The violence was intense, shocking. Members of the faculty who tried to hold the steps of Low, Fayerweather, Avery, and Mathematics were brutalized. Charles Parsons, associate professor of philosophy, felt they were bearing witness to their personal concern for the students: "our shame at the bankruptcy of University policies which was shown by this resort to force. . . ." Several professors reportedly ended the night in the hospital, although Bell says of the bleeding students, "not one required hospitalization."

The Civilian Complaint Review Board received 120 charges of police brutality. But there was give as well as take; a policeman was permanently paralyzed when a student jumped on him from a window ledge. A total of 705 arrests were made; of these, 181 were not connected with Columbia. Of the arrested Columbia students, 77 percent were undergraduates (of whom 21 percent were women from Barnard College, whose pupils received Columbia University degrees). "In effect, almost ten percent of the college student body was arrested" (Daniel Bell).

No force was needed against the blacks occupying Hamilton Hall; their evacuation was negotiated through Professor Kenneth Clark, an eminent black psychologist at the City University, with a son of his own in the building. The black students walked out quietly through the tunnels to the waiting police vans. On Wednesday, May 1, the police were still on campus, patrolling Low Plaza and checking identification cards. A rally that day ended in serious violence, with three policemen and ten students hospitalized.

The morning after the police bust, the Ad Hoc Faculty Group held a stormy meeting in McMillin Theater, joined now by a large number of incensed faculty members who had previously taken no part in the attempts at mediation. The chairman of the ad hoc group, Professor Alan Westin, read out a strong resolution expressing distress at the way the administration had handled the situation and declaring the group's intention to "respect" the student strike which had just been called. (Westin later had second thoughts and withdrew.) At 4 P.M. a meeting of the Joint Faculties of Morningside Heights was held in St. Paul's Chapel, with Kirk and Truman present. The atmosphere was highly emotional—on Amsterdam Avenue Mark Rudd was addressing a thousand students drawn from colleges all over the city. When Morton

Fried read out a pro-strike motion involving the resignation of Kirk and Truman, President Kirk vacated the chair. But the faculty was now divided into a plethora of unhappy factions.

The student strike was almost total, yet the schism within its ranks ran deep; about half of the Strike Coordinating Committee quit to form the more moderate Students for a Restructured University. The administration decided at this juncture to assert its authority by suspending four of the SDS leaders. SDS retaliated with a second occupation of Hamilton Hall on May 23 by about 250 students (no blacks were involved). SDS's leaders (Mark Rudd, John Shils, Juan Gonzalez, Ted Gold, Tony Papert, Stu Gedal, and Lewis Cole) now derived additional inspiration from contemporaneous events in Paris, but the "Restructured" moderates, claiming to represent 3,000 students, refused to take part. President Kirk—like Rector Roche of the Sorbonne—knew no greater wisdom than to call in the police yet again, on this occasion only ten hours after the occupation began. The effect was to reunite a student body whose sense of common purpose had been visibly disintegrating.

The assault came through the tunnels leading to Hamilton Hall, at 2:30 A.M. on May 21. There was no resistance; the occupiers had gathered in the lobby to sing. The first policeman to emerge from the tunnel immediately ripped down a poster of Mao. Mark Rudd was arrested and handcuffed. His bail was set at $2,500, and he was later charged with riot, incitement, criminal trespass, and criminal solicitation. A total of 131 people were arrested inside Hamilton Hall, but of these only 68 were Columbia students.

The scene across campus was again a violent one, with barricades at the gates on College Walk, bricks hurled through the windows of Low Library, and protracted beatings handed out both by plainclothes police and uniformed cops wearing no badges or with their numbers taped over. Barnard women standing on the roof of their dormitory across Broadway at 116th Street were screaming at the police, "Up against the wall, motherfuckers!" Arrests totaled 174, with 68 persons injured, including 17 policemen. Following this second police bust, no less than 3,500 students and faculty signed a demand that Kirk and Truman resign.

One incident that occurred during the police invasion of Hamilton Hall was later cited, time and again, to prove the barbarous spirit of the radicals. We already encountered Professor Orest Ranum valiantly attempting to dissuade the militants from running amok on April 23; he subsequently became one of the most outspoken critics of the insurrection. Now, as the police burst into Hamilton Hall, Ranum's office door was forced by students, his files ransacked, a fire started, and his irreplaceable notes and manuscripts on the history of Paris and the reign of Louis XIV destroyed. The Strike Coordinating Committee later disclaimed any responsibility, but the grim event was soon known in every faculty common room in America. Professor Ivan Morris, Columbia's authority on Japan, cited this act of barbarism as one reason why he, though active in Amnesty International, would not grant amnesty.

The university now suspended seventy-three students, most of whom had taken part in the second occupation. The SDS leaders considered most culpable by the administration were four of the IDA 6: Mark Rudd, Morris Grossner, Nick Freudenberg, and Ed Hyman. The registrar's office informed local draft boards that they were no longer enrolled and were eligible for conscription. (On the day Rudd was suspended, his parents received a copy of a letter to him from Acting Dean Harry Coleman congratulating him on "your fine scholastic record for the fall term.") There were hundreds of disciplinary summonses, with priority accorded to members of the senior class whose graduation depended on clearance. Probation was offered if the summons was answered, but most refused; the air was thick with talk of due process, double jeopardy, indictments unsupported by evidence.

Because there had been no regular classes at Columbia College or even in some of the graduate schools since April 23, and a complete shutdown since May 1, the decision was taken to call off final examinations and to award only two grades, Pass or Fail, on the basis of previous work. Any student requiring a more precise grade could arrange for a private examination.

As the term ended, the students made clear their sentiments by insulting hallowed traditions. Class Day, "the most intimate ceremony of Columbia College graduation," was called off when the marshals of the senior class informed the dean that they did not wish it to be held. Graduation ceremonies were normally held on the steps and plaza of Low Library, but this year the ceremonies were prudently transferred to the Cathedral of St. John the Divine, with Kirk yielding his traditional role as commencement speaker to Professor Richard Hofstadter. As Hofstadter stepped onto the podium, nearly three hundred students and a dozen members of the faculty walked out of the cathedral into the sunlight, pulled out red arm bands from under their academic gowns, and raised their arms in a V-sign to the cheering crowd lining the police barriers along Amsterdam Avenue. Meanwhile, a counter-commencement ceremony was staged at the foot of the statue of Alma Mater on the steps of Low Library. This was organized by the left-reformist Students for a Restructured University, at loggerheads with the administration but wary of SDS. The crowd here was small and rather dispirited.

President Kirk resigned and was replaced by Andrew Cordier.

The faculty licked its wounds, chastened by the erosion of classroom theories when confronted by mob action, rhetoric, disorder, and inflamed emotions. Professor Allan Silver, a member of the original Ad Hoc Faculty Group, concluded: "A faculty which had been as inert as Columbia's before the convulsion could not play a decisive role during it." The faculty suffered from "aridity, pedantry, and an insufficiently critical view of American society," while the university's Board of Trustees was "distant and staggeringly uninformed. . . ."

But, in general, sympathy for the students was highly qualified by the end of term. Eric Bentley discovered that he wanted "the kind of change that runs a good deal deeper than what is contemplated by Westin and his colleagues, yet can occur without the total social revolution which is what Mark Rudd has in mind." Hostile to President Kirk and unimpressed by the "value-free" mediating proposals of Professors Daniel Bell and Alan Westin, Bentley conceded that, "For my part, yes, I *fear* some of our little Robespierres. As Noam Chomsky told them, 'You'd rather Karl Marx had burned the British Museum down than worked on *Das Kapital* in it.' "

Daniel Bell himself concluded that during the last days of April, hundreds of students underwent a "conversion experience as a result of their impulsive commitment to action." The hothouse atmosphere, the sense of community, "made it difficult for doubters to leave," giving the most radical voices a psychological advantage and forcing moderates to prove their *bona fides* by suppressing doubts and staying with the rebels. Bell felt that Columbia's administration, lacking any feel for the "volatility of social movements, or for the politics of ideology," lost the opportunity to discriminate between reformist and revolutionary students. Bell himself loathed the "chiliastic" SDS (which he also found culpable of "antinomianism"): ". . . the guttering last gasps of a romanticism soured by rancor and impotence. . . . It lives on turbulence, but is incapable of transforming its chaotic impulses into a systematic, responsible behavior. . . ."

One perplexing feature of New Left revolts was the rapid escalation of demands. Dons accustomed to the constitutional pursuit of defined programs became exasperated: What is it you really want? Professors Peter Gay and Lionel Trilling found that some students would emphasize the IDA issue, some the gym, some the wider restructuring of American society, some the failure of the administration to communicate openly with the faculty and students. Diana Trilling could discern "no reasonable reason to tear the place to pieces"; after all, Columbia was not like the Sorbonne and Berkeley, "so gigantic and dehumanized." (But this is pass the parcel; she would not have found Berkeley's Mario Savio or Nanterre's Daniel Cohn-Bendit any more congenial than Mark Rudd.)

Among the most forthright condemnations of the insurrection was that of Herbert A. Deane, professor of government at the time of the crisis and subsequently vice-provost for academic affairs. As a liberal, Deane fully understood the anger of the young in the face of Vietnam, ghetto poverty, racism, the assassination of King; but what he could not stomach was "the posture of complete self-righteousness and of unyielding moral absolutism in the attitudes and actions of the radical leaders." The true believer did not deign to discuss, compromise, or negotiate. The vanguard elite was bent on polarizing society by the exercise of the pure, nonrational violence whose apostle had been Georges Sorel. (The allusion to Sorel was standard nonsense among professors of history and politics hostile to the New Left; one may search in vain for any favorable reference to Sorel in New Left ideology.) Offended by SDS's lack of respect for the civil liberties of those who wished to take part in ROTC or meet military recruiters on campus, Deane concluded with a warning that displays of radical lawlessness would inevitably lead to a right-wing backlash, hence the ominously rising popularity of Wallace and Reagan, not to mention the triumph of de Gaulle.

The Bureau of Applied Social Research questioned a random sample of 2,000 Columbia students and found a close correlation between dissatisfaction with the university and wider political attitudes as measured by opinions about Vietnam, Black Power, the Poor People's March, and presidential candidates. Of those classified as "left," 95 percent expressed high dissatisfaction with Columbia's administration; of the "medium left," 79 percent; of the "medium right," 41 percent; of those classified as "right," only 10 percent. Professor S. M. Lipset concluded from this and other surveys that general political orientation, rather than local campus grievances, explained university unrest. One could add that the perception of a campus grievance may depend on political orientation; conservative students regarded President Kirk's paternalistic regime, business connections, and defense contracts as the natural algebra of achievement rather than as symptoms of corporate America's unacceptable penetration of the university.

Liberal benefactors produced the approximately $100,000 required to keep Columbia's SDS out of jail (bail money, fines, lawyers); when the first day of registration arrived in September, SDS duly demonstrated on behalf of the thirty-odd suspended students. Acting President Andrew Cordier retaliated by refusing SDS a permit to hold the International Revolutionary Students Conference in McMillin Theater, to which SDS responded by liberating the auditorium. French, Italian, and British students heard Mark Rudd call for "action tonight"—a march around the campus which the foreign students prudently observed, but did not join. There was much discussion about how to support the Mexican students; the German SDS kept stressing the importance of planning. Finally Yippie Abbie Hoffman leapt onto the speaker's desk with a yo-yo and enchanted his audience with the best-received performance of the week.

The second occupation of Columbia, in the spring of 1969, brought contempt-of-court convictions for eight students given suspended sentences the previous year. Each spent thirty days in a New York City jail. Dr. Andrew Cordier, Kirk's successor as president, released the names of twenty-nine students and eight nonstudents to the Senate Permanent Committee on Investigations.

TO CHINA

By a dazzling concurrence, it was on April 23, 1968, the birthday of Columbia's student insurrection, that a parallel crisis struck Tsinghua University, set in five hundred acres of the northwestern suburbs of Peking. Distinguished *New York Times* correspondent Harrison E. Salisbury later wrote: "To Americans familiar with 'The Movement' at Columbia in 1968, or at Berkeley in 1966 [*sic*], or on any of the other campuses where the great wave of turbulence erupted . . . the story had a familiar ring."

But did it? The crisis at Tsinghua University, the epicenter of the Cultural Revolution launched by Mao Tse-tung in 1966, may indicate why—despite the inspiration derived from it by Western Maoists—the Cultural Revolution was a very different beast from the student revolts in America and Europe.

What occurred at Tsinghua on April 23 was a military battle between two factions of Red Guards: the Regiment and the Fours. Both proclaimed themselves the only true disciples of Mao and his teaching. Gunfire was exchanged, firebombs burned out the science building, and the factions started tunneling beneath each other's strongholds with explosives. A state of war persisted for a further three months—with the campus emptied of the rest of its 12,000 students—until some 30,000 Peking workers marched in to restore order (in the name of Mao). Such was the fanatical state of mind of the Red Guards that they fought their way out with machine guns and hand grenades, killing 5 workers (10 students had already died) and wounding 751 (according to Premier Chou En-lai himself). The Red Guards then wandered the countryside searching for true believers until, confronted by their own madness, they surrendered and were subjected to thought-cleansing processes not unlike those they had inflicted on almost the entire faculty and administration of Tsinghua since the day in August 1966 when Mao had sent them a message of personal support.

Mao had unleashed populist resentment (and the native intolerance of boys carrying sticks) against privilege, "foreign knowledge," and Western devils. The extraordinary crisis that had prevailed during the previous eighteen months also involved a power struggle between Mao's radicals and the threatened party cadres associated with President Liu Shao Ch'i. Liu's wife had led a team of five hundred senior party people to purge Tsinghua, but they had finally been sent packing. By the autumn of 1966, classes and curriculum had been abandoned; Tsinghua did not attempt to resume operations until 1970–72.

Professors were dragged before disorderly congregations, who hurled insults and forced them to kneel, to wear demeaning placards ("jackass," "stupid") and dunce's caps, and to engage in repeated self-criticism. The same was happening at neighboring Peking University, where administrators and staff were imprisoned in "the cowshed" (a faculty building) and treated as subhuman. Almost every member of the teaching staff was packed off to a May Seventh School (another of Mao's innovations) to engage in farm labor, shovel dung, and purge their bourgeois superiority complexes.

When Tsinghua did reopen, admission was restricted to students who had spent three years in factories, in fields, or in the People's Liberation Army. Instruction was confined to practical, vocational subjects. The sociology faculty, so dear to Western radicals, was closed; Mao wasn't having any of *that*.

It should be clear that the Cultural Revolution in China, whatever its social complexities, was an instrument from first to last of ruthless factional power play; it had little in common with the libertarian and internationalist culture of the New Left. No demonstration could have hopped through the streets of Chairman Mao's China chanting "Ho-Ho-Ho Chi Minh" or bearing aloft Che's image. Profoundly philistine (destruction of books, closure of theatres, parroting of a single text) and often chauvinist (attacks on foreigners), the Cultural Revolution foreshadowed the activities of the genocidal, Chinese-backed Khmer Rouge in Kampuchea (Cambodia)—the ultimate example of the somewhat abused term Red Fascism.

10

PRAGUE SPRING

"'We must not and we will not stop half way,' said Dubček."

OF OUR OWN FREE WILL

PRAGUE, May 1, 1968—A huge procession files through Wenceslas Square (Václavské náměstí), under a forest of flags. "Of our own free will, for the first time," announces a calico banner. Here, too, are people representing organizations that have been silenced for twenty years: veterans of the International Brigades, veterans of the Second World War, former political prisoners, even a group of small landowners and artisans wearing the costumes of their former guilds. The Party's official organ, *Rudé Právo,* celebrates "the springlike blossoming of our new public life, the breath of fresh air brought by democratic freedoms."

Watching the procession from the rostrum were the country's new leaders: Alexander Dubček, first secretary of the Communist Party; President Ludvík Svoboda, commander of the Czechoslovak forces in Russia during the war, arrested in 1952, but later rehabilitated as a hero of the Soviet Union; the dynamic liberal Josef Smrkovský, chairman of the National Assembly, a key figure in the Prague uprising of 1945, but later found "guilty" of being a Gestapo agent and imprisoned; Ota Šik, the economic brain of the reform movement; Prime Minister Oldřich Černík. Beside the politicians stood the great Olympic runner, Colonel Emil Zatopek.

The Prague Spring came in three phases: (1) from the resignation on January 5 of the all-powerful Antonín Novotný as first secretary of the Communist Party (after which Novotnýite forces remained strong enough to thwart full liberalization, despite the collapse of the censorship system in early March); (2) from Novotný's resignation as state president on March 21 to the end of June (the period of the Action Program and the most rapid liberalization); and (3) from July to the Soviet invasion on August 20–21 (when Dubček's regime was simultaneously trying to keep liberalization in check while fending off Soviet remonstrances and warnings).

Parliamentary democracy had been extinguished in Czechoslovakia exactly twenty years earlier, when twelve non-Communist ministers resigned from the coalition government in protest against Communist infiltration of the Interior Ministry and the police. The Communists responded by staging a coup in February 1948, taking over all mass communications, then holding rigged elections with only a single list of candidates. The Communist leader Klement Gottwald launched a purge, arrested thousands of "bourgeois nationalists," and suppressed the Catholic Church. Industry was nationalized and agriculture collectivized. It was the classic formula, and twenty years later Czechoslovakia was still writhing to unfasten the chains and to rediscover "socialism with a human face." Few Czechoslovaks could imagine its precise contours.

The police terror had soon turned in on the Communist Party itself. In 1951–52 eleven Party leaders were executed for alleged Titoism. The number of Communists persecuted in Czechoslovakia was three times higher than in all the other Soviet satellites taken together. The cycle of hysteria, denunciations, and confessions was unrelenting. According to Vladimir Kusin, over 100,000 people served time for political reasons in prisons and labor camps between 1948 and the early sixties. "Tens of thousands were physically tortured. Thousands died in jail. And perhaps three hundred were executed." In 1955, Gottwald's successor, Antonín Novotný, unveiled a huge statue of Stalin, reputed to be the largest of its kind in the world, on the heights of Prague overlooking the Vltava River.

Novotný ran the Communist Party (KSČ) along Stalinist lines. The function of the highest elected body of the Party, the Central Committee Plenum, was reduced to rubber-stamping decisions already made in the Presidium or by Novotný himself. Criticism was treated as a threat to "unity." Potential critics were usually not offered a chance to speak.

WRITERS AND STUDENTS

The first major challenge came from the country's students, writers and—indirectly—brilliant film directors. At the Fourth Congress of Czechoslovak Writers in June 1967, the young novelist Ludvík Vaculík, author of *The Axe,* set the tone when he declared that "not one human problem has been solved in our country for twenty years." He spoke of power, which "becomes more and more homogeneous, purging everything foreign to it until each part is a replica of the whole, and all parts are mutually interchangeable." With extraordinary courage he added: "This Congress did not take place when members of our organization decided, but when our master . . . gave us his kind permission. In return he expects, as has been the custom in the past thousands of years, that we shall pay tribute to his dynasty." Art and power, said Vaculík, could never "meet for a sing-song"; they were "not suited for each other."

Milan Kundera, author of *The Joke*, whose publication had been delayed by petty censorship, told the congress: "I am sometimes frightened that our present civilization is losing that European character which lay so close to the hearts of the Czech humanists and revivalists." He also spoke of freedom: ". . . in our case, the guarding of frontiers is still regarded as a greater virtue than crossing them."

The regime's cultural spokesman, Jiří Hendrych, delivered a violent counterattack. *Kulturní Tvorba*, cultural weekly of the KSČ Central Committee, accused Vaculík and other outspoken writers, including Pavel Kohout, Alexander Kliment, and Václav Havel, of demagoguery and anarchy. Ludvík Vaculík, A. J. Liehm, and Ivan Klima were expelled from the Party. Milan Kundera, Pavel Kohout, and Jan Prochazka received "Party punishment" (the last was dropped from the Central Committee), while other writers experienced reprisals in the form of refusals to publish their work. The National Assembly was instructed to condemn the dissident writers as a prelude to a demoralizing punishment: the Writers' Union weekly, *Literární Noviny*, was taken over by the Ministry of Culture.

FROM NOVOTNÝ TO DUBČEK

A plenum of the Central Committee opened on October 30, 1967. Alexander Dubček, at that time first secretary of the Slovak Party, launched an attack on the prevailing conservatism, largely under the guise of defending Slovak national interests: "Neither émigrés nor imperialist agents can cause us major problems, and therefore we should not devote such powerful, undeserved, and for us damaging propaganda to them." Although typically moderate in tone, Dubček offered the first systematic critique of Party behavior—the implicit target being Novotný himself. He also demanded separation of Party and state offices; Novotný was not only first secretary of the KSČ but also state president and commander of the armed forces and of the People's Militia.

But Novotný remained at ease in his own ice age, replying extemporaneously, in a sharp, excited manner: "We have had more than enough of democracy in life." He disparaged Dubček as too much a Slovak.

Prague's students now entered (or re-entered) the stage. With 19,516 students in twelve faculties, the Charles University was the largest—and most radical—in the country (whose total student population had risen steadily to 137,000 in 1967, with an impressive student-staff ratio of 8 to 1). The Novotný regime had kept students under tight political control through the official Czechoslovak Union of Youth (ČSM), which every student was required to join. No independent student magazine existed until 1966, when the weekly *Student* was first published. The top functionaries of the ČSM were mainly Party careerists already in their thirties, boorish creatures of routine. Discontent traditionally surfaced during the annual May Day processions (*Majáles*), a kind of carnival with allegoric figures, humorous placards, and improvised happenings. In 1965 and 1966, this event ended in turmoil. In 1965, they had crowned Allen Ginsberg King of the May; the authorities promptly expelled him.

According to the historian Milan Hauner, throughout 1965 the Prague University Student Committee (VOV), a branch of the official ČSM, had been infiltrated by radicals, whose most prominent figures were Lubomír Holeček, Jiří Holub, Jan Kavan, Karel Kovanda, Jiří Müller, and Miroslav Tyl. At the student conference in December 1965, Müller proposed that the ČSM "has even to play the role of the Party's opponent when it is necessary." This provoked an alarmed reaction; in December 1966, Müller was expelled from his faculty and conscripted for military service. His colleague Holeček met the same fate.

On May 1, 1966, students, apprentices, clerks, and workers—most of them between seventeen and twenty-three years old—had marched from Petrin across the bridge into the center of town, shouting "We want freedom, We want democracy," and "A good Communist is a dead Communist!" The crowd of a few hundred marched to Wenceslas Square, stopped some trams on the way, and came to a halt at the equestrian statue. On May 24, the municipal court in Prague sent twelve of the demonstrators to prison.

The Fifth Congress of the ČSM in 1967 echoed the rebellious mood of the Writers' Congress. Radical students expressed their solidarity with the writers and editors of the banned *Literární Noviny*. But the crucial event in spreading the spirit of militant discontent was the student march protesting the failure of the electricity supply for the umpteenth time at the large, bleak student hostel in the Strahov District of Prague. On Tuesday, October 31, the day after Dubček's clash with Novotný at the Central Committee Plenum, the lights went out again at about 10:30 P.M. There were the usual shouts and whistling, a few bits of lighted paper floated down from the windows, then the students emerged carrying candles, formed a procession, marched around the square, and set off in the direction of Dlabacov, shouting, "We want light! We want to study!"

Entering the upper part of Malostranské náměští, the crowd was stopped by the police, who advised the students to choose a few representatives who would be taken to register their complaint. This proposal was greeted by a roar of derisive laughter; the students knew that trick. Having summoned reinforcements, the police lashed out with their truncheons and tear-gas bombs, shouting, "There's your light!" The VOV, supported by some faculty and hostel councils, demanded an impartial investigation and the punishment of policemen who had inflicted severe injuries on several students. (It was to be one of the significant reforms of the Prague Spring of 1968 to require policemen to wear identification badges.)

The December 20 session of the Central Committee began with a Novotnýite counter-offensive, but ended with a rout of his loyalists; the shrewder conservatives now regarded Novotný as an embarrassment. On the morning of January 5, 1968, Novotný resigned as first secretary. Dubček was elected unanimously to succeed him—a display of unity around a compromise candidate whom the conservatives believed they could control, rather than a reflection of genuine consensus. Novotný remained state president and a member of the Presidium.

Alexander Dubček was born in 1921 in West Slovakia, the son of a Communist cabinetmaker who, after pre-1914 emigration to the United States, settled in the Soviet Union (Kirghizia) in 1925 as a member of a cooperative. Alexander attended secondary school in Frunze before returning to Slovakia with the family in 1938. He joined the Communist Party and worked as an apprentice locksmith at the Skoda munitions factory. In August 1944, when the Slovak national revolt began, he joined the partisan brigade of Jan Zizka and fought the Germans in the mountains. In November he was twice wounded and his brother Julius was killed. From 1955 to 1958 he attended the Higher Party School in Moscow; five years later he displaced Karol Bacílek as first secretary of the Slovak Party and as a full member of the KSČ Presidium. A quiet, shy, rather inarticulate man, whose strength of purpose was not immediately visible and whose idealism was masked by the routine phraseology of a Communist *apparatchik,* Dubček remained little known to the wider public outside Slovakia.

Four of Dubček's supporters were elected to the Presidium in January, most notably Josef Špaček, nominated secretary for ideology, and Josef Pavel, who was promoted to the key post of minister of the interior in March. But the first weeks of the Dubček era provided the general public with no sense of the far-reaching reforms ahead. The liberalization impetus seemed to lie outside the Party, in the cultural weeklies, then on radio and television.

What helped break the stalemate between reformers and entrenched conservatives was the Šejna affair. General Jan Šejna, the most powerful Party general in the Defense Ministry and a close associate of Novotný, was reported by Prague Radio on February 27 to have fled the country, charged with massive embezzlement. It was also made clear that Šejna, Colonel-General Vladimir Janko (deputy minister of defense), and other generals had plotted with Novotný to thwart the opposition within the Central Committee. Šejna, a close friend of Novotný's son, finally arrived in Washington, the highest-ranking Warsaw Pact officer ever to defect to the West. On March 14, General Janko shot himself in his official car.

The scandal was an unmitigated blessing for Dubček and the reformers. Petitions poured in from Party branches calling for Novotný's resignation as state president and member of the Presidium. Novotný finally resigned as president on March 21, and the purge of his closest associates began. During April the Spring began to open its buds. On April 4, a new Presidium was elected. The Action Program of the KSČ, published on April 9, listed in detail the material and moral shortcomings of the past years. People had grown bitter, demoralized, and disillusioned. The Party should abandon its self-appointed role as the universal caretaker of society; it should no longer "bind all organizations and every step taken in life by its directives." Although the Action Program expressed its good intentions in sometimes awkward phrases, the passionate desire for genuine reform could not be doubted:

> It is necessary to overcome the holding up, distortion, and incompleteness of information, to remove any unwarranted secrecy of political and economic facts, to publish the annual balance sheet of enterprises . . . and to increase the import and sale of foreign newspapers and periodicals. The Party press especially must express the Party's life and development along with criticisms of various opinions among the Communists, etc., and cannot be made to coincide fully with the official viewpoints of the state.

The public reaction was one of guarded approval. The old corps of functionaries feared where it might all lead; the new forces of liberalization—not the least the students—wanted far more.

In its issue of April 5, *Time* magazine put a benign portrait of Alexander Dubček on its cover and made the Prague Spring its lead story, listing the profound changes embodied in the proposed Action Program: The Communist Party's powers had undergone "a major shrinkage," the National Assembly would exercise genuine legislative authority, freedom of speech was guaranteed, Czechoslovaks would enjoy the right to travel abroad and emigrate, the economy had been liberalized, and a new federal constitution would give the Slovaks greater control over their own affairs. The transformation, said *Time,* was already remarkable. Almost everything could now be questioned and, if necessary, changed. Censorship had virtually disappeared, while "the press, television and radio have exploded in an orgy of free expression." Long-banned films, plays, and books were "blossoming into production."

Public feeling against the police now burst out into the open. On May 7, the Communists of the Criminal Investigation Department complained about the treatment they were receiving at the hands of the public. Several former employees of the courts, the Public Prosecutor's Office, and the Ministry of the Interior associated with the Stalinist purges committed suicide. At the end of May, it was announced that so far twenty-nine State Security interrogators had been "disciplined." The Procurator-General's Office now had its own Action Program and was responsible for pinpointing personal responsibility for the illegal actions of the past.

Meanwhile, the new minister of the interior, Josef Pavel, discovered a large number of Soviet agents in the counterespionage system, most of them Czechoslovak citizens reporting to the various Soviet "advisers" attached to Prague ministries. During the summer, about 150 were suspended on full pay. On June 7, it was announced that 250 State Security men had been dismissed. The Soviet leaders were alarmed. Had not Dubček told Brezhnev, at their first, cordial, meeting in January, that nothing much would be changed? Nor was Moscow happy about the broom wielded by the new minister of defense, General Dzúr. Officers known to pass information to Soviet intelligence outside official channels were either relieved of their posts or transferred.

While Novotný had remained master, the truth about the purges could never emerge in full; previous commissions of inquiry had been frustrated or rigged. The long suffering of the nation now generated an irresistible demand for the "rehabilitation" of the victims and for the punishment of the prosecutors, torturers, and executioners. The Piller Commission was appointed to produce a report on the trials and terror of 1950–1954 and the subsequent suppression of evidence.*

Simultaneously, a Commission of Inquiry was set up to investigate

---

*The commission set about its task with vigor, but the Soviet invasion in August ensured the suppression of its report. A provisional draft was smuggled out of the country and published, in translation, by Jiří Pelikán.

the death of the liberal Foreign Minister Jan Masaryk, the admired son of the founder of the Czechoslovak Republic, who had been found dead under the window of his flat in the Ministry on March 10, 1948, only a few days after the Communist coup. Masaryk's fate seemed to symbolize the whole nation's: suicide or murder? And if suicide, why? Czechoslovak Television ran its own parallel inquest. The press was full of letters about those unjustly accused, imprisoned, or executed. Late in July the minister of justice, Dr. Bohuslav Kučera, announced that "between sixty and seventy thousand Czechs, mostly victims of political trials held from 1950 until 1955, and former camp inmates would be rehabilitated under a ten-year program." Those unjustly imprisoned—or their relatives—would receive a reparation of up to 20,000 crowns (approximately a year's average earnings).

On June 3, Dubček promised: "One thing is clear; we must not and we will not stop half-way. If we are to be successful we must consolidate the democratization drive. . . ." But the old guard still had to be reckoned with: some forty Novotnýites in the Central Committee clung to their seats. "We talked to these comrades and wanted them to leave," Dubček told the nation. "But they did not understand." In fact they understood only too well; they were biding their time, relying on Moscow. Dubček was forced to call an Extraordinary Party Congress for September 9. Delegates to the Fourteenth Congress would be elected at regional and municipal conferences to be held between June 10 and 23, with one delegate elected by every 1,100 Party members. Dubček was in no doubt that his supporters would carry these elections; Moscow was in no doubt either: September 9 became a black spot on the Kremlin calendar.

TOO FAR, TOO FAST

"We must not and we will not stop half-way," said Dubček. Could this mean complete freedom of the press in a Communist, one-party state? For almost twenty years publishers had been forced to submit all manuscripts to the censors before sending them to the printers. Newspapers suffered resident censors. In mid-March the members of the Central Publication Board in the Ministry of the Interior had called for an end to "preventive political censorship" and sharply attacked Party Secretary Jiří Hendrych and Interior Minister Josef Kudrna for their repressive policies. A few days later Novotný had been ousted as president; Hendrych and Kudrna went with him.

By the beginning of June, however, the government was increasingly warning the liberals not to go too far too fast. During a Central Committee meeting at the end of May, the press was accused of sensationalism, subjectivism, a negative approach to the past, scandalizing, praising bourgeois democracy, fabricating anti-Soviet sentiment, and advocating a legal opposition party. Jiří Pelikán, director-general of television, and Miroslav Sulek, director-general of the national press agency, were both summoned to hear the Central Committee's recriminations. Dr. Čestmír Císař, head of the Party's ideological section, accused the media of jeopardizing the nation's foreign relations and of creating "a mass psychosis of a certain kind." (Writers were by now complaining of the daily pressure exercised by Císař on editors and directors of publishing houses.) The Slovak Party's Control Commission announced: "Freedom of expression and creation of public opinion are not tantamount to any freedom of expression and creation of any public opinion."

Nevertheless, with admirable boldness, the National Assembly finally abolished censorship on June 27. Any intervention against freedom of expression was forbidden. For the old guard this was too much to swallow; for the Soviet leaders, intolerable. The debate in the assembly was lively, even fierce, and a small minority of thirty conservative members voted against the press law, with seventeen abstaining.

THE INTELLECTUALS

The subject of censorship brings us to the intellectuals. How were they faring?

On April 1, Dubček recommended the annulment of a number of harsh decisions made after the 1967 Writers' Congress, including the transfer of *Literární Noviny* from the Writers' Union to the Ministry of Culture, the expulsion from the Party of Klima, Vaculík, and Liehm, the reprimand to Pavel Kohout, and the disciplinary action against Milan Kundera.

Before its forced closure in October 1967, *Literární Noviny* was printing in editions of 160,000 copies. When it was able to resume publication on March 1, 1968, under the name *Literární Listy,* such was the demand that it had to print 260,000 copies. Each edition was snatched up within hours. A taxi driver told a visiting professor, Z. A. B. Zeman, "Nobody talks about football at my local any longer." *Mladá Fronta,* the youth organization paper, was so popular that it was sometimes unobtainable in the center of Prague. When *Sesity* came out with a translation of Albert Camus's celebrated essay on capital punishment, the edition sold within hours. Czechoslovak periodicals grew bolder. In an article published on June 13 in *Literárni Listy*, "Another Anniversary," Osvald Machatka recalled the secret trial and execution of the Hungarian leader Imre Nagy, snatched by the Soviet secret police after he left the refuge of the Yugoslav embassy in Budapest. Praising the independent stand of the Yugoslav Communists against bullying from Moscow, Machatka drew the "lesson obvious to a country facing mounting Soviet pressure."

Heresies previously unprintable were now tolerated. The new magazine *Information Materials* reprinted extracts from a manifesto of the Fourth International, addressed to the Czechoslovak workers, while *Literárni Listy* published texts by Trotsky and Bukharin and began serializing extracts from Isaac Deutscher's latest work, *The Unfinished Revolution*. All this was carefully noted by the Soviet embassy and transmitted to Brezhnev in person.

On April 4, *Literárni Listy* published an article by Václav Havel, "On the Subject of Opposition," in which the playwright argued that "democracy is a matter not of faith but of *guarantees,*" allowing "public and legal *'competition for power.'*" (Havel was the author of *The Memorandum (Vyrozumeni)*, a subtle satire about the manipulation of language and the ultraconformity of the bureaucrat to whatever is the current Party line.) The democratization of the ruling party, he argued, did not of itself guarantee democracy: ". . . if the Communist Party does not make possible rapid development of strong outside control, it will have no guarantee that it will not soon enter into a gradual degeneration all over again." Havel ridiculed the puppet pluralism of the National Front. "To my mind the only truly logical, and indeed, in our circumstances, effective way . . . to reach the ideal of democratic socialism is a regenerated and socialist social structure patterned on the *two-party model.* As these, obviously, would not be parties based on class. . . ." (This was not, in fact, so obvious—nor would a genuine democracy necessarily limit itself to two parties.)

The Soviet press lashed out at Havel with its customary smears, pointing out that *The Memorandum* and its author had recently been warmly received in New York. (If the Bolshoi Ballet was warmly received at Lincoln Center that was something else.) More than ten years later, when Havel was imprisoned for his part in Charter 77, his plays continued to be widely performed in the West.

On June 6, a group of non-Party writers convened at the Union of Writers in Národní Street. Many of these men in their forties and fifties looked exhausted by the lost years, the Kafkaesque struggles with bureaucracy. Several were suffering from heart complaints. The meeting discussed a manifesto prepared by Havel, challenging the notion that Communists were necessarily endowed with superior moral qualities. Refusing to accept a liberty granted on sufferance, Havel sustained his demand for free and democratic elections. Most of those present nodded in agreement, but few of them believed it was possible.

The new, liberal chairman of the Writers' Union was Eduard Goldstücker, a Jewish professor of literature whose family had perished in Auschwitz. Returning to Prague after the war, Goldstücker had served as the Czechoslovak ambassador to Israel; arrested during the anti-Zionist campaign of the early fifties, he was lucky to escape with his life. Rehabilitated in 1956, he later became rector of the Charles University, leading a campaign to admit Franz Kafka into the pantheon of progressive writers acceptable to Marxism. Goldstücker's model of liberalism, however, did not extend to the genuine pluralism and free elections demanded by Havel. Early in June he repeated the Dubček line to the word; even after the Soviet invasion he still repeated it: "The Communist Party had all power firmly in its hands. It was responsible for the development of society over twenty years. Who else but the Communists would propose new ideas, a new program? . . . We could not from one day to the next go over to completely free elections, that was obvious." The revival of the Social Democratic Party would have been "a harmful step" because that party "could rely on one single thing, namely exploitation of dissatisfaction with the mistakes, failures, and actual crimes of the Communist leadership in the course of the past twenty years."

Students and academics were no less a force for liberalization than the writers were. After Novotný was replaced by Dubček, student leaders like Holeček, Kavan, Kovanda, and Müller moved into the vanguard of the reform movement. In March 1968, an assembly of 20,000 young people approved the Manifesto of Prague Youth, calling for a humanitarian, democratic socialism based on the U.N.'s Declaration of Human Rights: freedom of speech, of the press, of assembly, and of association. The student leader Jan Kavan wrote: "I have often been told by my friends in Western Europe that we are only fighting for bourgeois-democratic freedoms. But somehow I cannot seem to distinguish between capitalist freedoms and socialist freedoms. What I recognize are basic human freedoms."

Fresh air was blowing through the Charles University. Husserl, Heidegger, and existentialism generally became available to philosophy students. The May issue of the journal *Mezinarodni Politika* (International Politics) showed a girl sunbathing in a bikini under the question: *Je Svet Lidem Fuk?* (Do people care?). In the Political Science Department, far-reaching changes had taken place, with the inclusion in the curriculum of Western writers like Harold Laski, C. Wright Mills, and

Raymond Aron. The nationalist theme was supported by the reappearance not only of Czech liberal statesmen like T. G. Masaryk and Eduard Beneš, but also Ataturk, Gandhi, and Nehru. Yugoslavia had become a focus of attention, in both its political structure and its resistance to Stalin.

In the field of Marxist studies, the Czechs were following the direction pioneered by the Poles during the brief thaw of 1956, with emphasis on anthropological and existential questions. Alienation was no longer attributed exclusively to capitalism; the abuses of power under socialism, and the persistence of assembly-line alienation among workers offered no real participation in decision making, were now accorded keen attention.

Yet certain lines were drawn. While Milovan Djilas's *Conversations with Stalin* was considered suitable for students, his seminal work, *The New Class,* was rejected as "erroneous," although its American counterpart, C. Wright Mills's *The Power Elite,* was recommended as "objective." (Djilas's "error" was to have argued that the Communist system inevitably creates a new, privileged class of functionaries, managers, and integrated intellectuals; Dubček and his colleagues blamed "deformations" on abuses, insisting that the basic system was not at fault.) The syllabus remained at the service of the prevailing Party line; in this regard, the reforming professors were scarcely more liberal than their predecessors. A liberal-Marxist professor of political science told the present writer that naturally the old-guard dogmatists had to go; they were not objective.

In April a student parliament was established in Prague; in May the autonomous Union of University Students (SVS) was created, severing the cramping bond with the Party-controlled Union of Youth. The Czechoslovak student movement was less flamboyant and more "responsible" than its New Left counterparts in the West. Czech students behaved like adults and had no quarrel with adults. Once the Prague Spring was launched, many seemed satisfied with bureaucratic reforms, such as the breakup of the Party-dominated youth movement and the creation of autonomous student unions for Bohemia-Moravia and Slovakia. They thought in terms of unions, committees, commissions, delegates, appointments—a complex of organizations and pressure groups with a striking capacity to channel tensions away from the barricades. The popular student weekly *Student* ran features on political movements in the West, discussing the merits of such disparate socialist voices as Günter Grass and Rudi Dutschke (who lectured at the Charles University before a large, intense audience only a week before the attempt on his life in West Berlin). But the German student riots following that outrage and the May events in Paris evoked only a faintly sympathetic response in Prague. The Czechs could not avoid mild impatience with hotheads who did not know how to gain concessions by working within the system.

There was no demand for Student Power within the university. What they wanted was an open curriculum, sympathetic professors, freedom of expression, and a library worthy of the name.

The Czech students were not so passionately interested in the Third World as their Western counterparts, nor did they derive inspiration from Guevara, Fanon, and Debray. Maoism had few advocates; the Red Guards' Cultural Revolution was dismissed contemptuously as chaos. The Cubans maintained a large bookshop in the center of Prague where one could obtain magazines and revolutionary woodcuts, but the local interest was tepid. On the other hand, students traveled to the West during the spring and summer in unprecedented numbers. (At the time of the Soviet invasion, 1,500 students found themselves stranded in Britain alone.) The playwright David Mercer, who visited Czechoslovakia during the summer, reported that the Czech students saw no sense in the Paris barricades, and were too much interested in liberty to be concerned about technocratic alienation. Capitalism had "delivered the goods," but they remained wearily resigned to their own socialist destiny. In the words of a Czech scholar, Milan Hauner, they had "experience of manipulation in a far more primitive form than their Western counterparts could even imagine . . . student criticism of the present Czechoslovak society and its institutions never degenerated into purposeless destruction."

An insight into the bottom-line alliances and allegiances of the international student movements was provided by the World Youth Festival, held in Bulgaria at the turn of July and August. Here three species converged uneasily: (1) the hand-picked, regimented Youth Brigades and Komsomols from the Soviet bloc; (2) the Czechoslovaks, "high" on liberalism and keenly supported by the Yugoslavs; and (3) the New Left from Western Europe. The behavior of the festival organizers and Bulgarian police soon transformed the three camps into two: topics and chairpersons were fixed in advance; plainclothes police harassed and beat dissenters. The Czechoslovaks found themselves organizing unofficial teach-ins in collaboration with the German SDS, the Young Liberals from Britain, the Dutch, and the Yugoslavs.

The thaw was visible in the variety of entertainments available in Prague. Pop music was in vogue, although Western records were scarce. At the Olympic Club, young men with shoulder-length hair drank fruit juice and went home to bed early. Hemlines were above the knee, but discreetly so. The pill was not generally available, and doctors normally refused to fit unmarried women with diaphragms. Western films on release in Prague at the end of May were mainly out of the commercial can: *Cleopatra* (starring Elizabeth Taylorova), *Rio Bravo,* and *The Pink Panther* from the United States, *Hokus Pokus* and *Alaska* from West Germany, *Viva Maria* (starring Brigitte Bardotova) from France.

The indigenous culture, responsive to the wider ferment, had better things to offer. At the Theatre on the Balustrade the master of mime, Ladislav Fialka, presented *Buttons,* a charming, witty show reflecting the bouncing humor and satirical bite of the Prague Spring. Fialka's *The Clowns, The Dolls,* and *King Ubu* had been seen recently in London. The message of *Buttons,* conveyed by mime and motion rather than the spoken word, was clear: Human beings could break free of hermetic orthodoxy and recover their freedom if bold enough to do so.

The impact of the Western avant-garde was both exhilarating and dubious. In 1962 an exhibition of cubist and expressionist works had been closed an hour after it opened, but during 1963–64 the authorities had capitulated to modernism. Much of the Czech art on display in 1968 resembled a furiously erotic derivative of American anti-art. The work of J. Vozniak, showing at the Galerie Václava Spaly, bombarded the spectator with movie queens, Frankensteins, blood, Charles Addams weirdos, open vaginas, and football helmets—a ferment of experiment, a great shout of release, yet as indiscriminate as a spree in a duty-free shop.

PLURALISM

As the Spring progressed, so did the demands of the People's and Socialist parties, the emaciated ghosts who had for twenty years maintained a half-life within the shop-window National Front, each allotted a statutory twenty members (as if one for each year of impotent survival) in the National Assembly. The Socialist Party, with 652,000 members in 1947 (and not to be confused with the Social Democrats, who suffered a shotgun wedding with the Communist Party in 1948), boasted a mere 10,705 in 1967, but now it grew bold: on March 22 the Socialist Party paper *Svobodne Slovo* published an open letter to Dubček calling for a multiparty system; two days later the *Lidová Demokracie* argued that the People's Party "must rid itself as soon as possible of the complex of subordination and build up the position of a free citizen with equal rights. . . ."

Certain groups that now raised their heads were clearly "bourgeois" and regarded with acute suspicion by the government. Even so, they were not curbed and their spokesmen freely addressed meetings and appeared on television. Club 231, founded on March 31 and open to anyone who had been imprisoned under Law no. 231 of 1948, was headed by Jaromir Brodsky (whom the Soviet press termed a fascist), by Václav Paleček ("the former bourgeois general"), and Otakar Rambousek ("the imperialist intelligence agent"). According to the Soviet *White Book* (an indictment of Prague's permissiveness, published after the invasion), Club 231 had over 40,000 members, including former Nazis, wartime collaborators, and representatives of the reactionary clergy. Club 231 claimed that its only aim was the rehabilitation of its members and their return to normal life, plus the punishment of those responsible for transforming "defense of the Republic" (Law no. 231) into a pretext for massive repression.

The Club of Non-Party Activists (KAN), founded on April 5 at a gathering of some 150 persons in Prague, was headed by the popular and outspoken philosopher Ivan Sviták, described by the Soviet press as "a rabid reactionary working at the Academy of Sciences and earlier expelled from the Communist Party." His assistants were named as "Ryabeck, Musil, and Klementjev—agents of the international Zionist organization." Other groups that offended Moscow by their existence included the Circle of Independent Writers, the Club of Critically Minded Individuals, and the Organization for the Defense of Human Rights.

Outspoken advocate of a genuinely pluralistic democracy Ivan Sviták's lectures at the Charles University were frequently published in *Student,* upholding the social democratic tradition and accusing the Communist leadership of wanting to hang on to 100,000 elite jobs. Only free and secret elections could dispose of the "totalitarian dictatorship." Sviták's speeches castigated Communist leaders, notably Čestmír Císař, who had warned on April 27 that pluralistic politics would undermine the essence of socialism and create a need to defend it by force. The Slovak Party leader, Dr. Gustáv Husák, a deputy prime minister, warned a meeting of 3,000 Communists in Prague that if "certain elements" attempted to revive the pre-1948 system, then they would be answered with a new February 1948. Sviták's answer to Císař and Husák was "as you wish"—but Husák's ultimate answer to that has lasted almost two decades.

A MIDDLE-CLASS REVOLUTION?

What was the state of public opinion? On May 13, *Rudé Právo* published an extensive questionnaire prepared by its editors in collaboration with the Institute of Political Sciences. Thirty-eight thousand respondents had taken part. Ninety percent of the non-Party members wanted the establishment of free opposition parties, while 75 percent rejected the proposition that the Communist Party alone could achieve socialist democracy. Even among Party members there was considerable uncertainty: 55 percent of them favored equal legal status for all political parties, and one-third believed that a humane socialism could be achieved *without* the Communist Party.

At first sight this poll would seem to vindicate the bold claim by Pavel Tigrid, an émigré writer sentenced *in absentia* for his literary activities abroad: "The majority of the population demanded, not democratization of a system which—to say the least had proved inefficient—but rather an open, pluralistic society which would be both socialist and democratic, with guarantees to this effect built in." But the picture was more ambiguous. Another opinion poll indicated that only a narrow majority of 53 percent believed that liberalization benefited the whole community; 21 percent thought it served the intelligentsia better than "ordinary people."

Public opinion, in fact, was divided along class lines. The Dubček regime represented, initially, a middle-class revolution, a long-delayed fusion of the technocrats' insistence on economic reform with the alienation of the intelligentsia. The neo-Stalinist system—centralized, bureaucratic, unresponsive to market forces at home and abroad—was increasingly regarded as an obstacle to economic progress. A high proportion of industrial profits were absorbed into subsidizing an agricultural sector still at the 1937 level. The technocratic wing of the Party had been pressing for decentralization, for greater managerial initiative, but Ota Šik's reforms envisaged neither democratic decision making by elected workers' councils nor the effective right to strike. The working class reacted with acute suspicion, fearing a growth in the managers' power to fire workers, alter wage rates, and increase "labor discipline."

Wages and salaries provided another bone of contention. Under Novotný, pay differentials were unusually narrow. Taking the average wage index as 100, a young engineer might expect to earn 130 or 140 at the most. At the huge ČKD (Skoda) enterprise on the outskirts of Prague, the average wage in May 1968 was 1,800 crowns a month, while doctors working at the factory received only 2,500 crowns. Time and again the present writer was told by members of the middle class that this was a ridiculous situation; that skill, education, and long apprenticeship must be rewarded. Indeed, this point of view was firmly embedded in the Party's Action Program of April 1968: *"To apply the principle of remuneration according to the quantity, quality, and social usefulness of work we must put an end to income leveling."* Only a proper income differentiation could develop the resources required to raise the standard of living.

Jiří Pelikán, the liberal director-general of television, and himself an ultrareformer, conceded that from the ideological point of view the egalitarian wage system introduced in 1955 might be construed as progress: "But in the transitional period of development of a socialist society, I think it is necessary to use both moral and material incentives. Precisely because a socialist society should favor technical and scientific development more than a capitalist society does, its technical and scientific personnel should be paid accordingly."

The "revolt of the intelligentsia" under Dubček was also directed against the old, Stalinist hierarchy, which had ensured working-class loyalty by reducing wage differentials—except for themselves. The most ostentatiously prosperous figures in Czechoslovak society were the Party leaders with their black Tatra limousines, large apartments, and special shops selling foreign produce. Party Secretary Zdeněk Mlynář confessed that his salary was ten times the national average, while the first secretary of the Party and the premier earned almost twice as much as he—25,000 crowns per month. Mlynář's chauffeur-driven car was available for his private use: "All I had to do to get anything from a new suit to something from Paris was to indicate it in the morning to my aide or secretary, and the rest would be seen to by the director of the 'House of Fashion' or the Czechoslovak ambassador anywhere in the world."

On inspection tours, top functionaries were showered with expensive gifts from the directors of enterprises. Special apartment blocks and holiday villas and medical facilities were available at nominal rents. The source of wealth in the Soviet system is power; in order to raise their own standard of living, the professional and technocratic classes were compelled to take over the Party and the industrial enterprises—in two words, the Prague Spring.

The working class observed this process with suspicion and resentment. Novotný had constantly assured them that they constituted the nation's postrevolutionary aristocracy; they now feared an economic counterrevolution. Suspicion was most acute among the unskilled workers; at the ČKD works in Prague, the iron foundry workers displayed Stalinist intransigence, the locomotive workers were more open to change, and the electrical engineers the most "progressive."

If the technocrats and the intellectuals were united in their demand for higher pay differentials, there was no unanimity about the feasibility of pluralistic democracy. Many technicians demanding higher pay, higher status, and a more flexible, open system of government, nevertheless rejected pluralism as the gateway to capitalism. These people were the "good Communists," despite the attraction of beneficial trade and credit agreements with West Germany, where many of them traveled in 1968, either in delegations or as individuals. (The Ulbricht regime in the DDR sourly monitored the traffic and denounced any accommodation with "the forces of revanchism" *et cetera* in the Federal Republic.) Pluralism was less attractive to the technocrats who had grown up under communism than to the students and the elderly with memories of T. G. Masaryk and the old, bourgeois Republic.

It took the Soviet invasion of August 20 and 21 to rally the working class fully behind the reform program and the government. Only then did the workers perceive liberalization as synonymous with national independence.

TWO THOUSAND WORDS

Pavel Tigrid's judgment of the reformers who now led the Party is incontestable; they tried to renovate the system in the name of the ideology that had brought about the sclerosis. "They attempted to cure the effects rather than the causes of the disease. . . . They wanted to ration liberty." It was in this spirit that the Presidium decided to prohibit the rebirth of an independent Social Democratic Party (swallowed by the Communist Party after the coup of February 1948, but still the greatest potential threat to the KSČ's monopoly of power). On June 1, *Lidová Demokracie* carried a critical commentary on the Ministry of the Interior's ban on new political parties. As Dr. V. Pavlíček, of the Law Faculty of the Charles University, explained, the constitution did not lay down any conditions for the establishment of new parties, nor did it endow the Ministry of the Interior with any veto in this respect. Like its predecessor, the Dubček regime was resorting to state powers it did not constitutionally possess.

Addressing the Central Committee at the beginning of June, Dubček emphasised that the KSČ would take care of everything: "The Party as a whole is not guilty of the deformations of the past. . . . It was the Communists who initiated the current renaissance of socialism and they are therefore morally and politically entitled to claim the leading role. . . . The Party is the main guarantee of good relations with other Socialist countries. The Party is the unifying force of the two nations. . . . The greatest majority of the best creative minds in the country is in the Party. The Party cadres comprise the backbone of the administrative structure of society. . . . The Party will resolutely oppose views demanding a revision of the historic merger of the Communists and Social Democrats." Power of decision making would be shared in future, but democracy did not entail "bourgeois parliamentarianism." "The establishment of any opposition party outside the National Front will be opposed by all means. . . ."

The pluralists, however, did not lie down. A Social Democratic policy document widely circulated on June 12 not only claimed that the Party was returning to life after twenty years, but declared invalid the enforced merger with the Communist Party in June 1948. Pressing the challenge, delegates from Bohemia and Moravia began to establish local committees.

The most eloquent and famous challenge to the Dubček regime's half-cocked liberalization appeared on June 27 in *Literární Listy* under the title, "2,000 Words to Workers, Farmers, Scientists, Artists and Everyone." Written by the novelist Ludvík Vaculík, the manifesto carried seventy signatures (including some members of the KSČ Central Committee) and immediately became a *cause célèbre,* goading Brezhnev into an immediate telephone call of protest to Dubček.

Vaculík blamed "the present state of affairs" on those who had been the instruments of arbitrary rule by a party that spuriously claimed to represent the will of the workers. "Each worker knows that in practice the workers did not decide anything." And what sort of people dominated the Party apparatus? Egoists who itched to wield authority, cowards with an eye to the main chance, who had stepped into the shoes of the deposed ruling class: "They still wield the instruments of power . . . the season of astonishing revelations, dismissals from high office, and heady speeches couched in language of unaccustomed daring—all this over."

There were echoes here of Milovan Djilas's *The New Class,* but Vaculík's emphasis was psychological rather than structural, moral rather than managerial; his was the voice of the Czech Orwell. Power, explains Orwell's Party boss O'Brien in *1984,* is an end in itself.

Remedy followed analysis—and it was the remedy proposed in the "2,000 Words" manifesto that most offended the Kremlin. Ordinary citizens must press forward against the ruling class. "Ways must be found to force them to resign. To mention a few: public criticism, resolutions, demonstrations . . . strikes and picketing their front doors. But we should reject any illegal, indecent or boorish methods."

The "2,000 Words" precipitated a flood of supporting and dissenting articles. Josef Smrkovský, the most liberal spirit close to Dubček, published a reply notable for its moderate tone in *Rudé Právo*. At a private meeting with the signatories, Dubček himself explained that he had no alternative but to disown them. On June 29, the Party Presidium rejected the "2,000 Words" as likely to unleash conflicts and clashes that "could jeopardize our process of regeneration and further progress of socialist construction." But the good faith of the signatories was not called into question, and no measures were taken against them. Moscow fumed.

On August 10, the new Draft Statutes of the Czechoslovak Communist Party appeared. Although democratic centralism ostensibly remained their guiding principle, the minority was now guaranteed the right to formulate its own position, to continue to hold that position after a decision had been taken, and to demand periodic reassessments on the basis of new knowledge. This was a radical departure from the model of a Bolshevik party as defined at the Tenth Congress of the Soviet Party in 1921, which demanded the immediate dissolution of all groups with a separate platform on penalty of expulsion.

The new Draft Statutes were later attacked in the Soviet *White Book* as a formula for factionalism.

THE RUSSIANS ARE COMING

The Communist regimes most alarmed by the Prague Spring were Brezhnev's USSR, Gomulka's Poland, and Ulbricht's East Germany. Each abhorred the liberal contagion; each feared that communism would not survive in the popular democracies if free elections were allowed; each subscribed to a reverse form of the Johnson administration's domino theory: if one Warsaw Pact state "went," they might all go. The Soviet-style systems depended for their survival on the Party's absolute, monopolistic control of the state machine, the media, and the economy.

Dubček received his first serious hectoring on March 23, when he met the full company of Soviet-bloc leaders at Dresden. Returning to Prague, the Czechoslovak leader decided to conceal from his own public the extent and tone of the criticism he had suffered. On March 27, the East German Party organ, *Neues Deutschland,* published a speech by a member of the Politburo, Kurt Hager, attacking Josef Smrkovský and complaining that West German "propaganda centers" were quoting the attacks of Czechoslovak writers and journalists on the role of the Party, the Central Committee, and the *apparat.*

Relations between Prague and Warsaw were at a low ebb. The Czechoslovak press had freely criticized the anti-Semitic campaign in Poland and the purging of the Warsaw University faculty following the student riots in March. Two of the victims, Professors Leszek Kolakowski and Bronislaw Baczko, were invited to lecture at the Charles University. On May 6, the Polish ambassador formally protested against the "anti-Polish campaign." The presence of Jews among the leading liberals of the Prague Spring was not lost on the anti-Semites in Moscow and Warsaw, nor, indeed, on Novotný's supporters within Czechoslovakia. Eduard Goldstücker, chairman of the Writers' Union and a target of Soviet diatribes, received a number of anonymous letters, one of which he published in *Rudé Právo* on June 23: "Mr. Goldstücker—Zionist hyena bastard. . . . Why don't you set up some other party, an ISRAEL party? . . . But your time will come you despot—your days are numbered. You dirty Jew."

Goldstücker commented that this was the "pathological periphery" in which not only Nazism had prospered, but also the Communist State Security apparatus: "I know its vocabulary. . . . It is the speech of my Ruzyne investigators in 1951–1953, of my Pankrac, Leopoldov, and Jachymov prison guards from 1953 to 1955. . . ." Unlike the New Left in the West and particularly the Black Panthers in the United States, the progressive intellectuals in Czechoslovakia and Poland associated anti-Semitism with reactionary Stalinism. Pro-Israeli banners were paraded by Prague students on May 1; the magazine *Student* carried an appeal for the resumption of diplomatic relations with Israel, issued by the Academic Council of Students in the Philosophical Faculty of the Charles University.

On May 11, the Soviet paper *Izvestia* published an article by V. Stepanov on the subject of legal opposition parties who aspired to become "loud-mouthed back-benchers in the socialist parliament and, if a suitable opportunity were to arise, to oppose socialism outright." This theme was insistently hammered home in the Soviet press, but not until June 14 did the Soviet Party venture a direct attack on one of the new leaders of Czechoslovakia. *Pravda* complained that Čestmír Císař had spoken at a recent rally in Prague about "certain negative signs of Leninism." Such criticisms, said *Pravda,* had been heard before from Mensheviks and Social Democrats.

On June 20, Warsaw Pact exercises began in Czechoslovakia. On July 2, it was announced in Prague that the exercises had ended, but Soviet troops did not immediately withdraw. Tension rose. The Soviet withdrawal began, but slowly. The crisis became apparent to the world in mid-July, when Soviet, Bulgarian, East German, Hungarian, and Polish leaders summoned Dubček and his colleagues to attend an emergency meeting in Warsaw. The Warsaw Pact's brazen disregard for Czechoslovakia's national sovereignty was too much; stiffening its spine against a *diktat,* Prague refused to attend. On that day Soviet troops abruptly stopped their withdrawal from Czechoslovakia. On July 18, the five powers issued a harsh letter to the Czechoslovak Central Committee: "We are deeply disturbed by the course of events in your country. The offensive of reaction, backed by imperialism, against your party and the foundations of the social system . . . threatens the interests of the entire socialist system." The five powers recalled that they had expressed misgivings at Dresden in March, in bilateral meetings, and in exchanges of letters. But: "We were convinced that you were going to defend the apple of your eye, the Leninist principle of democratic centralism."

And what was happening in Czechoslovakia? Antisocialist forces had "gained control over the press, radio and television and transformed them into a tribune for attacks on the Communist Party . . . [and on] friendly relations between the Czechoslovak Socialist Republic and other socialist countries." Cited here was the "2,000 Words" manifesto—"an open appeal for strikes and disturbances . . . an attempt to implant anarchy." Normal Warsaw Pact exercises had been presented in the Czechoslovak media as a pretext for "groundless accusations of violation of [Czechoslovak] sovereignty. . . ." The five powers demanded "seizure by the Party of media of mass information," plus "a cessation of the activity of all political organizations coming out against socialism."

On July 19, the Czechoslovak Presidium replied, refuting the allegations. President Svoboda reaffirmed loyalty to the Warsaw Pact. (Unlike Hungarian prime minister Imre Nagy in 1956, the Czechoslovak leaders never hinted that they wished to leave the Warsaw Pact and invoke neutrality.) On July 20, the leaders of the Italian and French Communist parties, alarmed by the mounting Soviet hostility toward Prague, flew to Moscow to warn Brezhnev against a military solution. Luigi Longo and the PCI regarded the success of the Czechoslovak reform movement as relevant to their own fortunes in Italy. (When the Soviets did resort to force, the PCI was outspoken in its condemnation; even the neo-Stalinist French Communists took the historic step of expressing "reprobation.")

On July 23, Dubček bowed to Soviet pressure by replacing Lt.-General Václav Prchlík, head of the Central Committee's Department for Defense and Security. Prchlík had drawn up a contingency plan outlining alternatives in the event of a Soviet invasion. On July 15, he gave a press conference calling for real equality among the member states of the Warsaw Pact, and complaining that Soviet marshals alone ran the high command of the Pact. When Dubček got rid of Prchlík in a reshuffle, he effectively signaled to Moscow that Czechoslovak sovereignty would not be defended by force of arms.

On July 26, *Pravda* expressed fear that Czechoslovakia was about to re-establish "a bourgeois regime."

Three days later an armored train brought the top Soviet leadership to bilateral talks at Čierna-nad-Tisou, the Slovak railhead with the Soviet Union. The little railwaymen's club had been hastily transformed into a conference room. "There, amongst the tinted mirrors and long red curtains, the two sides sat opposite each other across a narrow table. . . . Brezhnev, declaring that he expected a counter-revolutionary attempt upon his life, insisted that the Russians sat facing the windows outside which Czechoslovak and Soviet troops . . . constantly patrolled." Brezhnev began abusively, recounting the crimes of the "counter-revolutionaries," citing offensive articles in the Czechoslovak press, and abusing such "bourgeois revisionists" as Šik, Goldstücker, and Císař.

Brezhnev urged Dubček to postpone the Fourteenth Party Congress, scheduled for September 9 and inevitably destined to oust the remaining pro-Soviet conservatives from the Presidium and Central Committee. Moscow realized that Prague had almost reached the point of no return. The alarm the Soviet leaders felt about the imminent Extraordinary Party Congress was reflected in *Pravda* on August 22. The election of delegates had been accompanied by "the defamation of cadres"—in plain language, the repudiation of the old guard.*

But whose business was it? The problem of Czechoslovakia's sovereignty remained. A new theory had emerged with the five-power letter from Warsaw in mid-July: the partial sovereignty of socialist states. This was spelled out more fully after the invasion: "Law and the norms of law are subordinated to the laws of the class struggle and the laws of social development. . . . The class approach to the matter cannot be discarded in the name of legalistic considerations."

The Russians were indeed coming.

*Moscow could not openly defend the dismissed State Security officials who had served Novotný, although General Kotov, the chief Soviet "adviser" to the Czechoslovak Ministry of the Interior, had fought a rearguard action on their behalf. Immediately after the invasion, a KGB official, Vinokurov, arrived at Prague's State Security Headquarters and complained that a number of high-ranking departmental security officers had been dismissed by Dubček's minister of the interior, Josef Pavel. Among those he listed were Houska (former chief of the first department), Kosnar (former chief of the second department), Klima (former chief of staff of State Security), and others.

11

FRANCE:
Students and Workers

"Maddened, the students tore up paving stones and formed parked cars into staggered barricades."

"That night St.-Germain was a battlefield."

"The Sorbonne was surrounded by gendarmes, the CRS [Compagnies Républicaines de Sécurité], and the *gendarmes mobiles,* a military unit."

"By the end of the night, 367 people had been injured, 460 arrested, and 180 cars had been damaged or destroyed."

THE STUDENTS

PARIS, May 3, 1968—The day starts like any other Friday, with no sign of the storm ahead. At noon a few activists from Nanterre, locked out of their own faculty, meet colleagues from the Sorbonne to discuss the disciplinary charges that eight of them, including Daniel Cohn-Bendit, are to face the following Monday. The previous day Dean Pierre Grappin has closed Nanterre under instructions from Paul Roche, rector of the University of Paris. But soon a larger crowd gathers in the courtyard of the Sorbonne in an angry mood. Also in the vicinity are members of the extreme right-wing movement, Occident, which has distributed pamphlets threatening to carry Cohn-Bendit to the frontier by the scruff of his neck and "to bring an end to Bolshevik agitation in the faculties by all means."

Rector Roche, a sixty-eight-year-old former professor of medicine, panicked and called the minister of the interior. By 4 P.M. the Sorbonne was surrounded by a massive police force headed by the notorious riot squads of the CRS—the Compagnies Républicaines de Sécurité, founded after the war and put through their baptismal fire in bloody battles with striking miners in the north. The police arrested all the political and trade-union representatives of the student movement they could identify, on the pretext that some of the five hundred students assembled in the courtyard were wearing helmets and had broken two tables in order to brandish the legs as clubs. The news spread. Students came from cafés, libraries, and everywhere to confront the police: "*Libérez nos camarades.*" Then the fighting began on a scale that persuaded Roche to close the Sorbonne, for only the second time in seven hundred years. The previous occasion had been been in 1940, when the Nazis took Paris.

Alexander Quattrochi, activist and journalist, expressed the prevailing view of the police, with audible social disdain: "By nine o'clock the Latin Quarter is virtually sealed off with peasants made watchdogs and clad in Martian plastic. They wear gloves over hands rescued from the obscure pains of the spade."

On the night of May 3–4, the National Union of Students (Union des Etudiants Français, or UNEF) and the lecturers' union, the Syndicaté Nationale de l'Enseignement Supérieure (SNESup), most of whose members were junior faculty, called their members out on strike, although as civil servants the university lecturers were legally bound to give five days' notice. The morning following the closure of the Sorbonne, the conservative newspaper *Le Figaro* thundered: "Students, these youngsters? Young guttersnipes, fit for the remand home, if not for a court of summary jurisdiction, rather than for the university." The magistrates worked through the Saturday handing out suspended sentences, but on Sunday four of the demonstrators were sent to prison.

The two unions now put forward three demands that the authorities refused to concede, resulting in the greatest popular insurrection ever experienced by a capitalist democracy in time of peace: (1) reopen the Sorbonne; (2) withdraw the police; and (3) release those arrested. These two unions were joined by the March 22 Movement in an action committee that subsequently enjoyed almost universal authority among students—hence the famous triumvirate of Jacques Sauvageot (UNEF), Alain Geismar (SNESup), and Daniel Cohn-Bendit (March 22).

The National Union of Students had attained the peak of its political influence and militancy during the final years of France's war in Algeria. At that time it claimed 100,000 members out of a total student body of 240,000. But after the war UNEF went into decline; by 1968, its membership was down to 50,000 out of 514,000 students. Even as a trade union UNEF had recently failed to become a partner in shaping policy toward student facilities and *cités universitaires.* Described by Cohn-Bendit as "moribund throughout the country and a complete farce at Nanterre," UNEF had played virtually no role in the turbulence there; indeed, its acting president, Jacques Sauvageot, confessed that he knew little about Nanterre until Cohn-Bendit filled him in when they both found themselves under arrest on May 3.

Yet immediately prior to the May events, UNEF had shown signs of life, campaigning against the more rigorously selective admission to universities proposed in the Fouchet Plan, demanding greater political freedom in the *cités universitaires,* and organizing demonstrations of solidarity with Vietnam, the German students, and Greek democracy. Discontent within the university system ran deep. France's student population had leapt in ten years from 170,000 to 514,000.* The system

---

*Despite this expansion, access to higher education remained largely confined to the middle classes. The children of peasant farmers accounted for only 6.6 percent of students; the children of workers, only 9.9 percent. (In class-ridden Britain, children from urban and rural working-class

could not cope with its human intake. Paris itself was crammed with 130,000 students. Libraries and laboratories were overrun; it was often impossible to get a seat in a lecture hall; and students were frequently compelled to listen to loudspeakers outside (an ideal model of alienation). Compelled to grant a place to any candidate who passed the national *baccalauréat* examination, the universities failed between a third and a half of all students before they finished the course. Professor Raymond Aron, who taught sociology at the Sorbonne, favored preentry selection on the English or American models. In Britain, each university department was at liberty to stipulate what grades on the national "A level" examinations were required to gain admission.

According to the Fouchet Plan of 1966, higher studies would be divided into several "cycles," offering both four-year degrees and inferior two-year degrees leading to junior jobs in teaching, industry, or the civil service. This proposal incensed students and bitterly divided the teaching staff. French students wanted an expansion of facilities (staff, lecture halls, libraries, dormitories), not a contraction of university places. When Fouchet's successor, Alain Peyrefitte, announced that a mere pass in the *baccalauréat* would not necessarily ensure entrance to a university, the *lycées* (high schools) also began to seethe with discontent, aware as they were that the *"bachot"* itself was a slaughterhouse eliminating about half the candidates.

French students found themselves in two contrasting situations. Many of those *de premier cycle* would not attain the first real grade of university studies, *la license;* their anxieties were basically careerist. It was the students who had reached the security of the *troisième cycle* (or of the *maîtrise*)—most notably those studying and rejecting empirical sociology, plus some teaching assistants—who could afford to challenge their destiny in the world of careers, joining political forces with students from the faculty of letters, whose conflict was less with technocracy than with outmoded syllabuses, remote professors, and bureaucratic authorities.

Edgar Morin noted the convergence, yet contradiction, between the pro- and anti-modern wings of the student revolt. On the one hand was the complaint that the curriculum was antiquatedly academic and irrelevant to the needs of employers; on the other hand was the denunciation of the university as a processing plant for industry and careerism. In Morin's view, what enabled these contradictory tendencies to cohere into a sense of communal struggle was "the Kerenskyism of the university authorities," their resort to repression after periods of vacillation.

---

homes accounted for a quarter of all university students.) In France, children of shop and clerical employees accounted for 8.5 percent of students. Despite comparable populations, the British university intake was less than half France's, but the number of students graduating was similar.

One thing that united the student generation was resentment against antiquated disciplinary rules. Political meetings and propaganda were normally forbidden on campus; men were not allowed into women's lodgings; students were not permitted to decorate their rooms; in many halls of residence, students could receive guests only in common rooms. It required only inspired leadership—the flair, humor, and courage of a Cohn-Bendit—to link the petty frustrations with the wider grievance against technocratic authoritarianism.

THE DEMONSTRATIONS

Monday, May 6, was to be one of the bloodiest days in the month. The Sorbonne was surrounded by gendarmes, the CRS, and the *gendarmes mobiles,* a military unit. The first clashes occurred in the morning as the Nanterre 8 passed through the police cordon, singing the "Internationale," to face the university disciplinary committee. That afternoon Minister of Education Peyrefitte indignantly asked the National Assembly: "What right does a union have to launch a strike which does not respect the legal formalities and, moreover, calls airily on teachers to abandon their mission, their students and their university tradition?"

Not yet ready for battle, the students crossed the river and marched through bourgeois Paris. The general public was mildly sympathetic, but the test came as they returned to the Latin Quarter. Approaching the rue St.-Jacques, they were suddenly charged by the police with stunning savagery. Maddened, the students tore up paving stones and formed parked cars into staggered barricades. Along the boulevard St.-Germain the air was thick with tear gas. The police called in reinforcements. The students now went south toward the Place Denfert-Rochereau, whose numerous outlets always presented a problem to the police. In the middle of the square, loudspeakers were set up on the plinth of the Lion of Belfort (which carries the unrevolutionary inscription, *"A La Défense nationale, 1870–1871"*). That night St.-Germain was a battlefield. The official score for bloody Monday was 422 arrests and 345 policemen hurt (the comparable figure for injuries to demonstrators could not be calculated, many preferring to nurse their wounds rather than risk falling into the hands of the police).

Tuesday's Long March followed. By the evening there were 20,000 to 30,000 demonstrators gathered around the Belfort Lion. The newssheet *Action* sold furiously. The young set off in a hurry, almost sprinting, responding to the *"hop, hop, hop"* of their cheerleaders. At the corner of the boulevard Montparnasse there was a moment of hesitation: eastward toward the working-class districts or westward toward the Champs-Elysées? The temptation to invade bourgeois Paris prevailed. But the bridge across the Seine was blocked by police. The students turned right and sprinted across another bridge and into the Champs-Elysées. By ten, they had reached the Etoile, red and black flags aloft, the massed demonstrators roaring the "Internationale" around the Arc de Triomphe.

By Wednesday, public opinion was shifting against the government. The middle classes were shocked by police brutality, and the workers were increasingly impressed by the fighting spirit of the students. From Toulouse and Marseilles in the south to Lille in the north, from Strasbourg in the east to Rennes in the west, came reports of solidarity meetings and demonstrations.

Again the Paris demonstration formed in the evening. It was raining. Geismar and Sauvageot confirmed that the three demands remained inseparable, but when the march reached the Luxembourg Gardens and the order to disperse was given, many groups lingered, fearful that the revolt had been betrayed. As the Communist loudspeakers urged dispersal "in calm, order and dignity," a student loudspeaker replied: "Those who want, go back to your tellies . . . students, young workers, down towards the boulevard Raspail!" Cohn-Bendit regarded the attempt to disperse the crowd as Communist treachery, but the UNEF was also responsible.

On Thursday, Cohn-Bendit proclaimed the street a lecture hall. With thousands just sitting down, the Boul' Mich' provided the setting for a lively teach-in. Geismar and Sauvageot admitted their mistake in dispersing the march the previous night. A vast meeting was held at the Mutualité that evening. Sectarian differences of approach and tactics led to long discussions.

On Friday evening, May 10, 30,000 demonstrators assembled at the place Denfert-Rochereau, blocking traffic for two miles. Cohn-Bendit and other leaders opened the debate: Where to march tonight? The targets chosen were the Santé prison, the Ministry of Justice, and the national broadcasting organization, ORTF (detested for its biased, insulting reporting of the week's demonstrations). The *lycée* students were now in the thick of it. The march took a new route, passing through the more popular quarters where people applauded from the pavements and opened windows. As the demonstrators moved down the boulevard St.-Germain toward the Latin Quarter, tensions rose. Each side street to the Sorbonne was filled with police deployed for combat. Derisively the students baited them: "CRS–SS!" Fearing an imminent attack, students began to rip up paving stones and build barricades (perhaps fifty in all) haphazardly. The police merely observed.

Negotations between the dean of the university and four representatives of the demonstrators, including Cohn-Bendit, made no progress. Jean-Jacques Lebel, noted practitioner of the "happening," reported on the opening moves before the battle: "1 A.M.: Literally thousands help build barricades . . . women, workers, bystanders, people in pyjamas, human chains to carry rocks, wood, iron. . . . Our barricade is double: one three-foot-high pile of wood, cars, metal posts, trash cans. . . . Of course the majority of people simply look on. We organize a cordon to keep photographers and bystanders away from us. . . ."

In many homes, transistor radios remained on all night. The two commercial stations, Europe One and Radio Luxembourg, rose to the occasion with courageous, on-the-spot, reporting. France stayed up to listen. The radio also served as a channel for negotiation between, for example, Rector Roche and Alain Geismar. Geismar made it clear that even though the government had now yielded on two out of three demands, there could be no compromise about the third: *"Libérez nos camarades!"*

Soon after midnight, acting Prime Minister Louis Joxe, deputizing in Georges Pompidou's absence, moved into the Ministry of the Interior to join Interior Minister Christian Fouchet, Bernard Tricot (de Gaulle's right-hand man), and Prefect of Police Maurice Grimau, who demanded, and got, a written order to clear the barricades.

The CRS rapidly cleared the barricades in the square facing the Luxembourg Gardens. But to storm the main obstacles in the rue Gay-Lussac, the police resorted to preliminary bombing, first with grenade throwers, then with hand grenades. In addition to tear gas, the CS grenades used in Vietnam were for the first time employed in France. The defenders of the barricades covered their faces with baking soda and handkerchiefs. To help the besieged, buckets of water were thrown from neighboring windows in the hope of clearing the atmosphere. Police battered the doors, shouting, *"Fermez les fenêtres."* Grenades were tossed through windows that remained open.

Jean-Jacques Lebel again: "2 A.M.: It is now obvious that police are preparing a powerful attack. Radio announces we are surrounded and that government has ordered police to attack. . . . In front of us we turn over cars to prevent police from charging with their buses and tanks (Radio said tanks were coming, but we never saw any). . . . I must insist again that the general mood was defense, *not* offensive; we just wanted to hold the place like an entrenched sit-down strike. . . . Their tactics are simple: at 100 yards distance they launch gas grenades by rifle which blind, suffocate, and knock us out. This gas is MACE

(Vietnam and Detroit Mace). Also explosive grenades. One student near us picked up one to throw it back; it tore his whole hand off. . . . But then police attack at three points simultaneously: at two extremities of Gay-Lussac, at our barricade, and at rue d'Ulm. . . . Finally we are forced back. Our barricade burns. At this point all I can remember is that I faint from lack of air."

Hospital orderlies had to brave police truncheons to get at the wounded. Professor Jacques Monod, *prix Nobel,* appealed for a truce so that the injured could be evacuated. Captured students knelt in the street, hands on heads. Even those already injured were assaulted. Professor Daniel Lacombe informed the Ministry of the Interior that police broke into a Red Cross post in the Institut Henri Poincaré and beat him up. Pasteur Roger Parmentier testified that injured people were dragged from stretchers.

Jean-Jacques Lebel, 6 A.M.: "Still fighting outside. . . . The police are searching house by house, room by room. Anybody with black hands and gas spots on clothes . . . or wounds is beaten and arrested. . . . Many people in cars and taxis volunteer to take us out of police zone. Everywhere we see enormous buses full of our people, tired, beaten, bloody prisoners."

There were no sanctuaries. Police stormed into private homes to drag out refugees whom they then clubbed into their vans. By the end of the night, 367 people had been injured, 460 arrested, and 180 cars had been damaged or destroyed.

On Saturday, convoys of troop carriers were booed and hissed as they hurtled along the boulevard St.-Germain. During the weekend, workmen with heavy machinery toiled to repave the streets, drag away burned-out cars, and remove mountains of charred debris. Returning from Asia the same day, Prime Minister Pompidou immediately put government policy into reverse, ordering the police out of the Sorbonne and the Latin Quarter. The police, who had suffered four hundred casualties in a week and required reinforcements from as far afield as Brittany, were bewildered and enraged. As Raymond Aron, himself an ardent Gaullist, reflected: "For a regime which for ten years has governed France with more authority than any other French Government has ever possessed, the discovery that there was such a fund of violence and indignation in the masses must have been both staggering and bitter."

THE POLICE

The greatest "fund of violence," however, belonged to the police and the regime that unleashed them. The painter Jean Hélion, who had been taken prisoner in 1940 and escaped from Pomerania in 1942, wrote to the minister of culture, André Malraux, complaining that both of his sons had been brutally beaten in separate incidents, and how he himself had been arrested while standing at the corner of the Boul' Mich', then thrown in a cage in the basement of the Opéra police station. The radical publisher François Maspero described how on May 6, injured people had taken refuge in his bookshop, La Joie de Lire, at 40 rue St.-Séverin, the unpleasant result being that police surrounded the shop, smashed the windows, and threw tear gas inside, badly burning the eyes of five of his assistants. Within six weeks of the street battles, Editions du Seuil published *Le Livre noir des journées de Mai,* detailing instances of brutal lawlessness by the *"services d'ordre"* between May 3 and 10 (corroborated by many foreign newspaper correspondents).

Police brutality had begun on May 3. Maddened by the historically charged taunt "CRS–SS!" (the main force of riot police belonged to the Compagnies Républicaines de Sécurité), infuriated by the hit-and-run tactics of the demonstrators, the police reacted with indiscriminate brutality and bitter xenophobia. (The German Jew Cohn-Bendit was often credited with masterminding the whole insurrection.) Entering a café in the place Saint-Sulpice on May 6, they ordered everyone out with kicks and blows. A young man protested, "I'm a foreigner." A cop of the CRS struck him: "Yes, and you've come to shit on us in France."

A student recalled the night of May 10: "I took my fiancée, who was choking and had burning eyes, to a house in the [rue Gay-Lussac]. With several comrades we took shelter with a woman who lived there. About six o'clock a plain-clothes policeman rushed in, revolver in hand. . . . He made us stand on the landing while he stationed about 30 CRS on the stairs, from the fourth floor to the ground floor, armed with batons. . . . Batons blows rained on us. . . . In the police station they went on beating us up."

A woman told how she took refuge in an empty flat with some others, including a young couple: "The wife was three months pregnant. They hid in the bathroom, and almost at once the CRS smashed the door and rushed at them, shouting furiously. . . . I could hear the young woman shouting 'I'm pregnant!' and being beaten up to the accompaniment of cries of 'You'll soon see if you're pregnant, you tart!' I skip the details. I could go on for ten pages. They beat her husband almost unconscious, beat up another boy and took them both off, leaving the pregnant girl . . . in a shocking state. . . ."

A nurse was arrested and taken to the detention center at Beaujon: "We got out of the bus and were beaten up; then, going between two ranks of CRS, I reached a stadium surrounded by barbed wire. I waited, standing in the rain. From time to time CRS buses delivered men and women, hit or gassed, with very bad head wounds, broken arms, etc. Chinese or Vietnamese and blacks especially were treated with great violence. Then we were taken indoors one by one. A CRS man said to me, 'Come along and I'll shave you, curly locks.' He hit me. An officer intervened, but the girl ahead of me had all her hair cut off. I was taken to a cell, three metres by six. After five hours, it contained 80 of us. We had to stand up. I could see the courtyard; a young man went by half naked, legs lacerated with baton blows, bleeding, holding his stomach, urinating everywhere. A young woman who'd been with him told me the CRS beat him till he fainted, then undressed him and hit his sexual organs till the flesh was in ribbons."

Le Livre noir also contained copious evidence about indiscriminate bombardments with the CS gas used by American forces in Vietnam. One witness reported seeing a policeman opening the unlocked doors of one house after another, throwing a gas grenade into each, then closing the doors again.

However, revolutionary Paris had seen worse: 2,596 people executed by the Jacobins; 20,000 to 30,000 Communards killed by the army of the Versailles government between March 28 and May 28, 1871.

On Monday, May 13, the students still detained were released, but the national trade unions had called a one-day strike and 200,000 demonstrators gathered shouting, *"De Gaulle assassin!"* and *"De Gaulle au musée!"* As the mass of demonstrators reached the place Denfert-Rochereau, the official terminus of the march, the order to disperse was given and promptly obeyed by the disciplined trade unionists, but the majority of students refused and finally found themselves on the Champ-de-Mars. It was here, as the students debated what to do with their movement, that an idea germinated from a murmur into a collective decision: Occupy the Sorbonne! The police had been withdrawn from the Latin Quarter, and the occupation was performed peacefully. The first night of the French cultural revolution began.

The following day, de Gaulle flew to Rumania for a scheduled state visit. Pompidou had advised him that the worst was over.

THE COMMUNISTS

During the first week of the disturbances the Communist Party (PCF) had condemned and belittled the Nanterre rebels. *L'Humanité* published a diatribe by the Party's future general secretary, Georges Marchais, "False Revolutionaries to be Unmasked": "Despite their contradictions, these splinter groups have united in what they call the March 22 Movement . . . led by the German anarchist Cohn-Bendit. . . . Not satisfied with agitating the students—to the detriment of the interests of the mass of the students themselves and to the delight of Fascist provocateurs—these pseudo-revolutionaries now have the impertinence to think that they can give lessons to the working class. More and more they have penetrated our factories or the hostels for foreign workers, distributing tracts and other propaganda material." Marchais warned that these playboys, "mostly sons of *grands bourgeois,* contemptuous toward students of working-class origin," would "quickly snuff out their revolutionary flames to become directors in Papa's business. . . ."

But on May 8, the Communists abruptly changed their tactics, attempting to take control of the uprising by urging Communist students and teachers to attend the mass meeting called by UNEF at the Faculty of Science. The Party also despatched France's most famous Communist writer, Louis Aragon, to address a street meeting outside the police-occupied Odéon. Reminded (as he put it) "so movingly of my own youth," Aragon was mercilessly heckled by Cohn-Bendit's group with cries of "Long live OGPU! Long live Stalin, the father of all the people!" When that evening's march moved off from the place Denfert-Rochereau, the Communist deputies and municipal councilors tried to head the procession, but the students weren't having it.

Aragon promptly issued a special edition of the Communist literary weekly, *Les Lettres françaises,* committing it fully to "the party of youth—if there is one." A printed box contained the PCF Political Bureau's statement of May 12, supporting the students' resistance to integration and calling for a university reform that would abolish social privilege and the technocratic regime of the monopolies. More credible was an article by the Communist writer Pierre Daix, recalling how his own generation had conformed to university rules and merit awards while waiting to make the revolution. Today the young changed the university in order to change the world. But Aragon's pages offered no hint of the tensions between the Party and the student movement. Instead he offered a poem of his own.

The most senior Communist dissident was Roger Garaudy, an intellectual and a member of the Political Bureau, who not only called for an alliance with the revolutionary students, but embraced their doctrine of economic self-management, autonomous councils, and decentralization. To compound this offense he applauded the Prague Spring and described the PCF's line as *la voie polonaise.* Finding only one ally in the Political Bureau and very few in the Central Committee, Garaudy would soon be expelled from the Party.

Police brutality on the night of May 10 forced the Communists to call a twenty-four-hour strike for Monday, May 13, but the PCF continued to belittle the entire ultra-Left as a petty-bourgeois cocktail of Bakunin, Trotskyism, and plain adventurism inclined to fantasies and brief outbursts of violence which soon gave way to apathy and submission to the ruling class. When the radical student-teacher leaders— Cohn-Bendit, Geismar, and Sauvageot—appeared on television, the PCF responded with a vehement protest. On May 22, an anonymous article appeared in *L'Humanité,* challenging the minister of youth on his "contacts" with Daniel Cohn-Bendit and the amount of subsidy he had granted to the March 22 Movement (a brazen invention). The following day the Communist trade-union leader, Georges Séguy, speaking at a press conference, further pursued this shameless campaign: "It seems that the warnings we had issued even before the Prime Minister hinted that the individual in question [Cohn-Bendit] belonged to an international organization are now being confirmed." In short, the greatest masters of red-baiting in France were the Communists themselves.

THE SORBONNE OCCUPIED

Repression having outraged the wider population, Pompidou had reversed government policy, hoping that a period of permissiveness would allow the insurrection to burn itself out. In the great courtyard of the Sorbonne, posters of Marx, Lenin, and Mao now gazed down (perhaps in astonishment) from the columns supporting the architrave inscribed in honor of Cardinal Richelieu. Trotsky, Castro, and Guevara were plastered along the walls beside the red, black, and Vietcong flags and the great flowering of slogans and hand-lettered posters, the programs for a better world, the collective manifesto of the Cultural Revolution:

- EVERYTHING IS POSSIBLE
- THE IMAGINATION TAKES POWER

- TAKE YOUR DESIRES FOR REALITIES
- IT IS FORBIDDEN TO FORBID

On May 13, a poster was attached to the main door of the Sorbonne: "The revolution which is beginning will call in question not only capitalist society but industrial society. The consumer society is bound for a violent death. Social alienation must vanish from history. We are inventing a new and original world. Imagination is seizing power."

On May 14, the General Assembly of the Sorbonne announced an Autonomous Popular University and elected a fifteen-person occupation committee, whose mandate was limited to twenty-four hours. The central amphitheatre was packed day and night for a nonstop debate. A Commission of Cultural Agitation, in almost permanent session, debated—and narrowly defeated—a motion to plaster over Puvis de Chavannes's fresco, *Ancient Greece Unveiling Herself Before Archaeology*.

The Sorbonne commune was desperately eager to explain its work to the outside world—to the workers, the press, the public. Students marched to the offices of *Le Figaro* shouting *"Le Figaro contre nous!"* They marched to the ORTF demanding an hour of television time a week to bring the cultural revolution to the people. Reporters from the independent Europe One and Radio Luxembourg, which provided energetic and fair coverage of the events, were welcomed as heroes.

In essence, there were two co-existing occupations of the Sorbonne (as, contemporaneously, of Columbia University): the revolutionaries; and the university reformers who established earnest commissions of inquiry to examine every aspect of the faculties. The reformers endowed the Sorbonne commune with its air of serious, practical endeavor; the utopians provided the vision of a far-reaching social transformation. Jean Lacouture contrasted *la Sorbonne basse* (continuous meetings in the amphitheatres) and *la Sorbonne haute* (rooms where groups restructured the university, with the women for the most part assigned to typing, stenciling, and domestic chores). Alain Touraine accepted the distinction, adding that *la Sorbonne basse* had as its sole function utopian discourse which permitted the pursuit of reform without the stigma of "reformist."

The self-assurance of the academic patriarchy had already been shaken before the student occupation of May 13, by the staff strike and the police violence of the night of May 10. On the evening of the 11th, for the first time in university history, the select *"professeurs titulaires"*—whose Conseil de Faculté, or senate, was the governing academic body of the Sorbonne—had been obliged to call an extraordinary meeting. As the 118 professors convened, some 800 junior faculty members were meeting next door in a state of high militancy. By a narrow vote of 65 to 53 the senior professors granted half the votes in the Conseil de Faculté to the lower academics and students.

The radicalism of their union, SNESup, undoubtedly affected the attitude of teaching staff who had been out on strike for a week. SNESup, representing only a quarter of the academic staff (predominantly junior ones), had been controlled by a radical coalition for the past year, allowing Alain Geismar, its secretary-general, to throw the union's weight behind the student strike despite the opposition of a substantial Communist minority within the union. Geismar regarded the mandarin professors, jealous of their powers and privileges, as "almost as much an enemy as the Government. . . ."

After May 13, the Sorbonne's ruling Conseil de Faculté was expanded into an Assemblée Plénière, with the participation of junior staff and students. In the majority of departments the same numerical balance was struck between the once all-powerful professors and equal numbers of students and lecturers; in some, the students secured equal voting power with the teachers as a whole. The most enthusiastic teachers were mainly younger ones, the *assistants* or *maîtres-assistants,* the majority of full professors with chairs having made themselves scarce. Departmental committees concluded that in the future deans, rectors, and administrators must be elected.

Raymond Aron, until January 1968 professor of sociology at the Sorbonne and a regular columnist for *Le Figaro,* was incensed that so many of the teaching staff had joined the revolt: "They were civil servants . . . yet they tried to overthrow the Government which allowed them all the liberties which they airily planned to remove from their French colleagues if victory would be theirs. . . ." It was all a "psychodrama . . . a verbal delirium." Bitterly he cited the fashionable intellectuals whose theories were washing around the corridors of liberation: Lévi-Strauss, Foucault, Althusser, Lacan, Sartre. Leftist emotionalism had sapped all resistance. If the young hated their fathers and their masters, then let them be faced by fathers and masters who stood erect instead of on their knees. Teachers must preserve their dignity and sense of responsibility: "Any election of professors . . . by an assembly which includes student members is incompatible with that dignity and responsibility."

Even further beyond Aron's pale, the utopian Critical University established within the Sorbonne proposed the abolition of all distinctions of rank among teachers, a revised relationship between teacher and pupil, and a new contract guaranteeing students prior agreement to curriculum, examinations, and other academic requirements. Students would acquire the inalienable *droit à la contestation,* the right to call everything into question and, indeed, to set up "counter courses."

At the elite Institut de Sciences Politiques ("Sciences Po") the students voted to occupy the buildings and not to take examinations. Heavy fighting followed a fierce attack by the right-wing group, Occident. In the entrance hall of the Faculté de Médecine on the rue des Sts.-Pères hung a large cartoon, "Down with the mandarins," depicting a senior surgeon gliding along, nose in the air, while junior surgeons bowed. Bowing to *them* were the general practitioners, and so on down the line to the humble students. The chief concern of the medical students was to revise their archaic teaching system and to loosen the stranglehold of an elite of overpaid, underworked surgeons.

The examination system was widely denounced as the rite of initiation into capitalist society; the March 22 Movement wanted to eradicate the distinction between workers and managers, rather than turn more workers' sons into managers. At the Ecole des Beaux Arts, the strike committee issued a manifesto denouncing social selection in education which penalized working-class and peasant children. "We want to fight the system of competitive examinations which is central to that selection." The departmental committees of the occupied Sorbonne concluded that in future the *agrégation* and similar national competitions must be eliminated, opening the universities to the workers in a massive program of adult education.

Yet the majority of students were torn between anti-careerist principles and personal anxiety to get a good job. When Alfred Willener asked seventy-seven students during the events what professions and occupations they considered worthy of esteem, only six mentioned proletarian labor, and only three, farming. The vision of workers crowding into libraries and lecture halls was far more attractive than the reverse journey of educated people to factories and fields. UNEF now denounced the examination system, but ambivalently; as a trade union, it feared that its members would emerge from the university of 1968 without degrees. "We are asking for a postponement," explained Sauvageot evasively. "The students in the various disciplines should work out the way the examinations can take place."

THE *LYCÉE* REVOLT

Schoolchildren formed Comités d'action lycéen (CAL), which called a strike, rather hopefully, in all the *lycées* of Paris on May 10. Many kids marched—or rampaged—in solidarity with the students. On May 11, pupils at the Lycée Paul-Eluard (named in honor of the Communist poet) in St.-Denis organized their own *"service d'ordre"* with the support of sympathetic teachers, set up pickets, and went marching. The smart Lycée Janson de Sailly was taken over by its pupils on Monday, May 20. Besieged by enthusiastic rebels from another school, the principal appealed to the minister of the interior, who merely advised him to lock the gates. But the whole school of 3,700 boys and girls was already in an uproar, egged on by teachers who had spent the weekend demonstrating. After each class had elected delegates to a central committee, four commissions set to work to discuss teaching methods, exams, and programs—joined by teachers, parents, and former pupils. Memoranda were duplicated on the school's machines and distributed to the general assembly.

The support of the teachers for the CAL was assured by their union, the Fédération de l'Education Nationale, representing 400,000 secondary-school teachers and influenced by the small political party closest in spirit to the student revolt, the Parti Socialiste Unifié. In Arras, capital of the Pas-de-Calais, where five *lycées* were occupied by pupils with the full support of their teachers, long discussions took place among senior pupils, teachers, and parents about reforming the *baccalauréat.* Such was the crisis and disruption in the *lycées,* that the *"bachot"* for 1968 had to be reduced to a brief oral examination.

THE WAR OF WORDS

Slogans covered Paris, hastily scribbled graffiti as well as highly professional posters from the Atelier Populaire of the Ecole des Beaux Arts (School of Fine Arts).

- LONG LIVE COMMUNICATION. DOWN WITH TELECOMMUNICATION.
- THE MORE I MAKE LOVE, THE MORE I MAKE THE REVOLUTION. THE MORE I MAKE THE REVOLUTION, THE MORE I MAKE LOVE.
- EVERY VIEW OF THINGS WHICH IS NOT STRANGE IS FALSE.
- AMNESTY—AN ACT THROUGH WHICH SOVEREIGNS FORGIVE THE INJUSTICES THEY HAVE COMMITTED.
- MANKIND WILL NOT LIVE FREE UNTIL THE LAST CAPITALIST HAS BEEN HANGED WITH THE ENTRAILS OF THE LAST BUREAUCRAT.
- PROFESSORS, YOU ARE OLD.

The Ecole des Beaux Arts (traditionally a fusty place, lacking in any spirit of political solidarity) went on strike on May 8, took physical control of the premises on May 14, and established its Atelier Populaire. Denouncing the domination of art education by corporate bodies like the Order of Architects, the students also called for an end to the sanctity of art and the fame or wealth accruing to the successful artist. Works of art should be anonymous, immediately responsive to life, and ephemeral. On May 21, the Atelier Populaire denounced the privileged status by which "bourgeois culture" isolated artists from other workers; the fetish of "artistic autonomy" was likewise exploited to wall off the artist in an ivory tower.

Rejecting electoral politics, class collaboration, and the tactics of the Communists, the Atelier Populaire urged artists to acquire first-hand experience of the workers' struggle in factories, workshops, and building sites. Marcel Cornu reported the key phrase cropping up in all discussions, *prise de conscience,* accompanied by a feverish desire to become the actor rather than the spectator of history.

Each morning during the May revolution a general assembly of the Ecole des Beaux Arts chose a few urgent themes from the many proposed. Designers worked on sketches that were submitted to general criticism. The silk-screen process enabled thousands of posters to be printed rapidly and cheaply, but overnight they became collectors' items with a commercial value. The Atelier Populaire responded indignantly: "The posters . . . are weapons in the service of the struggle and are an inseparable part of it. . . . To use them for decorative purposes, to display them in bourgeois places of culture, or to consider them as objects of asethetic interest is to impair both their function and their effect. . . . Even to keep them as historical evidence of a certain stage in the struggle is a betrayal. . . ."

- COMMODITIES ARE THE OPIUM OF THE PEOPLE
- RUN FORWARD, COMRADE, THE OLD WORLD IS BEHIND YOU
- THE GENERAL WILL AGAINST THE WILL OF THE GENERAL

The key weapon of the Beaux Arts posters was a grim humor based on subversive juxtapositions of familiar symbols: skulls in police helmets, barbed wire across the ORTF television screen, the same screen as the face of a traffic cop, de Gaulle as a robotic customs official, de Gaulle's profile as a workshop vise, Gaullist "participation" as a clamp screwing down the head of a worker, the press as a bottle of poison ("Do Not Swallow"), a road sign showing a microphone ("Attention! The Radio Lies"). This type of juxtaposition, called *détournement* by the Situationists and alienation by Brechtians, is, of course, the universal weapon of cartoonists.

Revolutionary wall newspapers appeared in the streets and markets and in the Métro, particularly at the Gobelins station in the 13th *arrondissement* and at Château Rouge in the 18th. Large, animated crowds gathered around them, exchanging views. Not only the official news was subverted but also, as Cohn-Bendit expressed it, "the threadbare explanations of the official party theorists who know everything, predict everything, and must needs organize everything." He shared the widespread belief that advanced capitalist society had developed unprecedented powers of manipulating consciousness to ensure uncritical acquiescence in the mindless, "value-free" cycle of production and consumption.

The high priests of this philosophy of spectacle and counter-spectacle were the American Yippies and the French Situationists. In 1966, a Situationist group, finding itself elected to a controlling position within the students' union of Strasbourg University, had promptly threatened to dissolve the union while cheerfully spending its funds on distributing 10,000 copies of a pamphlet called "Of Student Poverty...." Having disrupted the inaugural lecture of A. Moles, professor of psycho-sociology, the Situationists were evicted from office by court order, the judge complaining that the Situationist International was dedicated to "theft, abolition of work, total subversion, and a world-wide proletarian revolution with 'unlicensed pleasure' as its only goal . . . sinking to outright abuse of their fellow students, their teachers, God, religion, the clergy, and the governments and political systems of the world."

A Situationist text declared: "In the epoch of totalitarian control, capitalism has produced its own religion: the *spectacle*. . . . The world itself walks upside down. And like the 'critique of religion' in Marx's day, the critique of the spectacle is now the essential precondition [for the abolition of] . . . those pseudo-needs and false desires which the system manufactures daily in order to preserve its power. . . ." Henceforward the struggle must lie "in the banalities of everyday life, in the supermarket, and the beat club, *as well as* on the shopfloor. . . ." The main body of Situationist theory—which in notable respects runs parallel to Herbert Marcuse's—was contained in the twelve issues of *L'Internationale situationniste,* edited by Guy Debord, and in the writings of Debord and R. Vaneigem. According to Debord's *La Société du spectacle,* the "spectacle" had transcended its decorative function, becoming the heart and model of the system of production, constantly transmitting the message, "that which appears is good, that which is good appears." In short, total alienation.

Situationist theory also inherited from dada and surrealism the vision of a playful society in which individual self-expression would replace the solemn and false masks worn by those trapped in the productive process. Like the American Diggers and Yippies, the Situationists not only condemned all work, but ridiculed Trotskyists and Maoists for sinking into the "closed world of the sect," for constantly striving to re-enact an *a priori* scenario—a remake of 1917 without the errors. Held in reserve for this single, redemptive action, the "whole man" thus fell into a profound conservatism. Other "ridiculous dramas" lampooned by the Situationists included "the battle of the anaemic gods" like Louis Althusser, Roger Garaudy, and Claude Lévi-Strauss, each promoting his own theology. (The great structuralist was unimpressed by the events of May.) According to the Situationists, haphazard anarchism alone could foster a genuinely innovative state of mind and recover the precious gift of spontaneity.

The big show of spontaneity was at the Odéon Theatre, the home of Jean-Louis Barrault's Théâtre de France, which was expropriated by a cultural commando unit on May 15: "Since the National Assembly has become a bourgeois theatre, all bourgeois theatres should be transformed into national assemblies." Marxian paradoxes blossomed.

The French counterculture was more highly politicized (and less liberated) than the American: dropping out was despised, the slippery word "sacrament" was not in circulation, Zen mysticism was derided, and psychedelic acid trips were off the agenda. Anything that dulled the mind was regarded as counterrevolutionary. As a Situationist text aimed against the hippies explained: "The mass consumption of drugs is the expression of a real poverty and a protest against it; but it remains a false search for 'freedom' . . . a religious critique of a world that has no need for religion, least of all a new one."

Yet there was long hair to be seen at the Odéon and the Sorbonne, some hippie gear, and a few slogans suggestive of beatnik influences: "Cleanliness is the luxury of the poor, be dirty." At this juncture French students regarded American sexual liberation with some envy, and London was seen as the vanguard of libidinal release. Although obscene language was a less prominent feature of the New Left in Europe than in America, it did figure in the Situationists' semantic arsenal. In April the Vandals Committee of Public Safety in Bordeaux warned students that they would remain *"des cons impuissants"* (impotent cunts) until they had *"cassé la gueule à vos profs"* (beaten up your teachers) and *"enculés tous vos curés"* (buggered all your curates).

Daniel Singer described the occupied Odéon: "Almost all day and night anyone could stand up from his seat and declare what he pleased. As a nonstop happening, the show was unique. As a sign of people's urge for self-expression, it was interesting. . . ." Unplanned marathon discussions went on almost to daybreak. The student chairmen stood in the aisle yelling *"Silence! N'interrompez pas! Un peu d'ordre! Discipline!"* The climate was scrupulously democratic; even Gaullists and fascist spokesmen of the Occident movement were allowed a voice. Foreign visitors tended to mistake the eloquence for liberation, forgetting that the local tradition of diamond-bright rhetoric survives every regime. But this was a miraculous spring, and people talked day and night in the Odéon, the Sorbonne, the Censier, the Beaux Arts, the cafés, the institutes, the streets. A graduate student told Alfred Willener: "the important thing was to be able to express yourself. Foresight, practicality, etc., were quite secondary. Building the future, yes, but with words and for the sheer pleasure of it. This reminded me of the automatic writing practiced by the surrealists. Here, it was automatic speaking."

The Odéon was a permanent spectacle rather than a permanent revolution, and as such attracted its share of snobs, radical-chic fellow travelers, and *voyeurs.* Edgar Morin described the invasion of the university by the Old Left of St.-Germain-des-Prés: ". . . warm hearted, cuddling, visionary, humble, wishing at the same time to go on its knees before the student and to put him over its knees." Painters, actors, directors, and writers embarked on ritual discussions about art at the service of revolution and revolution at the service of art *(Je n'ai rien à dire, mais je veux le dire).*

The student assembly at the Odéon was generally quick to refuse a hearing to celebrities, but when Jean-Paul Sartre came to speak the theatre was so full that at first he could not reach the platform. Tiny and ugly, the lenses of his glasses thick as portholes, Sartre suggested that the vast audience should disperse into separate workshops; but they all wanted to hear Sartre. Interviewed for Radio Luxembourg on May 12, he had embraced the revolution: "These youngsters don't want the future of their fathers—our future—a future which has proved we were cowardly, worn out, weary, stupefied by total obedience. . . . Violence is the one thing that remains, whatever the regime, for the students. . . . The only relationship they can have to this university is to smash it." The message was distributed by leaflet in the Latin Quarter.

Sartre located the seedbed of the May events in Vietnam. "The fundamental impact of the war on European or American militants was its enlargement of the field of possibilities." On May 20, he debated in the great hall of the occupied Sorbonne with the inspirational spirits of the revolt, the incarnation of the historical force he had defined in the *Critique de la raison dialectique* as a "group-in-fusion"; those who "tried to devise liberty in action." (The crush was frightful, the corridors were jammed; 7,000 had crammed into the "ampi," built to house 4,000. "There were students sitting in the arms of Descartes and others on Richelieu's shoulders," recalled Simone de Beauvoir. Finally they got only Sartre of several invited writers into the hall, leaving his colleagues disgrunted at having waited for nothing. "I'm fed up with the star system," remarked Marguerite Duras.") Sartre utterly condemned the role of the Communist Party and the manipulative electoral politics of the Fourth and Fifth Republics. "When I vote," he wrote in *Les Temps modernes,* "I abdicate my power—that's to say the opportunity each person has of forming with everyone else a sovereign group which has no need of representatives. . . ." Sartre later concluded that the French youth of May 1968 had been unable to make a cultural revolution because they were incapable of making a real revolution, which he defined as "the seizure of power by violent class struggle." So long as the working class continued to support "the largest conservative party in France"—the PCF—no revolution would be feasible. On the other hand, added Sartre, "it is obvious that anarchism leads nowhere, today as yesterday."

Occupation fever gripped the intelligentsia. Radical doctors occupied the premises of the medical association, radical architects proclaimed the dissolution of their association, actors closed all the capital's theatres, writers led by Michel Butor occupied the Société des Gens de Lettres at the Hôtel de Massa. Even business executives got into the act, seizing for a while the building of Conseil National du Patronat Français, then moving on to the premises of the Confédération Générale des Cadres.

On May 18, the Cannes Film Festival ended abruptly a week early when several hundred filmmakers led by Jean-Luc Godard (who marched with the great Communist demonstration of May 29) and François Truffaut seized the festival hall in support of the national strike movement. There were fights in the hall and brawling on the stage, during which Godard was knocked down and an elaborate display of flowers crashed to the floor. Four members of the festival jury resigned in solidarity with the strikers.

Film workers responded to the events by convening their own Estates General of the French Cinema, which pooled all cinematographic resources and democratized filmmaking. Many productions were anonymous—no "cult of personality" was permitted. These "cinetracts," the equivalent of wall posters, were made quickly, designed for instant consumption, but generally to a high standard. The role of the working class in the strikes and demonstrations was recorded in such films as *Le Cheminot, Travailleurs émigrés,* and *Comité d'action.* In

Oser lutter, oser vaincre (Dare to Struggle, Dare to Conquer), Jean-Pierre Thou argued that the striking Renault factory at Flins had been betrayed by the unions in June. (The Communists hit back with compilations such as Paul Seban's *La CGT en Mai.*) The most gifted documentary filmmaker in France, Chris Marker—always clear, precise, objective, and witty—collaborated with Mario Marret to produce *A bientôt, j'espère,* a tribute to militant workers at Besançon.

The transformation was abrupt but short-lived. During the affluent mid-sixties, the French cinema had generally preferred a cool, laid-back glamour to the grimmer face of social conflict. Typical were Claude Lelouch's streamlined box-office hits, *Un homme et une femme* and *Vivre pour vivre.* Even Godard and Truffaut could not entirely avoid the demands of the pleasure principle. May '68 bred a new seriousness, as reflected in the *Cahiers du cinéma* (often marred by semiotic-structuralist jargon), and the films of Costa Gavras, a Greek-born Frenchman: *Z* (inspired by the Lambrakis scandal in Greece) and *L'Aveu* (based on Artur London's memoirs of the Stalinist trials in Czechoslovakia).

But France soon went back to work, abandoning itself to the romantic settings, lush women, sophisticated lovers, and pseudo-philosophical exchanges (Pascal rather than Marx) of Eric Rohmer's popular films, *Ma nuit chez Maud* (1969) and *Le Genou de Claire* (1970).

Among the revolution's detractors, Raymond Aron scoffed sourly at the writers' seizure of the Société des Gens de Lettres (Authors' Society) and the putsch staged by successful film directors at the Cannes Film Festival, both "typical of a certain kind of Paris intelligentsia which mixes 'Byzantism' with Castroism or Maoism." Jacques Ellul heaped elaborate contempt on modish postures and the cheap cult of the word "revolution," which had become "the daily fare of an affluent consumer society . . . just another timely topic of chatter" for the smart Parisian intelligentsia who liked to gossip about cultural revolution and Maoism along the Riviera. Ellul also savaged "Sigma Week" in Bordeaux: street theatre, underground films, *Marat-Sade,* music in motion, eroticism, excess—in his view a vain, pretentious imitation of the old carnival, the Mardi Gras, which recognized its simple purpose as entertainment and packed itself with genuine popular invention.

THE WORKERS

The strike wave began in western France. On May 14, workers at Sud-Aviation near Nantes occupied their factory. Renault followed, first at Cléon, then at Flins and Le Mans, then at Boulogne-Billancourt. At Cléon, in Seine Maritime, where Renault gear boxes were manufactured, two hundred young workers refused to leave the factory after their shift, locked the manager in his office, and stayed for the night.

On May 16, a few thousand students, led by Jacques Sauvageot and the Trotskyist Alain Krivine, marched to the Renault car factory at Boulogne-Billancourt, where 35,000 employees had stopped work. Traveling part of the way by Métro, they evaded the police waiting to intercept them on the Seine bridges, but found, on arrival, that the metal gates of the factory had been bolted by the Communist-dominated Confédération Générale des Travailleurs (CGT). A number of young workers standing on the roof shouted greetings, and a few came out of the gates to converse; small groups began a hesitant dialogue in the place Jules-Guesde. At the rear gate near the river, discussions took place through the iron railings.

The CGT's cautious and conservative posture mirrored that of German social democracy sixty years earlier, as described by Rosa Luxemburg in *The Mass Strike, the Political Party, and the Trade Unions.* With an estimated membership of 1.5 million, the CGT's strength was greatest in the traditional heavy industries: engineering, automobiles, aircraft, mines, railways, and docks. Narrowly dedicated to material demands—wages, hours of work, job security—the confederation had risked few political "adventures" since the 1950s. Outside the grimy Arras Mexei metallurgical works, the local CGT representative explained, "We keep apart from the students but we don't criticize one another. *On ne se mange pas le nez.*"

Second place among the union federations belonged to the Confédération Française Démocratique du Travail (CFDT), Roman Catholic in orgin, with 750,000 members. Its strongholds were in engineering and electronics, among technicians and salaried staff for whom the issue was alienation rather than exploitation. The third grouping, the Force Ouvrière, with 600,000 members and historically inclined toward the Socialist Party, generally displayed a friendlier disposition toward student activists than did the CGT.

Sit-in strikes spread through the engineering and chemical industries. Industrial Normandy closed down, as did the "red belt" of Paris and the Lyons region. On Saturday, May 18, the coal mines stopped production, while public transport in Paris and the major cities came to a halt. The national railways followed. Workers in the gas and electricity utilities took over their plants, but decided to maintain supplies to domestic consumers. Red flags hung from the tower of the huge shipyards of Penhoet at St.-Nazaire, which employed 10,000 workers and accounted for two-thirds of France's output. By the weekend of May 18–19, two million workers were on strike and 120 factories were occupied. It all amounted to a spontaneous chain reaction, unplanned and uncertain of its destination.

The postal service ceased. The prospect of a stoppage at the Bank of France and in the Central Savings Office precipitated a run on the banks, which had to limit withdrawals to 500 francs ($100). Drivers rushed to gasoline stations, which dried up. Garbage piled up in the streets. By Monday the 20th, none of the French cross-channel ferries was operating. At American Express offices tourists lined up for precious seats on sightseeing buses converted into evacuation coaches to Brussels, Geneva, and Barcelona.

The Citroën factory—whose work force included impoverished Portuguese, Spanish, North African, and Yugoslav migrant workers harassed by autocratic management, identification cards, and spot checks—produced the sleek Citroën DS, symbol of executive high tech. Student pickets were waiting outside the gates at 6 A.M. on May 20 when the shift arrived. Insecure and easily victimized, the foreign workers read the leaflets and hesitated under the gaze of the factory guards and foremen. Then young workers came marching from a nearby branch of the factory, already occupied, chanting, "Bercot [the owner] assassin!" Citroën joined the strike. On Tuesday the 21st, the textile mills came out, and the big Parisian department stores closed their doors.

A remarkable feature of the strike wave was the rapid involvement of skilled cadres and middle-class professionals. On May 17, the Orly Airport control tower and French Television (ORTF) both voted to come out. On May 20, the general assembly of ORTF demanded a forty-hour week, a lower retirement age, abrogation of the antistrike laws of 1963, a national minimum wage of 1,000 francs, and creation of enterprise committees. More important, the employees called for a radical revision of ORTF's structure and relationship to the government. The state television channel was confined to one news program a day, although hourly bulletins were maintained on state radio.

On May 22, teachers stopped work, although many heeded the call of their unions to go to school and keep in touch with their pupils. The stoppage extended even to the Atomic Energy Commissariat and several ministries, including Equipment and Social Affairs; civil servants in the Ministry of Finance paraded outside their office, chanting slogans. No general strike order was ever issued, and the unions had difficulty keeping pace with their members. By May 22, 9 million people were out. Nothing on this scale had occurred in France since the war.

"Threat of anarchy grows in France," announced the London *Times* on May 22. "Paris fears rats as garbage piles up in street." A correspondent reported: "Streets usually washed and swept almost round the clock are now filthy with litter. Crates of empty wine and soft drinks bottles and piles of refuse have overflowed from restaurants. . . ." On the doors and windows of the banks, office buildings, and shops the same sign was everywhere posted: *"Grève illimitée"* (Unlimited Strike). The workers of the Berliet enterprise, masters of the anagram, were inspired to alter the sign over the main door to *"Liberté."*

Three students from Nanterre produced a detailed, first-hand report on events at Nantes, which they euphorically entitled "An Entire Town Discovers Popular Power."

Militant students at Nantes had blazed a trail for those at Nanterre, first by dismantling sexual segregation, then by supporting the demands of the university's restaurant employees, and subsequently by invading the rector's office on February 14. The CRS were called in; their customary brutality only widened the base of the radical movement. Anarcho-Situationist students denounced American psychosociology. Teachers and students at Nantes University came out on strike in support of their colleagues at the Sorbonne as early as May 7. Even the conservative faculties—Law, Pharmacy, Medicine—supported the strike.

The Sud-Aviation factory at Bouguenais, west of Nantes, was the first to be occupied and acted as detonator to the general strike that followed throughout the Nantes region. The conflict at Sud-Aviation actually began before the student riots in Paris, when a demand for a reduction in working time without loss of salary was rejected. On May 14, the boss, Duvochel, was imprisoned in his office and forced to listen to revolutionary songs pouring from a loudspeaker outside his door. But the CGT leader, Georges Séguy, condemned such actions and Monsieur Duvochel's internment remained a divisive issue among the work force. Student delegations from the Faculty of Letters were not allowed inside the factory gates by distrustful CGT officials, so the link between workers and students was made at defense post no. 16, manned by workers belonging to Force Ouvrière.

The strike committee of the harbor of Nantes put forward its own demands, including no limitation on the right to strike, payment during the strike, more power for union delegates, creation of a works committee enjoying real power in the Port Authority, the democratic nationalization of the Merchant Marine, and equal leave and meals subsidies for officers and men. Striking seamen requisitioned all cargoes. This had never happened before.

The state electric power station in Chevire was also occupied on May 18. The 293 operatives elected a strike committee made up of delegates from each union, then cut the power supply to local industry, but maintained essential services. Everywhere the workers were keen to display their capacity to administer the means of production. The central strike committee in the ACB shift yards took over all aspects of administration, including the payment of wages and distribution of canned food. Having gone on strike, the transport workers established control of communications within the city, rationing gasoline, issuing coupons, and defending their roadblocks (set up on May 24) against the police. A battle took place with *gardes mobiles* who arrived from Nantes in an attempt to dismantle the barriers made of oil drums.

In Batignolles, a proletarian district of Nantes, the wives of the strikers had organized themselves into family associations, mainly concerned with food supplies. A supply committee elected from the striking factories contacted the local farmers and set up a distribution network to bypass the middlemen. Teams of workers and students helped pick the new potatoes. Prices were pegged to the cost of production; a litre of milk came down from 80 to 50 centimes, a kilo of potatoes from 70 to 12 centimes. The big dealers were obliged to close. Every morning the unionists checked the market prices, appealing by megaphone to the traders to remain honest. Free food coupons were distributed to those suffering hardship; children were automatically entitled to free coupons for milk and bread.

On Sunday, May 27, the central strike committee, which combined the unions of peasants, workers, and students, took the revolutionary step of installing itself in the town hall and assuming the powers of both the mayor and the prefect. The "people's republic" of Nantes lasted four days.

The strike came late to the port of Marseilles, the second largest city in France, but once it arrived it was embraced with enthusiasm. By May 21, 200,000 striking workers had brought 150 industrial concerns to a standstill. The port and naval shipyards were paralyzed—even the customs officers were on strike. The oil refineries were occupied, railway workers took over stations and goods depots, and the banks and postal services ceased to function. The police maintained a low profile, and there was no violence.

Ernest Mandel later listed examples of working-class militancy transcending the material demands to which the unions strove to limit the conflict. At the occupied CSF plant in Brest, workers produced walkie-talkies to assist the defense of the premises. At Caen, the strike committee forbade vehicles access to the town for twenty-four hours. In the Rhône-Poulenc factories, strikers established direct-exchange relations with farmers; they also discussed (but did not implement) an "active" strike—resuming production under cooperative management. At the Wonder batteries factory in St.-Ouen, the strike committee refused to admit CGT officials through the barricades. At the Rouen naval yards, the workers took under their protection young people who were threatened with arrest by the CRS for distributing revolutionary literature. Typesetters in Paris insisted on changes in headlines (*Le Figaro*) or refused to print a whole edition (*La Nation*). The student-worker-peasant liaison committee known as CLEOP organized convoys distributing food to occupied factories or selling it at cost (11 centimes for an egg, 80 centimes for a kilo of chicken). For Mandel, "the most eloquent case of all" was a form of silence: at the Atlantic yards, St.-Nazaire, workers occupied the plant for ten days while staunchly resisting union pressure to draw up a list of demands.

Inside the Renault factory at Boulogne-Billancourt, a large meeting of workers gathered each morning at 9 A.M. to discuss wage claims and working conditions. (But meetings were invariably dominated by the official CGT speakers on the platform. The worker on the floor had to get up and move conspicuously across the hall before he could make himself heard—if the chairman permitted.) Key demands were a minimum wage of 1,000 francs a month (a municipally subsidized apartment cost 300–400), a pension at sixty ("at present workers go straight from the factory to the cemetery"), payment during the period of the strike, and a forty-hour week ("we are the only country in Europe working a forty-eight-hour week"). Meetings ended with a recording of the "Internationale," but after that it was film shows, volleyball, and *pétanque* organized by the CGT.

12

FRANCE:
Agitators and Politicians

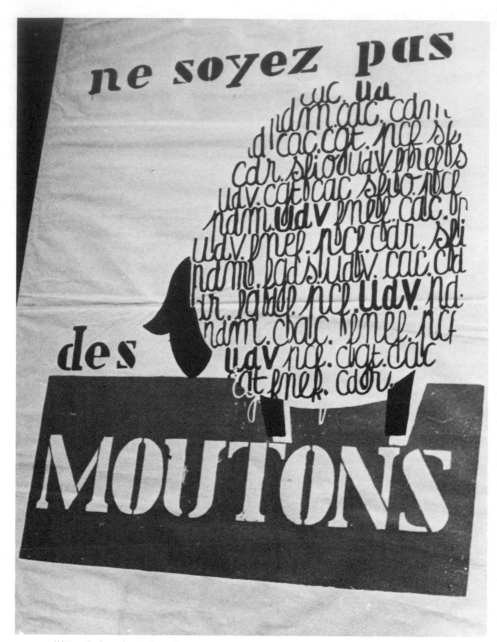

"'Don't be sheep'…Slogans covered Paris, hastily scribbled graffiti as well as highly professional posters from the Atelier Populaire…"

A KIND OF DELIRIUM

PARIS, May 22, 1968—The government survives a censure motion proposed by the Left in the National Assembly on its handling of the crisis. But the margin is narrow: eleven votes. That night the police block the passage of 5,000 students marching on the assembly to protest the order of banishment imposed two days earlier on Daniel Cohn-Bendit while he was outside France. In the Latin Quarter the cafés are jammed, collecting boxes for medical aid are passed around, and students in arm bands control traffic, clearing a path for the occasional car with *"Serrez, s'il vous plaît, camarades."*

Raymond Aron recalled: "In Paris at least, almost everyone was in the grip of a kind of delirium. The French people, and certainly the people of Paris, felt that the state had disappeared, that there was no more Government any more, and that once more anything was possible. Yet nothing serious happened."

The president addressed the nation on television on May 24. De Gaulle spoke of the need of "a mutation in our society . . . a more extensive participation of everyone in the conduct and result of the activities which directly concern them." He referred to "the crisis in the university . . . caused by the impotence of that great institution to adapt itself to the modern needs of the nation." This had "by contagion unleashed in many other places a tidal wave of disorders or of surrenders or of work stoppages." He therefore sought through a referendum a "mandate for renewal and adaptation."

The Conseil d'Etat (a constitutional watchdog) immediately ruled that the referendum would be unconstitutional.

The March 22 Movement and the action committees, having distributed pamphlets rejecting parliamentary solutions, negotiations which propped up capitalism, and referenda, organized five assembly points from which demonstrators could converge on the Gare de Lyon at 5 P.M. At 8 o'clock in the evening, the demonstration heard de Gaulle on transistor radios calling for a referendum. A column of 30,000 marched from the Gare de Lyon toward the place de la Bastille. Finding their passage blocked by police, they threw up barricades of paving stones, planks, and tree grilles. The police advanced under cover of a tear-gas bombardment. Police cordons protected the Hôtel de Ville, the Elysée Palace, and the ministries, but the Bourse (Stock Exchange) was undefended. A minority of demonstrators armed with axe handles, wooden clubs, and iron bars broke away from the main march, shouting, "Temple of Gold!" The Bourse was set on fire.

According to Daniel Cohn-Bendit, the night of the 24th "revealed a lack of political awareness among the masses and the narrowness of outlook of the different left-wing splinter groups." The invasion of the Bourse was the signal that the revolution had started "in earnest," but then the Trotskyist Jeunesse Communiste Révolutionnaire (JCR) lost its nerve and turned the demonstrators back toward the Latin Quarter, while UNEF and Parti Socialiste Unifié (PSU) cadres blocked the seizure of the Ministry of Finance and the Ministry of Justice. "As for us, we failed to realize how easy it would have been to sweep all these nobodies away. . . . It is now clear that if, on 25 May, Paris had woken to find the most important Ministries occupied, Gaullism would have caved in at once. . . ." And even if the ORTF in Paris was well guarded, "the authorities could not have defended or reoccupied the radio stations of Lille, Strasbourg, Nantes, Limoges, and elsewhere." (Despite the "we," Cohn-Bendit himself was in enforced exile on the night of the 24th.)

Later that night the fighting moved to the Latin Quarter. Plane trees showing their first spring leaves were axed down to reinforce barricades constructed out of uncollected garbage and overturned cars. During this ceremony no police were to be seen. However, the ritual dictated that once the barricades were up the police would emerge from their long, cratelike vans with thick wire netting over the windows "behind which," noted Stephen Spender, "they wait like mastiffs." The massed police phalanx advanced like "a thick wedge of mercury up a glass tube." Tear-gas shells that did not explode were hurled back, with a few homemade gasoline bombs. Yet an uncanny normality returned to the Latin Quarter during daytime. The cafés were crowded, people strolled along the pavements (including well-dressed *voyeurs*), and everything was lightly layered in dust from uncollected refuse.

In Bordeaux, normally a model of calm, 500 students had occupied the Grand Theatre on May 23. On Saturday, students attempting to storm the Hôtel de Ville were repulsed by the CRS using tear-gas grenades. This led to protracted violence and barricades in other parts of the city, notably the place Victor-Hugo, resulting in sixty-nine policemen and forty students injured. Finally, Gabriel Delaunay, prefect of Aquitaine, negotiated a "cease-fire"; of sixty-six persons arrested, thirty were students.

May 24 was the bloodiest night, with barricades not only in Paris but in Nantes, Bordeaux, Lyons, and several other cities. Widespread disturbances took place in Lyons on the nights of May 24 and 25, during which a police commissioner, René Lacroix, father of three, was mortally wounded by a truck driven by demonstrators, and twenty-nine other police were injured. In a style unique to France, the senior police officers' federation issued a statement that in any future society the most profound human aspiration would be "the peace so much demanded today." But the demonstrators wanted tomorrow's version of peace, not today's.

At Clermont-Ferrand, the CGT and the UNEF ended up marching separately after the Communists tried to ban placards demanding the return to France of Cohn-Bendit. During the night of the 25th, an attempt was made to set fire to the Palais de Justice in Rennes. At Brest, 20,000 marched to demand de Gaulle's resignation.

France's farmers mainly remained aloof from the unrest, or limited their demonstrations (as on May 24) to sectional claims.

PERMANENT REVOLUTION

Cohn-Bendit stressed that the March 22 Movement did not owe its ideology to any of the prestigious socialist philosophers, though the writings of Marx, Bakunin, and Sartre were familiar. To his knowledge none of the French militants had ever read Herbert Marcuse. What March 22 shared in common with other New Left movements was a general distrust of the state and government, a belief in "workers' control," a tendency to romanticize spontaneous action or "permanent revolution" as the pulsing heart of the future society, an aversion to entrenched leaders and blueprinted programs, and a mischievous sense of humor.

Implacably hostile to any version of state socialism, whether reformist or revolutionary, March 22's distrust of the Marxist factions, or *groupuscules,* was reminiscent of Bakunin's famous quarrel with Marx: how, Bakunin demanded, can a free society emerge from an authoritarian revolutionary movement? But the young French militants were not doctrinaire anarchists; there was no counterpart in France to the Spanish Anarchist Federation (FAI) and the anarcho-syndicalist trade unions (CNT) during the civil war. And if a number of commentators discerned in the May general strike a revival of pre-1914 revolutionary syndicalism, then it was an unconscious revival.

Cohn-Bendit agreed that "provocation"—which the old anarchists used to call "propaganda by deed"—was part of the armory. In his *Revolution in the Revolution* (1967), Régis Debray argued that the "small motor" of the guerrilla *foco* in Latin America would detonate the wider peasant insurrection. Debray anticipated the March 22 Movement's condemnation of Communist parties as betrayers of the struggle, but whereas Debray's model guerrilla band is unashamedly the vanguard elite of the revolution, March 22 rejected all such elites. According to Alain Geismar: "It has a number of 'leaders' in the sociological sense of the term, but no 'chiefs,' no executive, even less bureaucracy. Anyone in it can speak 'to the four winds'; the meeting does not vote, it sorts out a number of lines of force and any of the movement's militants can express them. A number of them are very well-known, because the press has put them in the headlines and the government stubbornly searches for scapegoats."

The boldest headlines belonged to Daniel Cohn-Bendit, who believed passionately in the revolutionary role of the working class—"No walk was too long to the factories"—and who measured socialist movements in terms of their "leftism." Thus "Marx was to the left of Proudhon and Bakunin to the left of Marx." After the Bolshevik Revolution, the center of integrity had shifted to the Workers' Opposition and the Ukrainian anarchists associated with Makhno, whom Trotsky and the Bolsheviks had reviled and crushed. Cohn-Bendit abhorred the repressive centralism of the Bolsheviks and quoted with reverence the libertarian manifesto issued by the Makhnovite army in the Ukraine, with its fierce opposition to state authority in any form.

On the night of May 10, leaving the university rectorate, and pressed by journalists determined to make him a leader and to challenge his right to be a leader, he said: "I am not mandated by anyone. I do not speak in the name of a movement. What I affirm is that I think what the mass of students think." On May 13 at the Champ-de-Mars he animated the general discussion among the groups, encouraging fresh thinking and the rejection of standardized Party slogans. His own slogan on that day was *"Occupons la Sorbonne"* (Let us occupy the Sorbonne).

On the extreme Left of French politics spun an exploding galaxy of doctrinaire sects, the *groupuscules*. The March 22 Movement encouraged freedom of initiative and insisted on action "here and now" within and against the university, whereas the Maoists and Trotskyists directed their gaze further afield. The Maoist Union des Jeunesses Communistes Marxistes-Leninistes (UJC-ML) had been launched when the Union des Etudiants Communistes (UEC) expelled six hundred members for pro-Peking factionalism in November 1966. Paradoxically, the UJC-ML was led by graduates of the elite Ecole Normale Supérieure, disciples of the dissident Communist philosopher Louis Althusser—hardly the prescription of Chairman Mao! Like the Maoists, the various Trotskyist factions believed in the necessity of the seizure of state power, a concept totally rejected by the libertarians of March 22. But in the heat of battle, as agitation at Nanterre led to the wider conflagration at the Sorbonne, the *groupuscules* learned to collaborate. Common enemies—the state, the university, the Communists, the parliamentary reformists—and the shared experience of violent repression brought the sects together through osmosis. So did the spirit of youth.

The Trotskyist JCR, led by Alain Krivine, a twenty-seven-year-old former history student who had been head of the Sorbonne-Lettres section of the Communist Student Union, was largely responsible for providing the student *service d'ordre,* whose duties included directing the traffic after the police withdrew from the Latin Quarter. The JCR "entered" the March 22 Movement, made contact with German radicals studying at Nanterre, and absorbed the crucial notion of youth as a vanguard (recently confirmed by Fidel Castro, no less, in *Les Temps modernes*). On the level of achievement, the JCR established a foothold in many of the 490 action committees that had mushroomed throughout the Paris region by the end of May. Wherever fighting occurred, the JCR were in the thick of it.

Yet there were serious frictions throughout the May events. A small Trotskyist faction, the Fédération des Etudiants Révolutionnaires (FER), had initially urged students to go home and wait until a massive demonstration of solidarity between workers and students could be organized. Later it advised its followers to steer clear of the debates at the Sorbonne, *"la kermesse* [village fair] *de Cohn-Bendit. "* The Maoists were obsessed by the need to prepare the masses ideologically (the masses were not yet ready in May 1968), recoiled from spontaneity, and stubbornly denounced the slogan "the Sorbonne for the students" as "petty bourgeois." The bitter diatribes against the "state power" sects unleashed by Cohn-Bendit after the events indicated the serious cracks beneath the surface unity.

The action committees of May–June regarded themselves as heirs to those formed in the forty-eight sections of Paris in 1790. During the French Revolution, the anarchist tendency had been overwhelmed by the centralizing Jacobin one (Cohn-Bendit and his friends called themselves *enragés* in tribute to Roux, Varlet, and the Left opposition of 1793), but the Commune of 1871 provided a more modern affirmation of revolutionary anarchism in practice—hence Trotsky's critique of its fatal lack of centralized direction. Geismar, embracing the new movement of *quartier* committees and factory committees, saw "no reason to 'cap' them in some way with union structures, which could only canalize this movement and restrict it." For their part, the Trotskyists of the JCR entertained their own vision of the action committees, as components of the transitional strategy of dual power, as soviets undermining the hegemony of the state and "raising class struggle to its highest and bitterest level" (to quote Ernest Mandel).

Daniel Cohn-Bendit, meanwhile, had become an "action committee in exile." Banished from France while abroad, Dany (as he was affectionately known) predicted in Amsterdam that he would return; the student council of the Free University of Strasbourg promised to seize the Kehl Bridge for the purpose. On May 24, hundreds of French riot police were waiting at the Forbach frontier as Cohn-Bendit arrived at the head of a thousand comrades, including Karl-Dietrich Wolff, leader of the SDS. The French subprefect duly served Cohn-Bendit with the expulsion order signed by Minister of the Interior Fouchet. In London, fighting broke out when a thousand radicals, including anarchists, marched on the French embassy in protest.

Cohn-Bendit complained that the press falsely made him into a "leader," yet his cheeky return to Paris in defiance of the banning order on May 29 (conveyed in a student volunteer ambulance with blackened windows and flashing lights) was immediately followed by a personal press conference in the Sorbonne during which he hinted that the revolution had betrayed him by sliding into a bureaucratic evasion of the required violence. His comrades of the original Nanterre pressure group promptly gave a rival press conference to denounce the "cult of personality."

By the last week of May, at least four hundred action committees had been formed in Paris alone. The issue of *Action* dated June 5 reflected the dilemma confronting the libertarian March 22 Movement. Spontaneity was still endorsed, but decisions had to be made and the working class was accustomed to advance its demands through large organizations. The population hesitated, uncertain of the horizons beyond the barricades, and Cohn-Bendit concluded that "the majority were not yet ready to run their own affairs. The most frequent question asked was 'What is going to happen?' and not 'What are we going to do?' "

But what were they going to do?

Cohn-Bendit was sceptical of an "overnight revolution." In his view the main task was to demolish "the myth that you can do nothing against the regime" and to open up a new field of possibilities by direct, escalating action. Sartre concurred. He congratulated the young: "Your movement is interesting because it puts imagination in power. . . . Something which astonishes, something which jolts, something which repudiates all that has made our society what it is today, has come out of your movement."

The problem was twofold: what kind of revolution, leading to what kind of socialism. The libertarians wanted *auto-gestion,* which meant the replacement of centralized political and union structures by factory and district *(quartier)* committees. Geismar called it the recovery of power by the producers at the point of production. (He rejected representative democracy and delegated power; the future class struggle could not be conducted in parliament.) He and Cohn-Bendit agreed that foreign models provided no guidance for an advanced society like France's. The latter's vision was of "a federation of workers' councils, soviets, a classless society where the social division of labor between manual and intellectual workers no longer exists. . . . As to the precise forms of organization, they cannot be defined. . . . The longer the strike continues, the greater the number of factories that have to be got going again. Finally the strikers will find themselves running the entire country."

But by what means? Anarchist ideology balks at this question like a frisky horse at a hedge of thorns. Saint-Simon had, famously, predicted the replacement of "the government of people" by "the administration of things." But how? And the Marxists ask: How do you suppress counterrevolution without resorting to state power?

POLITICAL MANEUVRES

On Saturday, May 24, at 3:00 P.M., representatives of the government, the unions, and the employers met in the Hôtel du Châtelet on the rue de Grenelle. The economic life of the country was virtually at a standstill with 9 or 10 million people involved in the work stoppage. The older generation remembered the Matignon agreements signed under the impact of the great strike wave that struck France in 1936 during the "crisis of expectations" detonated by the victory of Léon Blum's Popular Front coalition (which included the Communists). Benoît Frachon, of the Communist CGT, took part in both negotiations: capitalism had survived in 1936 and now, thirty-two years later, Frachon and the current CGT leader, Georges Séguy, would make sure it survived again.

After twenty-five hours of talks in the rue de Grenelle, Pompidou read out the terms of the agreement to the nation at breakfast time on Monday the 27th. The guaranteed industrial minimum wage was raised by 35 percent, affecting a million and a half industrial workers and some 500,000 in agriculture. There was also an all-around wage increase of 10 percent and a progressive reduction of the work week to forty hours. But what of participation, of workers' power? The package merely mentioned the outline of a potential accord on new trade-union rights within the firm.

The union bosses—Georges Séguy, Eugène Descamps of the CFDT, and André Bergeron of Force Ouvrière—emerged from the conference room smiling, thumbs up. Séguy drove straight to Renault at Boulogne-Billancourt, the heartland of the CGT's industrial constituency, brimming with confidence: "This is what we have snatched from them, after extreme difficulty, difficult talks. . . ." Booing started when he admitted that only half-pay for the duration of the strike would be granted; anger mounted, and Séguy left to a storm of whistles and catcalls. At Renault-Cléon the reaction was identical; at Orléans and Le Mans, even stiffer. A resounding no came from Citroën-Berliet, Sud-Aviation at Nantes, and Rhodiaceta at Lyons-Vaise. At Caen the unions blocked all the roads into the town. Almost everywhere the same story: No!

Opportunistic as ever, the parliamentary parties of the Left now maneuvred to divert the libertarian tide of youth into a patched-up coalition reminiscent of the Fourth Republic, which had perished with de Gaulle's assumption of power in 1958. François Mitterrand, the defeated presidential candidate of the Left in 1965, now proposed to replace de Gaulle and to appoint Pierre Mendès-France as caretaker prime minister of a broad-based coalition government extending from the Communists to the center—in short, dump the constitution. When the left-wing PSU and the CFDT unions staged a rally on May 27 in the university stadium at Charléty, euphoria swept through the ranks of the young idealists as the charismatic CFDT leader André Barjonet declared, "Today, revolution is possible." Revolution without revolution; it was the same pull as that exercised by Eugene McCarthy and Robert Kennedy in America. (At that moment Kennedy was a week short of death.) Cohn-Bendit, who regarded the gathering at Charléty with contempt, described Mendès-France as "the left-wing de Gaulle. . . . He is the man who appears to be above parties, above the mêlée."

The Communists, though boycotting the Charléty meeting, entertained ambitions of their own. The bright yellow Party posters which were plastered up every night now called for a Government of the People—but not for a general election. This was a time of extreme disarray and anxiety for the Gaullists; Raymond Aron tremulously wondered "if a regime which was based on one man's magic was going to collapse the moment that magic vanished." On May 29, the CGT marched under its enormous red and yellow banners, half a million workers on parade, sector by industrial sector. Discipline was total, and there were no incidents.

Just before 10 A.M. on May 29, ministers arriving at the Elysée learned that the scheduled council meeting was cancelled. In mid-morning de Gaulle and his wife left the Elysée by car. Their destination was given as Colombey-les-Deux-Eglises, the president's country home, but the president had vanished and the capital was in a fever of speculation. In fact, he had flown from the heliport at Issy-les-Moulineaux to a military airfield at Saint-Dizier, halfway to the Rhine, and from there to Baden-Baden, where he conferred with his top generals, including Jacques Massu, the commander of 70,000 French troops in Germany. De Gaulle returned to Paris assured of the military support he needed if it came to the crunch.

On May 30, de Gaulle reappeared on the nation's television screens at 4:30 P.M. The referendum was abandoned; he now intended to call elections within forty days. The National Assembly was promptly dissolved, and Pompidou was instructed to form a new cabinet. De Gaulle called on the French people—*"françaises et français"*—to undertake "civic action" against subversion and the threat of "totalitarian Communism." He also promised tough measures if "the whole French people were gagged or prevented from leading a normal existence, by those same elements that are being used to prevent the students from studying, the workers from working—that is to say by intimidation, intoxication, and tyranny organized by well-trained conspiracy within, and by a party which is the extension of a totalitarian enterprise." If this continued unchecked, he would not hesitate to resort to "other ways than an immediate vote." He offered his own model of "participation" and profit-sharing within the enterprise: "Discussion in common, followed by the action of one man by himself. This will be the character of participation as of all other sorts of behavior."

Mitterrand and Mendès-France were caught with their proposed Provisional/Popular Government of Public Safety at half mast. The Left leaders denounced the president's speech as "a call to civil war," with Mitterrand embellishing in fine style: de Gaulle's was "the voice of 18th Brumaire [1799] . . . the voice of 2nd December [1851] . . . the voice of 13th May [1958]." But the Parliamentary Left would now regret its attempt to steal into office in the shadow of barricades erected and defended by others.

The general had at last shown his mettle, and the great patriotic nation took courage, emerging from four weeks of humiliating paralysis into a vast *manifestation.* They marched up the Champs-Elysées as the sun sank behind the Arc de Triomphe, a forest of *tricolores* and arms raised in the Gaullist *V*-salute. Their cars sounded their horns to the famous rhythm of *"Algérie française!,"* while well-dressed people chanted "France back to work! Clean out the Sorbonne! We are the majority! . . ." There was also the notorious chant of "Cohn-Bendit to Dachau!" (to which the student demonstration of June 1 replied, "We are all German Jews!"). Stephen Spender witnessed "the triumphant bacchanal of the Social World of Conspicuous Consumption, shameless, crowing, and more vulgar than any crowd I have seen on Broadway or in Chicago."

CRS vans crossing the boulevards were cheered, *"La police avec nous!"* In the central courtyard of the Paris police school the cops had clustered around the radios to hear de Gaulle's broadcast. Exhausted and seething with discontent, at last they had something to smile about.

The CRS were swiftly dispatched to remove strike pickets from the oil refineries, gasoline stations were resupplied, and Parisians lined up to fill their tanks, then set out in hundreds of thousands for a three-day Pentecost holiday, creating traffic jams worthy of Jean-Luc Godard's film *Weekend.* The students were left behind in Paris to demonstrate once again, without the Communists. Circling around the Left Bank from Montparnasse, the column chanted: "Student-worker solidarity! Down with the bosses' state! Elections are treason! It's only a beginning!" Reaching the Austerlitz station, the students shouted to the railway pickets, "The strikes continue. Don't sign!" Workers returned their greetings with the clenched-fist salute, joined in singing the "Internationale"—and signed the improved terms offered by the government.

WHY DID IT HAPPEN?

Charles de Gaulle had been executive president of France for a decade. The Fifth Republic had brought unprecedented political stability. National production had risen by 63 percent, foreign trade had tripled despite the shift from colonial markets to the more competitive ones of the EEC. Gold and foreign reserves had never been higher, nor had France's international prestige. Inflation had been contained. By May 1968, two-thirds of French households owned a refrigerator, 60 percent a TV set. In the field of foreign affairs, the granting of independence to Algeria in 1962 had disposed of the last, major divisive issue. Gaullism offered the most stable regime for a century. There was no hint of what was to come. A report published in May 1967, based on a questionnaire sent to 280,000 young people aged between fifteen and twenty-four, showed a prudent, materialistic, "bourgeois" generation pursuing professional success and economizing to buy a car or to put together a trousseau. Despite an informed interest in current affairs, there was no desire for personal political involvement; indeed, 72 percent of the young thought that the present voting age of twenty-one should not be lowered.

With the wisdom of hindsight, historians have discovered ominous signs of student and working-class discontent in 1967, which no one took seriously at the time. In February 1967, the Rhodiaceta works at Besançon had been occupied in libertarian style; workers' *jacqueries* had broken out in Caen, Mulhouse, Redon, and Le Mans—yet each remained isolated and containable.

Among the most interesting analyses of the events was Alain Touraine's *Le Mouvement de Mai*. Touraine diagnosed the source of the crisis in the mutation from the old bourgeois order to the new technological society, which split the middle class and put nontechnical professionals in much the same position as skilled labor during early industrial capitalism. According to Touraine, May '68 was essentially a "cultural revolt" by the professionals, broadened by the French historical tradition of incorporating the proletariat in any "left" movement. Universities had become society's "higher nervous system"; the chain breaks where the links are weakest, where expertise and functional skills clash with relevance, humanism, and meaning.

The students' boldness appealed most deeply to the younger workers, those under thirty, not yet conditioned to the mutilating life, to *"la petite vie,"* and to young people exiled from the world of work, the *"blousons noirs, jeunes déclassés."* As Claude Lefort observed, what triggered the workers' revolt was not economic grievances, but the sudden realization that traditional power structures could, with boldness, be challenged. "In an instant one discovers that the claimed necessity of obedience is based on a relationship of force and that this relationship can be overthrown."

But in favor of what? Touraine argued that what the workers wanted was piecemeal structural reform of the kind demanded by the CFDT, whereas genuine workers' control sounded not merely unattainable but unimaginable. What was it? The March 22 Movement issued its own tentative formula for "self-management in the enterprise," but the phrases were vague and vaporous: ". . . power of the worker at the level of his work (opposition to technocracy) . . . break hierarchical clustering into cadres, and separation of technical, economic and financial functions." That was all very well (if one understood the jargon), but could you eat or drink it?

A REVOLUTION BETRAYED?

The student Left believed, passionately, that the Communist Party betrayed "the revolution." The Communists angrily denied that any such revolution existed. Georges Séguy denounced those—"most of them renegades"—who dared to insult the PCF by alleging it let the hour of revolution pass. On May 21, Séguy informed a press conference that "self-management is a hollow formula: what the workers really want is immediate satisfaction of their claims." The CGT's "highly responsible militants" were not in the habit of mistaking their desires for reality. "No, the ten million strikers did not seek power; all they wanted was better conditions of life and work." The economist André Barjonet, by contrast, resigned his post as secretary of the CGT's research unit on May 23, in protest against the Party's blinkered perspective on social change and Séguy's refusal to harness the strike movement to political change. There is no doubt that the Communist CGT discouraged fraternization between students and striking workers. As André Gorz wrote at the time, what the situation required was a strategy of "revolutionary reform," a series of advances irreversibly shifting the balance of power in favor of the workers. But the PCF, like Pietro Nenni in Italy, behaved as if the state machine was a neutral instrument that could be used by an elected working-class party to achieve the passage to socialism.

A partial apologia for the Communist line was offered by the British historian Eric Hobsbawm: having delivered an initial (May '68) salute to the students "in spite of the feet-dragging of the unions and party," Hobsbawm later insisted that the PCF had been correct not to advocate insurrection, because the May crisis was "not a classical revolutionary situation," and "the forces of revolution were weak, except in holding the initiative." Therefore "the best chance of overthrowing Gaullism" was "to let it beat itself." Hobsbawm assumed that the PCF *wanted* a revolution and was part of "the forces of revolution," but this is incorrect. The PCF and CGT were determined to keep the young militants at arm's length from the striking workers because workers' control was incompatible with the Party's reformist-statist program; the PCF feared that student "Castroism" would undermine its own grip on the working class while alienating the skilled cadres and technicians. Capitalism had long since become for the PCF a rather comfortable opponent; indeed, the Communist Party was profoundly Gaullist, devoted to "order," to authority, to transmitting commands from above, to the cult of personality, to channeling popular aspirations into tidy "agreements" (or "victories").

The Communist philosopher Louis Althusser, author of the globally influential *Lire le capital* and *Pour Marx,* was ill during the May events, but he later surfaced with an analysis in which history was smothered by theory. "The PCF presented things in their real order: the primacy of the general strike over the student actions." Althusser agreed that the student revolt came first, and indeed served as a detonator, yet Marxism-Leninism identified the proletariat as the sole revolutionary force, when it got itself into a revolutionary state of mind. Failing that, said Althusser, it was banal to blame the PCF or the CGT for the refusal to embark on an "adventure." However, "a real advance" had been made: "And, *above all,* the working class now had etched in its memory (and this is a definitive inscription) the knowledge that the bosses, the Government and the state apparatus had been thrown into stark fear overnight . . . and that action, one day, would lead to something that the working class had heard spoken of—since the Paris Commune, since 1917 in Russia and since 1949 in China: the *Proletarian Revolution.* "

Althusser's "one day," like Hobsbawm's "let [Gaullism] beat itself," reflected the impact of lifelong membership in the Communist movement on political philosophy. As André Glucksmann's *Strategy and Revolution in France* pointed out, the USSR feared that a revolution sparked by generational conflict and fired by democratic aspirations in Paris could spread east as well as west (*vide* Poland, Czechoslovakia, Yugoslavia), hence the essential congruity of interests between the Kremlin and the Elysée. Diamond-bright as was Glucksmann's analysis, it also embodied a central weakness in French political philosophy: the passion for abstraction. The only human beings mentioned by name (apart from de Gaulle) were Marx, Engels, Lenin, and other master thinkers long dead. None of the creatures of flesh and blood who populated the drama of May–June gained admission to Glucksmann's text, except on a single occasion in a single phrase taken from Nanterre: *"Tout le monde est Cohn-Bendit. "*

THE END

By June 5, the strike was drawing to an end on the railways, in the post office, in gas and electricity, and in the coal mines. France now experienced a resumption of "normality." Pockets of working-class resistance became the targets of severe repression. The situation in the auto industry remained particularly tense. Before dawn on June 7, riot police expelled strike pickets from the Renault works at Flins, where 11,000 workers were employed in an isolated, predominantly rural area west of Paris. Support and solidarity committees managed to reach Flins to reinforce strike pickets and get supplies through to the 260 militants occupying the enterprise. In a military-style operation, some thirty light-armored cars and half-tracks drove to the factory gates, smashing through the barriers, with the CRS following close behind. The pickets were driven out at gunpoint. For the next three days, young students and workers sustained a running battle with the CRS in the surrounding fields and woods.

Violence broke out at the Citroën plant southwest of Paris, where 4,000 workers reported for work, but were blocked by strike pickets and subjected to a hail of stones and water from fire hydrants. At the Michelin works at Clermont-Ferrand, pickets prevented nonstrikers from entering the shops. In St.-Nazaire, militant workers fought with security forces. At Peugeot's Sochaux works, pickets were expelled by police on June 8. On June 10, 95 percent of the labor force returned to work, but later that day production ground to a standstill and the factory was once again occupied. When gendarmes and the CRS launched an attack, workers retaliated with bolts and whatever weapons were to hand. The police opened fire; two workers were killed and several were wounded during a battle that lasted thirty-six hours. Not until June 17 did 60,000 Renault workers throughout France vote to return to work.

The PCF, desperately anxious to prove its law-and-order credentials before the coming general election, demanded the suppression of the action committees responsible for sustaining the guerrilla warfare in the striking factories: "These squads, trained in para-military fashion, act visibly as agents of the worst enemies of the working class—employers, government, police." Georges Séguy complained of "a strange complacency on the part of the authorities," toward "a specialist in provocation" like the SNESup leader Alain Geismar, implying that the government hoped to discredit the Left by associating it with continuing disorder.

The government, however, banned all streets demonstrations and, on June 13, outlawed eleven student groups (but not the right-wing Occident). More than 150 foreign student activists were expelled from France, including Schofield Corryell, who had taken part in the occupation of the Sorbonne as leader of a group of American draft resisters and army deserters. Séguy and the PCF congratulated themselves publicly on having forced the government "to remove the troublemakers on the eve of the elections." Public opinion, Séguy explained, "has come to look upon the CGT as a great force for peace and order." The general secretary of the PCF, Waldeck Rochet, pledged that the Communists would fight "the lack of national feeling that certain anarchist elements vaunt as a sign of their revolutionary ardor." "The colors of France" must be restored to the working class.

One by one the university faculties were recaptured. On June 12, the UNEF staged its last street protest. Two days later, the police expelled the students first from the Odéon and then, on the 16th, from the Sorbonne itself. Simone de Beauvoir had paid her last visit to the occupied Sorbonne on the 10th; the sociologist Georges Lapassade told her, "Terrible things are happening here." The cellars were teeming with rats; lice were everywhere; at night the buildings filled with hippies, whores, tramps, and drug pushers. The amphitheatres stank of hashish and pot. Mercenaries known as the Katangais had been allowed in, ostensibly to repulse potential attacks from Occident, but they were a law unto themselves. When the end came on June 16, a crowd which gathered in protest was dispersed with the usual mixture of truncheons and tear-gas grenades. The red and black flags over the main entrance were torn down. The Ecole des Beaux Arts did not "fall" until June 27.

The striking radio and television workers of ORTF—13,000 technicians, producers, and journalists—held out longest. Wages were not the issue at ORTF. The strikers' consistent demand was for more objective programs and less government interference in the fields of news and current affairs; and for a statute and an elected commission to guarantee ORTF's independence. But Information Minister Yves Guéna would not yield a centimeter. The technicians gave up toward the end of June, the journalists on July 12. By the end of the month, fifty-seven TV and radio journalists had been fired, thirty had been offered the option of jobs in the provinces or abroad, fifteen had been granted "early retirement." Among those dismissed were Emmanuel de la Taille, the leading economics reporter, and François de Closets, the outstanding expert on science and technology; both had acted as spokesmen for the strikers. On July 31, the new secretary of state for information announced reform of the ORTF, including abolition of the notorious Interministerial Liaison Service for Information. The government now promised to explain its policies by means of separate broadcasts, rather than by playing Big Brother on news bulletins.

The outcome of the general election was a sweeping victory for the Gaullists, whose campaign was masterminded by Georges Pompidou. To appease the extreme Right, General Raoul Salan and Colonel Antoine Argoud, champions of *Algérie française,* were released from prison. The same Old Left faces appeared on TV: the cynical Socialist veteran, Guy Mollet, the imperious François Mitterrand, the disenchanted Pierre Mendès-France. The Communists fixed their sights on symbolic enemies: personal rule, high finance, the "two hundred families," leftist adventurism, the danger of fascism. The Party presented itself as the true guardian of patriotism and social stability, but de Gaulle himself was master of that terrain.

The swing in the popular vote, compared to March 1967, was not dramatic—a mere 3 percent—but the two-ballot electoral system* enabled the Gaullists and their allies, Giscard d'Estaing's Independent Republicans, to squeeze the soft center and hand out a crushing parliamentary defeat to the Left: the Federation of the Left slumped from 118 seats to 57; the PCF from 73 to 34; the PSU (the party closest in spirit to the May events) from 3 to 0. The Gaullists leapt from 197 to 294; the Independent Republicans from 43 to 64. The Gaullists captured 60 percent of the National Assembly on the strength of 43 percent of the vote, but it was a famous victory, greater even than that of 1962. The ascendancy of Gaullism was further confirmed in 1969 by Pompidou's election as president following de Gaulle's sudden retirement. The Right was destined to govern France for thirteen years after the insurrection of May 1968.

CONCLUSION

France had come out on general strike by national reflex. French history and political culture endorsed a recurring scenario during which— but only during which—workers and intellectuals assumed the role of heirs and custodians of an "alternative" France. It was a validated ceremony with a hint of carnival, a reflexive eruption of "refusal" with antecedents in 1936, 1871, 1848, 1830, and 1789. But this occasion was a more cathartic ceremony than ever before. The strikers of May 1968 were playing Republicans against Kings on a historical board game that is not available, for example, in the British or German cultures, and still less in the American.

The Gaullist regime enjoyed the support of the army and security forces, while the working class was dominated by trade unions hostile to libertarian socialism. Yet by the last week of May, the country was paralyzed and the regime was thrown into a profound crisis of self-confidence. Let us imagine that the strike wave had been allowed to continue—had been actively encouraged and coordinated by the unions—and that provincial disorders had gathered momentum. Let us imagine that the action committees and workers' councils had carried the mass of workers beyond mere wage demands. Could the govern-

*The parliamentary system of the Fifth Republic was based on single-member constituencies. But where no candidate obtained an absolute majority of the votes cast in the first ballot, a rerun was held two weeks later, with electoral pacts normally reducing the field to two candidates.

ment have survived? Could de Gaulle have re-enacted the massacre of 1871? Could he have turned Paris into "Budapest 1956"? On May 30, he made his threats, but it was the trade-union leaders and the PCF who got him off the hook by driving the strikers back to work and swimming frantically into familiar electoral waters like sharks offered a rotting carcass. The hook changed mouths.

The national *langue* yielded to the international *langage,* the "infernal cycle" of production and consumption.

13

FILMS, SEX,
AND WOMEN'S LIBERATION

"No two American artists could have had less in common than Ginsberg and Warhol…"

"The women's movement was both a product and a repudiation of male-dominated radicalism in the late sixties."

GODARD: RADICAL POSITIONS, RADICAL POSES

The insurrections of 1968, not least the events in France, attracted—and indeed generated—the radical chic, the "Riviera revolutionaries" whom Jacques Ellul castigated: the *voyeurs* in the occupied Odéon, those who bought up the posters of the Atelier Populaire or boldly mingled with the *enragés* in the courtyard of the Sorbonne, the elegant people in leather who dined out on a whiff of tear gas in the Boul' Mich'. Radical chic was an international phenomenon; its smooth rails ran from the Ile Saint-Louis and the Crazy Horse in Paris through Chelsea and South Kensington to Max's Kansas City restaurant and the *New York Review of Books*. In the splendid apartments and penthouses overlooking Central Park, hostesses lavished "hellos!" on radical intellectuals and playwrights, on Jules Feiffer, Robert Lowell, Norman Mailer, Jean Genet, and Jean-Luc Godard. Radical chic was a form of moral tax deduction.

Godard, brawling at the Cannes and London film festivals, seemed to incarnate the spirit of 1968. Susan Sontag, writing in February, had called him "indisputably the most influential director of his generation. . . ." Godard, she said, had "destroyed" the rules of film technique on a scale to be compared with Schönberg's repudiation of tonal conventions in music or the cubist challenge to three-dimensional pictorial space. He had boldly introduced "alien elements" into film, including "abstract ideas." Story lines were often subverted by jump cuts, motives were left unexplained, and characters were inclined to embark on long, literary monologues direct-to-camera, as if transposed from a fictional story into a documentary. Brecht's influence on Godard was a powerful one. Like Brecht, also, Godard found inspiration in American B-movie melodrama, the world of gangsters and spies.

Godard played with ideas like toys. A toy for the child is a thing in itself, blotting out the surrounding world. A monologue from Saint-Just (in *Weekend*) or from Mao (in *La Chinoise*) would suddenly intrude as an obsessive distraction until it was equally abruptly discarded, like a toy, for another.

Radical politics loomed large in Godard's films, but where did he stand? A good artist, of course, is not obliged to "stand" anywhere. Susan Sontag suggested that Godard's basic allegiance was to "that other cultural revolution, ours, which enjoins the artist thinker to maintain a multiplicity of points of view on any material." But Bertolt Brecht's use of alienation techniques had rarely obscured the mature artist's own point of view; Godard was a brilliant boy wearing the urbane sophistication of a Parisian intellectual.

His films played off fundamental moral questions against the slick backdrop of urban life in the consumer society: fast cars, chic apartments, airports, pinball machines, fashion magazines, cafés, freeways, beautiful people. He also played off radical politics against the glamour of journalism, conspiratorial guerrilla groups, and beautiful people again. Sontag spoke of his "ambivalent immersion in the allure of pop imagery and his only partly ironic display of the symbolic currency of urban capitalism"; but her penetrating analysis avoided a harsher point: Godard himself was an eclectic consumer of whatever shone brightly in the world about him, with a gift for veneering his own naïveté in shock-tactic sophistication. Thus, in *Made in USA* (1967) a narrator remarks: "Already fiction carries away reality . . . already I seem to be plunged into a film by Walt Disney, but played by Humphrey Bogart— and therefore a political film." This is radical chic.

During the period immediately preceding the May 1968 insurrection in Paris, Godard became fascinated by the Marxist-structuralist ideological jargon of the *groupuscules.* To quote again from *Made in USA,* "The idea of a permanent revolution is only valid if the diversity and the determination of the teams of political economists allow them to overcome the uncertainties of the conjuncture." The clogged jargon persisted into *La Chinoise* (filmed a year before the May events), in which Godard further developed his distinctive expressionist style of abrupt transitions, staccato shots, and changes in pace and rhythm. Six characters form a Maoist cell in a borrowed bourgeois apartment, which they fill with Little Red Books and slogans conceived by Kirilov, a paranoid Russian painter: "Reaction + revision + police = Yankees." Or: "A minority with the correct revolutionary line is no longer a minority." "La Chinoise" herself is Véronique, a student at Nanterre, the Maoist daughter of a provincial banker. Godard pins his characters against the wall, forcing them to recite their lives in monologues and lecture each other on the perils of revisionism and Brezhnev's bourgeois line.

It was in *Weekend* that Godard came closest to a genuine film allegory of contemporary bourgeois society. A married couple set out for a weekend drive to visit her mother, casually deciding on the way to kill the old lady for her money. En route they encounter traffic jams, blazing cars, the frustration of bourgeois trying to escape from the city into the countryside, and attacks by cannibalistic guerrillas. The young technocrats display indifference to the scenes of carnage, in which the throats of human mothers and pigs alike are casually slit on camera. Bursts of savagery alternate with long-held shots during which dogmatists of the Front de Libération de la Seine-et-Oise quote Saint-Just and expound on Vietnam or the role of the Left. Their bestial violence, however, was entirely unprophetic of the libertarian Left's behavior in May 1968. Godard was feasting the appetite of urbane audiences for political *frisson.*

One Plus One, co-starring the Rolling Stones and Black Power leader Frankie Y, brought Godard storming onto the stage of the National Film Theatre in London on December 1, 1968. Complaining that his film had been mangled by the Canadian producer, Godard exhorted the audience to demand its money back and send it to the Eldridge Cleaver defense fund, or be condemned as "bourgeois fascists." Godard then punched the producer on the jaw.

Godard pursued ultraradicalism as other men chase skirts,* but he was not averse to merging the two. In *One Plus One,* a beautiful young woman in a long white dress is followed through woods by an interviewer, cameraman, and sound technician. She is asked a long list of questions about culture, sex, revolution, and politics, to each of which she answers, almost at random, yes or no—usually yes. Meanwhile, in a junkyard on the banks of the Thames, Black Power men bloodily execute three kidnapped white girls. This gratuitous sadism, reminiscent of *Weekend,* is again rendered respectable by torrents of rhetoric or by pseudojournalism, as when two chic black chicks interview the insipid Frankie Y. More random "meanwhiles" follow: in a Soho porn shop a young man in a purple suit reads *Mein Kampf* while customers slap the faces of two pro-Vietcong student "prisoners" and deliver Nazi salutes.

One radical-chic dimension of the era was conveyed in the March 26, 1969 issue of *Variety:* "Jean-Luc Godard, German student activist Daniel Cohn-Bendit, and rebel producer Gianni Barcelloni have picked

---

*The sceptical view of Godard's politics in this chapter would be widely challenged, as by Gerald Rabkin, who writes: "I think you underestimate the creativity and importance of Godard's work, particularly from *Breathless* to *La Chinoise* . . . [and] how it *evolved* from his amateurist, Hollywood-influenced early period, through his Maoist radicalization, to his abandonment of 35mm in his Dziga Vertov period . . . to his elliptical, poststructuralist feature-film return in the seventies."

up financing from capitalist tycoon Angelo Rizzoli's Cineriz Distribution Associates for an antiestablishment Western. . . ." In fact, Godard—seized by enthusiasm for the May '68 revolution—had been widely commissioned by television companies to cover the events, but very little of it was ever screened. In August he shot *Un Film commes les autres,* a discussion between workers and students intercut with footage from May, but not even the militants distributed it.

Clearly indebted to Godard was Bernardo Bertolucci's *Partner* (1968), on a theme from Dostoyevsky's story, *The Double.* A young, unassuming, bookish drama teacher discovers an alter ego, a wild revolutionary who finally bursts free after driving him to dementia. Gorgeous and inventive in its visual effects, *Partner* contrived to keep its Marxism safely within an elegant bourgeois environment. Unlike Vittorio da Sica and Roberto Rossellini after World War II, radical directors no longer regarded slums and working-class neighborhoods as box office. Bertolucci's central character never breaks out of himself; politics, Vietcong flags, a guillotine, the making of a Molotov cocktail—all are ingested into a private life which is both scandalous and surreal. At the end, the director addresses the audience to explain that to make films for the masses you first have to make films for the elite.

Bored and beautiful, Jean-Pierre Léaud and Anna Wiazemski, two of the principal faces of Godard's *La Chinoise,* reappear as the children of an ex-Nazi industrialist in Pier Paolo Pasolini's film *Pigsty,* the prize exhibit of the London Film Festival of 1969. The vagrant robber-rapists roaming bleak, volcanic countryside display the same pitiless ethic as Godard's cannibal hippies in *Weekend.* Meanwhile, in a parallel story set in post-Nazi Germany, the industrialist's son and his beautiful girl hold poker-faced conversations in which it is revealed that she is "political," he merely bored. The young man, it transpires, has a perverted appetite for pigsties and is finally consumed by the swine (survivors, no doubt, from Godard's *Weekend*). What these films offered the avant-garde public, apart from the striking artistic talents of their directors, was a sweet-and-sour cocktail of decadence, glamour, sadism, and pseudoradicalism. They sold themselves to (and on) the very qualities they affected to reject.

POP

Andy Warhol was a different kind of filmmaker, offering a different kind of radical ambiguity.

One evening, Jane Kramer reports, Allen Ginsberg was eating in

Max's Kansas City with his Beat colleague Gregory Corso and the "phantom of the underground," Andy Warhol. Situated at the corner of 18th Street and Park Avenue South, Max's had opened in 1966 and was quickly patronized by writers, artists, filmmakers, musicians, the underground, pop intelligentsia, and students. As Kramer describes that evening, Corso was snarling with resentment while Warhol—the famous lock of dyed silvery white hair drooping down his forehead, and wearing an expression of "relentless passivity"—sat in silence as Corso heaped insults upon him.

> "I know all about you pop people," said Corso. "How you use people. How you make them superstars of New York and then you drop them. You're evil. You and all those rich women and faggots and Velvet Undergrounds, and Allen with Swamis and Fugs—you've all lost me. . . . And you know what else? You never give anything away. The Diggers—you know the Diggers?—they give *everything* away. . . . You know what's wrong with you? Too many lovely women are in love with you. You use them. You give them dope and then you leave them. You don't *love* them."

When Corso had gone, Ginsberg hugged Warhol. " 'He *did* hurt your feelings. You've got *feelings!* what do you know—feelings!' "

Here lay a point. No two American artists could have had less in common than Ginsberg and Warhol, apart from homosexuality; the big, furry, warm Jew was all about values, while the pale, cool, silent Warhol was all about Actors Studio pauses and value-free art. Warhol had nothing against the world. Yet the radical culture of the time was a remarkably eclectic mix, and Warhol's underground films fascinated the young patrons of the Village cinemas who opposed the Vietnam War, while his art decorated the apartments of smart professional people who incarnated the "Consciousness II" later made famous in Charles Reich's *The Greening of America*. Warhol employed a dozen young artists to turn out pop art, which might just be interpreted as a hostile comment on the fetish of consumer products or, as with Roy Lichtenstein's famous *Whaam!* (purchased by the Tate Gallery), as a comment on America's juvenile, comic-strip war culture.

Warhol silk-screened and faintly mocked the fetishes of a wealthy, hedonistic society, which responded by buying him. When a Warhol exhibition opened at the Rowan Gallery in London in March 1968, he was already celebrated as the high priest of Campbell soup cans, electric chairs (with a sign on a nearby door enjoining "Silence"), Marilyn and Jackie, Brillo boxes, and helium-filled silver cushions. Warhol was the flaccid werewolf of "why not?" A film of a man sleeping? Why not? His subject was detachment, being a spectator confronted by what the art critic Robert Hughes called the "sense of glut and anaesthesia."

Warhol's films stared deadpan at objects indolently, insolently, interminably—eight hours at the Empire State Building. Another marathon, *Flesh,* became a triumph at the Garrick Theatre in Greenwich Village during 1968. Warhol passed no comment; he was a literalist of the banal, a plastic man hovering in an amphetamine heaven, a ticket-machine dealing out films called *Kiss, Haircut, Couch, Harlot, Screen Test, Vinyl Horse, Blow Job, The Chelsea Girls, Bike Boy.* Grove Press, patrons of both the political and artistic avant-gardes, brought out his coyly titled book *a;* the interwash of aesthetic elegance, of style, and a possible radicalism was beguiling. The same eclectic mix was on sale at any Village bookstore: Warhol and Guevara, op and pop, mother-fucker "comix" and Ho, Camus and cunt, Rolling Stones on soundtrack, Ginsberg and LeRoi Jones in cheap editions alongside Marilyn pouting. Everything seemed part of everything else.

In his essay "Protean Man," Robert Jay Lifton pointed to the tension between the young's urgent search for conviction (a rapid hopping from one belief or religion to another) and the underlying tone of mockery, the sense of absurdity, in pop and kinetic art. This detachment, this sense of it both mattering and not mattering, echoed in current jargon: "scene," "scenario," "making it," "cool it," "cop out," "play it cool." Yet the Left also sought a nonalienated world in which language, image, and meaning would be wholly married to the world.

Robert Hughes sardonically monitored the applause of late-sixties Marxist critics, particularly in Germany, where Warhol was honored as a radical who had broken with "elite art" by mass production. One critic even coined the phrase "anaesthetic revolutionary practice," but Hughes pursued Warhol's career into the seventies and eighties, by which time it had descended to owning a gossip magazine, society portraits from Polaroids, jetting between the Shah and the Reagans.

In June 1968, Warhol's charmed life almost ran out. Valerie Solanas, who had once played the lead role in a Warhol film, but had since been discarded, shot him, seriously but not fatally. "I just wanted him to pay attention to me," she explained. "Talking to him was like talking to a chair." To secure her fame, Solanas produced her one-woman *Scum Manifesto,* a raving indictment of the whole male sex.

SEXUAL LIBERATION AND WOMEN'S LIBERATION

If one quality united the New Left with the underground arts—magazines, theatre, films, music—it was rampant male chauvinism. When BBC Television summoned the leaders of the international student insurrection to its Wood Lane studios in June 1968, not a single woman was among them. Jim Haynes's autobiography reprints a "Who's Who in the Underground" of London during 1967–68. Of the sixteen boxed and photographed biographies, only one was a woman's: Caroline Coons, twenty-two, painter and coordinator of Release, which had assisted 150 hippies charged with drug offenses.

The underground counterculture was saturated in male chauvinism. In France the luminary of the radical happening was Jean-Jacques Lebel, who fought behind the barricades on the night of May 10; Jeff Nuttall recalled "the last and most dynamic" of Lebel's shows, which included a happening by Alexandro Jodorowsky "that left everyone stunned." Jodorowsky himself described it:

> I get inside the frame with my back to the audience.
> The woman lashes me with her whip.
> I draw a red line on her right breast with a lipstick.
> A second lash of the whip. I draw a line on her left breast.
> A last blow of the whip. The line begins at her solar plexus and goes down to her vagina.

Even to a poet as sensitive as Allen Ginsberg, women who displayed possessive traits were a bore. He recounted how a girlfriend became hysterically jealous because of his contemporaneous homosexual relationship with Peter Orlovsky. "It was a shame really, because Peter was bringing chicks home, so there was a lot of nice orgies going on." "Chicks" was the word. Dr. Joseph Berke, prophet of the counterculture and cofounder of New York's Free University, described a visit to Kommune I in Berlin: "From time to time [Dieter] Kunzelman would stop fucking the chick with whom he was sharing a mattress. . . . After a while Rainer Langhans drifted over, as did rather a cute little blonde girl who seemed to be his chick." Later the Kommunards promoted their book by distributing photographs of their copulations, plus a cartoon photo-fantasy of "two huge spades . . . fucking the archetypical superblonde in the ass and the cunt at the same time." These were sold under-the-counter, on request.

The name adopted by the Lower East Side Motherfuckers speaks for itself. A Yippie leaflet issued before the Chicago demonstrations cheerfully warned: "230 rebel cocksmen under secret vows are on

24-hour alert to get into the pants of the daughters and wives and kept women of the convention delegates." In February 1968, the San Francisco Diggers rallied the tribe after a police riot in these terms: "We're beautiful people. Our men are tough. They have style, guile, balls, imagination and autonomy. Our women are soft, skilled, fuck like angels; radiate [sic] children, scent and colors like the crazy bells that mark our time."

Male chauvinism was often decked out as sexual liberation, involving a gallop into pornography. The German underground press traded in such beguilingly radical terms as "sexpol," "politsex," and "politporn"; Klaus Rainer Rohl's magazine *Konkret* did nicely out of a hot goulash of revolutionary incantation and hard porn. Quoting both Wilhelm Reich and Herbert Marcuse (who in fact disparaged Reich), Rohl claimed he was breaking new ground among the high school students. In 1969 his wife, Ulricke Meinhof, took her leave of him on her way to the deranged terrorism of the Baader-Meinhof gang, imprisonment, and suicide.

By 1967–68, *Oz* had become the market leader among London's "liberated" underground publications, dependably delivering images of sexual sadism, obscenity, and theatre-of-cruelty (drawing heavily on American material) in a riot of polychrome newsprint and psychedelic topography, while presenting itself as the subverter of bourgeois repression. *Oz*'s editor, Richard Neville, described sexual liberation for the benefit of drooling squares in his book *Play Power:* "On festive occasions . . . a generous girl will 'put on a queue' behind the sand dunes for a seemingly unlimited line-up of young men." (But why *behind* the dunes?) Like a vending machine, Neville also offered a private style: "I ask her home, she rolls a joint and we begin to watch the mid-week TV movie. . . . Comes the Heinz Souperday commercial, a hurricane fuck, another joint. No feigned love or hollow promises. . . ."

In New York, the operation was even more flagrantly commercial. *Screw,* which appeared in September 1968, was originally conceived in the offices of the *New York Free Press* as a moneymaker for a serious political enterprise, but as circulation soared to 150,000, *Screw*'s editors went independent and forgot the politics. Two other *Free Press* editors founded the rival *New York Review of Sex.* Meanwhile, the *East Village Other* spawned *Kiss.* The editors of these porn mags occasionally talked pretentiously about the sexual revolution preceding the political one, but they were merely converting lust into money and by the time Kenneth Tynan's *Oh! Calcutta* began to cream its profits in London and New York, the bankers were fully at ease with the counterculture.

The women's movement was both a product and a repudiation of male-dominated radicalism in the late sixties.

Women's liberation—often disparaged by the Robin Hoods of the New Left as "pussy power"—had made slow progress; the massive physical confrontations of the era, on campus and on the street, merely boosted the male's self-congratulatory image of himself as bearded guerrilla fighter, the hero whom the sisters would loyally service with food, sex, and admiration. The New Left was a movement of male captains and female corporals, which belatedly and reluctantly accepted the terms "male chauvinism" and "sexism" in 1968–69. Jerry Rubin eventually repented of his male chauvinism, Yippie-as-Superman, after the trial of the Chicago 7 in 1969: "Having huge competitive egos, and being at the center of the media storm, we defendants did not try to overcome the hypocrisy in our lifestyle." The radical superstars had huddled in conclave, making all the decisions like a board of directors, while the women typed next door and filled their beds. On this one point, Tom Hayden was in agreement with Jerry Rubin: "The entire process by which leaders become known is almost fatally corrupting. Only males with driving egos have been able to 'rise' in the Movement or the rock culture and be accepted by the media and dealt with seriously by the Establishment."

In March 1968, Naomi Jaffe and Bernardine Dohrn published "The Look is You" in *New Left Notes*. This is a period piece insofar as it analyzes women's specific oppression (men define reality, women are defined in terms of men) as merely an aspect of the general oppression of capitalist commodity society—the position adopted at the turn of the century by the Polish-German Marxist Rosa Luxemburg. While showing how the new *Playboy* permissiveness reinforced the image of women as passive consumer objects, "The Look is You" referred neither to patriarchy nor to the male's innate biological imperialism—key concepts for later radical feminists. More ominous for male egos, 1968 saw the publication in the *New American Review* of Kate Millett's *Sexual Politics,* an attack on the attitude toward women found in the writings of Henry Miller and Norman Mailer.

At Halloween 1968, the Women's International Terrorist Conspiracy from Hell (WITCH) descended, heaping curses ancient and modern on the New York Stock Exchange. Their manifesto looked back to the "oldest culture of all—one in which men and women were equal sharers in a truly cooperative society, before the death-dealing sexual, economic and spiritual repression of the Imperialist Phallic Society took over again and began to shit all over nature and human life."

Unreconstructed women were also a prime feminist target. The "No More Miss America" campaign made nine points. The beauty competition was degrading, like a sheep fair. It was racist—only whites won. Miss America became a death mascot, touring the troops in

Vietnam. She was part of a consumer con game, a walking commercial. She incarnated the ethic of competition; there could be only one winner and forty-nine useless losers. She stood for Woman as Pop Culture obsolescence. She symbolized the male insistence that women be young and ripe, then tossed aside. She represented a combination of Madonna and Whore. Finally she symbolized mediocrity—the feminine duty to conform, to be empty-headed, without commitment, accepting her lot with a bland smile.

Although rebelling against the chauvinism of the New Left, many of the women had learned the craft of consciousness raising and direct action from the Movement itself. Susan Brownmiller, who had campaigned for civil rights in Mississippi, then attended her first feminist meeting in 1967 when she was working as a television network newswriter, has recently recalled how the women learned "Zen action" and mass-media publicity from the Yippies. A strong proponent of the right to abortion—she had had three—Brownmiller was one of two hundred women who staged a day-long occupation of the offices of the *Ladies Home Journal,* which regularly advised its 12 million readers how to please their husbands and rescue difficult marriages. Brownmiller was among those who thought divorce might be a better solution. She also campaigned against pornography and later wrote *Against Our Will: Men, Women and Rape.*

During 1969, British women's groups began to forge stronger links with the American movement. In January, *Black Dwarf* produced a special women's rights issue, and in February the International Marxist Group (IMG) launched *Socialist Woman.* But, during the Festival of Revolution conference at Essex University in the spring, women's discussions ran into disruptive opposition from male radicals. Barbara Koster, a German socialist feminist who lived with Daniel Cohn-Bendit for four years, has remarked how women excluded from the male hierarchy of the New Left tended to shriek their frustration at mass meetings—and were then accused of hysteria. Out of this painful experience emerged an outspoken generation of militant feminists: "We are still the movement secretaries . . . the shit-workers, we served the food, prepared the mailings . . . earth mothers and sex-objects for the movement men. We were the free movement 'chicks'. . . . If a woman dared conceive an idea that was not in the current limited ideological system, she was ignored and ridiculed. . . ."

When the faction-torn, final SDS convention met in June 1969, the rival groups rushed out tracts on women's liberation, competing for the allegiance of the women delegates, who constituted about a quarter of the 1,500 gathered in Chicago. But the Black Panther spokesmen— young bloods as male chauvinistic as farmyard cocks, touched by the male supremacy preached by the Muslims and often raised in ghetto matriarchies—equated rebellion with manhood and did not intend to defer to any white group, let alone women. Chaka Walls, of the Illinois Panthers, announced that women had their place in the Movement, "for love and all that . . . for pussy power," adding: "I'm glad to see there's enough women here for all the revolution. The way the women contribute is by getting laid." Faced with heckling and chanting from the hall, Walls tried to hold his ground: "Superman was a punk. He never even tried to fuck Lois Lane." After Walls left the rostrum, another Panther, Jul Cook, took the microphone to remind his outraged audience of Stokely Carmichael's nostrum: "The only position for women in the Movement is prone."

A young woman, who had lived for a number of years with a former president of SDS, responded in fury: "Here they come. Those strutting roosters, those pathetic male chauvinists, egocentric, pompous and ridiculous bastards."

In July 1969, the "Redstockings Manifesto" was published in New York: "Our oppression is total. . . . Every such [male/female] relationship is a *class* relationship. . . . racism, capitalism, imperialism, etc. are extensions of male supremacy." *All* men, claimed the manifesto, had always oppressed *all* women. As Marlene Dixon noted in an objective essay published in *Ramparts* at the end of the year, 1969 had seen a rapid development of a hard line, a new bitterness and rage. On January 24, 1970, radical women, including Redstockings and members of WITCH, took over *Rat* magazine in New York, blasting the assumption of its male editors that politics equaled whatever the Black Panthers and Young Lords were into, plus some porn, dope, rock, and movies.

In her celebrated "Goodbye to All That" (February 1970), Robin Morgan launched a ferocious onslaught on the sexist pornography preached and practiced by "the friends, brothers, lovers in the counterfeit, male dominated Left"; "the token pussy power or clit militancy articles"; and the Old Left parties that offered their female members "women's liberation caucuses." With caustic scorn, she took apart Paul Krassner, a fellow traveler of the Yippies, for his columns in *Cavalier,* his "Instant Pussy" aerosol can poster, his dream of a rape-in against legislators' wives, his locker-room delight in reeling off the names of the women in the Movement he had had.

Morgan also attacked the "Weather Sisters" for tolerating the machismo and gratuitous violence of their male colleagues, who had chosen as their hero Charles Manson, master of a harem who set his women to do all the shit work and to kill to order. "Goodbye," wrote

Morgan, "to the dream that being in the leadership collective will give you anything but gonorrhea."

Within the Movement, styles of appearance had begun to reflect the shift of consciousness. Dressed in miniskirts and go-go boots, women had been invited to identify their own project in life with the limbs they flashed, the heads they turned, the competition they overcame. Nothing new in this, except that it had thrived and throbbed within a notionally radical, nonconforming culture. Now came the colors of the earth, skirts like tents, baggy trousers, floppy shirts, heavy, flat-heeled boots, and the whole range of casual garments that the boutiques, quick as ever on the draw, called "unisex." This new style was itself a kind of manifesto.

14

RADICAL THEATRES

"The most famous guerrilla company was the Living Theatre...the company's productions...amounted to a frontal assault on the traditional separation between actors and audience."

"AMERIKA"

The ongoing war in Vietnam, the corruption and compromises of power politics, the endemic violence of American society, the cathartic and intensely theatrical counter-politics of the Chicago Mobilization—all this was the stuff of contemporary radical theatre, yet the performance often seemed a pale, affected shadow of the televised reality.

Theatre no less than film had to wrestle with the devil of the easy posture, the glib scattershot directed at every facet of the system (and therefore, finally, at none). Jules Feiffer, the celebrated cartoonist of angst and indecision, followed the success of his *Little Murders* with *God Bless,* which opened at Yale in October 1968. Feiffer aimed his fire at the powerlessness and irrelevance of the American liberalism in whose womb he prospered, wheeling onstage a president, a Black Panther, a Yippie, the TV newscasters, a potential nuclear holocaust, and generous doses of the absurd, in a shallow, unconvincing exercise tarted up by expressionist stage technology.

"Amerika" was now *the* target of the radical theatre; absolutely nothing was to be hinted in its favor. *Collision Course,* consisting of eleven short plays directed by Edward Parone, arrived at the Actors' Playhouse in 1968 from the Mark Taper Forum in Los Angeles. The authors included Jean-Claude van Itallie (whose *America Hurrah* enjoyed long-running success), Lanford Wilson, Jules Feiffer, and Israel Horovitz. The message was uniform: America was crippled by conformism; by lack of love; by guilt, hate, violence, and indifference; and by fear of the bomb.

Van Itallie stood at that moment the most celebrated author of antitexts—of choreographed and sculpted triangles of words designed for ensemble acting and "director's theatre." Open Theatre's major piece, *The Serpent* (text by van Itallie), retold the story of the Creation "through images of loss born of the assassination of JFK and Dr. King" (in Gerald Rabkin's description). First performed in Rome in May

1968—a memorable month in Europe—it moved to New York in December and exercised considerable influence on other ensemble productions.

The longest "serpent" in the theatre, as in the streets, was Vietnam. Barbara Garson's brilliant *MacBird!,* which opened in 1967, juxtaposed two myths: the Shakespearian sentiment of Macbeth and the hero-images of American politics. Lyndon Johnson was mercilessly satirized (to the delight of the New York intelligentsia), but the rampant humor of the piece and its well-sustained alienation effects did not detract from its passionate indictment of American imperialism and the Vietnam War.

Bread and Puppet Theatre's *Fire* was dedicated to three Americans who had immolated themselves in protest against the war. Peter Schumann, the company's German-born director, imparted to its productions an extraordinary combination of inventiveness and discipline, relying on improvised dialogue and, frequently, on no dialogue at all. Wearing chalk-white masks, achieving enormity with hidden stilts, Bread and Puppet's grotesque, lumbering figures paraded the streets and parks in pursuit of their agonized, half-human destiny before mesmerized passersby. In the spring of 1968, Bread and Puppet embarked on its first European tour, captivating audiences in England, France, Germany, and Holland.

More of Vietnam: In February 1968, the film version of Peter Brook's *US,* entitled *Tell Me Lies,* opened in London. The critics accounted it as great a disaster as the notorious Royal Shakespeare Company's production that had preceded it. The *New Statesman*'s critic, John Coleman, dismissed it as a "talkathlon . . . evincing its sincerity, Godard-fashion, by holding the camera interminably on the incoherent." Peter Brook described the hostile reception he had encountered in America during radio and television interviews: Why, he was constantly asked, had he ignored Vietcong atrocities?

That was not, however, the main problem. The original *US,* which opened at the Aldwych Theatre on October 13, 1966, had attempted to synthesize a critique of the Vietnam War with the director's own philosophy of ensemble improvisation—"experimental laboratory work," as Brook called it. Rehearsals lasted four months, exercises were devised in the spirit of the theatre of cruelty, Jerzy Grotowski was called in, Joseph Chaikin came over from New York, and the result was disastrous. As the critic Charles Marowitz put it, the first act, set in Vietnam, "was crammed with sloppy, demonstrational acting and familiar extracts from Vietnam folklore." The second act, which resorted more solidly to the spoken word, was about sitting comfortably in England, not really caring, a dialogue between a man on the point of suicide and an unorthodox liberal woman whose detachment was supposed to represent the audience's. What most infuriated the critics was the superior posture adopted by the company toward the audience. At the intermission, the actors put their heads in paper bags, clambered down off the stage, and groped up the aisles, bleating and flailing their arms for assistance. (This happening was excised from later performances.) The critic Hilary Spurling came out of the theatre disgusted by "hysterical clowning, self-righteous belligerence and mawkish attempts at solemnity. . . ." Arnold Wesker rebelled against the production's onslaught on the assumed indifference of the audience. "You can't stand on the sidewalk and attack others who do the same; and that play stands on the sidewalk because . . . all theatre is on the sidewalk. . . ." Marowitz, an American who contributed to the vitality of the British theatre as producer and critic, concluded that Peter Brook's directorial judgment had been seduced by his addiction to the theatre of cruelty, "replete with Artaudian effigies and theatrical stylizations, and studded with dazzling little thefts from old Happenings and contemporary Destructivist exercises." The war was real, and it was still going on; to cloak it in artistic ambiguities was an insult.

Vietnam inspired another theatrical disaster, written by Peter Weiss (whose *Marat/Sade* Brook had triumphantly directed for the Royal Shakespeare Company). Early in 1968, Weiss's *Vietnam Discourse* opened in Frankfurt, a tedious epic, neo-Brechtian dramatization of the history of Vietnam over a period of 2,400 years, groaning under a lead weight of statistics. Weiss celebrated his conversion to Marxism by abandoning plot, characterization, and dramatic instinct— indeed the most dramatic event of the evening came at the end, with an invasion of the Frankfurt stage by students carrying Vietcong flags. Author, director, cast, and students then settled down to discuss what it all meant—marathon upon marathon.

THE LIVING THEATRE

The American theatre of 1968 experienced the counterculture at its most rampantly aggressive. The playwright's theatre almost vanished off-Broadway; text was now regarded as an authoritarian, inhibiting imposition on the creativity of the acting company and on the necessary involvement of the audience in the action. By 1968, Robert Brustein's admiration for the "third theatre" had declined into depression, as it abandoned itself to disruptive and histrionic acts by juvenile revolutionaries peddling stereotyped assertions and simple-minded nihilism.

During the May revolution in Paris, a solemn declaration was made in the occupied Odéon, from which Jean-Louis Barrault and his company had been temporarily ousted: "The only theatre is guerrilla theatre. Revolutionary art takes place in the street."

Or on the campuses of the West Coast. In January 1968, not only the faculty council of California State College at Fullerton, but even the student senate had voted to refuse use of the campus quadrangle to the brilliantly inventive San Francisco Mime Troupe for a free performance of *Olive Pits*. While a drama professor, George Forest, went to court to reverse the ban (unsuccessfully), the troupe performed in an orange grove across the street from Cal State. The professor resigned, riots shook Haight Street, the Tac Squad assumed control, the Diggers reawakened, and life and theatre flowed together along the San Andreas Fault. When the Peace and Freedom Party held its founding convention in Berkeley during March, the San Francisco Mime Troupe staged its Gorilla Marching Band débuts. In May, El Teatro Campesino was awarded an Obie for "creating a workers' theater to demonstrate the politics of survival," following which came the company's first full-length play, *The Shrunken Head of Pancho Villa* by Luis Valdez, performed at the Radical Theatre Festival, which was held in September at San Francisco State College, soon to be torn apart by strikes and race riots. The festival brought together Bread and Puppet, El Teatro Campesino, Gut Theatre, Berkeley Agit-Prop, and the San Francisco Mime Troupe (whose inspirational figure was R. G. Davis).

The most famous guerrilla company was the Living Theatre, led (though leadership was definitely out) by Julian Beck and his wife, Judith Malina. The Living Theatre had staged two major Brecht productions before they were evicted from their New York City premises by the tax collectors and forced to leave for Europe. By the late sixties, the Becks were committed anarchists contemptuous of authorial texts. Returning from four years' exile, the company went into productions of *The Mysteries, Antigone,* and *Paradise Now,* in what amounted to a frontal assault on the traditional separation between actors and audience. How authentic was the anarchist dimension? Robert Brustein, dean of the Yale School of Drama, who lived to regret inviting the Living Theatre to Yale in the fall of 1968, was not convinced: ". . . it was constraint and control that remained most conspicuous. No spectator was allowed to violate the patterns of manipulated consent."

Soon after Brustein published these damaging comments he accepted an invitation to take part, with the Becks, in a New York symposium on Theatre or Therapy. During the discussion members of the Living Theatre seated in the audience became increasingly disruptive, until they took the whole thing over. A black actor, Rufus Collins, kept screaming, "Fuck Chekhov, fuck Shakespeare, fuck the universities" and "fuck technology." (A man asked him why he was wearing glasses.) Judith Malina then explained how everybody could act creatively and beautifully; when *Paradise Now* had been busted by the police at Yale, "it was a very beautiful and joyous moment, everybody was feeling like something beautiful was happening." But, she complained, Robert Brustein had remonstrated with her that all this freedom could lead to fascism. At this juncture, as if to confirm Brustein's fears, three Living Theatre actors, Rufus Collins, Ben Israel, and Jenny Hecht, began screaming and stamping. Collins seized the pocketbook of a woman in the audience and emptied it on the floor, whereupon Julian Beck, master choreographer of the seminar, announced: "Get used to this. It's happening all over America. . . . Get used to this. This is what is going to happen from now on." He then tore a fur coat from a woman's shoulders and threw her hat on the floor: "What are you doing about Vietnam, what are you doing about the black people?" As Brustein's disgust rose in his gorge, Richard Schechner, one of the young luminaries of the new radical theatre, came up on the platform and explained: "You've got to learn to groove with it. Let's all have five minutes of meditation to think about the beautiful thing that's happening here." But the drama critic Stanley Kauffmann did not need five minutes and did not groove; he accused Malina of having staged the whole performance, "You and your stooges."

"No, no," she demurred, "everybody should be allowed to do what he wants. That's what's so beautiful about freedom."

Irving Wardle, of the London *Times,* contrasted the "discipline and clarity" of the Living Theatre's old, 14th Street productions—*The Connection* and *The Brig*—with the "overblown and self-indulgent" style developed in exile. "They flog themselves into an evangelistic hysteria in the hope of touching an alien public . . . they spend as much time in the audience as on stage, enacting police state routines in the aisles and brandishing their fists in the spectators' faces. . . ." When the Living Theatre arrived at the Roundhouse in London, drama critics responded in much the same spirit of exasperation. Benedict Nightingale, of the *New Statesman,* commented: "The in-people this summer are those who have been trampled, shaken, spat at, deafened, or had the inside of their mouths inspected by men chanting 'holy teeth, holy gums.' " He found *Antigone* a more disciplined production than the others in the repertoire, despite a thirty-minute Bacchic ritual, but Malina's innocent, irreproachable Antigone and Beck's eye-popping Creon invited no reflection on the competing claims of law and conscience—merely a prepackaged conclusion to be accepted blindly, dumbly.

When Julian Beck explained himself in print, what mainly emerged was superficial self-contradiction. People (he asserted) could not begin to be free unless they shook off mammon, personal possessions, and the alienating experience of working for money. On the other hand . . . the Living Theatre had recently been shooting a film in Rome. Authority, also, must be destroyed. "I have to wither away as the founder and director." On the other hand . . . he hadn't. The company's recent productions *Mysteries, Frankenstein,* and *Antigone* had been attempts to destroy the authority of authors, directors, and leading actors. On the other hand . . . he and Malina had directed them.

Beck offered a tip to anyone aspiring to join the twenty Americans and thirteen Europeans who then constituted the traveling company. "If you can get a member of the company to fall in love with you, or if you're a chick and you can get impregnated—that's a very good way because we have a very bourgeois sense of responsibility."

A strong defense of the Living Theatre has been made by Gerald Rabkin, who points out that their 18,000-mile tour of the United States, from September 1968 to March 1969, "filled auditoriums, gymnasiums, churches, theatres with audiences who responded passionately—even if oftentimes negatively. . . ." Clive Barnes, of the *New York Times,* also defended the group's affirmation of "man's need for ritual and involvement" against Eric Bentley's angry attack, "I reject the Living Theatre," which castigated its "cult of intimacy," its guruism, and its avoidance of any real political dialectic. Attending *Paradise Now* (but prudently leaving his wallet at home), Rabkin finally surrendered to the Living Theatre's "passionate obliteration of the distinction between performers and spectators, between actors and acted upon. I went back four times to be disturbed."

THEATRE OF GESTURE

Elizabeth Hardwick noted that the Brechtian theatre of alienation was "too austere and intellectual for Hippydom"; the director Joseph Chaikin, formerly an actor with the Living Theatre, commented: "The New Left people would find the political terms of the *Lehrstücke* irrelevant, and the militant don't want to listen to anyone but themselves." Hardwick, although a woman of letters, clearly took pleasure in the new antiverbal theatre, where she discerned "reciprocal, unifying gestures, suitable to a peace-loving, radicalized mood." *Hair* and Tom O'Horgan's production of Paul Foster's *Tom Paine* incarnated these qualities.

She was also impressed by the "triumphant cunnilingus" of Michael McClure's *The Beard* (despite its shortage of words), and by the spectacle of Jean Harlow and Billy the Kid as "copulating essences, coarse, hoarse, solely occupied by cock and cunt in their blue velvet Heaven— or Hell." The meaning, as far as Hardwick could tell, was that "If we don't do what we want, we're not divine."

La Mama production of *Tom Paine* conveyed the political naïveté of the new ensemble theatre. Lightly basing itself on the life of Thomas Paine, it offered a succession of vigorous scenes dominated by inspired group choreography that reduced history to an animated chamber of horrors inhabited by waxwork grotesques. Philip French, a *New Statesman* critic increasingly alienated by the ahistorical, anti-intellectual posture of the new avant-garde, came away exasperated: "Unless tedium is the message nothing emerges from this brilliant display except a sense of wilful exhibitionism and self-indulgence." Charles Marowitz chided La Mama for "rigorously applying a fascinating acting style to second- and third-rate material. . . ." Not only did the athleticism of the company constantly "mickey-mouse" the dialogue, it also got them off the hook of playing credible individual characters.

A publisher responsible for the publication of many outstanding avant-garde texts, John Calder, complained in the autumn of 1968 that "the theatre of noise" (screams, yells, incoherent mumblings) was now in the ascendant. "The words have ceased to matter and the audience is caught up in movement and ritual, whose impact is made through surprise, shock and alienation rather than the projection of thought through language." Calder argued that art required the unity of vision that could come "only from one creative source." But, of course, directors like Peter Brook, Jerzy Grotowski, and Joseph Chaikin regarded themselves as nothing less than that; in essence they were claiming the role traditionally enjoyed by film directors. Chaikin defended "the radical exploration of voice, movement and behavior now being made in theatre laboratories" across Europe and America. "Actors play images as in a dream, men as primal creatures. There are disembodied voices, zombies, cartoons, gods, machines. There is a sense of alarm, a rediscovery of joy. . . . They all agree that we are stunned creatures living in an untenable world."

Such creatures inhabited the Théâtre de Panique which, supposedly performing Fernando Arrabal's *The Labyrinth* at the Mercury Theatre, Notting Hill Gate, distributed a notice to the audience: "We have been trying to purge our presentation during the past two weeks . . . of all elements in the play . . . that we feel to be dead or irreversibly conventional in structure. . . . The evolution, once begun, led us logically to the conclusion that in the end we would completely abandon the play by Arrabal." What they offered the audience instead was bedlam.

Ensemble acting increasingly involved the audience, whether they liked it or not. Even when a production was based on an author's text, as with Sam Shepard's *Forensic and the Navigators,* all hell soon broke loose: smoke blanketing stage and auditorium; a rock group pumping out songs about tolerance and drug addiction. Irving Wardle noted: "What started as a formal theatrical event melted into an amorphous union between performers and audience. . . ." Wardle also braved La Mama's production of Megan Terry's *Changes,* during which spectators were blindfolded and put through an elaborate mind-bending routine, assailed by loudspeakers and flashing lights, threatened, picked up and tossed in the air, forced to crawl on all fours, and thrust into a bed and mixed up with naked lovers. Wardle registered "despair" at the "absence of content."

The intrepid critic Nora Sayre reported in April: "Lately, the off-off Broadway actors' involvement with the spectators has so intensified that one fully expects to get laid during the next evening at the theatre." Five months later she described the charms of group therapy sessions (known as T-groups), and an authorless production, *The Concept,* improvised and acted by ex-addicts and "punctuated by yells, screams, mutual accusations, enough hostility to win a war, and sufficient tenderness to sink a whale." The trick was to yield the Self to the Group—to "blow your image" and find authentic shared experience. Gargling, incoherence, and repetition were taken as evidence of probity. Undaunted, Sayre visited Richard Schechner's *Dionysus in 69* and had an actor whisper in her ear, "Dionysus cannot bear a mocker or a scoffer." Perhaps he had read Sayre's theatre columns.

Visiting Ed Berman's *The Nudist Camps Grow and Grow* at the tiny Ambiance lunchtime theatre in Queensway, Sayre's colleague Philip French was invited to take off his clothes but "remained resolutely buttoned." At a higher level of mind and body, the audience found itself physically and morally besieged by Jerzy Grotowski's Laboratory Theatre production of *Acropolis,* the function of the spectators being "to sit still and symbolize the 'civilized' world, helplessly witnessing gross crimes against humanity." The Polish director's productions and his belief in a "poor theatre"—a nonliterary theatre of intense physical performance in austere and confined settings—exercised a major influence on Western directors and critics, but Grotowski's grim preoccupations belonged to a world of elemental stress distant from the flamboyant Western counterculture.

Hair silenced the critics. The show opened in 1968 both on Broadway and in London, magically summoning every appealing facet of the counterculture to a supreme feast. Directed by Tom O'Horgan, with lyrics by Gerome Ragni and a book by James Rado, *Hair* had it all: a rock-beat score by Galt MacDermot that sprang from the bones and nerves of young America; beautiful bodies; good-natured improvisational humor; spectacular kinetic and stroboscopic sequences; hippies dressed like American Indians (one of them stricken at the end when his hair is shorn and he is stuffed into khaki for shipment to Vietnam); suicidal Buddhists and miniskirted nuns pursued by coolie-hatted VCs pursued by Green Berets; corpses; brilliant ensemble work and deft reversals.

The enemies in *Hair* are the imperialists of middle age: parents, teachers, cops. Against this domineering superego, beleaguered youths, hugging their precarious freedom and capacity for love, huddle together for warmth. The middle-aged theatre critics were utterly captivated: "Primal innocence . . . fundamentally gentle . . . a great hymn to freedom and love . . . nothing like it can have been heard on the West End stage before"—to quote from the London *Times, Sunday Times, Observer,* and *New Statesman.* Benn Levy, an Old Left playwright writing in *Tribune,* called *Hair* "an extraordinary synthesis of Christian and pagan love," adding: "With those disarmed, exuberant kids up on the stage we can all feel safe, even the squarest, even the least deserving of us." Benn Levy (and *Tribune*) were so enthused that they even printed the word "fuck" instead of dots. For Charles Marowitz, *Hair* was one of those rare shows "which consolidates some part of the *zeitgeist* . . . the most powerful piece of anti-war propaganda yet to come out of America. . . ."

Such could hardly be said of the film industry's disenchanted *fin de siècle* romance *Easy Rider,* depicting two young men on a cool, hip, escapist journey out of the "system," fueled by pot, gun play, and rampant machismo. A late-sixties version of *On the Road* and *Rebel Without a Cause, Easy Rider* paid ironic tribute to the rebel as dropout pursuing self-fulfillment. Despite critical praise—the film has been described as "a kind of pastoral remake of the Chicago demonstration"—the rebellion had evaporated into style, gesture, and effortless violence.

LONDON

In London, the indigenous theatre remained allergic to the student revolution and the counterculture, although visiting American companies like La Mama, Open Space, the Living Theatre, and Bread and

Puppet—and the box-office bonanza *Hair*— played to packed houses. The year 1968 saw plays by Harold Pinter, Tom Stoppard, John Osborne, David Storey, Simon Gray, Peter Nichols, Alan Bennett, and Brian Friel, but these writers did not see 1968—or 1967. Even Arnold Wesker, Edward Bond, and other post-1956, left-wing playwrights associated with the Royal Court were nonplussed by the outbreak of theatrical politics and of a new, radical theatre which challenged the playwright's traditional primacy.

John Osborne recoiled fastidiously from the juvenile insurrection. On July 7, 1968, he was interviewed by Kenneth Tynan:

> I don't know any students and I certainly would not like to see a Negro minority taking over this country. A lot of nice bus conductors running the Government isn't my idea. . . . And student power is a very factitious thing. It always seems to me that, "What am I?" is a much more interesting question than, "What are we?" but now they're all "we-ing" all over the place. And acting as groups, which I find both uninteresting and ugly. . . . What happened at the Sorbonne seemed more animal than human to me. . . . Were they being exploited? I don't know. I thought they were expecting a great deal. In any case, disappointment is the salt of life. . . . I know this sounds very Blimpish—the prospect of rule by instant rabble doesn't appeal to me either.

The main source of political tension in the British theatre remained the censorship system. It was no coincidence that *Hair* opened in London on September 27—the day after the abolition of the Lord Chamberlain's role as theatre censor. A member of the Royal Household, the Lord Chamberlain had first been empowered in 1737 to forbid the performance of any play "for the preservation of good manners, decorum or of the public peace." He could also impose cuts or changes in the text; his decision was final and there was no appeal—as "Colonel Blimp" Osborne himself had recently discovered to his financial cost when his *A Patriot for Me* was unable to transfer from club performances at the Royal Court to the West End because of the Lord Chamberlain's disfavor.

In June 1967, a Joint Parliamentary Committee had recommended the abolition of theatre censorship; legislation was duly introduced. Lord Cobbold, however, while waiting to be "abolished," excelled himself. Receiving the text of Edward Bond's *Early Morning* from the Royal Court Theatre (not Lord Cobbold's royal court), his Lordship was horrified to discover that nothing was sacred: Bond had the Prince Consort plotting with Disraeli to assassinate Queen Victoria, the Queen persuading Florence Nightingale to poison Albert, then forcing the great nurse to submit to lesbian rape, while Gladstone drilled a group of thugs in the art of putting in the boot. Cobbold demanded no changes in *Early Morning;* he simply banned the play outright. In April 1968, the Royal Court threaded itself hopefully through the legal loophole of private club performances on Sundays only, but the police arrived in Sloane Square and performances stopped.

That nothing was any longer sacred was doubly impressed on Lord Cobbold when the text of Rolf Hochhuth's *Soldiers* landed on his desk. The new victim of sacrilege was Churchill himself—clearly held guilty by Hochhuth not merely of criminal bombing of German civilians, but also of arranging the assassination of Britain's wartime ally, the Polish leader in exile General Sikorski. Here the Lord Chamberlain could derive moral support from the Board of the National Theatre, which had adamantly vetoed *Soldiers* despite the recommendation of the theatre's artistic director, Sir Laurence Olivier, and its literary manager, Kenneth Tynan. An alternative production having been arranged, the Lord Chamberlain declared that he would not pass the play until he had the written consent of all the surviving relatives of all the historical characters portrayed. *Soldiers* finally opened in November, a few weeks after the Lord Chamberlain's demise as censor.

What continued to preoccupy socialist playwrights in 1967–69 was history, working-class culture, and the imperial decline of Britain. Charles Wood's *Dingo* directed its fire at Churchill and Montgomery; Edward Bond's *Early Morning* settled accounts with Gladstone and Disraeli; Peter Barnes's *The Ruling Class,* though contemporary in theme, was set in an allegorical ducal estate; Peter Terson's *Zigger Zagger* and *The Apprentices* brilliantly explored the subcultures of working-class youth; Charles Wood's *H* focused its disenchantment on the British Raj in India. Five years elapsed before Trevor Giffiths's *The Party* brought a serious dramatic assessment of 1968 and the New Left.

In the 1970s, a new generation of playwrights—David Edgar, Howard Brenton, David Hare, Howard Barker—emerged to confront contemporary political themes in the theatre and to reassert the claims of the written text. They were the angry children of '68 and not shy of the revolutionary heritage.

Two talents associated with the Royal Court did confront the contemporary insurrection of the young: Lindsay Anderson and John Arden. Anderson's film *If. . .,* which opened in the final month of 1968, brought the revolution to an English public school steeped in elitist values and authoritarian, sado-masochistic practices. The prefects are called "whips," the little ones, "scum." The masters affect liberal attitudes while delegating the brutal stuff to the ever-eager prefects. The headmaster, a smooth pseudoliberal keeping pace with the new media, cannot cope with a rebellious trio of dreamy nonconformists wrapped in surrealist dreams of love. Having insulted the head boy and been brutally caned, they plot a rebellion in the course of which they bayonet the school chaplain during an OTC field day, stick pictures of guerrillas and busty broads on their walls, escape into town on a motorbike, and end up by setting fire to the school on Prize Day, taking to the roof and machine-gunning everything that moves, in a dreamlike catharsis. Although allegorical in form, Anderson's *If...* remains the finest film about, or out of, the late sixties.

John Arden and his wife, Margaretta D'Arcy, devised and inspired a one-day, agit-prop Vietnam event in the East Village in May 1967, while Arden was teaching at New York University. A playwright supremely in control of the formal text, Arden was now turning away from "author's theatre" and Royal Court, "left-establishment" theatre toward street theatre and agit-prop, burlesque and cartoon. Arden noted that the so-called revolution at the Royal Court had been largely one of content, but "this new (or renewed) public was still expected to submit to exactly the same actor-audience relationships that had obtained at least since the start of the century."

Arden's *Harold Muggins is a Martyr,* written for the Cartoon Archetypal Slogan Theatre (known as CAST), was a cartoon parable about the takeover of a café (representing Britain) by Mr. Big. It opened in June 1968. Charles Marowitz was fascinated by Roland Muldoon's CAST, a guerrilla troupe that sought out working-class audiences to offer furious indictments of capitalism and the Labour government in a theatrical style that was more Brecht than Brecht and more Artaud than Artaud: chalk-white makeup, a brash delivery, and crude, earthy humor. CAST's comic *Mr Oligarchy's Circus,* in which the Labour government sold itself to capitalism, was still playing to radical student audiences in 1968, in constantly updated form, two years after its first production. CAST was eventually ejected from the Unity Theatre by its Old-Left Communist trustees for being too outrageous.

Arden, meanwhile, staged his own "cartoon" history play, *The Hero Rises Up,* at the Roundhouse, unmasking Lord Nelson without turning a blind eye to his heroic (if diminutive) stature. Arden's "conversion" was not, in fact, abrupt. Interviews he gave in 1966 indicated the co-existence of two Ardens: the mainstream professional playwright, jealously guarding his own text; and—influenced by his collaborator Margaretta D'Arcy—the "communal" artist working in Yorkshire and Ireland with part-timers and amateurs. Even so, the insurrectionary mood of the late sixties seems to have exerted a permanent change in his outlook. In 1966, Richard Gilman summed up Arden's achievement as "to have taken the social and political life of man and rescued it, as a subject for drama, from didacticism on the one hand and from impressionism on the other." But within two years of that comment the critics were berating Arden for unbridled didacticism. Parting company with the established repertory theatres after a flaming row with the RSC over its production of *The Island of the Mighty* in 1972, he and D'Arcy worked mainly with small, agit-prop groups and Irish Republican themes.

John Arden and David Mercer, the two established British playwrights who most conspicuously embraced the radical politics of the late sixties, attended a Revolutionary Be-In at the University of Essex in 1971. As Mercer recalled, a lad who threw a smoke bomb told the two disapproving writers that it was a more meaningful event than anything either of them could write. Mercer withdrew from the radical university circuit.

15

THE DEMOCRATS AT CHICAGO

"To liberal America, George Wallace was too bad to be true."

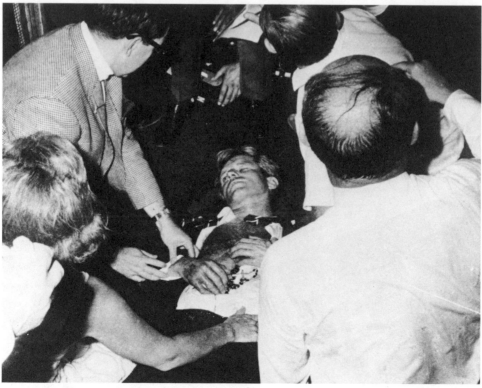

"Following a three-and-a-half-hour operation to remove the bullet, with the shocked nation at prayer for him, [Bobby Kennedy] died at 1:44 A.M., June 6, aged forty-two."

KENNEDY ASSASSINATED

LOS ANGELES, June 5, 1968—Robert Kennedy stands on the podium in the Embassy Room of the Hotel Ambassador, glowing with victory over McCarthy in California. Graciously, he congratulates his opponent on his long campaign since New Hampshire and for "breaking the political logjam." He pays tribute to his achievement in making "citizen participation a new and powerful force in our political life"— and appeals to McCarthy's people to join him. Kennedy also attacks Humphrey for steering clear of the primaries and avoiding the issues.

Bobby and his aides pushed through the jam-packed room, heading out of the hotel, then filed through a narrow kitchen passage almost blocked by two huge freezers. A man of Middle Eastern appearance, wearing a blue press badge, darted forward. Gun flashes lit up the passage. Sirhan Bishara Sirhan fired his .22 Iver-Johnson revolver eight times. Bobby was hit once in the shoulder and once in the head. The fatal bullet entered the right mastoid bone above the ear and lodged in the brain. His wife, Ethel, expecting their eleventh child, knelt over him.

Three others were wounded, including Paul Schrader, California head of the United Automobile Workers and the only labor leader to back Kennedy. The cramped kitchen passageway was boiling with people shouting to keep back, to give the victims air. Bobby lay on his back with his eyes open. Once, he licked his lips slowly. He was taken to the Hospital of the Good Samaritan but never recovered consciousness. Following a three-and-a-half hour operation to remove the bullet, with the shocked nation at prayer for him, he died at 1:44 A.M., June 6, aged forty-two. A curse lay upon the Kennedys. John Updike later remarked that God might have withdrawn His blessing from America.

Kennedy's body was carried to New York in an aircraft provided by the White House. On board with Ethel and Jacqueline Kennedy (who had flown with a coffin before) was another recent widow, Coretta King.

The assassin turned out to be a Jordanian currently living in Pasadena with his mother and brothers (Sirhan's father had returned to his Jordanian village in 1961). Found in his home was a notebook with the words: "Kennedy must be assassinated before June 5, 1968." It was the first anniversary of the disastrous Arab defeat in the Six-Day War. Sirhan's village on the West Bank had been occupied by the Israelis.

The present writer was in Czechoslovakia at the time—the euphoric summer of the Prague Spring—eating lunch in a restaurant patronized by writers and intellectuals. Someone came in and said, "They've assassinated Bobby Kennedy." A numbed silence fell across the restaurant; it was as if the air had been sucked out by all the reactionary forces, from racist bigots to Stalinist *apparatchiks*, ranged against the men of reason and liberality across the world.

Norman Mailer stood in vigil for fifteen minutes as a member of the honor guard around the coffin in St. Patrick's Cathedral in New York City. People waited in line for five or six hours, inching forward, including the poorest of the working class, blacks, Puerto Ricans, Irish washerwomen, old Jewish ladies: ". . . this endless line of people had really loved him, loved Bobby Kennedy like no political figure in ten years had been loved." For the funeral the high and the mighty took over under the tight protection of the Secret Service: the president, members of Congress, the Wall Street establishment. Mailer found St. Patrick's "dank with the breath of the over-ambitious offering reverence. . . ."

Perhaps a million people saluted the funeral train's slow passage from New York to Washington, its bell ringing incessantly, its whistle blowing in long, piercing blasts of melancholy. Under a blazing sun some waved, some knelt, some buried their faces in their hands. In Baltimore a silent mass, mainly black, had waited for hours; when the train pulled in, they joined hands to sing "The Battle Hymn of the Republic."

AFTER BOBBY

The question was now reversed: Would the Kennedy people join McCarthy? And would McCarthy's brittle dignity allow him to compete with Humphrey in bidding for their support? After California, McCarthy seemed to lose impetus. During the summer he displayed astonishingly little aggression toward Hubert Humphrey, the president's surrogate. When addressing the same state conventions, they decorously ignored each other and avoided debate. McCarthy's supporters in New York, the Committee for a Democratic Alternative, experienced difficulty in bringing their perversely proud candidate to the city for a rally at CUNY's Lewisohn Stadium on June 17. That the nomination was being "fixed by professional politicians oblivious of popular preference" (as Louis Heren of the London *Times* believed) was clearly demonstrated in the New York primary. Here McCarthy won 62 elected delegates against 30 for the Kennedy inheritance, 19 uncommitted, and only 12 for Humphrey, yet the party machine awarded McCarthy only 15 of 65 at-large delegates. The conclusion is inescapable that McCarthy had inwardly abandoned hope of the nomination, but could not resist haunting the machine's feast—and the White House.

Humphrey had already put the forthcoming Democratic Convention behind him and was competing with Richard Nixon for Middle America. Interviewed by *Look* in mid-June, the vice-president denounced "inflammatory" television coverage of ghetto riots and of the speeches of black leaders like Stokely Carmichael. "Negro youth particularly likes to get on television." So did HHH (as his campaign buttons described him, the outer *H*'s pressing their shoulders into the center "Humph").

The indefatigable Al Lowenstein spent the summer organizing the Coalition for an Open Convention in Chicago, a last-ditch attempt to bring together all the anti-HHH forces and the waverers. McCarthy's people were suspicious; was it a gambit to hand over their delegates to George McGovern or Edward Kennedy? The New Left accused Lowenstein of emasculating and manipulating dissent into conventional politics. A pre-Chicago meeting of the National Student Association reflected the virulence of New Left animosity toward this liberal caucus-corporal, inflamed by Lowenstein's nomination as candidate for Nassau County's fifth congressional district.

REPUBLICANS . . . WALLACE

The Republicans convened in Miami during the first week in August. Here was John Wayne, complaining about the left-wing press and the treatment of his film *The Green Berets.* Here was Tony Martin singing "The Glory of Love." Here were Midwestern faces in flat Nixon skimmers, ladies in rinsed hair, ambitious young Jaycees in corporation suits.

Of the three major Republican candidates, Richard Nixon arrived in Miami as the front-runner. Vice-president for two terms under Eisenhower, Nixon had been defeated in the presidential contest of 1960 by only a few thousand popular votes; his political fortunes later hit rock bottom when he lost the gubernatorial election in his home state of California. "Tricky Dick" had been universally written off; who would buy a used car from him? But Nixon had taken his lawyer's talents to Wall Street, worked patiently to regain lost ground, and now he would win the Republican presidential nomination for the second time. Of his two main rivals, Ronald Reagan had gained in stature since tear-gassing California's students; the speech nominating him promised that, "A man will confront the radicals on our campuses and the looters on our streets and say, 'The laws will be obeyed.' " But Reagan's hour was not yet.

Nelson Rockefeller, governor of New York State, had spent an estimated $10 million on his bid. Outside of New York, Republicans tended to regard Rocky with deep suspicion as a metropolitan liberal Democrat (like New York City Mayor John Lindsay) in drag. Mailer, the brightest commentator of this or any other year, noted that Rocky had an almost perfect face for the White House: Spencer Tracy's younger brother, virile, friendly, rough-hewn, marred only by "a catfish mouth." In the center of the mouth there seemed to be another mouth, which did the speaking. The *New York Times* estimated that 8,000 people came to the giant party he threw in Miami, but only 277 delegates voted for him as against 692 for Nixon and 182 for Reagan.

Nixon's acceptance speech was a homage to private enterprise, millions on payrolls rather than on welfare rolls. He offered black Americans their own homes and businesses, the chance to be managers and executives, "to have a piece of the 'action' in the exciting ventures of private enterprise." Six miles from the convention hall, in the area of Miami from 54th to 79th streets, the blacks rioted and the police exchanged fire with snipers, but Nixon's daughter Tricia was a vision in virgin white and Julie Nixon, sweet and neat and smiling, brought her David Eisenhower, grandson of a great man dying.

And Nixon said: "Let's win this one for Ike!"

Governor Spiro Agnew, of Maryland, was to be his vice-presidential running mate. Nixon had found a "veep" who would have to resign from office in disgrace before he did.

Winning against Hubert Humphrey was of course going to be easier than winning against Lyndon Johnson, but the lengthening shadow of George Wallace, former governor of Alabama, lay across the Republican camp. Several weeks before the convention, J. Strom Thurmond, of South Carolina, had endorsed Nixon and promised to stop Wallace in the South. A former Dixiecrat who had won 4 states and

39 electoral-college votes against Truman and Dewey in 1948, Thurmond had joined the Republicans during the ultra-Right Goldwater campaign of 1964. In November, 45 percent of Nixon's votes would come from the South.

Who was George Wallace? As governor of Alabama, in 1963 he had used state troopers to block the integration of schools, and state militia to stop federal marshals from serving a court order on him. "Of course, if I did what I'd like to do I'd pick up something and smash one of those federal judges in the head and then burn the courthouse down." In 1964, running as a Democrat, he launched his ambitious thrust into the North, picking up between 25 and 43 percent of the vote in primaries in Indiana, Wisconsin, and Maryland. Constitutionally barred from running again for governor of Alabama in 1966, he had invited the voters to elect his wife, Lurleen, which they did. In March 1967, she defied an order of the federal district court to establish a racial balance in Alabama's schools. In May 1968, Lurleen Wallace died.

Now, defying the party machines, he was running as head of the American Independence Party, offering a crusading campaign against the federal bureaucracy, Communists, anarchists, pot smokers, long-haired students, snobs, the press, and integration in housing and schools. "If anybody ever lies down in front of my car it will be the last car he ever lies down in front of in his life." He also suggested that, "We ought to turn this country over to the police for two or three years and everything would be all right."

To liberal America, George Wallace was too bad to be true. He might not qualify as a full-fledged fascist in a comparative government course, but he passed every other test. Wallace on welfare: idle parents of illegitimate children drinking moonshine whiskey while honest tax-payers were bled dry to pay for the welfare checks. Wallace on universities: spoiled, overprivileged college kids tearing up what their parents had worked to build. Wallace on crime: decent citizens afraid to leave their homes at night. Wallace on the Supreme Court: turning criminals loose while handcuffing the police. Wallace on the Enemy: big government, big parties, big labor, big business.

"You take all these pseudo-intellectuals, these sociologists, and they'll tell you, 'That man is a criminal—a rapist, a robber—because his daddy didn't give him a pony when he was a little boy.' Well, I was poor, too. My daddy didn't give me no pony—and I never rioted."

"They call you and me 'rednecks.' Well, if working for a living, working with your hands, working with the soil—if that's what they mean by 'rednecks,' then I'm proud to be one."

The Wallace line paralleled that of the Black Panthers: the same sense of exclusion by the System, the same demand for status, the same vision of a vast conspiracy, the same scorn for consensus, the same tribal celebration of "them and us." But whereas the Panthers spoke for a people trodden down, demeaned, and kept in poverty, Wallace spoke for the humbler, more insecure people who did the treading—not only the rednecks of the South, but many blue-collar workers in the North. After his death a lot of Bobby Kennedy's blue-collar support turned to Wallace as the only other candidate who was speaking to *them.*

The bewilderment and muffled resentment of his constituency demands, at least, consideration; and parallel constituencies extended to Europe. Three years later, Robert Coles reported a conversation with a policeman, but it would have served equally well in 1968: "Have you ever seen those college kids shouting at the police? I've never seen anything like them for meanness and cheapness. The language that comes out of their mouths. . . . They make insulting gestures at us. . . . I can't believe it's what they *say* it is, that they're just upset about injustice."

CHICAGO: THE DEMOCRATIC CONVENTION

The Democrats came to Chicago at the end of August, a week after the Soviet invasion of Czechoslovakia. By the time this most violent of conventions had run its course, the wits were talking of "Czechago"; Leonid Brezhnev was reported to have cabled Mayor Daley asking for 2,000 of his finest.

It was swelteringly hot. Cab drivers had joined the bus drivers on strike. Delegates emerged from a dozen hotels, wearing plastic badges around their necks on elastic strings, climbed into chartered buses, and followed squad-car escorts through streets patrolled by 12,000 police and 6,000 National Guardsmen. Delegates passed through at least six checkpoints before penetrating the barbed-wire ring surrounding the International Amphitheatre.

The Democratic primaries, conducted under different rules in each state (some delegates were elected by popular vote, others nominated by caucuses) culminated in a convention rank with sweat, intrigue, cries of betrayal, wheeling and dealing around favorite sons, and the Kennedy camp up for grabs after it became clear that the younger brother, Edward Kennedy, was not available for nomination. The formal proceedings began with seventeen separate challenges to nearly 1,000 out of 5,600 delegates and alternates. The 110-person credentials committee under Governor Richard Hughes, of New Jersey, rejected moves from the McCarthy camp to unseat delegations from Washington, Pennsylvania, Minnesota, Connecticut, Georgia, Texas, and Alabama.

Lyndon Johnson did not come to Chicago, but his men were in every key position and his friend Mayor Richard Daley ran the city. Hale Boggs, majority whip of the House of Representatives, sat on the Platform Committee; Carl Albert, majority leader of the House, was chairman of the convention with power over the floor; John B. Connally, governor of Johnson's home state, Texas, and Mayor Daley were seated in front of the rostrum with their loyal delegations. As Mailer noted, the rostrum was layered with pro-Humphrey delegations, while the opposition was relegated to the rear of the amphitheatre. Chairman Carl Albert was "taking his cue on what to do next by nods, fingers and other signs from Daley's henchmen, transparent in their signification— 'Let the boss speak' or 'Shut the guy up'—to thirty million TV viewers."

The McCarthy "children" arrived in Chicago, some of them in VWs covered in white and blue psychedelic flowers. As Mailer noted, "no one could claim that the loyalty of their effort had been equaled in many a year—certainly not since Adlai Stevenson, perhaps not since Henry Wallace. . . ." And they sang: "The GOP will cry in its beer, for here is a man who will change the scene. Gee-yene! Gee-yene!" Mailer did not feel at home with their "disinfected idealism," himself preferring the romantic, violent, ethnically charged idealism of the New Left or the Hollywood, prize-fight politics of the Kennedy campaign.

The liberal forces were further divided by the intervention of Senator George McGovern, former bomber pilot, university professor, and director of the Food for Peace program. Widely regarded as a "holder" for the Kennedy forces until Teddy Kennedy could emerge in his own right, McGovern told the Nebraska caucus that McCarthy "has taken the view that a passive and inactive Presidency is in order, and that disturbs me." As if to confirm his inactivity, McCarthy spent most of his time in his hotel room on the twenty-third floor of the Hilton. Despite many caucuses from state delegations wanting to meet him, he stood aloof and met only five. At a private meeting with the California delegation, he did not once mention Bobby's name. He refused, as David Halberstam noted, to glad-hand or pander; he choked on pride. He also refused to take the convention floor to argue for a general peace plank because, according to custom, no candidate addresses the convention until the nominees are chosen.

Questioned about Czechoslovakia, he slid into the cool, patrician detachment that frequently brought his staff close to despair. "I saw no need for a midnight meeting of the United States Security Council."

The Soviet action, he opined, was "likely to have more serious consequences for the Communist Party in Russia than in Czechoslovakia." These comments did McCarthy immense harm. Two days later he tried to repair the damage: "Our involvement in Vietnam is leaving us without tactical, moral and diplomatic power to be exercised in other parts of the world and other crises." Better—but a man of presidential caliber should strike the first pitch.

The peace plank was written by representatives of McCarthy, McGovern, and Kennedy after much haggling and loss of temper. The controversial passages of the final text called for an unconditional end to the bombing of North Vietnam, *the negotiation of mutual withdrawal from the South, and encouragement of the Saigon regime to negotiate with the NLF.* (Italics added; this formula would not have ended the war.) An additional paragraph was tacked on: "We are resolved to have no more Vietnams. . . . We shall neither assume the role of the world's policeman, nor lend our support to corrupt oppressive regimes unwilling to work for essential reforms and lacking the consent of the governed." Endorsed by former aides of the Kennedy administration, like Ted Sorensen and Pierre Salinger, this fine rhetoric sounded hollow when set against the record of 1961–63.

Speaking for the majority, Representative Hale Boggs quoted General Creighton Abrams, U.S. Military Commander in Vietnam: If the bombing of North Vietnam were to be suspended unilaterally, the enemy could, within ten days or two weeks, increase his capability in the DMZ fivefold.

The peace plank was defeated by 1,567 to 1,041. When the New York and California delegations began to sing "We shall overcome"—Wisconsin stood in support—the convention managers turned the New York microphones down and amplified the public address system for the convention band. The rear of the floor booed the front of the floor.

In an attempt to heal the rift, a movie was shown about the life of Bobby Kennedy. Everyone rose and applauded at the end. After five minutes of funeral-parlor unity, Chairman Carl Albert banged his gavel. The New York and California delegations began to sing the "Battle Hymn of the Republic," and again everyone joined in. Finally, after twenty minutes, Mayor Daley gave his signal and the gallery began to chant, "We love Daley." At Daley's disposal was the entire Illinois delegation, right under the podium, described by Mailer as "all those hecklers, fixers, flunkies and musclemen scanning the audience as if to freeze certain obstreperous faces, make them candidates for a contract and a hit." When HHH arrived to accept the nomination, he found the galleries packed with Daley's people and an enormous sign hanging from the gallery: "World's Great Mayor . . . Richard J. Daley."

Humphrey—described by Mailer as "an animal drenched in politics"—came to Chicago with nine-tenths of the machine behind him, including labor, the South, the president, and the Mafia. Everywhere was awash with Humphrey buttons, the big bold HHH. Mailer was disgusted by the vice-president's endless, loquacious speeches with their slovenly syntax and their phrases shunted back and forth "like a switchman who locates a freight car by moving everything in the yard."

And so the nomination went, inevitably, to Hubert Humphrey (1,761.75 votes), against 601 for McCarthy and 146.50 for McGovern. Humphrey chose as his running mate Senator Edmund Muskie of Maine.

16

THE OTHER CHICAGO— YIPPIES AND PIGS

"The noisy progress of the Yippie movement signaled the demise of the passive, flower-power motions cherished by the hippie dropouts."

"When Mayor Richard Daley's police were unleashed, it was not only the Yippies and the 'freaks' who suffered, but also convention delegates, campaign staff, reporters, concerned college kids, and bemused bystanders."

THE MOBILIZATION

Detailed planning for the Chicago Mobilization had begun on March 23, when a hundred antiwar groups gathered in a YMCA camp at Lake Villa, Illinois, under the auspices of the National Mobilization to End the War in Vietnam, whose leading organizers were David Dellinger, chief architect of the Pentagon demonstration; Rennie Davis, head of the Center for Radical Research; Tom Hayden of SDS; and Vernon Grizzard, a Boston draft-resistance leader. The target was the Democratic Convention.

The Chicago demonstrations would bring together the antiwar liberals, the concerned college kids, the radicals of the New Left, and the Bohemian apostles of the counterculture for the first time since the "levitation" of the Pentagon ten months earlier. What imparted a unique and traumatic quality to the demonstrations was the concurrence of the Democratic Convention—the climax to the long primary campaigns and the last hope of liberals committed to constitutional politics. When Mayor Richard Daley's police were unleashed, it was not only the Yippies and the "freaks" who suffered, but also convention delegates, campaign staff, reporters, concerned college kids, and bemused bystanders.

Nevertheless, the high-profile media attention accorded to the flamboyant apostles of the counterculture had a justification. Neither SDS nor the Yippies believed that the system could be redeemed by way of conventional liberal politics. Their intention was to prove that Vietnam was a manifestation of an inherently violent and repressive system—and to provoke that violence before a national audience. They succeeded. Although the counterculture was an international phenomenon, its heartland lay along the East and West coasts of America, with San Francisco and New York its twin Meccas.

Yippie leaders Abbie Hoffman and Jerry Rubin had been working on a vision of bringing 100,000 kids to Chicago to hold a youth festival—a "community of consciousness"—including music, theatre, witchcraft, and spontaneous disruption. The media stars of the revolution held a press conference on March 17 at the Hotel Americana in New York, during which Allen Ginsberg explained that the Chicago be-in would involve "a gathering together of younger people aware of the planetary fate that we are all sitting in the middle of . . ." and a search for an alternative to "competition, acquisition and war." To launch the search, Ginsberg chanted a Hare Krishna mantra for ten minutes to the television cameras.

The noisy progress of the Yippie movement signaled the demise of the passive, flower-power motions cherished by the hippie dropouts. Before arriving in the sweltering streets and parks of Chicago in August, we may plot the journey through the shifting terrain of the counterculture.

HIPPIE

The hippie enclaves had planted themselves across the country; an estimated 200,000 young people had left home to try the alternative life, and every national magazine ran eyewitness alarm stories about new cults of the bizarre and the occult, Jesus-freakery, the zonked flirtation with Zen, and acid. Papers like the *Oracle* and the *East Village Other* celebrated spiritual transvestism, the psychedelic supermarket of "sacramental" products offered to young people wandering in a transcontinental hallucination. Bodies and minds were damaged, though not always irreparably. Drug pushers, various maharishis, and the novels of J. R. R. Tolkien were on hand to pick up the profits, though the never-never land of the hedonistic Hobbits was no doubt stolen as often as purchased. In January 1967, there had taken place a "Gathering of the Tribes for a Human Be-in" in San Francisco with every kind of freaked-out hippie costume on display: colonial petticoats, buckskins and war paint, Arabian desert robes, paisley body stockings, Hopi tops and Hindu bottoms, bedspreads, togas. Allen Ginsberg lent his benign, soothing, and intensely corporeal presence. No one wanted to be "into" any kind of politics.

A number 7 bus from Market Street carried Richard Schlatter, an inquiring visitor from the square world, to Haight-Ashbury in about fifteen minutes. "I got off the bus and began to walk, and what I saw was incredible. This is an ordinary San Francisco neighborhood . . . with thousands of hippies sitting and wandering about, hair long and dirty, beaded, bearded, many with headbands, mostly with dirty bare feet. . . ." Schlatter entered an old movie theatre, where he found "everyone, including some stray dogs, wandering about genially and aimlessly." Garlands of marijuana leaves were being hung from the balcony. "Eventually some Indians in costume arrived and one man talked a great deal of nonsense about the teachings of the Great Spirit. . . ."

"The object of some polite interest since I was the only person in tie and jacket and shoes," Schlatter fell into conversation with an attractive couple, who continually pressed him to take some LSD. Harry, eighteen, was from the Bronx, a graduate actor of the New York City High School of Performing Arts and a dropout from City College. Kate, also eighteen, was from California, the daughter of motel keepers and harboring vague aspirations to attend San Francisco State College. Harry and Kate took Schlatter to a restaurant called the Macrobiotics, a vegetarian, natural-food-fetish hole-in-the-wall with meals of carrot and apple juice, soy beans, and brown rice, all for 50 cents. Harry and Kate told him about the virtues of nature and Thoreau, about Indian Great Spirits, Hindu mystics, immortality, and marijuana; and about the evils of alcohol and tobacco. They dismissed Schlatter's objections concerning the physical dangers of LSD as simply Establishment propaganda.

This ardent young couple lived by buying marijuana at $90 a kilo, making cigarettes worth $240, and selling them to high school kids. They entertained some fear of going to jail, but had so far escaped arrest. When Schlatter asked Harry about the draft, he said he would wait until he was called for his physical, take a dose of LSD, and tell the doctor he hoped to introduce soldiers to the benefits of pot and acid. Friends who had done this had apparently been let off.

By this time, 1968, the genuine hippies were drifting out of Haight-Ashbury in search of rural communes like Oneida Village and Brook Farm. The San Francisco scene increasingly belonged to specimens of cultural cross-pollination, wearing shaggy heads and carefully raggy clothes, but driving glistening Corvettes and Jaguars. Jefferson Airplane was being piped into office elevators and Greyhound Bus waiting rooms; suburban couples started taking off their clothes at parties and painting each other's bodies. San Francisco itself had become a self-parody for tourists, with topless nightclubs, topless shoeshine parlors, topless fortune-tellers, and topless lay psychiatrists. North Beach, on the fringes of Chinatown, had collapsed into commercialism, with Ferlinghetti's City Lights Bookstore the only authentic reminder of the old Beat scene.

DIGGERS

Out of the hippie counterculture sprang two movements that rejected the helpless lethargy of the stoned, freaked-out kids who lay about the streets and parks like *objets trouvés*. The Diggers and the Yippies offered contrasting models of compensating political aggression, the former embracing an ancient tradition of communal self-help (the first "Diggers" were disaffected soldiers from Oliver Cromwell's New Model Army, who attempted to create a genuinely communist colony on a Surrey hillside in 1649). The Yippies, on the other hand, sought a theatrical apocalypse on the national stage.

For both movements, the Dutch Provos, later reincarnated as the Kabouters, provided an inspirational example. The Provo of Amsterdam was *homo ludens,* reveling in play, magic, and provocative disruption; the message was directed at the "Provotariat," the alienated youth of the asphalt jungle. (The working class was condemned for watching television and joining the bourgeoisie in "a huge grey mass," the slave of the politicians.) The Provos' numerous White Plans blended seriousness with satire—like the White Chicken Plan to turn policemen into social workers. Other plans were ecological: the antipollution White Chimney Plan and the White Bike Plan, a proposal for free communal transport on two wheels. "The asphalt terror of the motorized bourgeoisie has lasted long enough." But the Provos shrewdly compromised on their own anarchist principles by running candidates in the Amsterdam city elections; the 13,000 votes they gained entitled them to one seat on the council. The Provos had disintegrated early in 1967 after the love-ins in Vondelpark, but later they were born again as the Kabouter (Elf) Party, which enjoyed remarkable electoral success in Amsterdam with the support of hippies, squatters, and visiting American Yippies.

The American Digger movement, born in 1966, flourished in two (predictable) cities: New York and San Francisco. Living in communes, tripping on LSD, cultivating the mumbling, inarticulate speech that signaled "no" to the brainwash of tidy semantics, the Diggers' strategy was to "pied piper" kids away from their bourgeois homes, then to hustle the authorities and local shopkeepers for free food, accommodation, and clinics. The other concern was to shield dropout kids with talent, such as musicians or painters, from the clutches of the commercial wolves. The New York Diggers created a free shop, distributed free stew in Tompkins Square, and transported a truckload of food to the Newark ghetto during the riots of 1967. They formed the East Side Service Organization to take runaways off the streets and to find them beds and jobs.

In October 1966, possession of LSD became illegal under California law. Denouncing this attempt to stop "the expansion of consciousness," the Diggers responded with a Love-Pageant Rally, threatening to present the mayor of San Francisco with "living morning glory plants and mushrooms. . . ." Free City was born partly in response to a social crisis in Haight-Ashbury, partly in rejection of the "straight" radicalism of SDS and the Maoist Progressive Labor Party. An early Digger leaflet warned: "Beware of leaders, heroes, organizers. Watch that stuff. Beware of Structure-freaks. . . . Any man who wants to lead you is the man. . . . *Fuck Leaders.*"

The Digger *Free News* traded in splash headlines and small-paragraph stories, an eclectic mix of the political and the communal: the arrest of Vietnam servicemen on drugs charges, the number of VC killed, Reagan saying the United States should take North Korean ships on the high seas, a crowd cheering the broken windows of the Haight Street branch of United California Bank, soul food dinners available at Bishop's Restaurant "for a quarter donation if you have it." A free cafeteria operated 11:30 A.M. to 12:30 P.M. daily at Saint Anthony's Church, Jones Street. Finally, "3 year old Andy and his papa Burt need a place to lay their heads they can contribute expenses."

Emmett Grogan, twenty-three, kingpin of the Diggers and blond, fair, with a freckled Brooklyn-Irish face, was in and out of jail (a tendency to hit cops) and had spent six years in Europe, on the road. Conscripted into the army on his return, he was soon in the psychiatric ward of Letterman Hospital, San Francisco, then out and into the San Francisco Mime Troupe. Grogan, who might have been written into a play by Sean O'Casey, took a look at the merchants profiteering off the hippie culture and declared war.

By the spring of 1967, the Diggers had come to the conclusion that despite six months of psychedelic social work, everybody in the neighborhood but themselves was either making money or holding on to what he or she already had. Set on a showdown, they convened a meeting in Glide Church, Haight-Ashbury: "The Diggers have a demand," screamed Grogan, "and that's that the rest of you—all the bands, stores, and people in *this* whole fucking hippie scene—go nonprofit. . . . We want you to start living this love shit you're always talking about." That meant barter, not money, for money, said Grogan, was guilt. Here Allen Ginsberg, who distrusted anger and self-righteousness, intervened to ask how he could possibly barter his poetry readings; he recommended the Diggers turn themselves into a foundation, as he had done. Himself the most generous of donors, Ginsberg taunted Grogan by saying he now rather fancied "a little something for myself," provoking the Digger to denounce him as "just a rich Jewish merchant."

Digger activity receded in the summer of 1967 when the area was overrun by imported flower children, but they re-emerged early in 1968 after the police rioted against the hippie remnants on Haight Street. Another hopeless verbal confrontation—this time between the helpless and the militants—took place in Straight Theatre. The Free City was as good as over, but a fascinating legacy was bequeathed in the shape of *The Digger Papers,* reflecting the utopian ideal rather than what had actually been achieved—an updated version of Gerrard Winstanley's *New Law of Righteousness,* written at the climax of the English Civil War 320 years earlier. (There was one crucial difference: Winstanley's Diggers asked only to work their communal fields in peace, whereas the San Francisco Diggers made a philosophy out of parasitism.)

"Our state of awareness demands that we uplift our efforts from competitive game playing in the underground to the comparative roles of *free families* in free cities. *Free Cities* are composed of Free Families (e.g., in San Francisco: Diggers, Black Panthers, Provos, Mission Rebels and various revolutionist gangs and communes) who establish and maintain services that provide a base of freedom for autonomous groups to carry out their programs without having to hassle for food, printing facilities, transportation, mechanics, money, housing. . . ."

The Digger vision, which took for granted the wider capitalist environment, had no thought of overturning the system as a whole, merely of digging radical enclaves within it. Private enterprise took care of production; hustling achieved expropriation; pure communism (to each according to his needs) was the principle of distribution.

Expropriation: The Free Food Storage and Distribution Center "should hit every available source of free food—produce markets, farmers' markets, meat packaging plants, farms, dairies, sheep and cattle ranches . . . and fill up their trucks with the surplus by begging, borrowing, stealing, forming liaisons and communications with delivery drivers for the left-overs from their routes. . . ." Pharmaceutical houses "should be hit for medical supplies."

Distribution: "Someone asked how much a book cost. How much did he think it was worth? 75 cents. The money was taken and held out for anyone. 'Who wants 75 cents?' A girl who had just walked in came over and took it."

The Digger philosophy was a peculiarly American blend of Arcadian simplicity and modern corporate realism, of "beat the system at its own game." Thus, in case anyone objected to the "begging, borrowing, stealing," there was to be Free City legal assistance "from top-class lawyers . . . first-class case-winners." Wheeling and dealing was to be conducted by "business-oriented cats" who, working with the lawyers, would "outmanoeuvre urban bureaucracies and slum landlords. . . ."

The vision was modernist. Everything would be "groovy . . .

everything with style. . . ." The Free City Environmental and Design Gang of artists would attack the slums and "comfortably construct environments for the community. Materials and equipment can be hustled from university projects and manufacturers, etc."

After the Digger movement disbanded, Emmett Grogan went off riding with the Hell's Angels and helped negotiate the fatal hiring of the Angels as "stewards" for the catastrophic Altamont rock festival in December 1969.

YIPPIE

The Youth International Party, whose followers were first called Yippees, but later, more commonly, Yippies, announced themselves as anyone who said, loudly, "Yippee!" According to Jerry Rubin, they were born at the Pentagon demonstration in October 1967, though "they have been developing in the womb of Mother America since the late 1950s." A Yippee was a "stoned-idealist, moved by the vision of a future utopia" and alienated by the vast and insane bureaucratic prison of America. The Yippie remedy was "happenings, community, youth power, dignity, underground media, music, legends, marijuana, action, myth, excitement, a new style."

A Yippie leaflet issued in 1968 warned: "All the gangs are coming out Saturday night at 11:00 to liberate St. Mark's Place between 2nd and 3rd Avenues. Yippie! St. Mark's Place is a fucking mess! We will restore it to its pristine state! Cadillacs, tourists' buses, cops with guns and clubs, private dicks chasing runaways and UPTOWN FREAKS will be REMOVED. Gem's Spa will be held under siege until the price of an ice cream cone is returned to 17 cents! Nach!"

Complaining of police harassment, the Yippies demanded "the freedom to stand around and do nothing," plus two free medical clinics in the city at Tompkins and Washington squares; otherwise there would be plagues of VD and hepatitis. "We will fuck the police and their horses! NOTHING will be SAFE from STREET FREAK GERM WARFARE if the city does not allow us to disarm ourselves!"

The Establishment took a sardonic view of the Yippies until the Chicago demonstrations in August 1968, but not thereafter. On April 5, *Time* magazine reported a recent Yippie happening in New York: "They poured into the vast main concourse of Manhattan's Grand Central Station 3,000 strong, wearing their customary capes, gowns, feathers and beads. . . . The Yippies—1968's version of the hippies— were celebrating spring. . . . A dozen youths scaled the information booth, ripped off the clock hands, scribbled graffiti and defiantly passed around lighted marijuana 'joints' in full view of the Tactical Purpose Force. The fuzz charged, billy clubs flailing, and arrested 61 demonstrators. . . ."

But the corporate liberals were not invariably amused. When Robert Kennedy attended a $500-a-plate dinner, the Yippies set up in the street outside the building offering free bologna sandwiches. "You scum, you dirt, you filth!" the liberals screamed at them. Rubin expressed equal contempt for those who tried to bridge the gap between Left liberals and the New Left: ". . . liberal fuck-offs who come on to revolutionaries real chummy-chum-chum."

Jerry Rubin was born into what he called the "Jewish subculture" of Cincinnati. When he visited his uncles and aunts, they complained about how hard they worked and how some people were living off welfare. Descended from Russian Jews on both sides, Jerry had graduated with the class of 1956 from Walnut Hills High School and got himself photographed—in short hair and bow tie, the neat collegiate look—with Adlai Stevenson. Nine years later, he had studied sociology at the Hebrew University in Jerusalem, met Che Guevara in Cuba, and become a leading light of the Free Speech Movement (and the Filthy Speech Movement) in Berkeley. After six weeks he had dropped out of a lecture course given by the neo-conservative political scientist Professor Seymour Lipset, then he dropped out entirely. Che Guevara had told him he'd like to fight in North America, "in the belly of the beast"—and Rubin began by messing up a Telegraph Avenue grocery store that didn't hire blacks.

In 1965 Jerry Rubin figured among a group of radicals, mainly from the Maoist Progressive Labor Party, who were subpoenaed by the House Un-American Activities Committee. At first he feared that he had been overlooked and suffered a bout of "subpoena envy," but within two hours of receiving his precious subpoena he was on the steps of San Francisco City Hall in front of "four television cameras, five photographers, four newspaper reporters, and seven radio stations. . . ." When cautious Old Leftists, habituated to legalistic stalling throughout the McCarthy era, advised him to refuse to testify and to cite the First Amendment, he yelled, "Fuck you! The worse the better!" Having hired an American Revolutionary War costume, he arrived at the hearing stoned in the August heat. While Progressive Labor witnesses gave Nazi salutes to the committee and called them "yellow-bellied, racist cowards," Rubin blew giant gum bubbles. The hearings were suspended before he could testify.

In December 1965, Rubin was sentenced to thirty days in jail for his part in a San Francisco demonstration against General Maxwell

Taylor. Soon afterwards, however, he was lured back into the belly of the beast via radical electoral politics, serving as manager for Robert Scheer, editor in chief of *Ramparts,* who was running for the California State legislature. Rubin later ran on his own behalf against the Republican mayor of Berkeley, Wallace Johnson, whom he loved to abuse, face-to-face, on platforms provided by church groups and PTAs. Inspired by the Dutch Provos, Rubin's mayoral campaign was an amalgam of scandalous demands: legalized pot, free heroin for addicts, legal abortion, the gradual disarmament of the police, and abolition of the draft. In pursuit of all this Rubin wore a long tie and a gold suit. He got 22 percent of the vote (but hardly any black votes), an honorable defeat.

Rubin's drug life began in 1965; he loved sex and movies under drugs. "For years I went to left-wing meetings trying to figure out what the hell was going on. Finally I started taking acid, and I realized what was going on: nothing. . . . Fuck left-wing meetings!" The solution lay in direct, frenetic action against every instance of repression. Praising theft and arson, he promised a world without clocks and barbers.

The year 1967 brought him into contact with Abbie Hoffman, also engaged in weaving webs of love between the political radicals and the zonked-out magic-mushroom hippies. Rubin fell in love with New York, roaming the city with Hoffman, Paul Krassner, Ed Sanders, and Keith Lampe, all of them male chauvinists for whom women would remain, before or after the apocalypse, simply "chicks." His need of drugs intensified. "Grass travels around the room like a continually moving kiss. Smoke grass in the morning. Stay high all day. . . . Marijuana is the street theater of the mind. . . ."

It was after the Six-Day War that Jerry Rubin rejected Zionism and adopted the Arab cause. Many Jews of the New Left followed this path, Daniel Cohn-Bendit among them.

Abbie Hoffman, who had worked in the civil rights movement in the South and North, set out his *credo* in the spring of 1968: "I am busy making my own revolution. I am busy building a new community. . . . Some call us hippies, yippies, dropouts, runaways, free men, flower children. The name doesn't matter. We are here to stay. We have our own civil war. . . . Long hair makes us the new niggers. It gives us high visibility. It is a symbol of rejection of the old order . . . the military, careers, university bullshit, outmoded mores and split-level living. . . ."

And what was freedom? "Freedom is the right to stand on the streetcorner and do nothing." Freedom was no censorship, an end to both poverty and property, to the draft as well. "Freedom is burning money. Freedom is the end of work. Our goal is full unemployment."

Reflecting upon himself (never a burden), Hoffman concluded: "I suppose all this energy results from being an anarchist, Jewish, bottle-fed, stubborn, beautiful, white, spoiled brat, dedicated male. . . ." By his own account Hoffman wrote and traveled frenetically: "I took about twenty acid trips, fucked about 856 times. . . . I managed to get busted only ten times and face a possible thirty-seven years or so in prison."

On June 13, 1968, New York narcotics detectives stormed into Rubin's Lower East Side apartment, angrily tore a Castro poster from the wall, and arrested him for alleged possession of three ounces of marijuana. They kept screaming about communism as they went through his papers: "If this was Cuba, you'd have no trial and they'd cut off your hands." Thrown into a cell, Rubin was kicked in the base of the spine, then taken to Bellevue Hospital's emergency ward. In December the Justice Department admitted in the U.S. Court of Appeals that it maintained electronic surveillance on Rubin.

Criticism from the orthodox New Left grew louder; radical leaders like Tom Hayden condemned the Yippie superstars for "media gamesmanship" and a devotion to motion, disruption, chaos, and rebirth. The systematic use of obscenity upset radicals raised in the climate of loving witness during the early sixties, but Rubin insisted that Puritanical repression was what the war in Vietnam was really about. (Obscenity, of course, is merely the reverse face of Puritanism.) His fantasies were crudely bullish: "Our tactic is to send niggers and long haired scum invading white middle-class homes, fucking on the living room floor . . . spewing sperm on the Jesus pictures."

The "authoritarian socialists," said Rubin, were itching to scrub the hippies, cut their hair, and send them to jail for using dirty words. Meanwhile, they were forever waiting for the working class. "The ideological left is made up of part-time people whose life-style mocks their rhetoric." The Yippies' capacity to offend the Old Left now outstripped their ability to freak the corporate liberals; when Rubin and Hoffman tossed dollar bills from the gallery of the New York Stock Exchange, they were greeted with amused applause from below, until the guards hustled them out; but when Rubin burned dollar bills during a debate with Trotskyists the audience hissed. "How can you burn money when poor people in the ghetto need it? You should join the circus!" Rubin told them that the goal of permanent revolution was to turn spectators into actors. Revolution was a permanent way of life, not a program for the next century.

The hip anarchism of the Yippies disgusted Progressive Labor and irritated Tom Hayden, yet beguiled a certain type of hard-Left intellectual. John Gerassi, an expert on American imperialism in Latin America, had explained the Cuban revolution to the Dialectics of Liberation conference in London: ". . . the one way to guarantee that their people are genuinely free is not elections, is not a free press, is not all the trappings of the so-called political democracy that we have, but simply to arm the people." Elsewhere, however, Gerassi grooved in with the do-your-own-thing spirit of Abbie Hoffman and the counterculture: "You want to turn on, turn on. You want to drop out, drop out. Groove to the MC5 singing John Lee Hooker's *Motor City is Burning* ('All the cities will burn. . . . You are the people who will build up the ashes') or the Lovin' Spoonful's *Revelation: Revolution '69* ('I'm afraid to die but I'm a man inside and I need the revolution')."

As for Hoffman's workless tomorrow, Gerassi could not quite put aside his knowledge of Third World realities: "I can teach. . . . Maybe I can hoe potatoes. . . . Well, not every day, maybe."

MOTHERFUCKERS

Intellectuals speculated about the Yippies' international heritage. For Gary Wills, dada held the key, with its death's heads, toy guns, mocking use of uniforms, incantations, and cult of nudity. Pigasus had first appeared at the International Dada Fair in 1920; during the Chicago Mobilization in August, the Yippies both loved and cursed their presidential candidate, their Père Ubu, the Pig. Wills diagnosed the Yippie phenomenon as the advance guard of an empirical pop culture currently sweeping the museums: kinetic art, programed action art, bleeping lights, "feel it" objects, and happening contraptions like Jean Tinguely's "Homage to New York." In fact, instant kinetics were up for grabs both for street fighters and the smart, moneyed people who patronized galleries and bought the new furniture.

Take the Lower East Side Motherfuckers. A bizarre hybrid of the political and cultural revolts, exhibitionistic delinquents reveling in the image of anarchistic lumpen scum, they mixed New York street talk with dada, surrealism, futurism, and French Situationist theory. The dada manifesto of 1919 was quoted in support of an end to work and the birth of a new, de-alienated man—but updated: "Today we offer automation, cybernation and free love on the streets."

In *King Mob,* a prototypical neo-pop "comix" produced in London but almost wholly focused on the New York scene, a muscular barbarian bellows, "Up against the wall. . . ." Beneath this, an esoteric caption: "Reich, Geronimo, Dada; American Revolutionaries with a Message for England." *King Mob* devoted itself to New York happenings, but its artwork copied nineteenth-century French cartoons: Death (Anarchy) with a rosette in his hat holding a torch of fire and a poster: "Mob Law. Paris Burns. Henry Returns, Tonite, St. Marx Pl." From the cover snarls the hideous specter of a black werewolf: "A M-M-M Mother Fucker is a WEREWOLF!" Highly recommended, also, was "Marinetti beating up Wyndham Lewis in an allnight urinal. . . . Marinetti imprisoning a bevy of wealthy culture vultures in a belltent and driving his motor bike over it full throttle time after time. . . ." The spirit of the Italian futurist was now revived (said *King Mob*) in the burning ghettos of America; art and life joined at last in the "insurrectionary carnival."

King Mob derided both passive, drugged hippies and the usual New Left rent-a-crowd who were forever "counting arseholes" and pursuing stale "issue politics." The "idiot Left" remained impervious to "the atrocious *modern poverty* of the over-developed countries. . . ." Work was to be avoided at any cost. The modern department store aroused the appetite for juvenile pandemonium (called creative violence) among anarcho-situationists in America and Germany. *King Mob* fantasized a "mill-in" at Macy's during the Christmas shopping rush of 1967: "Half-starved dogs and cats were let loose in the food department. A hysterical buzzard flew around the China section. . . . Decoys with flags and banners planted themselves in the middle of groups of straight middle-class shoppers who were promptly roughed up and hustled outside by cops and floor walkers. Utter chaos. . . ."

Early in 1968 the Motherfuckers reincarnated themselves as the Lower East Side chapter of SDS. Piles of refuse were set aflame during the New York City garbage strike, and stones were hurled at the firemen, the stated purpose being to "invert all the symbols and stereotypes in any given area" and to "exacerbate the contradiction between what people *apparently* feel and what they *really* feel." The Motherfuckers took over the Fillmore East during a performance by the Living Theatre (thus mau-mauing the Mau Mau) in October 1968, demanding an end to performances and "artistic exploitation" in the name of community self-expression. "Creative violence" was by 1968–69 becoming rather less creative; *King Mob* admiringly depicted the Motherfuckers "smashing windows . . . firing anything that would burn . . . using karate chops, brandishing knives and slashing with bicycle chains strapped to their wrists, screaming 'Up Against the Wall Motherfucker. . . .' "

London's Situationist *Arson News,* having wiped the Provos, hippies, and politicals off the revolutionary map, promised to mobilize skinheads, greasers, Angels, football hooligans, and factory thugs in a new "Spectre" that would "stop at nothing." Meanwhile, the White

Panthers, formed out of Detroit Artists' Workshop in 1968, was into rock, drugs, liberating high schools, and, in the case of their inspirational spirit, John Sinclair, into Marquette State Prison, Michigan. Given ten years for handing two (free) marijuana joints to an undercover narcotics agent, Sinclair was released in 1972, but not before he had poured out prison manifestos imbued with the mindless male chauvinism of the counterculture: "Fuck God in the ass. Fuck your woman until she can't stand up. . . . Our program of rock and roll, dope, and fucking in the streets is a program of total freedom for everyone."

CHICAGO STREET SCENES

Abbie Hoffman and Jerry Rubin had fruitlessly negotiated with Chicago's deputy mayor for a permit to hold their planned outrage in the city during the Democratic Convention. At the same time, David Dellinger's National Mobilization to End the War in Vietnam intended more conventional demonstrations, although now, as at the time of the Pentagon demonstration, Dellinger erected no barriers between the short- and long-haired soldiers of peace.

Sixty-six years of age and four times elected mayor, on the last occasion with 74 percent of the vote, Richard J. Daley walked behind a mighty barrel of a chest: though only 5 feet 8 inches tall, he was said to weigh 200 pounds. His were the jowls of the traditional city boss. A poor Irish boy, the son of a sheet metal worker who became a blacklisted trade unionist, Daley attended mass every day and kept his city machine—a complex web of patronage—in perfect shape. As Mailer put it, "No interlopers for any network of Jew-Wasp media men were going to dominate the streets of his parochial city, nor none of their crypto-accomplices with long hair, sexual liberty, drug license and unbridled mouths."

It was the last week of August. Less than a week after the Soviet tanks had rolled into Prague, the Democratic Convention delegations arrived in Chicago, a minority of them determined to confront their own country's imperialism. The Mobilization's supporters were arriving, SDS contingents, the Yippies, the intellectuals, and the artists. The media were out in force.

In Lincoln Park, on the Sunday afternoon of August 25, a rock group was playing to an orderly crowd of 1,000 or 2,000 seated kids and young adults, while others milled about, watching. "Vote Pig in '68" urged the Yippie placards. When the band stopped, Humphrey Dumpty was introduced in the shape of a painted egg with legs, striding through the crowd, "the next president of the United States." Other Yippie clowns followed: a hideous Miss America; a symbolic representation of Mayor Daley's political machine; and a Green Beret done in "some sort of wax vomit pop art," as Norman Mailer noted, strolling through the park.

The hostility of the System, the menace from Daley's police, welded the dissident groups, straight and freaky, into a community sharing platforms and bullhorns: David Dellinger, Rennie Davis, Tom Hayden, Abbie Hoffman, Allen Ginsberg, Norman Mailer. The programmatic battle was being fought within the convention amphitheatre, but in the streets and parks the complex stratifications of American society and the great variety of outlooks had—as in the Civil War—distilled themselves into two camps. As opinion polls were later to show, the majority of the nation loathed the people in the parks. The strength of the Yippies was that they reveled in this hostility.

Mailer picked up a Yippie throwaway in the park. It was headed *YIPPIE,* exhorted "VOTE PIG IN '68," and demanded: (1) an immediate end to the war in Vietnam; (2) immediate freedom for Huey Newton and "all other black people," plus "adoption of the community control concept in our ghetto areas."

Thus the Yippies began with standard Left political demands before arriving (point 3) at their own special base, the legalization of marihuana [so spelled] "and all other psychedelic drugs. . . ." From here it was a step to (5) "the abolition of all laws related to crimes without victims." This linked up logically with point 14, "An end to all censorship. We are sick of a society which has no hesitation about showing people committing violence and refuses to show a couple fucking." Point 15 followed without delay: "We believe that people should fuck all the time, anytime, whomever they wish." Anticipating what was to befall them in Daley's Chicago, the Yippies betrayed their white, middle-class background by demanding (6), "The total disarmament of all the people beginning with the police. This includes not only guns but such brutal devices as tear gas, MACE, electric prods, blackjacks, billy clubs, and the like." (The Black Panthers, by contrast, demanded the right to carry guns.) After that it was point 7, "The Abolition of Money" and point 8, "a society in which people are free from the drudgery of work"; in other words, "full unemployment. . . . Let the Machines do it."

The manifesto ended on an inflammatory note: "Political Pigs, your days are numbered. We are the second American revolution. We shall win. Yippie!" Mayor Daley had in mind a different scenario.

Tough Irish and Polish kids were circulating on the edges of the laughing crowd of radicals and long-haired Yippies. Mailer, who had a strong presentiment that trouble was coming, encountered other artists and intellectuals in the park: Allen Ginsberg, William Burroughs, Jean Genet, and Terry Southern. "They had the determined miserable look of infantrymen trudging to the front." Ginsberg gave him a friendly salute, while Genet, "large as Mickey Rooney, angelic in appearance," glanced at Mailer "with the hauteur it takes French intellectuals at least two decades to acquire."

Next day was LBJ's birthday. Three thousand youths converged on the Chicago Coliseum, an old and crumbling convention hall, to attend an anti-birthday party, with the Holocaust No-Dance Band playing at full volume. Phil Ochs sang, "It's always the old who lead us to war; it's always the young who fall," and the crowd rose, holding their hands high in victory signs and chanting "No, no, we won't go." Burroughs and Genet spoke of the police as mad dogs; the popular black comedian Dick Gregory wasted a dominant Puritan culture both racist and violent.

Around midnight on Tuesday, some four hundred clergy, concerned citizens, and other respectable persons joined SDS, the Yippies, and the National Mobilization committee to fight for the privilege of remaining in the park. Sporting black-cross arm bands and chanting pacifist hymns, the clergy exhorted the gathering to join in a nonviolent vigil. Half an hour passed before the police attacked. The police bullhorns gave the crowd five minutes to be out of the park. Mailer noted the rising fear. People all over the park were shyly introducing themselves to each other. The more enterprising rubbed Vaseline on their face and tied wet handkerchiefs around their nose and mouth. Someone announced over the speaker: "If it's gas, remember, breathe through your mouth, don't run, don't pant, and for Christsake don't rub your eyes."

Allen Ginsberg was chanting "Oom" in a hoarse whisper, with occasional tinkles from his finger cymbals. William Burroughs, wearing a felt hat, let his thin lips twitch in a half-smile. Jean Genet rubbed his nose on the sleeve of his leather jacket.

Huge tear-gas canisters came crashing through the branches, snapping them, and bursting in the center of the gathering. Some ministers began to retreat with their huge wooden cross, "carrying it like a fallen comrade." Gas was everywhere. People were running, screaming, tearing through the trees. "We walked along," Sol Lerner, of the *Village Voice,* reported, "hands outstretched, bumping into people and trees, tears streaming from our eyes and mucus smeared across our faces. . . ." The police advanced, swatting at the stragglers and crumpled figures; huge trucks swept along the street at the edge of the park, spraying more gas. Kids began ripping up the pavement and hurling chunks of concrete at the truck windows. Then they flooded out into the streets, blocking traffic, fighting with the plainclothes policemen who awaited their exodus from the park, and bombarding the patrol cars that sped through the crowds. Mobs roamed through the streets, breaking windows, setting trash cans on fire, and overturning patrol cars. Diving down into the subway, Lerner found a large group of refugees who had made the same escape.

Seventeen newsmen were attacked by the police, as well as cameramen from three television networks. Nicholas von Hoffman reported in the Washington *Post:* "Next, the cops burst out of the woods in selective pursuit of news photographers. Pictures are unanswerable evidence in court. They'd taken off their badges, their name plates, even the unit patches on their shoulders to become a mob of identical, unidentifiable club swingers." Later, at Henrotin Hospital, editors came to claim their wounded.

The kids didn't give up. Mailer wondered whether the tear gas served as a kind of catharsis for some of them, a purging of middle-class timidity. By three in the morning, several thousand had massed in Grant Park, listening to speakers, cheering, chanting, calling across Michigan Avenue to the huge, brooding facade of the Hilton, a block wide and twenty-five stories high, where most of the convention notables were staying. The police, though out in force, were not yet prepared to attack in full view of the Hilton.

A cheer went up as the National Guard replaced the police. "It was like a certificate of merit for the demonstrators. . . ." to see the rifles, army trucks, and Jeeps with barbed-wire gratings in front of their bumpers. From the fifteenth and twenty-third floors of the Hilton, the McCarthy campaign blinked all their lights on and off in salute, "like ships signaling across a gulf of water in the night." Convention delegates came out of the hotel in a spontaneous surge of fraternity, united by the sour odor of Mace, "the sighing and whining of the army trucks moving in and out all the time. . . ."

On Wednesday a meeting took place in Grant Park under the auspices of the Mobilization, drawing a crowd of 10,000 or 15,000. The mayor had granted a permit to assemble, but had refused to allow a march; the Mobilization was determined to march to the Democratic Convention amphitheatre—for that purpose they had come to Chicago. The worst violence was imminent.

When three demonstrators climbed a pole to cut down the American flag, a squad of police charged at them, but got into trouble themselves, choking on their own gas, fighting their way clear through a barrage of rocks. Then came a larger force of police, busting everyone and heading for Rennie Davis at the bullhorn. He was knocked unconscious, his head cut open. Tom Hayden, who had been moving about the city in disguise, suggested that the crowd break into small groups and go out into the streets of the Loop "to do what they have to do."

But many, including the apostles of nonviolence, simply remained. Ginsberg addressed them—the poet rich in hair and spirit but bald at the crown, his soft eyes magnified by horn-rimmed eyeglasses—croaking from an injured throat. Ginsberg had been gassed Monday night and Tuesday night, and had gone to the beach at dawn to read Hindu mantras to some of the Yippies. Now he led them in the deep chant of peace, "Ooom. . . ."

GINSBERG

The poet Allen Ginsberg provided the stoutest bridge between the counterculture and the New Left, between the wandering minstrels of existential self-discovery and the political battalions. Gifted and generous, tolerant but tough, Ginsberg commanded affection and respect throughout the Movement. He was the Jewish Daddy to thousands of "children," but he wanted none of his own. In July 1967, he attended the Dialectics of Liberation conference in London, spent the fall writing in Venice, and ended the year in a New York court after the End the Draft Week demonstrations outside the Whitehall Street Induction Center. Astonishingly, it was his first conviction.

In January 1968, Ginsberg turned up at a rally at Town Hall to protest the indictment of Dr. Spock, continued to lecture widely on the sins of American imperialism, joined in preparations for the Yippie counter-convention in Chicago, and duly manifested his broad, comforting presence during the savage week in August.

A decade had passed since Ginsberg was prosecuted for publishing *Howl,* a poem in 112 stanzas which by the late sixties had been officially translated into nine languages and run off in contraband editions in at least a dozen others. *Howl* went into its seventeenth legal printing in September 1966:

> Moloch! Moloch! Robot apartments! invisible suburbs!
> skeleton treasuries! blind capitals! demonic industries!
> spectral nations! invincible madhouses! granite cocks!
> monstrous bombs!

Ginsberg thrived on notoriety and loved to evoke recognition on street and campus without responding, his shining black eyes fixed straight ahead, rich locks of hair hanging to his shoulder, a prophet's beard, an Oriental carpetbag slung over his shoulder. As a viable alternative to one-dimensional American corporate man, Ginsberg offered a pantheism of disparate cultures, ranging from Yoruba dances to "the electric vibrations of the Beatles who have borrowed shamanism from Afric sources," from ganja, the hemp sacred to the Great Lord Shiva, to American Indian peyote ritual—all enlisted to help the young achieve "a peaceful natural community" and the cessation of "desire, anger, grasping, craving." Ginsberg recommended the enlarged family unit, matrilineal descent, children held in common, and sexual orgies. These he described as a "community sacrament—one that brings all people closer together." Unfortunately, "sacrament" was the most overworked and abused word of the era.

Travel, pilgrimage, discovery were in his blood, not only India and the Orient, but Europe, too. On May Day 1965, a vast crowd of Czech students had crowned Ginsberg King of the May and borne him through the streets in a rose-covered chariot. But then someone handed a Ginsberg notebook to the police and four hours later he was on a plane, accused of having "grossly violated the norms of decent world behavior." Arriving in London, he took part in a huge poetry-reading marathon at the Albert Hall, returned to America, and set about awakening his fellow countrymen to the possibilities of nonviolent confrontation with authority—as when he negotiated a truce of sorts between a Berkeley antiwar demonstration and hostile police and Hell's Angels. His invariable advice to demonstrators was to perform "outside the war psychology"; Ginsberg was the pioneer of "flower power."

He was also a passionate advocate of the drug culture. Monogamous sex and antidrug laws were all part of the repressed system's "big jealous arrangement." He assembled a thick, erudite, documentary file on all aspects of drugs and their use, having in mind one day to bring a legal case arguing that existing statutes violated the legal rights of artists to the necessary tools of their trade. Much of his poetry was written when high. Giving evidence to a special Senate Judiciary Subcommittee hearing on narcotics legislation, he suggested that the terror preceding an LSD breakdown was not an effect of the drug itself, but of threatening laws and unfriendly social circumstances.

Appearing on the same platform as famous music groups like the Fugs, and now confronted by Moloch in the form of a $30,000 income, Allen Ginsberg turned himself into a charitable, tax-exempt foundation, appointed himself treasurer, and began handing out money freely as one spiritual emergency after another occurred (for example, the police bust of the London *International Times* or the straitened circumstances of Beat poets). At Marquette, the Jesuit fathers imposed a ban on a Ginsberg reading, generating a spiritual shoot-out on the campus and a minor national scandal. A few days later campus police at Michigan State stopped the sale of Ginsberg's books at a benefit reading he gave for a student literary magazine.

Ginsberg was the central casting office of the underground. A fat address book in his purple bag contained the names of kindred spirits across the world, and one of his pleasures was to put them in touch with one another so as to advise about local statutes, bail fund sources, pot peddlers, and where (in Jane Kramer's words) "the best sex and the best conversation can be found." A gifted operator and fixer, with effective contacts in city halls, law firms, and American Civil Liberties Union offices, Ginsberg was patient and persevering with the protocols of the square world, avoiding the irate, scornful style common within the underground—"coming on like some spooky superexclusive angry beatnik egomaniac madman," as he expressed it.

Persuasion was always preferable to violence; Ginsberg regarded the language of politics as comic-strip fantasy, hypnosis, "an outrage against feeling," yet he was increasingly involved in political protest, the body language of the war dance, partially persuaded that withdrawn meditation could not alter the operational norms of the real world, the Pentagon, and the police. He needed the esteem of the radicals and admired their bravado, but his "better half" belonged to those, like the hippies, committed to "a community of awareness, to control of anger, to the preservation of the planet, to art, to tolerance, to sexuality . . . to the entire body rather than just that part called the cerebral cortex. . . ."

Despite the antiauthoritarian, antibureaucratic emphasis of the New Left, his suspicions remained: politics was a bad trip. "I propose civil liberties and the individual right to speech and sex as against a police state. I propose the sexual commune as an intelligent, spiritual way of life as against a kind of dinosaur socialism run by a bunch of sexually and spiritually perverted Marxists. . . . I propose that Tim Leary and Stokely Carmichael get together and cook up something for Mississippi and Alabama."

THE POLICE RIOT

CHICAGO, Wednesday, August 28, 1968—The demonstrators in Grant Park break through the police cordons and out into the city at 6:30 in the evening. On the Loop they encounter and greet the mules and wagons of Ralph Abernathy's Poor People's Campaign. Spreading across Michigan Avenue, the demonstrators begin to move forward in the gray early dusk of late summer, pushing toward the Hilton. At Balbo Avenue they are blocked by police. Half an hour later the police attack with tear gas, with Mace, and with clubs.

". . . They attacked like a chain saw cutting into wood . . . lines of twenty and thirty policemen striking out in an arc. . . . Seen from overhead, from the nineteenth floor, it was like a wind blowing dust. . . ." The observer on the nineteenth floor of the Hilton was Norman Mailer.

Police violence had hitherto been confined to young demonstrators, the dropouts and attendant reporters, but now the police riot overflowed and no one was immune. The police chased people into the park, ran them down, beat them up, "maddened," wrote Mailer, "by the uncoiling of their own storm." Tourists standing behind the police barriers in front of the Hilton were crushed against the windows of the Haymarket Inn, a ground-floor restaurant in the hotel. Finally the window gave way, sending screaming women and children through the broken shards of glass. The police then burst into the restaurant and ran riot.

Sol Lerner wrote in the *Village Voice:* "To fall down in the crush was just as terrifying as facing the police. Suddenly I realized my feet weren't touching the ground as the crowd pushed up onto the sidewalk. I was grabbing at the army jacket of the boy in front of me; the girl behind me had a stranglehold on my neck and was screaming incoherently in my ear."

A member of McCarthy's staff, Jeremy Larner, watched the police riot from the fifteenth floor of the Hilton: "You could hear the sudden *thuck* of club on skull. . . ." He saw cops pursuing terrified kids into the park and out of sight, saw them return, one cop dragging a boy or girl by the leg while another clubbed the victim in the groin. A man attempting to pull a bleeding woman into the hotel was clubbed and thrown into a police wagon along with the woman. When people ran up to plead with cops beating kids on the ground, the cops turned around and clubbed them. They clubbed men in white who knelt to assist the injured, and they clubbed anyone carrying a camera. It was as bad as Paris, perhaps worse.

Many young demonstrators were convinced that they had "won" the battle of Michigan Avenue because the brutal clubbings had been seen on television. On Wednesday the 28th, Walter Cronkite told prime-time television viewers: "I want to pack my bags and get out of this city." Middle-aged, middle-ground reporters were generally more outraged by the tactics of the police than by the demonstrators. The London *Times*'s Louis Heren, observing the National Guard driving into the crowd in jeeps equipped with steel frames, across which were stretched strands of barbed wire, commented: "It was worthy of any Wehrmacht Einsatz Kommando in Poland, the unhappy land from which most of the guardsmen's families had come." Roy Lewis, also of the London *Times,* wrote: "The crowd (in a land of free speech) was vociferous and (in a permissive age) often profane and obscene but never, that I saw, violent. It obeyed its own often ad hoc leaders—notably when they yelled: 'Cool it,' 'Back off the road,' and 'Sit down now.' "

Nevertheless, aspects of the New Left's behavior were acutely alienating even to sympathetic middle-aged observers like I. F. Stone. He had walked around Grant and Lincoln parks and on the streets, talking at random. His conclusion: ". . . in revulsion against the war the best of a generation was being lost—some among the hippies to drugs, some among the radicals to almost hysterical frenzy and alienation." The New Left was abandoning dialogue with the silent majority, the "non-people." To play with revolutionary tactics, to hurl obscenities instead of arguments, would precipitate the reign of the Storm Troopers.

Jerry Rubin (who did not rank high in I. F. Stone's esteem) claimed he was hounded around the clock by three shifts of plainclothes policemen. At 10:30 P.M. on Wednesday, August 28 (the day of the most spectacular police brutality), Rubin was snatched off a downtown street by the police. On October 29, a Cook County Grand Jury indicted him on two counts of "solicitation to commit mob action," the main witness against him being an undercover cop, Robert Pierson, alias Bob Lavon, whose disguise had been convincing enough to enable him to infiltrate the Yippie ranks and get himself taken on as Rubin's bodyguard. Pierson testified that Rubin had said, "We should isolate and kill a cop." Rubin claimed he had really said, "It's amazing with all the violence here that no one kills a cop," but later he celebrated the physical attacks on the Chicago police, "the rhythm of rocks rending copcar metal and shattering windshields." The undercover agents were everywhere; Irv Bach, of the Chicago police, even got himself put in charge of the Mobilization's marshals.

VIOLENCE AT THE CONVENTION

The Democratic National Convention delegates supporting McCarthy and McGovern—and many in the Kennedy camp—were outraged by the behavior of Richard Daley's police. Was this meant to be Prague or what? The Wisconsin delegation decided to march to the hall in protest at police brutality, but after walking two of the six miles they were turned back by the police. On Thursday, the 29th, the chairman of the New Hampshire delegation was set upon by three guards and hustled in a headlock out of the hall. Paul O'Dwyer, the Democratic candidate for senator from New York, was dragged from the hall while coming to the aid of a protesting delegate. Mike Wallace of CBS was punched on the jaw when he tried to raise questions about the suppression of dissent. When Senator Abraham Ribicoff came up to the podium he criticized Daley's methods with unexpected candor: "And with George McGovern as President of the United States we wouldn't have those Gestapo tactics in the streets of Chicago." Daley leapt to his feet, shaking his fist at the podium, mouthing words. Robert Maytag, chairman of the Colorado delegation, interrupted on a point of order: "Is there any rule under which Mayor Daley can be compelled to suspend the police state terror being perpetrated at this minute on kids in front of the Conrad Hilton?" Carl Albert ruled Maytag out of order. Frank Makiewicz, speaking for McGovern, denounced "the night sticks and mindless brutality on Chicago streets and on this convention floor." The young Julian Bond, the only black elected to the Georgia State Legislature, but denied his seat, rose to second McCarthy's nomination. Never, said Bond, had he seen police behavior like this in Mississippi, Alabama, or Georgia.

Finally the police invaded McCarthy's campaign headquarters on the fifteenth floor of the Hilton at 5 A.M. on Friday, August 30, dragged McCarthy's staffers from their beds, and beat them. The pretext? Someone had allegedly dropped beer cans out of a window.

Mayor Daley issued an encyclical claiming that terrorists had planned to disrupt the convention and paralyze the city. Humphrey came in behind Daley, claiming he had evidence from the FBI that he had been targeted by an assassination team. (Thomas Foran, of the attorney general's office in Chicago, denied any knowledge of such a plot.) The vice-president had also witnessed "hard core agitators" throwing stink bombs, uttering disgusting obscenities, and coming into the Hilton to spread filth and manure on the rugs. On September 16, Daley's own, hour-long version of the Chicago disorders was broadcast by 142 television stations. Thomas Lyons, of the Chicago Police Intelligence Department, solemnly reported threats of mass sit-ins, public fornication, LSD in the water supply, and ground glass in the delegates' food. The narrator concluded: "You be the judge. It could happen in your city."

A nationwide Sindlinger telephone survey taken soon after the convention discovered overwhelming support for the Chicago police. The University of Michigan's Survey Research Center reported two months later that only 19 percent of a national sample thought "too much force" had been used by the police; even among citizens who preferred Eugene McCarthy, only 36 percent answered that "too much force" had been used; among those who would have preferred the late Robert Kennedy, only 29 percent.

On December 1, the National Commission on Violence, chaired by Dr. Milton Eisenhower, released its report, prepared under contract by ninety full-time investigators and based on 20,000 pages of eyewitness statements, 180 hours of film, and 12,000 photographs. The commission found that the police had indeed been provoked by obscenities, stones, and missiles, but their response had been "unrestrained and indiscriminate." It was "a police riot" and it had taken place with the backing of the city's officials. Three days later, Daley answered the commission by announcing a huge, 22 percent salary increase for experienced police and firemen.

17

CZECHOSLOVAKIA: THE SOVIET INVASION

"Czechoslovakia, August 20–21, 1968—The largest Soviet military force on the move since the Second World War crosses the nation's [Czechoslovakia] frontiers by night."

THE RUSSIANS ARE COMING

CZECHOSLOVAKIA, August 20–21, 1968—The largest Soviet military force on the move since the Second World War crosses the nation's frontiers by night.

Shortly after midnight on Tuesday, August 21, two gigantic airplanes with Soviet markings touched down at Ruzyně Airport, Prague, disgorging Soviet commandos who immediately seized the main airport building, herding staff and tourists into a confined area. Liaison officers from the Soviet embassy in Prague soon arrived at the airport to coordinate the operation with two key Czechoslovak collaborators, Colonel Elias, commander of the Ministry of the Interior Security Air Squadron, and Colonel Rudolf Stachovský, chief of passport control at Ruzyně. Then came the main airborne invasion, carried in An-12 transport planes.

Every invasion requires a pretext; as with Hungary in 1956, the Kremlin claimed that "party and state leaders" had requested urgent assistance against "counter-revolutionary forces." But the Soviet news agency Tass was unable to name the Czechoslovak party and state leaders. The fake "Appeal," which appeared in *Pravda* on August 22, declared: "Citizens! Today everything that our working people have created in the past 20 years is at stake; all the gains of socialism are at stake." But there were no signatories.

As the Warsaw Pact forces (initially a quarter of a million men—Soviets, Poles, East Germans, Hungarians, and Bulgarians) crossed the frontiers of Bohemia, Moravia, and Slovakia, the Presidium of the Czechoslovak Communist Party was in routine session. At 11:40 P.M. on the 20th, Prime Minister Oldřich Černík returned from the telephone to inform the Presidium that Czechoslovakia had been invaded. Party Secretary Zdeněk Mlynář recalls a confusion of voices and one of the Soviet collaborators, Vasil Bil'ak, pacing back and forth and shouting, "All right lynch me! Why don't you kill me?" Suddenly

Alexander Dubček, first secretary of the Party, announced that he had received a letter from the Soviet leader, Leonid Brezhnev, three days before; Dubček stammered more than usual as he read it aloud. One of the pro-Soviet conspirators tried to censure him for keeping the letter a secret, but this got no support. "The impossibility of defending ourselves militarily . . . was discussed, but it was hardly a debate. . . ."

The Presidium's formal proclamation was not the one the Soviet leaders wanted. Shortly after 1 A.M. a statement was issued denouncing the invasion as "contrary to the fundamental principles of relations between socialist states and a denial of the basic norms of international law." There were four dissenting votes: Vasil Bil'ak, Drahomír Kolder, Emil Rigo, and Oldřich Švestka (editor in chief of *Rudé Právo,* who later that night tried to prevent distribution of the Presidium's resolution).

The Soviet command now had no alternative but to seize the leading figures of the Party and government. The prime targets were Alexander Dubček, Oldřich Černík, Josef Smrkovský (chairman of the National Assembly), František Kriegel (chairman of the National Front), Minister of the Interior Josef Pavel, and the secretary of the Prague Party, Bohumil Šimon. Premier Černík was arrested at 3 A.M. in the government Presidium building and led to the cellar at bayonet point by Soviet troops who also destroyed the telephone switchboard and took the Czech civil servants' wristwatches (so that they might forget they were living in the twentieth century, as one Prague joke had it).

After 4 A.M. the first Soviet armored cars reached the building housing the Secretariat of the Central Committee. An hour later the building was occupied. Party Secretary Mlynář describes it:

"Suddenly the doors of Dubček's office flew open and about eight soldiers and low-ranking officers with machine guns rushed in, surrounded us from behind around a large table and aimed their weapons at the backs of our heads." A dwarfish colonel arrived, wearing a row of medals, and began to issue commands, roaring at his captives, "No talking! Sit quietly! No talking Czech!" Mlynář says this broke his own temper and he shouted in Russian, "Where do you think you are anyway? You are in the office of the First Secretary of the Communist Party. Do you have orders to silence us? Of course you don't! So obey your orders." Without a word the flabbergasted colonel left the room.

The Soviet soldiers cut the telephone lines and closed the windows so that the Czech crowd, which had gathered beyond the cordon of paratroopers, could not be heard singing the national anthem and chanting Dubček's name. František Kriegel lay down on the floor and went to sleep; his powerful snores set the eight Soviet soldiers on edge.

Nothing further happened for about three hours. At 9 A.M. the dwarfish colonel returned with collaborators of the Czechoslovak State Security, one of whom arrested Dubček, Smrkovský, and Kriegel "in the name of the revolutionary tribunal led by comrade Alois Indra." Shortly afterwards, Šimon was also relieved of his liberty. Čestmír Císař, a secretary of the Central Committee and chairman of the Czech National Council, was taken from his home to State Security Headquarters in Bartolomejska Street.

The leaders of an independent, sovereign nation not at war were bundled unceremoniously to the airport in handcuffs and after a longish wait flown via East Germany and Poland to the Ukraine in eviscerated transport planes. Thirty-six hours passed before they were offered a proper meal. Smrkovský, the most intensely disliked in Moscow, was left moldering in the Carpathians for a further twenty-four hours after Dubček and Černík were taken to Moscow. Had the Soviet Union succeeded in installing a puppet government, Dubček and his arrested colleagues would most probably have suffered the same fate as Imre Nagy: phoney charges, a secret trial, execution.

The pro-Soviet collaborators worked hard to serve the invasion forces through the night and following day, in particular Viliam Šalgovič, deputy minister of the interior, certain section chiefs within the ministry, including the Prague State Security chief, Lt.-Colonel Bohumil Molnar, and a number of Stalinists who had been dismissed under Dubček: the former head of the sixth department; the former head of the first department; Colonel Houska; the former chief of the second department, Spelina; and the former chief of inspection, Kral. These men—for whom liberalization had been both a personal and an ideological disaster—now operated without legal authority from the liberal interior minister, Josef Pavel, who was forced underground.

Pavel had served as a commander in the International Brigade during the Spanish civil war. After 1948 he had been implicated in the purges as head of the Central Committee Security Department and deputy minister of the interior, but in 1951 he, too, had been arrested. Refusing to confess to fabricated crimes, he escaped the stage-managed political trials. By 1968 he was fiercely committed to liberalization. Mlynář recalls how after the Čierna meeting with the Soviet leaders at the end of July, Prime Minister Černík had telephoned Pavel, ordering him to confiscate the latest issue of *Reporter,* which carried a cartoon that had enraged Brezhnev. Pavel refused, advising Černík to find himself a new minister of the interior. Mlynář thought that in the tense situation Černík was right, but Pavel replied, "If I break the law once, I'll break it again, and we're right back where we started."

But Viliam Šalgovič, a long-standing KGB agent, had been imposed on Pavel as deputy minister, by the wish of Dubček himself; it was Šalgovič who now functioned as the senior collaborator in State Security.

The occupation forces also moved to silence the state broadcasting system, whose personnel were among the most liberal in the country. Karel Hoffman, director of the Central Communications Administration, acting under instructions from the collaborator Alois Indra, a secretary of the Central Committee, intervened to prevent transmission of the Presidium's defiant proclamation, which began to go out over the air at 1:55 A.M. on the 21st. Hoffman ordered the technicians to switch off all transmitters. At 1:58 people still listening to Prague Radio heard: "Yesterday, on August 20, 1968, at about 2300 hours, . . ." then silence. The radio went off the air. But programs broadcast on several short and long waves were able to continue, informing the outside world of the grim event.

At 4:30 Prague Radio came to life again: "Wake up your friends, wake them up right now, early as it is, wake up your neighbors and all other citizens. . . ." The announcer then read the Appeal to All the People of Czechoslovakia issued by the Presidium.

The 210-meter wavelength radio station Vltava, sited in East Germany, began broadcasting communiqués of the Soviet news agency Tass, insisting that "Personalities of the Czechoslovak Communist Party" had requested military assistance against counterrevolutionary forces within and "outside forces."

Ladislav Mnacko described the night of August 20–21, in Bratislava. He found a solitary tank on what used to be called Stalin Square. A group of "hippies" were throwing cobblestones and park benches at it while the gunners stood in their turrets, fending off the youngsters with rifle butts. "A salvo of machine-gun fire cut through the night. As though it was a prearranged signal, guns spoke from all over the city. They stopped as suddenly as they had begun." In front of the Reduta, on the riverbank, an armored car was surrounded by dozens of young people in lively discussion with the crew: "An officer drove up in a jeep and ordered them to disperse; his voice was arrogant, domineering and cruel. They did not disperse. He ordered the men to fire a warning shot. They still did not disperse. The officer went away with a gesture of helpless fury."

The following day the Soviet tank crews sat behind their machine guns, gazing into the middle distance, patiently suffering the names they were being called; they even allowed youngsters to paint slogans on their tanks. People shouted *"Smotri v glaza . . . nu, smotri"*—"Look me in the eye, come on, look."

At 7:35 A.M. on the 21st, Czechoslovak Radio reported that troops approaching the radio building on Vinohradska Street in Prague were firing tracer bullets and live ammunition while several hundred people tried to stop the advancing tanks with their bodies. The building, which had been hit by dozens of shots, was being buzzed by aircraft of the Antonov type and by larger fighter planes. The announcers of Czechoslovak Radio fell silent as Soviet troops occupied the building. The radio relayed the national anthem along with the sound of gunfire.

At 10 A.M. the editorial offices of *Rudé Právo* were occupied. At 1 P.M., following an ultimatum, all editors, typesetters, and printers were forced to leave the building.

On August 21, the National Assembly demanded "the release from detention of our constitutional representatives": President Ludvík Svoboda, Prime Minister Oldřich Černík, Chairman of the National Assembly Josef Smrkovský, First Secretary of the Party Alexander Dubček, Chairman of the National Front František Kriegel, and Chairman of the Czech National Council Čestmír Císař. The National Assembly also demanded "immediate withdrawal" of the invading armies and full respect for the sovereignty of the Czechoslovak Socialist Republic. This appeal, which was directed to "the parliaments of all countries and world public opinion," was transmitted by the majority of Czechoslovak embassies abroad.

The printing presses had been seized, but newspapers kept appearing several times a day with full freedom of expression. On the evening of the 21st, Soviet troops took over the editorial offices and the printing plant of *Mladá Fronta* in Panska Street. "They forced us into one room and held us there at gunpoint throughout the night. They confiscated the final edition." The editorial board later issued a statement: "In 1945 *Mladá Fronta* was born in the spirit of freedom. It will never abandon or betray this ideal."

During the night of August 21–22, some fifty collaborators in the Central Committee, including Alois Indra, Drabomír Kolder, Vasil Bil'ak, Karel Mestek, Vilem Novy, Miloš Jakeš, and Jan Piller, met in the Praha Hotel in the presence of Soviet officers. But none of those attending was as yet prepared to form an alternative government or state publicly that he approved of the military occupation. Vladimir Kusin has written: "The pro-Moscow faction showed pitiful half-heartedness. . . . In reality they did nothing of substance, except staff a propaganda radio station in East Germany, a silhouetted television screen from the Soviet Embassy in Prague, and a pro-invasion newspaper distributed by Soviet soldiers and burned on the spot by the public."

The national institutions rallied. They spoke with one voice and without flinching. With astonishing speed, the Presidium of the Academy of Sciences convened in extraordinary session on the night of the invasion and adopted a strong statement that was broadcast on television at 8:12 A.M. and sent to UNESCO in Paris. At 7:30 A.M. on the 21st, the editorial board of *Rudé Právo* issued a statement of "unequivocal" support for the Party Presidium and its overnight proclamation. At 7:45 A.M. the radio reported that the Ministry of Foreign Affairs, surrounded by troops, was repeating that the occupation was unjustified.

At 12:25 P.M. on the 21st, Czechoslovak Radio broadcast an appeal in several languages, signed by the professional unions representing writers, plastic arts, architects, film and television workers, and journalists. Stalinism, they declared, precluded any prospects for a humane socialism. Progressive figures across the world were urged to protest against the invasion and come to the defense of Czechoslovakia.

The clandestine radio stations became the lifeline of the Republic. On the morning after the invasion the Slovaks were still broadcasting from their regular studios in Bratislava. One nonconforming local citizen invited to record an interview was the pugnacious writer-journalist Ladislav Mnacko, who had broken with his Stalinist past and won fame in 1964 by publishing a hard-hitting exposé of Party hacks and bureaucrats, *Belated Reports* (which sold 300,000 copies and led the reviewer in *Literárni Listy* to declare, "At first my heart almost stopped beating, so unbelievable seemed the daring of the author . . ."). Mnacko reached the radio studio, but had scarcely begun ("Behave as though you haven't seen them, haven't heard them—as though they were not here . . .") when armed troops arrived and he was cut off.

A dozen full-strength medium-wave transmitters were operating.* If forced off the air they could be replaced within the hour by another transmitter in another town. In Vienna the radio ether was crowded with Czech voices. According to Mnacko, clandestine transmitters were sited on the edges of forests, on islands in the Danube, in camouflaged trucks. Within a few days the original three had increased to thirteen, assisted by the Czechoslovak army, who lent transmitters intended for the call-up of reservists in case of war with the West. This was what baffled the Soviets troops—how it was done. The Soviet emissary Vasili Kuznetsov later complained to Smrkovský about it. The Czech replied: "I should like to explain to you that we already have more than 2,000 transmitters at the disposal of our official organization 'Svazarm' and the People's Militia. They are not secret transmitters. . . . No one has yet found any secret transmitters in our country."

A radio reported: "I saw how a young soldier started to cry when

---

*Including Radio One, Radio Danube, Radio North Slovakia, Radio East Slovakia, Radio Brno, all broadcasting on the same wavelength, 6.075 MHz in the 49-meter band and just below 10 kilocycles in the medium wave.

an old woman asked him: 'Does your mother know that you, her son, have murdered peaceful people?' However, let us not think, because of such episodes, that the occupation soldiers would somehow hesitate if they were ordered to start firing at us with all their weapons. . . . And so, let us just show them again and again that they are unwelcome guests here . . . let them eat only what they brought along themselves, let us give them nothing to drink, let us not show, even by the slightest gesture, any momentary pity over their situation."

Ladislav Mnacko reported that "Not a drop of water for the invaders" became the chief slogan on the radio waves. Citizens were urged to avoid provocation. "Show the invaders your scorn in silence; do not attempt to discuss or argue with them. . . ." Calling for unity in resistance, the stations read out the car license plates of known collaborators. Some broadcasts were alarmist: "Citizens! Šalgovič's secret police have got lists of people they are out to arrest with the help of advisers from the occupying forces. Help them to hide!" The esteemed Olympic gold medallist, Emil Zatopek, was warned on the radio not to return to his apartment.

Even more urgent was this message: "Calling all railwaymen! A freight train is approaching Prague from Chocen, carrying radio location equipment to be used in locating our transmitters and jamming our broadcasts. Railwaymen, you know what you have to do!" On August 27, *Politika* reported a fascinating conversation with a railroad worker who knew about the adventures of the Soviet train carrying radio-jamming equipment. It was subtly sabotaged all along the line: "Near Olomouc, it got ahead of a long freight train. Then it accidentally broke up into three sections, and it took four hours to fix it. Then it moved on to Trebova, and, with repair work going on all the time, as far as Chocen. From there we wanted to steer them into Poland, but by that time they had maps. Suddenly they were in no great hurry because they had eaten up everything they had in their two parlor cars. . . . The Russians were quite nervous. . . . But such a Schweik-type operation cannot last indefinitely."

THE FOURTEENTH PARTY CONGRESS

A quarter of a million troops had invaded Czechoslovakia to prevent the newly elected Fourteenth Congress of the Communist Party from convening on September 9. Moscow knew that the congress would elect a new Central Committee totally committed to the April Action Program and Alexander Dubček's leadership. The instinctive and immediate reaction of the ultraliberal Prague City Committee of the Party on the night of the Soviet invasion was to convene the Fourteenth Congress ahead of schedule and without delay. Telephone contact was maintained throughout the night and morning with Bratislava and the regional secretariats, urging them to locate delegates elected to the Party Congress, and to assure their arrival in Prague. The Prague Committee also issued an appeal "To the Communist and Workers' Parties of the Entire World!" protesting against "this unprecedented violation of socialist internationalism . . . [this] act of lawlessness." At about 6 P.M. that evening the committee's secretary, Bohumil Šimon, a close colleague of Dubček's, was taken by a Soviet military vehicle to an unknown destination. Šimon soon found himself in Moscow.

Despite roads and railways clogged by invasion forces, the majority of delegates reached Prague with remarkable speed. The Extraordinary Fourteenth Congress was opened, under the protection of the working class, at the giant ČKD plant in the suburb of Vysočany, on the morning of August 22—only thirty-six hours after the invasion began. By a considerable feat of organization, 1,290 out of 1,543 elected delegates managed to reach the factory by the end of the day (935 when the first session started). The Slovak delegates who were prevented from making the journey sent a telegram of support.

Although deprived of its leaders, the congress lost no time in establishing its authority as the supreme organ of the Party. The urgent task of electing a new Central Committee, to establish definitively that the Prague Spring represented the will of the nation, brought anxious inquiries from all over the hall: how have our leaders behaved during the past thirty-six hours? Who has proved himself worthy of trust? Who a traitor? Information was fragmentary and rumor abounded, but soon a reliable picture emerged. A passionate debate identified the hated collaborators: Piller, Indra, Jakeš (chairman of the Central Control and Audit Commission), Jozef Lenárt, Kolder, and Bil'ak had recommended collaboration with the Soviet forces and attempted to prevent the convening of the Party Congress. The chairman announced that Party secretaries Lenárt, Kolder, and Indra were now working inside the Soviet-occupied Central Committee Building and were convening a meeting of the old Central Committee in the Praha Hotel. To massive applause, the chairman insisted that the old Central Committee was now dissolved and that supreme authority resided in the congress itself.

Jiří Pelikán, the liberal director of television, appealed for the re-election of all Central Committee members who had behaved patriotically, even those suspected of conservative tendencies. The 144 members elected did not include a single collaborator. The congress elected as members of its working Presidium all the comrades who had been arrested and humiliated by Soviets officers (and whose fate was unknown): Dubček, Černík, Kriegel, Smrkovský, Císař, Šimon, as well as Minister of the Interior Pavel, who arrived to address the congress before once again going underground.

Demanding the departure of all foreign troops, the congress declared: "There was no counter-revolution in Czechoslovakia, and socialist development was not endangered. . . . Czechoslovakia's sovereignty, the bonds of alliance . . . were trampled underfoot."

The congress called a one-hour national protest strike for 12 noon the following day, August 23.

At the end of the session the chairman warned delegates that the Soviet military commandant, Lt.-General I. Velichko, had imposed a curfew from 10 P.M. to 5 A.M. Buses were waiting in the factory yard to transport delegates to all parts of the country. They would leave "by various gates, not only by gate No. 2, at intervals, so that it should look as if the afternoon shift was going home." The Prague District Committee would find overnight accommodation for those who needed it.

And the workers of ČKD who had not gone home? A reporter from the Union of Youth's paper, *Mladá Fronta,* described that warm August night at the plant employing 20,000: "People do not talk, but every so often they hiss and spit out, 'the sons of bitches.' Sons of bitches, swine, and even cruder, more fitting terms. I stop by an arc-oven spewing flames and talk to the man who has been a member of the Communist Party for 23 years. He presses my hand, clenches his fist, and shouts that the people who committed treason are not human beings at all. . . . Dubček should have put them all behind bars in January . . . or strip them of their positions. Why did he coddle them? Why did he trust them? . . ."

PASSIVE RESISTANCE

The morning that the Party Congress met, Hradčany Castle, the official residence of President Svoboda, was still hermetically sealed by tanks, but the president was allowed freedom of movement within it. During the morning of the 22nd he was visited by General Ivan Pavlovsky, commander of the occupation forces, and Soviet Ambassador Stepan V. Chervonenko, who were pressing hard for a "workers' and peasants' government" composed of the collaborators already holding official positions. The talks were inconclusive. Later that day Svoboda received a pro-Soviet delegation led by Indra, Kolder, and Bil'ak, who also invited him to appoint an alternative government. Svoboda adamantly refused. Zdeněk Mlynář quotes the president: "If I were to do anything of the sort, the nation would have to drive me out of this Castle like a mangy dog." Svoboda decided to fly to Moscow to join his deported colleagues in facing Brezhnev.

On August 22, *Rudé Právo* declared belligerently: "Our determination to create a highly humane and democratic socialist society, to return to socialism its human face, was not understood. In fact it could not be understood. It had to be misunderstood . . . out of fear that the nations of the socialist states might perceive in the Czechoslovak example a course worthy of imitation." On August 23, *Rudé Právo* published the names of the newly elected Central Committee.

Wenceslas Square stretches up a mild incline to the huge, imposing National Museum of Bohemia. Standing below is a statue of the patron saint of Bohemia, Prince Václav (Wenceslas). During the first days of the Soviet invasion the area around the statue became the focal point for symbolic resistance. An eleven-year-old boy was shot dead on the steps of the statue as he tried to push a Czechoslovak flag down the barrel of a Russian tank. The statue then became a kind of shrine, covered with flowers and pictures of Dubček, Svoboda, Smrkovský.

On August 22, a lone marksman in one of the high windows shot the commander of a Soviet tank; nine Soviet machine guns at once raked the building, shattering all the windows and sending chips of stone flying. *Rudé Právo* reported the scene at 5 P.M.:

> Wenceslas Square is surrounded by occupation tanks. Near the museum they form a perfect wall. The gun barrels are aimed down the sidewalks. The faces of the soldiers are sombre and hard. At Mustek [at the foot of the Square] and on the sidewalks the groups of people, especially young boys and girls, grow in size. . . . Will there be a massacre? The legal radio repeats its warnings. . . . On Jindřišská Street, a tank turret swivels as if searching for a target. Then slowly, unwillingly, the groups start dispersing. . . .

At noon on August 23, began the hour-long national protest strike called by the Fourteenth Party Congress.

The first issue of *Politika* (August 24) reported scenes the previous day: "I missed the usual lines in front of food stores. Instead, there was a long one in the park next to the Children's Home. Thousands were signing a petition to have Czechoslovakia declared neutral. . . . Do the occupiers feel any shame? They do, obviously. Their eyes are always on the move, trying to avoid looking at the faces of the people around."

"Prague changed overnight," wrote a journalist. "The occupiers were tearing down slogans, posters, and appeals to citizens. To no avail! New ones were up by morning. Prague is like one huge poster. 'Occupiers, go home!' And still another change occurred in Prague during the night [of the 23rd]. On the suggestion of Czechoslovak Radio, all street and building signs were torn down. Instead, inscriptions appeared on the walls: Dubček Avenue and the like. . . . Prague has simply been transformed into Dubček Avenues."

The deputies of the National Assembly had pledged that they would not voluntarily leave the building, which was surrounded by Soviet troops, but not occupied. On August 24, the assembly's Presidium issued an instruction that all persons taking their orders from the occupation forces, or working outside the framework of Czechoslovak law, should be dismissed. On Sunday, August 25, the assembly sent a letter to President Svoboda in Moscow: "Our people resolutely reject the occupation as illegal, unconstitutional, and groundless and demand the departure of the occupation armies."

On the Sunday, at about 2:00 P.M., the occupiers tried to play the collaborationist radio station over the public address system in Wenceslas Square, but as soon as the first words were heard there was a deafening barrage of whistling. The same day the interior minister, Josef Pavel, was interviewed on Czechoslovak Radio. Pavel did not feel free to disclose his movements: "As you can see, I cannot telephone from here. . . . I have a number of work places like this, and I keep shifting from one to another all the time." He insisted that "I do, in fact, run security." But Pavel's days were numbered; the Kremlin would demand his head.

On August 25, Czechoslovak Radio broadcast a protest by professors and students against the occupation of Charles University. *Rudé Právo* simultaneously published an Open Letter from the Officers of the Prague Garrison: "You came at night, you pounced on a country that was asleep and on an army that was turned to face the enemy on the western border. . . . Whether you like it or not, your posture in our country is that of an aggressor! . . . Go back home!"

The Writers' Union Building had been seized, along with many others, but on August 26 the union issued a scalding resolution by democratic vote: "The long uncertainty as to whether the Soviet Union is to play the role of an apostle or of a gendarme in the socialist camp has finally been overcome. The great socialist power is returning to the tried and tested traditions of Cossack diplomacy. By this retrograde and fascist-like action, the Soviet Union has deprived itself of any right to play a leading role in the international Communist movement." Addressing the world, the union urged a complete boycott of Soviet activities and cultural agreements, films, shows, and plays.

On Monday the 26th, from 9:00 to 9:15 A.M., Czechoslovak Radio relayed a fifteen-minute demonstration during which all the sirens and car horns in Prague sounded, and church bells rang. At the main railroad station, Soviet officers with drawn pistols threw themselves on an engineer sounding the whistle of his locomotive. During the demonstration a young woman was shot at Klarov. She died in the hospital. *Lidová Demokracie* reported another incident: "It happened on the Cyril and Methodius Square in the Karlin district of Prague. An armoured car . . . approached a house where a boy about 15 years of age was painting on the wall in the Russian alphabet the most common sign of these days: 'Go home!' The machine-gunner riding on the vehicle pointed his gun toward the boy. This was observed by a woman pushing a baby carriage. In the naive hope that the occupiers might be compassionate, she took her six-month-old child in her arms and stood by the boy. The occupier murdered all three with a single burst of his gun."

Rudé Právo opened its columns to distinguished friends of the USSR who were now bitterly disenchanted. Jarmila Glazarova had first written for *Rudé Právo* in May 1945, at the moment the Soviet forces came as liberators, when the paper was only, as she recalled, "a buff-coloured sheet printed in haste. . . . Could anyone in the darkest, most fantastic dream, foresee that 23 years later I would be writing . . . a confession of my grief and disillusionment? . . . " The tone of the liberal press was savage. On the 28th, *Literární Listy* published a Commentary of the Day describing the occupation as a "political fiasco." A story entitled " 'Brothers' with Peasant Faces" described how Soviet soldiers had shot teenage boys carrying leaflets in Podolí, in front of the waterworks. The Czech Public Security Commander had been refused all documentary information, including the names of the Soviet soldiers involved. "World, tremble with helpless terror, with desperate anger, with revulsion and shame for . . . murderers of defenceless children!"

On the whole the behavior of the occupying forces was restrained; had the Czechs offered armed resistance like the Hungarians in 1956, it would have been different. One important aspect of the restraint was the absolute ban on the confiscation of food. Vladimir Kusin reports: ". . . we can still recall the two Soviet soldiers with dangling submachine guns who walked into a bakery store full of fresh and nice-smelling bread and asked humbly to be given some. When the request was turned down they walked out again, disappointed and visibly moved by the unmistakable hostility of the customers and staff." The story, of course, also works to the credit of the Soviet commanders.

According to *Svoboda* (August 25), "In the first two days [August 21 and 22] there were 307 wounded and 18 dead in Prague." The government's official survey of casualties during the first twelve days of the occupation, which was never published, recorded 72 deaths as a direct result of actions by the invading forces, including 45 shot dead and 25 killed by military vehicles. Of these, 23 died in Prague, the remainder being distributed fairly evenly around the country. In addition, 267 persons suffered serious injury. The historian Vladimir Kusin interprets these low figures as the result of a policy of restraint by the invaders, and of their crucial decision not to enter factories.

Armed resistance against the Warsaw Pact invasion forces would doubtless have been futile and immensely destructive to Czechoslovakia. Among intellectuals and students, however, there was immense frustration about the nation's failure to defend its independence for a second time in thirty years. Now, as in the Munich crisis of 1938, Czechoslovakia possessed a modern army it had failed to use. Calculations of prudence had again prevailed; did Czechoslovakia suffer from an excess of caution? The émigré writer Pavel Tigrid believed that armed resistance would have driven the Party underground and transformed it into an immensely popular force. But this option was not feasible; for the generation which led the Party, the government, and the army, friendship with the Soviet Union could not be converted during a single, catastrophic night into war.

MOSCOW

President Svoboda had flown to Moscow on August 23. Jiří Pelikán has described attempts by liberal circles to persuade him not to go—to remain entrenched in Hradčany Castle, a president on his own soil, to draw strength from the solidly anti-Soviet resolutions passed by the Fourteenth Party Congress and the National Assembly; in short, to let the Soviets stew in their own juice. But Svoboda went to Moscow. Telephoning his wife from the Kremlin (with Brezhnev's permission), he was told: "There is shooting here in Prague . . . it's a blood bath, but the people are with you. Ludvík, don't be afraid, don't budge an inch. . . ." But Svoboda wasn't with his people and he had already budged the crucial "inch"—Moscow lies 1,000 miles east of Prague.

In the Kremlin they confronted him alone, urging him to assume the functions of first secretary and prime minister, but he refused to negotiate without colleagues whom he had not seen since they were bundled into captivity.

At noon on August 25, a tiny group of Soviet human rights activists gathered in Red Square and unfurled placards in the hope that the Czechoslovak leaders in the Kremlin would take heart. One placard said, "For your and our freedom!" The seven demonstrators were seized and sentenced to varying terms of prison banishment and forced psychiatric treatment. In January 1969, two of them, Pavel Litvinov and Mrs. Yuli Daniel, were sent to Siberia for publicly protesting against the invasion of Czechoslovakia.

Dubček, who was ill during much of the negotiations, did deliver an impassioned speech, in Russian, defending the "revival process" in Czechoslovakia. Brezhnev responded by castigating Dubček for conducting domestic politics without seeking his prior approval. Zdeněk Mlynář, who was present during this exchange in the Kremlin, quotes the Soviet leader: "From the outset I wanted to help you against Novotný. . . . I asked you, 'Are his people threatening you? . . . Do you want to replace the Minister of the Interior? And the Minister of National Defence? . . .' But you said no, they're good comrades. And then suddenly I hear that you've replaced the Minister of the Interior, of National Defence, and other ministers, and that you replaced secretaries of the Central Committee."

Brezhnev then spoke of the Soviet losses during the war; this was the heart of the matter, the unalterable division of Europe. "I asked President Johnson if the American Government still fully recognizes the results of the Yalta and Potsdam conferences. And on 18 August I received the reply: as far as Czechoslovakia and Rumania are concerned, it recognizes them without reservation. . . . So what do you think will be done on your behalf? There will be no war."

The brutal negotiations within the Kremlin culminated in the Moscow Protocol, which was signed by every member of the Czechoslovak delegation except František Kriegel (who had been kept in solitary confinement and whom Brezhnev wanted to detain even after the other Czechs had left for Prague). In one sense it was a defeat for the Kremlin: Dubček, Černík, and Smrkovský remained in their posts. But the terms were draconian: the Fourteenth Congress of the KSČ was declared invalid (on the ground that members of the Presidium and secretaries of the Central Committee had not been present); Warsaw Pact troops would remain in Czechoslovakia until "the threat to socialism [in Czechoslovakia] and to the security of the countries in the socialist community" had passed; measures would be taken as a top priority for "controlling the communications media . . . by preventing anti-socialist elements on radio and television. . . ." The press would be purged, and the Social Democratic Party banned. Czechoslovaks who had collaborated with the invading forces would not be victimized.

The Soviet negotiators also insisted that Czechoslovakia's delegates at the United Nations must protest against attempts by other nations to raise the issue and must insist that the country had not been invaded in any sense that violated the U.N. Charter. Finally, the text of the Moscow Protocol itself would not be disclosed—such was the confidence of the Kremlin in its own values.

Dubček came home. On August 27, he addressed the nation on the radio. He begged the people to have faith and to respect the Moscow agreement, even though he was not at liberty to disclose its terms. At moments his voice cracked; he wept. Kriegel was dismissed, Císař was removed as a Party secretary (Mlynář resigned in November), Pavel obviously had to go as minister of the interior, Jiří Hájek as foreign minister. The directors of Prague Radio and Czechoslovak Television, Zdeněk Hejzlar and Jiří Pelikán, were unacceptable. The Social Democratic Party was banned along with the anti-Soviet groups KAN and K231. Dubček postponed the Fourteenth Party Congress indefinitely, but otherwise kept the visible damage to a minimum, allowing Czechoslovak democracy to die a slow death.

Ten years later Milan Hauner published a pamphlet in exile, likening Dubček's post-Moscow performance to that of Richard II:

> Mine eyes are full of tears, I cannot see.
> And yet salt water blinds them not so much
> But they can see a sort of traitors here.
> Nay, if I turn mine eyes upon myself . . .

Momentarily, the spirit of national resistance spilled over into a waterfall of defiant resolutions, the most outspoken of which came from 2,000 workers at the all-enterprise assembly of ČKD, Prague, who described the USSR as "an imperialist state with all its characteristic attributes. Therefore, it is neither the homeland of socialism nor a shield of socialism. . . ." Czechoslovakia's leaders had been dragged to Moscow "as slaves" and treated as slaves. The occupying forces were described as "people of Asiatic manners and low culture." Defiant protests poured in—from the Revolutionary Trade Union Movement at ČKD Foundries; from the Czechoslovak Youth League, which demanded a national plebiscite; from the CP District Committee of Prague, which refused to accept the Moscow communiqué as representing "the free will" of the Czechoslovak leaders; from the Naradi (Tools) Enterprise in Prague 10, whose 7,061 employees felt "bitterly disappointed and betrayed"—and stood by the work of the Fourteenth Party Congress. The Elektrocas National Enterprise and the Lokomotiva-Sokolovo Plant agreed, insisting that the occupation forces must be withdrawn immediately and all collaborators dismissed.

The editors of *Student,* accusing the Czechoslovak negotiators of capitulation, betrayal, and treason, demanded that the National Assembly immediately reject the agreement. But later the editorial staff apologized for their initial comments, adding, in despair, that they would no longer publish their magazine.

Autumn came to Prague. Winter—the replacement of Dubček by Gustáv Husák—was deferred for a further six months.

18

BRITAIN:
The Student Revolt

"Nevertheless, the LSE offers a classic model of a New Left student elite in aciton—most notably the strategy of institutional confrontation as an assault course for the wider war against capitalist imperialism."

LEICESTER, ESSEX, AND HULL

British universities were in turmoil throughout 1968. The student insurrection in Great Britain had begun in the autumn of 1966 at the London School of Economics (LSE), but did not take root beyond that hothouse of radical ferment until the turn of 1967–68. In December 1967, students at the Regent Street Polytechnic and the Holborn College of Law and Commerce staged sit-in demonstrations on the issue of student representation. A month later the council of Aston University, Birmingham, was besieged by 250 students singing and clapping in the corridor.

A sit-in began at Leicester in February, after the senate rejected student union proposals for representation on governing bodies. Sleeping bags filled the corridors while a senate committee met to discuss demands for representation. The union voted 449 to 235 to boycott the catering facilities and to refuse to sign lecture attendance sheets until their demands were met. The vice-chancellor, T. A. F. Noble, remarked that he and the senate were not impressed.

It all sounded outrageous to the public: on March 10, the London *Sunday Times* spoke of "anti-student hysteria," the *Sunday Telegraph* of an "almost vindictive hostility to the student population" (to which the *Telegraph* papers themselves had made a significant contribution —"pretentious adolescents, generally of small intellectual ability . . ."). Ten days later the Police Federation attacked the tolerance of academic staff and magistrates for "the mob violence which now goes unchecked at our universities." Yet the reported conflicts usually broke into the headlines only after the students' persistent petitions for representation in the government of the university had encountered stubborn stonewalling by a middle-aged administration hyperconscious of its own dignities and impervious to changing expectations. The press ignored the months of peaceful pressure and only took note when it spilled over into occupations or strikes; the long-suffering taxpayer was financing undisciplined hooligans to assault policemen and insult ministers of the Crown.

In June the much respected *Universities Quarterly* noted how little student representation was provided for in British universities, the vast majority of which still allowed no student members on the executive bodies of the senate or council. (Among the radicals, however, formal representation was never the main issue, merely the cutting edge of wider political concerns.)

Of varying influence in these disturbances was the Radical Student Alliance (RSA), founded in November 1966 to challenge the reformist leadership of the National Union of Students (NUS) and to provide a militant vanguard for student action. A loose coalition of left-wing Labour, CP, and Young Liberals, and closely allied to the Vietnam Solidarity Committee, the RSA demanded a student voice in the shaping of courses and staff appointments and the democratization of education in general. The alliance never achieved a membership in excess of eight hundred, but its inspirational figures, notably David Adelstein of the LSE, and David Triesman of Essex, commanded widespread respect. In April, the RSA challenged the right-wing Labour leadership of the National Union of Students at its annual convention in Leicester, but the radicals' motion of censure was defeated and moderates handsomely won the elections to the executive.

Police with dogs were called to the "model" new campus at Essex on May 7, after 150 students—some no doubt inspired by news from Paris—had broken up a meeting addressed by Dr. T. A. Inch, of the chemical defense experimental establishment at Porton Down. Preventing invited speakers from speaking was already an established tactic at Essex among members of the RSA. In March a meeting addressed by Enoch Powell, MP, had been broken up and his car damaged on the campus, but the student union—which had disaffiliated itself from the reformist National Union of Students—adopted the surprising position that this should be a matter for the police and the civil law, not for university discipline. (The campaign at Berkeley against "double jeopardy"—punishment by both the courts and the university—was possibly an influence; yet the cry of students the world over was "Police—out!" However, the essence of guerrilla warfare is flexibility.)

Essex's vice-chancellor, Dr. Albert Sloman, reacted to the disruption of Dr. Inch's lecture by suspending three of the alleged ringleaders on May 10—without a hearing. The vice-chancellor argued that he could not refer the case to the normal staff-student disciplinary committee because "breaking up a lecture" had not been listed as a forbidden activity. He had therefore translated the affair into an attack on academic freedom, of which he himself was the custodian. The 250 protesting students who came marching to his private residence on the campus did not agree.

Nor did the seven hundred who met and called a strike. At this juncture members of the academic staff sympathetic to the students' case helped to ensure that no violence occurred. Professor Peter Townsend, the sociologist, was impressed by the orderly atmosphere prevailing.

The three suspended students declined to leave the pleasantly landscaped, semirural campus. Ralph Halberstadt, a first-year student, sported a cotton cap over long, unkempt hair and a full beard, whereas David Triesman, the inspirational radical at Essex and a leading figure in the RSA, wore the short hair more typical of the British New Left. Press photographs remind us that ties were still widely worn by students about to "overthrow society" (as the *Daily Telegraph* put it). In France, Dany-the-Red was short-haired; today Dany-the-Green has let it grow. To the generally quiescent but casually attired student generation of the 1980s, the firebrands of 1968 might look like schoolteachers.

On May 15, with all classes at a standstill, the senate met under strong pressure to reinstate David Triesman, Ralph Halberstadt, and Pete Archard and, in addition, to postpone all examinations until one month after their reinstatement. (Exams were scheduled to begin in two weeks' time.) But the eleven-hour meeting of the senate ended by supporting the vice-chancellor, although 98 out of 167 academic staff, highly critical of Sloman's action, approved a resolution setting up a committee to investigate the affair and the operative principles of free speech. (According to Triesman, the senate belonged to a generation "which is paranoid about both Communism and Fascism on the grounds that they inhibit 'free speech'—a mystified absolute." Triesman identified himself with "a post-CND [Campaign for Nuclear Disarmament] generation, taught our final lessons in Grosvenor Square.")

The "Three" were reinstated on May 17, but peace was not restored. The plea for the postponement of examinations became a demand to abolish all examinations. The students also demanded representation in the senate. A "free," or alternative, university surfaced, attracting at its peak up to 1,000 staff and students. Professor Peter Townsend called it "the most rewarding experience of my whole university career." A significant role was played by a scattering of Situationists, who enlivened the proceedings with spray-painted slogans declaring that "Ubu cares."

Many of Essex's professors loathed the whole experience. According to Professor Jean Blondel, of the Department of Government, the radicals were determined to "have their pound of flesh" from Dr.

Sloman. Richard Lipsey, founding professor of economics, was not impressed by complaints about inaccessible hierarchies; he customarily spent two hours a day in the bar talking, most of the time, to students. "We all came for Dr. Sloman—he is Essex." Lipsey was soon to join other professors disgusted by the behavior of students abusing (as they believed) a free education by signing an appeal for the creation of Britain's first private, fee-paying—and therefore properly industrious—university. Alasdair MacIntyre, a Catholic-Marxist philosopher who had been serving as dean of students, made way for Dr. Ian Cook, reputed to be stronger on discipline. MacIntyre explained: "Ironically, our mistake was to be so liberal. . . . They have no real practical injustices to fight against; so they had to rebel on ideological issues like germ warfare and Vietnam—and these we were powerless to alter." MacIntyre wrote a book debunking Herbert Marcuse and subsequently moved to the United States.

During the summer, David Triesman committed his energies to the international insurrection, in particular the American scene, confiding to *New Left Review* some strategic thoughts that were rapidly quoted by S. M. Lipset and others as evidence of radical diabolism but which, in reality, merely registered a strain of infantilism. "What we should do," wrote Triesman, "if the situation were to arise again, would be to behave as provocatively as necessary and to effectively sanction the University to the extent that they *need* to use force, probably the police." At this masterminded conjuncture, the normally myopic sector of students and staff would enter the fray ("a situation already politically structured"). The aim, Triesman explained, was to combat "the whole nauseating apparatus" by which universities turned out new generations of capitalist managers.

Late in May the administrative wing of the University of Hull was occupied by two hundred students led by Tom Fawthorp, who had returned from Paris inspired by the May events and then walked out of his final examinations in protest against the exam system. When the Socialist Society convened on May 30, it formulated eight demands, including an end to exams. On June 8, they were back in the administrative wing demanding equal representation on all governing bodies, with full voting powers, plus student control of halls of residence. Twenty-six members of the staff registered their sympathy by signing the visitors' book; a hundred faculty members called for reforms.

On the subject of examinations, the International Socialist (IS) group—a Marxist faction with a strong student component—issued a pamphlet, "Education, Capitalism and the Student Revolt": "What awaits students is not the kingdom of the mind they were promised . . . but participation in or apologetics for the world of money and militarism, poverty and police forces. Instead of being offered a chance to understand the world and society they themselves are subjected to a crude quantification; in place of an exploration of reality they get exams."

THE ANTI-UNIVERSITY

One institution where students were tortured neither by exams nor any other form of assessment was the Anti-University of London, love child of the Free School of New York. In the fall of 1967 the redoubtable Allen Krebs took off for London to help set up the Anti-University at 49 Rivington Street, on the shabbier fringe of the city, in seven rooms rented from the Bertrand Russell Peace Foundation. Wiry, affable, and dependable, Krebs became the "Anti's" coordinator, and gave his own course called Life in a Television Set—Passivity and Devitalization in a Consumption-Oriented Society.

"Anti" was a hypnotic notion: Joseph Berke, M.D., offered a course on anti-universities, anti-hospitals, anti-theatres, and anti-families, while the artist John Latham styled his course "Antiknow." According to an eyewitness, Dr. Berke asked his class: "How can we discuss how we can discuss what we want to discuss?" The silence that followed was broken by someone saying, "Maybe we don't need to discuss it." Berke said very little and after a while announced he wasn't feeling well. The class continued for an hour after he left. John Latham's general drift was the need "to behave without knowing. Knowledge is an illusion that people have." Latham promised to reveal "what is going on, seen as sculpture . . . a hard edged non-rhetorical picture that will burn the edges of all textbooks."

Richard Martin (who was announced in the catalogue as "well-known Sorbonne anarchist, youngest member of College de Pataphysique . . . currently described by Clause Daussot as 'Hegel revenging himself on Christ' ") offered an antilogical course on the subject of Alchemists and Hallucinations from de Nerval to Joyce. Gustav Metzger lectured on A Theory of Auto-Destructive Art, with special reference to "large self-destructive sculptures, made with the latest technologies, that rot and fall apart in public" and which can undermine "a suicidal faith in the benefits of technology." Jeff Nuttall, poet and artist, presented Day Long Group Mind Merger and Jeff Nuttall Is Fat, scheduled to last "one entire weekend." The acid-tripping novelist Alexander Trocchi came to talk about "the urgencies of the invisible insurrection," while Yoko Ono was advertised as giving "an irregular course" on connecting people to their own reality by means of "brain sessions and ritual."

The conventional Left was also represented: C. L. R. James on workers' power in history, Juliet Mitchell on literature and psychology, Tony Smythe on civil liberties, David Mercer on drama and social values, Ruth First (later murdered by a South African parcel bomb in Maputo) on African politics, Ken Coates on workers' control, Robin Blackburn and Nicholas Krasso on the Cuban revolution. The "Anti" embraced all leftward spirits, hard and soft, cerebral and instinctive, rational and mind-blown, verbal and performance, overground and underground. There were those who argued that the teachers shouldn't be paid—indeed, should pay to teach but should not teach, since the distinction between teacher and student was the root of all evil. The composer Cornelius Cardew, though a professor at the Royal Academy of Music, dismayed some of his Anti-University class by refusing to teach them. When this happened, the less liberated students tended to think about the fee of eight pounds a quarter.

The local white working class of Shoreditch was not friendly. The long-haired intellectuals were shunned in the pub across the street and even by the building workers who were engaged in bitter labor disputes on the huge Barbican project—although students affiliated with the IS group took part in the Barbican picket lines, and the Socialist Society at the London School of Economics collected money for the strikers. There was also the problem of who was to look after the "Anti's" premises, which had been inherited from the Vietnam Solidarity Committee. Three communal groups succeeded one another as caretakers, each less caretaking than its predecessor. By July 1968, the building itself had degenerated into a squatter camp with blocked toilets and broken windows; soon afterwards it was reclaimed by the landlord, the Bertrand Russell Peace Foundation.

The Free School of New York and the Anti-University of London—the present writer did service at both—attracted much of what was half-baked in the counterculture. Ritual phrases strung together in predictable chains too often served as substitutes for genuine analysis. The CIA was the bogey of the moment, its malign tentacles the cause of just about every social affliction (a strange reversal of Marxism), and the term "bourgeois" was tossed about promiscuously, like the verdicts of an eccentric hanging judge. Despite the history courses, History was Now. The real bourgeoisie, meanwhile, was hard at work learning languages and electrical engineering.

COLLEGES OF ART IN REVOLT

Inspired by the Ecole des Beaux Arts, students at the Hornsey College of Art in North London rebelled at the end of May. The immediate demands were autonomy for the student union and a guaranteed sabbatical year for its presidents, although a deeper cause of unrest was a government plan to incorporate the College of Art into a new polytechnic. On May 28, a teach-in to discuss grievances was transformed into a permanent occupation under the leadership of the Student Action Committee (whose meetings were open to interventions from all students). Nonstop discussion followed; no one slept. The students occupied the principal's office, manned his switchboard, and spent the Whitsun weekend printing their charter and spring-cleaning the college. Most of the nonadministrative staff reacted positively, enjoying this outbreak of creative effort. (On June 5, a day-long meeting of the Hornsey staff passed six resolutions and came out in support of the students.)

A torrent of memos poured forth: Document no. 11 had thirty-one clauses and called for a radical revision of the entire structure of art education. The demands included flexible "network" courses based on individual projects to replace specialized linear ones based on fixed curricula, and an end to compulsory examinations. Some of the ideas attracted the serious attention of leading figures in art and design. The college was alight with new excitement and energy. The canteen was now open twenty-four hours a day, stew was available at 1/9d (21 cents), pies at 1/3d (15 cents), tea at 4d (4 cents). Guitar music in the manner of Andrés Segovia was beamed through the building. Tom Nairn, a lecturer at the college, noted that the Hornsey students refused to let themselves be politicized by the professionals of the New Left.

The excitement did not extend, however, to the good citizens of the borough of Haringey, whose council was the responsible authority for the Hornsey College of Art. An editorial in the Wood Green, Southgate and Palmers Green *Weekly Herald* offered the most succinct of commentaries on the "1968 phenomenon":

> ... a bunch of crackpots, here in Haringey, or in Grosvenor Square, or Paris, or Berlin, or Mexico, can never overthrow an established system. ... They may dislike having to conform to a system in which they are required to study, and follow set programmes, and take examinations or their equivalents; and acknowledge that in doing so they are through the indulgence of others preparing themselves for a lifetime of earning. ... The system is ours. We the ordinary people, the nine-to-five, Monday-to-Friday, semi-detached, suburban wage-earners, we are the system. We are not victims of it. We are not slaves to it. We are it, and we like it.

Does any bunch of twopenny-halfpenny kids think they can turn us upside down? They'll learn.

Haringey Council, the responsible education authority, was under Conservative control and Alderman George Cathles, chairman of Haringey's education committee, was no less incensed than the editor of the *Herald*. Finally, on July 4, eight days before the summer vacation, when only two dozen students were occupying the building, Cathles sent in security guards with dogs. The principal now reoccupied his office, offering a commission of inquiry and other conciliatory gestures. A meeting of Hornsey students eventually accepted the package, although the more militant ones took themselves off to join the occupation of the Guildford Art College.

Returning on the first day of the autumn term, September 23, Hornsey students found themselves locked out. Students and part-time staff implicated in the revolt were dismissed. After a sit-down protest outside Haringey Town Hall, about two hundred students voted to establish their own college.

The scale of the reprisals against staff as well as students in the British art colleges appears to have had no counterpart in any Western country during the campus insurrections of 1968. The reason lay in a decentralized structure of finance and employment; unlike the universities, colleges of art and technology operated under local authorities controlled by councilors hostile to academic strikes and unmoved by considerations of academic autonomy. (The Conservatives had made sweeping gains in the local council elections of 1968.) Influenced by emissaries from Hornsey, students at the Croydon College of Art began an occupation during the first week of June. At the Guildford School of Art the second and third weeks of the month were abandoned to a nonstop talk-in. The outraged governors closed the college and cut off the gas and telephone. Surrey County Council then expelled the students involved, while dismissing a total of forty-five full- or part-time members of the staff. When the term opened in September, thirty of them were picketing the gates. At least twenty-five new staff people had been taken on. The courses in foundation and contemporary studies were destroyed.

One of the Hornsey manifestos, a critique of art education, had been written by Paul Harris, a part-time lecturer at both Hornsey and Guildford, for the head of the Visual Research Department. Harris took part in the Hornsey sit-in debates and was dismissed without notification. Workless, he went on supplementary benefit.

Not all the staff of the art colleges sympathized with the rebellion. Rosalind Pulvertaft, of the Guildford School of Art, found that teaching had become impossible: "One cannot even explain a technical fact like the working of the iris diaphragm of a lens without an hour-long discussion on whether or not it is necessary to understand a lens to succeed as a photographer. . . ." However, her sympathies altered and in June 1969 she rashly wrote to the Surrey Education Committee supporting an inquiry. Three weeks later she was sacked.

The Hornsey manifestos revealed an internal contradiction within the "academic revolution." While the March 22 Movement and SDS in America complained of *vocational* education, of "processing" students to operate as cogs of the capitalist wheel, the Hornsey students were in rebellion against the new, broad-based, humanistic Diploma in Art and Design, which required specialization in one of four areas (fine arts, three-dimensional design, graphic design, or textile design) supplemented by such liberal studies as English or sociology. This, the rebels complained, did not equip them for the "total environment" (polite radical language for getting a job). Their own preferred solution was a new, self-directional "network" system under which the student would choose a personal project requiring learning in a range of skills and materials, to be acquired from the various departments dispensing equipment and teaching on an ad hoc, "service unit" basis. The objections, both educational and administrative, were obvious.

A number of students expelled from Hornsey put their talents at the disposal of Poster Workshop, at 61 Camden Road, NW1, which turned out posters for tenants' associations, squatters, Angry Arts, the young Irish Republican MP Bernadette Devlin, the Ford strikers and the firemen, Anti-Apartheid, the anti-Vietnam movements, for colleges, for *Black Dwarf, King Mob,* Schools Action Union, Stop-It, the CP, and YCL—the entire gamut. Schools Action Union reminds us that the *lycée* revolt in France and Italy had its counterpart among British teenagers. A rash of school action groups appeared in Manchester and London; the National Union of Students began to recruit sixth-formers. Even public school boys truculently experimented with hair long enough to tickle their ears.

On Whit Monday, June 3, some two hundred students invaded the Clarendon Building, the administrative center of Oxford University, and occupied the office of the proctors, demanding the withdrawal of a regulation forbidding the distribution of leaflets without prior permission. Ninety students (the Committee of 90, whose spokesman was Trevor Monroe) had broken the proctors' rules by handing out leaflets, outside a car factory, attacking the Wilson government's incomes policy. Naturally the proctors did what proctors have to do, whereupon the demonstrators congregated outside the Clarendon Building—and then inside. Senior Proctor Charles Smith—dressed in gown, mortar board, and white tie and supported by a bowler-hatted university constable ("bulldog")—confronted the demonstrators but capitulated after a five-hour occupation and agreed to rescind the rules about distributing leaflets.

The next day, over a thousand undergraduates signed a manifesto deploring the occupation; this was the work of the Conservative Association. Professor Max Beloff (the Raymond Aron of the British summer of discontent) argued that even if the proctors' rules on leafleting should be withdrawn, it was wrong of the proctors to yield to force.

The university set up a committee under Professor H. A. L. Hart to investigate grievances and possible reforms. The college junior common rooms submitted recommendations, mainly moderate in substance, asking for representatives of a student council to sit on university bodies affecting junior members, and for legal machinery to deal with disciplinary offenses. (A year later the university sent every graduate and undergraduate a copy of Professor Hart's "Report on Relations with Junior Members," containing complicated proposals for joint consultative committees to be negotiated with the Student Representative Council. But that fragile body had already begun to disintegrate and interest in the whole issue had abated.)

In October, a socialist faction at Oxford sent an "ultimatum" to the academic rotten borough of the national Establishment, All Souls College, whose devious resistance to an era of educational reform had been condemned by a University commission of inquiry. Its warden, John Sparrow, had recently described radical students as unwashed "sluts" whose sex could not readily be determined. The "sluts" responded with three demands: All Souls must (1) admit undergraduates for the first time in its five-hundred-year history; (2) publish the college's accounts (huge surplus revenues from real estate had been hoarded); and (3) hold "democratic" elections to fellowships. One wall slogan read: "Chairman Mao say, maybe sparrows into birds-nest soup." But neither the Cultural Revolution nor undergraduates succeeded in penetrating All Souls.

The vast majority of British students continued to believe that revolution was appropriate for France and points further afield, but not for Britain. On the eve of the major Vietnam demonstration of October 27, in London, the Cambridge Union debated the morality of violence. Arguing for it, Richard Kirkwood (of the Vietnam Solidarity Committee, IS, and the London School of Economics) described British democracy as choosing every five years between "one group of bourgeois fakirs and another lot." Unpersuaded, the union rejected violence by a majority of more than three hundred.

LONDON SCHOOL OF ECONOMICS

October 25, 1968—Eight hundred students occupy the London School of Economics, which the school's director, Dr. Walter Adams, has already "closed." Two large banners adorn the front portal in Houghton Street: "Victory to Vietnamese Revolution" proclaims one; "Adams Closed It We Opened It" announces the other. The purpose of the occupation is to provide a place of sanctuary, medical assistance, and discussion for anyone taking part in Sunday's major Vietnam demonstration. On the Saturday night there are an estimated 2,000 demonstrators camping in the LSE.

More than 1,500 members of the Students' Union had convened on October 23 to debate an emergency resolution calling for the occupation. Professor Meghdad Desai, who was chairing the meeting on that occasion—as members of staff frequently did—recalls that the assembly was spread through three different halls, inevitably involving difficulties if the voting was close. The motion was defeated by 780 votes to 727. People were already leaving the hall (it was sports afternoon) when the radicals called for a recount. This time the motion was carried by 798 votes to 792, an astonishing increase in the aggregate vote of 83! The president of the union, Colin Crouch, declared its neutrality, and the radicals went ahead with the occupation. Repeated votes, or one meeting after another, had become a familiar radical tactic to bypass a moderate majority.

The rift between revolutionaries and reformists now widened further when the National Union of Students appealed to its members to boycott the Vietnam demonstration scheduled for October 27. Geoffrey Martin, outgoing chairman of the NUS, expressed strong hostility to the insurrectionary tactics of the radicals on the campus, in the streets, and—not least—within the NUS. In July the NUS and the Committee of Vice-Chancellors had issued joint proposals on student representation, a major reformist triumph for Martin, whom the radicals cordially detested.

THE DEMONSTRATION

The Vietnam Solidarity Campaign demonstration planned for October 27 had excited a fever of speculation. On September 5, the London *Times* came out with a front-page headline, "Militant plot feared in London," followed by a story claiming that "a small army of militant extremists plans to seize control of certain highly sensitive installations and buildings in Central London next month. . . . This startling plot has been covered by a special squad of detectives. . . ." The extremists were apparently manufacturing Molotov cocktails and "amassing a small arsenal of weapons." Scotland Yard promptly denied knowledge of any such plot and the *Times* did not speak of it again, but when the day arrived more than one hundred police were stationed around Broadcasting House; the BBC even took the precaution of sending duplicate tapes to Birmingham in case the London studios were occupied by Tariq Ali and the ghost of Che Guevara.

Before the march began there was a bitter dispute about tactics between the moderates of the ad hoc organizing committee (a strange mix of Trotskyists, some constituency Labour Parties, trade-union branches, and the Communists) on the one hand, and the Maoist-anarchist faction known as the Britain Vietnam Solidarity Front, who hotly denounced Tariq Ali and "the revisionist clique pressuring the heroic Vietnamese people to surrender to American imperialism." (All rather confusing to the man in the street.) The upshot was that the march split, the moderate majority proceeding down Whitehall, then on to Hyde Park, while some 3,000 ultras galloped up Regent Street toward Grosvenor Square, chanting "Victory to the NLF!" and "U.S. Embassy!" to charge the massed police in Japanese fashion. Meanwhile, a group of anarchists arrived at the entrance to 10 Downing Street chanting "Wilson We Want You . . . Dead!" and tossed a few fireworks at the police cordon. Even the general secretary of the National Council for Civil Liberties praised the tactics of the metropolitan police as "exemplary." There were only eleven arrests in the course of the entire day, but twenty-five police and twenty-two marchers were given medical attention.

According to a survey of 147 demonstrators conducted by *New Society,* 64 percent were aged between eighteen and twenty-four, and 75 percent were students. In descending order of radicalism, 13 percent described themselves as anarchists, 46 percent supported ultra-Left Marxist groups, 17 percent were Communists, while only 23 percent declared an allegiance to the Labour Party. Condemnation of American policy was almost universal, but there were nevertheless divisions of aim. Fifty-six percent hoped for an outright NLF military victory, but 38 percent wanted a compromise settlement, no doubt reflecting the view of the Campaign for Nuclear Disarmament (CND) and *Tribune* (the weekly voice of the Parliamentary Left) that the war could be ended only by negotiation. (CND had refused to join the ad hoc committee which planned the demonstration.)

THE LSE IN TURMOIL

The London School of Economics is an elite college of London University, with one of the highest academic entrance standards in Britain. For the past two years it had been in a condition of almost continuous insurrection, the brightest of a generation confronting administrators anchored to the habit of unchallenged authority. Less sensational than its "rivals in outrage," the LSE could not stage confrontations to compete with those on Sproul Plaza at Berkeley; it did not set a capital alight and threaten a government, as in France; its police busts lacked the savagery displayed at Columbia; there was no mob violence to compare with that at San Francisco State College. Nevertheless, the LSE offers a classic model of a New Left student elite in action—most notably the strategy of institutional confrontation as an assault course for the wider war against capitalist imperialism.

Trouble had begun in the autumn of 1966 with the announcement that the next director of the school would be Dr. Walter Adams, previously principal of University College, Rhodesia (UCR). Following the Unilateral Declaration of Independence by Ian Smith's white minority regime the previous year, and the subsequent inability of the Wilson government to do anything about it, Rhodesia was a trigger issue within the student Left. The LSE Students' Union had even voted in favor of British military intervention. A Socialist Society pamphlet, mainly the work of Steve Jefferys, appeared on October 17, denigrating Adams's record as principal of UCR. The president of the Students' Union sent a copy to the chairman of the LSE's governors, inquiring whether the allegations were correct.

These two protagonists perfectly embodied the conflicting political cultures of the 1960s: in the red corner, David Adelstein, nineteen years of age and Jewish–South African by birth, a pupil of Manchester Grammar School, and an inspirational figure in the movement for participatory democracy (commonly called Student Power); in the blue corner, the chairman of the governors, Lord Bridges, former secretary to the war cabinet and head of the civil service, marinated in Establishment values. Bridges responded to Adelstein's inquiry in time-honored fashion, citing the twin deities of Authority and Confidentiality, and declining to discuss the appointment of Dr. Adams. The school's director, Sir Sydney Caine, and the academic secretary, Harry Kidd, insisted that the body that had appointed Adams as future director was "not answerable to anyone." Lord Bridges, however, decided to reply to the allegations by means of a published letter to the London *Times,* representing Adams as a splendid chap who had done an excellent job in Rhodesia.

Colin Crouch, soon to become president of the Students' Union, recalls a meeting at this time with a group of senior members, including Caine. A radical graduate student, Ben Brewster (a member of the editorial board of *New Left Review*), explained that, "People must take part in all decisions which affect their lives." Caine could neither comprehend nor concede this.

The Students' Union Council drafted an answer to Bridges's letter, but Sir Sydney Caine forbade its publication over the name of the Students' Union, citing an LSE regulation. Advised by two junior members of the Law Department that the director's interpretation of the rules was invalid, the union then resolved by 306 votes to 23 that Adelstein should sign and send the letter to the *Times* in his capacity as union president. The letter was published on October 29. It was the first act of open defiance.

The LSE's Board of Discipline now convened for only the second time since 1945. Adelstein, facing charges, responded with an un-British demand for due process (legal representation, cross-examination of hostile witnesses, and the like). The union staged a demonstration in Houghton Street; lectures and classes were boycotted. One banner proclaimed: "Berkeley 1964: LSE 1966: We'll bring *this* School to a halt too." Members of the Socialist Society sang songs from the civil rights repertoire. Adelstein was not punished. The students greeted this as a triumph and one victory deserves another.

The Adams issue was revived when a Stop Adams meeting was called for January 31, 1967, in the Old Theatre. Caine and Kidd marched around the corridors pulling down posters they considered libelous of Adams; then, discovering leaflets in circulation threatening "direct action," Caine decided to ban the meeting. Having ordered the electrical fuses removed from the Old Theatre, Caine confronted a large crowd gathering outside its closed doors. Caine explained that his intervention was not directed against free speech but against violent action. Adelstein, however, insisted that the issue was indeed now one of free speech and of arbitrary action by the director.

At this juncture the choreography became complicated and uncertain. According to Kidd: "Caine was asked whether he would change his decision, and again refused. There was a movement towards one of the doors of the theatre. Caine and I moved to stand in front of the porters in the doorway, and a number of students, including Marshall Bloom [the American president of the Graduate Students' Association] and Adelstein, are said to have formed a line to hold the crowd back."

While Adelstein was taking another vote, somebody hit a porter and the porter hit him back. In the general scuffle another porter, Edward Poole, aged sixty-four, slipped, fell, and died of a heart attack. According to Kidd, Adelstein said: "This is more serious. Don't go in.

Someone is hurt. Sir Sydney has given us an assurance that there will be no victimization of those already in the Old Theatre. Will everyone please go to the bar?" But the crowd insisted on pushing into the (darkened) Old Theatre. Caine was punched in the mêlée. A few candles were lit; small points of light illuminated agitated, gesticulating human forms as the Old Theatre filled. Caine climbed onto the platform: "The man has now died. Does that satisfy you?" There were enraged screams of "No!" from all sides. Then the mood changed dramatically. The students began to leave.

Once again the disciplinary machinery went into operation, this time against Adelstein, Bloom, and four members of the Students' Union Council, on the ground that they had been responsible for going ahead with the meeting after the director had banned it. Three members of the Law Department, including the redoubtable civil libertarian, Professor J. A. G. Griffith, appeared for the accused. The trial dragged on for some weeks. Adelstein was finally adjudged to have encouraged disobedience by putting to the vote a proposal that the students should "storm the Old Theatre" in defiance of the director's ban, even though it was accepted that Adelstein did not favor that course of action himself. The board also concluded that a meeting called to prevent Adams's taking up his post as director was "a denial of academic freedom" and could not be defended on terms of free speech.

Four of the accused students were acquitted, but Adelstein and Bloom were suspended for the rest of the academic year. Dragons' teeth had been sowed; the administration was now confronted by a formidable display of student power. At five o'clock on March 13, more than two hundred students streamed out of a union meeting and sat down in the corridors and lobbies of the school. The occupation was to last nine days. Encouragement came from several members of the academic staff, notably political scientist Dr. Ralph Miliband, and a telegram of support arrived from Bertrand Russell, no less.

At 4:30 on the following Wednesday morning there was a knock on the door of Connaught House, the administrative building. The night porter asked, "Who is it?" A voice answered, "Cleaners." The porter opened the door and was swept aside by a raiding party that grew to sixty-five. This occupation of the administrative wing dissolved Caine's scruples about bringing in the police; the occupiers were ejected (without the brutality displayed at Berkeley and Columbia) after Kidd had sentenced them all, summarily, to three months' suspension for repeated refusal to vacate the premises. Kidd's published account adds: "Their suspensions were not in fact enforceable; the photographer did not send the promised photographs."

Being situated in the heart of the capital, the occupied LSE was naturally a center of attraction for radicals unconnected with the school. (Their presence was suspected of swelling the militant vote at union meetings.) More than 1,500 students from other colleges and universities joined the LSE contingent on the "Daffodil march" that took place on Friday the 17th, threading its way down Fleet Street between Morris Minors, Minis, and taxis, with a strong escort of police. One banner warned: "Beware the Pedagogic Gerontocracy." Photographs of the march reveal few cases of long hair and none of extravagant costume; it was a sober gathering of the young elite later destined to administer and teach, if not govern, the nation. Thirty-nine percent of the LSE's students took part.

The Students' Union voted by 347 to 116 to continue the protest and to send a letter of explanation to all members of staff: "We deeply resent being branded irresponsible (truants, Provos, American agitators, hard-core dissidents, etc.). . . ." Stressing their desire to communicate and discuss, they also pointed out that they had forbidden violence and destructive actions: "We even organized our own policing to prevent any irresponsible behaviour by insiders or outsiders."

The Easter vacation intervened. By a compromise formula, Adelstein and Bloom wrote letters of regret, allowing the Court of Governors, "on an act of clemency," to suspend the penalty conditional on good behavior. Bloom returned to America, ran an underground press agency, retreated from disputes to a hippie communal farm, and committed suicide in 1969.

Four members of the school's staff, two of them lecturers in social administration, two of them statisticians, later conducted a highly professional survey of student attitudes and actions during the crisis. A questionnaire was sent to all 2,806 students on the registry list. Eighty percent (2,239) sent usable replies. The LSE's students had arrived overwhelmingly from private or academically selective secondary schools. Only 4 percent had attended "secondary moderns" or the newly emerging "comprehensive" schools (even though 22 percent came from working-class homes). By standard academic criteria, the level of the LSE's intake was impressive. The percentage of entrants with at least three A or B grades in the advanced-level examinations was twice the national university average, indicating that the academic level of the LSE's social science students was the highest in Britain (though comparable figures for Oxford and Cambridge were not available).

The survey discovered that 36 percent of the LSE's students had taken part in the sit-in on one or more days; 62 percent took no part at all. Twenty-one percent had braved the discomfort of at least one whole night in the school. A few had carried the major burden: 7 percent had spent four to six nights on the premises, and a heroic 1 percent, seven or more whole nights. Twenty percent said they had acted as pickets outside the entrances and the lecture halls.

Regarding the boycott of lectures and classes, 56 percent of undergraduates and 40 percent of graduates missed "at least some" academic sessions, and of the "strikers," about three-quarters had missed them all.

Questioned about Vietnam, Rhodesia, antiracist legislation, forms of secondary education, and party allegiances, the LSE student body emerged as exceptionally radical and conspicuously to the left of other London colleges such as University and Imperial. The survey revealed a clear correlation between left-wing political attitudes and criticism of the school (as at Columbia a year later). Forty-five percent of Conservative students had attended lectures and classes as usual during the boycott, compared to 30 percent of Liberals, 23 percent of Labour supporters, and only 4 percent of the Marxists.

What kind of powers did the LSE's students, *reflecting each in isolation,* demand? The responses show a pattern far from contemptuous of age and experience; the rules governing their own facilities and rights, rather than academic policy, were the main bone of contention. Sixty-nine percent wanted effective student power in the running of the library, 54 percent in questions of school discipline, 43 percent in teaching arrangements; but only 34 percent in course content, only 28 percent in relation to examination policy, only 13 percent in appointing the LSE's director (despite the seminal role of the Adams affair in launching the troubles), and only 9 percent wanted a voice in academic appointments. In short, quite a moderate profile. Postgraduates, particularly those with a first-class honors degree, were the most sceptical about student involvement in academic appointments and examination requirements.

Another significant variable was field of study. A survey of attitudes at Berkeley in 1965 showed support for the Free Speech Movement varying from 75 percent of social science majors to 42 percent of those majoring in business administration, engineering, and architecture. At the LSE, only 38 percent of sociology/anthropology undergraduates took *no* part in the occupation or boycott, yet the corresponding percent for those reading history, economic history, geography, and the industrial subjects was up to 66 to 75 percent.

As for student protest tactics, about 70 percent of LSE students condoned picketing, boycotts, and sit-ins, *provided they did not immobilize the school.* But action that did immobilize the school (and therefore robbed other students of freedom of choice) was condemned by 53 percent, partly justified by 18 percent, and wholly justified by 22 percent.

In September 1967, the LSE's controversial new director, Dr.

Walter Adams, took up his post with scarcely a murmur of protest from the student body. At the end of February 1968, the Students' Union rejected official proposals for student representation on the school's three main governing bodies; the union wanted a staff-student senate possessing full and final authority in all fields.

On May 23, 1968, two hundred LSE students dramatized their solidarity with the French Left by means of an all-night vigil overhung with red and black flags. The union president, however, condemned the gesture as inconsiderate to students preparing for their exams. The *Guardian*'s correspondent, Dennis Barker, positioned himself on the steps of St. Clement's Building and asked a dozen students for their reactions. He concluded that sympathy for yet another Socialist Society demonstration would be minimal unless the authorities reacted repressively. John Pritchard (first-year sociology) thought that British students were probably better treated than French ones; Lawrence McDonald (second-year economics) sympathized with the French students but saw no purpose in the sit-in; Winston Murray, a Ghanaian reading economics, was sceptical about the relevance of such actions to Britain; Brian Beagan (third-year international politics) did not believe students possessed a valid political role or a consistent outlook. Pamela Hart (third-year economics) said: "I think what has been going on here is very foolish. Well—the idea of an anarchist 'society' sounds a bit odd, don't you think? All the activity seems to have dried up here." Michael Cooke (first-year economics) regarded the whole thing as "futile," as letting off steam during exam time; he was all in favor of inviting dock workers to speak at the school, but revolutionary circumstances did not exist in Britain. James Gill (first-year economics) said, "It's all a bit pointless." Ian George (first-year economics) added: "I have examinations in a fortnight. That is more important to me. I've got sympathy with the ideal. . . ." Rhys Hall, a graduate reading history, thought "It could possibly catch on later. It depends on the reaction of the School authorities. If they move against people, then it will catch on. . . ."

Barker's ad hoc survey was not necessarily representative; the more radical students distrusted the press and often refused to be interviewed. But the impression of scepticism in the wider student body is inescapable. Rhys Hall's comment would have been equally valid at other university flash points: "It all depends on the reaction of . . . the authorities."

On June 15, 1968, a new national grouping, the Revolutionary Socialist Students Federation (RSSF), held its inaugural conference at the LSE in the volatile atmosphere generated by events in France. ("Students of the world IGNITE," exhorted a poster.) The conference, which rejected parliamentary politics outright, was attended by two leaders of the French insurrection, Daniel Cohn-Bendit and Alain Geismar, both clearly exhausted (Geismar had been fighting the police outside the Renault factory at Flins). A humorous report of these sessions by David Widgery portrays the intervention of Chris Harman, a Trotskyist who habitually began his speeches, "We have to be absolutely clear about this." Greeted with friendly groans, Harman brandished his moped crash helmet: "We must be quite clear what's happening. 1968 is a year of international revolution no less than 1789, 1830, 1848, 1917 and 1936." Militants with *Black Dwarf* in their laps were to be seen conferring about what did actually happen in 1830.

The RSSF was a serious body, claiming a paid-up membership of 2,500 by the end of the year, reflecting the deepening estrangement from parliamentary politics, but burdened with the usual quota of egoists, sectarian tyros, and Americans who'd seen it all. (Paul Hoch and Vic Schoenbach, prominent activists at the LSE, had brought their radical outlook from Brown and Columbia, respectively; they complained that they were branded "ultra-left adventurists" because they wanted to *do* something.) The following dialogue, reported by David Widgery, is taken from an RSSF meeting at Cambridge University:

> "What you guys need is a trip and a fuck. When did you last have a fuck?"
> "What the hell has fucking got to do with socialism?"
> "What happened in France happened because some guys felt that they didn't like being told when they could and when they couldn't have a fuck."

The first plenary conference of the RSSF, held at the Round House in November 1968, was marred by monotonous and ritualized speeches about imperialism, but it did pass a statement of aims calling for "red bases" in the universities, with all power to be vested in a general assembly of students, staff, and administrative workers.

THE LSE CRISIS OF 1968–1969

As earlier described, eight hundred students occupied the LSE in support of the major Vietnam demonstration on October 27, 1968. Within the radical camp there were tensions between the ultras and the more responsible Marxists who controlled the occupation steering committee. The committee's decision to terminate the occupation after the Vietnam demonstration was challenged. In the London University student paper *Sennet* (November 20), the Situationists complained about the dictatorial "Committee of Public Safety" at the LSE and about the persistence of "relationships, language and bodies [which] were the reincarnation of the authoritarian ghosts who have buggered us all once already." Martin Shaw, a leading student activist, recalls that the International Socialist group generally recommended physical moderation against Maoists, anarchists, and American freewheelers. This tactical moderation was not, however, to be confused with the reformist outlook of successive Conservative and social democratic union presidents, Peter Watherston, Colin Crouch, and Francis Keohane.

By his own account, Crouch increasingly regarded himself as committed to an ideological struggle: "I had really lost interest in acting as the political representative of those to whom I was responsible. As tensions mounted over various issues I was too engrossed in defending the university as an institution against the attacks from the Left to voice student concerns." (Crouch later became a don at the LSE and a member of the Court of Governors.)

A new threat now dominated the landscape. After Adams had attempted to close the school, the new chairman of the governors, Lord Robbins, intervened. More sympathetic to the "Continental manifestations" of the student movement, Robbins believed that, "You can't have a democracy paying the money for youngsters to do what they like." As for the radicals' critique of the bourgeois content of the curriculum, he found this position "as hideous and remote from me as the ideals of the Hitlerjugend." In November Robbins issued a strong statement warning academic staff that they risked dismissal if they encouraged or took part in disorderly conduct. He referred to "certain junior members of the staff who are alleged to have encouraged and participated in the unauthorised occupation." This was thought to be the first such public warning to academics in a British university. Seventy-six members of the LSE's academic staff (one-quarter of the total) signed a letter drawing Robbins's attention to Article 28 of the school's Articles of Association: No member was to be punished for expressing *opinions* on any subject.

The Students' Union responded immediately by passing a motion proposed by Victor Schoenbach deploring the governors' threats and promising resistance in the form of direct action. (The union also censured its own executive for "their abysmal failure to actively counter the governors' and directors' autocratic behaviour.") A disgusted Colin Crouch resigned as president of the union and came out with a Young Fabian pamphlet alleging that the extreme Left wanted only revolutionary Marxism to be taught at the LSE. In a straight fight for control of the union between revolutionaries and reformists committed to constitutional action, the reformists captured all the seats on the council, although the election for president was won by the narrowest of margins: 716 votes to 677. But the radicals were on the warpath regardless of elections.

BIRMINGHAM AND BRISTOL

The specter haunting Europe came to Birmingham University with an eight-day occupation at the end of November. The vice-chancellor, Dr. Brockie Hunter, was imprisoned in his office, where he was joined by the registrar. After long negotiations, students had been offered membership of most committees but not a vote. By early December even the Federation of Conservative Students was behind the sit-in. Hunter then refused to negotiate until the occupation (involving about 400 students out of 6,000) ended. On December 3, a huge meeting of the Guild of Undergraduates voted by 2,346 to 1,542 to end the six-day sit-in, but the guild's council, forgetful of "participatory democracy," then voted by 71 to 42 to continue it; Ray Phillips, president of the guild, explained that the mass meeting had not applied "enough thought" to the matter. Two days later the sit-in ended with a promise of no victimization.

In December students at Bristol opened their new union building to those from less favored colleges. The university said no. The Senate House (which accommodates not only administrative offices but the senior common room, and enjoys a fine view of the residential suburbs of Clifton) was occupied for four days. The confrontation was a tense one, with reinforcements "flown" in from Birmingham, Hull, and Cardiff. Two hundred engineering students counter-demonstrated outside, some of them dressed for rugby or worse. The university obtained a legal writ against eight of the occupiers it could identify, whereupon 1,500 others signed a declaration of complicity and the confrontation moved to the law courts in the Strand. Finally a large meeting of the union voted by 773 to 215 to discontinue the sit-in.

SHOWDOWN AT THE LSE

At the LSE, Dr. Walter Adams now faced the school's most severe crisis. On January 8, 1969, the director addressed a teach-in on Rhodesia and was immediately confronted with three demands anticipatory of American campus action in the mid-1980s: that the school publish a list of its holdings in Rhodesia and South Africa; that the school's governors should resign from the boards of companies trading with white southern Africa; and that such companies should not be allowed to recruit on the school's premises. Adams came back two days later, predictably failed to meet most of the demands, was shouted down, and left. Tempers rose. A delegation was sent to bring the director back to face the music, but he refused. Incensed, a large section of the meeting surged through the school and up the stairs toward the administrative building, where they were confronted by locked fire doors. The drawbridge was up. So they invaded the senior common room instead, pursued by a photographer from the London *Times,* which reported that the students had voted to bar the Court of Governors from the school "by force if necessary." An explosion was imminent.

The locked fire doors turned attention to the iron gates recently installed by the administration at strategic points in the corridors. On January 23, 1969, the Students' Union Council called an emergency meeting to debate a motion postponing direct action over the gates on the ground that the administration had agreed to negotiate. The motion was passed by 365 to 322 with 76 abstentions, and six negotiators were appointed. But the following day the radicals, following a familiar tactic, engineered a second union meeting; this time the vote was 282 to 231 in favor of removing the gates there and then. Almost immediately a crowd of militants attacked the gates with a sledgehammer, crowbars, and pickaxes. There were angry scenes as members of the academic staff tried to hinder the demolition gangs. Professor Desai recalls that he and Professor J. A. G. Griffith (both of the Left) were urging the students not to do it. Paul Hoch and Victor Schoenbach, the leading American ultras at the LSE, later described with relish the pushing aside of staff who were defending the gates by passive physical resistance.

Adams summoned the police, who at first refused to turn out, on the ground that it did not constitute a public disorder. Finally they arrived, bringing students up from the Three Tons Bar in the basement—but some of the culprits escaped by a back entrance—for identification by members of the teaching staff, a traumatic moment for all who believed in the self-governance of a scholarly community. ("So much for your value-free methodology," remarked a militant to a Hungarian exile.) Students who had been "identified" were taken to Bow Street magistrates' court, where a further demonstration took place, resulting in more arrests. Staff members who collaborated with the police were marked down as "academic spies."

Adams closed the school. This time the lockout was enforced with police support and lasted until February 19—four weeks out of a ten-week term. A crowd of outraged students from the LSE arrived at the University of London Student Union Building to establish an LSE in exile. Sympathetic staff members came to offer courses on conventional subjects, supplementing the "radical alternative" seminars. Laurence Harris, an economist on the LSE staff who took part, believes that the "mob" aspect of radical conduct has been exaggerated; in his view it was a time "of great rationality and consideration" leading to important theoretical developments in social science departments during the 1970s.

The university administration reacted with hostility. "I have rarely been so depressed as when I looked out from the window of my room in the Senate House at the various processions," reported Sir Douglas Logan, principal of London University. "My mind was irresistibly taken back to Germany in the days after Hitler seized power. . . ."

Four days after the gates had been pulled down two letters appeared in the London *Times*. Mary Tiffen, an LSE graduate student wrote: "Most students do not want to spend all their time attending meetings. . . . By democracy I understand the right to elect representatives. . . . The Socialist Society . . . are attempting to impose change on the nature of the community by calling continual meetings until, by the weariness of the other students, they are able to get a majority at one particular meeting." But the cocky voice of ultra-Jacobinism was heard from Jeff Olstead, secretary of Queen's College Union, Cambridge, deriding the "whimpering of the so-called 'moderates' " who "will presumably exhibit the same bovine capacity when released into the greater and sicker society of this country."

In the House of Commons, the Labour secretary of state for education, Edward Short, came out in support of Adams and vice-chancellors in general, denouncing "this squalid nonsense." He thought it high time "that one or two of these thugs are thrown out on their necks." Wreckers of society, they operated by means of "lies, defamation, character assassination, intimidation, physical violence." The LSE, meanwhile, had taken out court injunctions against thirteen* (only nine of whom were currently LSE students), restraining them from entering the school.

In February internal disciplinary charges were brought against three members of the academic staff. Laurence Harris, a twenty-six-year-old economics lecturer, was charged with (1) on January 24,

*Including the "hard core": David Adelstein, former president of the Students' Union, Paul Hoch, Victor Schoenbach, David Slaney, and Richard Kuper, a graduate of the University of Witwatersrand, Cambridge, and the LSE, a founding member of the RSSF, and a student representative at negotiations with the standing committee of the Court of Governors during the 1967 occupation.

applauding a speech advocating forcible removal of the gates; (2) being present at their removal; (3) having taken the chair at the teach-in of January 10, then allowing a vote on a resolution that the governors should be forcibly kept out of the school and the director barricaded in his room; (4) having on January 25 or 26, at the University of London Union, made or supported proposals to enter the LSE by force and set up a tribunal to try staff who had assisted the police.

A huge meeting of the LSE Students' Union, perhaps 2,000 strong, convened in the Friends Meeting House in Euston Road, excluded journalists and photographers, and, from several proffered motions, passed one proposed by Martin Shaw on behalf of the Socialist Society. It demanded no victimization, no more informing by members of the staff, and the reopening of the LSE minus the iron gates and minus the police. A motion deploring the violence of those who removed the gates was defeated. The *Observer* came out on Sunday with a feature, "How Soc Soc whips up trouble at LSE."

Robin Blackburn, an assistant lecturer in sociology who had traveled to Bolivia for the Bertrand Russell Peace Foundation on Régis Debray's behalf, was charged with a speech made after the pulling down of the gates and with a similar statement on BBC-TV—both construed as incitement to similar behavior in the future. Blackburn had been attending a seminar when the union voted to remove the gates, but he later took part in a great debate in Central Hall, Westminster, between the Old Left (Michael Foot, Eric Heffer) and the New (Tariq Ali, Bob Rowthorne). During the discussion period, Blackburn supported the pulling down of the gates, allowing himself (as he now puts it) to get "carried away by the occasion." His comments were reported in the press.

The third lecturer facing disciplinary proceedings was Nicholas Bateson, a Maoist teaching in the Psychology Department, described by Blackburn as a "workerist" dedicated to serving the people and also a leading firebrand in the Britain Vietnam Solidarity Front, which had broken from the main march on October 27 and headed for Grosvenor Square. Bateson had reportedly equated the removal of the LSE's iron gates with the liberation struggle in Rhodesia, Thailand, and Palestine.

On March 7, the director of public prosecutions took out criminal summonses against eight students and two lecturers (Bateson and Harris), accused of committing willful damage. On March 10, the union responded by supporting (355 to 206) a Socialist Society resolution calling for a new occupation. Spray-painted slogans covered the corridors and the doors of academic staff involved in the disciplinary action. Students forced their way into the office of Dr. Percy Cohen, dean of undergraduate studies (a liberal who had spoken up for Adelstein in

1967), spilled paint on his desk, and stole draft exam papers together with minutes of certain school committees. Members of IS then cleaned up the office (to the scorn of Hoch and Schoenbach).

On April 18, it was announced that Blackburn and Bateson would be dismissed without appeal. Professor J. A. G. Griffith protested that Blackburn had been punished for advocacy rather than action, which was contrary to the LSE's articles of association. Under criticism from staff and students, the school agreed to set up an appellate tribunal consisting of a Queen's Counsel and two law professors. The tribunal found that Blackburn's statements were a direct encouragement to further violence, though none took place: ". . . he is a committed believer in violence as a means of reforming the School, at any rate where the School authorities do not meet student demands." The dismissals of Blackburn and Bateson were confirmed.

What Blackburn did believe was that the prevailing social science texts and lectures reinforced capitalist values by presenting them as the only imaginable rationality. The revolutionary impulse was translated into sterile equations, like Chalmers Johnson's "Multiple dysfunction + elite intransigence = Revolution." According to Blackburn, the economics and sociology texts dominating the syllabus—Paul Samuelson, R. G. Lipsey, Alvin Gouldner, Talcott Parsons, Raymond Aron—induced "a morbid paralysis of social will." The crucial concept of messianic totalitarianism was presented as the alternative to bourgeois democracy. Blackburn's colleague on *New Left Review,* Perry Anderson, added that Britain produced "empirical, piecemeal intellectual disciplines" that "corresponded to humble, circumscribed social action"; the native culture gratefully welcomed and honored foreign-born scholars who reinforced the prevailing conservatism, notably Ludwig Wittgenstein in philosophy, Lewis Namier in history, Isaiah Berlin in political theory, Karl Popper in social theory, Hans Eysenck in psychology. "Every insular reflex and prejudice," wrote Anderson, "was powerfully flattered and enlarged in the magnifying mirror they presented to it." Members of this White Guard duly received their knighthoods: Sir Lewis, Sir Karl, Sir Isaiah. . . . By contrast the foreign-born Marxist, Isaac Deutscher, was "reviled and ignored by the academic throughout his life. He never secured the smallest university post."

That, too, was to be the fate of Robin Blackburn and Nicholas Bateson. Blackburn was offered a post in the Sociology Department at Essex but (he recalls) Vice-Chancellor Sloman intervened to veto the appointment. He became a publisher, author, and journalist. Bateson was in the wilderness until he joined a branch of the civil service; he was never able to pursue his career as a social psychologist.

The dismissal of Blackburn and Bateson was greeted with indignation by an emergency union meeting, which voted by 468 to 42 to support an academic boycott of lectures. Some freelancers took matters into their own hands: the word "spy" was painted on certain office doors, tubes of metal glue were applied to the locks of "academic assassins," lectures by Professors A. C. L. Day and M. Freedman were disrupted, and the senior common room was briefly invaded by 150 who marched in with a megaphone. Day had a pitcher of water emptied over his head in the Old Theatre on April 22. During a second invasion of the senior common room, the quasi-Yippie Hoch and Schoenbach took down a portrait of Lord Robbins. Some of those responsible for this guerrilla warfare had disregarded a court injunction restraining them from entering the school and refused to promise good behavior when brought before a High Court judge. Eight members of the LSE staff testified in support of a move to commit them to Brixton Prison, but the judge thought it would do more harm than good.

Forty-five members of the teaching staff, including ten full professors, protested the dismissal of Blackburn and Bateson and called for an independent inquiry into the administration of the school. In the House of Lords the socialist economist Lord Balogh announced that academic freedom at the LSE had been violated by a "small oligarchy of conservative professors and conservative laymen." Despite the massive confrontations in France and Italy, Balogh knew of no instance of a university teacher losing his job. One hundred members of the LSE branch of the Association of University Teachers asked London University to set up a tribunal on the dismissals, but on May 7, the academic board voted 125 to 36 in support of the governors' actions to stamp out violence before it became standard practice.

The internal disciplinary proceedings against Laurence Harris began after the Blackburn and Bateson rulings—and after Harris's legal indictment had been thrown out by a Bow Street magistrate. The tribunal recommended no action against him, but in 1970 he left the school and took a nonacademic job. Today he is a professor of economics at the Open University, which broadcasts degree courses for adults. Like Blackburn and the majority of LSE radicals of the late sixties—and also their opponents—he remains unrepentant.

A period of conservative reaction lay ahead, the prevailing faculty values being those expressed by the sociologist David Martin, who described Blackburn (one of his former pupils) and Anderson as "fast, slippery" minds engaged in "slippery evasion" of the facts. The school's former director, Sir Sydney Caine, flew his pennant at the masthead of counterrevolution in a book called *British Universities: Purpose and Prospects,* which denounced ". . . the decay of standards which removes any presumption of respect for existing authority and institutions, elevates novelty to the level of the principal criterion of values and encourages the tendency of intellectually arrogant young people to believe whatever ideas are currently in their minds to be the last word in human wisdom." In Sir Sydney's view university government was not the business of undergraduates, or graduates, or even junior staff—because of "their essential incompetence."

Administrative structures were destined to change very little. In 1982–83 only six of the LSE's one hundred governors were nominated by the Students' Union.

— 19 —

MILITANT STUDENTS, ANGRY PROFESSORS

"At close range the spectacle of students suddenly and self-righteously engaged in 'liberation' reminded many dons of mob rule or worse."

THE STUDENT ACTIVISTS

The student revolution in the United States was to gather momentum into 1969–70. The distinctive quality of campus unrest in 1968 was its relationship to the national power structure at a time when bitter divisions over Vietnam and race relations were reflected in the primaries, the party conventions, and—courtesy of George Wallace—in the presidential campaign itself. The candidacy of Eugene McCarthy presented liberal and radical students with both a dilemma—to work within the system or to reject it outright—and an opportunity to reshape national policy. Neither the dilemma nor the opportunity survived the nomination of Hubert Humphrey and the election of Richard Nixon, yet campus rebellion continued to expand from the minority of colleges affected in 1967–68 to the broader spectrum of 1969–70.

R. E. Peterson's investigations of 859 colleges and universities in 1967–68, based on questionnaires submitted to deans of students, yielded interesting data on the pattern of campus unrest. If we make an initial distinction between external (national or global) and internal (campus) causes of dissidence, we find the percentage of colleges reporting various forms of protest as follows: (1) *external:* the Vietnam War, 38 percent; civil rights, 29 percent; the draft and military recruitment on campus, 25 percent; (2) *internal:* disciplinary regulations, 34 percent; participation in policy decisions, 27 percent; curriculum dissatisfaction, 15 percent.

In general only a minority of students in the affected colleges involved themselves in direct action; according to one estimate, not more than a quarter of a million out of a national student population of 7 million were politically active in 1967–68.

Thus listed, the two sets of statistics might suggest an approximate balance between external discontents and internal ones. In practice, however, it was the wider political consciousness that generated a critical attitude toward patterns of authority within the college. Moreover, challenges to internal disciplinary regulations were not presented in the abstract, but normally arose from clashes arising out of demonstrations against the war or draft. These in turn put Student Power on the agenda. Draft exemption was dependent on course grades and the collaboration of colleges with Selective Service, a further cause of tension and protest. It was as a result of the general radical culture that colleges came to be regarded as integral units of corporate capitalism, dehumanized technocracy, war research, racism, and authoritarianism. The demand for black studies was inspired less by the desire to learn Swahili or discover the religions of the Niger than by a transplantation of ghetto experience to the white-dominated academy.

Kenneth Keniston, the distinguished Yale social psychologist, demonstrated that student revolt was rarely caused by a specific failing of the university affected. The radical vanguard was generally populated by the brightest kids endowed with a keen awareness of the wider world and its values. In its campaign for national prominence, Michigan State at Lansing decided to attract National Merit Scholarship winners by offering special scholarships and honors programs; as a result the campus was transformed from somnolence into radical activity, with a flourishing SDS, cultural alienation, and drugs.

Elaborate schemes for student participation had no effect. Antioch College, where students had been involved, in Keniston's phrase, "to the eyeballs in governance," and even in faculty appointments, nevertheless experienced alienation and protest. The more energetically that Berkeley attempted, during the years 1964–68, to democratize its administration and offer flexible study options, the *lower* the proportion of students who expressed satisfaction.

This perspective is confirmed by the statements of the New Left theoreticians themselves. Carl Davidson of SDS derided the traditional forms of student government precisely because they rehearsed the competitive careerism required by a society increasingly divided between managers and managed. Had not that notorious corporate liberal, President Clark Kerr of the University of California, spoken of capturing students for the system? Davidson regarded the teaching staff as paradigmatic of the wider society: The top level of professors and administrators should be regarded as "managers" whose interests were tied to those of the ruling class. The "traditional academics" should be seen as "middle-class professionals in the classic sense." However, the third and largest group, the assistants and junior faculty, who were most engaged in teaching on the "mass production line," should be treated as members of the new working class, despite their tendency to false consciousness. Campaigning for student power was not an end in itself, but a means of mobilizing mass consciousness. "For the most part, it will be difficult to determine whether or not a reform has the effect of being anti-capitalist until it has been achieved."

What kind of young people were most inclined to become political activists? According to Keniston, they had normally accepted their parents' *values* but not necessarily their *performance*. The typical profile of the New Left activist showed high academic achievement, a liberal home (often Jewish, Unitarian, or Quaker) sustained by a healthy income and less status anxiety than typically afflicted conservative students. The activists' parents tended to be either thirties-Marxists or, more often, Adlai Stevenson Democrats. Many of the young activists interviewed by Keniston retained from early childhood a sense of the family holding distinctive views not shared by the community. They had frequently championed unpopular causes in school.

Keniston concluded that ". . . what was most impressive was not their rebellion against their parents or American society, but their ultimate fidelity to both. . . ." Relationships with the mother were normally warm, but attitudes toward the father were ambivalent—a split image, a tension between admiration and hostility, between identification and rejection; the father's life-style did not necessarily match his professed ideals. Paul Jacobs and Sol Landau went further than Keniston—and perhaps too far—in identifying the young radicals as the children of homes where performance and professed values were in conflict: ". . . their parents are the once-poor scholars who head rich academic institutes; the ex-union organizers who run their own large businesses; the former slum dwellers who develop segregated real-estate tracts; the families once on the WPA who live in suburbia—all those who have made it."

Keniston found that radical activism emerged logically from the domestic ethos; few reported a sudden conversion and none suffered from anxiety about the personal consequences of radical activism; the "great fear" of the Joseph McCarthy period had vanished. After ten years of interviewing students from middle- or upper-middle-class backgrounds, Keniston had not yet discovered one who was worried about finding a job and relatively few who were worried about securing a *good* job.

In addition, a psychological pattern emerged alongside the sociocultural one. Keniston noticed that the radicals' adolescence had tended to follow the European rather than the American pattern—introspection, a shy, guilty feeling about sex, intensive reading and writing, and an active fantasy life—whereas the more typical American adolescent turned away from the family to seek his norms in the peer group. These findings led to a further line of inquiry. Following the work of Jean Piaget and Lawrence Kohlberg, Keniston identified three stages of moral reasoning: the preconventional (dominated by egocentric gratification); the conventional (dominated by the moral standards of the community); and the postconventional or "ethical" stage (as Erik Erikson termed it). We may conclude that an introspective, studious childhood would be likely to foster personal or postconventional values informed by wide reading and relatively critical of the tribal wisdom of the majority.

A study of students at Berkeley and San Francisco State College undertaken by Brewster Smith, Jeanne Block, and Norma Haan during the traumatic campus upheavals found that only 12 percent of nonprotesting students had reached the postconventional moral stage, compared with 56 percent of protesting students. (The ranks of the protestors also included a higher proportion of moral "primitives" who had not yet reached conventional standards; 10 percent of protestors fell into this category, compared with 3 percent of nonprotestors.) But any such psychological analysis must be subordinated to the wider persuasions of history, meaning both objective events and the "epidemic" factor. Protest itself may become, in certain circles, a conventional posture; abstainers may include not only the "unthinking" football player or fraternity buff, but also the most discriminating intelligences on the campus. History rather than individual psychology must account for the relative political passivity of the student generations of the 1950s and 1970s.

THE PROFESSORS

The professors—what did they make of it all?

S. M. Lipset reported: "A comprehensive analysis of demonstrations which occurred at 181 institutions during 1967–68 found that faculty were involved in the planning of over half of the students protests which occurred. In close to two-thirds of them, faculty bodies passed resolutions approving of the protests." On the other hand "the existence of basic tensions between student radicals and faculty supporters" resulted in "faculty backing being short lived for student protest on any given campus." This was made abundantly clear by a Gallup poll taken in the spring of 1969 (when some 4,000 students were arrested), in which 76 percent of university faculty members approved of the expulsion of disruptive students.

From the thin ranks of veteran university presidents who had defended academic freedom during the congressional inquisitions of the 1950s, a few survived to champion the spirited kids of the late sixties.

Robert Hutchins, former chancellor of the University of Chicago, was one; Harold Taylor, former president of Sarah Lawrence College, was another. There was something of the mischievous old man's winking collusion with his grandchildren against their dad about Hutchins's comment on the Columbia uprising: not only should the students be granted amnesty for taking over five college buildings in six days, "but should be honored at special graduation ceremonies for forcing open the door to university reform." Harold Taylor did in fact turn out for the Columbia "counter-Commencement." George Wald, a Harvard professor of biology and a critic of the war, explained that "the cure for student unrest is *adult* unrest."

The supportive voices from the academy were frequently heard in the *New York Review of Books,* where Henry David Aitken celebrated "The Revolting Academy" in July 1968 and where Frederick Crews, of the University of California, came out in support of the demands of black students; their "insistence on connecting identity to learning and learning to committed action" was of significance to all students in "the self-estranged knowledge industry." Aitken hailed the arrival of "shadow universities" where young scholars were now discussing man as a moral agent rather than as a petrified object of behavioral research. He wanted "off-beat, cross-generational dialogue in which it is not assumed in advance that only teachers have professorial rank."

Kenneth Keniston wrote: "I am far more worried about police riots and American military violence than I am about student violence, and I consider the radicalism of a minority of today's college students a largely appropriate, reasonable and measured response to blatant injustices." Martin Duberman, professor of history at Princeton, attested that the SDS members he knew were "far more knowledgeable and sophisticated, far less imprisoned by myth and ideology, than the average undergraduate." Duberman believed that emotion and commitment were the essence of education. James S. Ackerman, professor of fine arts at Harvard, described the activists as superior students who had enriched the atmosphere "by contrast to . . . the passive and dreary years of the McCarthy era." Answering George F. Kennan's equation of genuine scholarly endeavor with "a certain remoteness from the contemporary scene—a certain detachment and seclusion," Charles S. Fisher, of Brandeis, wondered whether Kennan would have advised the Negro students of the South "to leave the lunch counters to return to their campuses for well-argued, heavily footnoted debates."

But the academic friends of the New Left were far outnumbered by its enraged critics. The most authoritative anathema was delivered early in 1968, through the *New York Times,* by George F. Kennan. Intellectually, it was a dubious, self-contradictory performance; at one point in his polemic Kennan claimed that the politically obsessed, revolutionary students of Tsarist Russia "never really learned anything in their university years," but in a later passage they "read extremely widely"—unlike contemporary American students—"in fiction, science and philosophy."

Kennan accused the New Left of everywhere destroying the pure academy of learning. But did it exist? Admitting university involvement in defense contracts and commercial ventures, he argued that no one forced students to talk with the recruiters from the Marines or Dow Chemical. In practice, however, the total environment produced by such subordination deeply affects students. Collaboration with defense-related projects involved sociologists, psychologists, and political scientists as well as scientists. Michigan State had accepted $25 million in federal funds to render varieties of assistance to South Vietnam. As the coordinator of that project, Stanley K. Scheinbaum later admitted, "The struggle for status, recognition and money is an irresistible lure . . . the new breed professor . . . orbits in the university's stratosphere of institutes, projects and contracts. The student is lowest among his colleagues."

Among Britain's new universities, Warwick presented a model of collaboration with local, Midlands industries, notably Rootes Motors. The vice-chancellor, J. B. Butterworth, told the university treasurer, "I still think we are giving too much away to them, not only in Warwick but in universities generally." He was referring, of course, to students: "them." When a headmaster wrote "in confidence" to denounce one of his own pupils, a candidate for Warwick, as a militant activist, the young man was promptly turned down and the informing headmaster received a letter of thanks from the registrar on behalf of the vice-chancellor. Derogatory information about an American lecturer at the university was sent to the vice-chancellor by Rootes's director of legal affairs, who accused the lecturer of "a very definite bias against employers in general. . . . [His] students would most certainly be exposed to a most undesirable indoctrination." None of this would have been revealed had not Warwick's students invaded the administration block and opened the files.

Defense contracts and business patronage did not exhaust the list of pollutions clouding the crystal waters of scholarship. In Britain the busy don groaned under his "teaching load"; apparently the taxpayer subsidized the student on sufferance; but on what terms did he finance the don? With nine new universities it was bonanza time with unprecedented opportunities for academic employment and advancement. Television, an expanding quality press, and fattened foundations provided what Peter Wiles, professor of Russian social and economic studies at the LSE, described as "the golden age of the don. He was free to research, to publish, to broadcast, to travel; he sat on Royal Commissions. The BBC, the Ford Foundation, the University of California, and the United Nations paid him substantial sums to air his views." L. G. Sykes, professor of French at Leicester, regretted that the more energetic and ambitious dons now turned aside from "the ungrateful task of academic teaching" to the more congenial pastures of television studios and the Sunday newspapers. Came the student revolution, and with it unwelcome public criticism of the universities, and the dons hastily resubscribed to scholarly values and responsible conduct.

The basic flaw in Kennan's *Democracy and the Student Left* lay in the attempt of a highly political intelligence to argue that the campus was no proper place for politics. As his argument progressed it became clear that nostalgia for dreaming spires and pure scholarship masked a conservative desire for continuing consensus about national institutions and America's role in the world. Student demands that universities should divest themselves of securities in companies operating in South Africa were "absurd"; so, too, were moves to boycott the Olympic Games if South Africa participated; likewise, student protests against Portuguese rule in Africa or Ian Smith's white regime in Rhodesia. Here the professor descended into casuistry. Had not the Left always demanded African independence from Britain? So why did it complain about Smith's Unilateral Declaration of Independence? Why was it that those who "are so suspicious of the will of the majority at home . . . are the ones who show the most uncritical enthusiasm for the immediate establishment of 'majority rule' " in southern Africa? As for Vietnam, Kennan complained that America was given no credit for resisting a brutal Communist dictatorship.

Clearly Kennan felt insulted by attacks on his own generation. Why should "the fathers" be blamed for the Bay of Pigs or the invasion of Santo Domingo? If only the radical students had combined genuine intellectual curiosity with a proper detachment, they would have discovered that "the decisive seat of evil in this world is not in social and political institutions, and not even, as a rule, in the will or iniquities of statesmen, but simply in the weakness and imperfection of the human soul itself. . . ." (However, the same argument did not seem to apply to "brutal Communist dictatorships" in Russia or Vietnam.) Edward Shils's lament for authority ceded and authority abdicated was underpinned by the same paternalistic anger as Kennan's. Himself a student of intellectual history, Shils was now provoked to attack the arrogance of intellectuals who brazenly exploited "the supineness of authority, academic or governmental." Shils's theory of student dementia was a variant of the "menstrual cycle" approach: Look out when examinations loom on the horizon. To the rebels he would concede no higher motive than the nursery tantrum: the aim was to frustrate and bewilder and enrage and degrade authority. The key term in Shils's vocabulary was now "authority," the key failing was abdication. "This is what happened in the Spring of 1968" (everywhere). What Western society was confronting was "the ethos of the expansive ego, free from constraint and from sanctions. . . ."

Hostile professors attributed the student disorders to a variety of noxious influences: Lewis Feuer referred to the intervention of nonstudents suffering from "prolonged adolescence," "lumpen agitators" advocating narcotics, sexual perversion, and collegiate Castroism; Louis Halle blamed the influence of "nihilistic" thought (Sigmund Freud, Konrad Lorenz, and so on); Arthur Schlesinger, Jr., looked back more than half a century to the malign message of the French syndicalist Georges Sorel and sideways at the no less malign message of Herbert Marcuse. Schlesinger devoted part of his commencement oration at City College of New York in June 1968 to denouncing the radicals' vulgar existential politics—feel and act before you think—as "fakery and fallacy . . . preposterous and depraved." Irving Howe concluded that 150 years of paternalism had been supplanted by "a psychology of unobstructed need" which now combined unpleasantly with the "authoritarianism" of a Tom Hayden, a Daniel Cohn-Bendit, and a Rudi Dutschke.

Howe was not the only socialist professor of the Old Left who learned to loathe the student revolt. Professor H. Stuart Hughes, president of SANE for many years and a third-party candidate for senator from Massachusetts, warned the American Historical Association in 1969 that, "if you lose the 'ivory tower,' you've lost the university. . . ." Given the military-industrial pressures on the universities, the urgent task was to de-politicize them, otherwise the faculty and campus would become polarized and the intellectual atmosphere would degenerate. Addressing the same gathering, Professor Eugene Genovese was more strident in tone: "The pseudo-revolutionary middle-class totalitarians . . . support demands for student control as an entering . . . wedge for a general political purge of faculties. . . ."

Although Eugene Genovese and Christopher Lasch complained that "higher education has become another form of industrial apprenticeship" dominated by the technological anticulture, they nevertheless urged students to jettison demands for Student Power and relevant courses, which merely reinforced the "vulgar instrumentalism underlying bourgeois ideology and practice." The New Left had simply "inverted the terms" of this vulgar instrumentalism by seeking "to have the universities serve the poor rather than the rich." Genovese and

Lasch had a point; on the other hand, the Old Left intellectual, vociferous in print and proud of the "critical perspectives" he or she offered the pupils, sometimes resembled the academic marzipan on the military-industrial cake.

Professor Noam Chomsky, of MIT, the distinguished linguist and relentless critic of American global policies, also defended "our legacy of classical liberalism . . . the commitment to a free marketplace of ideas. . . ." Speaking at a Columbia panel during the occupation of April 1968, Chomsky assured an increasingly hostile audience that MIT had never interfered with his freedom of speech, despite receiving funds from the Institute for Defense Analysis. "Furthermore, it is quite probable that the choice of research topics, in the sciences at least, is influenced very little by the source of funds, at least in the major universities. . . ."

In Britain, too, many socialist dons were disenchanted. Professor Bernard Crick was adamant that the university cannot function as an agency of political change: "Every time a students' union wracks itself with resolutions and counter-resolutions on world politics, it both diverts its members from their interests as students, and weakens its authority. By all means let students be politically active . . . but active as members of the community in groups catering for all ages and interests—like, for instance, political parties." This sounded like an exhortation to the New Left to be the Old Left. A central proposition of the New Left was that "no" must begin at the place of work or study (just as feminism must begin at home, with personal relationships, if it is to make sense of its demand for equality in the wider world). According to the New Left, the seminal experience of power, bureaucracy, and ideology cannot be gained at a remove; the student discovers the fake tolerance of liberalism, which freely awards As to clever Marxist essays, only by harnessing actions to beliefs.

The "leave-the-university-out-of-it" approach of the Old Left (Hughes, Genovese, Lasch, Crick) also conflicted with another central component of New Left ideology: the university's special function within technological capitalism. As argued by Gareth Stedman Jones, a young Oxford academic of the New Left, contemporary capitalism required not only engineers (technicians of production), but also a new elite of social engineers—market researchers, media specialists—to serve as technicians of consumption. Add to that a third category trained in the universities, the technicians of consensus (journalists, television editors, personnel managers), and Stedman Jones had made his case for launching the struggle in the classrooms and administrative corridors of the university itself. Only collective action demanding democratic control over the curriculum, reading lists, the appointment of teaching staff, and examinations, could challenge the elitist self-serving of hierarchical liberalism.

The question arises: are students qualified to establish their own curricula and appoint their own teachers? How often must the syllabus change if today's students disagree with yesterday's? How can lecturers teach effectively unless able to fashion their own priorities? Is Student Power as relevant to electrical engineering as to sociology? If exams are abolished, does human laziness simultaneously disappear? If universities must establish capability and performance at the point of entry, how can they justify abandoning the same competitive criteria at the point of exit? Such were the invisible graffiti on the walls of senior common rooms.

A good cause does not always make good men. At close range the spectacle of students suddenly and self-righteously engaged in "liberation" reminded many dons of mob rule or worse. The sociologist Peter Berger, who had been active in SANE as well as in various protests against the Vietnam War, recalled his youthful experience of Nazi stormtroopers, the godheads of "the movement" *(die Bewegung)*, hurling themselves at "the system" *(das System)*—the one absolutely noble and embodying the wave of the future, the other absolutely corrupt and representing nothing but decaying stasis. "Anyone who remembers the Nazi use of *Saujuden* (Jewish pigs) should stop to reflect about the human implication of the current usage of the term 'pigs.' "

Irving Louis Horowitz, literary executor of C. Wright Mills, a seminal influence on the New Left, finally concluded that "Fascism returns to the United States not as a right-wing ideology, but almost as a quasi-left ideology. . . ." (Despite the contrast between the confident tone of "fascism returns" and the two qualifying adverbs, "almost" and "quasi.") Like Berger and Horowitz, Robert Nisbet, professor of sociology at the University of California at Riverside, was reminded also of the Hitler Youth: ". . . shouted obscenities, humiliation of teachers and scholars, desecration of buildings, and instigation of various forms of terror." Dr. Marie Jahoda, professor of social psychology at Sussex, told a Commons Select Committee that radical students were employing Nazi techniques, including pornographic caricatures of faculty members. She condemned "misplaced democracy."

Horowitz reissued his study of Georges Sorel in February 1968, explaining how the ghost of the French syndicalist was haunting the campus corridors. Moralism, the unbridled exercise of the will, the cult of violence, exultant irrationality, and abhorrence of politics—the whole package had been passed across six decades to the New Left. But it hadn't. For Sorel the central revolutionary force was the unionized proletariat. He harbored no fear of technology; he was not alienated by totalitarian state machines of the Left (there were none); the bearded Third World guerrilla did not figure in his vision. Groping for glue, Horowitz even stuck "the Sorelian moral vision" on "the so-called 'hippies' or 'street people.' " In those awkward quotation marks resided the arthritis of the academy.

Many professorial voices choked with unfiltered scorn and disgust. John W. Aldridge, professor of English at the University of Michigan (the scene of SDS demonstrations against defense contracts), suffered from a wounded ear: ". . . their speech is a sort of patois of most of the major sounds ever uttered by human lips within their hearing: Mississippi Negro dialect, Appalachia hillbilly, the jargon of technology, the jargon of political science, the jargon of psychiatry, the jargon of the ghetto, the jargon of rock-music culture, the jargon of the dope addict, and the jargon of Madison Avenue."

In June 1968, Max Beloff, Gladstone Professor of Government at Oxford, wrote to the London *Times* explaining that rapid university expansion had produced a minority of teachers and students incapable of self-discipline. Such troublemakers should be removed. A week later G. R. Elton, professor of history at Cambridge, wrote to express his scorn for student protestors who had no time for scholarship or learning yet demanded the appointment of teachers by student-dominated bodies. Hugh Trevor-Roper, Regius professor of history at Oxford, was no more clement in his verdict: "They talk of 'student democracy.' In fact such demands are not only illogical; they are also unattainable. The radicals who exploit them do not believe in them at all. They are generally foreigners . . . and they simply take advantage, as demagogues, of a captive mass of immature persons. . . . Students may—if governors are foolish enough to yield to fashionable parrot cries—push their way on to governing committees, but they will never do more thereby than minister to their own self-importance and waste everyone's time."

Beloff later became vice-chancellor of Britain's first and only private university, the call for which was issued on January 3, 1969, by a formidable phalanx of dons demanding more discipline, "experience of gainful employment," and orientation toward "the changing market for graduates and research." The list of signatories included no less than eleven professors from the riot-torn LSE, including Donald MacRae, M. J. Oakeshott, and Maurice Cranston.

One of the signatories, Professor Donald MacRae, having experienced two years of student occupations and strikes at the LSE, sighed wearily: "I am never told *how* to cope with a revolutionary movement that is determined not to be appeased, has . . . no scruples, and wants to bring the place to a halt." MacRae saw the typical university don as someone who had learned "disillusion and self-control, usually at the cost of emotional enrichment; whereas the quintessence of the New Left is the principled rejection of self-control." This motif also appealed to MacRae's colleague in the LSE sociology department, David Martin: "If the student kicks the policeman it arises from spontaneous revulsion; if the policeman kicks the student it is evidence of systematic brutality." Student anarchism sprawled luxuriantly on a waterbed of indulgent hypocrisy. (And more vivid imagery.) Kenneth Minogue, a political scientist at the LSE, put the New Left away with the reminder that, "The life of the mind is Rodin's motionless thinker and the courteous Socrates, not men on balconies or demonstrators in the streets." (But do we think creatively with elbow on knee, chin in hand? Rodin's statue may belong to the doctor's waiting room rather than the Platonic academy.)

American sociologists emerged from their campus traumas no better disposed toward their tormentors. Robert Nisbet, professor of sociology at the University of California at Riverside and author of *The Sociological Tradition* and *The Degradation of Academic Dogma,* detested the turmoil that had begun at Berkeley in 1964, the era of Mario Savio and the Free Speech Movement: ". . . destructive, vandalistic action proceeding from adolescent boredom . . . simple, stark, grabbing for power by a small minority of cynical, if usually bright, delinquents whose objective was, instead of money or automobiles, rule of the campus . . . a combination of adolescent power-thrust and colossal permissiveness by faculty and administration."

A no less embittered view was expressed by John R. Searle, who had joined the Berkeley philosophy faculty in 1959 and later served as an administrator in charge of student affairs. Initially supportive of the Free Speech Movement, his outlook later plunged into the sardonic antipathy conveyed in his book, *The Campus War.* The soft acquiescence of faculty liberals in radical disorder exasperated him, the smug penitence of voices like this: "While no one can endorse [some recent violent act or occupation] let us remind ourselves that as we stand here people are dying in Vietnam, children are starving in the ghettos." Or a student activist might say: "You object to the violence of the demonstration. What about the violence in Vietnam?" To Searle such disjunctions were the quintessence of a prevailing illogicality, as if two wrongs made a right.

In Searle's opinion participatory democracy was a sham. The Free Speech Movement at Berkeley was so averse to bureaucracy that it elected neither president nor secretary; in consequence it was dominated by a *de facto* elite of dedicated activists who were formally responsible to nobody and who could always get their strategy endorsed at mass meetings.

Searle also blamed the media's saturation coverage of the juvenile carnivals, the television cameras seeking out the most charismatic demagogues, the most exotic hippies in the crowd, the most beautiful women—all played back on the television screens in an orgy of narcissism. Searle had watched the Third World Liberation Front playing war games with the police on Sproul Plaza at Berkeley almost every lunch hour, when the crowds were biggest and there was still time to process the film for the evening news. Bernard Crick complained about the "extravagant exoticism of nearly all the new leaders. . . . The role of fantasy can hardly be exaggerated. Why do people dress like Castro or Guevara . . . ?"

Sir Eric Ashby, author of works on the history of education and vice-chancellor of Cambridge University from 1967 to 1969, offered his fellow administrators the tactical prescription: aggressive tolerance. This meant refusing to respond to provocation with force, while vigorously launching an intellectual counter-offensive through fact sheets, news bulletins, and statements from "young members of staff known to have liberal views." This would ensure that tolerance looked like an act of conviction rather than of weakness. If the students demanded amnesty (as during the University of Chicago sit-in which began on January 30, 1969), the best thing was to get all the chapel deans and chaplains to join forces to quote Martin Luther King, Jr., on accepting the legal consequences of civil disobedience. The whole purpose, wrote Ashby and his co-author Mary Anderson, was "to cut the demonstrators down to size, so they appeared to be adolescents seeking a painless martyrdom. . . ."

And the future? Edward Shils—an advocate of "efficiency, competence, selection on the basis of past and prospective accomplishment, and differential rewards"—was chillingly optimistic: "Widespread enthusiasm has never persisted before in human history. . . . Most students will return to their studies and will reenter the body of moderates. . . . Some student consultation in the government of academic institutions will occur and it will be, as the student radicals fear it will be, 'incorporated' in the governing system of most universities."

The bafflement aroused by the New Left in the antique liberal imagination was expressed with measured charm by Lionel Trilling, the distinguished literary critic. Having tried to make sense of what happened at his own university, Columbia, Trilling came to the conclusion (like Professor Peter Gay) that the rebels were more sympathetic as individuals than in the mass. Trilling recalled his own undergraduate outlook: "Like all my friends at college, I hadn't the slightest interest in the university as an institution. I thought of it, when I thought of it at all, as the inevitable philistine condition of one's being given leisure, a few interesting teachers and a library. I find it hard to believe that this isn't the natural attitude. . . ."

20

A SEASON OF VIOLENCE:
Mexico, Europe, and Japan

"...students engage in bloody clashes with riot police (*granaderos*) only three weeks before the scheduled opening of the Olympic Games in [Mexico City.]"

MEXICO

MEXICO CITY, September 23, 1968—In the Tlatelolco neighborhood students engage in bloody clashes with riot police (*granaderos*) only three weeks before the scheduled opening of the Olympic Games in the same city.

Two months earlier, on July 26, Mexico's students had laid on a vast demonstration in honor of Fidel Castro's July 26 Movement and the Cuban revolution. They were dispersed with at least ten dead. In broad daylight, close to one hundred plainclothes police wearing face masks and driving unmarked cars had machine-gunned the facade of Vocational School No. 5. At night they returned, entered the school, and beat up the students still occupying it. The same evening police broke into the printing office of the Communist Party and destroyed it. The following day a protest strike extended to all universities and high schools. Demands included the implementation of constitutional rights, an end to police repression, and the release of political prisoners.

As with other Third World countries, Mexican students were more concerned about exploitation and repression than about alienation. The 160,000 students crammed into the institutes of higher education in Mexico City demanded genuine national democracy, the enforcement of the constitution, an end to corruption in government and the unions, and a campaign against unemployment and rural misery. The Institutional Revolutionary Party had by 1968 been uninterruptedly in power for thirty years. President Gustavo Díaz Ordaz was deeply distrusted by the students.

On August 27, a demonstration estimated at 300,000 marched from the National Museum of Anthropology to the Zócalo, the plaza which commemorates the revolution. On this occasion students had been joined by parents, workers, and some peasants, their banners celebrating Mexican heroes like Emiliano Zapata. The march was repeated on September 13 in total silence, a tribute to the discipline of those taking part, but the size of the crowd had fallen by two-thirds.

On the night of September 18, troops sealed off the Ciudad Universitaria (University City), invaded the National Autonomous University, and took 3,000 prisoners, including professors, teachers, and parents. The Ministry of Internal Affairs justified the operation as safeguarding the autonomy of the university against outside agitators. The army had already moved into the National Polytechnic Institute. The press now carried pictures showing soldiers gleefully shaving off the hair of student prisoners.

On September 22, students decided to make a last stand in Vocational School No. 7, situated in the Tlatelolco suburb (where the Indians had staged a final, heroic resistance to the conquistadores). Having captured a dozen buses to form a barricade, they sealed off all the approach streets, siphoned gasoline out of cars and buses, and went from house to house collecting bottles and rags. At 6:30 *grenaderos* and troops began closing in with helicopters overhead. For seven hours the night echoed with shouts of "*¡Abajo Asesinos!*" and "*¡Muera Díaz Ordaz, Asesino!*" The students were not alone. As in Spain, poverty and exploitation had forged links between students and working people. The inhabitants of the Tlatelolco apartments reserved for low-income government workers fought the police for two hours, setting the Ministry of Foreign Affairs on fire. At 9 P.M. the forces of law and order decided to withdraw. At dawn the following day thousands streamed into the barrio of Tlatelolco bringing food, gasoline, and expressions of solidarity with the local people and students.

By the last week of September, shortly before the start of the Olympic Games, some 2,000 foreign athletes had arrived to condition themselves to the high altitude. On October 2, another peaceful meeting at Tlatelolco was attacked by tanks and shock troops, but fighting continued during the first few days of the month, leaving twenty dead and seventy-five wounded. This—and thousands of arrests—prompted Sartre and Russell to call for an Olympic boycott. Students in Paris and Berlin held rallies to demonstrate support, but the Olympic Games began punctually on October 12—to the relief of millions of television viewers around the world. One voice conspicuously silent throughout the Mexican students' ten-week struggle was that of Fidel Castro. Not a whisper of support came from Havana; Mexico City provided Cuba's only air link with Latin America.

GERMANY AGAIN

FRANKFURT, September 22, 1968—Daniel Cohn-Bendit is arrested as he attempts to pass a police barrier and enter St. Paul's Church, where a special peace prize is to be presented to Léopold Senghor by the organizers of the annual Frankfurt Book Fair. Senghor, president of Senegal and famous as a poet of "negritude," is regarded as a neo-colonialist by the SDS—having called in French troops to quell his own students.

Where had Dany been since setting Paris on fire? Arriving in London at the invitation of the BBC (boldly determined to put all the most dangerous young radicals in the world in a single studio), but granted only a twenty-four-hour pass by a suspicious Home Office, Cohn-Bendit had staged a caper with the comrades at the BBC's television studios, got his permit extended, attended a conference of revolutionary students at the LSE, then departed. The English smiled; it was Ascot week and the ladies were wearing miniskirts with the traditional, broad-brimmed hats. After a two-week holiday with an actress in Sardinia, Cohn-Bendit turned up at an anarchist conference at Carrara. Here, in a run-down theatre, bearded figures in black berets and bow ties protested that Cohn-Bendit was not a true believer (having treacherously collaborated with Marxists in Paris) and should not be allowed to address the congress. After some pushing and shoving, Dany got the floor, defended a broad libertarian church, and ridiculed purists who despised the compromises required by mass action.

And so to Frankfurt during Book Fair week. A violent street clash ensued when police turned tear gas and water cannon on students protesting Senghor's prize. Cohn-Bendit was bundled into Butznach Prison, brought into court handcuffed, and given a suspended sentence for breach of the peace. But it was not suspended for long: five weeks later he interrupted the trial of four radicals accused of arson. Fighting broke out in court and Dany went to jail. Three of the four arsonists later became famous as members of the Baader-Meinhof terrorist gang: Andreas Baader, Gudrun Ensslin, and Thorwold Proll. Their elitist "Red Army Faction" tactics in the 1970s might have alienated Cohn-Bendit (he was an agitator, not a bomber), but hostility to state repression led him to act as interpreter and intermediary in 1975 when Sartre gave a press conference after visiting Baader in prison.

The German SDS had arrived at an impasse, torn by a quarrel between the libertarians and the organization men. The congress held in Frankfurt in September was unable to produce an agreed text, no executive bureau was elected, and a hyperfeminist accused men of tyrannizing women "in the movement as well as in bed." The conservative press rejoiced. "How the devil did the Bundestag seriously fear that a revolution could be born from this?" asked the *Frankfurter Allgemeine Zeitung*.

The temperature began to pick up in October when the trials began in West Berlin of some four hundred demonstrators arrested during the year. Fifty protestors gathered in the cold, a police photographer snapped them, a scuffle broke out within the court building. "This is freedom," cried a young Berliner with a new beard. "The Shah is free, Johnson is free, the Berlin police are free. They are all free to kill and bully anyone they want." Another shouted, "What is civilization? Is it a Mercedes? A nice house? Is it an easy conscience? I ask you again, comrades, what is civilization?" Gastau Salvatore, a Chilean friend of Rudi Dutschke, and recently expelled from the Free University, expressed himself in terms destined to become familiar in the 1970s: "Bombs are the only language people with power understand. Bourgeois humanists only deplore the system and do nothing about it."

Fritz Teufel, the stuntman of Kommune I, was sentenced in October to seven months in prison for a string of offenses. Squinting through thick, round glasses, he told the court, "I request you to give me a hard and unjust sentence."

Horst Mahler was a radical lawyer who had taken part in the anti-Springer demonstrations in April, been given a suspended two-year sentence, and now, in November, was summoned before a "court of honor" of the Bar Association convened to consider the prosecutor-general's request that Mahler's license to practice be revoked. A thousand students attempted to storm the court, and 120 people were injured in heavy fighting involving a hail of stones, bottles, truncheons, tear gas, and water cannon. Mahler was not disbarred. During the 1970s he was to become involved in the terrorism of the Baader-Meinhof gang as both lawyer and practitioner.

The Berlin Kommunes were by the end of the year somewhat depleted. Penetrating the working-class and Bohemian area of Moabit, where the notorious Kommune I occupied a three-story, brown-brick building, Ralph Blumenthal of the *New York Times* found only one female Kommunard still in residence in December. Teufel had departed, but Rainer Langhans, cofounder of the Kommune, was still there with Dieter Kunzelmann and Ulrich Enzensberger, brother of the distinguished writer, "stonily examining his red-painted fingernails."

Interview fees had become a primary source of income (as for the American Yippie media stars). A five-minute filmed sequence was said to have cost CBS $750. Volker Gebbert, another cofounder and now the backbone of the Linkeck (Left Corner), insisted that Kommunards were not hippies. But it was hard to be sure. The hard core, some seventy-five scattered through ten Kommunes, had become little more than freaks of the media.

During the winter of 1968–69 university violence in Germany, especially Frankfurt, reached its climax. Classes at the Free University were disrupted by the SDS in December, the previous year's scuffles in the Kaiser Wilhelm Memorial Church were repeated, Rudi Dutschke stayed abroad to avoid trial for his part in them, and twenty police wearing white riot helmets were now posted in front of the altar. In January 1969, 150 students at the Free University caused havoc by smashing doors, emptying filing cabinets, and manning fire hoses, after the dean threatened to close the Drama Institute which they were threatening to occupy. When Nixon visited West Berlin in February, students burned flags, chanted *"Sieg heil,"* and bombarded the presidential procession. Sixty thousand respectable West Berliners, meanwhile, gave him the tumultuous welcome they accorded all American presidents.

FRANCE AGAIN

FRANCE, October 1968—Militant students are back on the streets.

Under the huge crystal chandeliers of the Salle des Fêtes in the Elysée, de Gaulle had held a press conference early in September. Contemptuously ignoring the reporters' questions, the president denounced the media for promoting whatever was "scandalous, painful, violent, destructive" at the expense of whatever was "normal, national and regular." The detritus of May thus swept into the gutter, the imperial avenue was cleared for the new minister of education, Edgar Faure, to introduce his University Orientation Bill, which guaranteed freedom of political debate and association in universities, accepted the principle of student participation in university government, and proposed a degree of autonomy for universities which would have been regarded as derisory in Britain. For example, the exact number of teaching staff in every department would still be decided by the ministry in Paris.

Militant students came back on the streets, the Ecole des Beaux Arts was once again occupied, art students invaded an examination hall at the Faculty of Medicine, and the *lycée* action committees (CAL) grew bolder, unappeased by the government's instruction to head teachers to set aside a room for political debates. (The head, however, retained the right to veto speakers and subjects, with a duty to provide political "balance.") The militant CAL were having none of it: "We will take what political rights we please. . . . The events of May demonstrated the uselessness of Parliament—why then introduce a parliamentary system into schools?"

In mid-December there were new attempts to halt classes at Nanterre. At Nantes, the Faculty of Letters was reoccupied. On the 15th, the minister of education issued a decree endowing rectors with emergency powers. At Toulouse police expelled two hundred students from an administrative building. On January 23, 1969, the office of Rector Paul Roche at the Sorbonne was occupied and vandalized. In February, after thirty-four students had been expelled from the University of Paris, Jean-Paul Sartre and Michel Foucault spoke at a protest meeting at the Mutualité. Sartre, who had attacked the *Loi d'orientation,* of October 1968, was given a huge ovation by the students. Interviewed by *Nouvel observateur,* he described them as "simply youngsters caught in a trap, refusing an education designed to make them servile." For the few years of active life remaining to him Sartre maintained his commitment to the extraparliamentary Left, mainly in its Maoist version. His insistence on selling the banned Maoist paper, *La Cause du peuple,* in the streets brought him close to the open jaws of the law, but de Gaulle and Pompidou believed it was folly to lock up Voltaire; Sartre's appearances in court were mainly on behalf of young militants such as Alain Geismar, one of the guiding spirits of May–June 1968, who was sentenced to eighteen months' imprisonment in 1970 for exercising the eroded right of free speech.

But the students had long since exhausted the patience of the wider population: "Is it never going to end? . . . Some people are never satisfied." As R. W. Johnson observed, "To stroll through Paris in this period was to experience the lingering power of the Events. The new battlegrounds were the *lycées,* where hordes of latter-day Cohn-Bendits flourished briefly in a welter of sit-ins, strikes, protests and, above all, graffiti. One passed street corners where little knots of concierges stood gazing with bleak fear and hatred at the antics of twelve- and thirteen-year-olds as they emerged from their schools through menacing cordons of police. . . . The events had been so sudden and shaking and yet, in a sense, so causeless that it was feared they could return as quickly, rather as the plague had paid recurrent, fearsome visits to medieval cities."

ITALY AGAIN

The political vanguard—and also the intellectual avant-garde—of the Italian student movement was strongest at the Faculty of Architecture at Milan. Partly inspired by events in France, the faculty celebrated 1968 by replacing the traditional examinations with a seminar for political analysis and pedagogic experiment. Outraged, the minister of education, Giovanni Batista Scaglia, took action in August, dismissing the dean of the Faculty of Architecture, Professor Carlo de Carl, for a "series of illegal acts." But illegal acts abounded; on October 10, 150 Florentine radicals barged into a faculty meeting that was on the verge of electing a new rector, then read out a resolution refusing any collaboration in the running of the university. The University Reform Bill, meanwhile, continued not to happen. The bill proposed in September was almost identical to the abortive effort of the defunct Center-Left government (professors would no longer be entitled to serve as parliamentary deputies or to hold public office). But the grim economics of the situation remained unalleviated: one lecturer for every forty of Italy's 530,000 university students. On November 20, the Leone government resigned, and the reform bill returned to cold storage until a new Center-Left government led by Mariano Rumor emerged before Christmas.

During the last quarter of the year a wave of strikes hit Italy, with Catholic, Socialist, and Communist unions working in collaboration. On December 5, a general strike brought Rome to a standstill. In Genoa, Venice, and Milan workers and students now fought together against the police.

The high schools had joined in the turmoil. Schools in Palermo were paralyzed by striking pupils demanding rights of assembly and free debate (the Communist-led Confederation of Labor jumped on the bandwagon). In Bologna, 4,000 high school students staged a march against "authoritarianism" on November 9, followed in turn by pupils in Bari, Ferrara and Florence, Pistoia (Tuscany) and Campobasso (Abruzzi), all demanding rights of assembly. The minister of education decided to postpone national examinations indefinitely. He also informed head teachers that henceforth pupils could hold their own assemblies in school halls.

A perceptive commentary by Chiara Ingrao reminds us that behind the superficial uniformity of demands and slogans joining the youth movements of Europe there lurked specific tensions peculiar to each country. Italian secondary education followed a two-stream system which had its French counterpart but was about to yield to the "comprehensive" school in Britain. The Italian *licei,* or grammar schools, prepared kids for university, while the most talented working-class children generally found themselves in technical schools preparing at best for industrial or clerical diplomas or badly paid teaching careers. (Resentment was heightened by the confinement of higher education to the universities.) It was these working-class children who now displayed the most embittered militancy. "Down with the class school!" was the common slogan. The radicals from the *licei* concentrated on the free-speech issue, but generally failed to carry the majority of their colleagues into demonstrations and strikes.

What Minister of Education Scaglia offered in any case fell short of the full "right of assembly" demands; his proposed assemblies would (1) be confined to one or two delegates from each class, (2) be closed to outsiders, and (3) take place under strict supervision. The radicals wanted general assemblies open to the neighborhood.

Unappeased, 6,000 high school pupils in Rome marched from the Coliseum to the Faculty of Architecture on December 3, having set up strike pickets outside their schools and parading up the Via Nazionale before the horrified gaze of the older generation. The spirit of the thing was jovially reflected in the disruption of a performance of Verdi's *Don Carlos* at La Scala, Milan, and by the distribution of tracts: "Enjoy yourselves, patricians, it's the last time." On December 20, thousands of high-school pupils clashed with police in the Piazza S. Maria Maggiore, Rome. The editor of the socialist paper, *Avanti,* while critical of the police, urged the pupils to discard slogans taken from the sacred texts of "infantile confrontationism."

The year ahead was to be one of mounting violence in Italy, with scenes of destruction in Turin, strike waves in the summer, massive scandals involving corruption, metal workers marching in Rome with red flags and clenched fists, and a bomb planted by unidentified terrorists in a Milanese bakery, which killed fourteen people. Italy was approaching the era of the Red Brigades.

SPAIN AGAIN

In September, Franco's new, "liberal" education minister, Villar Palasi, persuaded the Spanish cabinet to recognize independent student associations. But political parties remained unlawful in Spain, and the student associations legitimized by a decree of September 23 were expressly forbidden from engaging in politics. The government had given too little too late, and the upshot was mounting turmoil.

On the last day of October, 1,800 students went on a rampage in

Madrid, sacking the dean's office in the Law Faculty, burning a portrait of Franco, stoning cars, and going ahead with a banned meeting to ridicule the government's educational reforms. The university was closed for three days, until police stormed the campus, tearing down posters. Unrest continued throughout November; by the end of the month three faculties were closed and the campus witnessed heavy rioting, followed by 150 arrests. At the beginning of December, strikes closed classes in Political and Economic Sciences, in Philosophy and Letters, and in the Faculty of Architecture.

In Bilbao, a student assembly demanded the resignation of the rector and the dismissal of three professors in the Economic Sciences Faculty, all of them members of Opus Dei. Violence returned to Barcelona, where Dr. Juan Maluquer, dean of the Faculty of Philosophy, was burned as he tried to put out a fire started during a riot—and was then inadvertently clubbed by the police. He resigned the following day. On December 6, the government dismissed Barcelona's rector, Francisco Valdecasas, replacing him with a more liberal professor. University education in Spain had almost come to a halt by December. The worsening crisis led the government to declare a state of emergency on January 24, 1969. Eighteen university professors and lecturers from Madrid were banished by decree to remote villages. Professor Gregorio Peces-Barba, who had been involved in drafting a resolution of the Madrid College of Lawyers on behalf of political prisoners, was exiled to a mountain village in Burgos.

POLAND AGAIN

Called off in July with an admission of "excesses," the official anti-Zionist campaign resumed in September; on the 28th, the *New York Times* reported that 2,000 Jews had left since 1967. Ida Kaminska, sixty-eight-year-old director of the Warsaw State Yiddish Theatre, fled with her husband, the director Marian Melman. Madame Kaminska had fled once before—to the Soviet Union to escape the Nazis. According to the Institute of Jewish Affairs in London, 14,000 out of 25,000 Polish Jews had "registered for emigration."

Ninety-nine university teachers had been dismissed since the March revolt for "revisionism" and "non-fulfilment of duties." The trials of the activists arrested during the March demonstrations followed. First into court was Krzysztof Topolski, a Jew and the son of a former government minister. He was sentenced to eighteen months in prison for alleged remarks such as "only Jews are fit to govern

Poland" and "all famous people are of Jewish origin." (One can imagine such phrases on the lips of police interrogators, prefaced by a sneering, "I bet you think that. . . .") Two other student leaders, Jozef Dajczgeward (age twenty-four) and Slawomir Kretkowsku (age twenty-one), were put away for two years and eighteen months, respectively, then four from Lodz were also despatched. Two alleged Warsaw ringleaders, Jan Litynski and Sewereyn Blumszatjn, both twenty-two, were sentenced to thirty months and two years, respectively, under a special section of the penal code, "Offenses especially dangerous in the period of the reconstruction of the state." Foreign reporters were not admitted to the trials.

Perhaps the most distinguished, and certainly the most dangerous, of the March dissidents to go on trial were two former Warsaw University lecturers, Jacek Kuron and Karol Modzelvski, who had only recently been released from prison following their subversive Open Letter (1965) to the Warsaw University branch of the ruling Polish United Workers Party. They argued that the "central political bureaucracy" in Poland constituted an exploiting class that imposed on the population "production for the sake of production." Again imprisoned for their agitational role in March 1968, Kuron and Modzelvski later worked within the Workers' Defense Committee (KOR), a precursor of Solidarity, after the workers' riots of 1970.

The Warsaw branch of the Writers' Union, which on February 29 had incurred the Party's wrath by boldly coming out against the banning of Adam Mickiewicz's play *Dziady,* had by now been brought to heel: when it met in December to elect delegates to the next National Writers Congress, the list presented by the Party was voted through without qualification.

JAPAN AGAIN (AND CHINA)

Unprecedented violence spread across the university campuses of Japan. In July no less than fifty-four universities were locked in disputes of various kinds. The Chinese news agency, Hsinhua (the voice of the Cultural Revolution that had closed down China's universities), hailed the heroic struggle of the Japanese students against "brutal suppression by American-backed Japanese reactionaries." Hsinhua delighted in denouncing the pro-Soviet "Miyamoto revisionist clique" in Zengakuren, the radical student body.

Although the Cultural Revolution in China had as its purpose a leveling of material possessions and social status—whereas Japan was

set for affluence, high technology, and social stratification—the scenarios played out on the campuses of the two countries closely resembled one another. The public degradation of professors by the young
(Red Guards or Sampa Rengo), the enforced self-criticisms, the recurring psychotic violence, were common to both cultures. In China, of
course, the whole process enjoyed the support and promotion of the
chairman of the Party, Mao; in Japan, of the Opposition. Even so,
another common phenomenon emerged: outbreaks of factional fighting
among the left-wing groups.

The Cultural Revolution and the Red Guard phenomenon of
1966–69 do not, however, properly fit into the category of student
revolution. Although students and schoolchildren formed the backbone
of the Red Guards, their purpose was to smash all thought other than
Mao's, to put all professors possessing Western perspectives in "the
cowshed," to eradicate the examination system which penalized workers and peasants, to ban and burn foreign publications. The kids mobil-
ized by Chairman Mao, helmsman and teacher, were instruments of the
state, or of one radical faction competing for domination of the state.

By contrast, the events in Japan made no impact on the deep-
rooted paternalism of the ruling Liberal-Democrats, whose education
research council concluded that students were not fit to participate in
the government of universities; the administration should enjoy absolute authority. Japanese students believed otherwise. On July 5, a meeting of 3,000 students at the Hiyoshi campus of Keio University, Tokyo,
began a boycott of indefinite duration to protest the acceptance of funds
for medical research from the U.S. Army. The university rapidly
acceded, but the students were not satisfied; they wanted mass collective bargaining in public. Nobuo Hara, the president of the Keio student body, justified this by explaining that the process of decision
making was more important than the decision itself. And he added:
"All over the world." In fact the students had acquired a taste for
humiliating their administrators in public. The strike at Keio did not
end for four months, until the beginning of November, when threats of
nonadvancement to the next academic year because of nonattendance
apparently did the trick.

Kyushu University, formerly the Imperial Palace of Learning,
happened to lie directly under the U.S. Air Force approach run to
Itazuke Air Base. On June 2, a warplane crashed into the new computer
center under construction. President Takaaki Mizuno led the protest
and demanded the removal of the base—for twenty years, staff and
students had been maddened by the noise. On July 2, the university
administration decided to clear the wreckage of the jet plane so that
building could proceed, but the militants wanted it to remain as a

reminder and symbol of oppression. The upshot was a bloody fracas on August 27, with a hundred militants swinging staves at their classmates and teachers, injuring twenty-one, including Professor Joji Kajiwara.

Students at the private Nihon University (the largest in Japan, with 80,000 students) imprisoned officials in their offices as part of a protest against a decision to build a new library instead of a student union building. It also emerged that 2,000 million yen ($5.5 million) had been paid from 1963 to 1967 to administrators and professors for unexplained purposes. There were other grievances: huge classes, too many part-time teachers, the censoring of the student press, bans on certain meetings. On May 25, the Student Joint Struggle Committee was created at Nihon.

On June 11, the right-wing athletics club dropped steel desks, chairs, and ashtrays on a dense crowd below, resulting in serious injuries. Massive strikes and a seizure of buildings followed. Early in July seven faculty councils at Nihon joined the students in calling for the resignation of the entire executive board. On August 4, Chancellor Jujiro Furuta and other senior administrators broke a pledge to attend a collective bargaining session, on the ground that it would be a kangaroo court. On September 4, 500 riot police cleared out students who had been occupying Nihon University for three months; 132 were arrested. The Chinese news agency jubilantly hailed the struggle in the economics and law faculties, and also a street demonstration against Chancellor Furuta during which 6,000 students clashed with 1,200 police; a record 154 were arrested. A reporter for Hsinhua claimed to have seen an employee of a bookstore in the street waving a banner, "Long live Mao Tse-tung's Thought." Within eight days of the police action the students had regained possession of the buildings.

Groups of helmeted students could regularly be seen running in phalanx across the campus while their leaders blew whistles. On September 19, the radical students demanded the resignation, en masse, of Nihon's directors; an end to censorship; and an opening of the university's accounts. Four days later, Chancellor Furuta announced a revision of the code of management, promised to resign, and withdrew all threats of punishment. Furuta, a friend of Premier Eisaku Sato, was finally forced to bow deeply in abject contrition and admit negligence before an audience of 10,000. The government of Premier Sato had been observing events with mounting anxiety. At a cabinet meeting on September 3, it was decided not to intervene in disputes affecting fifty-one universities and colleges, but the fate of his friend Furuta prompted Sato to denounce publicly the habit of "mass bargaining," a form of trial and humiliation by people's court, which had led to a collapse of authority not only at Nihon University but elsewhere. This was all the more traumatic in a society schooled in civic discipline, obedience, and deference to elders. But Japan was also the country of the warrior, whose dedication to an idealistic cause could assume hypnotic force, whether defending the emperor's honor or destroying a corrupt oligarchy. The arrival of Marxism was only one motion in Japan's long and destabilizing encounter with the modern. The constant humiliation of authority was widely resented; it generated the fanatical right-wing backlash associated with the private-warrior army of the novelist and filmmaker Yukio Mishima.

The struggle at Tokyo University (17,000 students) also assumed ritualistic shape among the regiments of the Left. It began the previous winter with corporate demands from medical students demanding (1) a closed shop for the Society of Young Physicians, (2) the right to determine their own curriculum, (3) the right of graduate students to practice medicine before receiving their license. Speaking on behalf of the administration, Professor Kunio Oota insisted that medical standards could not be compromised, even though all the other medical schools (Oota said) had surrendered except for the National Dental College. He blamed the influence of the Trotskyist Sampa Rengo. In March 1968, penalties were inflicted on one researcher, four interns, and twelve students after a professor had been taken prisoner and maltreated. The commencement ceremony on March 28 had to be cancelled when the entrances to the Yasuda Auditorium were blockaded.

Tokyo University's "medics" did not arouse much sympathy among other students until President Kazuo Okochi called in the riot police on June 17 to evict those who had occupied the administration building. The response was predictable: on June 25, a full-scale strike spread beyond the medical school, affecting 6,000 students. The strength of student solidarity and the numbers involved put university administrations under intense pressure; on August 10, the university, in another abrupt capitulation, offered the students the "heads" of the dean of the Faculty of Medicine and the director of the University Hospital. This gesture appeased 118 moderate medics, who deserted the strike, but 200 others persisted in demanding the total withdrawal of punishments handed down the previous March. The wider strike in other faculties continued.

By the end of September, Tokyo University faced the worst crisis in its ninety-one-year history. Most classes had been closed since June; half the students faced imminent disqualification from advancing to the next academic year owing to nonattendance. It was a time of mounting violence. During the preplanned riots at Shinjuku Railway Station, Tokyo, on October 8, 150 were arrested and over 800 police and students injured. Six days later a riot at Nihon's Fukushima campus resulted in arson and considerable damage.

By now several university administrations were in disarray and headlong retreat. On November 1, the senate of Tokyo University not only rescinded the punishments decreed in March, but, in a gesture of collective hara-kiri, promised to resign en masse. Nothing to parallel it had occurred in Europe or America. (The Medical School of Osaka University, no doubt impressed by these events, accorded its students the right to veto any future decision—including appointments, facilities, and curriculum. This was the first agreement of its kind, in any country.) Tokyo University's president, Kazuo Okochi, resigned. A week later students released Kentaro Hayashi, a fifty-six-year-old dean, who had been held prisoner in the Faculty of Letters for eight nights and subjected to what the students euphemistically called "collective bargaining," during which he refused to budge on disciplinary action against a student who had assaulted a faculty member. Doctors were eventually called in, and the exhausted Dean Hayashi was taken to hospital on a stretcher.

"Nonsense" was the favorite term of rebuttal among radicals. Amid huge scenes and scenarios negotiations broke down as Tokyo's acting president, Ichiro Kato, and the two professors who bravely flanked him, left a packed auditorium amid cries of "Nonsense!," "Get out!," and "Go!" One problem for the administration was whom to negotiate with; the moderate Communists (JPC) were not on speaking terms with the radicals (some four hundred of whom regularly drilled with staves and steel pipes), and both factions insisted on separate negotiations with the administration. The radicals even demanded that acting President Kato apologize for negotiating with the moderates. An obsessive notion of honor apparently lay behind this obsession with formal apology; the result was vertigo.

On Tuesday, November 19, after the radicals seized the library building, the two groups of left-wing students massed into rival armies, each some 6,000 strong and each reinforced by students from other universities. Professors and assistant professors joined nonaligned students in negotiating a compromise. On November 29, acting President Kato tried to address 10,000 students gathered in front of the library, but was physically harassed by the All-Campus Struggle Committee, who insisted that their seven demands be accepted unconditionally. The Communist faction, meanwhile, used loudspeakers to hurl abuse at the radicals. Kato tried to escape, but was forced to stand on the library steps and suffer interrogation. Whenever he tried to explain his position, the student standing next to him would snatch the microphone and demand that he confine himself to answering the questions.

The spirit of concession having failed, Kato resorted to threats. On December 2, he issued an ultimatum warning that there would be no graduations if the dispute was not resolved by the 10th. It was not resolved, and on December 22 the minister of education suggested that Tokyo University close indefinitely and cancel the following year's entrance examinations. On December 24, fifty were injured as rival groups did battle yet again. Strikes at the Faculties of Law and Economics had ended, but the College of General Education was still out. The climax arrived on January 18, 1969: throughout that day, beginning shortly after dawn and lasting into the next afternoon, thousands of riot police laid siege to buildings that had been occupied for six months. The ensuing battle, involving firebombs, tear gas, and the ritual *geba* style of combat, did not prevent many of the combatants from later accepting disciplined, dedicated employment with the capitalist giants—Sony, Hitachi, Toyota, Datsun, and Sanyo. Others, fewer in number, became the most fanatical exponents of international Red terrorism.

21

THE USA:
Black Students, White Teachers

"The American presidential campaign, alight with idealism, dramatic conflict, and tragedy during the Democratic primaries, had degenerated into a dull, routine contest between two gray men..."

"Receiving their medals... [Tommie Smith and John Carlos] defiantly raised clenched fists clad in black leather gloves while the U.S. national anthem was played."

THE OLYMPICS: BLACK POWER

The issue of racism in sport had been simmering throughout the year. In February, British students had three times invaded Gosforth rugby pitch, covered in snow, to disrupt a match against the Orange Free State university team. A few days later, Kenya joined thirteen other African and Arab nations promising to boycott the 1968 Olympics if South Africa took part. On April 21, the Executive Board of the International Olympic Committee (IOC) recommended that the invitation to South Africa be withdrawn. President Avery Brundage invited the seventy-one member-nations of the IOC to endorse this decision by postal vote. South Africa was expelled.

Meanwhile, in the United States, racial tension in athletics had become acute. A key figure of the anti-Establishment was Harry Edwards, a young professor of sociology at San Jose State College, who had made it out of the ghetto through a sports school and was now campaigning against colleges' exploitative recruitment of black sportsmen who, in many cases, never graduated. "Blacks are brought in to perform. In most cases their college lives are educational blanks."

Edwards's star pupils included the black sprinters Tommie Smith and Lee Evans. On Wednesday, October 16, Smith and John Carlos won gold and bronze medals, respectively, in the 200-meter run (Smith's time of 19.83 seconds was a world record). Receiving their medals, they stood on the podium wearing black scarves and socks, then defiantly raised clenched fists clad in black leather gloves while the U.S. national anthem was played. The IOC protested and the U.S. Olympic Committee apologized, indignantly suspending the offending athletes and expelling them from the Olympic Village. Lee Evans had announced that he would repeat the gesture if he won a medal in the 400 meter—and win he did, with another world record time, 43.80 seconds (still standing). Silver and bronze also went to black Americans, Larry James and Ron Freeman. The three filed onto the victory podium wearing black berets and civil rights badges on their chests; as each athlete's name was read out he raised a clenched right fist.

WALLACE

In the United States, race was the raw, wide-awake issue during the fall. September and October belonged to the apostle of the backlash, the former governor of Alabama, George Wallace, who was on the ballot of every state. John Leonard reported: "There isn't a white taxi-cab driver, bartender or newspaper composing room worker I have talked to who doesn't intend to vote for him." The polls showed Wallace's popularity rising from 9 to 20 percent. On September 30, wearing his customary black silk suit, Wallace was confronted by a sea of banners and placards at a big rally in Chicago: "America—Love it or Leave it"; "For Wallace, Daley and the Chicago Police"; "Save our Schools"; "Poles for Wallace," "Lithuanians for Wallace," "Italians for Wallace."

Precisely how Wallace would win the war in Vietnam became revealed when, early in October, he presented as his running mate General Curtis Le May, a former chief of the Air Force, who now told a press conference that he saw no difference between being killed by a rusty knife and a nuclear weapon. Given the choice, he would lean toward the latter; a nuclear war would not mean the end of the world. Twenty years after Bikini, the fish were back in the lagoons and the rats were bigger than ever. "We must be willing to continue our bombing until we have destroyed every work of man in North Vietnam, if that is what it takes to win this war." Wallace nodded in agreement.

The backlash against militant blacks and revolting students was in full swing. The annual riot season had been up to standard and suited Wallace nicely. Police patrolling the black areas of Seattle, Gary, Cleveland, and Peoria were subjected to sniper fire and incendiary bombs. John Harrington, president of the Fraternal Order of Police, complained that the public was not concerned about dead or injured policemen, only about the civil rights of the accused. In October the FBI's annual report warned that the New Left had "mushroomed into a major security problem, with some of its adherents talking about sabotage. . . ." The FBI also detected "growing foreign involvement" in black militancy. Wallace was now advocating "fear of the constabulary" as the only way to curb anarchy; he would "let the police stop it like they know how to stop it."

On October 25, George Wallace came to Madison Square Garden

in New York City to greet 17,000 of his fans. Protected by a bulletproof lectern, he assured them, "Ah's not spending your tax money to educate students to raise money for the Communists." Their faces contorted with rage and ecstasy, and waving Confederate flags and singing "Dixie," his supporters leapt up and down screaming, "White Power!" and "Down with niggers!" Wallace always liked to have a few students and blacks heckling him to rouse the blood lust of his followers before having them thrown out with maximum brutality. His quips to hecklers were part of the routine: "Come on down. I'll autograph your sandals," and "Hey sweetie pie, oh sorry, ah thought it was a she but it's a he."

NEW YORK SCHOOLS ON STRIKE

As Wallace arrived in New York, the city was in the grip of a long, bitter, racially charged dispute. The clenched fist of Black Power, seen by millions watching the Olympic ceremonies, had also been raised within the New York City school system. The crippling teachers' strike in the fall of 1968 was about several issues, not least the rapidly deteriorating relationship between American blacks and Jews.

The Six-Day War of June 1967 had raised the temperature of racial animosity. That month's issue of *Black Power* (published by the Panthers of northern California) carried a poem, "Jew-Land": "The Jews have stolen our bread/Their filthy women tricked our men into bed/So I won't rest until the Jews are dead. . . ." The poem also promised to "burn their towns and that ain't all/We're gonna piss upon the Wailing Wall. . . ." It would be "ecstasy, killing every Jew we see in Jewland." In 1968, Stokely Carmichael promised a fight to wipe out Zionism "wherever it exists, be it in the ghetto of the United States, or in the Middle East." LeRoi Jones came out with a poem vilifying the "dangerous germ culture" of the Jews; the Panthers settled for the formula "Zionism (Kosher Nationalism) + Imperialism = Fascism." "Fascist Zionist pigs" headed the sty.

Such sentiments shock decent opinion, and rightly, but decent opinion is not always aware of the persistent bias of its own culture—for example, the tone of American news reports during the Six-Day War, when objective reporting of Israeli military victories was underpinned by a blatant jubilation reaching beyond understandable relief at Israel's survival to a deeper celebration of White-Western supremacy when it counted. But the root of the antagonism between blacks and Jews lay within the American ghettos themselves. Malcolm X had complained that, "in every major ghetto, Jews own the major businesses. Every night, the owners of those businesses go home with that black community's money, which helps the ghetto to stay poor." This theme was to figure prominently in the socialist rhetoric of the Black Panthers. The hostility was mutual; in 1968, Rabbi Meir Kahane formed the Jewish Defense League, ostensibly to defend Jews in low-rent neighborhoods, usually black ones (Kahane later became a fundamentalist zealot of Israeli settlement on the occupied West Bank). After Leonard Bernstein and his wife gave a party to raise money for Black Panthers facing trial, he received an avalanche of threatening mail; in Miami, Jewish pickets forced the withdrawal of a film of Bernstein conducting the Israel Philharmonic on Mount Scopus in celebration of Israel's victory in the Six-Day War. Finally the conductor released a statement condemning the Panthers' violence, their support of Al Fatah, "and other similarly dangerous and ill-conceived pursuits."

The manifest issue which precipitated the teachers' strike was local community control (or not) of education. The latent issue was racial tension. The scene of the confrontation was the predominantly black Ocean Hill–Brownsville (henceforward OH-B) district of Brooklyn. In the fall of 1967, the United Federation of Teachers (UFT) had joined with its traditional antagonist, the Council of Supervisory Associations, in a suit to declare illegal the appointment of four school principals by the board of OH-B. One of the new appointees, Herman Ferguson, had been indicted for conspiracy to murder two prominent moderate black leaders, Roy Wilkins of the NAACP, and Whitney Young of the Urban League. Ferguson was subsequently convicted and sentenced. Dwight Macdonald, a prominent *New Yorker* writer and a partisan of the OH-B school board during the subsequent dispute, admitted that Ferguson's appointment was "disgraceful, irresponsible, inexcusable."

Boss of the OH-B board was its burly and sometimes flamboyant black unit administrator, Rhody McCoy, often seen with a pipe jammed between his teeth. McCoy hit back by firing nineteen teachers and supervisors most closely involved in the UFT's suit. On May 8, 1968, the teachers received a letter summarily dismissing them from their posts and advising them to report to 110 Livingston Street for reassignment by the New York City Board of Education. The teachers were denied any form of due process.

When 350 of the dismissed teachers' colleagues went on strike in protest, they were fired by the OH-B board. The city's Board of Education subsequently held hearings on charges brought by the OH-B board; Judge Rivers, the appointed arbitrator, exonerated the teachers. The city's Central Labor Council, AFL–CIO, came out in support of the UFT, largely to protect the jobs of plumbers and technicians working for the school board.

The majority of New York's teachers were both white (90 percent) and Jewish (60 percent). The teachers argued that the quality of education in the city would be compromised if local communities acquired the power to hire and fire. The UFT insisted that it favored the right kind of decentralization—but not "a cheap sop to ethnic minorities," as the UFT's spokesman, Reuben W. Mitchell, put it. The UFT's president, Albert Shanker, had advocated independent funding for local boards, and the union supported the Marchi bill, which was passed by the state legislature in the spring of 1968, giving increased powers to New York City's thirty-three school districts. But the UFT did not agree that local boards like OH-B should be empowered to appoint school principals and assistant principals.

The teachers were defining the "quality" of education in white, middle-class terms; indeed the Jews of New York were fighting school busing no less fiercely than the Irish, the Italians, and the Protestants. Each side in the school dispute charged the other with racism. There was plenty to go around in New York and elsewhere. During the last week of September, black teenagers in Boston roamed the streets after a Black Power rally, while white pupils were demanding segregation of East Boston High School (where only twenty-three black pupils were enrolled out of 1,300). In Chicago, black kids demanding more black teachers had been staging walk-outs and sit-ins. Trenton High School in New Jersey—where more than half of the 3,500 pupils were black—was closed for the fourth time in nine months on account of racial violence. Four hundred white pupils demonstrated in a park, many of them wearing "Wallace for President" buttons and carrying White Power placards.

Back in New York, a small radio station that appealed to the hip-radical underground invited a black schoolteacher from High School 271 to read an anti-Semitic poem written by a fifteen-year-old black pupil and "dedicated" to Albert Shanker, the outspoken president of the UFT.

> Hey, Jew boy, with that yarmulka on your head,
> You pale faced Jew boy. . . . I wish you were dead.

The "poem" also commented on Israel:

> They hated the black Arabs with all their might and you, Jew
>   boy, said it was all right.
> Then you came to America, land of the free,
> And took over the school system to perpetrate white supremacy.

According to I. F. Stone, himself a Jew, the teachers' union was deliberately exploiting any bit of anti-Semitic drivel it could lay hands on. By sticking together passages taken from different sources, said Stone, the union made the school board of OH-B responsible for statements it had never made.

With the Ocean Hill–Brownsville dispute unresolved and an Ad Hoc Committee to Defend the Right to Teach established, the UFT staged three successive strikes from September to November, affecting the whole city. Nine hundred schools closed down and 1.1 million kids went without schooling. The chief aim was to remove Rhody McCoy, his OH-B school board, and the principals he had appointed.

The strikes were accompanied by intense bitterness and some violence; there were fights with police outside schools. Many parents were panicked into a rush on private schools; house prices in the suburbs leapt by 10 to 15 percent. Condemning racism of any stripe, Mayor John Lindsay gained the enmity of all parties. In mid-October, Lindsay was booed and cursed by 1,500 whites in a Brooklyn synagogue. Claiming that the city had raised teachers' salaries by over 50 percent in five years, the mayor accused both sides of illegal action. The United Federation of Teachers inserted a full-page advertisement in the press, blaming Lindsay for "vacillation, indecision, permissiveness and backtracking."

The dispute sharply divided the city's intellectuals; radicals who had broadly supported the New Left, like Dwight Macdonald, tended to rally to the black cause, while liberals and socialists of the Old Left remained hostile. In a classic statement of the liberal position, the Socialist Party chairman, Michael Harrington, supported the teachers because they had been denied due process, because the OH-B board's actions lent unwitting support to the conservatives, and because autonomous neighborhood school boards might embark on witch-hunts. Harrington argued that autonomy would merely institutionalize segregation.

Rhody McCoy, the peppery administrator of OH-B, continued to defy the school board by refusing to accept eighty teachers who were union members. Early in October, the superintendent of New York City schools, Bernard Donovan, not only dismissed McCoy but also fired seven of the eight school principals he had appointed. McCoy marched into his office before 7 A.M. to announce to reporters that he would stay at his post. It took armed police to keep the dismissed principals out of their schools. On November 15, the appellate court ruled that the Board of Education had acted illegally in appointing four school principals in OH-B. The proposed compromise involved the appointment of a trustee named by the state education commissioner to supervise OH-B. On November 18, New York's teachers voted to end their third successive strike. Most of the city's children had received only eleven days' schooling since the beginning of September.

A report by a faculty research group at Columbia University estimated conservatively that 2,000 high school rebellions took place in the United States between November 1968 and April 1969. The flash-point in New York City schools was ethnic, but Vietnam also figured, as did disputes over censorship, discipline, educational reform, and stuffy codes of dress.

The High School Student Union (HSSU) produced the anticapitalist *New York High School Free Press,* which opposed the teachers' strike "because it was racist," yet welcomed it because it "rescued us from Mickey Mouse." Supported by the college-level black bodies, the Afro-American Student Association (A-ASA), and the Black Students Union (BSU), the HSSU tried to open up strike-bound schools and establish "community control"—though easier said than done.

Out of the New York City strike flowed occasional alliances of radical teachers and pupils. James Horelick, an untenured teacher of English at Washington Irving High School, was not retained by the superintendent of schools after refusing to join the teachers' strike and also lending help to the kids' underground paper, *Weakly Reader* (so spelled). Horelick was said to have sold it in school, made his apartment available as an editorial office, and given financial support. In August 1969, the Board of Education rejected the findings of Superintendent Donovan and transferred Horelick (with tenure) to another school.

A spectacular campaign of violence was unleashed in the schools on April 21, 1969, continuing until May 19 and involving arson and clashes with the police. The demonstrations were coordinated by the BSU, A-ASA, and the HSSU. Police roamed the corridors. According to the *New York High School Free Press,* by June at least 40,000 students were suspended in the city's schools—a 300 percent increase over 1968. The *Press* complained that school principals often broke the rules by handing down oral suspensions without reporting them in writing, thus sidestepping the required hearings. But even the kids' underground press began to gag on the interminable violence. *Smuff,* a radical sheet from Hackensack High School, New Jersey, which advocated antiwar demonstrations and draft-dodging, was upset when two members of SDS beat up a Columbia professor with a club, calling him "pig." By now SDS was into Weatherman territory, and *Smuff* had no appetite to follow.

Free speech was the cry of *Freethinker* of La Puente, California—but does the First Amendment apply to minors? As for the Fourth Amendment, these young legal stars were on to it in a flash whenever school administrators penetrated unlocked PE lockers in search of cigarettes or pot, then handed out the lesson, "Lock your locker!" Often written to a high standard, the school underground papers reported fascinating clashes with authority involving long hair, clothes, refusal to pay fines, use of obscene language, and censorship. Out of Southampton, New York, came *Up Against the Wall,* complaining you couldn't even go to the lavatory without begging for permission and telling the teacher it really was "necessary." "In short," sighed the editorialist, "the school allows you all the personal freedoms that any well-run prison would." Pupil Power was needed, but that wouldn't happen (he explained) until kids arrived at school—literally in the hundreds—wearing the forbidden species of slacks and blue jeans.

Then there was the cultural revolt against Middle America. *T.R.I.P.,* of Long Beach, California, was aghast at the sophomore assembly of Millikan High School chanting, "We're number one! We're number one!" punctuated—can you believe it?—by the boom of a bass drum. "For a moment I could have sworn it was 1984, and the middle of the Two Minutes Hate." As for orthodox student government—what a pain! All that careerism and conformity! *Minstrel,* of Waukegan, Illinois, uncovered the fact that less than 20 percent had voted in the student council election.

The radicals were children of the counterculture and mostly self-consciously hip: recover the music of the youth culture from Columbia Records, know about Paris '68, stage free rock shows in Central Park's Sheep Meadow, scatter four-letter words like confetti.

The feminist dimension was there (as was every dimension). With the support of the Emergency Civil Liberties Committee, fourteen-year-old Alice de Rivera broke all barriers by demanding a transfer to New York City's boys-only Stuyvesant High School. The local patriarchy lived up to expectations by vetoing the project. The court ruled she could take the exam, which she duly passed, a victory (as she put it) for women's liberation. Alice was clearly something: editor of *The Streetfighter* at John Jay High School, she recommended Dick Gregory for president and his autobiography, *Nigger,* for reading. She also liked the Doors, Jimi Hendrix, the Rolling Stones—and graffiti generally. Interviewing Alice, the *Weakly Reader* could not resist mentioning her good looks and clearly had to struggle to suppress the chauvinist caption, "Lucky Boys at Stuyvesant!"

AMERICA: THE PRESIDENTIAL CAMPAIGN

The American presidential campaign, alight with idealism, dramatic conflict, and tragedy during the Democratic primaries, had degenerated into a dull, routine contest between two gray men, Hubert Humphrey and Richard Nixon; the excitement of the spring had given way to machine-consensus politics, with Humphrey generally trailing in the polls.

Eugene McCarthy, recently the idol of so many "sweetie pies," as George Wallace called them, had relapsed into what looked like a sulk. Although only fifty-two years old, he now announced he would not seek re-election to the Senate in 1970—as if, like de Gaulle, his country could either have him on his own terms or none. Irving Howe wrote: "Some disastrous streak of cultural snobbism or intellectual perversity overtook this very intelligent man." At the end of October, McCarthy endorsed Humphrey belatedly and with reservations. The depression among liberals was universal.

The Kennedys came back on stage on October 20, when Jacqueline Kennedy and the Greek millionaire Aristotle Onassis were married according to the rites of the Orthodox Church at Skorpios, his island retreat. The Vatican condemned the marriage on account of Mr. Onassis's divorces; others worried about the imprisonment and torture of Greek democrats by the military dictatorship (recognized by the United States since January) ruling Mrs. Onassis's new homeland.

By way of a final election gambit, President Johnson ordered a halt to the bombing of North Vietnam on October 31, announcing that delegates of the NLF and the Saigon government would join the peace talks, though neither would be formally recognized by the other side. To balance the political ledger, Johnson ordered an intensification of the bombing along the Ho Chi Minh Trail in Laos.

Humphrey conceded defeat at noon on Wednesday, November 6. Both candidates had won 43 percent of the popular vote, with Wallace taking 14 percent. Wallace had faded at the tape (as third-party candidates do), taking only five Southern states. Nixon won thirty-two states, including California. Humphrey gained thirteen, plus the District of Columbia. Republican control of the Senate (58 seats) was assured by a net gain of five seats. The Democrats remained in the majority in the House, with 244 seats to 191. The 91st Congress would almost exactly resemble the 90th. *Plus ça change. . . .*

SAN FRANCISCO STATE COLLEGE

SAN FRANCISCO, November 6, 1968—Humphrey concedes and the Black Students Union at San Francisco State College, supported by the Third World Liberation Front and white radicals, calls a strike. Humphrey's defeat is of no relevance, but Nixon's victory may be.

A vicious circle of black student violence and police violence had taken hold since two were killed and forty were wounded in February 1968, when police opened fire on South Carolina State College students protesting segregated facilities in the town of Orangeburg. Also in February, police and National Guard used tear gas to break up a demonstration by both black and white students demanding a black studies program at the University of Wisconsin. Early in May, sixty black students at Northwestern University seized the finance building and locked out the staff. At Duke University in North Carolina, black students occupied the administration building and threatened to burn the records unless they were granted black studies, a black dormitory, and other demands.

Martin Kilson, a black professor of government at Harvard, contrasted the behavior of blacks studying in predominantly white colleges (70 percent of black students) with those attending the more conservative, all-black institutions of the South. It was the former who insisted on the new Afro-American identity—dress, names, hairstyles, black studies, violent rhetoric, and "not infrequently" guns. According to Kilson the new style was deeply affected by an influx of black students from the ghetto who were adept at "the quick and facile manipulation of others for short-run benefits . . . 'rapping,' 'conning,' 'put-on,' etc." Virtually every aspect of life at white colleges was interpreted in racial-political terms and was frequently resolved by resort to "violence bordering on the pathological." Clearly, black students were also affected by Black Panther ideology. The demand for separate, autonomous black institutions, funded but not governed by the white parent body, echoed the Panthers' call for a separate black American Republic. Unless separate, never equal.

By 1968, San Francisco State College had 20,000 students. Throughout 1967 the white student activists of SDS and the Marxist Progressive Labor Party had sustained agitation about Vietnam, ROTC, and the college's collaboration with the Selective Service system. The new president of San Francisco State, John Summerskill, a laid-back liberal of some charm recently recruited from Cornell, played it cool. Although the Academic Senate twice advised the president not to provide the Selective Service with students' rank in class (which determined eligibility for draft deferment), Summerskill was directed by his superior in the state college system, Chancellor Glenn S. Dumke, that he was obliged by law to do so. Largely on this issue the radicals effectively disrupted Summerskill's formal inauguration as president in May 1967.

The San Francisco–Oakland area was home territory for the Black Panthers and other militant black groups. Racial tension was reflected in the student elections of 1967. The new officers of San Francisco State's student union and the student newspaper, *Gater,* accused the Black Students Union (BSU) of planning to import Black Power to the campus. On November 6, 1967, the San Francisco State blacks showed their hand at violence when the editor of *Gater,* his editorial staff, and a faculty adviser were badly beaten in the paper's office. "Provocation" was one motive for the attack, but the ultras in the BSU also aimed to radicalize their own ranks by provoking a white backlash. The assault party included George Murray, a part-time English instructor and minister of education in the Black Panther Party. Of him, more later. Those responsible were arrested; Summerskill suspended them. The BSU leader, Jimmy Garrett, accused the president of liberal rhetoric, smiles, and stabs in the back.

The counterculture now intervened to sharpen Summerskill's misery. After an obscene poem about a cat appeared in the semiunderground student paper, *Open Process,* Summerskill suspended the paper, its editor, and the author of the poem. The San Francisco *Examiner* congratulated the president on finally taking a firm stand on something. But, faced with an outcry from liberal faculty and students, Summerskill climbed down in front of a heckling crowd and television cameras: "I was mad and impatient and I acted improperly," he admitted. The San Francisco *Examiner* apologized to its readers for having praised Summerskill: "He is a high priest of the cult of permissiveness."

Among those heckling the president was John Gerassi, a temporary member of the faculty, an expert in Latin American affairs, and a principal speaker at the Dialectics of Liberation conference held in London in July. Gerassi, who had toured North Vietnam on behalf of the Russell War Crimes Tribunal, wanted to know why Summerskill did not have the courage of his professed convictions on Vietnam and Selective Service. War tension had risen during October 1967 with violent demonstrations at the Oakland Induction Center during Stop the Draft Week. As in 1965, Berkeley's radicals were in the van; when Chancellor Roger W. Heyns first gave his consent to a teach-in but was later forced to cancel it by a county court injunction, Berkeley students responded with a series of rallies. Two were suspended. To protest, 1,000 took part in a "mill-in" for three days from November 29, choking Sproul Hall and Sproul Plaza, the bottleneck where administration, student union, campus police, speakers, and pamphleteers converged. Heyns suspended four more students and confiscated $42.5 million in assets from the student government. The unrest spilled over to San Francisco State, where Marshall Windmiller, of the International Relations Department, persuaded the college to put its facilities at the disposal of a War Crisis Convention held during normal class time.

The liberal Summerskill had backed the nation's first black studies program, appointing as its director Dr. Nathan Hare, a sociologist and ex-boxer, who had been dismissed by Howard University. But liberal gestures merely fed the panther. Supported by the BSU, Dr. Hare demanded an autonomous Black Studies Institute, whose faculty and students would be exclusively black. Summerskill and a majority of the faculty balked at so alien a proposal; among its most energetic opponents was the chairman of the Political Science Department, John Bunzel, who was later to suffer slashed tires, an unexploded homemade bomb, and an attack on his office by men in stocking masks (after security guards had warned him to leave the building).

On December 6, 1967, San Francisco State was hit by a violent demonstration. Again Gerassi was in the vanguard; the two issues of race and the war were coalescing. The BSU sent raiding parties to close down classes and promised a "community" demonstration, which it duly delivered in the form of high school students rampaging around the campus, ransacking the cafeteria, starting a fire in the bookstore, and destroying photographers' cameras. (Like almost every other happening at the college, this one was played out before television cameras and was relayed to an increasingly appalled public on the six o'clock news.) Summerskill decided not to call in the police. Eight hundred members of the faculty praised his restraint and endorsed his leadership.

The nine blacks who had assaulted the editor of *Gater* the previous month were found guilty in court, fined, and put on probation. The college re-suspended four of them.

At this stage the radical specter at San Francisco State was expanded by a new force, the Third World Liberation Front (TWLF), composed of Orientals and Latinos, and led by a temporary instructor, Juan Martínez, whose contract had not been renewed. Demanding their own counterpart to the black studies program, the TWLF occupied the YMCA's office space on campus and imported their own "community" demonstration—more high school students roaming around the administration building.

On May 21, 1968, the faculty voted 282 to 250 to retain the ROTC program on campus; many liberals who deplored the Vietnam War nevertheless regarded the issue as freedom of choice. As they deliberated, SDS and the TWLF were already occupying the administration building. Summerskill wandered in and out of offices, up and down halls, available to anyone with any idea for resolving any conflict. The president and the police tac squad finally worked out a plan to accept a token twenty-nine volunteers for arrest, but an ugly confrontation developed outside the gates, resulting in a new occupation during which Summerskill agreed to all sorts of SDS and TWLF demands before abruptly quitting the scene in search of a new job.

This chaotic mill-in lasted eight days; inevitably the demand for an amnesty now headed the list. Robert Smith, a senior member of the staff and a moderate liberal who was appointed acting president, declined to recommend an amnesty to the courts or to hold a college referendum on the ROTC issue. Meanwhile at Berkeley, police used tear gas on June 28 to quell students demonstrating their solidarity with the comrades in Paris. The following two nights it was barricades and gas masks.

Racial tension was constantly rising in the Bay Area. On September 9, the Panther leader, Huey Newton, was sentenced for shooting a policeman the previous year. A day later the Panthers' headquarters were shot up by two off-duty policemen. Fires, beatings, and chaos swept through fifteen high schools. In October black students seized the computer center at the University of California at Santa Barbara and threatened to blow it up. A community college, San Mateo, was closed down by riots. The director of San Francisco State's bitterly embattled black studies program, Dr. Nathan Hare, told the National Conference on Black Power, "We should develop tactics for physically taking over or disrupting racist learning whenever the situation demands."

Now the issue of George Murray came to a boil. Given a six-month suspended sentence for his part in the attack on the editor of *Gater* the previous November, Murray had been allowed to continue at San Francisco State both as a graduate student and as part-time instructor in the Educational Opportunities Program (which admitted four hundred nonwhite students at below the normal entrance standard)—even though he had delivered a speech advocating that Summerskill and Provost Donald Garrity be taken "out of this world." Murray had further inflamed conservative hostility by announcing his enthusiasm for the Cuban revolution after a visit to the island during the summer of 1968. His reappointment by San Francisco State in September 1968 raised a wall of protest from the press, encouraged by Governor Ronald Reagan's office, which was concurrently raising a hue and cry over the appointment of Eldridge Cleaver as an external lecturer at Berkeley.

The national elections were only two weeks away, and the hottest political issue in California was campus chaos. It went to the gut: racial discrimination, ghetto deprivation, the proverbial taxpayer, authority, loss of parental control over children, violence, law and order, and the ancient duel between liberals and conservatives.

During the last week of September, President Smith of San Francisco State and his senior administrators were summoned to Los Angeles for a crisis meeting with the outraged trustees. As Smith later recalled, they were kept waiting for an hour and a half: "The twenty-plus trustees and Chancellor's staff members were crowded around a horseshoe-shaped dinner table. There were no extra places for our group. No one moved to find a place for us. We stood. . . . We surveyed the debris of a seven-dollar dinner with cocktails, wine, and the smell of good cigars and none but Caucasians in the room. . . ." Against Smith's advice, the trustees voted eight to five to "request" George Murray's removal as a part-time instructor at San Francisco State.

Wearing "shades" and a scraggly beard, his mouth twisted in anger, the twenty-three-year-old Murray (son of a Christian minister) appeared on television to blast racist pigs. "What we need is killers, political assassins . . . armed revolutions . . . [they had] guns back in 1776." On October 30, Chancellor Dumke ordered Smith to suspend Murray immediately. Smith complied. Murray left his classroom peacefully, but violent black demonstrations on his behalf shook nearby colleges.

Despite the nominal solidarity between the white New Left radicals and the black students, the latter were less impressed by participatory democracy than by "democratic centralist" leadership. Writing in the BSU's *Black Fire,* a student leader explained that the BSU had elected a central committee whose decisions would be binding on the entire BSU membership. To poll all black students on strike action would, he warned, merely lead to chaos and no strike. (Indeed many white campus radicals were inclined to act first and count votes later; it was the action—and the reaction of the authorities—which created majorities.)

The BSU had ten demands on the table including the reinstatement of George Murray and the promotion of Dr. Nathan Hare to full-professor status, with tenure; the Third World Liberation Front added five more. The strike called by the BSU began on November 6 and was supported not only by Nathan Hare but also by the black dean of all undergraduate studies, Joseph White. Black squads burst into classrooms, faculty members were outraged, there were fights. The TWLF, employing what it called "the tactics of the flea," despatched commandos in stocking masks into departmental offices to scatter the staff and destroy equipment. Five thousand people swarmed about in the middle of the campus.

Now came a new turn. The American Federation of Teachers

Local 1352 (representing only 120 out of 1,300 faculty members) voted to support the black student strike, although it did not endorse all the BSU demands. On November 13, sixty members of the faculty set up a picket line. The same day an appalling running fight broke out between the mobile police squads which were now stationed on the campus (supported by plainclothes policemen), and a large crowd of students. Finally the sixty picketing faculty bravely marched between them and managed to cool the temperature. One of the faculty spokesmen, William Stanton, professor of economics and a former legislator, told the rally that followed: "There are no more classes at San Francisco State! And we're not taking any more horseshit from the fucking trustees!"

Smith closed the campus. Governor Reagan immediately accused him of capitulation to rioting students and striking faculty, and of having "kindled the fires of violence" by his handling of the George Murray case.

At this stage an investigating team from the American Council on Education found that: (1) the trustees and chancellor were detested by faculty and students alike; (2) the college was perceived by the trustees as "rebellious, unreasonable, sick . . . egomaniacal . . ."; (3) the chancellor regarded President Smith as deceitful, evasive, and defiant, while the students saw Smith as "a tool of the repressive power structure." Smith was widely liked, but "his every decision is considered fair game for debate and review by the multitude."

Smith resigned on November 25, after the trustees and the chancellor directed him to keep the campus open at whatever cost, despite bomb threats and the fact that the safety of 20,000 people must now depend on the president's hour-by-hour judgment. Smith was replaced as acting president by the noted semanticist S. I. Hayakawa, a leading light in the right-wing Faculty Resurrection Group at the college. During the first week of Hayakawa's administration, Murray was arrested and imprisoned.

Most days from noon onward there were confrontations and running battles with the police tac squads in front of the cameras. Hayakawa would speak through the public address system: "This is an unlawful assembly. Please disperse. If you want to make trouble, stay where you are and the police will see that you get it." At the age of sixty-two, Hayakawa took on the rebels with a gusto and a flair for publicity that rapidly brought him to the top of the Gallup poll as the nation's most popular educator. At a Washington Gridiron dinner he was seated between General Westmoreland and Senator Edward Kennedy, and when Hayakawa appeared for a VIP-media celebrities softball game, bat in hand and wearing a tam-o'-shanter, 10,000 spectators gave him a long standing ovation. Hayakawa publicly described the striking students as "anarchists, gangsters, hooligans, yahoos, Maoists"; as for the striking faculty (now 300 out of 1,300), they were "crypto-commies." On one occasion he climbed onto a student truck and pulled out the wires from the sound equipment he had banned. "This is a tough neighborhood," he said. "The more policemen I see, the more relieved I feel."

Striking students frequently assaulted those who tried to attend class. Classes were invaded and brought to a halt, provoking white counter-violence from the "blue-bands," mostly students in the Physical Education Department. During January, Nathan Hare and other members of the Black Faculty Union climbed onstage to disrupt a speech by Hayakawa and were arrested. Hare later described this as "a contradiction"—why hadn't the president been arrested for pulling the wires on the students' sound equipment? Dr. Hare told a press conference that the staff he intended to recruit for the (future) independent Black Studies Department would be revolutionary nationalists. "I don't want assimilationists." Hare was also scornful of the reformist tactics of the AFT, their wheeling and dealing with the San Francisco Labor Council, their good relations with the police, and their picket lines which tried to keep students off the campus.

The big bust came on January 23, 1969, when a BSU-TWLF rally on campus refused a police order to disperse. It was Hayakawa's moment: 453 people were arrested. Fearing a collapse of their movement, the BSU and TWLF leaders resorted to more serious acts of violence. Tires were slashed and Edwin Duerr, Hayakawa's administrator for student discipline, barely escaped from his firebombed home. A BSU student, Tim Peebles, was injured when a pipe bomb he was planting in the Creative Arts Building on March 5 exploded prematurely.

The AFT claimed 80 percent student nonattendance at classes, while the Hayakawa administration put the figure at 40 to 50 percent; but by the end of February the faculty strike was faltering. Personal financial problems were beginning to bite and on March 6 they voted, by a bare majority of 112 to 104, to go back to their classrooms, mollified by a reduction in their work load and the reinstatement of those who had been fired. None of the BSU–TWLF demands had been met. The climate of opinion in California, as in the nation, remained hostile: a state poll showed 72 percent agreeing "strongly" that "students who challenge and defy university and college authorities should be kicked out to make room for those who are willing to obey the rules." A year previously, only 58 percent had adopted this position.

Hayakawa had won. For the best part of a year the defense of those arrested in the major bust of January 23 would absorb the funds and energies of the Movement. San Francisco State refused amnesty to 384 of the students arrested during the past four months. By the end of the year, 109 had been convicted and given jail sentences, while 242 others had pleaded no contest in return for suspended sentences and probation. Nathan Hare was dismissed as chairman of the black studies program, George Murray was in jail for parole violation. When Hayakawa announced that the number of black students to be admitted through the Educational Opportunities Program was to be cut from the 400 authorized in 1968 to 150, four black administrators resigned in protest. Hayakawa waved them goodbye.

The trustees of San Francisco State voted by 16 to 2 to make Hayakawa permanent president.

CORNELL

ITHACA, New York, December 1968—At Cornell University, eighteen armed blacks take over an administration building.

Of the upheaval at Cornell, two eyewitnesses in the English Department offered conflicting versions, each embodying classical attitudes of the time. Matthew Hodgart, professor of English at Sussex University, was spending the year at Cornell; Mike Thelwell, whose subject was black literature, had contributed to *William Styron's Nat Turner: Ten Black Writers Respond.* Perhaps the only sentiment they shared was contempt for Cornell's liberal-Quaker president, James A. Perkins. Hodgart regarded Perkins as a master of the self-defeating concession; Thelwell, as a master of anticipatory compromise. Perkins had held the job since 1963.

Cornell had only 250 black students out of 12,000, almost all of them members of the Afro-American Society (AAS), renamed the Black Liberation Front. Following the assassination of Martin Luther King, they had demanded a black studies program; Perkins responded with "Yes, let's appoint a committee to study it." For four months (said Thelwell), the university *pretended* to listen; meanwhile the black students themselves had to listen to visiting black speakers taunting them with having escaped from the ghetto into the Man's academy of assimilation.

So, as at San Francisco State, Cornell blacks upped their demand to an autonomous black college. To make the point they disrupted the library, the cafeteria (they wanted separate eating facilities), and the clinic (they wanted a black psychiatrist). In December 1968, armed blacks took over an an administration building, ejected its occupants, and turned it into the headquarters of the AAS. Emboldened, a group burst into President Perkins's office brandishing guns—toys, as it turned out. When charges were brought against six of them, that became a new issue; 150 blacks showed up to explain why "the Six" would not attend the disciplinary hearings (only blacks can sit in judgment on the "political activities" of blacks, including gunplay in the president's office). Right on, noted Mike Thelwell, who sneered at white America's paranoid hysteria when guns were held in black hands.

More was to come. When blacks disrupted a symposium on South Africa, protesting Cornell's holding stock in Chase Manhattan (of whose board Perkins was a member), a student seized President Perkins by the scruff of the neck and threw him from the platform; even Thelwell thought that a bit unmannerly. Professor Matthew Hodgart was appalled by Perkins's willingness to capitulate; the AAS had extracted $1,700 from the administration to buy bongo drums for the celebration of Malcolm X Day, then used them to disrupt the meeting at which the president was manhandled from the platform.

On April 17, a fiery cross was burned on the campus in the vicinity of the black women's dormitory. Two days later black students occupied Willard Straight Hall. Hearing a false report that armed whites were on the way, they sent out for guns of their own. By now "the Six" had been reduced to "the Three," who were let off with the mildest of reprimands, but Tom Jones of the AAS went on local radio to threaten violence against named professors and administrators, plus the destruction of the university within three hours if the reprimands to "the Three" were not withdrawn. According to Hodgart, nine separate assaults by blacks on whites took place within a few days. On May 11, a black freshman was arrested while holding a loaded gun at a student's head and demanding money. Charged with first-degree robbery and possession of a deadly weapon, he was suspended; a thousand students and faculty promptly convened to demand that his suspension be reversed: "no double jeopardy!"

President Perkins, still knuckling under to every militant demand, withdrew the reprimands and promised that no criminal action would be taken against the armed occupiers of Willard Straight Hall. In addition the trustees voted $240,000 for an all-black college, the Afro Center. Three professors of government and one of history, who had opposed Perkins's concessions, resigned after receiving personal threats from the AAS. About twenty members of those departments suspended their teaching in protest, including a disgusted Hodgart. "The University degenerated into a banana republic; brain-washing by fear and by liberal guilt produced weird euphoria analogous to the after-Munich days." Hodgart later wrote a Swiftian parable on the theme of *Gulliver's*

Travels, subtitled "Wherein the Author Returns and Finds a New State of Liberal Horses and Revolting Yahoos." According to Edward Shils, such was the influence of the *bien pensants* in New York publishing that twelve houses turned down Hodgart's satire before it was accepted.

Despite the racial tension and the physical threats, there was no doubt that a majority of students at Cornell were swept along in a euphoric tide of permanent revolution. The Anthropology and Psychology departments restructured themselves as "communes" with daily meetings of all professors and students. Mass meetings were held in Barton Hall to set up a large constituent assembly modeled on the Estates-General of 1789, with the full backing of the president and administration.

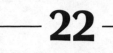

22

PRAGUE WINTER

"Husák's speech on the day he took command of the Party condemned all manifestations of anti-Soviet feelings, even at the time of the military invasion."

"...some 80,000 citizens of all ages and professions who filled Wenceslas Square sang, wept, and cried aloud the name of Dubček...until the police moved in with batons, water cannon and tear gas."

JAN PALACH

PRAGUE, January 16, 1969—At 3:30 on a drizzling afternoon a battered Skoda comes to a halt at the top end of Wenceslas Square. The three occupants of the car are all students at the Charles University's Philosophy Faculty, bitterly resentful of Soviet domination of their country.

On Sunday, November 17 (the 29th anniversary of the execution of nine Czech student leaders by the Nazis), the strike committee of the Philosophical Faculty had organized a sit-in protest strike which was joined by 60,000 students throughout Bohemia and Moravia. The Soviet invasion had dispelled the latent distrust between workers and liberal intellectuals which had persisted during the Prague Spring. Many workers and more than 1,000 journalists and writers openly supported the ten-point resolution that the students sent to the Central Committee, demanding the abolition of censorship, the restoration of the right of assembly, the establishment of self-managing workers' councils, and the Party's commitment to the liberal reforms promised in its Action Program of April 1968. All factories throughout the country blew their sirens for fifteen minutes in a demonstration of solidarity.

One of the philosophy students climbed out of the Skoda, carrying a small can of gasoline. The car drove away. The student turned toward the huge National Museum, its dirty stonework now pockmarked by hundreds of white bullet scars. Blocks of stone lay about in the mud behind flimsy metal barriers. Jan Palach sat down on one of the blocks, took off his coat, which he laid carefully on the stone, picked up the gasoline can, and poured most of the contents over his head and shoulders, splashing the rest against his chest and trousers. He then flicked a lighter and set his clothes on fire.

A tram was passing up the hill toward the cemetery at Olsany. The driver, Jaroslev Spirek, saw a young man aflame from head to foot, running into the road screaming. The driver braked, jumped down from the tram, pulled off his overcoat, and threw it over the human torch, stifling the flames.

Jan Palach had left in his own neatly folded overcoat a letter:

> Seeing that our nations are on the brink of despair we have decided to make our protest and arouse the people of this country in the following way.
>
> Our group consists of volunteers who are resolved to let themselves be burnt alive for our cause.
>
> I have the honour to draw the first lot and thus obtain the right to draft this first letter and become the first torch.
>
> Our demands are: (1) The immediate abolition of censorship. (2) A ban on the distribution of *Zpravy* [a Soviet occupation sheet featuring venomous attacks on Czechoslovak liberals].
>
> Unless our demands are met within five days, i.e., by 21 January 1969, and unless the public demonstrates adequate support (i.e., by an indefinite strike), further torches will burst into flames. Signed: Torch No. 1.
>
> PS: Remember August! Czechoslovakia has obtained room for manoeuvre in international affairs: let us exploit the fact.

Palach suffered third-degree burns on 85 percent of his body. He continually asked the hospital staff to describe the nation's reaction to what he had done, and was informed that thousands of flowers had arrived at the hospital and the Central Committee had been inundated with resolutions supporting his demands. Palach reportedly managed to smile before he died.

On the day after his death thousands of students filled Red Army Square, in front of the Philosophy Faculty Building where Jan Palach had been a student. Speakers urged the crowd to stiffen resistance against the occupation forces; Alexander Dubček was now described as little better than a collaborator. The demonstrators then tore down the street signs and renamed the square after Palach. Demonstrations took place throughout the Czech lands, although, ominously, Gustáv Husák, Party boss of Slovakia and Dubček's eventual successor in the national post, forbade any such displays in that province. In Bohemia and Moravia black flags were flown from all public buildings.

An estimated 120,000 people came to Prague for Jan Palach's funeral. His body lay in state in the Carolinum, a beautiful old court-yard of the university. About 350,000 people lined up in the narrow streets of the Old Town to pass by the coffin where it lay under the statue of Jan Hus, the great religious martyr of medieval Bohemia. When Palach was buried on Saturday the 25th, the funeral procession was reckoned at 800,000. The police remained out of sight, leaving all policing to the students; everyone conducted themselves with dignity. But the following day police used tear gas to disperse crowds around Wenceslas Square.

This vast display of patriotic solidarity momentarily encouraged certain illusions. In its immediate aftermath, radical student leader Lubomíř Holeček addressed the Bertrand Russell Peace Foundation Conference in Stockholm: "What are the plans of my generation for 1969? (1) To pursue a current of political thought opposed to all forms of Stalinism and yet not indulging in dreams. For us it is necessary to reject some of the dreams of the New Left in the West . . . (2) To maintain our links with the working class and trade union organizations. We speak daily in factories to gatherings of up to a thousand workers. . . ." In reality, Holeček's optimism was not justified. As Milan Hauner has pointed out, the postinvasion patriotic unity was stronger on sentimental rhetoric than on effective political action. The rhetoric also masked serious divisions—for example, the trade unions were unable to accept the radical students' rejection of the National Front (by which the Communist Party controlled the electoral process under a thin disguise of pluralism).

On February 25, another student, Jan Zajic, also burned himself to death in the same square. According to student sources, he belonged to Palach's group. An epitaph for Palach and Zajic had already been written, on October 31, 1968, by the Prague section of the Writers' Union: "By force it is possible to annihilate men, but not ideas. During this century alone we in Bohemia have three times seen monolithic systems crumble before resuscitated truth."

THE FALL OF DUBČEK

In March 1969, the Czechoslovak ice hockey team defeated the Soviet Union's twice during the world championships in Stockholm. The anti-Soviet demonstrations that followed finally brought Dubček down. Under ultimatum from the Soviet leaders, Dubček asked the Central Committee on April 17, 1969, to relieve him of his post as first secretary, and to elect Gustáv Husák as his successor. The massive purge had at last begun.

Authoritarian by temperament and conviction, Husák had himself been a victim of the Stalinist excesses of the early 1950s. Although one of the communist organizers of the Slovak uprising against the Nazis, he was later purged as a "bourgeois nationalist" and sentenced to life imprisonment. Released in 1960 after nine years, he was rehabilitated three years later. Deputy premier under Černík, Husák became Party boss in Slovakia after the Soviet invasion and pressed successfully for Smrkovský's dismissal as chairman of the National Assembly. Repeatedly Husák attacked the liberal media, which had "introduced various radical slogans into the people's heads and thus caused ideological and political confusion. . . ." The Party must resume its complete control. Husák's speech on the day he took command of the Party condemned all manifestations of anti-Soviet feeling, even at the time of the military invasion. "The problem of freedom and democracy is for us a class problem. There can be no freedom for people who in crisis situations such as today's . . . abuse freedom and democracy against the interests of the state and socialism."

On June 11, addressing the World Conference of Communist Parties in Moscow, Husák denounced the Czechoslovak reform movement for "naïveté and political romanticism, cheap gestures and slogans not based on a class viewpoint, about democracy, freedom and humanism and the so-called will of the people. . . ." (The Italian and Spanish Communists took the opportunity to reaffirm their condemnation of the Soviet violation of Czechoslovak national sovereignty; the Italians in particular spoke up passionately for the liberal reforms of the Dubček era.)

On August 21, the first anniversary of the Soviet invasion, the whole nation walked to work as a gesture of protest. The trams and trains were empty; at midday a five-minute strike was observed throughout the country; some 80,000 citizens of all ages and professions who filled Wenceslas Square sang, wept, and cried aloud the name of Dubček, *"At zije Dubček!"* until the police moved in with batons, water cannon, and tear gas. The demonstrators rallied. At six in the evening seventy-five tanks were ordered into the city—so fierce and protracted was the street fighting that 1,387 were arrested in Prague. In Brno, where the battle continued until the 23rd, four people were killed. On the following day the Presidium promulgated Emergency Laws suspending the normal safeguards (frail as they were) under the rule of law.

In September, Dubček was dismissed from the Presidium. Twenty-nine liberals, including Smrkovský, were removed from the Central Committee, which—in the most soul-wrenching act of obeisance—now fully endorsed the Soviet invasion as "motivated by the interests of the defence of socialism . . . by the class interests of workers and the communist movement." On October 15, Dubček was dismissed as chairman of the National Assembly. In January 1970, he was exiled to Turkey as ambassador—a clear invitation to defect, which he declined. In June he was expelled from the Party.

All exit permits to the West were declared invalid in October 1969, and the frontiers were closed. Those living abroad were summoned to return home within fifteen days or face prison sentences. Perhaps 50,000 chose to remain in the West.

The workers' councils which, paradoxically, had gained real momentum only after the Soviet invasion, growing in number to five hundred by June 1969 and embracing over 1 million workers, were extinguished. In October 1969, Husák denounced the councils as an anarcho-syndicalist threat to "social" (that is, state) property and central planning; the following June they were banned outright.

The purges gutted the country. An estimated one-fifth of Communists in the armed forces were expelled from the Party—some 11,000 persons. Of 136 generals in August 1968, at least 20 were dismissed. The universities, the Military Political Academy, Prague Radio, Czechoslovak Airlines, and certain departments of the Academy of Sciences were decimated. Forty institutes were either disbanded or merged. The onslaught on the social sciences was brutal: "revisionists" were eliminated from the scene and their publications withdrawn from circulation. In a nation of only 14 million, 70,217 screening groups were set up, comprising 235,270 interviewers to test the credentials of every Party member. The screeners themselves were screened, and the interviewers interviewed, in a process worthy of Kafka's homeland.

Those expelled from the Party, or otherwise condemned by the loyalty tests, almost invariably lost their jobs and were barred from the professions. The writer Václav Havel took a job in a brewery, the philosopher Julius Tomin in a zoo, other intellectuals worked on roads, as night porters, as ancillary staff in hospitals. According to Husák, 21.67 percent of Party members were expelled—about 460,000 people, of whom 30 percent lost their jobs. After the Journalists' Union was purged in December 1969, about half of its 4,000 members could no longer work.

On September 15, the new minister of education, Professor Jaromir Hrbek, wrote to all employees in the universities, enclosing a questionnaire. The questions in Section A concerned the respondent. For example:

> Question 6: If you are a member of the Communist Party, have you displayed throughout the years 1968 and 1969 a consistent Party attitude . . . have you not allowed yourself to be broken by the attack of the rightist and anti-socialist forces?
>
> Question 8: In which anti-Party and anti-Soviet actions have you participated against the true adherents of Marxism-Leninism and socialist internationalism? Which pressure-resolutions have you signed or voted in favour of? (Neutrality of CSSR, abolition of People's Militia . . . the entry of Allied troops. . . .)

Question 13: On what points do you not agree with the present policy of the Party and National Front; where are you uncertain, and have doubts?

Are you aware that you will also be evaluated by a collective of coworkers, and eventual contradictions in data will be investigated?

The questions in Section B concerned people other than the respondent: "Which are honest and capable? (Name at least ten.) Which have been discredited by anti-socialist, anti-Soviet deeds and attitudes?"

Husák's political trials were not "show trials" in the mold of the 1950s—no bogus confessions to fabricated conspiracies. The leaders of the Prague Spring were not imprisoned, let alone executed. Husák's aim was an authoritarian regime that avoided the excesses of the Gottwald-Novotný era, yet his was nonetheless a police state which turned legal dissent into a crime. Many of the charges were unashamedly political, without even a veneer of legal wrongdoing. Thus General Prchlík was accused of having on July 15, 1968 "criticized organs [i.e., the Warsaw Pact] and their activity in impermissible form, and adduced information which he must have known would aggravate not only the already acute internal political situation but above all the friendly relations with the USSR." The New Left group led by Peter Uhl received prison sentences because they had "compiled and duplicated various printed matter and leaflets whose contents could arouse disagreement with and resistance to the socialist social order. . . ."

In conclusion, there is the heroic case of Jiří Müller. In 1965, when a twenty-one-year-old student at Prague's Institute of Technology, he had disrupted the stage-managed National Student Conference by calling for a democratic reform of the Union of Youth, and by demanding that freedoms guaranteed by law should be practiced rather than mutilated by "custom." His reward followed: expulsion from the Institute and military conscription. He reappeared during the Prague Spring and became, in the words of his radical colleague Karel Kovanda, "the principal architect and moving force of the amazingly successful worker-student coalition, anchored in the new works councils. . . ." In 1971, Müller joined others urging citizens to abstain or vote against the single slate of National Front candidates in the rigged elections (the first since 1968) to the National Assembly. One of hundreds arrested by the infuriated authorities, he was sentenced to five and a half years in prison.

Jiří Müller belonged to a different sort of student revolution—one that united people of all generations and classes in defense of the wheat and water of the human spirit.

23

DECLINE OF THE NEW LEFT

"On October 29, Seale was chained hand and foot to a metal chair and gagged with muslin."

"The Woodstock Music and Art Fair, staged in Bethel, New York, in August 1969, had offered a charming, idyllic image of the youth culture..."

THE END OF SDS—WEATHERMEN

By the end of 1968 the United States had lost 30,500 in Vietnam, nearly half of them during the previous twelve months. Expenditures on the war were running at $30 billion per year, with a troop commitment of 550,000 and no chink of light from the Paris peace talks. Martin Luther King, Jr., and Robert Kennedy were dead and Eugene McCarthy was politically buried. Richard Nixon would inherit the White House in the New Year and not one Western European government would pose any serious challenge to American policy in Vietnam. De Gaulle, the German Grand Coalition, and the Wilson government all sat secure. Likewise, the dictatorships of Franco in Spain, Caetano in Portugal, Papadopoulos in Greece, and Ian Smith in Rhodesia.

A history of the New Left in 1968 cannot tidily sew up its hems on December 31 of that year. It was during 1969 that the American Movement embraced dogmatism, virulent rage, violence—and its own disintegration.

By the turn of 1968–69, SDS had reached the peak of its strength, with between 60,000 and 100,000 members in local chapters, compared with only 8,000 three years earlier. After the Columbia rebellion in April 1968, the Movement spread to almost every campus in America, including the smallest of junior colleges. Many of the new recruits knew little of the Movement's founding philosophy, of the Port Huron Statement, of the community projects in the ghettos; they enlisted as children of the war—and of the media.

In May 1969 the Permanent Subcommittee on Investigations reported 471 disturbances at 211 colleges during the previous two years, including 25 bombings, 46 cases of arson, 598 injuries, 6,158 arrests, and 207 buildings occupied.

As SDS gained in influence on the campuses the Marxist-Leninist Progressive Labor Party (PLP) increasingly bent its energies to absorbing student radicalism into its ranks through a front organization, the

Worker-Student Alliance, whose strength was concentrated in the campuses of New England. Founded in 1964 by former Communists who rejected Soviet revisionism, the PLP had fervently embraced Mao's Cultural Revolution. The Leninist organization of the party, and its insistence that all conflicts are subordinate to the class struggle, was clearly alien to the gentle, Emersonian, participatory, pot-eased radicalism of the early New Left. Its capacity for savaging New Left icons was prodigious. It condemned the 1968 Chicago Mobilization and the Yippies; it condemned the Black Panthers for "nationalism" and "adventurism"; it (now) condemned Castro's regime as "a personalistic and paternalistic" one-man show; it condemned Ho Chi Minh and the NLF for Soviet-style revisionism and for talking peace with the United States; it attacked hippies and the drugs scene. The climax to this relentless sectarianism came after Nixon's visit to Peking when the PLP broke with China herself for seeking a rapprochement with the United States. Only Albania remained, in all the world, wholly admirable.

Despite its numerical strength, by 1969 SDS was in a state of terminal fission. Even the enemies of the Maoist Worker-Student Alliance were split between increasingly doctrinaire sects styling themselves Revolutionary Youth Movement I and II. Local chapters broke away, accusing the national office of "bureaucratic Stalinism." History had at last caught up with the New Left.

The SDS convention met in Chicago's Coliseum on June 18, 1969. After the press had been excluded, the 1,500 delegates were handed a six-page article, "You Don't Need a Weatherman to Know Which Way the Wind Blows"—a line taken from a Bob Dylan song. The work of SDS militants belonging to a new faction calling itself Revolutionary Youth Movement (RYM) I, notably Bernardine Dohrn, Mark Rudd, and Terry Robbins, the document castigated the Worker-Student Alliance's deviations from the true SDS line, of which two were fundamental: (1) SDS granted the blacks the leading role in the struggle, whereas for the PLP the blacks were merely a segment of the proletariat; (2) SDS granted a special place to youth as a vanguard class, whereas the PLP assigned this role exclusively to the working class. But the Weatherman Manifesto also marked the end of SDS's dedication to participatory democracy and Emersonian persuasion. Born out of SDS's experience of insurrection at Columbia and on the campuses of the Midwest, it called for the creation of a revolutionary organization under a single general staff (regarded by the Maoists as foolish adventurism).

The convention proceedings immediately became embroiled in crazy factionalism. The Black Panther spokesmen first offended the women delegates with a truculent display of male chauvinism, then denounced the PLP as "counter-revolutionary traitors." Such was the uproar that Mark Rudd proposed an hour's recess for cooling off, but the flamboyant Bernardine Dohrn strode to the microphone and led a walkout by RYM I.

Born in 1942, her father a Hungarian Jew, her mother of Swedish descent, Dohrn had studied law in Chicago and helped poor tenants in legal battles with landlords. After graduating she worked for the National Lawyers' Guild, advising draft resisters and defending members of the Movement. Dohrn did not join SDS until early in 1968, but soon moved into its leadership as an ultraradical whose admiration for Martin Luther King had rapidly been supplanted by a commitment to violence. Of the Manson murders she had this to say: "Dig, first they killed those pigs, then they ate dinner in the same room with them, and they even shoved a fork into a victim's stomach. Wild!" Dohrn herself was later featured in the FBI's Most Wanted posters.

The day following her walkout, Dohrn led her contingent back into the main conference room of the Coliseum to confront the Worker-Student Alliance (who at that moment were dispersed in workshops) and to insist on their expulsion from SDS as "racists" (among other things). The Maoists rushed back and Dohrn's motion failed; she then stormed out of the building, followed by hundreds, leaving the Worker-Student Alliance to proclaim themselves the one and only SDS.

The coalition between the RYM-Weathermen and the Black Panthers was also doomed. The disastrous New Politics Conference of September 1967 was virtually replayed in July 1969, a month after the SDS convention, when the Panthers staged a conference in Oakland for a "united front against fascism." The white New Left was invited but not consulted. During three days of disorganized rhetoric and hectoring, the Panthers segregated themselves behind a roped-off section at the back of the auditorium and allowed no workshops or floor discussions until the final night. What they wanted was white endorsement of a demand for locally elected councils to control all police forces across the nation. To SDS this made sense in black and brown neighborhoods, but not in white ones, where such a devolution would merely pass control of the police to vigilantes and bigots. But the Panthers weren't listening. "We're not going to let SDS worm their way out of their revolutionary duties," announced the Panthers' chief of staff, David Hilliard. Another disaster.

As a minor mass movement with a coherent ideology the American New Left was a spent force after the SDS convention; only the futile "days of rage" and the bombings followed. In October 1969, Weathermen came storming out of Lincoln Park, Chicago, in paramilitary fashion, demolishing parked cars and smashing windows. Two days later they attacked the business section of the Loop. Arrests on the two occasions totaled 287, but all were set free when $2.3 million was posted in bail, mainly by parents. Tom Hayden concluded that the New Left had been wrong in the early sixties to focus, with Marcuse, on the co-optive powers of liberal society. The civil rights and antiwar movements had not been seduced or co-opted, but clubbed, tear-gassed, and jailed. But Hayden could not follow the Weathermen into artificial terrorist violence devoid of any wider constituency. While on trial as one of the Chicago 7, Hayden was invited to address two hundred Weathermen gathering in the park for the "days of rage." He wrote: "They looked exactly like the people we were accused of being; helmeted, wearing heavy jackets, carrying clubs and NLF flags, they stood around a fire of park benches exactly like a primitive, neophyte, nervous army. . . ." Bernadette Dohrn and the women armed themselves with helmets, clubs, and poles, worked themselves to a fever pitch in a Chicago park, then sped off chanting the piercing "oy" of the Arab women they'd heard in the enormously influential film, *The Battle of Algiers.*

Many went underground. Weatherman commando units stormed into high schools, threatened teachers, shouted "Jail break!" and preached revolution to surprised students. Mark Rudd, of Columbia fame, was in on this. "It's a wonderful feeling to *hit* a pig," he avowed during the Weatherman conference held in Flint, Michigan, at Christmas 1969. "It must be a really wonderful feeling to *kill* a pig or blow up a building."

Jane Alpert, once a bomber of corporation buildings, later explained herself: "I was young, in love, naïve." Family misfortune had pitched her into adolescent rebellion; an affair with a Weatherman hero did the rest. But she was also motivated by exceptional political pressures: spectacular bomb blasts seemed like the way to bring home to the American public that the Vietnam War could reach out to threaten the streets and corporate elites of the United States. In Jane Alpert's case there was an additional, self-hating, urge to violence; Jewish, she adopted the Palestinian cause. Today she writes publicity for nonprofit social agencies.

Between August 1969 and March 1970, seven major companies were bombed in New York. Revolutionary Force 9 claimed credit for the simultaneous explosions at GE, Mobil, and IBM on March 12. At one point, 30,000 people were evacuated from buildings in midtown Manhattan, with threats coming in at the rate of one every six minutes. All Washington, D.C., schools were evacuated after explosions in the capital and in Pittsburgh. ROTC buildings from Oregon to Texas were attacked. On March 6, a Weatherman group blew itself up while manufacturing bombs in a townhouse on 11th Street in New York City. Two women escaped naked, were given clothes by unsuspecting neighbors, and vanished. Three others, one a woman, died in the explosion. From January 1969 to April 1970, bomb blasts caused forty-three deaths (mainly novice saboteurs) and caused $21.8 million in damage.

Ten years had passed since the day in February 1960 when four Negro students entered the F. W. Woolworth store in Greensboro, North Carolina, sat down at the whites-only lunchcounter, and made their famous request to be served coffee. The New Left had come—and gone—a long way.

THE CHICAGO EIGHT (SEVEN)

Judicial retribution for the riots during the Democratic Convention of August 1968 was duly exacted. The trial of the Chicago 8—subsequently reduced to 7—began on September 24, 1969 on the 23rd floor of the Federal Building in Chicago's Loop. It lasted four months, with full television coverage, and further polarized an already divided public. Arraigned before the U.S. District Court in Illinois, the eight were charged under an amendment to the Civil Rights Act of 1968 with conspiring to cross state lines with intent to incite riot. Seven of the eight defendants began the trial free on bail; the exception was the Black Panther leader, Bobby Seale, whose case, like that of Huey Newton, became an international *cause célèbre*.

Bobby Seale had been in Chicago for only two days during the Democratic Convention, a last-minute substitute for Eldridge Cleaver, who had been forbidden to attend by his parole board. Robert Pierson, an undercover agent, testified that Seale had made a speech in Lincoln Park calling on those present "to barbecue some pork." Returning now to Chicago in chains, and facing a possible death sentence in Connecticut where he was charged with having ordered the execution of a police informer, Seale asked to be defended by Charles Garry, the San Francisco lawyer who also acted for Newton and Cleaver. But Garry was due for a major operation, and Judge Julius Hoffman refused to delay the trial. Seale then demanded to defend himself, but Hoffman refused on the ground that Seale had already accepted William Kunstler as a substitute for Garry—even though Kunstler insisted he could not defend an unwilling client. Seale called Hoffman a racist, a fascist, a pig. "You begin to oink in the faces of the masses."

Such was the burning acrimony between Seale and Hoffman that the judge charged Seale with sixteen counts of contempt, for which he was given four years in jail. On October 29, Seale was chained hand and foot to a metal chair and gagged with muslin. Under the gag his mouth was taped. Kunstler called it "medieval torture" and "a disgrace." The following morning the gag was further strengthened by an elastic bandage, and Seale's mouth was stuffed with some kind of cotton which the marshals had managed to insert by holding his nose. Then Seale choked and they had to remove it. Some of the marshals were black. Seale called them "fascist dogs" and "sons of bitches."

A group of lawyers filed suit before another federal judge on behalf of Seale's right to defend himself, but the suit was denied. Eventually Judge Hoffman declared a mistrial for Seale and set the new trial for April 23, 1970. The Chicago 8 became the Chicago 7. They were: Rennie Davis and David Dellinger, organizers of the National Mobilization to End the War in Vietnam; John Froines, assistant professor of chemistry at the University of Oregon; Tom Hayden of SDS; Abbie Hoffman and Jerry Rubin of the Youth International Party; and Lee Weiner, a graduate student at Northwestern University.

Julius Hoffman was the prosecution's judge. (Seventy-four years of age, five feet four inches tall, dainty in manner, with a mobile, elastic mouth and a gift for impersonation, Hoffman was the villain of the piece.) When former Attorney General Ramsey Clark offered to testify for the defense, the Republican assistant attorney general, Richard Schultz, objected and Hoffman refused permission, directing the defense lawyers to say nothing about this within hearing of the jury. The *New York Times* later called this "the ultimate outrage" of the trial. The Washington *Post* commented: "The judge is doing a frightening job on people's faith in the integrity of the federal courts." In the course of the trial (as *Life* pointed out), the judge casually sent lawyers to jail without bond, admitted hearsay evidence from government witnesses, and quashed almost every motion offered by the defense, whom he treated to "a running litany of insult."

On December 11, Allen Ginsberg took the witness stand, wearing white tennis shoes and walking with a bouncing gait, a large woven purse slung over his left shoulder. The New Left and the counterculture embraced for the final time in the remarkable spirit of this poet. Ginsberg testified for one and a half days, while Special Agent Stanley of the FBI sat at the government's table searching for discreditable passages in Ginsberg's poems. What seemed to obsess Prosecutor Thomas Foran was sex and "faggots"—he cross-examined Ginsberg as to whether he had "intimate" relations with Hoffman and Rubin. Foran also asked Ginsberg to recite three poems clearly regarded by the prosecution as obscene. Ginsberg calmly obliged, then explained about Walt Whitman, tenderness, and natural sexuality. Foran muttered under his breath, "Goddam faggot."

When Ginsberg recited *Howl,* it was at the invitation of the defense, on redirect examination. At the climax he wheeled in his chair and pointed at the judge: "Moloch the vast stone of war! Moloch the stunned governments! Moloch whose ear is a smoking tomb! Moloch whose blood is running money!"

The defendants mocked the court and the judge at their daily press conferences and speeches. The oldest among them, David Dellinger, editor of *Liberation,* had been imprisoned during World War II as a conscientious objector. When Judge Hoffman instructed him to stop making speeches outside the court, he refused and a fight broke out as Hoffman suspended Dellinger's bail and his protesting daughters were dragged from the gallery by marshals. Defense attorney William Kunstler went on his knees, crying: "Your Honor, take me now. You've destroyed everything I believe in." Even Tom Hayden lost his restraint on this occasion; the ensuing brawl weighed heavily against them all when the contempts were finally totaled.

On the following day the two Yippies, Hoffman and Rubin, screamed epithets at the judge in an attempt to get themselves jailed, but Judge Hoffman merely noted it all down in what Hayden called his "doomsday book." When marshals moved to physically restrain Jerry Rubin, he shouted: "Don't hit me in my balls, motherfucker."

Subpoenaed by HUAC after the Chicago riots of August 1968, Rubin had showed up in a Black Panther beret set rakishly on his exploding hair, his face streaked in Indian war paint, and a Mexican bandolier of real bullets (removed by the congressional guards) across his bare chest; he also clutched a toy gun (which the guards let pass). Abbie Hoffman's favorite gimmick was to drape himself (illegally) in the U.S. flag; for this offense he was arrested during the HUAC hearings in September 1968, and blacked out by CBS when he appeared on the Merv Griffin show wearing the Stars and Stripes. Viewers saw Griffin talking to a half-blank screen.

But for the Yippies it wasn't all fun and games. Immediately prior to the Chicago trial, Rubin, already sentenced in Virginia as a result of the October 1967 Pentagon demonstration, was serving thirty days in Santa Rita Rehabilitation Center, California. Federal marshals drove him across the nation for five days, handcuffed to two other convicts, and dumped him in Cook County Jail, Chicago. Released on bail, he spent most of the trial at liberty—and made the most of it. He and Abbie Hoffman succeeded in penetrating the exclusive club where Judge Julius Hoffman customarily took luncheon, hounding him from table to table, after which the two Yippies appeared in court garbed in judge's apparel; Abbie duly disrobed to reveal the white shirt of a Chicago policeman and got six extra days in jail.

Hayden despised their "self-marketing" as mythic media models for kids. Abbie Hoffman and Jerry Rubin may have wanted to abolish money, but not yet—the hype surrounding the publication of the Yippie stars' books was worthy of *Valley of the Dolls*. Marketing Abbie Hoffman's *Woodstock Nation,* Random House depicted its own trademark building being blown up on the cover. Simon & Schuster advertised Rubin's *Do It!* as "a Molotov cocktail in your very hands." In May 1969, Dial Press placed a half-page ad in the *New York Review of Books* for Hoffman's *Revolution for the Hell of It* (fourth big printing), capitalizing on the author's indictment for conspiracy. The selling blurb was "Warning! Possession of this book may make you part of a conspiracy." The film rights were sold to MGM. According to Tom Hayden, the Yippies also wanted to sell the movie rights of the Chicago conspiracy trial: "Let them have Washington, D.C.," declared Abbie Hoffman, "we're going to take over Hollywood." (But the trade was also nervous; Rubin listed the leading publishers who had turned down his books or backed out of agreements.)

The jury, mainly composed of Cook County housewives, and a young lady who later sold her story to the *Sun-Times* before marrying an official in the County Sheriff's Department, deliberated for five days. Froines and Weiner were acquitted. The other five were found not guilty of conspiracy, but guilty of crossing state lines to riot. The contempt sentences handed down by Judge Hoffman were to be served concurrently with the main prison sentences. Defense lawyers were also punished. William Kunstler, the most flamboyantly outrageous (and arguably influential) radical lawyer in America, received a jail sentence of four years; his colleague Len Weinglass, two years. Appeals would follow.

At the end of the trial Rubin got five years for incitement to riot plus two years for contempt (Abbie Hoffman felt "put down" to have earned only eight months for contempt, less even than the sober Hayden). Threatened by the state of Illinois with a new trial under state laws, Rubin took his lawyer's advice and pleaded guilty on an assurance he would get only sixty days, half of them to run concurrently with the sentence imposed in Virginia as a result of the Pentagon demonstration in October 1967. Rubin affected to adore the Weatherman bombs: "brilliant attacks on key capitalist symbols"—clearly no outrage could ever be too "outasight" for Jerry. Leaving one prison, he visited the multiple-murderer Charles Manson in another at Manson's request. Rubin described Manson as ". . . one of the most poetic and intense people we ever met . . . his words and courage inspire us . . ."—though he was nonplussed by Manson's "incredible male chauvinism." "Is Charlie innocent or guilty? What is innocence and guilt?"

Rubin traveled to Amsterdam to meet kindred spirits, the Kabouters, who had won five seats on the city council and seized a number of city-owned houses for homeless squatters. In Amsterdam you could smoke pot anywhere, even in front of a cop, though it was illegal. After a meeting with Cohn-Bendit in Frankfurt and a passage to England by sea, the Yippies disrupted a live David Frost television show, met Bernadette Devlin, MP (an honorary Yippie since going to jail for inciting riot), in the House of Commons, evaded the home secretary's expulsion order, went underground in Belfast, city of "pigs" and soldiers (Bernadette had explained that the troubles in Ireland had "nothing" to do with religion), got arrested, and were shipped home.

ROCK NEMESIS

ALTAMONT, California, December 6, 1969—The rock counterculture meets its nemesis, as the trial of the Chicago 7 reaches its climax.

The Woodstock Music and Art Fair, staged in Bethel, New York, in August 1969, had offered a charming, idyllic image of the youth culture; *Time* magazine tuned up its prose to hail "history's largest happening . . . one of the significant political and social events of the age." Woodstock was subsequently made into a $4 million movie whose immense popularity extended the Woodstock aura across the nation.

Then came Altamont, a disused racetrack thirty miles east of Berkeley, the hastily improvised and ill-prepared site for a free rock concert starring the Rolling Stones at the climax of their American tour. The Stones were not every young person's heroes. Sol Stern quoted a young woman in a café on Berkeley's Telegraph Avenue: "Those fuckers are making 2,000,000 dollars on the tour and Mick Jagger practically spit [*sic*] in Abbie Hoffman's face when Abbie asked him for some bread for the Chicago 8."

Whereas Woodstock had been a predominantly middle-class affair, there were enough working-class street kids at Altamont to bury the dream of universal love. Collection buckets for the Black Panthers' defense fund were ignored with sullen hostility. A vast crowd of 300,-000 to half a million was packed like sardines before the stage and seven hundred people were treated at the site for nightmarish acid trips.

The fatal move had been to hire the Hell's Angels as stewards and praetorian guards of the platform. From noon until well after dark less than a hundred Angels, tanked up on free beer and LSD, vicious, fearless, and totally dedicated to the ruthless exercise of tribal power, wreaked havoc in the crowd. The Jefferson Airplane was about to begin

"We Can Be Together" when a terrified black man leaped onstage pursued by Angels. He was beaten to the ground, coughing up blood and teeth. When Marty Balin of the Jefferson Airplane attempted to intervene, he was knocked unconscious onstage by an Angel wielding a pool cue. The loving community of *Hair* was disintegrating into Hobbes's state of nature. Zonked by drugs, kids stripped off their clothes and repeatedly crawled toward the stage, offering themselves as sacrifices to the Angels.

Arriving by helicopter, the Stones deliberately allowed ninety minutes to elapse between the previous rock group and their own appearance, even though the December night had grown bitterly cold and the crowd was into catatonic exhaustion. A film was being made (*Gimme Shelter*) and Jagger wanted complete darkness before he strode on, in his red satin cape glowing under the beautiful lights, surrounded by Hell's Angels.

Leering, Jagger had started into "Sympathy for the Devil" ("Permit me to introduce myself, I'm a man of wealth and taste . . .") when six Angels began beating a naked girl who had clambered onstage. Jagger broke off in mid-verse, mildly rebuked them, started again, then stopped, sure that he had seen a black man in a green suit pointing a gun at him from the audience. The Angels plunged into the crowd and grabbed Meredith Hunter, an eighteen-year-old black youth who had come to the show accompanied by a pretty blonde. It was he who had the gun and now he was ritually stabbed to death in a frenzy of racial hatred. Jagger tried hip talk through the superb amplification system: "Brothers and sisters, come on now. That just means everybody just cool out . . . we can groove." Meredith Hunter lay dying. "Hey, we need a doctor here. . . ." murmured Jagger.

Four died and hundreds were injured at Altamont. The counterculture fell into deep shock. The *Berkeley Tribe,* the most widely read underground paper in the Bay Area, announced: "Stones Concert Ends It—America Now Up for Grabs."

THE WAR CONTINUES

President Nixon's accession brought to the antiwar movement a broader liberal base and a new respectability. On Sunday, April 6, 1969, 70,000 marched down the Avenue of the Americas in New York City while middle-aged Easter shoppers applauded and gave *V*-signs. Parades in a number of cities were attended by servicemen wearing white paper overseas caps (GIs Against the War), by mothers with children, and by members of the older generation. Four years of demonstrations reached their climax in the fall of 1969; the Moratorium of October 15 (mainly organized by a revived fraternity of graduates from the McCarthy and Kennedy campaigns) was endorsed by town meetings across the country and by sixty-five members of Congress. Fifteen separate resolutions were before Congress, demanding troop withdrawals. More radical was the New Mobilization demonstration in Washington on Saturday, November 16, which drew more people—perhaps half a million—to the Washington Monument than any other gathering in history, but which received no live coverage on television, following Vice-President Spiro Agnew's blanket attack on the networks, the press, SDS, Weathermen, and Yippies. Governor Reagan said it was all planned in East Berlin and Attorney General John Mitchell moved 9,000 troops into federal buildings. The Weathermen duly unleashed their violence.

On the last day of April 1970, Nixon announced that he had ordered a military incursion into Cambodia. An unprecedented wave of protest struck the universities and colleges. On May 4, the Ohio National Guard opened fire on demonstrating students at Kent State University, killing four and wounding nine. Two students were shot at Jackson State College, a black campus in Mississippi. Students at 350 colleges went on strike, ROTC buildings were burned on thirty campuses, the National Guard was called out in sixteen states.

By the fall the rioting was over and with it died the momentum of student protest. The campus insurrection that had begun at Berkeley in 1964 faded and was replaced by the reassuring contours of normality. The war continued.

AFTERWORD

"Tom Hayden (who married the actress Jane Fonda)…[said,] 'We made a mistake then—we came ten years too early.'"

The new decade opened with a best-selling book written by a Yale law professor, Charles Reich's *The Greening of America*. While paying tribute to Herbert Marcuse (and to virtually every other radical idol), Reich splendidly illustrated Marcuse's thesis about the system's capacity to absorb, domesticate, and profit from radical challenges; heaping praise on a decade of protest, Reich contrived to render it harmless. Corporate liberalism? Bad. Electoral politics? Bad again. The Vietnam War? Very bad. The condition of the blacks? Intolerable. Police brutality? Unacceptable. The new communalism? Excellent. Taking responsibility and doing what you believe in? Right on. Expanding consciousness through drugs? Why not? On each and every topic Reich's position echoed that of the New Left and/or the counterculture.

But Reich was selling an Arcadian idealization to book-club America. The package came prettily wrapped as "Consciousness III," like a spacecraft. Put behind you Consciousness I—the old backwoods frontiersman, overtaken by events, suspicious of change, seeking scapegoats in foreign enemies. Wrestle down the seductive demon of Consciousness II—the post–New Deal, corporate executive or professional, wedded to "progress" and reform (if in fashion), separating his private beliefs from his career obligations, jealous of his privileged, atomized private life and recreations (no sense of community), and displaying slightly avant-garde tastes (not necessarily his own).

Reich then "sold" Consciousness III—the recovery of "self." It was a masterly contribution to the "How to Improve Yourself" tradition. You too can achieve Consciousness III! You may be old, you may be square, you may even be rich and successful, but you too can recover your real self—painlessly. Without giving up anything. "For older people, a new consciousness could rest on growing a garden, reading literature, baking bread, playing Bach on a recorder, or developing a new sense of family, so long as it represents a true knowledge of self rather than false consciousness."

Deep into the book Reich began to chide the New Left for attempting confrontation, for displaying hostility, for proselytizing. It was all
counter-productive. "Bob Dylan did what he wanted to do, lived his
own life, and *incidentally* changed the world; that is the point the
radicals have missed." Reich offered Consciousness III free of the
burdens of action or sacrifice: "Only the person who feels himself to be
an outsider is genuinely free of the lures and temptations of the Corporate State. Only he can work in a bank or go to a cocktail party in
'safety' because he will not be taken in."

It's a long, long process, but, in the end: "When self is recovered,
the power of the Corporate State will be ended, as miraculously as a
kiss breaks a witch's enchantment."

In Europe the communal idealism of the New Left yielded to the
fanatical violence of small, embittered factions. The 1970s became the
decade of Red terrorism: bombs, kidnappings, hijackings, assassina-
tions. The Red Brigades in Italy, the Red Army Faction (Baader-
Meinhof) in Germany, the Angry Brigade in Britain, Action Directe in
France—all engaged in a murderous battle with the State, supposedly
to arouse the working class from its torpor, in reality to play out social
frustrations and personal fantasies. One of the kidnappers of Aldo
Moro, a former Italian prime minister, later admitted that he had
watched too many films.

Yet Marxists and anarchists have accounted for a miniscule proportion of the terrorism and civil violence practiced in the world since
1970. From a Marxist perspective the past two decades have witnessed
not only a consolidation of capitalism but a regressive recycling of
mutinous energies into separatist nationalism (Ireland, the Basques,
Quebec, Sri Lanka) and religious fanaticism (Ireland again, Lebanon,
Iran, the Punjab). In black Africa, tribalism has frequently carried all
before it, obliterating the socialist perspectives of the anticolonial era.

The American Black Panthers were both Marxists (of a kind) and
black nationalists. They discovered not only the penalties of gunplay
against superior force but also the hostility of the ghetto population
toward a self-appointed people's police manned by arrogant youths. As
in other wars of liberation, it was easier for the Panthers to harass
"collaborators" than to defeat the enemy. In 1971, Huey Newton admitted: "We thought of ourselves as a vanguard . . . when we looked
around we found we were not the vanguard for anything, we lost the
favor of the black community and left it behind."

Black radicalism began to refocus its energies on coalition politics
and maximizing the electoral bargaining power of the black vote. The
initiative passed to a black leadership that spoke neither of Leninism
nor of separatism. Eldridge Cleaver returned to America in 1975, was

arrested, and was released on bail after a spell in prison. He denounced communism, called for a strong America, and appeared on a platform with his old persecutor, Ronald Reagan.

Today black poverty and deprivation persist, but so does the process of assimilation. Blacks began moving into the corporate structures. Black studies courses and institutes became less popular with students who no longer pursued a separatist identity with the vigor of their brothers during the Black Power era. The emphasis now was on equality of opportunity; indeed, behind the Black Panther rhetoric that was always it. In the mid-eighties Bobby Seale was interviewed on film by Daniel Cohn-Bendit while practicing his vocation as a cook and preparing a barbecue party for the mayor of Philadelphia. In retrospect he portrayed the Black Panther movement as a logical extension of Martin Luther King's SCLC: "The issue wasn't about violence or nonviolence. Oppression is violent." Panther separatism had also got lost in the mists of time: "We promoted a lot of politicians subsequently elected." Seale's radical spirit, however, was not quenched: "Chase Manhattan runs things, not the people." To raise money for various enterprises promoting social change, he was writing a cookbook.

The young rebels came of age, though with difficulty. When the Democratic Party held its 1972 Convention, Abbie Hoffman and Jerry Rubin were seated inside the hall. Camped in a nearby park, the last of the true believers complained that Jerry and Abbie had sold out. But Hoffman got into more trouble on a charge of drug dealing, jumped bail in March 1974, went into hiding near the Canadian border on the St. Lawrence River, and reportedly underwent plastic surgery three times. A fugitive for the remainder of the 1970s, his return cost him a few months in prison by prior agreement with the Justice Department. In 1987, he was back in the headlines as a participant in demonstrations and minor acts of civil disobedience directed against American policy and CIA operations in Central America. In April of that year, Hoffman and Amy Carter, the nineteen-year-old daughter of former President Jimmy Carter, and thirteen others were brought to trial in Massachusetts after obstructing CIA recruiters at Amherst the previous fall. The radical lawyer Len Weinglass, defense attorney in the Chicago 7 trial, cemented the link with the 1960s: what was now different was the defendants' acquittal.

Amy Carter herself had been born in 1968. In 1985 she had been arrested at the South African embassy in Washington, D.C., and again the following year at the IBM office in Providence, Rhode Island. A student at Brown University, she was studying feminist theory, plant biology, and American literature—a combination hard to imagine without the intervening counterculture of the sixties.

Twenty years after revolutionary Cuba fired the imagination of the New Left, Washington's hostility to Marxist Nicaragua aroused the energies of an aging Left, but in a less utopian mold. Following his successful military intervention in Grenada, President Reagan seemed pulled toward both his own Bay of Pigs in Nicaragua and his own Watergate (the revelation that congressional curbs on aid to the Nicaraguan contras had been circumvented in secret by the executive). Reviving the spirit of the Vietnam War Mobilization, 75,000 demonstrators marched in Washington on April 25, 1987. Two days later more than four hundred were arrested, including Daniel Ellsberg, when protestors blocked the entrance to the CIA building in Virginia.

But the underpinning assumptions of the sixties could not be revived. Contemporary protests against the impoverishment of the Third World are no longer inspired by the New Left's chiliastic vision of revolutionary renovation. The new elites of Africa and Asia have manipulated single-party constitutions to consolidate power and privilege. Completing his third decade in power, and life president in all but name, Fidel Castro has forfeited his hold on youthful imaginations.

It is white rule in South Africa that has recently awakened the student conscience from its long hibernation. Anti-apartheid has also served to reintegrate the race question with a wider challenge to American foreign policy; the Reverend Jesse Jackson brackets the defense of Nicaragua with the liberation of South Africa, as Martin Luther King finally linked Vietnam with civil rights at home. The anti-apartheid agitation of the eighties has generally preferred peaceful and constructive strategies designed to persuade colleges, public authorities, and businesses to disinvest—although violence returned to the Berkeley campus in April 1986, when police stormed barricades manned by students protesting the university's huge investment in companies doing business in or with South Africa. In clashes described as the most violent since the 1960s, nearly one hundred demonstrators were arrested and twenty-nine were injured. But sanctions and disinvestment have become the received wisdom of the Establishment. The National Conference of Catholic Bishops endorsed the policy. Only three months after the Berkeley clashes, California's governor, George Deukmejian, reversed his previous opposition to disinvestment, and the University of California's Board of Regents began to divest itself of $3.1 billion in South African related investments. One hundred major U.S. corporations and banks had responded to pressure by the end of 1986; so, too, had 20 states, 68 cities, and 119 universities. On October 2, the Senate followed the House in overriding a presidential veto on a congressional package of economic sanctions against South Africa.

In South Africa itself white students at the universities of Witwatersrand and Cape Town demonstrated vigorously against apartheid during the all-white parliamentary election campaign of April–May 1987, suffering campus invasions and beatings by the riot police. Even in the academic heartland of the Afrikaner culture, Stellenbosch, students and teachers demanding rapid political reform broke with a long tradition of allegiance to the ruling National Party.

There is, however, no disguising the triumph of the capitalist ethos in the advanced nations during the past twenty years. The popular materialism that re-elected Reagan, Thatcher, and Kohl has also infected the young. The loudest voice belongs to money. Even among the veteran radicals of the sixties, some have been bewitched.

In 1976 Jerry Rubin published *Growing (Up) at Thirty-Seven,* describing his voracious shopping expedition in the spiritual supermarket: gestalt theory, bioenergetics, jogging, health foods, hypnotism, acupuncture, Reichian therapy. In short, the "awareness" craze described by Rubin as "the inner revolution of the seventies." From the "awareness" craze it was a short step to the "success" craze. Rubin became a stockbroker on Wall Street and serviced Yuppies by setting up and "networking" their social events. Installed in an elegant New York apartment, severely barbered and wearing a crisp white collar, tie, and tailored sports jacket, Rubin was interviewed by Daniel Cohn-Bendit, to whom he proudly displayed the pill bottles and exercise routines of a health fetishist. Peddling a reconditioned *zeitgeist,* Rubin explained to his bemused interviewer that "the way to fight the state is to become the state. We, the doctors, dentists, managers—we are the state." What about the poor? "You go to talk to poor people, what do they want? They want to be successful. They don't want a revolution. We have to have a philosophy of success." But—protested Cohn-Bendit—had Rubin not burned dollar bills in the sixties? Rubin's response choked with contradictions. The sixties, when all the best ideas belonged to the Left, had been the time to show people that there was more to life than money; but now in the eighties, when all the best ideas belonged to the Right, such iconoclasm must yield to the pursuit of success. According to this bizarre logic, "the burning of money is now in people's consciousness"—Rubin taps his forehead—"and we have to build on that." By making money.

The leap from the radical Left to the radical Right is a validated motion among American intellectuals; the "God that Failed" seems to fail more drastically in the United States. Jerry Rubin stalls at endorsing Reaganism, although he believes that the invasion of Grenada in 1981 may have been necessary to prevent "another Cuba"—the revolutionary island he once loved. No such hesitations inhibit the conversion of former editors of *Ramparts,* David Horowitz and Peter Collier, who in their ultra-Left days had been roughed up by Governor Reagan's troopers in Berkeley and tear-gassed by the National Guard. "The system cannot be revitalized," they had written. "It must be overthrown. As humanly as possible, but by any means necessary." Horowitz, the author of a classic New Left text, *Containment and Revolution* (1967), voted for Reagan in 1984 in order to repudiate the sixties and "the self-aggrandizing romance with corrupt Third Worldism . . . the casual indulgence of Soviet totalitarianism . . . the hypocritical and self-dramatizing anti-Americanism which is the New Left bequest to mainstream politics." These reflections were published in *Encounter,* the magazine whose CIA connections *Ramparts* had documented in 1967. The culpable founding editor, Melvin Lasky, was still at *Encounter*'s helm in 1985 to publish the conversion of Horowitz and Collier.

In Europe such dramatic defections are less common. A handful of Red terrorists apart, few of the European leaders of the New Left later embraced the wilder fads of the seventies. Those who jettisoned their revolutionary romanticism generally settled for the mellower pastures of social democracy or environmental concern—the Greens. But a certain constancy of purpose also survived within the more Puritan platoons of the American New Left. Tom Hayden (who married the actress Jane Fonda) became active in the liberal wing of the Democratic Party and founded the Campaign for Economic Democracy. Although his primary campaign for the Senate in 1976 was unsuccessful, he was elected to the California legislature. Questioned about his socialist past, Hayden replied: "The radicalism of the sixties has become the common sense of the seventies." And: "We made a mistake then—we came ten years too early." By surrendering to machine politics Hayden lost few enemies; in 1980 Abbie Hoffman wrote of his co-defendant in the Chicago conspiracy trial, "He had a movement reputation for sending others to face the cops while he backed out the back door. He avoided all collective decisions where he could be outvoted. He was absolutely without humor."

The eclipse of the New Left in Europe after 1968–69 did not initially diminish Daniel Cohn-Bendit's radicalism. More than ever convinced that the dormant proletariat must be aroused, in the early seventies he joined the young intellectuals who were attempting to revolutionize the workers of the Opel car plant in Russelheim, near Frankfurt. Later he taught preschool children, but became disillusioned with "anti-authoritarian" education—"if that means that the kids do whatever they like."

The leaders of the German SDS went their various ways. Helmut Schauer, chairman from 1964 to 1967, became an official in the metal workers' trade union. In 1986 he chaired a reunion of 1,000 former members of the SDS, including Cohn-Bendit, under the self-mocking conference title of Wonderful Weather. Pinned to the speaker's podium was a famous old SDS poster showing Marx, Engels, and Lenin with the caption: "Everyone's talking about the weather. We're not." A regretted absence at the reunion was Rudi Dutschke, who had died in Denmark ten years after being shot down in Berlin—and after a shameful expulsion from Britain by the Heath government in 1971, despite universal support from his academic supervisors at Cambridge. Missing also were those members of the SDS who had later embraced the terrorism of the Red Army Faction, including Ulrike Meinhof and Andreas Baader. Cohn-Bendit told the conference that "without their turn to violence we could not have switched so firmly to the philosophy of non-violence."

The Green movement in Germany (founded in 1979 and an electoral force since 1983) inherited many of the demonstrational strategies of the New Left, including mass charges against nuclear installations, siege tactics, and the most effective form of televised demonstration, the resolutely passive sit-down under attack from police water hoses and drag-away snatch squads. The German Greens are the only significant political force in Western Europe today who can lay claim to a substantial portion of the New Left legacy.

In a four-part television film, *Revolution Revisited,* Cohn-Bendit has charted his own journey into middle age. "Today I am a militant of the German Green Party but I hate the countryside. I love the aggressivity of the big city." He lives in Frankfurt and edits an "alternative libertarian" magazine. Filmed in a Paris bar in conversation with a veteran of 1968, he was interrupted by a well-groomed young woman who had been eavesdropping. "We don't need a label to exist," she said. "The idea of bosses doesn't mean anything. There are bosses everywhere—we're all bosses." Identifying herself as a marketing manager for whom 1968 had been a "holiday," she explained how she could smoke a joint any time, make money, feel good, not give a damn about politics, and still make sense of life.

From Paris to Peking students have recently resurfaced as a significant political force. In France the demonstrations of December 1986 persuaded the Chirac government to withdraw university reforms quite similar to those proposed by the Gaullist government in 1967. The student agitation of 1986 again triggered sporadic working-class strike action, notably among transport and electricity workers as well as among schoolteachers, but the union confederations were divided and no concerted movement to stop work took place. Strikes and demonstrations by workers and students in Spain during 1987 were directed against the economic policies of a socialist government, rather than against the authoritarian regime of the late General Franco.

Within the Communist world, the most dramatic changes have taken place in China following the death of Mao, the trial of the Gang of Four, President Teng Hsiao-ping's Four Modernizations, and the official repudiation of the Cultural Revolution. The Peking students who congregated on January 5, 1987, to burn the Peking *Daily* represented the liberal avant-garde of the Chinese intelligentsia—a far cry from the xenophobic sloganeering of the Red Guards. The Chinese students had arrived at the position of their Polish and Czechoslovak colleagues twenty years earlier. But the reaction of the Chinese leadership indicated that it was Gomulka rather than Dubček who was alive and well in Peking. The octogenarian Teng cracked down on the demonstrations, dismissed leading liberals and delivered two speeches claiming that foreigners were more interested in China's stability than in its human rights record. He also praised General Jaruzelski's iron-fisted suppression of the Solidarity movement in Poland.

Poland has endured the upheavals of 1970, 1976, and 1980–81. The emergence of Solidarity, a beacon for democracy, was met with repression and martial law after a brief interlude of semitolerance. In Czechoslovakia the Husák regime has for two decades sustained the winter which followed the Prague Spring. Novotný's police state soon reclaimed its inheritance. Intellectuals prominent in 1968 suffered again, ten years later, for participation in the Charter '77 movement. On January 6, 1987, the playwright and prominent Chartist Václav Havel, imprisoned from 1979 to 1982, was prevented from leaving his house to attend a press conference.

On March 11, 1987, Havel was among a hundred supporters who filled the courthouse when the chairman of the Czechoslovak Jazz Section, Karel Srp, was sentenced to sixteen months in prison. He and four others were found guilty of "economic crimes"—in reality, publishing and distributing uncensored literature after the dissolution of the Musicians' Union in 1980. The Jazz Section's friends boldly cheered the defendants and sang John Lennon's "Give Peace a Chance." A visit by Soviet leader Mikhail Gorbachev to Czechoslovakia the following month raised hopes that the new spirit of *glasnost* (openness) might present a powerful challenge to Prague's arthritic conservatism, but in May the appeal court confirmed the sentences of the Jazz Section.

The growth of unemployment among college graduates in the West has fostered a more cautious, conforming, competitive attitude among students. As the economy reduces its demand for graduate skills, the students become less, not more, radical: self-confidence yields to anxiety. Student Power is a slogan asleep. Despite greater student representation on academic committees, the administrators and faculty remain in control. The freeze on academic appointments since the mid-seventies has also cooled the radicalism of the faculties; the professors recruited during the sixties may be more radical than their juniors, though there is no shortage of conversions, both to the Right and the middle ground.

The emphasis on relevance and consumer demand in colleges reached its peak in the mid-seventies: not only did black studies and women's studies flourish, but Third World studies, Comparative Imperialism, and the like. In 1975 a master's degree in women's studies could be obtained in 112 American colleges and universities. Since that time there has been a revival of traditional academic values, a rebirth of narrative history, and a weakening of the all-powerful, post-sixties "critical sociology."

No excessive cynicism is involved in imagining the conduct of a university or corporation president who was an ardent member of the New Left twenty years earlier. What lessons may he or she have learned? When challenged, do not make an issue of authority and avoid punishing the ringleaders. Keep the police out of it. After a decent interval—the rebels need to feel they have won a hard-fought victory—accept many of their demands. In principle. Allow time and inertia to dissipate the principle into practicality. Even if a few ultraradicals pursue their demands, their following will decline as the rebels experience the inconvenience of their own disruption. Our president will know that participatory democracy is a part-time activity much eroded by the claims of the pleasure principle: food, sleep, sex, rock, and poetry among them. For the president, on the other hand, the exercise of power in an emergency overrides every competing claim on his or her energies.

The major radical movement to have emerged during the past twenty years is feminism. As we have seen, the women's movement was both a product and a rejection of the New Left. While there are socialist feminists as well as nonsocialists, it must be obvious that a crusade on behalf of half of the human race against the other half inevitably subverts the universal radicalism of the New Left (not overlooking its unthinking male chauvinism). It also places a large question mark on such universalism—as did Black Power ideology—by locating *the* primary exploitation in gender (or race). But the gains have been great: more women in work they desire, more women in positions of authority, a spreading awareness of sexist assumptions. On the whole, however, white males, middle-aged or elderly, still hold the levers of political and corporate power.

The battle for sexual-erotic liberty in life, literature, and the arts has been largely won in the West, despite inevitable backlashes. AIDS is now the deterrent, not Judge Argyle. On the West Coast of the United States, the Gay Rights movement has fully politicized itself, running candidates for office. "Equal opportunities" has become the watchword of progressive employers, and there are laws to enforce it.

The long-term impact of the New Left has been "cultural" in the broad sense. The distinctive challenge of 1968 to the State, the political system, and corporate capitalism was defeated. The counterculture became acceptable, provided it abandoned its political cutting edge. The spirit of the Movement shows itself in local action, tenants' associations, ecology groups, squatters' communes. There are more "people's lawyers" today, more "people's architects," and not a few business people keen to place entrepreneurial skills at the service of poor communities. Journalists and media people who grew to maturity in the sixties are less respectful of state power and state secrecy. The Greenpeace antinuclear and antipollution vessels are today's guerrillas. But greens are not reds. Live-Aid for starving Africa is a far cry from "Viva Che!"

Drugs, hair of any length, and extravagant costumes came to stay. Sheer style no longer upsets middle-aged sensibilities as it did twenty years ago, though the fear of heroin and cocaine (crack) remains acute. Long hair and jewelry became absorbed into machismo; it even goes with executive briefcases. Many wires got crossed, with hip tycoons everywhere. We may expect a professedly gay heavyweight champion of the world. Rock music still hypnotizes the young and "top of the charts" is top of the world. Capitalist culture became more eclectic: the ideal TV talk show confronts Miss America with a militant feminist, and then has the former reveal she's a "feminist," too. So that's all right. This constant cultural neutering of dissent, the eclecticism which treats all ideas as short-lived merchandise, has reinforced the triumph of the profit motive and the idolization of market forces in the era of Reagan and Thatcher.

CHRONOLOGY
OF MAIN EVENTS
——— 1967-1969 ———

1967

January

Cultural Revolution continues in China (officially launched in August 1966). Universities, institutes, and scientific research cease to function. Few books available apart from Chairman Mao's "Thoughts." Teachers are pilloried and sent to May Seventh farm schools for re-education. Spreading violence and faction fighting, as Red Guards "struggle against the black line of Liu Shao Ch'i."

Student violence at the London School of Economics. A porter dies of a heart attack.

March

London School of Economics is occupied for nine days.

April

1,500 draft cards are burned or returned in United States. Wave of antiwar demonstrations in American universities. Half a million people take part in marches.

United States bombs Haiphong.

Arrest and trial of Régis Debray in Bolivia. (November: sentenced to 30 years' imprisonment.)

Greek military seizes power in coup before scheduled May elections. Arrest of George and Andreas Papandreou.

May

Russell-Sartre War Crimes Tribunal opens in Stockholm after de Gaulle refuses permission to hold it in Paris.

Black Panthers demonstrate at California State legislature, Sacramento.

Muhammad Ali (Cassius Clay) is sentenced to five years in prison for refusing induction.

June

Disturbances in West Berlin follow the shooting of a demonstrator during a state visit by the Shah of Iran.

Six-Day War between Israel and Arabs. (New Left will adopt Palestinian cause.)

Black rioting in Florida, then in Atlanta and Buffalo.

July

Black rioting in Kansas City. 23 killed in Newark riots. 36 killed and $1 billion damage in Detroit riots.

Dialectics of Liberation Conference at Roundhouse, London.

Organization of Latin American Solidarity Conference opens in Havana. Che Guevara elected honorary president in absentia. Call for seizure of power through armed struggle in the region.

September

Newark Black Power Conference attended by 1,100 delegates. Huey Newton is jailed for murder. Eldridge Cleaver's *Soul on Ice* is published in the United States. 5,000 attend New Politics Conference in Chicago.

Thieu elected president of South Vietnam.

Anti-University of London is founded.

October

The United States bombs Haiphong harbor.

Stop the Draft Week in Oakland and New York. Picketing of induction centers. 2,000 draft cards turned in. Sit-in at University of Michigan to stop military research.

50,000 take part in Pentagon demonstration.

Baltimore 4 destroy draft files.

First Grosvenor Square anti-Vietnam demonstration in London. Vietnam Solidarity Campaign is founded in Britain.

Che Guevara is killed in Bolivia.

Students and police clash in Prague. Struggle between reformers (Dubček) and conservatives (Novotný) at Central Committee meeting.

Students riot in Madrid.

November

Student strike at *cité universitaire* of Nanterre in the suburbs of Paris.

Student insurrection in Italy begins at Trento.

Berkeley mill-in by 1,000 students.

December

300 arrested during New York antidraft demonstrations.

Violent demonstrations at San Francisco State College.

1968

January

Alexander Dubček elected first secretary of Czechoslovak Communist Party, replacing Novotný.

Daniel Cohn-Bendit confronts French minister of youth at Nanterre.

Madrid's Faculty of Philosophy and Letters is closed.

Demonstrations in Japan against U.S.S. *Enterprise.*

Havana Cultural Conference attended by European and American intellectuals.

Johnson's State of Union Message reiterates readiness to talk to North Vietnam on San Antonio formula of September 1967.

U.S. intelligence vessel *Pueblo* is seized by North Koreans.

Communist Tet offensive begins in Vietnam. Vietcong hold part of U.S. embassy in Saigon for six hours.

Martin Luther King, Jr., launches Poor People's Campaign.

Dr. Benjamin Spock, Reverend W. Sloane Coffin, and colleagues indicted by a federal grand jury for conspiracy to counsel evasion and violation of the Universal Military Training and Service Act.

Disruption at Aston University, Birmingham.

Polish students and intellectuals protest banning of a play by Mickiewicz.

February

Bobby Seale and other Black Panthers are arrested.

Battle of Hue and siege of Khe Sanh in Vietnam.

Senator Eugene McCarthy contests New Hampshire primary against President Johnson.

Commonwealth Immigration Act in Britain. Unrest at Leicester University.

March

Student riots in Italy lead to closure of Rome University.

Czechs commemorate 20th anniversary of death of Jan Masaryk. Novotný replaced by Svoboda as president of Czechoslovakia.

Zengakuren (Sampa Rengo) students fight police at Nurita, Japan, in opposition to new airport.

10,000 join Vietnam Solidarity March in London.

Polish students invade Ministry of Culture, followed by students' protest strike against police treatment of demonstrators. Authorities retaliate with expulsions, arrests, and anti-Zionist campaign.

General Westmoreland is replaced as U.S. commander in Vietnam by Creighton Abrams. Partial bombing halt.

Robert Kennedy enters Democratic primaries.

March 22 Movement is formed by Cohn-Bendit and colleagues in France, following continuing unrest at Nanterre.

Dubček is criticized by Soviets, Poles, and East Germans at Dresden Conference.

University of Madrid is closed by Franco after violence.

McCarthy does well in New Hampshire primary and defeats Johnson in Wisconsin by 57 to 35 percent. In Gallup poll, only 36 percent of American people support Johnson's conduct of affairs. Johnson announces he will not seek his party's renomination.

April

Johnson calls partial bombing halt of North Vietnam.

Smrkovský is elected chairman of Czech National Assembly. Party publishes Action Program, promising fundamental reforms; rehabilitation of political prisoners; freedom of press, assembly, and religion.

Martin Luther King is assassinated in Memphis. Nationwide black rioting follows; National Guard called out. Eldridge Cleaver is arrested during a shoot-out.

German student leader Rudi Dutschke is shot. Anti-Springer demonstrations in Germany and in London.

Anti-American riots in Tokyo; 110 injured, 179 arrested.

Nanterre is closed as a result of mounting student unrest.

Columbia University is occupied by SDS and black students; police clear buildings with extreme violence.

Heavy fighting takes place as Red Guard factions battle at Tsinghua University, Peking.

Enoch Powell delivers speech in Birmingham warning of "rivers of blood." London dock workers march in support.

Protracted rioting begins in Madrid as students and workers join forces.

May

Poor People's Campaign, led by Rev. Ralph Abernathy, marches from Memphis to Washington, D.C.

Clashes in Britain between students and Powellite workers.

Czechoslovak government presses ahead with reforms.

Police occupy Sorbonne in Paris. Ten days of demonstrations by students follow. Night of the barricades; extreme police brutality. Students reoccupy Sorbonne. General strike spreads throughout France; workers occupy factories. Cohn-Bendit is expelled from France. Clashes in provincial cities. Attack on the Bourse. Tension between libertarian action committees and Communists. Grenelle Agreement rejected by workers. De Gaulle calls general election; Gaullist counter-demonstration is held.

Unrest at Essex University.

Vietnam peace talks begin in Paris. (NLF delegation arrives in November; procedural wrangling till end of year.)

American forces lose 562 in a single week. Spock trial opens in Boston. Catonsville 9 burn draft records.

Demonstrations against West German Emergency Laws.

Italian general election ends Center-Left coalition government.

Eugene McCarthy fails in Indiana and Nebraska, but wins in Oregon. He and Kennedy are neck-and-neck in California primary. Both trail behind Hubert Humphrey in delegate votes.

Unrest at universities of Hull, Bradford, and Leeds. Hornsey and Guildford colleges of art are occupied. Dismissals of staff and students follow in the autumn.

Occupation at San Francisco State College.

June

Kennedy-McCarthy television debate. Kennedy wins California 45–42 and is immediately assassinated in Los Angeles by Jordanian Arab.

Student demonstrations in Belgrade.

Police enter Tokyo University in attempt to end occupation. Disruption of Japan's largest university, Nihon, and of Keio University, Tokyo.

Czechoslovak government warns against excessive liberalization, rejects "bourgeois pluralism," and insists that Communist Party must retain power. "Two Thousand Words" manifesto appears in Prague, calling for democratic socialism. Warsaw Pact military maneuvres in Czechoslovakia. National Assembly abolishes censorship.

French strikes end. Police storm occupied factories. Left-wing groups banned. In general election, Gaullists secure absolute majority in National Assembly.

Berkeley students clash with police.

July

Spock trial; four out of five defendants are convicted.

Power struggle between radical factions at Chio University, Japan.

Prague refuses to attend Warsaw meeting of Warsaw Pact. Soviet bloc leaders condemn Czechoslovak revisionism, and warn that it is their common concern. Czech army commanders demand revision of Warsaw Pact. Czechoslovak and Soviet leaders meet at Čierná.

Students clash with police in Mexico.

August

Meeting of Soviet bloc leaders in Bratislava virtually concedes Czechs' right to pursue own path.

At Miami, Richard Nixon completes comeback by securing Republican nomination, defeating Rockefeller and Reagan. Chooses Spiro Agnew as running mate. Rioting and gunfire in black Miami during Convention. George Wallace, running as third-party candidate, spearheads racist backlash.

Student occupation of Tokyo University enters third month. Bloodshed on Kyushu University campus.

Warsaw Pact armies invade Czechoslovakia. Dubček and colleagues are taken prisoner and flown to Moscow. Czech National Assembly and

Extraordinary Party Congress declare occupation illegal. Soviet Union fails to form puppet government, but imposes secret Moscow Agreement ending liberalization. Dubček returns to preside over "Prague Autumn."

30,000 join protest demonstration in Mexico City.

Democratic National Convention in Chicago. Liberal forces split and Humphrey is nominated. Running battles between Mayor Daley's police and young demonstrators. National Guard is called out.

September

Huey Newton is sentenced. Violence between police and Black Panthers intensifies.

Milwaukee 14 destroy 10,000 draft records.

Cohn-Bendit is involved in Frankfurt riots.

Chancellor of Nihon University, Japan, capitulates before 10,000 students.

Heavy fighting and many deaths in Mexico on eve of Olympics.

October

Law reforming French university system leads to renewed demonstrations.

Black American athletes give Black Power salute from Olympic rostrum.

Trials of Polish students and intellectuals begin.

Jacqueline Kennedy marries Aristotle Onassis.

Tokyo students demonstrate for return of Okinawa from United States. Tokyo University president resigns.

Vietnam Solidarity Campaign march in London. London School of Economics is occupied and "closed." Occupations at Birmingham and Manchester universities. Prosecutions and fines follow demonstrations at Oxford.

Johnson calls for bombing halt on eve of presidential election.

GIs march in San Francisco; case of the Presidio 27.

November

Nixon elected president.

Eldridge Cleaver jumps bail, flees United States.

Teachers' strike and student anarchy at San Francisco State College. Black unrest at Cornell. Over 1,200 campus arrests in United States.

Tokyo University in turmoil.

New York teachers' strike ends.

Czechoslovak students strike in support of national freedom.

Occupation at Birmingham University.

December

Occupation of student union and Senate House at Bristol University.

Armed blacks occupy Cornell's administration building.

Further disruption in French universities and schools.

1969

January

Suicide of Jan Palach in Prague, followed by national day of mourning.

Franco imposes martial law and closes Madrid University; 300 arrests.

Agitation at LSE over school's holdings in South Africa. Radicals smash iron control gates; arrests, injunctions, prosecutions. LSE is closed.

Further violence at the Free University of Berlin and the Sorbonne.

Vietnam peace talks open (again) in Paris.

February

34 students expelled from University of Paris.

400 soldiers stage peace march in Seattle.

Riotous demonstrations in European capitals against Nixon's visit.

March

Acting President Hayakawa establishes control at San Francisco State College after violent clashes and mass arrests.

New occupation of LSE. Select Committee of Commons harassed at University College of Swansea, then Essex.

Anti-Soviet demonstrations in Czechoslovakia result in final Soviet ultimatum threatening new military occupation.

April

Dubček replaced by Gustáv Husák as first secretary of Czechoslovak Party. Press censorship reimposed.

Two LSE lecturers dismissed.

Antiwar demonstration in New York.

Continuing violence at Cornell. Harvard SDS occupies University Hall; police are called in. Columbia occupied again.

De Gaulle resigns after referendum.

May

North Vietnam rejects Nixon's eight-point offer of military withdrawal.

People's Park conflict at Berkeley reaches violent climax.

Berrigan brothers and others burn draft records.

High school rebellions in United States. Black Power violence at New York's City College. Columbia reoccupied.

June

Fort Dix Stockade rebellion.

SDS Convention in Chicago splinters after PLP challenge. Weathermen emerge.

Pompidou elected president of France.

July

Third World strike at Berkeley.

August

Weathermen bombings begin.

Woodstock Rock Festival.

Anti-Soviet demonstrations in Prague on anniversary of invasion. Husák government takes emergency powers. Purge continues.

September

Death of Ho Chi Minh.

Chicago 8 conspiracy trial begins.

Dubček expelled from Czechoslovak Party Presidium.

General election in West Germany results in SPD-FDP coalition led by Chancellor Willy Brandt.

October

Antiwar demonstrations (Moratorium) in United States and at army bases. Weathermen "Days of Rage" in Chicago.

November

New police offensive against Panthers.

New Mobilization antiwar demonstration in Washington.

December

Weathermen conference in Flint, Michigan.

Nixon announces a further withdrawal of 50,000 troops following a previous withdrawal of 25,000.

1970

January–March

American SDS disintegrates as Weathermen bombings intensify.

April–May

United States attacks Cambodia. Massive student demonstrations. National Guard shoot students at Kent State and Jackson State.

REFERENCES AND
——— SOURCES ———

Abbreviations used in the references:

BD *Black Dwarf*
CSM *Christian Science Monitor*
DT *Daily Telegraph*
FT *Financial Times*
IHT *International Herald Tribune*
IT *International Times* (renamed *IT*)
LM *Le Monde*
LLF *Les Lettres françaises*
LTM *Les Temps modernes*
NLR *New Left Review*
NS *New Statesman*
NYRB *New York Review of Books*
NYT *New York Times*
PR *Partisan Review*
ST *Sunday Times* (London)
S.Tel *Sunday Telegraph*
Times *The Times* (London)
TLS *Times Literary Supplement*

PROLOGUE: THE PENTAGON

For contemporary reports of the Pentagon demonstration, see Norman Mailer, *The Armies of the Night,* New York, 1968; Andrew Kopkind, "The Siege of the Pentagon," *NS* 27 October 1967; Louis Heren, "10,000 Besiege the Pentagon," *Times* 23 October 1967.

On the Grosvenor Square demonstration: *Times* 23 October 1967.

CHAPTER 1: THE VIETNAM WAR—TET

Comprehensive, if partisan, on the war is Gabriel Kolko, *Vietnam: Anatomy of a War 1940–1975,* London, 1986, pp. 305–10. (New York, 1968)

On Tet: *I. F. Stone's Weekly* 19 February 1968.

On the War Crimes Tribunal: *Prevent the Crime of Silence: Reports from the Sessions of the International War Crimes Tribunal Founded by Bertrand Russell,* ed. by Peter Limqueco & Peter Weiss, London, 1971, p. 240.

On Vietnam in the 1950s: Dwight D. Eisenhower, *Mandate for Change,* London, 1963, p. 372. (New York, 1963). Eisenhower's speech is quoted in John Gerassi, *North Vietnam: A Documentary,* London, 1968, p. 10. (New York, 1968)

On military policy and atrocities in Vietnam: Gerassi, *North Vietnam,* pp. 76, 85, 137, 188; *Prevent,* pp. 112, 171–73, 245, 270; Orville & Jonathan Schell quoted by Noam Chomsky in a preface to *Prevent,* pp. 11–12.

Johnson's fears are quoted by Arthur Schlesinger, Jr., *Robert Kennedy and His Times,* London, 1978, p. 742. (Boston, 1978)

CHAPTER 2: THE ANTIWAR MOVEMENT: AMERICA, EUROPE, AND
JAPAN

On student opinion: S. M. Lipset, *Rebellion in the University: A History of Student Activism in America,* London, 1972, pp. 39–43. (Boston, 1972)

On the VDC in California: Paul Jacobs & Sol Landau, *The New Radicals,* New York, 1966, p. 254.

On the Old Left and the war: Irving Howe, *Steady Work: Essays in the Politics of Democratic Radicalism, 1953–1966,* New York, 1966, pp. 96–199.

On the War Crimes Tribunal: *Prevent,* pp. 185, 363–65.

Conor Cruise O'Brien's statement is in his foreword to Gerassi, *North Vietnam,* p. 28.

Nigel Young's comment on Vietnam is from his *An Infantile Disorder? The Crisis and Decline of the New Left,* London, 1977, p. 173.

On visits to North Vietnam: Susan Sontag, *Trip to Hanoi,* London, 1969 (New York, 1968); Andrew Kopkind, *NS* 31 May 1968; Julius Lester, *Search for the New Land,* New York, 1969, p. 127; Daniel Berrigan, *Night Flight to Hanoi,* New York, 1968, p. 45.

On television coverage of the war: Robert MacNeil, "The News on TV and How It is Unmade," *Harper's* October 1968.

On anti-American student demonstrations in Japan and the radical student organizations: *Japan Times* 4, 20 January; 2, 18, 22 March; 10, 12 July; 11 November 1968. Also: *NYT* 12 January, 27 October 1968; *IM* 19 June 1968.

Speculative is Murray Sayle, "Japan's Secret Student-backers," *ST* 30 November 1969. In general, see Fred Halliday, "Students of the World Unite," in A. Cockburn & R. Blackburn (eds.), *Student Power,* London, 1969, pp. 294–98.

CHAPTER 3: THE NEW POLITICS OF THE YOUNG

Jürgen Habermas, *Toward a Rational Society: Student Protest, Science and Politics,* London, 1977, p.28.

On the contrasting moods of the 1950s and 1960s: Jack Newfield, *A Prophetic Minority,* New York, 1966, p. 41; Massimo Teodori, *The New Left:*

A Documentary History, London, 1970, p. 412 (New York, 1970); see also: James O'Brien, "The New Left 1967–68," *Radical America,* November–December 1968, pp. 42–43.

On the nuclear threat: Theodore Roszak, *The Making of a Counter Culture,* London, 1968, p. 47. (New York, 1969)

Staughton Lynd's NL strategy is quoted in Jacobs & Landau, *New Radicals,* p. 314. For the Old Left view, see Irving Howe, *A Margin of Hope: An Intellectual Biography,* London, 1983, pp. 291–94. (New York, 1982)

On SDS: Howe, *Steady Work,* p. 60.

On the CIA connection: Christopher Lasch, "The Cultural Cold War," in *The Agony of the American Left,* London, 1970 (New York, 1969); Diana Trilling, "Liberal Anti-Communism Revisited," in *We Must March My Darlings,* New York, 1977, p. 61.

For Dwight Macdonald's experience of revolution, see "An Exchange on Columbia," *NYRB* 11 July 1968, p. 42. A rejoinder: Edward Shils, *The Intellectuals and the Powers and Other Essays,* Chicago, 1972, p. 265. See also Trilling, *We Must March,* pp. 56, 59, 156, 148.

On Irving Howe, Tom Hayden, and New Left violence: Howe, *A Margin of Hope,* pp. 305–6, 308, 310–11, 326; *Times* 6 December 1968. On Herbert Marcuse, see Teodori, *New Left,* pp. 468–73; Herbert Marcuse, *An Essay on Liberation,* London, 1969, pp. 35, 36, 56, 68. (Boston, 1969)

On the January 1968 Havana Cultural Congress: Andrew Salkey, *Havana Journal,* London, 1971, p. 24; Alexander Cockburn, "Culture in Havana," *NS* 26 January 1968; Arnold Wesker, *NS* 4 May 1968.

For American perceptions of Cuba, see Mailer, *The Armies,* pp. 87–88; Howe, *Steady Work,* p. 201.

For Susan Sontag on Cuba, see Marianne Alexandre (ed.), *Viva Che,* London, 1968, p. 109; Susan Sontag, "Some thoughts. . . ." in Ramparts, *Divided We Stand,* New York, 1970, pp. 164–70.

For uncritical enthusiasm, see Julius Lester, *Revolutionary Notes,* New York, 1968, p. 177, as quoted by Paul Hollander in *Political Pilgrims,* New York, 1981, p. 239.

CHAPTER 4: CHILDREN OF PLEASURE—THE COUNTERCULTURE

Joan Baez's "To Bobby", from her album *Come from Shadows*, is quoted by Klaus Mehnert, *The Twilight of the Young: The Radical Movement of the 1960s,* London, 1976, pp. 261–2 (New York, 1978); also Ellen Willis, "The Sound of Bob Dylan," *Commentary* November 1967, p. 74.

On the Beatles and Rolling Stones: *Times* 20 February 1968 and 1 August 1967; Hunter Davies reviewed by Philip French, *NS* 4 October 1968; *BD* 15 October 1968; Alan Brien, *NS* 26 July 1968.

On folk and rock music: Morris Dickstein, *Gates of Eden: American Culture in the Sixties,* New York, 1977; Simon Frith, *The Sociology of Rock,* London, 1978, p. 145.

On Mick Jagger as revolutionary: Tony Sanchez, *Up and Down with the Rolling Stones,* New York, 1979, p. 122; *BD* 15 October 1968.

On students and drugs: Kenneth Keniston, *Youth and Dissent: The Rise of a New Opposition,* New York, 1971, pp. 235–38.

Generally on drugs: Brian Inglis, *The Forbidden Game: A Social History of Drugs,* London, 1975, pp. 189, 204; Tony Sanchez, *Up and Down,* p. 75; Warren Hinckle, "The Coming of the Hippies," in Ramparts, *Conversations with the New Reality, Readings in the Cultural Revolution,* New York, 1971, p. 10.

On LSD: Tom Wolfe, *The Electric Kool-Aid Acid Test,* New York, 1969; Dr. Hoffman interviewed in *Everyman,* BBC-TV 13, 16 November 1986; Timothy Leary quoted in Peter Lomas, "Acid Bath," *NS* 20 February 1970 and by Hinckle, "Coming of Hippies," p. 19. See also Timothy Leary, *The Politics of Ecstasy,* New York, 1968; Trilling, "Celebrating with Dr. Leary," in *We Must March,* pp. 13–38. On Leary's arrest and escape: David Zane Mairowitz, *The Radical Soap Opera,* London, 1976, pp. 185, 240, 270.

Jerry Rubin on heroin, etc.: *Do It!,* London, 1970, p. 168. (New York, 1970)

A key text on (and of) the underground is Jeff Nuttall, *Bomb Culture,* London, 1968. (New York, 1968)

IT on psychedelics is quoted in Robert Hewison, *Too Much: Art and Society in the Sixties,* London, 1987, p. 128. Also on drug culture: Joseph Berke & Calvin Hernton, *The Cannabis Experience,* London, 1974, pp. 257–58; (New York, 1974); Joseph Berke, *Counter Culture,* New York, 1969; Nuttall, *Bomb Culture,* p. 142; William S. Burroughs, "Kicking Drugs: A Very Personal Story," *Harper's* July 1967, p. 40; Peter Stanshill & David Zane Mairowitz, *BAMN: Outlaw Manifestos and Ephemera, 1965–70,* London, 1971, p. 45; Jerry Rubin, *We Are Everywhere,* New York, 1971, p. 118.

On R. Laing and the virtues of the counterculture: Nuttall, pp. 225–27, 212–16, 148–49.

On *IT* and the New Left: David Widgery, *The Left in Britain,* London, 1976, p. 378.

Jim Haynes describes the late sixties in *Thanks for Coming! An Autobiography,* London, 1984.

On obscenity charges against *IT* and *Oz:* John Sutherland, *Offensive Literature: Censorship in Britain, 1960–1982,* London, 1982, p. 99.

For sex and the New York theatre: *Times* 26 March 1969; see also Margot Hentoff, "Notes from Above Ground," *NYRB* 22 May 1969; Nora Sayre, "Rapture Unwrapped," *NS* 12 December 1969.

A sociological approach to the counterculture is provided by Stuart Hall (ed.), *Resistance through Rituals: Youth Subcultures in Post-War Britain,* London, 1975. Lighter is Mark Crispin Miller, "What Happened in the Sixties?" *NYRB* 4 August 1977, pp. 17–21.

The quotation from Louis Kampf is from his "Notes Toward a Radical Culture," in Priscilla Long (ed.), *The New Left,* Boston, 1969, pp. 424, 432.

The classic text is Roszak, *Making of Counter Culture.*

On the Free School of New York: Berke, *Counter Culture,* p. 225. Raymond Mungo is quoted in Teodori, *New Left,* pp. 385–87.

CHAPTER 5: INSURRECTION IN EUROPE, I

Poland

For the student riots and allied events of February and March 1968, see *IHT* 1 February, 20 March 1968; *Guardian* 12, 14, 20, 21, 26 March 1968; *NS* 13 March 1968; *Times* 2, 9, 11, 13, 14, 16, 20 March 1968; *DT* 14 March 1968; *FT* 14, 15, 20 March 1968; *Observer* 17 March 1968; *LM* 27 March 1968; K. S. Karol, "The Czech Spring Could Spread," *NS* 22 March 1968.

For the aftermath, dismissals, anti-Semitic campaign, and purge, see: *Guardian* 4 May, 13 July 1968; *LM* 11 April; 3, 5, 12 May; 28 June 1968; *Observer* 5, 19 May 1968; *NYT* 21, 24, 29 April; 19 May; 15 July 1968; *Times* 31 May 1968; *IHT* 15 May 1968; see also Jacek Kuron & Karol Modzelewski, *Solidarinodsc: The Missing Link,* London, 1982.

Italy

For the period from late 1967 to the general election of May 1968, see *LM* 2, 17 March, 12 April 1968; *NYT* 10 February; 2, 17 March; 25 April 1968; *Corriera della Sera* 17 February, 28 April 1968; *NYT* 4 March, 25 April 1968; *S. Tel.* 28 April 1968; Bruce Renton, "Violence and Apathy in Italy," *NS* 17 May 1968.

For two Communist perspectives on the student movement, see Rossana Rossanda, "Les etudiants comme sujet politique," *LTM* No. 266–67, August–September 1968, pp. 206–30; Maria Antonietta Macciocchi, *Letters from Inside the Italian Communist Party to Louis Althusser,* London, 1974, pp. 269–70, 275.

For the events of the summer, see *Times* 30, 31 May; 10 June; 11 September 1968; *NYT* 4, 7, 9 June 1968; *LM* 18 June 1968; *Guardian* 3 June, 16 September 1968; *IHT* 3, 5 June 1968.

In general, see Halliday, in Cockburn & Blackburn, *Student Power,* pp. 303–7.

Spain

For the student riots up to April 30, and the student movement in the 1960s, see *NYT* 12, 17, 21 January; 4 February; 28 April 1968; *DT* 21 January; 7 February 1968; *Times* 15 December 1967; 22 January; 16, 19 February 1968; *LM* 9, 21, 26, 30 January; 20, 22, 24 February; 1, 8, 12 March; 22 April 1968; *IHT* 12, 13 January; 7, 16, 26, 28 March; 5 April 1968; *Guardian* 16 January 1968.

For the period May–June, see *IHT* 20 May 1968; *DT* 24 May 1968; *NYT*

30 May 1968; *LM* 6, 23 May 1968; *Guardian* 3 June 1968; *Times* 5, 6 June 1968.

In general, see Halliday, in Cockburn & Blackburn, *Student Power,* pp. 307–10.

Nanterre

See Daniel & Gabriel Cohn-Bendit, *Obsolete Communism: The Left-Wing Alternative,* London, 1968, p. 50 (New York, 1969); Herve Bourgès (ed.), *The Student Revolt,* London, 1968, pp. 131–32 (New York, 1968); Alain Touraine, *Le Mouvement de Mai ou le communisme utopique,* Paris, 1968, pp. 35, 102–4.

Britain (Vietnam)

On the March 17 demonstration, see *Times* 19, 22 March 1968.

On CND and the New Left, see Frank Parkin, *Middle Class Radicalism: The Social Bases of the British Campaign for Nuclear Disarmament,* Manchester, 1968; Michael Rustin, "The New Left and the Present Crisis," *NLR* May–June 1980. The May Day Manifesto is quoted in Mehnert, *Twilight,* p. 158.

On the Dutschke-Springer demonstration, see *Guardian* 16 April 1968; *Observer* 21 April 1968; *Tribune* 19 April 1968.

On Tariq Ali, see his *1968 and After,* London, 1978, pp. 140, 198; also *BD* 1, 15 May; 5, 19 July 1968.

Britain (Race)

See *NYT* 16 February 1968; *Times* 27, 28 February; 26 April; 15, 20 June 1968; *NS* 1 March 1968.

CHAPTER 6: INSURRECTION IN EUROPE, II

Germany

On the attempt on Dutschke and the Peter Brandt case: *NYT* 13–16, 20 April 1968; *Times* 2 January, 18 April 1968; *Observer* 14 April 1968; *Guardian* 16, 19 April 1968; *ST* 21 April 1968; *CSM* 19 April 1968; *IHT* 21 April 1968; *Sun* (London) 17 April 1968; *LM* 18 April 1968; Corinna Adam, "The Riddle of the Berlin Riots," *NS* 19 April 1968; *Guardian* 14 December 1968.

On the first quarter of the year in Berlin and the Federal Republic: *Times* 21 January; 14, 22 February 1968; *Observer* 11, 18 February 1968; *NYT* 10 February; 13 March 1968; *IHT* 24 February 1968; *LM* 12 March 1968; *Neue Zurcher Zeitung,* 13 March 1968; Corinna Adam, "West Germany's Young Ones," *NS* 29 March 1968.

Habermas's comments are in *Toward a Rational Society,* pp. 16–19, 24,

32, 45. For a detailed study of the Berlin student movement, see Serge Bosc & Jean-Marcel Bouguereau, "Le Mouvement des etudiants berlinois," *LTM* No. 265, July 1968, pp. 41–48.

On students and workers: Mehnert, *Twilight,* p. 298; *Times* 31 May 1968.

On the Kommune and future terrorism: Mehnert, *Twilight,* p. 108; Jillian Becker, *Hitler's Children,* London, 1977, pp. 27, 44, 54–56; Berke, *Counter Culture,* pp. 121–42.

On the Emergency Laws and the riots of May: *Times* 13 May, 28 June 1968; *CSM* 27, 28 May 1968; *LM* 29 June 1968; *Guardian* 11 July 1968.

Belgium

See *IHT* 15 April, 1 July 1968; *Guardian* 23, 24, 30 May; 5 December 1968; *NYT* 25, 26 May; 5 December 1968; *LM* 17 June 1968.

Yugoslavia

See D. Plamenic, "The Belgrade Student Insurrection," *NLR* No. 54, March–April 1969, pp. 61–71; *Times* 5, 6, 7, 10 June 1968; *LM* 23 April 1968; *Guardian* 4 June 1968; *NYT* 4, 7, 12, 20 (Jonathan Randal) June 1968; *Radio Free Europe Research* (Slobodan Stankovic), 4, 5 June 1968; Lajos Lederer, *Observer* 9 June 1968; Anatole Shub, *IHT* 13 June 1968.

CHAPTER 7: THE USA: THE DEMOCRATIC PRIMARIES AND DRAFT RESISTANCE

First-hand accounts of the Kennedy campaign are found in Jack Newfield, *Robert Kennedy: A Memoir,* London, 1970, p. 204; Schlesinger, *Robert Kennedy,* pp. 835, 756.

On the controversy over Al Lowenstein: Richard Cummings, *The Pied Piper: Allard Lowenstein and the Liberal Dream,* New York, 1985; Hendrik Hertzberg, "The Second Assassination of Al Lowenstein," *NYRB* 10 October 1985; "Allard Lowenstein: An Exchange," *NYRB* 30 January 1986.

On the campaign in the New Year: *Times* 9 February, 23 March 1968; David Halberstam, "Travels with Bobby Kennedy," *Harper's* July 1968; David Halberstam, "Politics 1968," *Harper's* March 1968; Jeremy Lardner, "Reflections on the McCarthy Campaign," *Harper's* April, May 1969. Robert Lowell's lines are quoted by Schlesinger, *Robert Kennedy,* p. 821.

On Kennedy's campaign style: *Time* 5 April 1968. On Kennedy's choices and his appeal: Newfield, *Robert Kennedy,* pp. 245, 258; Andrew Kopkind, "All Fool's Eve," *NS* 5 April 1968. On the cartoonists' LBJ: *Harper's* February 1968.

On Vietnam after the partial bombing halt: *Times* 20 May, 27 July 1968; *NYT* 11 June 1968.

Kennedy in Indiana is described by Halberstam in *Travels.*

On the Democratic party machine: *Times* 24 April 1968.

On enmity between Kennedy and the liberal intellectuals: Schlesinger, *Robert Kennedy*, pp. 896, 907; Newfield, *Robert Kennedy*, p. 268.

On the California TV debate: *Times* 3 June 1968.

The class and racial patterns of conscription are discussed in Young, *An Infantile Disorder*, p. 364; Blair Clark, "What Kind of Army?," *Harper's* September 1969. See also John Gregory Dunne, "The War that Won't Go Away," *NYRB* 25 September 1986 (Mr. Dunne reviews *Chance and Circumstance: The Draft, The War and The Vietnam Generation*, by Lawrence M. Baskir & William A. Strauss, New York, 1986).

On draft resistance during 1967–69, see Mehnert, *Twilight*, p. 35; Jessica Mitford, *The Trial of Dr. Spock*, London, 1969, p. 21 (New York, 1969); Michael Ferber & Staughton Lynd, *The Resistance*, Boston, 1971, p. 281.

The impact of General Hershey's initiative is discussed in Mitford, *The Trial*, p. 55.

For the mood early in 1968, see Nora Sayre, "Fighting the Draft," *NS* 22 March 1968.

On those who went to prison: Long, *The New Left*, p. 458; Michael Lerner, "Anarchism and the Counter-Culture," in D. Apter & J. Joll (eds.), *Anarchism Today*, London, 1971, p. 49. (New York, 1972)

A portrait of Coffin at work is in Mitford, *The Trial* p. 39. From the protagonist himself: William Sloane Coffin, *Once to Every Man: A Memoir*, New York, 1977, p. 310.

For the prosecution of Spock, see Mitford, *The Trial*, p. 271; Joseph W. Bishop, Jr., "The Reverend Coffin, Dr. Spock, and the ACLU," *Harper's* May 1968, p. 58.

On the defense's trial tactics: Letter from J. Rubin, *NYRB* 10 April 1969; on the outcome, *NS* 13 February 1970.

For Kennan's onslaught on civil disobedience, see George F. Kennan, *Democracy and the Student Left*, London, 1968, pp. 18, 107, 167–69. (Boston, 1968)

On the constitutional arguments for civil disobedience: Sayre, "Fighting the Draft."

The Noyd case: Jeremy Larner, "The Court-Martial of Captain Noyd," *Harper's* June 1968.

On rebellious servicemen: Vera Brittain, "GIs Fight for Peace," *NS* 9 May 1969, p. 643.

On the Catonsville 9: *I. F. Stone's Weekly*, 21 October 1968. The best account of the Catholic ultra-Resistance is by Francine du Plessix Gray, *Divine Disobedience: Profiles in Catholic Radicalism*, London, 1970, pp. 140, 160–70. (New York, 1970). See also Francine du Plessix Gray, "The Ultra Resistance," *NYRB* 25 September 1969.

Daniel Berrigan's sentiments are from *America is Hard to Find*, London, 1973, pp. 21, 51. (New York, 1972)

On the run, Daniel Berrigan was interviewed by Robert Coles, *NYRB* 11 March 1971.

For a brilliant account of the Milwaukee 14, see Gray, "The Ultra Resistance."

CHAPTER 8: THE USA: BLACK POWER

On the riots after King's assassination: Louis Heren, *Times* 6 April 1968; Alan Brien, *NS* 12 April 1968.

On King's turn to the northern cities and to the left: David Halberstam, "The Second Coming of Martin Luther King," *Harper's* August 1967; C. Vann Woodward, "The Dreams of Martin Luther King," *NYRB* 15 January 1987, p. 8.

On the bugging and FBI surveillance of King: Schlesinger, *Robert Kennedy*, p. 878; Woodward, "The Dreams," p. 6; David Wise, "The Campaign to Destroy Martin Luther King," *NYRB* 11 November 1976.

On the Poor People's Campaign: *I. F. Stone's Weekly*, 15 April 1968.

On the Muslims and Malcolm X: E. U. Essien-Udom, *Black Nationalism: The Rise of the Black Muslims in the USA*, London, 1966, p. 78; *The Autobiography of Malcolm X*, London, 1965 (New York, 1965); Stokely Carmichael & Charles V. Hamilton, *Black Power: The Politics of Liberation in America*, London, 1968. (New York, 1967)

On the poverty programs and the gangs: Tom Wolfe, *Mau-Mauing the Flak Catchers*, London, 1971. (New York 1970)

On Black Power theory, see Lasch, *Agony of the American Left*, pp. 122–56; *PR* Spring 1968, reporting the views of Hoffman on p. 108, Kelley on p. 217, Mailer on p. 219. See also Peter Schrag, "The New Black Myths," *Harper's* May 1969, p. 40.

On Eldridge Cleaver's *Soul on Ice* (New York, 1968), see Wolfe, *Mau-Mauing*, pp. 127–29.

On Stokely Carmichael, see Jack Newfield, *A Prophetic Minority*, pp. 107–8; on Carmichael's conflict with Cleaver, Teodori, *The New Left*, pp. 276–79, 287–92; Peter Buckman, *The Limits of Protest*, London, 1970, pp. 252–53; Hollander, *Political Pilgrims*, p. 202.

On friction between the Panthers and the police: *Times* 6 September 1968; Nora Sayre, "America on the Eve of Race Revolution," *NS* 2 May 1969; Murray Kempton, "The Panthers on Trial," *NYRB* 7 May 1970.

Eyewitness accounts of the National Conference for New Politics include: Richard Blumenthal, "New Politics at Chicago," *Nation* 25 September 1967, pp. 274–76; Martin Peretz, "The American Left and Israel," *Commentary* November 1967, pp. 27–28; Anthony Howard *NS*, 13 June 1969.

On Cleaver's flight and exile: Kathleen Cleaver, "Concerning My Husband," and Eldridge Cleaver, "An Open Letter to Stokely Carmichael," both in Ramparts, *Divided We Stand*.

Foreign observations of white liberal masochism are conveyed by Ben Whitaker, MP, letter to *Times* 23 February 1968; also Irving Wardle's theatre column in *Times* 14 February 1968.

The radical chic issue is variously contested in: Tom Wolfe, *Radical Chic*, London, 1971; Jason Epstein, "Journal du Voyeur," *NYRB* 17 December 1970, p. 4.

On *Big Time White Buck:* Irving Wardle, *Times* 14 February 1968; Robert Kotlowitz's comment on Kramer's film: *Harper's* January 1968.

The controversy over William Styron's *The Confessions of Nat Turner*, London, 1968: the quoted sentence is on p. 428; see also Eugene Genovese, "The Nat Turner Case," *NYRB* 12 September 1968; William H. Grier & Price M. Cobbs, *Black Rage*, New York, 1968; Cleaver, *Soul on Ice*.

CHAPTER 9: COLUMBIA

On President Kirk and the New Left, see Steve Halliwell, "Columbia: An Explanation," in Long, *The New Left*, p. 208; Jerry L. Avorn, *University in Revolt: A History of the Columbia Crisis*, New York, 1968, p. 25.

The Linda St. Clair incident: *Times* 13 April 1968.

On the gymnasium issue and SDS: Daniel Bell, "Columbia and the New Left," *The Public Interest*, No. 13, Fall 1968, pp. 64–65; *Times* 2 May 1967; Trilling, "On the Steps of Low Library," in *We Must March*, p. 141.

On the occupation of Hamilton Hall and Low Library: Bell, "Columbia and the New Left," p. 72.

Tom Hayden is discussed by Newfield in *A Prophetic Minority*, pp. 121, 142; Jacobs & Landau, *The New Radicals*, p. 34; Teodori, *New Left*, p. 346; Newfield, *Robert Kennedy*, pp. 303–4; Schlesinger, *Robert Kennedy*, pp. 770, 915; Trilling, *We Must March*, p. 143; Larner, "Reflections on McCarthy," p. 79; Howe, *A Margin of Hope*, p. 293; Murray Kempton, "Three Who Didn't Make a Revolution," *NYRB* 7 February 1971, pp. 37–39.

On tensions within the strike committee: Bell, "Columbia and the New Left," p. 97.

On documents discovered in Kirk's files: Avorn, *University in Revolt*, pp. 64, 68, 111, 120–21.

On outside sympathizers: Bell, "Columbia and the New Left," p. 92; Stephen Spender, *The Year of the Young Rebels*, London, 1969, p. 4. (New York, 1969)

Herbert Marcuse's statement is in *PR* Summer 1968, p. 375; see also Trilling, *We Must March*, p. 93.

Mark Rudd and Dotson Rader are quoted in Avorn, *University in Revolt*, pp. 292, 373–75; *Times* 29 May 1968; Trilling, *We Must March*, p. 102; Lipset, *Rebellion*, p. xxi; Spender, *The Year of the Young Rebels*, p. 28.

On student opinion and Ad Hoc Faculty Committee proposals, see Bell, "Columbia and the New Left," pp. 75–79.

For the black militants: *PR* Summer 1968, pp. 376–77, 380; Trilling, *We Must March*, p. 87.

For a variety of faculty views: *PR* Summer 1968, pp. 354, 361–62, 367, 389; Allan Silver, "Who Cares for Columbia?" *NYRB* 30 January 1969, p. 22.

On the police bust, strike, suspensions, and second occupation: Bell, "Columbia and the New Left," pp. 83, 84, 89; "An Exchange on Columbia," *NYRB* 11 July 1968, p. 41.

On commencement and counter-commencement: Trilling, *We Must March,* p. 114.

Daniel Bell's views: Bell, "Columbia and the New Left," pp. 87, 91, 93, 95, 100; other faculty critical of the rebels, including Gay and Lionel Trilling: *PR* Summer 1968, pp. 366–69, 360; Diana Trilling, *We Must March,* pp. 99, 122; Herbert A. Deane, "Reflections on Student Radicalism," in Avorn, *University in Revolt,* pp. 287–90.

The September international students' meeting at Columbia is reported in *BD* 15 October 1968.

On new penalties in 1969, see Columbia parents' letters, *NYRB* 11 September 1969.

On events at Tsinghua, China, see Harrison E. Salisbury, *To Peking and Beyond: A Report on the New Asia,* London, 1973, pp. 32–36. (New York, 1973)

CHAPTER 10: PRAGUE SPRING

The most complete general narrative is H. Gordon Skilling, *Czechoslovakia's Interrupted Revolution,* Princeton, 1976.

On the 1967 Writers' Congress: Robin Alison Remington, *Winter in Prague: Documents on Czechoslovak Communism in Crisis,* Cambridge, Mass., 1969, p. 4. On the Czechoslovak student movement: Milan Hauner, "Czechoslovakia," in Margaret S. Archer (ed.), *Students, University and Society,* London, 1972, pp. 36–56.

On the displacement of Novotný: Pavel Tigrid, *Why Dubček Fell,* London, 1971, pp. 19–20; Remington, *Winter in Prague,* pp. 21, 26.

The Action Program is printed in Remington, *Winter in Prague,* p. 105.

On replacing security personnel: Tigrid, *Why Dubček Fell,* p. 64.

The Piller Commission Report was published in the West: Jiří Pelikán (ed.), *The Czechoslovak Political Trials, 1950–1954,* Stanford, 1971.

On the public desire for justice and rehabilitations: Z. A. B. Zeman, *Prague Spring,* London, 1968, pp. 134–40.

The government begins to warn against irresponsible use of freedom: David Caute, "Czechoslovakia in the Balance," *NS* 21 June 1968, p. 826.

On the abolition of censorship: *Times* 28 June 1968; Remington, *Winter in Prague,* pp. 182–83; Tariq Ali, *1968,* p. 38.

Havel's arguments in favor of pluralism: see Václav Havel, *The Memorandum,* London, 1967 (New York, 1968); Havel, "Politics and the Theatre," *TLS* 28 September 1967.

Eduard Goldstücker's interview: "Lessons of Prague: A Conversation with Edward Goldstücker," *Encounter* August 1971, p. 80.

On the Czech student outlook: Spender, *Year of the Young Rebels,* pp. 65–67; David Mercer, "Czechs Mated," *BD* 19 July 1968. The World Youth Festival is reported by Peter Broderick in *Times* 13 August 1968.

The claims of non-Communist parties to an independent existence are discussed in William Shawcross, *Dubček,* London, 1971, p. 225. (New York, 1971)

On K 231 and KAN: Milan Hauner, letter to the author, February 1987; Remington, *Winter in Prague,* p. 318.

Ivan Sviták's criticisms of the government are found in his *Czechoslovak Experiment, 1968–1969,* New York, 1971. For public opinion, see Shawcross, *Dubček,* p. 229.

On class attitudes and wages, see Jiří Pelikán, "The Struggle for Socialism in Czechoslovakia," *NLR* January–February 1972, p. 20; Zdeněk Mlynář, *Night Frost in Prague,* London, 1980, pp. 128–30. (New York, 1980)

On government resistance to pluralism: Tigrid, *Why Dubček Fell,* pp. 48, 198.

"Two Thousand Words," a new translation, *TLS* 18 July 1968, pp. 747–48.

Czechoslovakia's relationship with the USSR and the Warsaw Pact is discussed in Remington, *Winter in Prague,* pp. 61–62, 189–92, 214–23, 308, 400; *Times* 19 July 1968; Shawcross, *Dubček* p. 170; Tigrid, *Why Dubček Fell,* pp. 83–84; Vladimir Kusin, *From Dubček to Charter 77,* Edinburgh, 1978, p. 38.

CHAPTER 11: FRANCE: STUDENTS AND WORKERS

Quattrochi's comment on the CRS is in Angelo Quattrochi & Tom Nairn, *The Beginning of the End,* London, 1968, p. 23.

The university system and varying student attitudes are discussed by Touraine, *Le Mouvement,* p. 24; Sartre's view of the competitive exam system is in "An Interview with Sartre," *NYRB* 26 March 1970, p. 30.

On the demonstration of May 6–10: Cohn-Bendit, *Obsolete Communism,* pp. 61–62, 120; Quattrochi & Nairn, *The Beginning,* p. 48; Jean-Jacques Lebel, "The Night of 10 May," *BD* 1 June 1968; Paul Johnson, "The Night of the Long Batons," *NS* 17 May 1968.

For a Gaullist view of the riots, see Raymond Aron, *The Elusive Revolution: Anatomy of a Student Revolt,* London, 1970, p. 9. (New York, 1969)

On police brutality: Mervyn Jones, "De Gaulle's Police State in Action," *NS* 5 July 1968.

On the decision to occupy the Sorbonne: Peter Brooks, "Fourth World," *PR* Winter 1969, pp. 15–16.

For the PCF line, see Louis Aragon and Pierre Daix in *LLF* 15–21 May 1968; Richard Johnson, *The French Communist Party Versus the Students,* New Haven, 1972, pp. 82, 96–97, 103–5, 108–9; Daniel Singer, *Prelude to Revolution: France in May 1968,* London, 1970, pp. 116, 122, 133. (New York, 1970)

On the occupation of the Sorbonne: Patrick Seale & Maureen McConville, *Observer* 19 May 1968; Edgar Morin, *La Brèche,* Paris, 1968, p. 27; Touraine, *Le Mouvement,* p. 48.

On SNESup and the faculty: Singer, *Prelude,* pp. 96–97; Bourgès, *Student Revolt,* p. 50; Aron, *Elusive Revolution,* pp. 125, 176–85.

On faculty reform and examinations, see Alfred Willener, *The Action-Image of Society,* London, 1970, pp. 37–65 (New York, 1971); Bourgès, *Student Revolt,* p. 90; *LLF* 15–21 May; 7 June 1968.

On the *lycée* action committees: *Times* 20, 21, 25 May 1968.

On posters and wall newspapers: Cohn-Bendit, *Obsolete Communism,* p. 80.

On the Situationists: one text is cited by Buckman, *Limits of Protest,* pp. 248–50; another by Tom Nairn, "The Last Comedy of Capitalism," in Quattrochi & Nairn, *The Beginning,* p. 111.

On structuralism and the May events, Richard Johnson, *French Communist Party,* pp. 87, 84. The classic Situationist text is Guy Debord, *Society of the Spectacle,* Detroit, n.d. See also Richard Gombin, "The Ideology and Practice of Contestation . . . in France," in Apter & Joll, *Anarchism Today,* p. 21.

The Bordeaux "Vandals" are quoted in Stanshill & Mairowitz, *BAMN,* p. 276.

On the pleasures of talking: Willener, *Action-Image,* p. 27.

On artists and intellectuals: Singer, *Prelude,* p. 166; Morin, *La Brèche,* pp. 29–30; Simone de Beauvoir, *All Said and Done* (*Tout compte fait*), London, 1977 (Paris, 1972), p. 460. (New York, 1974)

Sartre's position: "An Interview with Sartre," *NYRB* 26 March 1970; Ronald Hayman, *Writing Against: A Biography of Sartre,* New York, 1986, pp. 393, 418.

For the French film industry in 1968, see Roy Armes, *The French Cinema,* London, 1985.

Hostile to it all were Aron, *Elusive Revolution,* p. 124, and Jacques Ellul, *Autopsy of Revolution,* New York, 1971.

The student delegation to Renault (Boulogne-Billancourt) is described in Quattrochi & Nairn, *The Beginning,* pp. 60–61.

On ORTF, see *LLF* 7 June 1968.

The Nantes region is described in Cohn-Bendit, *Obsolete Communism,* pp. 30–31, and a mimeographed article from Nanterre.

A Trotskyist view of workers' aspirations is: Ernest Mandel, "The Lessons of May 1968," *NLR* November–December 1968, pp. 22–23.

Inside Renault at Boulogne-Billancourt: William Millinship, *Observer* 2 June 1968.

CHAPTER 12: FRANCE: AGITATORS AND POLITICIANS

For the mood of the last week in May, see Mervyn Jones, "That Week in Paris," *NS* 7 June 1968; Aron, *Elusive Revolution,* pp. 25, 33.

On Daniel Cohn-Bendit's version of May 24: Cohn-Bendit, *Obsolete Communism* p. 71. Other versions are: Spender, *Year of the Young Rebels*, pp. 40–56; Halliday, "Students of the World Unite," p. 320; *LM* 28 May 1968.

On provincial unrest: *LM* 27–29 May 1968. In general from *Le Monde* on the last 10 days of May, see: Frédéric Gaussen, "Les comités d'action," 24 May 1968; Jean Lacouture, "Une république libertaire," 21 May 1968; Pierre Viansson-Ponte, "Participation, le mot-miracle," 23 May 1968; "Nouvelles scènes d'émeute à Paris et en province," 26–27 May 1968; Joanine Roy, "Le raidissement ouvrier," 29 May 1968; Jean Lacouture, "Charléty: tout est possible," 29 May 1968; Josée Doyère, "Usine occupée," 30 May 1968; "Les Champs-Elysées en blue, blanc, rouge," 1 June 1968.

Geismar on the March 22 Movement: Bourgès, *Student Revolt*, p. 54.

Touraine on Cohn-Bendit: Touraine, *Le Mouvement*, p. 114–15.

For Cohn-Bendit's anarchism and anti-Leninism, see Cohn-Bendit, *Obsolete Communism*, pp. 200–1, 220–22; see also Morin, *La Brèche*, p. 47.

On the various *groupuscules:* Richard Johnson, *French Communist Party*, pp. 91–93, 163–67, 174–78, 181.

On the action committees: Morin, *La Brèche*, p. 17 and following; Geismar and Cohn-Bendit on the committees and socialist perspectives, in Bourgès, *Student Revolt*, pp. 52–63, 68–80; Cohn-Bendit, *Obsolete Communism*, p. 104.

On the situation after Grenelle: *Nouvel observateur* 28 May 1968.

On anarchism in France: Daniel Guérin, "Mai, une continuite, un renouveau," *Le fait public* 6 May 1969; Jean Maitron, "Anarchisme," *Le mouvement sociale* October–December 1969.

Cohn-Bendit's scorn for the Charléty meeting: Cohn-Bendit, *Obsolete Communism*, pp. 72–73.

Raymond Aron's despair: Aron, *Elusive Revolution*, p. 122.

On the Gaullist counter-demonstration: Quattrochi & Nairn, *The Beginning*, p. 155; Spender, *Year of the Young Rebels*, pp. 57, 117; Brooks, "Fourth World," in *PR*, p. 18; Mervyn Jones, *NS* 7 June 1968.

For a general analysis close to the events, see Edgar Morin, Claude Lefort, Jean-Marc Coudray, *Mai 1968: La Brèche*, Paris, 1968; Touraine, *Le Mouvement*, p. 54; *Tribune du 22 Mars* 9 June 1968; see also *Nouvel observateur* 26 June–2 July 1968.

On the role of the PCF and the CGT during the strikes: Richard Johnson, *French Communist Party*, p. 82; André Barjonet, "CGT 1968," *LTM* July 1968, p. 103; Eric Hobsbawm writing in *BD* 1 June 1968; Eric Hobsbawm, "Birthday Party," *NYRB* 22 May 1969; Althusser appears in Macciocchi, *Letters from Inside*, pp. 304–16. Cohn-Bendit's view of the CGT and PCF is in Cohn-Bendit, *Obsolete Communism*, pp. 161–67.

For socialist perspectives on where the strikes might have led, see Mandel, "Lessons of 1968"; André Gorz, "The Way Forward," and André Glucksmann, "Strategy and Revolution in France," all in *NLR* November–December 1968, pp. 22, 49–55, 83–115.

On the end of the strikes and the repression in June: K. S. Karol, "France: The Violence Grows," *NS* 14 June 1968; Cohn-Bendit, *Obsolete Communism*, p. 75.

De Beauvoir, *All Said,* p. 463, describes the last days of the occupied Sorbonne.

On the ORTF strike: "ORTF La véritable action civique," *LLF* 19 June 1968; Andrew March, "France's TV Purge," *NS* 9 August 1968.

CHAPTER 13: FILMS, SEX, AND WOMEN'S LIBERATION

Sontag's essay on Goddard is in Susan Sontag, *Styles of Radical Will,* London, 1969, pp. 149–50, 152, 158, 160, 164, 168, 181–82 (New York, 1969); Quotation is from Jean-Luc Godard, *Made in USA,* London, 1967, p. 50.

Jacques Ellul's attack on Godard is in Ellul's *Autopsy of Revolution,* p. 182. Gerald Rabkin's appreciation of Godard, letter to the author, February 1987.

On Warhol: *Times* 11 June 1969. On Ginsberg and Warhol: Jane Kramer, *Paterfamilias: Allen Ginsberg in America,* London, 1970, pp. 177–79 (New York, 1969). See also Robert Mazzocco, "aaaaaa . . . ," *NYRB* 24 April 1969, p. 34; Robert Hughes, "The Rise of Andy Warhol," *NYRB* 18 February 1982.

On engagement and disengagement: Robert Jay Lifton, "Protean Man," *PR* Winter 1968, p. 23.

Jodorowsky's "happening" is described in Nuttall, *Bomb Culture.*

On the "chicks" syndrome, see Kramer, *Paterfamilias,* p. 45; Berke, *Counter Culture,* pp. 121–42; Mehnert, *Twilight,* pp. 240–41; Richard Neville is quoted by Mervyn Jones, *NS* 20 February 1970.

For the general male chauvinism of the New Left, see James Gilbert, "The Left Young and Old," *PR* Summer 1969, p. 354; Stanshill & Mairowitz, *BAMN,* p. 84; Jerry Rubin, *We Are Everywhere,* New York, 1971, pp. 110, 131; Tom Hayden, *Trial,* London, 1971, pp. 70, 109; see also *NYRB* 16 January, 27 March 1969.

Jaffe and Dohrn are reprinted in Teodori, *New Left,* pp. 355–58. The activities of WITCH are reported in Betty & Theodore Roszak, *Masculine/ Feminine: Readings in Sexual Mythology and the Liberation of Women,* New York, n.d., p. 260. The Miss America campaign is reported in Stanshill & Mairowitz, *BAMN,* p. 203. Susan Brownmiller and Barbara Koster are interviewed by Daniel Cohn-Bendit in *Revolution Revisited: A Journey with Dany the Red,* a film by Steven de Winter and Daniel Cohn-Bendit, Belbo Film Productions, 1987. Disillusioned movement women are quoted by Mehnert, *Twilight,* p. 68; Robin Morgan is reprinted in Roszak & Roszak, *Masculine/ Feminine,* pp. 241–44

CHAPTER 14: RADICAL THEATRES

On the Open Space company in 1968: Gerald Rabkin, letter to the author, January 1987.

Barbara Garson, *MacBird!,* New York, 1967; on Bread and Puppet, see interview with Peter Schumann, *The Drama Review* Winter 1968.

On Peter Brook's *US: NS* 16 February 1968; *Times* 17 February 1968; Hilary Spurling, "Mr. Brook's Lemon," *Spectator* 21 October 1966; Arnold Wesker in *US,* London, 1968, pp. 139–43; Charles Marowitz, "The Royal Shakespeare's 'US'," *Tulane Drama Review* Winter 1966, pp. 173–75.

On Peter Weiss: Michael Stone, "Weiss/Vietnam," *NS* 12 December 1968.

On radical theatre and the Living Theatre: Robert Brustein, "The Third Theater Revisited," *NYRB* 13 February 1969; Robert Brustein, *Making Scenes,* New York, 1981, pp. 66–69; Robert Brustein, "Monkey Business," *NYRB* 24 April 1969; Irving Wardle, *Times* 21 October 1967; Benedict Nightingale, "Anarchs," *NS* 20 June 1969; Julian Beck, "Money Sex Theatre" in Berke, *Counter Culture,* pp. 91–94. Gerald Rabkin, "The Return of the Living Theatre: Paradise Lost," *Performing Arts Journal* Summer 1968, p. 8.

Joseph Chaikin is quoted from *TDR. The Drama Review* Winter 1968, p. 147. See also Elizabeth Hardwick, "Notes on the New Theater," *NYRB* 20 June 1968.

On La Mama's *Tom Paine:* Philip French, *NS* 27 October 1967; Charles Marowitz, *Confessions of a Counterfeit Critic: A London Theatre Notebook 1958–71,* London, 1973, pp. 133–34.

John Calder's protest against antitext theatre: "The Theatre of Noise," *Flourish* (RSC broadsheet) Autumn 1968.

On Nora Sayre's adventures: "Further Off Broadway," *NS* 5 April 1968; "New York Therapy Theatre," *NS* 6 September 1968; Sayre in *NS* 6 September 1969.

Philip French on Ed Berman: *NS* 26 July 1968; Benedict Nightingale on Grotowski: *NS* 30 August 1968.

On *Hair:* Robert Kotlowitz, *Harper's* September 1968; Nightingale in *NS* 4 October 1968; Benn Levy in *Tribune* 18 October 1968; Marowitz, *Confessions,* p. 144. John Osborne speaks his mind: *Observer,* 7 July 1968.

On British stage censorship: Sutherland, *Offensive Literature,* pp. 79–87. On John Arden: "Who's for a Revolution? Two Interviews with John Arden," and Richard Gilman, "Arden's Unsteady Ground," both in *Tulane Drama Review* Winter 1966, pp. 41–53, 62.

Mercer and Arden visit Essex University: Widgery, *The Left in Britain,* p. 354.

CHAPTER 15: THE DEMOCRATS AT CHICAGO

The scene in St. Patrick's is described by Norman Mailer, *Miami and the Siege of Chicago,* New York, 1968, p. 194; the funeral train by Schlesinger, *Robert Kennedy,* pp. 1–2.

On the summer campaign and opinion polls: *Times* 1 July, 23 July, 2 August 1968; on Humphrey, *Times* 25 June 1968.

At the Republican Convention: Mailer, *Miami,* p. 71.

On Wallace: Andrew Kopkind, "The Real Significance of Wallace," *NS* 2 August 1968; Tom Wicker, "George Wallace: A Gross and Simple Heart,"

Harper's April 1967, pp. 45–46; Charles Longstreet Weltner, "The Heritage of Wallace," *NS* 12 September 1968.

The complaining policeman is in Robert Coles, "A Policeman Complains," *NYT Magazine* 13 June 1971, pp. 11, 75.

The manuevres at the Democratic Convention: *Times* 22 August 1968; Mailer, *Miami,* pp. 104, 106.

On McCarthy and McGovern: Larner, "Reflections on McCarthy." McCarthy on Czechoslovakia: *Times* 29 August 1968. Defeat of the peace plank: Mailer, *Miami,* pp. 154–55. Daley's Convention operation: Mailer, *Miami,* pp. 195–96. Mailer on Humphrey, *Miami,* p. 113.

CHAPTER 16: THE OTHER CHICAGO—YIPPIES AND PIGS

For Ginsberg at the March 1968 press conference: Jason Epstein, "The Chicago Conspiracy Trial: Allen Ginsberg on the Stand," *NYRB* 12 February 1970, p. 28.

On West Coast hippies: Richard Schlatter, "California Letters," *PR* Winter 1968, pp. 110–13; Kramer, *Paterfamilias,* p. 46.

On the Diggers: Nora Sayre, "Among New York's Diggers," *NS* 24 November 1967; Stanshill & Mairowitz, *BAMN,* p. 51; Kramer, *Paterfamilias,* pp. 102–4; "The Digger Papers," *The Realist* August 1968; Sol Stern, "Altamont: Pearl Harbor to the Woodstock Nation," Ramparts, *Conversations with the New Reality,* p. 65.

Oz, March 1968, no. 11, is quoted by Buckman, *Limits of Protest,* pp. 245–46.

The New York Yippie leaflet is from Stanshill & Mairowitz, *BAMN,* p. 107.

Rubin on Jerry Rubin: *Do It!,* p. 256.

Hoffman on Abbie Hoffman: *PR* Spring 1968. Also Abbie Hoffman, *Woodstock Nation: A Talk-Rock Album,* New York, 1969, pp. 11–12.

The June 1968 bust: Rubin, *Do It!,* p. 171; Rubin, "An Emergency Letter to my Brothers and Sisters in the Movement," *NYRB* 13 February 1969.

Rubin burning money: Rubin, *Do It!,* pp. 111, 114, 138.

John Gerassi arms the people in "Imperialism and Revolution in America," in David Cooper (ed.), *The Dialectics of Liberation,* London, 1968, p. 93; Gerassi "grooves" in Berke, *Counter Culture,* pp. 64–71.

On the Yippies' dada heritage and pop culture: Gary Wills, "The Making of the Yippie Culture," *Esquire* November 1969.

On the Werewolves: Mairowitz, *Radical Soap Opera,* p. 227.

On Mayor Daley: David Halberstam, "Daley of Chicago," *Harper's* August 1968; see also Hayden, *Trial,* pp. 13–18.

The "Vote Pig" manifesto is reported by Mailer, *Miami,* pp. 127–31.

Chicago street scenes: Mailer, *Miami,* pp. 134, 138, 140.

Ginsberg's credo is in *IT* January 1967. He is widely quoted in Kramer, *Paterfamilias.*

On riots and police violence: Sol Lerner is quoted by Mailer, *Miami,* pp. 142–43, 168; Nicholas von Hoffman is quoted by Mailer, *Miami,* pp. 139–40; see also Mailer, *Miami,* p. 149; Larner, "Reflections on McCarthy," p. 92.

Two middle-aged views of police and rebels: *Times* 31 August, 4 September 1968; *I. F. Stone's Weekly,* 9 September 1968.

Violence within the Democratic Convention: Mailer, *Miami,* p. 168; Paul O'Dwyer, letter in *NYRB* 10 April 1969; John Leonard, "The Democratic Happening," *NS* 6 September 1968.

On Daley's counterclaims and public opinion: *Times* 2, 17 September 1968. The National Commission on Violence report: *Times* 2 December 1968.

CHAPTER 17: CZECHOSLOVAKIA—THE SOVIET INVASION

The diplomatic background to the Soviet invasion is recounted in Karen Dawisha, *The Kremlin and the Prague Spring,* Berkeley, 1984. The most important source for events inside Czechoslovakia after the invasion is: Robert Littell, *The Czech Black Book,* London, 1969 (New York, 1969); See also Kusin, *From Dubček,* p. 329.

An eyewitness account of the Czech Presidium meeting is Mlynář, *Night Frost,* pp. 146–49, 179–85.

On the arrests of the leaders on August 21: Shawcross, *Dubček,* p. 182; and Mlynář (who was with Dubček), *Night Frost,* pp. 112–14.

On the initial radio transmission: Tigrid, *Why Dubček Fell,* pp. 99, 105.

Ladislav Mnacko's description of Bratislava is in *The Seventh Night,* London, 1969, pp. 17–18, 43. (New York, 1969)

On Soviet troops and the maneuvres of the collaborators, *Black Book,* pp. 32, 36, 61, 72; Kusin, *From Dubček,* p. 22.

Czech Radio broadcasts appeals of professional groups: *Black Book,* p. 46. On clandestine radio activity, see letter from Edwin Hayes in Vienna, *NS* 30 August 1968; Mnacko's attempt to broadcast is described in Mnacko, *Seventh Night,* pp. 39–42, 85, 95.

On clandestine radio stations: Tigrid, *Why Dubček Fell,* p. 228; *Black Book,* pp. 152, 215–16.

The Prague Party convenes the 14th Congress: *Black Book,* pp. 41–42.

On the 14th Congress, the Soviets, the collaborators, and Svoboda: *Black Book,* pp. 80–81, 178; Mlynář, *Night Frost,* pp. 191, 194–97; Kusin, *From Dubček,* p. 19; Jiří Pelikán, *The Secret Vysočany Congress,* London, 1971.

Rudé Právo on August 22 is quoted in *Black Book,* p. 100.

On street scenes and shootings: *Black Book,* pp. 93, 112, 144, 203–4, 192, 229.

On Joseph Pavel: Tigrid, *Why Dubček Fell,* p. 10.

Statement of the Prague Garrison: *Black Book,* pp. 179–80.

Glazarova quoted in *Black Book,* pp. 235–37. *Literární Listy* quoted in *Black Book,* pp. 154–55.

Casualty statistics are in Kusin, *From Dubček* p. 11.

On the Moscow negotiations and Protocol: Pelikán "Struggle for Socialism," p. 30; Tigrid, *Why Dubček Fell,* pp. 112–14; Mlynář (a participant in the Moscow negotiations), *Night Frost,* pp. 233–45.

On Dubček's radio broadcast and the popular reaction: Kusin, *From Dubček,* p. 50; Hauner, letter; *Black Book,* p. 277 and following.

CHAPTER 18: BRITAIN: THE STUDENT REVOLT

On Aston University: *Times* 17 January 1968. On Leicester: *Times* 27 February 1968; *BD* 15 October 1968.

Universities Quarterly is cited by Boris Ford, "What is a University?" *NS* 24 October 1969.

On Essex: Peter Wilby, "Crisis Days for 'Dream' University," *Observer* 19 May 1968; *Guardian* 24 May 1968; *ST* 13 October 1968; *BD* 15 October 1968; David Triesman, "Essex," *NLR* July–August 1968, pp. 70–71; *Times* 14 January 1969.

On Hull: *Times* 31 May, 10 June 1968; *BD* 15 October 1968.

The IS pamphlet is quoted by Colin Crouch, *The Student Revolt,* London, 1970, p. 159. On the RSA: letters to the author from Martin Shaw and Richard Kuper, February 1987.

The Anti-University of London: Richard Boston, "Anti-University," *New Society* 16 May 1968.

On Hornsey and the art colleges: *Times* 7 June 1968; Tom Nairn, "The Crouch End Commune," *NS* 7 June 1968; Nairn, "Hornsey," *NLR* July–August 1968, pp. 65–69, 112–13; *Times* 1 October, 4 December 1968; letters from R. Pulverhaft, *NS* 1 November 1968, 22 August 1969; Peter Wilby, "What the Art Students Want," *Observer* 6 October 1968.

On the Schools Action Union: Christopher Price, "The Spectre of Pupil Power," *NS* 28 March 1969.

On Oxford: *Times* 4 June 1968; Max Beloff in *S. Tel* 9 June 1968; *Guardian* 12 June 1968; see also David Caute, "Crisis in All Souls," *Encounter* March 1966.

On the Cambridge Union debate: *Times* 27 October 1968.

On the vote to occupy the LSE in October 1968: conversation with Prof. Meghdad Desai, February 1987.

Fears before the demonstration of October 27: *Guardian* 5 July 1968; *ST* 13 October 1968; Mervyn Jones, "Prospects and Dangers for 27 October," *NS* 4 October 1968.

A statistical study of the demonstrators is found in James D. Halloran, Philip Elliott, Graham Murdock, *Demonstrations and Communications: A Case Study,* London, 1970; see also Mervyn Jones, "Britain's New Model Army," *NS* 1 November 1968.

Colin Crouch's recall is in Joan Abse (ed.), *My LSE,* London, 1977, p. 199.

On the Adams affair and the occupation of 1967: Harry Kidd, *The*

Trouble at L.S.E., 1966–1967, London, 1969, pp. 51–52, 80–81, 86, 96–97, 101; Crouch, *The Student Revolt,* p. 184.

The academic study based on the LSE questionnaire is by Tessa Blackstone, Kathleen Gales, Roger Hadley, Wyn Lewis, *Student Conflict in the L.S.E. in 1967,* London, 1970, pp. 21–24, 27–28, 42, 56, 120, 175, 181–83, 189–92, 205, 211–13, 269.

Students' Union rejects proposed reforms: *Times* 2 March 1968.

On the impact of the May events in France, the Soc Soc occupation, and the meeting of the RSSF at the LSE; *Times* 24 May 1968; Dennis Barker in *Guardian* 25 May 1968; *BD* 3 December 1968; Widgery, *The Left in Britain,* pp. 341, 357.

Lord Robbins is quoted in *Guardian* 20 November 1968.

For an "ultra" account of the autumn of discontent: Paul Hoch & Victor Schoenbach, *The Natives are Restless,* London, 1969; see pp. 25–26 on the decision to end the October occupation.

On the reaction to governors' threats and the struggles between radicals and reformists: *Times* 1, 6, 15, 27 November 1968.

On Birmingham: *Times* 4, 6 December 1968.

On Bristol: *Times* 9 December 1968.

On the Rhodesia/South Africa resolutions at the LSE, direct action against the director, and the pulling down of the iron gates: conversation with Desai; conversation with Blackburn, January 1987; Hoch & Schoenbach, *The Natives,* pp. 25–26, 64, 87; letter from Shaw; Kidd, *The Trouble,* p. 94; *Times* 31 January 1969.

On the closing of the school, the "LSE in exile," legal charges, internal disciplinary action, and the dismissal of two lecturers: conversation with Blackburn; letter to the author from Laurence Harris, February 1987; letter from Shaw; Hoch & Schoenbach, *The Natives,* pp. 129, 132–44, 164; J. A. G. Griffith, "Opinion and Punishment," *NS* 5 September 1969.

On the radical critique of the university syllabus: Robin Blackburn, "A Brief Guide to Bourgeois Ideology," and Perry Anderson, "Components of the National Culture," in Cockburn & Blackburn, *Student Power.*

Caine's book is quoted by Ford, "What Is a University?," p. 561.

Composition of the Court of Governors: *LSE Calendar 1982–83.*

CHAPTER 19: MILITANT STUDENTS, ANGRY PROFESSORS

Petersen's survey (R. E.) Petersen, *The Scope of Organized Student Protest in 1967/68*) is cited by Blackstone et al., *Student Conflict,* p. 235.

Keniston's findings on student radicalism are contained in: "Harvard on My Mind," *NYRB* 24 September 1970; Keniston, *Youth and Dissent,* pp. 148–248.

Carl Davidson's "Campaigning on Campus," is in Cockburn & Blackburn, *Student Power.*

On the family background of young radicals: Jacobs & Landau, *New Radicals,* p. 5.

On stages of moral awareness: Keniston, *Youth and Dissent,* pp. 257–73.

On faculty attitudes to dissent: Lipset, *Rebellion,* p. 198; Mehnert, *Twilight,* p. 42.

On sympathetic dons: Hutchins is quoted by Hollander, *Political Pilgrims,* p. 190. See also: Henry David Aitken, "The Revolting Academy," *NYRB* 11 July 1968; Frederick Crews, "The Radical Students," *NYRB* 24 April 1969; Keniston, *Youth and Dissent,* p. 271.

The hostile view is expressed by Kennan, "Democracy and Student Left," pp. 1, 10, 141, 173–74, 192, 201.

Scheinbaum's admission is in *Ramparts* April 1966, quoted by Buckman, *Limits of Protest,* pp. 38–39; see also Silver, "Who Cares for Columbia?" The British version of university-as-corporation is in E. P. Thompson (ed.), *Warwick University, Ltd.,* London, 1970, pp. 111–12, 106–8, 124.

More examples of professorial hostility: Shils, *The Intellectuals,* pp. 188, 287, 293–97; Arthur Schlesinger, Jr., "America 1968: The Politics of Violence," *Harper's* August 1968.

The Old Left's hostility: Genovese is quoted in Lipset, *Rebellion,* pp. 211–12; see also C. Lasch & E. Genovese, "Education in the University We Need Now," *NYRB* 9 October 1969. Noam Chomsky is quoted by Lipset, *Rebellion,* p. 214. Bernard Crick is in David Martin (ed.), *Anarchy and Culture: The Problem of the Contemporary University,* London, 1969, p. 164.

For the New Left critique, see: Gareth Stedman Jones, "Meaning of the Student Revolt," in Cockburn & Blackburn, *Student Power.*

On the "Sorel industry": Irving Louis Horowitz, *Radicalism and the Revolt against Reason: The Social Theories of Georges Sorel,* New York, 1968 edition, pp. vi–xvii; Shils, *The Intellectuals,* p. 275.

Professors reminded of the Hitler Youth are cited by Lipset, *Rebellion,* pp. 116–17; Marie Jahoda is reported in *Times* 19 March 1969.

John W. Aldridge, "In the Country of the Young," *Harper's* November 1969.

Beloff and Elton are reported in *Times* 5, 12 June 1968. Signatories of an appeal for a private university are in *Times* 3 January 1969. Trevor-Roper is in *Observer* 22 June 1969, quoted in Hoch & Schoenbach, *The Natives,* p. 31.

Kenneth Minogue is in Abse, *My LSE,* p. 178. Donald MacRae is in Martin, *Anarchy and Culture,* pp. 199, 212.

On hostile Californians: Robert Nisbet, "Who Killed the Student Revolution?" *Encounter* February 1970, pp. 10–18; John R. Searle, *The Campus War,* London, 1972, pp. 26–101. (New York, 1971)

Lionel Trilling is in *PR* Summer 1968, p. 391.

The liberal Machiavellians: Eric Ashby & Mary Anderson, *The Rise of the Student Estate in Britain,* London, 1970, pp. 136–37.

CHAPTER 20: A SEASON OF VIOLENCE: MEXICO, EUROPE, AND
JAPAN

Mexico

On the unrest of July–October 1968: *Times* 4 October 1968; *BD* 12
October 1968; K. S. Karol, *Guerrillas in Power: The Course of the Cuban
Revolution,* London, 1971, p. 502. (New York, 1970)

Germany

The mood in Berlin during the student trials is reported by John Heilpern,
"The Student Revolt: Where It All Started," *Observer* 27 October 1968.

For the events of the autumn, see *Guardian* 8 October, 5 November 1968;
Times 5 November 1968; *IHT* 7 November; 12, 26 December 1968; *LM* 6
October 1968.

The Berlin communes were visited by Ralph Blumenthal, *NYT Magazine*
1 December 1968.

On further occupations, demonstrations: *Times* 24 January, 28 February
1969.

France

On de Gaulle's press conference and Faure's educational reform: *Times*
10, 19 September 1968; Margot Lyons, "De Gaulle Bangs His Drum," *NS* 13
September 1968.

Sartre is quoted in *Observer* 10 November 1968. On continuing *lycée*
unrest: R. W. Johnson, *The Long March of the French Left,* London, 1981,
pp. 63–64. (New York, 1981)

Italy

On university and schools strikes and demonstrations: *LM* 17 August; 10
November; 3, 4, 23 December 1968; *Times* 11 September 1968; *Guardian* 11
October, 28 November 1968; *NYT* 13 November 1968.

For an analysis of the schools insurrection, see Chiara Ingrao, "The
School Movement in Rome," *NLR* March–April 1969.

On Italy in 1969: Bruce Renton, "The Splintered Left," and "Whose
Funeral in Italy?" *NS* 11 July, 26 December 1969.

Spain

On continuing unrest despite reforms: *NYT* 15 September 1968; *Guardian* 1 November, 9 December 1968; *LM* 15 November 1968; *DT* 16, 28, 30
November; 5, 7 December 1968.

Poland

On the revival of the anti-Semitic campaign: *LM* 28 August 1968.

On trials of students: *NYT* 17 October, 2 December 1968; *LM* 15 November, 15 December 1968; *Guardian* 13 December 1968; *IHT* 13 December 1968; Neal Ascherson, *Observer* 15 December 1968.

Japan

On Nihon and Tokyo universities: *Japan Times* 2 March; 7 July; 27, 29 September; 10, 19 October; 2, 3, 11, 13, 17, 19, 23, 30 November 1968; *NYT* 5 September; 25 December 1968; *Times* 3 October 1968.

On the Chinese view: Hsinhua News Agency, 8 July, 8 September 1968.

For historical background, see Henry Dewitt Smith II, *Japan's First Student Radicals,* Cambridge, Mass., 1972.

CHAPTER 21: THE USA: BLACK STUDENTS, WHITE TEACHERS

For the Black Power issue in U.S. athletics, quoting Harry Edwards, see Neil Allen in *Times* 13 July 1968.

On the Wallace campaign: *NS* 13 September 1968; *Times* 2, 4, 26 October 1968.

For the New York City teachers' strike—hostility between Jews and blacks, see Wolfe, *Radical Chic,* pp. 83–84, 90, 92; Mehnert, *Twilight,* p. 307.

On the Herman Ferguson appointment in OH-B: Dwight Macdonald, "A Reply to a Non-Reply," *NYRB* 16 January 1969.

On the UFT position: letter from Reuben W. Mitchell, *NYRB* 21 November 1968.

The anti-Semitic poem is quoted by Nora Sayre, "Breakdown of a Metropolis," *NS* 14 February 1969. I. F. Stone is quoted in letters page, *NS* 21 February 1969, p. 256.

Answering Macdonald: Michael Harrington, "A Reply," *NYRB* 2 February 1969.

The settlement: *Times* 10 October, 19 November 1968.

On the U.S. presidential election: Howe, *A Margin of Hope,* p. 312.

On riots and disturbances in American schools: *Guardian* (New York) 17 May 1969. Material on the schools' underground press and activities is from John Birmingham (ed.), *Your Time Is Now: Notes from the High School Underground,* New York, 1970.

On the pattern of black student radicalism: Martin Kilson, "The Black Student Movement," *Encounter* September 1971, pp. 83–89; October 1971, pp. 81–85.

On unrest at Berkeley in 1968: Roger Rapoport, "Status Report," *Harper's* June 1968.

On the San Francisco State College mill-in: *Times* 1, 2 July 1968. The most comprehensive account of San Francisco State's chaotic year is: Robert Smith, Richard Axen, DeVere Pentony, *By Any Means Necessary: The Revolutionary Struggle at San Francisco State College,* San Francisco, 1970, pp. 49, 94, 141, 165, 197–98.

On the AFT strike and violence on the campus: the exchange between Andrew W. Rosen and Andrew Kopkind, *NS* 7 March 1969.

On California politics, Smith's resignation, and Hayakawa's victory: Smith, et al., *By Any Means,* pp. 260, 272, 282, 301; Dr. Nathan Hare, "From Francisco State," in Ramparts, *Divided We Stand,* pp. 17–20; and A. J. Langguth, "San Francisco State," *Harper's* September 1969.

On Cornell: Matthew Hodgart's letter and a reply, *Times* 17, 23, 26 May 1969; also Michael Thelwell, "From Cornell," in Ramparts, *Divided We Stand,* pp. 14–16.

Matthew Hodgart published *A New Voyage to the Country of the Houyhnhmns,* New York, 1969; on this, see Shils, *The Intellectuals,* p. 187.

CHAPTER 22: PRAGUE WINTER

On the Czech student demonstrations in November 1968: "A. J.," "Prague Winter," *PR* Winter 1969, pp. 36–56; Gabriel Lorince, "Moscow Finds its Czech Stooges," *NS* 15 November 1968; Lorince, "Smrkovský's Last Stand," *NS* 3 January 1969.

On Palach: Kusin, *From Dubček,* pp. 50–59. The Writers' Union statement of October 31, 1968 is quoted in Jiří Pelikán, *Ici Prague: L'Opposition intérieure parle,* Paris, 1973, pp. 90–97.

On the fall of Dubček and Husák's accession: Remington, *Winter in Prague,* pp. 444–47, 454–55; Shawcross, *Dubček,* p. 261, 264; *Times* 10, 11 February, 12 June 1969; Kamil Winter, "The Czechs' Grim Anniversary," *NS* 15 August 1969; Edward Dean, "Dubček's Last Chance," *NS* 3 October 1969; Hans J. Morgenthau, "Inquisition in Czechoslovakia," *NYRB* 4 December 1969.

On student-worker unity and the workers' councils: Hauner, "Czechoslovakia," pp. 51–55, and Vladimir Fisera, "Workers Councils in Czechoslovakia," *NLR* September–October 1977.

On Hrbek's witch-hunt, see Kusin, *From Dubček,* pp. 95–98. On Husák's political trials, Kusin, *From Dubček,* p. 118. On the purges generally, Kusin, *From Dubček.*

CHAPTER 23: DECLINE OF THE NEW LEFT

On the scale of campus violence in 1967–69: Mairowitz, *Radical Soap Opera,* p. 243; Young, *An Infantile Disorder,* p. 200.

On the 1969 SDS convention: Mehnert, *Twilight,* pp. 43–45; Roger Kahn, "The Collapse of SDS," *Esquire* October 1969; Dohrn is quoted in Howe, *A Margin of Hope,* p. 313.

On SDS and the Panthers: Ronald Steel, "Letter from Oakland: The Panthers," *NYRB* 11 September 1969; Young, *An Infantile Disorder,* p. 129.

On the Days of Rage: Hayden, *Trial,* pp. 92-94; Mairowitz, *Radical Soap Opera,* p. 264, 268.

On Weatherman bombings: Vera Brittain, "Bombing the Bourgeoisie," *NS* 20 March 1970; Jane Alpert is interviewed in the film *Revolution Revisited.*

On the Chicago 8 trial: "The Trial of Bobby Seale," *NYRB* 4 December 1969; Jason Epstein, "The Chicago Conspiracy Trial," *NYRB* 12 February 1970; Rubin, *We Are Everywhere,* pp. 37, 126, 131, 218; Hayden, *Trial,* pp. 57, 69–72, 109–10; J. Anthony Lukas, "The Making of a Yippie," *Esquire* November 1969.

On Altamont: Sol Stern, "Altamont," in Ramparts, *Conversations with the New Reality;* Sanchez, *Up and Down,* pp. 174–89.

On the Moratorium and Mobilization, October–November 1969: Vera Brittain, *NS* 21 November 1969; Murray Kempton, "Washington after Dark," *NYRB* 18 December 1969; Lipset, *Rebellion,* p. 43; Coffin, *Once to Every Man,* pp. 295–99.

AFTERWORD

Charles Reich, *The Greening of America,* New York, 1970, pp. 263, 215, 233, 246, etc.

Where are they now? See Peter Clecak, *Radical Paradoxes: Dilemmas of the American Left, 1945–1970,* n.p., 1973, p. 267. On Abbie Hoffman's plastic surgery: Mehnert, *Twilight,* p. 208, based on Jeff Nyghtbyrd, "The Many Noses of Abbie Hoffman," San Francisco *Examiner,* 5 December 1975. Also on Hoffman: Christopher Lasch, "The Narcissist Society," *NYRB* 30 September 1976.

Cohn-Bendit's interviews with Hoffman and Rubin are in his film, *Revolution Revisited.*

On anti-CIA demonstrations in 1986–87; *IHT* 16, 29 April 1987.

On sanctions against South Africa: *Times* 5 April 1986; *IHT* 21 July; 18 August; 13, 14, 18, 29 September; 3 October 1986.

On Tom Hayden: Mehnert, *Twilight,* p. 358; Nicholas von Hoffman, "Seize the Day," *NYRB* 6 November 1980.

For Peter Collier and David Horowitz's revised position, see "Who Killed the Spirit of '68?," *Encounter* September–October 1985, pp. 69–72.

On Cohn-Bendit in the 1970s: Mehnert, *Twilight,* pp. 360–61. For Cohn-Bendit's statement of his position as a German Green, see his film *Revolution Revisited.*

On the Czech Jazz Section and Polish underground: *Guardian* 12 March 1987.

INDEX